D1520325

Federal Civil Service Law and Procedures
A Basic Guide

Second Edition

Federal Civil Service Law and Procedures
A Basic Guide

Second Edition

Ellen M. Bussey, Editor

Carl D. Moore
Sandra H. Shapiro
Kathryn A. Bleecker
Michael J. Riselli

R. John Seibert
Robert T. Simmelkjaer
David L. Feder
Stuart R. Horn

Jerome P. Hardiman

The Bureau of National Affairs, Inc., Washington, D.C.

Copyright © 1984, 1990
The Bureau of National Affairs, Inc.

Library of Congress Cataloging-in-Publication Data

Federal civil service law and procedures : a basic guide / Ellen M. Bussey, editor. —
2nd ed.
  p.   cm.
  ISBN 0-87179-634-1
  1. Civil service—United States.   I. Bussey, Ellen M.
KF5337.F38   1990
342.73'068—dc20
[347.30268]   89-23996
                                                                               CIP

Authorization to photocopy items for internal or personal use, or the internal or personal use of specific
clients, is granted by BNA Books for libraries and other uses registered with the Copyright Clearance
Center (CCC) Transactional Reporting Service, provided that $0.50 per page is paid directly to CCC,
27 Congress St., Salem, MA 01970, 0-87179-634-1/90/$0 + .50.

Published by BNA Books, 1231 25th St., N.W.
Washington, D.C. 20037

Printed in the United States of America
International Standard Book Number 0-87179-634-1

Introduction

This Second Edition of *Federal Civil Service Law and Procedures* constitutes a much enlarged version of the original book published in 1984. Not only are we exploring many additional areas, but the greatly expanded case law in federal employee and labor relations dispute resolution has required a very different approach, which has resulted in new content and organization of the material. These substantial changes make this volume particularly important to those wishing to be informed and up-to-date while coping with the problems faced by management, employees, and unions in what has become a highly complex field since the promulgation of the Civil Service Reform Act in 1978.

The Act, which did not become fully effective until the early 1980s, was strongly motivated by considerations that federal civil servants had become too secure. It was felt by many that along with job security had come entrenched positions no longer responsive to the political system. But, although one ostensible purpose of the Reform Act was to make it easier for managers to terminate poor performers, the rights and procedural safeguards for employees were also strengthened in the process, complicating the existing system.

It is the editor's intention that this volume serve two purposes. It should make the enormous detail and complexity of existing civil service law clear to anyone who is affected by it or working with it professionally. Thus, emphasis has been put on making the text readable and direct, so that each employee, union steward, supervisor, and labor relations official should be able to pick up the book and know what course of action is open to him or her. At the same time, however, this volume addresses the needs of expert litigators in federal civil service law by referencing approximately 1,700 cases related to the material covered by the chapter contributors.

As stated in the Introduction to the first edition, the book grew out of the need encountered by all of its contributors for a single, comprehensive statement on federal personnel law—something to which they could turn quickly for specific answers to the great variety of questions with which they were constantly confronted. And to the extent that the two editions have taken some of the enigma out of the system of civil service law and procedures for the average civil servant with a problem, and facilitated research for practitioners and attorneys, we will have accomplished our purpose.

The legal structure described in this book evolves around several organizations. Personnel actions in the federal civil service are currently coordinated by the Office of Personnel Management (OPM) under Title II, Section 201 of the Reform Act. It is headed by a Director and Deputy Director, each appointed by the President for a four-year term and confirmed by the Senate. The OPM has five regional offices and 24 area offices throughout the country. (See Appendix 2 for the location of federal offices for organizations discussed in the book.)

Adjudicating a variety of employee appeals and overseeing the application of merit principles throughout most of the system is the responsibility of the Merit Systems Protection Board (MSPB) with its Special Counsel (Title II, Section 202). The term "merit system principles" is defined in Title I, Section 101 and discussed in the book's Chapter 3. The MSPB is headed by three Members appointed on a bipartisan basis to seven-year, nonrenewable, terms. It hears and decides employee appeals as described in Chapters 1, 2, and 3. It also has oversight responsibilities for the merit system as a whole and is charged with reporting annually to Congress on how that system is functioning. The Board has 11 regional offices in addition to its Washington, D.C., headquarters.

To assure the implementation of the merit system principles as spelled out by the law, 11 prohibited personnel practices have been defined (Title I, Section 101). Allegations of such practices are prosecuted by the Special Counsel of the MSPB (see Chapters 1, 2, and 4). A prohibited personnel practice that has received wide attention is the one barring reprisals against whistleblowers—individuals who disclose information that suggests illegal agency action or a gross waste of funds, abuse of authority, gross mismanagement, or a substantial danger to public health and safety. The Special Counsel is appointed by the President for a five-year term. There are four field offices throughout the country in addition to the national headquarters in Washington, D.C.

The Equal Employment Opportunity Commission (EEOC), created by the Civil Rights Act of 1964 to administer Title VII of the Act, is the Federal Government's chief civil rights watchdog. Along with Title VII, which prohibits employment discrimination on the basis of race, color, religion, sex, or national origin, it is also responsible for the enforcement of the Age Discrimination in Employment Act, which protects workers between the ages of 40 and 70; the Equal Pay Act, which protects against pay discrimination based on sex; and Section 501 of the Rehabilitation Act of 1973, which prohibits discrimination against the handicapped. Chapters 1, 2, and 5 present a detailed description of EEO in the Federal Government. The EEOC has five Commissioners and a General Counsel appointed by the President and confirmed by the Senate for five and four years, respectively. Its headquarters is located in Washington, D.C., while 23 district offices handle full services in the field. In addition, two area offices provide complaint examiners for federal sector cases.

The Federal Labor Relations Authority (FLRA), with three permanent Members, administers the federal labor-management relations program including union elections and representation (see Chapter 7), unfair labor practices (see Chapter 8), negotiability of labor/management issues (see Chapter 9), collective bargaining and impasses (see Chapter 10), and arbitration in the federal sector (see Chapter 11). The Authority also encompasses the Federal Service Impasses Panel (FSIP). At the request of either party, collective bargaining impasses may be resolved by the FSIP, or by the binding arbitration decision of an independent neutral, if this was adopted as a procedure by the parties to the collective bargaining contract and was approved by the FSIP (see Chapter 10).

Of the Authority's three Members, not more than two may be of the same political party. Appointments are for five-year terms, made by the President with the consent of the Senate. Within the FLRA, a General Counsel, appointed by the President with the consent of the Senate, investigates unfair labor practices and prosecutes them before the Authority. The General Counsel may be removed by the President at any time. The FLRA has nine regional offices in addition to its national headquarters in Washington, D.C. The FSIP is located in Washington, D.C., only.

Overall, the new edition contains six new chapters, expanding the first edition's discussion of labor relations, investigating a new area of supervisory liability, and examining remedies available and not available in the federal sector. The first two chapters of the book describe who may challenge a personnel action, what types of action may be challenged, and the proper forum in which the case may be heard. The subsequent four chapters deal with the evolving law regarding employee relations in terms of actions that may be appealed to the MSPB (Chapter 3), prohibited personnel practices and whistleblowing (Chapter 4), equal employment opportunity (Chapter 5), and a new chapter that looks at the extent to which supervisors can be held liable in the event they are found to have acted incorrectly and disadvantaged a subordinate (Chapter 6).

The six chapters dealing with employee relations are followed by five chapters on labor relations, four of which are new in this edition. Chapter 7, "Representation and Elections," deals with the status of unions in the federal system and the processes by which elections and unit determination may take place. Chapter 8, "Unfair Labor Practices," is the only chapter in the labor relations section that also appeared in the first edition. But, like the other updated chapters, this one needed to be considerably expanded and encompasses many new developments. The subsequent chapter (9) deals with negotiability issues that arise in federal labor-management collective bargaining. It describes the appeals process unions must follow when in disagreement with management and highlights specific issues that have been of major concern to both parties and how these have been decided. The actual process of collective bargaining is discussed in greater detail in Chapter 10, "Collective Bargaining and Impasses." And since the law permits the parties to a negotiated agreement in the federal sector to call on outside neutrals for assistance in the event of disputes, the book also contains a chapter (11) entitled "Arbitration of Grievances in the Federal Sector." It discusses some of the special problems facing labor arbitrators in the federal sector and highlights the most important issues that have come before them. In the federal sector the arbitrator is confronted with myriad laws, rules, and regulations, and appeals from arbitral awards are common.

One of the remedies available to successful grievants in the federal sector is the right to attorney's fees under certain conditions, a new concept with the Civil Service Reform Act. Situations in which attorney's fees may be granted have been carefully defined in the past decade in a substantial body of case law and administrative decisions. Thus, Chapter 12, "Attorney's Fees in the Litigation of Federal Personnel Disputes," has inevitably grown to nearly 50 pages in this edition as compared to its 15 pages in the first edition. The last chapter of the book summarizes remedies available and not available in the federal system so an employee and his or her representative, before initiating an action, will be fully aware of what the employee can in fact expect to gain if successful and the standards that must be met before various types of remedies that are available under the law can be applied to the particular case.

I would like to take this opportunity to thank "the team" who contributed with such dedication to this arduous effort throughout the many stages of coordinating, writing, and editing characteristic of the process of creating a book of this nature. All of the contributors hold more than full-time positions but were willing to give many, many hours of their scarce free time to help clarify a system with which they are associated for others affected by it, or professionals involved with it. For three of the chapter contributors, Carl D. Moore, Sandra H. Shapiro, and David L. Feder, this was a second round and their endurance deserves to be cited as particularly remarkable.

All chapters were written in the authors' private capacities. No official support or endorsement of any government agency is intended or should be inferred.

All of us who worked together on the first edition have warm memories of John B. Zimmerman as a friend and colleague. His untimely death at the age of 38 came as a shock and loss to each of us. We dedicate this Second Edition to his memory.

March 1990   Ellen M. Bussey

Contents

**4. Prohibited Personnel Practices and the Office of the
    Special Counsel**
    Kathryn A. Bleecker

8. Unfair Labor Practices 231
David L. Feder

Appendices

Employee Relations

I. Challenging Agency Actions

1. Personnel Actions That May Be Challenged

CARL D. MOORE

Employees in the Federal Government and applicants for employment may challenge a variety of management's personnel actions before various adjudicatory authorities. Each of these authorities hears only certain categories of challenges. Selecting the proper authority to hear a challenge requires an understanding of the various appeals, grievances, and complaints that may be raised as well as an understanding of the employment status of the individual protesting a personnel action.

Since the early days of the Federal Government, it has been acknowledged that federal employment is not contractual but rather appointive in nature.[1] An appointment is not effective until an authorized official (usually the personnel officer for the agency or the agency subdivision), signs an Office of Personnel Management, Standard Form 50 (SF-50) appointing the individual to the position.[2] By definition, every federal employee has in his or her official personnel folder an SF-50, effecting appointment to his or her present position. The SF-50 contains all the information necessary to determine an employee's status.

There must be statutory authority for each appointment, i.e., Congress must have given the employing agency permission to make the appointment. Such authority also defines the nature of the appointment, including the rights and benefits afforded to the employees. For example, a "competitive service" employee may challenge an adverse action, such

---

[1]*Marbury v. Madison*, 1 Cranch 137 (1803).

[2]Nonappropriated fund (NAF) employees are defined as civil service "employees" for only limited purposes. Therefore, their appointment is not effected with an SF-50. See also *infra*, note 6.

as a removal or reduction in grade, before the Merit Systems Protection Board (MSPB). However, an "excepted service" employee may not challenge an adverse action before the MSPB unless the employee is a "preference eligible."[3] This should make it apparent that some of the basic terms involved in explaining employment status deserve a brief definition.

In the Federal Government, the "civil service" refers to all appointive positions in the executive, judicial, and legislative branches except for the uniformed services.[4] Throughout this book, we will be concerned with civil service "employees." This refers to individuals who are—

1. appointed in the civil service,[5]
2. engaged in the performance of a federal function under authority of law or an executive act, and
3. subject to the supervision of an individual listed in footnote 5.[6]

---

[3]5 U.S.C. 7411(a)(1); *Wren v. MSPB*, 681 F.2d 867 (D.C. Cir. 1982). Until a recent court decision, it was well established that excepted service employees could organize and collectively bargain a grievance-arbitration procedure that provides protections similar to those enjoyed by competitive service employees. *Department of the Treasury v. FLRA*, No. 88-1159 (D.C. Cir. May 2, 1989). The point to this discussion, however, is that the rights and protections created for employees by statute, as opposed to those collectively bargained, may vary substantially depending upon the type of appointment under which an employee is serving.

[4]The term "uniformed services" includes the armed services (Army, Navy, Air Force, Marine Corps, and Coast Guard), the commissioned corps of the Public Health Service, and the commissioned corps of the National Oceanic and Atmospheric Administration. 5 U.S.C. 2101(2) and (3).

[5]The appointment must be by one of the following:
   (A) the President;
   (B) a member of Congress, or the Congress;
   (C) a member of the uniformed service;
   (D) an individual who is an employee under this section;
   (E) the head of a Government controlled corporation; or
   (F) an adjutant general designated by the secretary concerned under section 709(c) of Title 32.
5 U.S.C. 2105(a)(1).

[6]5 U.S.C. 2105(a). The statute also specifically defines as an "employee" an individual employed at the U.S. Naval Academy in the midshipmen's laundry, the midshipmen's tailor shop, the midshipmen's cobbler and barber shops, and the midshipmen's store, except an individual employed by the Academy dairy. For limited purposes, the statute also includes in the definition of "employee" individuals paid from nonappropriated funds of the Army and Air Force Exchange Service, Army and Air Force Motion Picture Service, Navy Ship's Stores Ashore, Navy Exchanges, Marine and Coast Guard Exchanges, and other instrumentalities of the United States under the jurisdiction of the armed forces conducted for the comfort, pleasure, contentment, and mental and physical improvement of the personnel of the armed forces. 5 U.S.C. 2105(c). For example, nonappropriated fund employees cannot appeal to the MSPB. *Taylor v. Department of the Navy*, 2 MSPB 6 (1980).

Civil service "employees" may be further divided into (1) those in the "competitive service," and (2) those not in the competitive service. "Competitive service" refers to all positions in the executive branch other than—

- positions specifically "excepted" from the competitive service (e.g., attorney positions are in the "excepted service");
- positions in the Senior Executive Service; or
- positions to which appointments are made by presidential nomination for confirmation by the Senate.

To determine whether an employee is in an excepted or competitive position, refer to block 35 on the SF-50, which effected the employee's appointment to the position in question. Civil service positions outside the executive branch also may be competitive service positions, but only if they are specifically included in the competitive service by statute.[7]

Another category of employees is the "preference eligible," that is, certain veterans, their wives, or mothers.[8] Preference-eligible employees receive certain advantages in initial appointment actions. Furthermore, preference-eligible employees who are in the excepted service are generally accorded the same rights in challenging personnel actions as employees in the competitive service. (See Chapter 3 regarding the persons covered under appealable actions.)

The rights accorded to Federal Government employees may vary depending upon the employee's category of appointment as reflected on the SF-50 (e.g., competitive service, excepted service, Senior Executive Service); the employee's special status (e.g., preference eligible, member of a bargaining unit); and the agency in which the person is employed (i.e., some agencies and government corporations are not subject to some of the statutory appeals procedures discussed herein). In the discussions throughout this book of the various actions that may be challenged and of the procedures in which such challenges may be raised, we will note the groups of employees who are covered and those who are not covered.

Appealable Actions

"Appealable actions" is a term in federal personnel work, which refers to actions that may be reviewed by the Merit Systems Protection

---

[7] 5 U.S.C. 2102.

[8] "Preference-eligible employee" is defined at 5 U.S.C. 2108. Generally it refers to individuals who have served in the Armed Forces of the United States and who were discharged under honorable conditions. It also includes certain wives and mothers of some disabled or deceased veterans. Preference eligibles are discussed by the MSPB in *Jacaruso v. Department of the Army*, 1 MSPB 360 (1980).

Board. The MSPB is not necessarily the exclusive reviewing authority for all "appealable actions." They may be reviewed in the negotiated grievance procedure and, when an equal employment opportunity violation is also alleged, the Equal Employment Opportunity Commission may participate in the review (see Chapter 2, "Using the Negotiated Grievance Procedure" and "Mixed Case Processing After the MSPB Decision").

Appealable actions have an important characteristic that distinguishes them from other categories of management actions. With most appealable actions, the employee need not guess whether he or she has been the object of a personnel action that may be challenged. Management is required to notify the employee of the action and of the employee's right to challenge it.

There are five major categories of appealable actions: (1) adverse actions, (2) performance-related actions, (3) within-grade increase denials, (4) reduction-in-force actions, and (5) retirement-related actions.[9] A detailed discussion of the agency procedural requirements for

---

[9]The "appealable action" jurisdiction of the MSPB is recited at 5 C.F.R. 1201.3. It may be summarized as follows:

Appeal Right	Authority
Performance-based removal or reduction in grade	5 C.F.R. Part 432
Conduct-based removal, reduction in grade or pay, suspension for more than 14 days, or furlough for 30 days or less	5 C.F.R. Part 752
Removal or suspension for more than 14 days of career appointee in Senior Executive Service (SES)	5 C.F.R. Part 752, Subparts E and F
Reduction in force of a career appointee in SES	5 U.S.C. 3593
Negative determination of competence for a general schedule employee	5 C.F.R. 531.410
Determinations regarding retirement	5 C.F.R. Part 831
Suitability determinations	5 C.F.R. 731.401
Termination during probation or first year of VRA appointment where discrimination based on political affiliation or marital status is raised	5 C.F.R. 315.806 and 307.105(b)
Supervisor's probationary period	5 C.F.R. 315.908(b)
Reduction in force (RIF)	5 C.F.R. 351.901
Furlough of career appointee in SES	5 C.F.R. 359.805
Restoration following injury, military duty, or RIF	5 C.F.R. 353.401, 302.501, and 330.202
Foreign Assistant Reemployment Rights	5 C.F.R. 352.508
Emergency Reemployment Rights	5 C.F.R. 352.209
International Organization Reemployment Rights	5 C.F.R. 352.313
Indian Reemployment Rights	5 C.F.R. 352.707
Taiwan Service Reemployment Rights	5 C.F.R. 352.807
Employment Practices	5 C.F.R. 300.104

Also see the Whistleblower Protection Act of 1989, P.L. 101-12, 103 Stat. 16, (April 10, 1989).

taking such actions and of the substantive law and regulations relevant to appealable actions appears in Chapter 3.

EEO Violations

An equal employment opportunity (EEO) violation arises when an employee or applicant for employment is the object of discrimination with regard to some employment matter. An individual or group of individuals may allege that they were treated differently from others or other groups in some kind of employment matter due to race, color, religion, sex, national origin, age, handicapping condition, or reprisal for EEO activity. Chapter 5 discusses in greater detail the elements of an EEO case. It also describes the types of relief available when discrimination is found to exist. EEO allegations may be appealed through the EEO complaints procedure or the negotiated grievance procedure and brought to the attention of the Special Counsel of the Merit Systems Protection Board (see Chapter 2).

Mixed Cases

Cases alleging an EEO violation are usually reviewed by one administrative authority (EEOC), while cases involving an appealable action are usually reviewed by another authority (MSPB). In passing the Civil Service Reform Act, however, Congress recognized that these two categories of cases often merge into one. This occurs, for example, when an employee alleges that his or her removal was motivated by race or sex discrimination. When an "appealable action" is combined with an alleged "EEO violation," it becomes a so-called "mixed case."[10] The procedure for processing a mixed case is unique and will be discussed in Chapter 2.

Prohibited Personnel Practices

With passage of the Civil Service Reform Act, Congress identified 11 personnel practices, each of which represents a serious breach of the merit system upon which the federal civil service is based. For a prohibited personnel practice to exist, there must first be a "personnel action," such as an appointment or a promotion[11] (see Chapter 4).

---

[10]5 U.S.C. 7702.
[11]5 U.S.C. 2302(a).

A prohibited personnel practice occurs when a federal employee, who, in connection with his or her authority to take, direct another to take, or approve a personnel action—

- discriminates;
- solicits or considers recommendations based on factors other than personal knowledge or records of job-related abilities or characteristics;
- coerces the political activity of any person;
- deceives or willfully obstructs any person from competing for employment;
- influences any person to withdraw from job competition;
- gives unauthorized preferred treatment or advantage to improve or injure the prospects of any particular person for employment;
- engages in nepotism (hiring or promoting relatives);
- takes reprisal for *bona fide* whistleblowing;
- takes reprisal for exercise of an appeal right;
- discriminates on the basis of personal conduct that is not adverse to the performance of the employee, applicant, or others;
- violates any law, rule, or regulation implementing or directly concerning merit system principles.[12]

Three special aspects of prohibited personnel practices are worth noting. First, an appealable action taken by an agency must be reversed upon review if the employee can show that the agency decision resulted from a prohibited personnel practice.[13] Second, when an employee represented by an attorney can demonstrate that an agency personnel action involving a prohibited personnel practice adversely affected him or her, the agency may be required to reimburse the employee for the attorney's fees[14] (see Chapter 12). Third, prohibited personnel practices constitute a major portion of the jurisdiction of the Special Counsel of the Merit Systems Protection Board. Therefore, the existence of a prohibited personnel practice may provide a basis for the Special Counsel to become involved in an employee's case. (See Chapter 4 for a detailed discussion of the Special Counsel's role.)

Unfair Labor Practices

Unfair labor practices arise within the context of the relationship between unions and management. Integral to the statutory scheme for

[12] 5 U.S.C. 2302(b).
[13] 5 U.S.C. 7701(c)(2)(B).
[14] 5 U.S.C. 7701(g)(1).

labor relations in both the public and private sector of this country is the concept that unions and management must refrain from infringing upon each other's basic rights as well as from violating the basic rights of employees. Consistent with this concept, the statute, which establishes labor relations in the Federal Government, creates eight unfair labor practices for management and eight unfair labor practices for unions.[15]

It is an unfair labor practice for an agency—

1. to interfere with, restrain, or coerce any employee in the exercise by the employee of any right under 5 U.S.C. Chapter 71;
2. to encourage or discourage membership in any labor organization by discrimination in connection with hiring, tenure, promotion, or other conditions of employment;
3. to sponsor, control, or otherwise assist any labor organization, other than to furnish, upon request, customary and routine service and facilities if the services and facilities are also furnished on an impartial basis to other labor organizations having equivalent status;
4. to discipline or otherwise discriminate against an employee because the employee has filed a complaint, affidavit, or petition, or has given any information or testimony under this Chapter;
5. to refuse to consult or negotiate in good faith with a labor organization as required by this Chapter;
6. to fail or refuse to cooperate in impasse procedures and impasse decisions as required by this Chapter;
7. to enforce any rule or regulation (other than a rule or regulation implementing 5 U.S.C. section 2302) which is in conflict with any applicable collective bargaining agreement if the agreement was in effect before the date the rule or regulation was prescribed; or
8. to otherwise fail or refuse to comply with any provision of this Chapter.[16]

It is an unfair labor practice for a labor organization—

1. to interfere with, restrain, or coerce any employee in the exercise by the employee of any right under 5 U.S.C. Chapter 71;
2. to cause or attempt to cause an agency to discriminate against any employee in the exercise by the employee of any right under 5 U.S.C. Chapter 71;

---

[15]The labor relations statute is found at 5 U.S.C. Chapter 71. The unfair labor practices are at 5 U.S.C. 7116.
[16]5 U.S.C. 7116(a).

3. to coerce, discipline, fine, or attempt to coerce a member of the labor organization as punishment, reprisal, or for the purpose of hindering or impeding the member's work performance or productivity as an employee or the discharge of the member's duties as an employee;

4. to discriminate against an employee with regard to the terms or conditions of membership in the labor organization on the basis of race, color, creed, national origin, sex, age, preferential or non-preferential civil service status, political affiliation, marital status, or handicapping condition;

5. to refuse to consult or negotiate in good faith with an agency as required under 5 U.S.C. Chapter 71;

6. to fail or refuse to cooperate in impasse procedures and impasse decisions as required under 5 U.S.C. Chapter 71;

7. a. to call, or participate in, a strike, work stoppage, or slow-down, or picketing of an agency in a labor-management dispute if such picketing interferes with an agency's operations, or

   b. to condone any activity described in subparagraph (A) of this paragraph by failing to take action to prevent or stop such activity; or

8. to otherwise fail or refuse to comply with any provision of 5 U.S.C. Chapter 71.[17]

An unfair labor practice complaint may be brought—

• by an employee against a union and/or management;
• by a union against another union and/or management;
• by management against a union.

Unfair labor practice complaints are heard by the Federal Labor Relations Authority. The procedure for initiating an unfair labor practice charge is discussed in Chapter 2. Details regarding the types of action which constitute an unfair labor practice appear in Chapter 8.

Actions Reviewable by the Office of Personnel Management

The Office of Personnel Management (OPM) reviews or reconsiders six types of decisions.

---

[17]5 U.S.C. 7116(b).

1. Position Classification Appeals

Employees, who are in General Schedule or Federal Wage System positions, may challenge the classification of their positions. Typically, this challenge is initiated by an employee who believes that the actual duties and responsibilities of his or her position deserve a higher grade classification than that assigned to it.

2. Life Insurance

When an agency or OPM denies regular or optional life insurance coverage, the affected employee, retired employee, or survivor may request that OPM review or reconsider the decision.

3. Health Insurance

When an agency or OPM issues a decision regarding registration or enrollment matters under the Federal Health Benefits Program, the affected employee (active or retired) or employee's survivors may request that OPM review or reconsider that decision.

4. Examination Ratings

An applicant for employment may be required to take an examination. The applicant may challenge the resulting rating by appealing to OPM.

5. Retirement

All claims for benefits and refunds under the civil service retirement system must be adjudicated by OPM before appealing to MSPB.

6. Fair Labor Standards Act (FLSA)

The FLSA sets certain compensation standards for private and public sector employers.[18] The provisions relating to the private sector are administered by the U.S. Department of Labor. The provisions relating to

---

[18]29 U.S.C. 204(f). However, the Equal Pay Act amendment to the FLSA is administered for both the private and public sector by the EEOC. See 29 U.S.C. 206(d) and 29 C.F.R. Part 1620. See Chapter 2, "Using the EEO Complaints Procedure," and Chapter 5, "The Equal Pay Act," for a discussion of the Equal Pay Act.

federal employees are administered by OPM.[19] The FLSA sets minimum wage requirements and prohibits employers from allowing employees to work overtime without compensation. The FLSA covers all "civil service employees," as defined in the introductory material to this chapter, and any other employee of an agency who is not specifically excluded from coverage of the Act.[20]

Other Agency Actions

This final category contains a variety of miscellaneous agency actions, both disciplinary and nondisciplinary. An employee may raise these actions in the agency administrative grievance procedure, unless the employee is a member of a bargaining unit. In that case, these actions would have to be raised in the negotiated grievance procedure (see Chapter 2, "Using the Negotiated Grievance Procedure" and "Agency Administrative Grievance Procedures"). The only disciplinary actions in this category are minor ones—suspensions from work for less than 14 days and reprimands. Employee challenges to performance appraisals usually fall into this category. However, an allegation that a low performance appraisal was based upon prohibited discrimination, a prohibited personnel practice, or an unfair labor practice could shift a performance appraisal challenge out of the agency administrative grievance procedure and into the EEO complaints process, into the Special Counsel investigation of a prohibited personnel practice, or into an unfair labor practice complaint, respectively. However, the typical case involving a disputed performance appraisal, more often than not, involves factual disputes such as the nature of the work assigned, the judgment of the supervisor, or the quality of the employee's work product. Such challenges belong in this category of "Other Agency Actions."

Any other complaints an employee may have regarding general working conditions also fall in this category. Examples might include a challenge to—

- a decision to reassign or transfer an employee to another position without a loss of pay or reduction in grade,

---

[19]OPM regulations at 5 C.F.R. 551 provide for OPM review of alleged violations of the FLSA. However, review by OPM is not a mandatory prerequisite to a lawsuit in federal district court challenging an agency's failure to comply with the requirements of the FLSA.

[20]5 C.F.R. 551.103. Coverage includes, e.g., employees of nonappropriated fund instrumentalities of executive agencies or military departments. Some agencies excluded from coverage are the Library of Congress, the Postal Service, the Postal Rate Commission, and the Tennessee Valley Authority. 5 C.F.R. 551.102(b) and (d).

- a decision to prohibit the use of individual floor fans in an office,
- a decision denying an employee's request for training,
- a decision changing an employee's work assignments or tour of duty.

If the reason for a management decision or action regarding a condition of employment represents prohibited discrimination or is intended, for example, to discourage or encourage membership in a labor organization, then the decision or action is not properly categorized as an Other Agency Action, but rather an EEO violation or an unfair labor practice, respectively. Like performance appraisals, some of the above management decisions constitute "personnel actions." (See Chapter 4 for a definition of "personnel action.") If the reason for the personnel action is a prohibited personnel practice, the employee may elect to appeal it as an Other Agency Action or as a prohibited personnel practice or both (see Chapter 2, "Prohibited Personnel Practices," "Agency Administrative Grievance Procedures," and "Using the Negotiated Grievance Procedure").

2. Where and How to Challenge an Agency Action

CARL D. MOORE

In the previous chapter we discussed the seven categories of agency actions that may be challenged. The seven adjudicatory systems responsible for reviewing these categories have very specifically defined jurisdictions. The administrative forums for appealing the various categories of agency actions generally are:

Category of Agency Action	*Adjudicatory Systems*
Appealable Actions	(a) Merit Systems Protection Board
	(b) Negotiated Grievance Procedure
EEO Violations	(a) Agency EEO Complaints Procedure
	(b) Negotiated Grievance Procedure
Mixed Cases	(a) Merit Systems Protection Board
	(b) Agency EEO Complaints Procedure
	(c) Negotiated Grievance Procedure
Prohibited Personnel Practices	(a) Special Counsel of the Merit Systems Protection Board
	(b) Negotiated Grievance Procedure

14

Category of Agency Action	*Adjudicatory Systems*
Unfair Labor Practices	(a) Federal Labor Relations Authority
	(b) Negotiated Grievance Procedure
Actions Reviewable by the Office of Personnel Management	(a) Office of Personnel Management
Other Agency Actions	(a) Agency Administrative Grievance Procedure
	(b) Negotiated Grievance Procedure

This chapter discusses the procedures for filing challenges in each of these adjudicatory systems. It also discusses two circumstances in which the areas of responsibility of the above forums overlap, that is, occasions when two or more systems have jurisdiction over the same case. These are (1) "mixed cases," and (2) situations where a member of a bargaining unit is raising an EEO allegation or an unfair labor practice allegation in conjunction with an "appealable action" or a member of a bargaining unit is challenging an adverse action or a performance-related action. In these instances, the individual, particularly a member of a bargaining unit, may have a choice of forums in which to pursue a case. The conditions under which such alternative procedures may be followed will be discussed under the appropriate section of this chapter.

Appealable Actions and the Merit Systems Protection Board

The Merit Systems Protection Board (MSPB) was created by Congress with jurisdiction limited to specific subjects. These subjects are referred to as "appealable actions."[1] Employees who are not members of bargaining units must use the MSPB procedure for review of appealable actions. However, employees who are members of bargaining units may elect, in certain circumstances, to use the negotiated grievance procedure,[2] the unfair labor practice procedure,[3] or the MSPB procedure.

---

[1]See Chapter 1 for a definition of "appealable actions" and Chapter 3 for a discussion of the law of appealable actions.

[2]See "Using the Negotiated Grievance Procedure," *infra*, for a definition and description of this procedure.

[3]See "Processing an Unfair Labor Practice Charge," *infra*, for a definition and description of this procedure. The substance of the unfair labor practices is discussed in Chapter 8.

The circumstances in which members of collective bargaining units may have an election between these various procedures is discussed elsewhere.[4] In this discussion, we assume that the employee has decided to file in the MSPB process.

What to File

The MSPB has a standard appeals form.[5] Use of this form is not mandatory, however. An individual may properly appeal to the MSPB by simply writing a letter stating the following:

1. his or her name, address, and telephone number and the name and address of the acting agency;
2. the action taken by the agency and its effective date;
3. whether a hearing is desired;
4. the reasons why the appellant believes the agency action to be wrong;
5. the corrective action the appellant would like the administrative judge[6] to order;
6. the name, address, and telephone number of the appellant's representative, if any; and
7. whether the appellant or anyone acting on his or her behalf has or has not filed a grievance or complaint with any agency regarding this matter.

The letter must be signed by the appellant (and by the representative, if there is one) and it must have attached any relevant documents, such as the notice of the proposed action, the employee's response, and the notice of the final action.[7]

Where to File

The petition for appeal must be filed with the MSPB regional office in the area where the appellant's duty station was located when the agency action was taken.[8]

---

[4]See "Using the Negotiated Grievance Procedure," *infra*, for a discussion of these various elections open to bargaining unit members.

[5]See Appendix I in 5 C.F.R. 1201.

[6]In 1986 the MSPB changed the name of the officials that conduct hearings for the Board from "Presiding Official" to "Administrative Judge."

[7]5 C.F.R. 1201.24(a).

[8]5 C.F.R. 1201.4(e) and 1201.22(a). Filing with appellant's agency rather than with the MSPB is improper and could lead to an untimely filing. *Auzenne v. Postal Serv.*, 83 FMSR 5006 (MSPB 1983). However, misdirecting an appeal to MSPB headquarters is still an effective filing. *Jackson v. Department of the Army*, 7 MSPB 362 (1981). See Appendix 2 of this volume for a listing of the MSPB regional offices and their addresses. The official listing is found at Appendix II in 5 C.F.R. 1201.

When to File

The petition for appeal must be filed within 20 calendar days of the effective date of the action.[9] This is easily determined because the employee receives written notice of the effective date of the agency action. The time limit may be waived by the MSPB when there is no prejudice to the agency and when good cause is shown for such waiver.[10]

The agency has 15 days from the date of receipt of the petition of appeal from the MSPB to respond.[11] After the initial petition for appeal is distributed by the Board, the parties' are required to serve copies of any further pleadings upon each other.[12]

---

[9]5 C.F.R. 1201.22(b).

[10]5 C.F.R. 1201.22(c). See also *Moschner v. Postal Serv.*, 7 MSPB 375 (1981); *McAdory v. Department of Justice*, 6 MSPB 106 (1981); *Alonzo v. Department of the Air Force*, 4 MSPB 262 (1980); *Booker v. Postal Serv.*, 5 MSPB 267 (1981). The MSPB subsequently recited the following criteria which, though not all-inclusive, are to be considered by administrative judges in these cases:

> the length of the delay, whether the appellant was notified of the time limit or was otherwise aware of it, the existence of circumstances beyond the control of the appellant which affected his ability to comply with the time limits; the degree to which negligence by the appellant has been shown to be present or absent; circumstances which show that any neglect involved is excusable neglect [which is more than mere forgetfulness, but rather is behavior expected of a reasonably prudent person]; a showing of unavoidable casualty or misfortune [which could not have been prevented by the exercise of reasonable skill and diligence]; and the extent and nature of the prejudice to the agency which would result from waiver of the time limit [including whether the agency's ability to defend its action has been impaired by the appellant's untimely filing].

Alonzo v. Department of the Interior, 4 MSPB 262, 264 (1980).

For cases in which untimeliness was waived, see also *Smith v. Postal Serv.*, 40 MSPR 201 (MSPB 1989); *Shiflett v. Postal Serv.*, 839 F.2d 669 (Fed. Cir. 1988) (time limit must be waived when agency fails to inform employee of applicable time limit); *Mirach v. Postal Serv.*, 84 FMSR 5139 (MSPB 1984) (agency failed to provide notice of time limits); *Stroup v. Department of the Air Force*, 6 MSPB 155 (1981) (agency misrepresented appeal rights to employee); *Meehan v. Postal Serv.*, 7 MSPB 106 (1981) (MSPB officials misled appellant); *Darrah v. Department of the Navy*, 3 MSPB 455 (1980) (medication that caused some confusion was good cause); *Nagel v. HHS*, 5 MSPB 303 (1981) (short delay excused where evidence showed employee diligently attempting to retain legal counsel but was having considerable problem doing so).

For cases in which untimeliness was not excused, see also *Buttram v. Postal Serv.*, 83 FMSR 5013 (MSPB 1983) (erroneous advice from union that confuses appellant is not good cause); *Phillips v. Postal Serv.*, 695 F.2d 1389 (Fed. Cir. 1982) (negligence of selected representative is attributable to appellant); *Hines v. TVA*, 4 MSPB 492 (1980) (delay caused by working another job while preparing to file appeal not excusable); *Gray v. Interior*, 40 MSPR 155 (MSPB 1989) (attorney's secretary's "belief" that letter would be postmarked same day she deposited it in mail does not represent ordinary prudence in ensuring petition was timely filed).

[11]5 C.F.R. 1201.26(b) and (c).

[12]5 C.F.R. 1201.26(b).

Right to Representation

The appellant has a right to an attorney or other representative in MSPB proceedings.[13] However, that provision merely means that the appellant has a right to obtain representation.[14] It does not mean that, as in criminal proceedings in this country, the MSPB has an obligation to provide representation.[15] The rules of the MSPB require that the appellant designate his or her representative in writing, give notice of any changes or revocation in writing, and serve the other parties with such notice.[16] The only restriction on the selection of a representative is that the representative cannot serve if it would constitute a "conflict of interest or conflict of position."[17]

A challenge to a representative must be filed with the administrative judge within 15 days after the agency receives notice of the designation.[18] Most of the reported cases from the MSPB involve situations in which a union representative has been designated to represent a management official. The argument has been that being represented by the union would compromise the official's position in later dealings for management with the bargaining unit members. The decisions have focused on whether there was an "actual" conflict of interest or merely a very remote possibility of a conflict.[19]

Intervenors

An intervenor is someone other than the employee-appellant and the agency who claims to have an interest in the outcome of the proceedings. The law recognizes the Director of the Office of Personnel Management (OPM) and the Special Counsel of the MSPB as having a right to intervene in a case before the Board. Any other individual must petition for permission from the MSPB to participate as an intervenor and demonstrate that the proceeding will affect them directly. The latter is referred to as a "permissive intervenor."[20]

---

[13] 5 U.S.C. 7701(a)(2).
[14] *Feathers v. OPM*, 85 FMSR 5229 (MSPB 1985).
[15] *Marsheck v. Department of Transp.*, 83 FMSR 5142 (MSPB 1983).
[16] 5 C.F.R. 1201.31(a).
[17] 5 C.F.R. 1201.31(b).
[18] *Id.*
[19] In *Shorter v. Department of the Air Force*, 85 FMSR 5370 (MSPB 1985) and *Alberio v. Hampton*, 433 F. Supp. 447 (D.P.R. 1970), the union representatives were disqualified. On the other hand, the union representative was not disqualified in *Sweeney v. Department of the Treasury*, 81 FMSR 5370 (MSPB 1981).
[20] 5 C.F.R. 1201.35(a).

An intervenor is a party to the case and, for the most part, enjoys the same rights as the principal parties. There are two exceptions to this rule. Intervenors do not have the right to a hearing and permissive intervenors may participate in the hearing only on issues that directly affect them.[21]

The Director of OPM has a right to intervene either while the case is at the regional office or when it is before the Board. To be timely, the Director must intervene within 20 days of the date of service of the response to the petition for review or within 20 days of the date of service of the cross-petition in response to the petition for review.[22] The Director of OPM may intervene on the grounds that the decision is erroneous and will have a substantial impact on any civil service law, rule, or regulation under the jurisdiction of OPM.[23]

The Special Counsel of the MSPB also has a right to intervene in cases either when they are before the regional office or when they are before the MSPB. The time limit for intervention is the same for the Special Counsel as for the Director of OPM.[24]

Among those who are recognized by the rules as potential permissive intervenors are individuals who are alleged to have committed a prohibited personnel practice in the appellant's case.[25] Since the law allows the Special Counsel to prosecute those responsible for prohibited personnel practices,[26] an employee's allegation that a particular supervisor or manager committed a prohibited personnel practice could warrant allowing the supervisor or manager to become a permissive intervenor in the employee's appeal to the MSPB. If the motion to intervene is denied by the administrative judge, the most appropriate challenge would be an interlocutory appeal.[27]

Discovery

The director of the MSPB regional office assigns each case to an administrative judge who has the sole responsibility for processing it until he or she issues a decision. The administrative judge conducts most of the appeals hearings for the MSPB. This includes setting a hearing date when

[21]5 C.F.R. 1201.34(d).
[22]5 C.F.R. 1201.114(g).
[23]5 U.S.C. 7701(e)(2).
[24]5 C.F.R. 1201.114(g)(2).
[25]5 C.F.R. 1201.114(g)(3).
[26]5 U.S.C. 1206(g).
[27]*Crumbaker v. Department of Labor,* 7 MSPB 15 (1981). For the lay reader, an interlocutory appeal is a challenge to a ruling that goes to the MSPB before the case itself is decided. See 5 C.F.R. 1201.91–1201.93 for an explanation and description of the procedure.

a hearing is requested and overseeing the discovery process. Under its regulations the MSPB has provided for a discovery process similar to that of federal courts. This may include taking depositions of witnesses, requesting relevant documents, and requesting written answers from witnesses to questions presented in writing. Although not bound by the Federal Rules of Civil Procedure,[28] administrative judges are to use the Rules as a guide in discovery matters.[29]

Like the Federal Rules of Civil Procedure, the MSPB Rules anticipate that the parties will engage in voluntary discovery. This means that the parties are to begin the process of exchanging information and should turn to the administrative judge only when they disagree regarding the discovery process.

The process begins when one party serves on the other a request for discovery. The MSPB Rules anticipate that discovery will move quite rapidly. The initial request for discovery must be served within 25 days after the date of issuance of the Board's order to the agency to respond to the petition for appeal, and discovery is to be completed no later than 65 days after the filing of the petition for appeal.[30]

Discovery from a person or federal agency that is not a party to the proceeding should also begin as a voluntary process.[31] Therefore, like discovery between the parties, discovery from another person or from a federal agency should require attention from the administrative judge only when there is disagreement regarding the discovery process.

In the event that the party or nonparty to whom a discovery request is made fails or refuses to respond in full or in part to a discovery request, then the party seeking the information should file a motion with the administrative judge to compel the nonresponding individual to comply with the discovery request. The motion to compel should be accompanied by the following:

1. a copy of the original request and a statement showing the relevancy and materiality of the information sought;
2. a copy of the objections to discovery or, where appropriate, a statement with accompanying affidavit that no response has been received.[32]

---

[28]For the layman, the Federal Rules of Civil Procedure are the rules used by U.S. District Courts in the processing of civil cases. It is available in any law library or may be purchased in paperback from any legal bookstore.
[29]5 C.F.R. 1201.72(a).
[30]5 C.F.R. 1201.73(d)(2) and (5).
[31]5 C.F.R. 1201.73(b).
[32]5 C.F.R. 1201.73(c)(2).

This motion to compel discovery must be filed with the administrative judge within 10 days of the date of service of the objections from the other party, or within 10 days of the expiration of the time limit for response when the other party has failed to respond.[33]

Administrative judges are empowered to order parties and nonparties to provide all relevant information to the requesting party. Relevant information is defined by the MSPB as information "which appears reasonably calculated to lead to the discovery of admissible evidence."[34] Therefore, discovery can include not only admissible evidence, but also facts which might lead to discovery of admissible evidence.[35] Anyone failing to comply with an order of an administrative judge to provide evidence may be subject to the following sanctions by the judge:

1. draw an inference in favor of the requesting party with regard to the information sought,
2. prohibit the party failing to comply with such order from introducing evidence concerning or otherwise relying upon testimony relating to the information sought,
3. permit the requesting party to introduce secondary evidence concerning the information sought, and
4. strike any appropriate part of the pleading or other submissions of the party failing to comply with such order.[36]

Hearing Before the Administrative Judge

The employee has a right to a hearing as long as it is timely requested[37] and as long as the MSPB has jurisdiction over the matter.[38] However, the agency has no right to a hearing. Whether an administrative judge grants an agency's request for a hearing is within the discretion of

---

[33]5 C.F.R. 1201.73(c)(4).

[34]*Supra* note 29.

[35]*Bize v. Department of the Treasury*, 3 MSPB 261 (1980).

[36]5 C.F.R. 1201.43. This section of the MSPB rules states that sanctions are imposed where the ends of justice require it, including where a party fails to comply with an order, where a party fails to prosecute or defend an action, or where a party fails to make a timely filing. See also *Stone v. OPM*, 5 MSPB 142 (1981). Sanctions are available for disobeying the MSPB's rules in any material way. *Johnson v. District of Columbia Bd. of Educ.*, 7 MSPB 481 (1981) (agency unreasonably fails to respond to appeal resulting in reversal of challenged action). However, absent repeated violations, such sanctions are not appropriate. *Conner v. Postal Serv.*, 5 MSPB 194 (1981).

[37]5 U.S.C. 7101(a)(1); *Ensminger v. Department of the Army*, 4 MSPB 367 (1980); *Sweat v. OPM*, 40 MSPR 84 (MSPB 1989) (MSPB will hold hearings at locations more convenient than its regional office cities and will hold telephone hearings).

[38]*Wizi v. Department of the Treasury*, 6 MSPB 169 (1981).

the respective judge. In denying the request, however, the judge must provide the reason for the denial. A denial without explanation is not acceptable to the Board.[39]

MSPB hearings are relatively formal administrative proceedings. The parties make opening statements, testimony of witnesses is taken, documentary evidence is received, and closing arguments are made.[40] The parties may subpoena witnesses for the hearings.[41] Federal employees who are called as witnesses, by the appellant or by the agency, must be made available at the respondent agency's expense, while all other witnesses should be subpoenaed and paid witness fees.[42]

Burden of Proof

In most cases before the MSPB, the agency has the burden of showing that, based on the evidence in the applicable law, the action it took against the appellant was more likely correct than incorrect.[43] If the agency action is based on the appellant's failure to meet the performance standards of his or her position, it has a lower burden of proof. The agency must show that based upon the evidence and applicable law, the action taken by the agency appears reasonable.[44] If an appellant is appealing the denial of an application for disability retirement, OPM is obliged to come forward with evidence and an explanation for its determination. However, the appellant has the ultimate burden in this instance of persuading the MSPB by a preponderance of the evidence.[45] An appellant who has received an overpayment from the Civil Service Retirement and Disability Fund has the burden of proving by substantial evidence that he or she is eligible for a waiver or adjustment.[46]

---

[39]*Thompson v. Department of Transp.*, 82 FMSR 5040 (MSPB 1982). See also *Schoenberg v. Department of the Army*, 40 MSPR 89 (MBSB 1989) (administrative judge abused discretion in terminating hearing when employee was reasonably incapable of proceeding).

[40]5 C.F.R. 1201.51 *et seq*.

[41]5 C.F.R. 1201.81.

[42]5 C.F.R. 1201.37(b). It should be noted that the rules provide that the employees of any federal agency or corporation testifying in any proceeding before the MSPB or making a statement for the record shall be in an official duty status and not receive witness fees. Payment of travel and per diem expenses are governed by the applicable law and regulation.

[43]Technically this standard of proof is referred to as the "preponderance of the evidence." See 5 U.S.C. 7701(c)(1)(B); 5 C.F.R. 1201.56(a)(1)(ii); *Parker v. Defense Logistics Agency*, 1 MSPB 489 (1980).

[44]Technically this standard is referred to as "substantial evidence." 5 U.S.C. 7701(c)(1)(A); 5 C.F.R. 1201.56(a)(1)(i); *Parker v. Defense Logistics Agency, supra* note 43.

[45]*Chavez v. OPM*, 6 MSPB 343 (1981).

[46]5 C.F.R. 1201.56(a).

If issues arise in the case regarding jurisdiction of the MSPB or timeliness of the employee's filing with the MSPB, the appellant must prove by a preponderance of the evidence that the MSPB has jurisdiction over the case or that the filing with the MSPB was timely. [47] If the appellant raises affirmative defenses, the appellant has the burden of proving those defenses by a preponderance of the evidence. [48]

In general, the appellant may raise three types of affirmative defenses in order to overturn the agency action. First, the agency action will be overturned if the appellant demonstrates that the agency committed a prohibited personnel practice in taking the action. [49] Second, the appellant may prove that the agency committed a procedural error in taking the action. For a procedural error to be the basis for overturning an agency action, however, the appellant must show that this error substantially prejudiced his or her ability to defend against the action. [50] Third, the appellant may prove that the agency's "decision was not in accordance with law." [51]

After receiving evidence and holding a hearing (when one is requested), the administrative judge closes the record [52] and issues a decision, which is referred to as the "initial decision."

Review of the Initial Decision by the MSPB

The initial decision becomes final 35 days after it is issued unless one of the parties files a request with the MSPB to reconsider the decision. [53] A petition for review may be filed by either party with the Clerk of the MSPB either by personal delivery during business hours or by mail addressed to the Clerk of the Board. [54] The parties have 35 days from the time the initial decision is issued to file a petition for review with the

[47] 5 C.F.R. 1201.56(a)(2).
[48] Id.
[49] 5 U.S.C. 7701(c)(2)(B); Gerlach v. Federal Trade Comm'n, 8 MSPB 599 (1981).
[50] This is referred to as "harmful error." 5 U.S.C. 7701(c)(2)(A); Hug v. Department of the Army, 4 MSPB 209 (1980). The burden is on the employee to show that absent the agency's procedural error, "a different result might have been reached." The burden, however, is not on the employee "to prove that the [absence of the procedural error] would have changed the result." Mercer v. HHS, 772 F.2d 856 (Fed. Cir. 1985) (emphasis in original). See also Parker v. Defense Logistics Agency, 1 MSPB 489 (1980); Huston v. Department of the Air Force, 6 MSPB 223 (1981).
[51] 5 U.S.C. 7701(c)(2)(C); Lovshin v. Department of the Navy, 767 F.2d 826 (Fed. Cir. 1985), cert. denied, 475 U.S. 1111 (1986).
[52] It must be clear from a formal notice or from other actions of the administrative judge that the record is being closed on a certain date. Meehan v. Postal Serv., 7 MSPB 106 (1981); Martinez v. Defense Logistic Agency, 5 MSPB 16 (1981).
[53] 5 U.S.C. 7701(e); 5 C.F.R. 1201.111 and 1201.113.
[54] 5 C.F.R. 1201.114(c). See Appendix 1 for the address of the MSPB Headquarters.

Board. Any response to a petition for review or a cross-petition for review must be filed within 25 days after the petition for review is served on the party.[55] An extension of time to file a petition for review, a cross-petition for review, or a response may be granted only upon a showing of good cause.[56]

In order to persuade the MSPB successfully to reconsider an initial decision, the party must show either that new and material evidence exists which was not available at the time of the hearing,[57] or that the administrative judge erred in the initial decision in interpreting a statute or regulation.[58] However, the MSPB is not limited to these two criteria in deciding whether to reconsider an initial decision. Since the MSPB can "[t]ake any other action necessary for the final disposition of a case"[59] and since the MSPB "may affirm, reverse, modify, or vacate the decision [of the administrative judge] in whole or in part,"[60] the MSPB has broad discretion in reviewing initial decisions.[61]

In reviewing an initial decision, the Board acts as a Court of Appeals. It reviews briefs filed by the parties and occasionally hears oral argument. If the Board concludes that additional evidence or testimony should be received, however, such evidence is not submitted to the Board. Rather, the case is remanded to the administrative judge.[62]

Settlements in MSPB Cases

Even though a case is appealed to the MSPB, the parties are still free to resolve the case without litigation. If the case is withdrawn as a result of a settlement, but the settlement agreement is not entered into record, the MSPB loses jurisdiction over the case.[63] There is good reason for both the employee and the agency to enter the settlement into the record. When it is entered, the settlement is subject to enforcement proceedings before the

---

[55]5 C.F.R. 1201.114(d).

[56]5 C.F.R. 1201.114(e).

[57]Evidence that the agency elects not to submit at the hearing is not "new evidence." *Powell v. Department of the Interior,* 4 MSPB 35 (1980); *Wakeland v. NTSB,* 6 MSPB 44 (1981); *Wheeler v. Department of the Navy,* 4 MSPB 225 (1980). To be "material," the new evidence must be of sufficient weight to warrant a different outcome from that of the initial decision. *Callahan v. OPM,* 6 MSPB 284 (1981); *Russo v. VA,* 3 MSPB 427 (1980).

[58]5 C.F.R. 1201.115.

[59]*Connolly v. Department of Justice,* 766 F.2d 507 (Fed. Cir. 1985), citing 5 C.F.R. 1201.116(a)(4).

[60]*Id.,* citing 5 C.F.R. 1201.117.

[61]*Id.*

[62]5 C.F.R. 1201.116.

[63]*Banks v. Postal Serv.,* 8 MSPB 124 (1981). A settlement agreement must be reduced to writing in order for it to be enforced by the MSPB. *Robertson v. Postal Serv.,* 37 MSPR 512 (MSPB 1988).

MSPB.[64] This protection is important for the employee and agency alike. For the employee, who is later dissatisfied with the agency's execution of the agreement, there is an available enforcement forum. On the other hand, since the administrative judge is involved in the process and makes some inquiry into the extent to which the settlement is voluntary, it is more difficult for the employee to later challege the voluntariness of the agreement. Thus, when an employee challenges a settlement agreement, it is very difficult for the employee to establish that it was invalid due to fraud by the agency or mutual mistake, because the administrative judge has reviewed the agreement with the parties before entering it into the record.[65]

Attorney's Fees and Enforcement Issues

After a decision becomes final, the administrative judge still retains jurisdiction for certain purposes. Two of these are entertaining a request by the appellant for attorney's fees and processing any petition for enforcement.[66]

A motion for attorney's fees must be filed within 20 days from the date an initial decision becomes final or within 25 days of the date a decision of the full Board becomes final. The agency may file a responsive pleading to a motion for attorney's fees within 20 days of the date it receives the motion.[67] The subject of attorney's fees is discussed in depth in Chapter 12.

The MSPB has authority to order an agency or agency employee to comply with decisions and orders of the MSPB.[68] In general, the agency is to communicate promptly with the employee regarding compliance efforts and advise the employee when compliance is completed. Likewise, the employee is to cooperate with the agency by providing whatever information the agency needs to effect compliance.[69] The petition for enforcement is to be filed with the regional office that processed the original case. The petition should state the reasons for believing compliance has not occurred and detail any communications with the agency about compliance.

---

[64]*Richardson v. EPA*, 5 MSPB 289 (1981).

[65]*Hazlett v. Department of Justice*, 85 FMSR 5015 (MSPB 1985); *Koury v. Small Business Admin.*, 40 MSPR 172 (MSPB 1989).

[66]5 C.F.R. 1201.112. The other purposes for which the administrative judge retains jurisdiction after issuing an initial decision are to rule on proposed corrections to the transcript and to rule on exceptions to the requirement of payment for the transcript.

[67]5 C.F.R. 1201.37(a).

[68]5 U.S.C. 1205(a)(2); 5 C.F.R. 1201.181.

[69]5 C.F.R. 1201.181(b).

If the petition is filed more than 30 days after the agency's notice of compliance, it must include a statement and evidence showing good cause for the delay and requesting an extension of time to file. [70] Within 15 days of receipt of the petition, the agency must respond detailing the nature of its compliance or demonstrating good cause why there is noncompliance or incomplete compliance. [71]

A hearing on the matter is at the discretion of the regional director or the administrative judge, either of whom may hear the case. [72] If it is found that there has been compliance, then a decision is issued. That decision is subject to appeal to the MSPB or to the Court of Appeals for the Federal Circuit just as an initial decision is. [73] If it is found that the agency has not complied with the order, a recommendation is issued. The agency either accepts the recommendation and files a notice of compliance within 15 days or it files a brief with the MSPB arguing why it disagrees with the recommendation. [74] The MSPB considers the agency's argument and any response filed by the employee. It then issues a decision, [75] which is appealable to the courts. [76]

Two points are of particular interest. The enforcement jurisdiction of the MSPB is broader than its appellate jurisdiction. For example, a prohibited personnel practice, which is not accompanied by an appealable action, cannot be heard by the MSPB under its appellate jurisdiction. However, if in taking, or failing to take, compliance action, an agency commits a prohibited personnel practice (i.e., takes reprisal against the employee for having pursued an appeal right), the MSPB will review the allegation even though no appealable action is involved. [77] Second, contrary to its earlier rulings, the MSPB determined in 1984 that it does have authority to adjudicate back pay disputes. Thus, it will instruct the agency to calculate and pay the amount of back pay due, rather than direct the parties to file with the Comptroller General. [78]

Judicial Review of MSPB Decisions

If an initial decision is not challenged and is, therefore, allowed to become final, the appellant has exhausted administrative remedies. If the

---

[70] 5 C.F.R. 1201.182(a).
[71] 5 C.F.R. 1201.183(a).
[72] 5 C.F.R. 1201.183(a)(2).
[73] 5 C.F.R. 1201.183(a)(3).
[74] 5 C.F.R. 1201.183(a)(6).
[75] 5 C.F.R. 1201.183(b).
[76] 5 C.F.R. 1201.183(b)(3).
[77]Meier v. Department of the Interior, 3 MSPB 341 (1980); Anderson v. Department of Agric., 84 FMSR 5527 (MSPB 1984).
[78]Spezzaferro v. FAA, 84 FMSR 7049 (MSPB 1984). For a discussion of back pay issues, see Chapter 13.

initial decision is challenged, the appellant has exhausted administrative remedies when the MSPB denies the petition for review or when it issues a final decision. Once administrative remedies have been exhausted, the appellant or the agency may seek judicial review.

The appellant may appeal an MSPB decision to the Court of Appeals for the Federal Circuit within 30 days after the date the appellant receives the notice of the final decision. [79] However, the appeal of "mixed cases" is very different (see discussion in "Processing a Mixed Case," *infra*).

If an agency wishes to appeal an MSPB final decision to the courts, it must do so through OPM. If the Director of OPM did not intervene in the case while it was pending before the Board, the Director must first petition the Board for reconsideration of its decision and have the petition denied, before appealing to the courts. The Director's appeal of a Board decision to the courts is limited to circumstances where the Director attempts to establish that the Board erred in interpreting a civil service law, rule, or regulation affecting personnel management, and that the Board's decision will have a substantial impact on a civil service law, rule, or regulation, or policy directive. [80]

Using the EEO Complaints Procedure

An employee, or applicant for employment, may file an individual EEO complaint seeking some relief or remedy applicable solely to his or her employment status. Also, an employee, or applicant for employment, may initiate a class action seeking relief or remedies for everyone who may be allegedly suffering from particular discriminatory practices. The procedures for filing individual and class complaints differ in many ways. [81]

Individual EEO Complaints

The EEO complaints procedure is regulated by the Equal Employment Opportunity Commission (EEOC). Each agency is required to issue

---

[79] The Civil Service Reform Act provided for appeals to the circuit courts and the Court of Claims. However, with the creation of the Court of Appeals for the Federal Circuit, all jurisdiction for MSPB cases rests with that court. The Court of Appeals for the Federal Circuit became effective on October 1, 1982. 28 U.S.C. 1295(a)(9).

[80] 5 U.S.C. 7703(d).

[81] This discussion is limited to the procedures used to raise an EEO allegation in the EEO complaint process. For a discussion of substantive EEO law in federal employment, see Chapter 5. Also note that at our publication time, the EEOC had approved proposed rule changes that would replace 29 C.F.R. Part 1613 with a new Part 1614. The proposed changes represent a dramatic departure from the procedures described here. At the same time, bills are being considered in Congress that would radically change the EEO complaint process.

regulations establishing a complaints procedure in line with the EEOC regulations.[82] When a collective bargaining agreement does not exclude EEO allegations from the negotiated grievance procedure, members of the bargaining unit may use the negotiated grievance procedure rather than the EEO complaints procedure. The members of a bargaining unit may file an "informal complaint" or consult with an EEO counselor without sacrificing their election between the negotiated grievance procedure and the EEO complaints procedure. However, filing a grievance in the negotiated grievance procedure or filing a "formal" EEO complaint constitutes an election that the bargaining unit member cannot change[83] (see also "Using the Negotiated Grievance Procedure," infra). This discussion assumes that the employee has elected to use the EEO complaints procedure.

Consulting an EEO Counselor

When an employee, or applicant for employment, believes that he or she has been discriminated against on the basis of race, color, religion, sex, national origin, handicapping condition, or reprisal for a protected EEO activity, the first step in the complaint process requires consultation with an agency EEO counselor.[84] Contact must be made with the counselor within 30 calendar days of the date that the complainant knew or reasonably should have known of the discriminatory event or personnel action.[85] The complainant has a right to be accompanied, represented, and advised by a representative of his or her own choosing. If the complainant is an agency employee, he or she is entitled to a "reasonable amount of official time" to present the complaint. The complainant may select another employee of the agency as a representative, unless the representation role would conflict with the official or collateral duties of the representative. If the complainant selects another agency employee as a representative, the representative is also given a "reasonable amount of official time" to present the complaint.[86]

The EEO counselor is required (1) to make whatever inquiry he or she believes is necessary into the matter, (2) to seek a solution to the

---

[82]29 C.F.R. 1613.211–1613.222.

[83]29 C.F.R. 1613.219.

[84]Note that there is no requirement that the administrative procedure be exhausted for an allegation of sex discrimination under the Equal Pay Act or for age discrimination. See "Processing Allegations of Equal Pay Act Violations" and "Processing Allegations of Age Discrimination in Employment Act Violations," infra. See also note 135.

[85]29 C.F.R. 1613.214(a)(1)(i).

[86]29 C.F.R. 1613.214(b).

matter on an informal basis, and (3) to counsel the individual who is raising the complaint.

During the counseling stage the counselor may not reveal the identity of the complaining party, unless authorized to do so by that individual. As a practical matter, the counselor can rarely do more than listen to and counsel the individual if such authorization is withheld. In most situations, investigation or settlement efforts by the counselor require that the individual's identity be revealed.

The regulations prohibit a counselor from attempting in any way to restrain an individual from filing a complaint.[87] The agency is required to assure that full cooperation is provided by all employees to the counselor in the performance of his or her duties. The regulations dictate that counselors are to be free from restraint, interference, coercion, discrimination, or reprisal in connection with the performance of their duties.[88]

No later than 21 calendar days after the individual contacts the counselor, the latter is to conduct a final interview. If the matter is not resolved to the satisfaction of the individual within that 21-day period, he or she is to be notified by the counselor in writing of his or her right to file a formal complaint of discrimination.

This notice from the counselor informs the individual of three important matters. First, it advises that a formal complaint of discrimination must be filed within 15 calendar days. Second, it identifies the agency official with whom the complaint must be filed. Finally, it requests that the agency be informed immediately if the individual retains legal counsel or any other representative.

Rejection or Cancellation of a Complaint

Once the formal complaint is filed, the EEO officer[89] will receive from the counselor a written report summarizing the counselor's actions and advice. The complainant will receive a copy of this report.[90] The EEO officer must make a decision as to whether to reject or accept the complaint. The complaint may be rejected or, if it is accepted initially, it may be canceled later if it is in one of the following seven categories:

---

[87]29 C.F.R. 1613.213(a).
[88]29 C.F.R. 1613.213(b) and (c).
[89]The EEO Officer is the official designated to represent the agency or agency subdivision in EEO complaints. The EEO Counselor, on the other hand, is an agency employee designated to hear the informal complaint, attempt resolution of the informal complaint, and assist the employee in filing a formal complaint.
[90]29 C.F.R. 1613.213(a).

1. It fails to state a claim of discrimination based upon race, color, religion, sex, national origin, age, or handicapping condition[91] or it states a claim that is pending before or has been decided previously by the agency;
2. It alleges that an agency is "proposing" to take action that may be discriminatory;
3. It is the basis of a pending civil action in a U.S. District Court in which the complainant is a party;
4. It is filed untimely;
5. It is a matter that the complainant first filed under the negotiated grievance procedure (see "Using the Negotiated Grievance Procedure," *infra*);
6. It is a matter the complainant has failed to prosecute; or
7. The complainant refuses an offer of full relief in settlement of the complaint.

The last two categories require some further comment. Before canceling a complaint for lack of prosecution, the agency must notify the complainant in writing that the complaint will be canceled unless the complainant provides certain information or otherwise proceeds with the complaint. If the complainant fails to respond within 15 days after receipt of this notice, the agency may cancel the complaint or the agency may issue a decision on the complaint if sufficient information is available.

Likewise, the agency may cancel a complaint if the complainant refuses to accept an offer of full relief. The complainant must have 15 days to consider the offer and the appropriate agency official must have certified in writing that the agency's offer constitutes full relief.[92] The offer need not contain the decision whether disciplinary action is appropriate. However, the agency must make such a decision and record the basis for that decision separately from the complaint file.[93] In transmitting the decision to reject or cancel a complaint to the complainant and to the complainant's representative, the agency must state the time limit for filing an appeal with the EEOC and state the complainant's right to file an action in federal court (see "Appealing to the EEOC" and "Filing in Federal Court," *infra*).[94]

---

[91]29 C.F.R. 1613.212 also notes that a complaint may be filed by an organization on behalf of an aggrieved person with the person's consent. Finally, 29 C.F.R. 1613.212 incorporates by reference the definition of a class complaint, which is found in Subpart F of the regulations (see "EEO Class Complaints," *infra*).

[92]The scope of available remedial action is defined by the EEO at 29 C.F.R. 1613.271.

[93]29 C.F.R. 1613.215(a).

[94]29 C.F.R. 1613.215(b).

Investigation of a Complaint

If the agency accepts the complaint, someone must be appointed to investigate the allegation of discrimination. The investigator may not occupy a position that is directly or indirectly under the jurisdiction of the head of that part of the agency in which the complaint arose. The agency must provide to the person conducting the investigation written authorization to (1) investigate all aspects of complaints of discrimination, (2) require all employees of the agency to cooperate with the investigator in the conduct of the investigation, and (3) require employees of the agency having any knowledge of the matter complained of to furnish testimony under oath or affirmation and without giving employees a pledge that their statements will be in confidence.[95]

The investigator compiles an investigative file, which includes written statements (affidavits) from the complainant and witnesses, together with copies of records, policy statements, or regulations that may relate to the complaint.[96]

At the conclusion of the investigation, the complainant and his or her representative are given a copy of the investigative file. The complainant is given an opportunity at this time to discuss the file with appropriate agency officials. If the agency or the complainant agree to settle the matter at this point, it is referred to as an "informal adjustment." The settlement must be reduced to writing and included in the investigative file.[97] If the parties agree on an adjustment of the complaint, but cannot agree on attorney's fees or costs, the issue of whether to award fees or costs, or the issue of the amount of fees or costs may be severed. In other words, the substance of the complaint may be resolved by agreement between the parties and the complainant may still pursue the issue relating to attorney's fees or costs to the EEOC (see "Appealing to the EEOC," infra).[98]

Decision Without a Hearing

If there is no informal adjustment of the complaint, then the agency must notify the complainant of its proposed disposition. The agency must also advise the complainant that he or she has a right to a decision by the agency head or designee, either with, or without, a hearing. If the complainant does not reply within 15 calendar days, the proposed dis-

[95] 29 C.F.R. 1613.216(b).
[96] 29 C.F.R. 1613.216(a).
[97] 29 C.F.R. 1613.217(a).
[98] Id. and 29 C.F.R. 1613.231(a)(3).

position can be adopted as the final agency decision. If the complainant does not respond, or if the complainant elects not to have a hearing, the agency head or designee issues a decision letter stating the findings, analysis, and decision of the agency.[99]

Decision With a Hearing

If the complainant elects to have a hearing, the person who conducts the hearing, an administrative judge, is selected by the EEOC from its staff or from the staff of an agency not involved in the complaint.[100] The administrative judge first receives the investigation file and determines whether further investigation is necessary, prior to holding a hearing. If the administrative judge determines that further investigation is needed, he or she may either remand the case to the agency for further investigation or call the witnesses needed to supply the necessary information at the hearing.[101] The administrative judge has the power to conduct an orderly hearing and collect evidence relevant to the complaint. These powers include authority to:

1. administer oaths or affirmations;
2. regulate the course of the hearing;
3. rule on offers of proof and receive relevant evidence;
4. order the production of documents, records, comparative data, statistics, and affidavits or the attendance of witnesses;
5. limit the number of witnesses whose testimony would be unduly repetitious; and
6. exclude any person from the hearing for contempt or misbehavior that obstructs the hearing.[102]

The complainant and the agency may call witnesses and cross-examine them. Testimony is taken under oath or affirmation.[103] The hearing is recorded and a verbatim transcript made.[104] While the judicial rules of evidence do not apply in these hearings, the administrative judge is expected to exclude irrelevant or unduly repetitious evidence.[105] If either party in bad faith refuses or fails without adequate explanation to

---

[99]29 C.F.R. 1613.217(c) and (d) and 1613.221(b)(3).
[100]29 C.F.R. 1613.218(a).
[101]29 C.F.R. 1613.218(b).
[102]29 C.F.R. 1613.218(d).
[103]29 C.F.R. 1613.218(c)(2). See Also *Jordan v. Hudson*, 47 FEP Cases 583 (E.D. Va. 1988) (federal employee who testifies against supervisor regarding alleged sexual harassment is immune from being sued in state court for allegedly false testimony).
[104]29 C.F.R. 1613.218(h).
[105]*Supra* note 103.

respond fully to proper requests for information, the administrative judge may take appropriate action, including—

1. drawing an adverse inference that the requested information would have reflected unfavorably on the party refusing to provide the requested information,
2. considering the matters to which the requested information pertains to be established in favor of the opposing party,
3. excluding other evidence offered by the party failing to produce the requested information, and
4. taking such other action as the administrative judge deems appropriate.[106]

Employees of the Federal Government who are called by the agency, the complainant, or the administrative judge as witnesses are to be in a duty status for pay and travel purposes during the time they are made available as witnesses.[107]

Although it provides the administrative judge, the EEOC does not assume jurisdiction over the complaint. This is still the "agency EEO complaints procedure." It is designed to provide the agency with sufficient information to render an agency decision. It also creates a record for EEOC review in the event that the employee appeals the agency decision to the EEOC.

Following the hearing, the administrative judge sends the agency (1) the "complaint file," which includes the investigative file and the hearing record;[108] (2) the findings and analysis of the administrative judge; and (3) the administrative judge's recommended decision. The administrative judge advises the complainant of the date on which this was done. In addition, by separate letter to the agency, the judge provides whatever findings and recommendations the administrative judge considers appropriate with respect to conditions in the agency that do not bear directly on the matter but either gave rise to the complaint or bear on the general environment out of which the complaint arose.[109]

---

[106]29 C.F.R. 1613.218(e).

[107]Although administrative judges do not have subpoena power, they can require agencies to make federal employees available as witnesses unless it is "administratively impracticable." Even when it is administratively impracticable for a federal employee to appear at the hearing, the administrative judge can make arrangements to otherwise secure the testimony of the employee. 29 C.F.R. 1613.218(f).

[108]The documents that are required to be in the "complaint file" are recited at 29 C.F.R. 1613.222. It includes such things as the counselor's report, the formal complaint, and the investigative file. One important provision is that no document may be included in the complaint file unless it has been made available to the complainant. 29 C.F.R. 1613.222(b).

[109]29 C.F.R. 1613.218(i).

If the agency does not issue a decision within 60 days after receiving the administrative judge's recommended decision, the recommended decision becomes the final decision and is binding on the agency. In this circumstance, the agency is still responsible for furnishing the complainant with the administrative judge's decision, a copy of the record, and with notice of the complainant's right to appeal to the EEOC or to file in federal court.[110]

When the agency does issue the complainant a timely decision, it must contain a copy of the administrative judge's recommended decision and a copy of the hearing record. It must be remembered, however, that the administrative judge's decision is only a recommendation to the agency. The final decision of the agency may adopt, reject, or modify the recommended decision of the administrative judge.[111]

If the final agency decision rejects or modifies the administrative judge's recommended decision, the agency decision must state in detail the specific reasons for rejecting or modifying the findings or conclusions of law in the recommended decision and advise the complainant of the right to an EEOC appeal or to file in federal district court.[112]

If the agency decision finds discrimination, it must take the appropriate remedial action (see discussion below) and provide notice that any request for attorney's fees or costs must be documented and submitted within 20 calendar days of receipt of the agency decision. Separate from the communication with the complainant, the agency must determine whether disciplinary action is appropriate for the managers or supervisors responsible for the discriminatory action against the complainant. The basis for the agency's decision to take, or not to take, disciplinary action must be recorded separately from the complaint file.[113]

An agency decision finding discrimination creates a presumption that attorney's fees and costs should be awarded (see Chapter 12). A decision of the agency on the complaint is not final until the decision on attorney's fees and costs has been made.[114] In the event that the agency denies all or any part of the requested fees or costs, it must state the specific reasons for its decision and advise the complainant of the right to an EEOC appeal or to file in federal district court.[115]

---

[110]29 C.F.R. 1613.220(d).
[111]29 C.F.R. 1613.221(b)(2).
[112]29 C.F.R. 1613.221(b)(1) and (2) and 1613.221(e).
[113]29 C.F.R. 1613.221(c). When the agency accepts the recommended finding of discrimination, it must, no later than 60 days after receipt of the recommendation, provide "to the fullest extent possible, make-whole relief and issue its final agency decision on all isues with specificity." *Kalra v. Skinner*, 89 FEOR 1067 (EEOC 1989).
[114]29 C.F.R. 1613.233(a).
[115]29 C.F.R. 1613.221(d) and (e).

Appealing to the EEOC

The complainant may appeal to the EEOC[116] by filing a "notice of appeal" within 20 calendar days after receipt of the agency decision. The 20-day time limit will not be extended unless the Commission decides at its discretion that the complainant was not notified of the time limit and was not otherwise aware of it, or that circumstances beyond the complainant's control prevent the filing of a notice of appeal within the limit.[117]

A "notice of appeal" is merely a statement identifying the complainant and the agency and stating that the complainant is going to appeal the agency decision. The notice is deemed filed on the date of the postmark or, if delivered in person, on the date it is received by the EEOC.[118] If filing by mail, address it to the Director, Office of Review and Appeals, EEOC, 5203 Leesburg Pike, Suite 900, Falls Church, Va. 22041.[119] Complainants would be wise to use certified mail so that they have proof of the date of mailing. If the complainant wishes to submit written argument, it must be sent to the EEOC (with a copy to the agency) within 30 calendar days of filing the notice of appeal.

Appeals to the EEOC are handled by the Office of Review and Appeals. Although there is no provision in the rules for the agency to file a response to the complainant's appeal, the rules do provide that the Office of Review and Appeals will consider "all relevant representations submitted by either party."[120] While there is no right to a hearing at this stage, the Office of Review and Appeals has the authority to remand the case to the agency for further investigation or a rehearing if it deems such action necessary, or it can order additional investigation by EEOC staff.[121]

Once the Office of Review and Appeals issues a decision, either the complainant or the agency may request the Commissioners of the EEOC to reopen and reconsider the decision. Such a request must be filed within 30 days of receipt of the decision from the Office of Review and Appeals,[122] and it must be supported by written argument or evidence

---

[116]In addition to appealing the agency decision on the merits to the EEOC, the complainant may also appeal to the EEOC an agency decision (1) to reject all or part of the complaint, (2) to cancel a complaint for failure to prosecute, or (3) on an award of attorney's fees. 29 C.F.R. 1613.231(a). The complainant may also appeal the agency's failure to comply with the terms of a settlement agreement (see 29 C.F.R. 1613.217(b)). The complainant may also appeal a decision from the negotiated grievance procedure to the EEOC (see "Using the Negotiated Grievance Procedure," *infra*).

[117]29 C.F.R. 1613.233(c).
[118]*Id.*
[119]29 C.F.R. 1613.232.
[120]29 C.F.R. 1613.234(a).
[121]*Id.*
[122]29 C.F.R. 1613.234(b)(1).

that tends to establish that (1) new and material evidence is available that was not readily available when the previous decision was issued, (2) the previous decision involves an erroneous interpretation of law or regulation or misapplication of established policy, or (3) the decision is of such exceptional nature as to have effects beyond the actual case at hand.[123] Argument regarding the request to reopen and reconsider must be filed with the Commissioners and with the opposing party within 20 days of receipt of the request.[124] Once the Commissioners issue a decision, it is final and there is no further right by either party to request reopening.

Enforcement by the EEOC

The rules, promulgated by the EEOC in 1987, contained important new provisions regarding corrective action ordered by the EEOC.[125] For example, when the EEOC has reinstated an employee in a case involving removal and the agency requests reopening, the agency is required to comply with the EEOC decision by temporarily, or conditionally, restoring the employee to duty status pending the outcome of the agency request for reopening.[126] Once an EEOC decision ordering corrective action becomes final, the agency must comply within 60 days.[127]

When a complainant believes that the agency is not complying with the EEOC decision, the complainant should file a petition for enforcement with the EEOC Office of Review and Appeals. The Office is required to determine whether the agency is implementing the EEOC decision. Three avenues are open to the Office of Review and Appeals. First, in the course of investigating the matter, it may determine that there is satisfactory compliance. Second, in appropriate circumstances, it may issue a clarification of the prior decision. Such a clarification cannot change the result of the prior decision or enlarge or diminish the relief. It may only explain the meaning or intent of the original decision.[128] Finally, the Office of Review and Appeals may advise the Commissioners that it could not

---

[123]29 C.F.R. 1613.235(b). Copies of the request must be served on all other parties along with proof of delivery. 29 C.F.R. 1613.235(c). It is important to note that there is some case law to the effect that requesting reconsideration by the commissioners does not toll the 30-day filing period for the federal courts. *Brunda v. Secretary of the Navy*, 31 FEP Cases 1072 (D.N.J. 1982). However, since that case, the EEOC rules have been amended so that filing in court terminates administrative processing of the complaint. The rules also state that the commissioners' decision on the request to reopen and reconsider is "final." 29 C.F.R. 1613.235(d). Therefore, unlike the facts in *Brunda*, the rules appear to mean that a request to reopen and reconsider tolls the time limit for filing with the court.

[124]29 C.F.R. 1613.235(c)(2).

[125]52 FED. REG. 41920 (1987).

[126]29 C.F.R. 1613.237(b).

[127]29 C.F.R. 1613.237(c).

[128]29 C.F.R. 1613.238(c).

obtain satisfactory compliance and make recommendations to the Commissioners for enforcement.[129]

The Commissioners can require the agency to explain why there has not been compliance with its prior order.[130] When the Commissioners determine that the agency is not complying with the prior decision or when the agency fails to submit a report of corrective action, the Commissioners notify the complainant of a right to seek judicial review of the agency's refusal to implement the prior decision.[131]

Retaliation for Filing a Complaint

The law and regulations prohibit reprisal against those who participate in virtually any way in the EEO complaint processing system.[132] Allegations of reprisal can be filed in the same manner as any other EEO complaint.[133] However, when a complaint alleges retaliation in connection with a complaint that is still in process, the complainant may request that the agency or the administrative judge consolidate the retaliation allegation with the pending complaint. The agency or the administrative judge may grant the request provided it is made within 30 calendar days of: (1) the act that forms the basis of the allegation, or (2) the effective date of the alleged discriminatory personnel action, or (3) the date the complainant knew or should have known of the retaliatory act.[134]

Filing in Federal Court

In almost all cases, a person must file a complaint in the agency EEO complaint process before going to federal court.[135] The complainant may

---

[129]29 C.F.R. 1613.238(d).
[130]29 C.F.R. 1613.239(a).
[131]29 C.F.R. 1613.239(c).
[132]29 C.F.R. 1613.261.
[133]29 C.F.R. 1613.262(a).
[134]29 C.F.R. 1613.262(b).
[135]Complaints under Title VII of the Civil Rights Act, 29 U.S.C. 2000e-16(c), dealing with race, color, religion, sex, or national origin or with retaliation for exercising Title VII rights and complaints under the Rehabilitation Act, 29 U.S.C. 791, dealing with a handicapping condition must begin in the agency EEO complaint procedure. However, complaints under the Age Discrimination in Employment Act (ADEA) and the Equal Pay Act (EPA) are treated differently. While resort to the administrative procedures is allowed for ADEA complaints (see 29 C.F.R. 1613.212(a)), resort to the administrative procedures is not required before filing in court under the ADEA. The ADEA complainant is required to give the EEOC at least 30 days' notice of an intent to file in court. That notice must be given to the EEOC within 180 days after the alleged discriminatory event, 29 U.S.C. 633a(d). A trial de novo has been held to be available in ADEA cases. Hall v. United States, 436 F. Supp. 505, 18 FEP Cases 335 (D. Minn. 1977). Neither notice nor resort to the

file suit in federal district court if any one of four conditions has been met:

1. If after 180 calendar days from the date of filing a complaint with the agency, the agency has issued no decision;
2. No more than 30 calendar days have elapsed since receipt of notice of the agency's final decision;
3. If after 180 calendar days from the date of filing an appeal with the EEOC, there has been no EEOC decision; or
4. No more than 30 calendar days have elapsed since receipt of notice of the EEOC decision.[136]

Once the individual files in federal court, the administrative processing of the EEO complaint ceases.[137] Discrimination cases go to the appropriate federal district court, which will conduct a trial *de novo*.[138]

EEO Class Complaints

EEO class complaints are processed in a manner slightly different from individual complaints of discrimination. A class complaint may be filed by an individual, who is called the "agent" of the class, alleging that a group of agency employees, former employees, and/or applicants for employment have been, are being, or may be adversely affected by an agency policy or practice and that the adverse effect or impact discriminates against the group on the basis of their common race, color, religion, sex, and/or national origin.[139]

Consulting an EEO Counselor

An employee or applicant who wishes to be a class agent must contact a counselor within 30 calendar days of (1) the matter giving rise to the allegation, (2) the effective date of the personnel action, or (3) the date the employee or applicant knew or reasonably should have known of the discriminatory event or personnel action.[140] The final interview by the

---

administrative procedures is required before filing suit under the Equal Pay Act. 29 U.S.C. 216(b). See *Edmondson v. Simon*, 24 FEP Cases 1031 (N.D. Ill. 1978). See "Processing Allegations of Equal Pay Act Violations" and "Processing Allegations of Age Discrimination Violations," *infra*.

[136]29 U.S.C. 2000e-17; 29 C.F.R. 1613.281.
[137]29 C.F.R. 1613.283.
[138]*Chandler v. Roudebush*, 425 U.S. 840, 12 FEP Cases (1976). For the layman, a trial *de novo* means that in addition to reviewing the administrative record, the court actually conducts a trial, which may include a hearing, receiving documentary evidence, hearing witnesses, and receiving argument from the parties.
[139]29 C.F.R. 1613.601(a).
[140]29 C.F.R. 1613.602(a).

counselor must be within 30 calendar days after the initial contact. The individual then has 15 calendar days in which to file a complaint. An agent, who is an employee, is entitled to "a reasonable amount of official time" to prepare the complaint. Likewise, if the agent designates another agency employee as the class representative, the representative must be given "a reasonable amount of official time" to prepare the complaint. Furthermore, both the agent and the representative, when they are agency employees in a pay status, must be on official time when their presence is required by the agency or the EEOC during the investigation, informal adjustment, or hearing on the complaint.[141] The complaint must state in detail:

1. the personnel management policy or practice giving rise to the complaint, and
2. the resultant personnel action or matter adversely affecting the agent.[142]

Acceptance, Rejection, or Cancellation of a Class Action Complaint

The agency has 10 days after receipt of the complaint to forward it to the EEOC. The counselor's report and any other information pertaining to timeliness or any other relevant circumstances related to the complaint must be included. The EEOC assigns an administrative judge to the complaint.[143] As noted above with regard to individual complaints, although the EEOC assigns the administrative judge, the EEOC does not at this point assume jurisdiction of the case. The administrative judge develops a record and provides recommendations to the agency. The agency renders a decision, which the class agent may then appeal to the EEOC.

The administrative judge has a preliminary role in class complaints. The administrative judge first recommends whether the agency should accept, reject, modify, or cancel the complaint. The judge may recommend that the agency reject the complaint or any part of it for any of the following reasons:

1. It was not timely filed;[144]

---

[141]29 C.F.R. 1613.603(g).
[142]29 C.F.R. 1613.603(b).
[143]29 C.F.R. 1613.604(a).
[144]The administrative judge may recommend that the agency extend the time limits for filing a complaint and for consulting with a counselor when the agent or representative shows that they were not notified of the time limits and were not otherwise aware of them or that they were prevented by circumstances beyond their control from acting within the time limit. 29 C.F.R. 1613.604(e).

2. It consists of an allegation identical to an allegation contained in a previous complaint filed on behalf of the same class which is pending in the agency or which has been resolved or decided by the agency;

3. It fails to state a proper claim;

4. The agent failed to consult a counselor in a timely manner;

5. It lacks specificity and detail;

6. It was not submitted in writing or was not signed by the agent;

7. It does not meet the following prerequisites:
   a. The class is so numerous that a consolidated complaint of the members of the class is impractical;
   b. There are questions of fact common to the class;
   c. The claims of the agent of the class are typical of the claims of the class;
   d. The agent of the class, or class representative, will protect the interests of the class fairly and adequately.[145]

If the class fails to provide information or otherwise fails to cooperate with development of the process, the administrative judge may recommend that the agency cancel the complaint.[146] If the administrative judge determines that the complaint meets the criteria for a proper class complaint, he or she must recommend that it be accepted. When appropriate, the administrative judge may also recommend that a class be divided into subclasses and that each subgroup be treated as a class.[147]

The administrative judge transmits the recommendation to accept, reject, modify, or cancel the complaint to the agency, the agent for the class, and to the agent's representative. Unless the agency rejects or modifies the judge's recommendation within 30 calendar days from its receipt, the recommendation becomes the decision of the agency.[148]

In any event, the agency must notify the agent's representative and the administrative judge of its decision to accept, reject, modify, or cancel the complaint. If the complaint is rejected or canceled, the agent has a right to appeal to the EEOC's Office of Review and Appeals and a right to file an action in federal court.[149] If the agency accepts the class complaint, it must immediately notify the members of the class. The notice explains the basis of the complaint and advises the members of the class that they may remove themselves from the class by contacting the agency

---

[145]29 C.F.R. 1613.604(b).
[146]29 C.F.R. 1613.604(g).
[147]29 C.F.R. 1613.604(f).
[148]29 C.F.R. 1613.604(j).
[149]Id. and 1613.631(a)(1).

within 30 days. The ultimate decision on the complaint is then binding on all those who remain in the class.[150]

Hearing the Merits of a Class Action and Appealing to the EEOC

The discovery process, the hearing, the issuance of a recommended decision, the process by which the agency must issue a final decision, and the process the agent must follow to appeal to the EEOC are the same for class actions and individual actions.[151]

Agency Finding of Class Discrimination

When the agency finds class discrimination, each class member still must take action on his or her own behalf. Each class member has 30 calendar days in which to file a written claim stating that he or she would have received an employment benefit "but for" the existence of the discrimination.[152] If the agency cannot resolve the individual claim within 60 calendar days, it is referred to the administrative judge. The individual claimant has a right to a hearing before the administrative judge. The agency makes a final decision on the individual's relief based upon the recommendation of the administrative judge. Again, the agency may accept, reject, or modify this recommendation.[153]

As noted in the discussion of findings of discrimination in individual complaints of discrimination, attorney's fees are normally available for the successful class complaint and for the individual members of the class, who must litigate to establish their right to a remedy (see Chapter 12).

Processing Allegations of Equal Pay Act Violations

The Equal Pay Act prohibits discrimination in salary due to sex.[154] Therefore, when men and women are paid different salaries for the same job, two laws may be violated—Title VII of the Civil Rights Act and the Equal Pay Act. The EEO complaints procedure described above applies to all violations of Title VII of the Civil Rights Act, including discrimina-

---

[150]29 C.F.R. 1613.605 and 1613.612(f).

[151]See 29 C.F.R. 1613.603–1613.614, 1613.631, and 1613.632. See also "Individual EEO Complaints: Decision With a Hearing" and "Appealing to the EEOC," *supra*, for details on these procedures.

[152]29 C.F.R. 1613.614. See Chapter 5, "Determining the Remedy," for a discussion of the "but for" test.

[153]*Id.*

[154]29 U.S.C. 204 (f) and 216.

tion based on sex. An Equal Pay Act violation also may be raised in the EEO complaints process.

A separate enforcement procedure for alleged violations of the Equal Pay Act also exists. Suspected violations may be reported directly to the appropriate EEOC district office, which will undertake any necessary investigation and subsequent prosecution.[155] There is no requirement that an employee exhaust either of these administrative remedies before filing in federal district court for an alleged Equal Pay Act violation[156] (see Chapter 5, "The Equal Pay Act").

Processing Allegations of Age Discrimination Violations

A federal employee who is alleging age discrimination may use the EEO complaints procedure or may file suit directly in federal district court.[157] If the employee elects to file in the EEO complaint process, but later decides to file suit in court, the filing of the court action terminates the processing of the EEO administrative complaint.[158] If the employee files in the EEO complaint process and pursues the administrative process through to a decision from the EEOC, the employee then has 30 days from receipt of the EEOC decision to file in federal district court.[159]

On the other hand, if the employee elects not to file an EEO complaint, but rather to file directly with the court, the employee must give the EEOC a notice of intent to file the court action not less than 30 days prior to the court filing. Furthermore, the notice must be given not more than 180 days after the alleged unlawful act occurred.[160]

Processing a Mixed Case

A mixed case involves both an "appealable action" and an EEO allegation. Typical cases would be when an employee's grade is being

---

[155]29 C.F.R. Part 1620.
[156]29 U.S.C. 216(b).
[157]29 U.S.C. 633a(c) and (d); 29 C.F.R. 1613.213(a).
[158]29 C.F.R. 1613.513.
[159]*Caraway v. Postmaster Gen.*, 45 FEP Cases 1815 (D. Md. 1988).
[160]29 U.S.C. 633a(d). The courts have not been uniform in their interpretation of the requirement to exhaust administrative remedies or of what statute of limitations applies to the federal sector provisions of the Age Discrimination in Employment Act (ADEA). The discussion above assumes that if the complainant first files an ADEA case in the administrative process, then the procedures and limitation periods of Title VII should apply. On the other hand, if the complainant first files an ADEA case in federal court, then the procedures and limitation periods of the private sector ADEA should apply. For a more authoritative and detailed discussion of these issues, see the comments of the GAO Personnel Appeals Board in 54 FED. REG. 24131, 24134–24136 (June 6, 1989).

reduced or employment is being terminated and the employee alleges that the real motive for the action is prohibited discrimination.[161] Such cases may be filed either in the EEO complaints process or as an appeal to the MSPB.[162] An employee in a collective bargaining unit has the further option of raising the case in the negotiated grievance procedure, unless the negotiated agreement specifically excludes EEO, appealable actions, or mixed cases from coverage of the negotiated grievance procedure.[163] The employee may initiate a mixed case in only one of these procedures, however. Generally, the first procedure in which the employee files is the procedure which must be pursued.[164]

Once the employee selects the forum (EEO complaint, MSPB appeal, or negotiated grievance procedure), the filing requirements of that forum apply. However, after a mixed case has been properly initiated, unique processing requirements are applicable. For example, regardless of the administrative forum in which a mixed case is initiated, the employee can eventually reach the MSPB and the EEOC for review.[165] Furthermore, there are numerous opportunities for the employee to opt out of the administrative process in order to file in federal court.

Therefore, this section will discuss the special processing requirements for mixed cases in the EEO complaints process, in the negotiated grievance procedure, and in the MSPB process. Regardless of the process selected, the mixed case eventually makes its way, at the election of the employee, to the MSPB for a decision by the full Board. Thus, after discussing the special mixed case process in each forum, the discussion then deals with the process that begins after the MSPB issues a Board decision. Along the way, the various points at which the employee may opt out of the administrative processes and file in federal court will be noted.

Mixed Case in the EEO Complaints Process

The following discussion, describes the process for pursuing a mixed case in the EEO complaints procedure.

---

[161]See Chapter 1 for a statement of the actions that constitute appealable actions and for a list of the forms of prohibited discrimination in the Federal Government.

[162]5 U.S.C. 7702(a).

[163]5 U.S.C. 7121(a) and (d).

[164]*Rodriguez v. MSPB*, 804 F.2d 673 (Fed. Cir. 1986); *Whitaker v. MSPB*, 784 F.2d 1109 (Fed. Cir. 1986); *Duncan v. MSPB*, 795 F.2d 1000 (Fed. Cir. 1986).

[165]*Ogden Air Logistics Center and AFGE Local 1592*, 6 MSPB 531 (1981) ("Thus a 'mixed case' can receive varied consideration under 7702, which balances the respective expertise of the Board and the EEOC in an effort to protect the integrity of each.").

What Constitutes an Election to Use the Complaints Process

The first process in which the employee files represents an irrevocable election. Consulting with an EEO counselor, however, does not constitute an election to use the complaints process; that is, it is not "filing an EEO complaint."[166] For purposes of identifying when the EEO complaint process was initiated, the date the formal EEO complaint is filed is controlling.[167] If the employee files first with the MSPB and raises the discrimination issues in that appeal, the agency must cancel any subsequent EEO complaint that involves the same facts.[168] If the employee files first in the MSPB, but fails to raise the EEO issues in that appeal, the agency must reject the subsequent EEO complaint and advise the employee that the EEO issue must be brought to the attention of the MSPB.[169] If the employee files the EEO complaint first and subsequently files an appeal with the MSPB, the agency must notify the MSPB of the earlier complaint filing and request that the MSPB dismiss the appeal so that the EEO complaint can proceed.[170]

When an agency proposes taking an appealable action, such as termination of employment or reduction in grade, the employee cannot appeal the proposal to the MSPB. Only the final action that is taken by the agency may be appealed to the MSPB. However, a proposed action can be the subject of an EEO complaint. Once the agency takes the action, however, the EEO complaint cannot continue without being joined with the appeal or complaint over the agency action. Thus, if the employee elects to challenge the appealable action before the MSPB, the agency must cancel the EEO complaint involving the proposed action. If the employee elects to file an EEO complaint on the appealable action, that complaint, and the earlier complaint involving the proposed action, are to be consolidated into one complaint.[171] If the employee files nothing in

---

[166]29 C.F.R. 1613.403; *Christo v. Postal Serv.*, 3 MSPB 145 (1980); *Cardenas v. Postal Serv.*, 1 MSPB 560 (1980). See also *Chamberlain v. VA*, 1 MSPB 540 (1980) (a letter complaining to the agency did not initiate formal EEO proceedings and was not sufficient to divest MSPB of jurisdiction); *Ritchards v. HHS*, 84 FMSR 5966 (MSPB 1984) (where there was not EEO counseling prior to filing of formal complaint, the formal complaint did not divest MSPB of jurisdiction because formal complaint filing was premature and, therefore, invalid). The Federal Labor Relations Authority has also ruled that filing an informal EEO complaint does not constitute an election that precludes a later filing in the negotiated grievance procedure. *Department of Justice, Marshals Serv. and Marshals Serv. Locals, AFGE*, 23 FLRA 414 (1986).
[167]29 C.F.R. 1613.403.
[168]29 C.F.R. 1613.404(a).
[169]29 C.F.R. 1613.404(a) and 1613.405(a).
[170]29 C.F.R. 1613.405(b).
[171]29 C.F.R. 1613.406(a)(1) and (2).

response to the appealable action, the complaint on the proposal is automatically treated as if it includes the final agency action and is processed as a mixed case.[172] Finally, if the ultimate agency action does not result in an appealable action,[173] then the complaint involving the proposal is processed using the standard EEO process rather than the mixed case process.[174] However, it has been held that when an EEO complaint is filed challenging a proposed disciplinary action, the employee is precluded from later filing a grievance over the decision to take the disciplinary action.[175]

When the issues involve the same personnel action and the same set of facts, then the case is treated as a mixed case and the filing requirements discussed above are applied.[176] The major difficulties with the filing requirements arise when an EEO complaint and an MSPB appeal involve related, but arguably different matters. Thus, an EEO complaint challenging the denial of a promotion due to alleged discrimination, which made no mention of a reduction in force and downgrade, did not divest the MSPB of jurisdiction over a contemporaneous downgrading action taken through the reduction-in-force procedures.[177]

When the agency cancels or rejects an EEO complaint because it is a mixed case that was first filed with the MSPB, then there is no appeal of the cancellation or rejection. There is one exception to this rule—that is, the employee may appeal the cancellation or rejection when the employee argues that the EEO complaint at issue is not really related to the MSPB appeal.[178]

Processing the Mixed Case in the Complaints Procedure

Once the EEO complaint is properly filed in the complaints procedure, the processing is identical to that of the standard EEO complaints procedure, discussed above, with three important exceptions. First, the

---

[172]29 C.F.R. 1613.406(a)(3).

[173]For example, the agency "proposes" to terminate the individual's employment, but eventually decides to suspend the employee for five days, the five-day suspension is not appealable to the MSPB.

[174]29 C.F.R. 1613.406(b).

[175]*Department of Justice, Marshals Serv. and Marshals Serv. Locals, AFGE, supra* note 166. The FLRA distinguished this decision from *AFGE Local 3230 and EEOC,* 22 FLRA 448 (1986), in which "there was no express reference in the EEO complaint to the suspension action over which the grievance was filed and no requested corrective action in the complaint relating to the suspension."

[176]*Allen v. Department of Agric.,* 85 FMSR 5413 (MSPB 1985); *Lewis v. IRS,* 2 MSPB 181 (1980).

[177]*South v. Department of the Air Force,* 7 MSPB 579 (1981).

[178]29 C.F.R. 1613.405(c).

hearing, which the employee has a right to request in the standard EEO complaints procedure, is deleted from the mixed case EEO complaints procedure. The hearing will come later when, as described below, the case goes to the MSPB.[179] Second, if the agency has not issued a decision within 120 days after the formal EEO complaint was filed, the employee may take the case out of the EEO complaints procedure by appealing the case to the MSPB.[180] Third, once the agency issues a decision, the employee does not appeal to the EEOC, as in an EEO complaint which is not a mixed case. Instead, the employee's appeal from the agency's decision is to the MSPB. The employee has 20 calendar days from receipt of the agency decision to file with the MSPB.[181]

Thus, when a mixed case is filed in the EEO complaints procedure and is not resolved to the satisfaction of the employee, he or she may, on the one hand, opt to appeal to the MSPB, as described above. When the complainant elects to appeal to the MSPB, the appeal is filed like any other appeal with the appropriate MSPB field office. The case is heard by an MSPB administrative judge and proceeds to a final decision of the MSPB.[182] (For a description of the next step in the administrative processing of a mixed case, see the discussion in "Mixed Case in the MSPB Process," *infra*.)

On the other hand, when a mixed case is filed in the EEO complaints procedure and is not resolved to the satisfaction of the employee, he or she may opt to file suit in the appropriate federal district court at two different times. First, if there is no decision by the agency within 180 days from the filing of the formal EEO complaint, the employee may file suit in a federal district court.[183] Second, when the agency issues a decision, the employee may file in federal district court within 30 days after receipt of the agency decision.[184]

---

[179] 29 C.F.R. 1613.405(e).

[180] 29 C.F.R. 1613.406(a). The EEOC regulation states that appealing to the MSPB without an agency decision must occur between 120 days after the formal complaint was filed, "but not later than one year from the filing of the formal complaint." 29 C.F.R. 1613.405(e). This one-year limit should have been changed in 1987 when the EEOC amended its complaints procedure rules. 52 FED. REG. 41920, 41930 (1987). However, this was apparently an oversight. While the MSPB originally had the one-year limitation on appeals without an agency decision, that provision was subsequently deleted from its rules. 5 C.F.R. 1201.154(a)(2).

[181] 29 C.F.R. 1613.405(e); 5 C.F.R. 1201.154(a)(1). See also *Hobson v. Department of the Navy*, 3 MSPB 79 (1980).

[182] 5 C.F.R. 1201.153.

[183] 29 U.S.C. 2000e.

[184] 29 C.F.R. 1613.405(e).

WHERE AND HOW TO CHALLENGE AN AGENCY ACTION 47

Mixed Case in the Negotiated Grievance Procedure

The employee who is a member of a collective bargaining unit may elect to appeal a mixed case through the negotiated grievance procedure (NGP),[185] unless the negotiated agreement specifically excludes EEO cases, appealable actions, or mixed cases.[186] The following discussion, describes the process for pursuing a mixed case in the NGP.

What Constitutes an Election in the Negotiated Grievance Procedure

As noted above, the first forum in which the employee files represents an irrevocable election to pursue that procedure. However, where the employee files in the NGP before the effective date of the appealable action, the MSPB has ruled that such a filing did not represent a knowing exercise of the election.[187] Other limited circumstances have led the MSPB to conclude that the employee's act of filing in the NGP did not result in a knowing election by the employee.[188]

The details of NGPs are discussed elsewhere in this chapter.[189] For our purposes here, it is sufficient to say that an NGP usually consists of two or three steps in which progressively higher management officials review the grievance and issue a decision. Following the last such step, the union has the option of invoking arbitration. This is necessary background information to understand the review of mixed cases that originate in the negotiated grievance procedure.

---

[185]5 U.S.C. 7121(d); 5 C.F.R. 1201.154(b).

[186]5 U.S.C. 7121(d).

[187]*Riddick v. OPM*, 85 FMSR 5368 (MSPB 1985); *Johnson v. Department of Labor*, 85 FMSR 5091 (MSPB 1985).

[188]*Blanshan v. Department of the Air Force*, 84 FMSR 5768 (MSPB 1984) (where employee files grievance due to misleading information from the agency, filing does not deprive MSPB of jurisdiction when employee subsequently files with MSPB); *Carreno v. Department of the Army*, 84 FMSR 5713 (MSPB 1984) (grievance filed on proposal to remove does not prevent employee from later filing with MSPB over decision to remove unless there is clear showing that grievance was intended to apply to removal action); *Smith v. Department of Transp.*, 84 FMSR 6038 (MSPB 1984) (after filing grievance, decertification of union, an event beyond employee's control, makes filing in the negotiated grievance procedure an invalid election and filing with MSPB is appropriate). See also *Department of Justice, Marshals Serv. and Marshals Serv. Locals, AFGE, supra* note 166.

[189]See "Using the Negotiated Grievance Procedure," *infra*.

Review of the "Final Decision" of the Negotiated Grievance Procedure

The law provides that once the employee receives a "final decision" in the NGP, he or she may elect to have the MSPB review that decision.[190] It is not clear what the reference to final decision means. While there are, arguably, three final decisions in the NGP, the MSPB has recognized only two possible final decisions.[191] First, if the case goes to arbitration, then the arbitrator's decision is a final decision. Second, if the arbitrator's decision is appealed to the Federal Labor Relations Authority (FLRA), the Authority's decision is a final decision.[192]

The first final decision, that of the arbitrator, may be challenged by filing suit in federal district court,[193] by appealing to the MSPB,[194] or, in

---

[190]5 U.S.C. 7121(d).

[191]The first of the "final decisions" is the decision made by the agency at the end of the grievance process and prior to the arbitration proceeding. While the EEOC has recognized this agency decision as a final decision (29 C.F.R. 1613.231(b)(1)), the MSPB has ruled repeatedly that an employee must follow the negotiated grievance procedure through arbitration if the agreement provides for arbitration. *Gillman v. Department of the Air Force*, 7 MSPB 192 (1981); *Garland v. Department of Labor*, 12 MSPB 171 (1982); *Ogden Air Logistics Center and AFGE Local 1592*, 6 MSPB 531 (1981); *Clark v. EEOC*, 86 FMSR 5294 (MSPB 1986). See also 5 C.F.R. 12101.157, which refers to a final decision as issuing from an arbitrator, but does not refer to the agency decision. In none of these decisions has the MSPB offered any explanation for its position nor described the circumstances that led the employee to appeal to the MSPB rather than go to arbitration. What the MSPB decisions fail to recognize is that the union, not the employee, invokes arbitration. If the employee is coming to the MSPB before the union makes a decision as to whether to invoke arbitration, there is some basis for the MSPB position. However, if the union refuses to invoke arbitration, the agency decision is the final decision for the employee. To date, nothing in MSPB decisions or rules has recognized this fact. Until this procedent is clarified, employees, who have a mixed case and who wish to avail themselves of the complete mixed case administrative processes, should be aware that they file in the negotiated grievance procedure at their peril. As the MSPB law stands at this moment, the union's decision not to invoke arbitration will apparently cut off the employee from complete administrative process that the Reform Act created.

[192]5 C.F.R. 1201.157.

[193]Nothing in the statute, MSPB regulations, or EEOC regulations states that the employee has a right to file a civil suit in federal district court after receipt of an arbitrator's decision. We base our conclusion here upon an analysis of 5 U.S.C 7702 and of the EEOC regulations as they address pure discrimination cases. To the extent that § 7702 and the EEOC regulations provide for recourse to federal court after the agency has issued a decision, there is nothing to suggest that the employee's access to federal district court should be lessened when the negotiated grievance procedure is chosen over the EEO complaints procedure or the MSPB procedure. At least one federal district court has apparently recognized by inference that the decision of the arbitrator represents an exhaustion of administrative remedies for purposes of filing in federal court. *Clark v. EEOC*, 86 MSPB 5294, n.5 (1986).

[194]5 U.S.C. 7121(d); 5 C.F.R. 1201.157.

certain circumstances, by appealing to the FLRA.[195] In the MSPB review of an arbitrator's award, the request for review must be filed with the clerk of the MSPB and the case is to be heard by an administrative law judge, a Board member, or the full Board.[196]

The second final decision, that of the FLRA, may be challenged by filing suit in a federal district court[197] or by appealing to the MSPB.[198] As with the arbitrator's decision, the request for review must be filed with the clerk of the MSPB and the case is to be heard by an administrative law judge, a Board member, or the full Board.[199]

If the employee decides to appeal the final decision from the NGP to the MSPB, the employee must file a request for review with the MSPB within 20 days of receipt of the final decision.[200] The request must include the following:

1. A statement of the grounds on which review is requested;
2. Evidence of record or rulings bearing on the issues before the MSPB;
3. Arguments in support of the stated grounds with specific reference to the pertinent documents and citations of authority; and
4. A legible copy of the final decision and other pertinent documents which may include a transcript or hearing tape recording.[201]

The MSPB review of an arbitrator's award is limited, because the MSPB gives the arbitrator's award deference. Thus, the MSPB review of

---

[195]Arbitration awards relating to an adverse action or a performance-based action (see Chapter 2) may not be appealed to the FLRA. However, any other arbitration decision, including mixed cases that involve other appealable actions, may be appealed by either party to the FLRA. 5 U.S.C. 7122. That would mean, e.g., that a within-grade increase denial or a reduction-in-force action that included an allegation of discrimination could be appealed to the FLRA. Ordinarily, appeal to the FLRA would only occur if the employee/union thought that the circumstances of the case also raised an unfair labor practice. In most cases, the employee will probably elect to appeal the arbitrator's decision to the MSPB or initiate action in federal district court.

[196]5 C.F.R. 1201.154(b) and 1201.157. In practice, it appears that appeals from arbitration awards are usually reviewed by the full Board. See, e.g., *Robinson v. HHS*, 86 FMSR 5121, X-198 (MSPB 1986); *Carr v. Department of the Air Force*, 87 FMSR 5185 (MSPB 1987).

[197]See *supra* note 193 regarding federal district court filing.

[198]5 U.S.C. 7121(d); 5 C.F.R. 1201.157.

[199]5 C.F.R. 1201.154(b) and 1201.157.

[200]5 C.F.R. 1201.154(b). See also *Henderson v. HHS*, 40 MSPR 101 (MSPB 1989).

[201]5 C.F.R. 1201.154(b). There is no requirement that a transcript or other verbatim record of the arbitration hearing be submitted to the MSPB. *Denson v. Veterans Admin.*, 86 FMSR 5122 (MSPB 1986). In *Denson*, the MSPB also rejected the contention that lack of a transcript or other verbatim record of the arbitration hearing entitled the employee to a hearing before the MSPB.

an arbitrator's decision is intended only to determine whether the arbitrator erred in interpreting civil service law, rules, or regulations.[202] By way of contrast, the MSPB scope of review for decisions by its own staff is extensive. It reviews not only interpretation of law, rules, and regulations, it also can review and modify or reject findings of fact and, in certain circumstances, can modify or reject credibility determinations made by the administrative judges or the administrative law judge.

This discussion has traced the progress of a mixed case through the negotiated grievance procedure to the point where the employee has appealed to the MSPB for review and the MSPB has conducted its review of the final decision from the negotiated grievance procedure. (For a description of the next step in the administrative processing of a mixed case, see "Mixed Case Processing After the MSPB Decision," *infra*.)

Mixed Case in the MSPB Process

The following discussion assumes that the employee has decided to file a mixed case appeal in the MSPB process rather than in the EEO complaints process or in the negotiated grievance procedure. As was noted above, if the employee files first in the EEO complaints process, there is no hearing provided for mixed cases. Such a mixed case is subject to a hearing when the case is appealed to the MSPB. Therefore, much of what is said in this section will apply to the mixed case that originates in the EEO complaints procedure, because the appeal to the MSPB begins at this level. However, also as noted above, if the employee files first in the negotiated grievance procedure, the subsequent review by the MSPB does not include provision for a hearing. Therefore, nothing that is said in this section will apply to the mixed case, which was filed originally in the negotiated grievance procedure. (For the next step in the process for such a case, see "Mixed Case Processing After the MSPB Decision," *infra*.)

With only minor differences, the process for a mixed case appeal to the MSPB is identical to that described in the discussion above, "Appealable Actions and the Merit Systems Protection Board." We briefly discuss below only the modifications that are necessary in the process for a mixed case.

In filing the petition for review in a mixed case, the appellant must (1) state that there was discrimination and provide examples of how the appellant was discriminated against, and (2) state whether the appellant has filed a separate complaint or grievance on the discrimination alle-

---

[202]*Robinson v. HHS, supra* note 195; *Carr v. Department of the Air Force, supra* note 196.

gation, including the date and action taken on such complaint or grievance.[203]

If, after filing a petition for review, the appellant discovers that he or she may have been subject to discrimination not raised in the petition, the administrative judge may allow the discrimination allegation to be heard if the appellant did not know of the existence of the basis for the discrimination allegation at the time the petition was filed. The administrative judge may exclude the discrimination issue from consideration, however, if the agency can show (1) that consideration of the issue would prejudice the rights of the agency and unduly delay the proceedings, or (2) that the discrimination issue is not directly related to the appealable action. In any event, if the administrative judge excludes the discrimination issue from consideration, it must be remanded to the agency for appropriate consideration under the EEO complaints procedure or under any other applicable law or regulation.[204]

The MSPB recognizes in its regulations that discovery may be very necessary to properly develop the record in a mixed case. However, it also notes that due to the statutory mandate to reach a decision within 120 days, the time for discovery may have to be shorter than in a simple appealable action.[205] Therefore, both the appellant and the respondent should be prepared to move through discovery procedures expeditiously.

As noted in the previous discussion of MSPB appeals, once the administrative judge renders a decision, either party may request that the MSPB reopen and reconsider the decision of the administrative judge. If no such request is made, the administrative judge's decision becomes the final decision of the MSPB 35 days after it is issued. If a request to reopen and reconsider is made, then the MSPB considers the record and the briefs filed by the parties and issues the final decision of the MSPB.

Mixed Case Processing After the MSPB Decision

The previous discussions illustrate that administrative review of a mixed case can commence in the MSPB appeals process, the EEO complaints process, or the negotiated grievance procedure at the election of the employee. However, unless the employee opts out of the administrative process by filing in federal district court following an admin-

---

[203]5 C.F.R. 1201.153. The MSPB has a form for filing petitions with the MSPB. See Appendix 4. Completion of Questions 24 and 25 on that form constitutes compliance with this filing requirement. See also *Anderson v. Veterans Admin.*, 3 MSPB 188 (1980).

[204]5 C.F.R. 1201.155(a). See also *Anderson v. Veterans Admin.*, supra note 203.

[205]5 C.F.R. 1201.155(b).

istrative decision or by filing in the federal court after the passage of 180 days without some administrative decision, each of the three administrative procedures ultimately leads to a decision from the MSPB. The employee who is dissatisfied with the MSPB decision may, within 30 days from notice of the decision, elect to file suit in federal district court or to appeal to the EEOC.[206]

If the employee appeals to the EEOC, the Civil Service Reform Act directs that within 30 days the EEOC must determine whether to consider the appeal. If it decides not to consider the appeal, the administrative process is concluded and the employee has 30 days in which to file suit in federal district court. If the EEOC decides to consider the appeal, the law directs that, within 60 days, it issue a decision that concurs or differs with the MSPB decision.[207] As a practical matter, EEOC has not yet been able to comply with those time limits and its decision as to whether to consider the appeal is usually merged with its decision to concur or differ with the MSPB decision. Since the Reform Act makes no provision for recourse when these time limits are not met, it would appear that the employee who has not received an EEOC decision must wait 180 days after filing with the EEOC before moving to the federal district court.

If the EEOC decision ultimately concurs with the MSPB decision, then there is, at long last, no further administrative recourse. The dissatisfied employee can only proceed further by filing in federal district court.[208]

If the EEOC decision differs from the MSPB, it automatically refers the case back to the MSPB,[209] which must concur or differ with the EEOC decision within 30 days. The MSPB is required to adopt EEOC findings with regard to discrimination issues unless the EEOC decision has incorrectly interpreted a provision of civil service law, rule, or regulation or unless the EEOC decision involving a provision of civil service law, rule, or regulation is not supported by the evidence in the record as a whole.[210] If the MSPB concurs with the EEOC decision, then again, there is no further administrative recourse and the dissatisfied employee may file suit in federal district court.[211]

If the MSPB differs from the EEOC, the MSPB automatically refers the case to a "Special Panel," which consists of a member of the MSPB, a member of the EEOC, and a chairman appointed by the President. The

[206]5 U.S.C. 7702(a) and (b).
[207]Id.
[208]Id.
[209]Id.
[210]Ector v. Postal Serv., 84 FMSR 5916 (MSPB 1984).
[211]5 U.S.C. 7702(c).

Reform Act requires that the Special Panel permit the employee and the agency to submit written argument and to appear before it to present oral argument. It also requires that the Special Panel issue a final decision within 45 days after it receives the record from the MSPB.[212]

Filing in Federal Court

Since the decisions of the MSPB are subject to review by the Court of Appeals for the Federal Circuit but EEO cases require a trial at the federal district court level, there was initially some confusion as to whether mixed cases could be filed directly with the court of appeals. It is now well established that the proper judicial form for a mixed case is in the federal district court.[213]

Prohibited Personnel Practices

The Special Counsel of the MSPB receives allegations of prohibited personnel practices, which it may investigate on its own initiative.[214] In certain circumstances the Special Counsel may elect to prosecute a case before the MSPB or to intervene in a case which an employee has already appealed to the MSPB.[215] However, unlike the other administrative authorities who are required to adjudicate or resolve all complaints, appeals, or grievances that are brought before them, the Special Counsel has discretion to determine whether to pursue allegations of prohibited personnel practices. The Special Counsel is not an adjudicator, but rather a prosecutor and, like all prosecutors, has the discretion to select the cases that will be prosecuted. Therefore, where a prohibited personnel practice may be involved, an individual, who has a right to challenge an action through one of the appeal procedures discussed above, should

---

[212]5 U.S.C. 7702(d). It is worth noting at this point that the mixed case procedure is extremely complex and convoluted. After the first mixed case worked its way through the entire system, a member of the MSPB wrote that there was a "need for Congress to bring some order to this chaos created by the convoluted maze of overlapping jurisdiction written into the Civil Service Reform Act. Unless this unwieldy appellate structure is streamlined, even the best efforts of employees, agencies and the judicial administrative tribunals charged with deciding these cases will be forever wanting." He concluded by characterizing the system of almost unending litigation as the "Twilight Zone." *Federal Times*, Mar. 31, 1986, p. 9.

[213]*Wiggins v. Postal Serv.*, 653 F.2d 219 (5th Cir. 1981); *Williams v. Department of the Army*, 715 F.2d 1485 (Fed. Cir. 1983); *Christo v. MSPB*, 667 F.2d 882, 29 FEP Cases 1012 (10th Cir. 1982); *Hayes v. United States*, 684 F.2d 137 (D.C. Cir. 1982).

[214]5 U.S.C. 1206(a)(1).

[215]5 U.S.C. 1206(c) and (i).

pursue that right, in addition to filing an allegation with the Special Counsel. The procedures for pursuing an allegation through the Office of Special Counsel and the prosecution of prohibited personnel practices are so closely intertwined, that a detailed discussion of those procedures is presented in Chapter 4.

Processing an Unfair Labor Practice Charge

The Federal Labor Relations Authority (FLRA) consists of three Members and a General Counsel, all of whom are appointed by the President. The General Counsel is responsible for receiving and investigating unfair labor practice charges (see Chapters 1 and 8) and for prosecuting unfair labor practice complaints. The three members and the administrative law judges of the FLRA adjudicate the unfair labor practice complaints brought by the General Counsel.

An unfair labor practice charge may be filed by any person against an agency, agency subdivision, or labor organization.[216] A charge against an agency or activity should be submitted on FLRA Form No. 22. A charge against a labor organization should be submitted on FLRA Form No. 23. The person initiating the charge is the "charging party." The agency, agency subdivision, or labor organization which allegedly committed the unfair labor practice is the "charged party."

An unfair labor practice charge, which also involves one of four kinds of appealable actions—adverse actions, performance-based actions, denial of a within-grade salary increase (WIG denial) and reductions in force—is subject to special rules. Adverse actions and performance-based actions cannot be raised in the unfair labor practice procedure. They may only be raised in the MSPB procedure or, if they are not excluded from its coverage, in the negotiated grievance procedure.[217]

With respect to WIG denials or reductions in force, in which an unfair labor practice is alleged, the procedure is different. When the collective bargaining agreement does not exclude WIG denials or reductions in force (or all appealable actions) from the negotiated grievance procedure, then a WIG denial or a reduction in force may be raised, at the employee's election, either in the unfair labor practice procedure or in the negotiated grievance procedure. On the other hand, when the negotiated grievance procedure excludes WIG denials or reductions in force (or all appealable actions) from the negotiated grievance procedure, then only

---

[216]5 C.F.R. 2423.3.
[217]5 U.S.C. 7116(d). See also discussion *infra* notes 301 and 302.

the MSPB procedure is available, even if the alleged reason for the WIG denial or reduction in force constitutes an unfair labor practice.[218]

What to File

FLRA Forms No. 22 and No. 23 require the following information:[219]

1. The name, address, and telephone number of the person(s) making the charge;
2. The name, address, and telephone number of the activity, agency, or labor organization against whom the charge is made;
3. A clear and concise statement of the facts constituting the alleged unfair labor practice, a statement of the section(s) and subsection(s) of Title 5, Chapter 71 of the U.S. Code alleged to have been violated, and the date, place, and occurrence of the practicular acts; and
4. A statement indicating whether any other procedure has been invoked involving the subject matter of the charge and the results, if any, including whether the subject matter raised in the charge—
   a. has been raised previously in a grievance procedure;
   b. has been referred to the Federal Service Impasses Panel, the Federal Mediation and Concilation Service, the EEOC, the MSPB, or the Special Counsel of the MSPB for consideration or action; or
   c. involves a negotiability issue raised by the charging party in a petition pending before the Authority pursuant to Title 5, Part 2424 of the Code of Federal Regulations.

When to File

An unfair labor practice charge must be filed with the respective regional director of the FLRA within six months after the alleged unfair labor practice occurred. The statute provides for only one exception to this time limit, that is, a situation in which the charging party was prevented by the charged party from discovering the alleged unfair labor practice during the six-month period. In such circumstances, a charge must be

---

[218]*Id.*
[219]5 C.F.R. 2423.4.

filed within six months of the date that the alleged unfair labor practice
was discovered.[220]

Where to File

A charge (original and four copies) should be filed with the regional
director of the Authority in the region in which the alleged unfair labor
practice occurred.[221] If more than one party is named, an additional copy
of the charge should be filed for each party. The charging party must
include supporting evidence and documents in its submission to the
regional director. However, to protect the identity of individuals involved
in the process, this evidence is confidential and is not shared with the
charged party.[222] Also accompanying the original charge should be a
statement of service. This simply informs the regional director that the
charging party served a copy of the charge (without the supporting
evidence and documents) on each charged party.[223]

Investigation

Once a charge has been filed, the regional director, on behalf of the
General Counsel of the FLRA, conducts whatever investigation he or she
deems necessary. This investigation will normally not commence until the
parties have had a reasonable amount of time, not to exceed 15 days from
the filing of the charge, in which to attempt to resolve informally the unfair
labor practice allegation. All parties are given an opportunity to submit
evidence and arguments. Furthermore, the parties are encouraged to
communicate and to settle the dispute voluntarily throughout the process.
To this end, the rules establish procedures for formal and informal
settlements at various stages, that is, precomplaint or postcomplaint
either prior to the hearing or after opening of the hearing.[224]

Upon completing the investigation, the regional director may pursue
one of the following courses of action:[225]

1. approve a request by the charging party to withdraw a charge;
2. refuse to issue a complaint;

---

[220]5 U.S.C. 7118(a)(4).
[221]5 C.F.R. 2423.6(a).
[222]5 C.F.R. 2423.7(d).
[223]5 C.F.R. 2423.6.
[224]5 C.F.R. 2423.2, 2423.7, and 2423.11.
[225]5 C.F.R. 2423.9.

3. approve a written settlement agreement in accordance with the provisions of 5 C.F.R. 2423.11;
4. issue a complaint;
5. upon agreement of all parties, issue a complaint and transfer the case to the Authority for decision based upon a stipulation of facts in accordance with the provisions of 5 C.F.R. 2429.1(a).

Refusal to Issue a Complaint

If the regional director determines that formal proceedings should not be pursued, he or she may request that the charging party withdraw the charge. In the absence of a withdrawal in a reasonable period of time, the regional director may decline to issue a complaint. In the latter case, the regional director issues a written statement to the parties setting forth the reasons for not issuing a complaint.

The charging party may appeal the regional director's decision to the General Counsel within 25 days after receipt of the decision. The appeal must include a complete statement of the facts and argument on which the appeal is based. It must be filed with the regional director, and the charged parties must be notified by the charging party that the appeal is being taken. Only the notice of appeal is provided to the charged party. The appeal itself, which may contain reference to evidence revealing the identity of persons involved in the process, should not be sent to the charged party. Any request for an extension of time to file an appeal must be in writing and filed with the General Counsel no later than five days before the appeal is due.

The General Counsel may uphold the decision of the regional director or may direct the regional director to take further action. The decision of the General Counsel is final and is not subject to further appeal.[226]

Issuance of Complaint

If, following the investigation, the regional director determines that formal proceedings should be pursued, then all of the parties are served with a formal complaint. It describes the basis of the alleged unfair labor practice and notes the date of the hearing.[227] Normally, the party against whom the complaint is issued (the respondent) has 20 days after its receipt to file an answer (one original and four copies) with the regional

---

[226]5 C.F.R. 2423.10.
[227]5 C.F.R. 2423.12.

director. A copy of the answer must also be served by the respondent on the chief administrative law judge and on all parties.[228]

The administrative law judge (ALJ) conducts a hearing and issues a decision. If neither party files an exception, the FLRA adopts the decision. However, unlike other Authority decisions, such a decision is not precedent, that is, the decision is binding on the parties in that case, but is not binding on future cases with similar facts or issues.[229]

Decision by the FLRA

When a party disagrees with any of the findings or conclusions of the ALJ decision, an exception to the decision may be filed with the Authority within 25 days of receipt of the decision.[230] The latter may affirm or reverse the ALJ decision, in whole or in part. If the Authority finds no violation, it dismisses the complaint. If the Authority finds a violation, it may issue an order (1) to cease and desist from whatever unfair labor practice it has found the agency or labor organization to have engaged in, (2) requiring the parties to renegotiate a collective bargaining agreement in accordance with the Authority's order and requiring that the new agreement be given retroactive effect, (3) requiring reinstatement of an employee with back pay in accordance with 5 U.S.C. 5596(b), or (4) including any of the above in combination or calling for such other action as may carry out the purpose of the federal labor relations statute.[231] When an FLRA order directs payment of back pay and a controversy arises over the back pay issue, the regional director can initiate formal proceedings to resolve the matter.[232]

Judicial Review and Enforcement of Authority Decisions

The law provides for review of the Authority's unfair labor practice decisions by the U.S. courts of appeal.[233] These same courts are available for the Authority to seek enforcement of its orders and for appropriate temporary relief or restraining order.[234]

---

[228]5 C.F.R. 2423.13(a).
[229]5 C.F.R. 2423.29(a).
[230]5 C.F.R. 2423.26(c).
[231]5 C.F.R. 2423.29.
[232]5 C.F.R. 2423.31.
[233]5 U.S.C. 7123(a).
[234]5 U.S.C. 7123(b).

Appealing to the Office of Personnel Management

As noted in Chapter 1, "Actions Reviewable by the Office of Personnel Management," some actions that the employee may challenge are adjudicated by the Office of Personnel Management. In most cases, the OPM decision is final. In a few instances, such as retirement, the OPM decision is subject to review by the Merit Systems Protection Board. The purpose of this section is to outline the procedures for appealing to OPM.

Position Classification Reviews

Jobs in the Federal Government are put into classes according to the similarity of work performed. The class distinctions allow not only for job differences such as clerical positions and secretarial positions but also differentiate between various kinds of secretarial and clerical positions.

Grade levels are established within each job classification according to (1) the level of difficulty and responsibility, and (2) the level of qualifications required by the work.[235] Basic salary levels correspond to grade levels.

There are, generally speaking, three reasons an employee might wish to challenge the classification of his or her position. First of all, an employee may wish to argue that the duties of the position correspond to another job type or job series that has greater promotion potential than the job type or job series he or she currently holds. More often, however, employees argue that the level of difficulty and responsibility for their respective positions has increased. Therefore, the grade level, which determines the pay level, should be increased. Finally, an employee may wish to challenge an agency action that has changed the classification of an employee's position, resulting in a loss of grade.

The grade and pay retention provision of the Civil Service Reform Act specifies that a loss of grade or pay as a result of a reclassification is not appealable to the MSPB.[236] Unless the reclassification is the result of

---

[235] 5 U.S.C. 5102.

[236] 5 U.S.C. 5366; 5 C.F.R. Part 536; and FPM Supplement 990-2, Book 536. An employee is entitled to the grade or pay retention provisions of the Civil Service Reform Act when placed in a lower graded position due to reclassification or reduction-in-force action, provided such placement is not for cause or at the employee's request. Under the grade-retention provision, an employee retains his or her current grade for two years beginning on the date the employee is placed in the lower graded position. During the two-year period, the employee's retained grade is treated as the employee's actual grade for all pay administration purposes. To be eligible for grade retention due to reduction in force, the employee must have served for 52 consecutive weeks in one or more positions at a grade or grades higher than that of the new position. To be eligible for grade retention due to a

a reduction in force, the only appeal is to the OPM.[237] In taking such an action, the agency is required to notify the employee of the right to appeal the agency's classification decision and of the time limits for the appeal.[238]

Most employees in the following agencies may appeal the classification of their positions to OPM:

- an Executive agency,
- the Administrative Office of the United States Courts,
- the Library of Congress,
- the Botanic Garden,
- the Government Printing Office,
- the Office of the Architect of the Capitol, and
- the government of the District of Columbia.[239]

The statute does not exempt from coverage some employees within these agencies, such as Foreign Service employees, whose pay is fixed under Chapter 14 of Title 22 of the U.S. Code and certain other Department of State employees, certain employees in the Veterans Administration, and the National Security Agency.

---

reclassification action, the position being downgraded must have been classified at the higher grade for a continuous period of at least one year immediately before it was downgraded. If the 52 consecutive weeks or the one-year requirement is not met, the employee is only entitled to pay retention.

At the end of the two-year grade-retention period, the employee is placed in the lower grade. At that time the employee is entitled to the lowest rate of basic pay in the lower grade which equals or exceeds his or her rate of basic pay immediately prior to placement in the lower grade. If the rate of basic pay can be accommodated in the rate range for the lower graded position, pay retention does not apply. If the employee's rate of basic pay exceeds the maxium step rate in the lower grade, the employee is entitled to pay retention. Under the pay-retention provisions, the employee is entitled to his or her rate of basic pay or 150% of the maximum step rate in the lower grade, whichever is less. While on pay retention, the employee is entitled to 50% of all comparability increases to the maximum step of the lower grade until such time as the employee's rate of basic pay can be accommodated in the rate range for the lower graded position. For example, an employee in grade GS-14, step 6 is downgraded to GS-13 through either a qualifying reclassification or reduction-in-force action. At the end of the two-year grade-retention period, the employee is placed at GS-13, step 10. The employee will receive only 50% of the comparability increases until his or her income equals the salary of a GS-13, step 10. Thus, such downgrading does not reduce current income for the majority of individuals, but rather reduces their future potential income.

[237]*Id*. As described in *supra* note 236, most employees would not suffer a loss in pay. Rather, the rate at which their pay increases through "comparability" adjustments would be cut in half for a period of time. However, an employee who suffered a radical reduction in grade from a GS-14 to a GS-7, e.g., would experience a real reduction in pay. See 5 U.S.C. 5363(b)(2).

[238]5 C.F.R. 511.602.

[239]5 U.S.C. 5102.

A classification appeal may be filed at any time. If an employee is challenging a reduction in grade or loss of pay, however, the appeal must be filed within 15 calendar days after the effective date of the reduction in grade for the employee to be eligible for back pay in the event the appeal is successful.[240]

The appeal may be to the employee's agency, or to OPM directly, or to OPM through the employee's agency. If the appeal is made through the agency, the agency must forward it to OPM within 60 days of its receipt if the agency chooses not to act on the appeal or if it does not act favorably on the appeal.[241] The appeal must be in writing and must contain the reasons why the employee believes the position to be improperly classified.

The agency is required to furnish OPM with all relevant facts concerning the position and the agency's justification for its decision.[242] OPM conducts whatever investigation it deems necessary to render a decision. There is no right to a hearing in these cases.[243] An employee may be represented in an appeal before OPM.[244]

When an employee successfully challenges a downgrading or loss of pay, the decision is retroactive, which means that the employee receives back pay.[245] However, when the employee is arguing that the nature of his or her position has changed, requiring a higher grade, a favorable decision cannot result in a retroactive promotion and back pay.[246] An OPM determination in favor of the employee is only a decision that the employee's present duties constitute a higher grade level. If the duties remain unchanged after the OPM determination, then the agency is obliged to promote the employee. If the agency removes the grade-enhancing duties from the employee's position, then it is not obliged to promote the employee.

The Director of OPM has discretion to reopen and reconsider any decision when the party making the request submits written argument or evidence which tends to establish that:

1. new and material evidence is available that was not readily available when the previous decision was issued;
2. the previous decision involves an erroneous interpretation of law or regulation or a misapplication of established policy; or

---

[240]5 C.F.R. 511.605.
[241]5 C.F.R. 511.604.
[242]5 C.F.R. 511.606.
[243]5 C.F.R. 511.607.
[244]5 C.F.R. 511.603.
[245]5 C.F.R. 511.703.
[246]*United States v. Testan*, 424 U.S. 392, 399 (1976); *Wilson v. United States*, 229 Ct. Cl. 510 (1981).

3. the previous decision is of a precedential nature involving a new or unreviewed policy consideration that may have effects beyond the actual case at hand, or is otherwise of such an exceptional nature as to merit the personal attention of the Director.[247]

Appeals regarding wage grade positions (Federal Wage System, which covers blue-collar positions in the Federal Government) are subject to procedures essentially the same as those described above except that appeals may not be submitted directly to OPM but must go through the agency first.[248]

Whether OPM decisions on classification appeals are judicially reviewable is not a completely settled question. There is authority for the argument that a violation of the Classification Act is a prohibited personnel practice and that resort to the Office of the Special Counsel is the only appropriate forum to challenge such an OPM decision. However, as long as the Special Counsel conducts an adequate inquiry, there is no recourse to the federal courts when the Special Counsel refuses to pursue corrective action proceedings.[249] On the other hand, at least one court has rejected this line of argument and accepted jurisdiction over a classification dispute.[250] Unfortunately, the Supreme Court declined to accept the case that arguably put the issue forward.[251]

Fair Labor Standards Act Violations

OPM is responsible for reviewing allegations of violations of the FLSA in the federal sector.[252] Violations of the FLSA, which may apply to

---

[247]5 C.F.R. 511.612.

[248]FPM Supplement 532-1.

[249]*Barnhart v. Devine*, 771 F.2d 1515 (D.C. Cir. 1985). The court, citing *Wren v. MSPB*, 681 F.2d 867 (D.C. Cir. 1982), stated that if the Special Counsel utterly failed to perform its statutory duty to investigate, then a mandamus action could be used to compel the Special Counsel to perform its duty. The court did not explain and it is not clear how a classification appeal necessarily constitutes a violation of the Classification Act. Violation of the Act is a prerequisite for the matter to be a prohibited personnel practice. In this regard it is worth noting that the General Accounting Office (GAO) Personnel Appeals Board (a parallel agency to the MSPB) has ruled that mere disagreement over a classification decision does not constitute a violation of the position classification law or regulation. However, a showing that the misclassification was "arbitrary, capricious, or lacking a reasonable basis in law" would constitute a prohibited personnel practice. *Patrick v. GAO*, 25-100-17-83 (PAB 1/12/84), *reconsideration denied*, (PAB 8/6/84).

[250]In *Burroughs v. OPM*, 764 F.2d 1300 (9th Cir. 1985), *reh'g denied*, 784 F.2d 933 (9th Cir. 1986), the court accepted jurisdiction over the classification issue and ruled in favor of the employee.

[251]*Gray v. OPM*, 475 U.S. 1089 (1986).

[252]5 C.F.R. 551. OPM jurisdiction for FLSA violations does not include the Library of Congress, U.S. Postal Service, Postal Rate Commission, or the Tennessee Valley Authority. 29 U.S.C. 204(f).

federal workers include (1) an employee being allowed to work overtime without compensation, and (2) an employee being improperly exempted from coverage of the Act.

The FLSA covers all employees of an agency other than:

1. a person appointed under appropriate authority without compensation,
2. a trainee, or
3. a volunteer;[253]
4. certain executive, administrative, and professional employees;[254]
5. employees serving in certain foreign areas are exempt from the overtime provisions of the FLSA.[255]

Complaints alleging FLSA violations are filed with the appropriate OPM regional office (OPM headquarters is the regional office for Washington, D.C.). It investigates and issues a compliance order if violations are found. The Director of OPM has discretion to reopen and consider any case decided by OPM. An employee who alleges a violation of the FLSA may sue in federal district court either originally or after receiving the OPM decision on the allegation.[256] Agencies must pay retroactive wages for up to six years.[257]

Retirement

OPM adjudicates virtually all claims for Civil Service Retirement System and Federal Employee Retirement System benefits and refunds.[258] Any decision rendered in writing by OPM that refers to the

---

[253]5 C.F.R. 551.103.
[254]5 C.F.R. 551.203.
[255]5 C.F.R. 551.208.
[256]29 U.S.C. 216(b).
[257]This 6-year limitation is not tolled by filing an FLSA claim with OPM. It is tolled by filing a claim with the GAO. Once a claim is filed with GAO, the agency may subsequently pay the claim for up to 6 years prior to the date the claim was filed with GAO. The employee should still file with OPM first. However, as the claim approaches the 6-year limit, a prophylactic filing with GAO is both appropriate and necessary. *In the matter of Spurr,* 60 CG 354 (1981). See also FPM Letter 551-18 (July 1, 1982).
[258]5 C.F.R. 831.109(a) and (c). See 5 U.S.C. 8347 and 5 C.F.R. 841.301 *et seq.* for claims processing under the Federal Employee Retirement System (FERS). See also Chapter 3, "Civil Service Retirement." The exception to OPM's jurisdiction over retirement claims is for the Central Intelligence Agency (CIA). The law that created FERS provided that, under both the Civil Service Retirement System (CSRS) and FERS, the CIA is to carry out many retirement functions, including determinations of entitlement to benefits and defense of MSPB appeals when a CIA employee is involved. The scope of the CIA responsibilities are to be determined by agreement negotiated between OPM and CIA. 5 U.S.C. 8347(n); 5 C.F.R. 8461(j).

right to reconsideration is an "initial decision" and is not reviewable by the Merit Systems Protection Board. Any person affected by an initial decision with regard to retirement rights or benefits may request reconsideration by OPM of its decision.[259] Requests for reconsideration must be filed within 30 days from the date of the original decision, be in writing, and include the individual's name, address, date of birth, and claim number, and must state the basis for the reconsideration request.[260] The final decision is issued by a representative of the OPM Associate Director for Compensation.[261]

An appeal to the MSPB of the OPM final decision must be filed within 20 days after the decision's effective date.[262] The appeal to the MSPB is subject to the MSPB appellate procedures (see "Appealable Actions and the Merit Systems Protection Board, *supra*).[263]

Decisions of the MSPB in nondisability and disability retirement cases are subject to review by the Court of Appeals for the Federal Circuit. However, in disability retirement cases the review of the court does not include the factual bases of the administrative decision, but rather is limited to legal and procedural questions.[264] In nondisability cases, on the other hand, restriction on the scope of review does not exist. Review in nondisability cases includes a review of the facts to determine whether the decision was, for example, arbitrary and capricious or whether the decision was supported by substantial evidence.[265]

---

[259]Other than the exception discussed above, adjudications of FERS claims are vested in OPM and the standards imposed by statute and regulation and the right to MSPB review of decisions are basically similar to the CSRS standards. One noteworthy exception is the FERS provision that makes an employee ineligible for disability retirement if the employee declines a "reasonable offer of reassignment to a vacant position if the position . . . is one in which the employee would be able to render useful and efficient service." 5 U.S.C. 8451(2)(A).

[260]5 C.F.R. 831.109(d) and (e). This discussion deals with retirement rights and benefits in general. There are other procedures dealing with reconsideration (1) of termination of annuity payments under 5 U.S.C. 8311 *et seq.* (see procedures at 5 C.F.R. Part 831, subpart K), (2) of a decision to collect an erroneous annuity overpayment (see procedures at 5 C.F.R. 831.1303(b), and (3) of an initial decision on an application for disability retirement (see procedures at 5 C.F.R. 831.1204(c)).

[261]5 C.F.R. 831.110. Final decisions regarding termination of annuity payments under 5 U.S.C. 8311-22 are not appealable to the MSPB. *Id.*

[262]5 C.F.R. 1201.22.

[263]5 U.S.C. 8347(d). See also *Chavez v. OPM*, 6 MSPB 343 (1981).

[264]*Lindahl v. OPM*, 470 U.S. 768 (1985). The narrow scope of review is due to language found at 5 U.S.C. 8347(c).

[265]*Cheeseman v. OPM*, 791 F.2d 138, 140 (Fed. Cir. 1986). The language of 5 U.S.C. 8347(c) restricting the scope of review in disability cases does not apply to nondisability cases. Therefore, the scope of review found in 5 U.S.C. 7703(b), which is much broader, applies to nondisability cases.

Life Insurance Reviews

Individuals may challenge determinations regarding life insurance coverage,[266] but such action must be brought against the insurance company rather than the Federal Government, unless a breach of its obligation is alleged against the United States.[267] However, federal agencies and OPM are responsible for making determinations as to basic life insurance coverage. Agencies must make the initial decisions on such questions for active employees and for former spouses not receiving annuities. OPM and other respective retirement systems[268] will make the initial decisions for annuitants and for former spouses who are receiving annuities. An employee, annuitant, or former spouse may request reconsideration by OPM of the initial denial of basic insurance coverage, regardless of whether that initial denial is made by the agency, OPM, or other respective retirement system. Employees, annuitants, and former spouses are entitled to only one reconsideration decision from OPM.[269]

When an employee's agency denies basic insurance coverage, the employee may request OPM to reconsider the agency decision.[270] The agency's written decision must carry notice of this right to reconsideration in order to be regarded as a final agency decision.[271]

An initial decision by OPM denying basic coverage may be appealed when it is rendered by OPM in writing and when it states the right to reconsideration. If an initial decision is rendered by the highest level of review available within OPM, it will not be subject to reconsideration.[272]

The OPM decision must be in writing and must state findings and conclusions.[273] The OPM decision may be challenged by filing suit in a federal district court or with the U.S. Court of Claims.[274]

---

[266]5 U.S.C. Chapter 87 is the statutory basis for life insurance coverage in the Federal Government.

[267]5 C.F.R. 870.101.

[268]Other retirement systems that are responsible for making the initial decision for participants of their retirement systems and for the their former spouses include the Central Intelligence Agency Retirement and Disability System and the Foreign Service Retirement and Disability System.

[269]52 FED. REG. 21597 (1987).

[270]5 C.F.R. 870.205(a).

[271]5 C.F.R. 870.205(b).

[272]5 C.F.R. 870.205(c).

[273]5 C.F.R. 870.205(f).

[274]5 U.S.C. 8715.

Health Insurance Reviews

When an individual is not permitted to register for health insurance or to change health insurance enrollment or to enroll a person as a family member, the individual may request OPM to reconsider that determination. Furthermore, an individual may request OPM review of a health plan's denial of a claim. The former issue is dealt with first.

Health Insurance Enrollment

Agencies must make the initial decisions on enrollment questions for active employees. OPM and other respective retirement systems[275] will make the initial decisions for annuitants and for former spouses who are receiving annuities. An employee, annuitant, or former spouse may request reconsideration by OPM of the initial denial on these health insurance issues regardless of whether that initial denial is made by the agency, OPM, or other respective retirement system. Employees, annuitants, and former spouses are entitled to only one reconsideration decision from OPM.[276]

When an agency refuses to permit registration for health insurance or to permit a change of health insurance enrollment or to permit enrollment of a person as a family member, the employee may request OPM to reconsider the agency decision.[277] The agency's written decision must carry notice of this right to reconsideration in order to be regarded as a final agency decision.[278]

An initial decision by OPM denying basic coverage to an annuitant or former spouse may be appealed when it is rendered by OPM in writing and when it states the right to reconsideration. If an initial decision is rendered by the highest level of review available within OPM, however, it will not be subject to reconsideration.[279]

Legal action to compel enrollment in a health plan should be brought against the employing agency.[280]

Denial of a Health Insurance Claim

When a health plan denies a claim, the individual has one year after notice of the denial in which to file with the health plan a request for

---

[275]See *supra* note 268 for examples of "other retirement systems."
[276]*Supra* note 269.
[277]5 C.F.R. 890.104(a).
[278]5 C.F.R. 890.104(b).
[279]5 C.F.R. 890.104(c).
[280]5 C.F.R. 890.107.

reconsideration of the denial.[281] The request for reconsideration must be in writing and must state the reason the claim should not have been denied.[282] Within 30 days of receipt of the request for reconsideration, the health plan must do one of three things: (1) affirm the denial in writing to the individual, (2) pay the bill or provide the service, or (3) request additional information on the claim.

If the plan requests additional information, it must (1) specifically identify the information needed, (2) state the reason the information is needed, (3) specify that the time limit for responding is 60 days from the plan's request, and (4) state that failure to respond will result in the determination being made based upon the information the plan already has available.[283] A plan may extend this time limit for providing additional information in two circumstances: (1) when there is evidence that the individual was not notified of the time limit, or (2) when circumstances beyond the individual's control prevented the individual from submitting the additional information within the time limit.[284] If the additional information is provided, the plan must within 30 days of receiving the information either affirm the denial of coverage, or pay the bill or provide the service.[285]

If the plan affirms its denial of the claim, it must explain in writing the detailed and specific reasons for the denial.[286] When the plan affirms the denial of the claim or fails to respond within 30 days,[287] the individual may request that OPM review the plan's claim denial.[288] The individual has 90 days after receipt of the plan's affirmance of its denial to request OPM review.[289] When the plan fails to respond to the individual, then the individual has 120 days, after requesting reconsideration by the plan, to request review by OPM.[290]

In response to a request to review a plan's claim denial, OPM may gather evidence by requesting additional information from the individual or by obtaining an advisory opinion from a physician.[291] OPM is to then

---

[281]5 C.F.R.   890.105(b)(1).
[282]5 C.FR.   890.105(c)(1).
[283]5 C.F.R.   890.105(c)(2).
[284]5 C.F.R.   890.105(b)(4).
[285]5 C.F.R.   890.105(b)(2).
[286]5 C.F.R.   890.105(c)(3).
[287]The failure to respond is measured from the date the plan receives the request for reconsideration or within 30 days after the plan receives additional information from the individual. 5 C.F.R. 890.105(b)(3).
[288]5 C.F.R.   890.105(b)(3).
[289]5 C.F.R.   890.105(d)(1).
[290]Id.
[291]5 C.F.R.   890.105(d)(2).

provide a decision to the individual and to the plan within 30 days after receipt of the evidence.[292]

Suit may be filed against the carrier of the health benefit plan to recover on a claim for the benefits. A suit against OPM is not proper, unless the action challenges OPM's regulations or unless the action challenges an OPM decision.[293] Suit may be filed on life insurance claims in a federal district court or with the U.S. Court of Claims.[294]

Review of Examination Ratings

An individual who seeks employment in a competitive service position within the Federal Government submits to an examining system which is conducted by OPM. The examining system generally consists of a review of the applicant's work and educational experience. For some positions, a written test is also required.

When this process is completed, the applicant is notified of his or her rating. If the applicant is dissatisfied, OPM will reconsider the original examination decisions upon reasonable demonstration that the review is warranted.[295] The request for reconsideration must be in writing and should state why it is believed that the original decision was not proper, what factors were not considered, and any other pertinent information which will support the request and enable the reviewing office to reevaluate the decision.

Requests for reconsideration of original examining determinations are submitted to the OPM office that made the decision. If the applicant is dissatisfied with the reconsideration decision, further review may be requested as follows:

- by the Associate Director, Staffing Group, OPM, Washington, D.C. 20415 for the Washington, D.C. metropolitan area;
- by the Director of the OPM regional office having jurisdiction of the examining office for reviews made outside the Washington, D.C. metropolitan area.

Using the Negotiated Grievance Procedure

A negotiated grievance procedure is part of a collectively bargained agreement between a union and the agency. Negotiated grievance pro-

---

[292]5 C.F.R. 890.105(d)(4).
[293]5 C.F.R. 890.107. The regulation provides that when OPM's decision concurs in the plan's denial of a claim, the subsequent legal action lies against the carrier, not OPM.
[294]5 U.S.C. 8715.
[295]Federal Personnel Manual Supp. 337, paras. 2–7.

cedures vary from one agreement to another. Therefore, an employee or manager must consult the labor agreement for guidance on a particular procedure. This chapter discusses the circumstances in which a bargaining unit member has an election between using a statutory appeals procedure or the negotiated grievance procedure. It also discusses the specific avenues for challenging arbitrators' decisions. The grounds upon which an arbitrator's decision may be challenged and other details relating to the grievance/arbitration process are discussed in Chapter 11.

Statutory Appeals and the Negotiated Grievance Procedure

The negotiated grievance procedure covers statutory appeals such as appealable actions and EEO violations, unless the collective bargaining agreement specifically excludes them from coverage. When the collective bargaining agreement excludes appealable actions and/or EEO violations from the negotiated grievance procedure, members of the bargaining unit are limited to the same procedures that are avilable to employees who are not in bargaining units (see "Appealable Actions and the Merit Systems Protection Board," "Using the EEO Complaints Procedure," and "Processing a Mixed Case," *supra*).[296]

However, when the collective bargaining agreement does not expressly exclude appealable actions and/or EEO violations from the negotiated grievance procedure, members of the bargaining unit have a variety of choices as to where they may initiate their cases.

Appealable Actions

When the collective bargaining agreement does not exclude appealable actions from a negotiated grievance procedure, members of the bargaining unit have the following elections. For an adverse action[297] or performance-based action,[298] the employee may use the negotiated grievance procedure or the MSPB procedure.[299] Even if the apparent reason for the action constitutes an unfair labor practice, the employee cannot use the unfair labor practice procedure.[300] Only the negotiated grievance procedure and the MSPB procedure are available for these particular

---

[296]5 U.S.C. 712(d).

[297]5 U.S.C. 7512 (suspension of more than 14 days, reduction in grade, removal under adverse action procedures).

[298]5 U.S.C. 4303 (reduction in grade and removal based on unacceptable performance).

[299]5 U.S.C. 7121(e). See "Appealable Actions and the Merit Systems Protection Board," *supra*, for a description of the MSPB procedure.

[300]5 U.S.C. 7116(d).

actions. If the employee elects to use the negotiated grievance procedure, there is no subsequent appeal to the MSPB. The only appeal is to the Court of Appeals for the Federal Circuit (see "Appealing the Arbitrator's Decision," *infra*).

The rule is different, however, for a reduction in force (RIF) and a denial of a within-grade salary increase (WIG denial). For both of these appealable actions, the employee must use the negotiated grievance procedure,[301] unless the alleged reason for the RIF or the WIG denial constitutes an unfair labor practice. In that case the employee may elect either the negotiated grievance procedure or the unfair labor practice procedure.[302] In other words, the employee in a bargaining unit, who wishes to challenge a RIF or a WIG denial has no right to appeal to the MSPB. The only statutory appeal process open to such an employee is the unfair labor practice process. If the RIF or WIG denial does not raise an unfair labor practice issue, the only method of appeal is through the negotiated grievance procedure. If the RIF or WIG denial involves an unfair labor practice issue, it is important to raise that issue, even though the employee elects to use the negotiated grievance procedure. Without the unfair labor practice issue being raised, the RIF or WIG denial cannot be appealed to federal court (see "Appealing the FLRA Review of the Arbitrator's Decision," *infra*).

When the collective bargaining agreement excludes reductions in force or within-grade increase denials (or all appealable actions) from a negotiated grievance procedure, then the members of the bargaining unit have no choice of forum. Such bargaining unit members are then like any other federal employee. They must use the MSPB procedure (see "Appealable Actions and the Merit Systems Protection Board," *supra*).[303]

Alleged EEO Violations

When the negotiated grievance procedure does not exclude EEO violations, bargaining unit members may use the negotiated grievance

---

[301]*Sotak v. HUD*, 84 FMSR 5168 (MSPB 1984) (MSPB without jurisdiction over reduction-in-force appeal when negotiated grievance procedure covers the subject); *Lovshin v. Department of the Army*, 83 FMSR 5187 (MSPB 1983) (MSPB without jurisdiction over appeal of denial of a within-grade salary increase when negotiated grievance procedure covers the subject).

[302]5 U.S.C. 7116(d). See "Processing an Unfair Labor Practice Charge," *supra*, for a description of the unfair labor practice procedure.

[303]Sometimes it is not clear whether the negotiated agreement excludes one or more of the appealable actions from coverage of the negotiated grievance procedure. *Bonner v. MSPB*, 781 F.2d 202 (Fed. Cir. 1986).

procedure or the EEO complaints procedure.[304] The law provides that when an employee raises an EEO allegation in the negotiated grievance procedure, the employee may appeal the final decision to the EEOC. The EEOC recognizes the following three possible final decisions in the negotiated grievance procedure:

1. the decision of the agency head (or designee),
2. the decision of the arbitrator, and
3. the decision of the FLRA.[305]

A notice of appeal must be filed within 20 days after receipt of the final decision with the EEOC Office of Review and Appeals. Any statement or brief in support of the appeal must be filed with the EEOC and the agency within 30 days after filing the notice of appeal. There is no right to a hearing at this stage of the process.[306] It appears that the traditional judicial deference to the finality of arbitration awards is used by the EEOC in this review process.[307] The other provisions for appealing to the EEOC, for requesting reconsideration of the case by the full Commission, and for enforcement by the EEOC are the same for the standard EEO complaints procedure and are discussed above under "Using the EEO Complaints Procedure."

Alleged "Mixed Case" Violations

When the negotiated grievance procedure does not exclude appealable actions or EEO violations, bargaining unit members may use the negotiated grievance procedure, the EEO complaints procedure, or the MSPB procedure. An unusual feature of the mixed case election is that the employee who elects to use the negotiated grievance procedure may later seek MSPB and EEOC review of the case (see "Processing a Mixed Case," *supra*).[308]

---

[304]5 U.S.C. 7121(d). See "Using the EEO Complaints Procedure," *supra*, for a description of the EEO complaints process. See also "Mixed Case in the EEO Complaints Process: What Constitutes an Election to Use the Complaints Process," *supra*.

[305]29 C.F.R. 1613.231(b)(1).

[306]29 C.F.R. 1613.234.

[307]This is a conclusion based upon interviews with EEOC staff reported in William V. Luneburg, THE FEDERAL PERSONNEL COMPLAINT, APPEAL, AND GRIEVANCE SYSTEMS: A STRUCTURAL OVERVIEW AND PROPOSED REVISIONS, Administrative Conference of the United States (1988).

[308]See "Processing a Mixed Case," *supra*, for a thorough description of the options available to an employee who is raising mixed case allegations.

Electing to Use the Negotiated Grievance Procedure

When an employee has a choice between procedures, the procedure in which the employee files first is the procedure which the employee must pursue.[309] He or she cannot use more than one procedure. The remainder of this section assumes that the employee elects to seek relief through the negotiated grievance procedure and discusses the procedural alternatives that exist once that election is made.

Generally speaking, negotiated grievance procedures will have certain things in common. There will be a time period within which grievances must be initiated following the complained-of action. There are usually two or three decision levels. The grievance is normally presented in writing at the lowest possible managerial level. It is then subject to a second and sometimes third level of management review. The final level of management review issues what will be the final decision in the matter, unless the union invokes arbitration.

In a mixed case, the employee apparently cannot appeal the final decision of management to the MSPB. If the union does not invoke arbitration, it appears that the only recourse for the employee is to file suit in federal district court.[310] In a pure EEO case (an EEO allegation that is not combined with an appealable action), the final decision of management may be appealed by the employee to the EEOC if the union does not invoke arbitration.[311]

Appealing the Arbitrator's Decision

When the arbitration process is invoked, the union and management select an outside, private, neutral party to decide the dispute and the arbitrator issues a decision (see Chapter 11 for further discussion of the arbitration process).

In general, an appeal from an arbitrator's decision by either party must be directed to the Federal Labor Relations Authority.[312] There are three exceptions to this general rule.

First, if the case concerns an appealable adverse action[313] or a

---

[309]*Id.*

[310]See "Mixed Case in the Negotiated Grievance Procedure: Review of the 'Final Decision' of the Negotiated Grievance Procedure," *supra.*

[311]29 C.F.R. 1613.231(b)(1). The employee has 20 days from receipt to appeal any decision from the negotiated grievance procedure to the EEOC. 29 C.F.R. 1613.233(b).

[312]5 U.S.C. 7122(a).

[313]Suspensions of more than 14 days, reductions in grade, and removals based upon conduct. 5 U.S.C. 7512.

performance-based action,[314] the FLRA may not review the arbitrator's decision.[315] The only review available is in the Court of Appeals for the Federal Circuit.[316] The agency does not have a right of direct appeal to the court from an MSPB decision. The law requires that the Director of OPM appeal on behalf of the agency. The Director may appeal only if the Board erred in interpreting a civil service law, rule, or regulation affecting personnel management and if the Board's decision will have a substantial impact on a civil service law, rule, or regulation, or policy directive.[317] Since the arbitrator is acting in the place of MSPB in decisions regarding appealable adverse actions and performance-based actions, the Director of OPM must follow the procedure required for an MSPB decision of intervening in the proceeding or, in the alternative, asking the arbitrator to reconsider the decision, before the Director may file in the court of appeals.[318]

Second, if the employee's case alleges an EEO violation, the employee may elect to appeal to the FLRA or the EEOC or to file suit in the appropriate federal district court.[319] The employee electing the FLRA may later appeal that decision to the EEOC or file suit in the appropriate federal district court.[320] As noted earlier, this employee has the option of using the statutory procedure for EEO complaints rather than the negotiated grievance procedure. But electing to use the negotiated grievance procedure for an EEO case does not preclude the employee from ultimately seeking review by the EEOC. After taking the case to the EEOC, the employee may still file suit in the appropriate federal district court (see "Using the EEO Complaints Procedure: Individual EEO Complaints: Filing in Federal Court," *supra*).

---

[314]Reductions in grade or removals based upon unacceptable performance. 5 U.S.C. 4303.

[315]Read 5 U.S.C. 7121(f) and 7703 together. See also *Department of Justice, Bureau of Prisons and AFGE Local 3882*, 22 FLRA 928 (1986).

[316]5 U.S.C. 7121(f). The Reform Act language, which provides for review in the appropriate court of appeals or the Court of Claims, was changed with the creation of the Court of Appeals for the Federal Circuit. See *supra* note 79.

[317]See text at note 80, *supra*, for a discussion of this requirement and a description of the process that the Director of OPM must follow.

[318]*Devine v. Nutt*, 718 F.2d 1048, 115 LRRM 2427 (Fed. Cir. 1983), *rev'd on other grounds sub nom. Cornelius v. Nutt*, 472 U.S. 648, 119 LRRM 2905 (1985); *Devine v. Sutermeister*, 724 F.2d 1558, 116 LRRM 2495 (Fed. Cir. 1983); *Devine v. Pastore*, 732 F.2d 213, 116 LRRM 2196 (D.C. Cir. 1984); *Devine v. Levin*, 739 F.2d 1567 (Fed. Cir. 1984).

[319]This discussion assumes an EEO allegation that is not combined with an appealable action. When the EEO issue is combined with an appealable action, it is a mixed case and the appeal process for a mixed case decision by an arbitrator is different from the process described here for an EEO allegation alone.

[320]29 C.F.R. 1613.233(b).

The third exception to FLRA review of arbitrators' decisions has already been discussed in this chapter under "Processing a Mixed Case." Briefly, the FLRA may review mixed cases except those involving an adverse action or a performance-based action. As a practical matter, mixed cases are rarely appealed to the FLRA. The only reason for doing so is when the case also raises unfair labor practice issues or other uniquely labor-related matters.

Appealing the FLRA Review of the Arbitrator's Decision

Most decisions by arbitrators can be reviewed by the FLRA, unless the decision falls within one of the three categories described above. In most cases, the FLRA review of an arbitrator's decision is final and not subject to further judicial review. FLRA review of an arbitrator's decision is subject to judicial review in only three circumstances, two of which are discussed above—the EEO decision that may be appealed to the FLRA and the mixed case decision that may be appealed to the FLRA. The only other category of arbitrator's decisions that may be subjected to judicial review after FLRA review is when the grievance "involves an unfair labor practice."[321] This situation arises when arbitration has been selected to resolve the grievance, the FLRA reviews exceptions to the arbitrator's decision, and an unfair labor practice is either an explicit or a necessary ground for the final order issued by the FLRA.[322] It is not enough that the issue could have been treated as an unfair labor practice. The allegation must be "characterized . . . and . . . pursued, by whatever route, as a statutory unfair labor practice, not as something else" such as a contract violation.[323]

Enforcement of Arbitration Awards

The FLRA has suggested that where there is a question as to the interpretation of an arbitration award or where there is need to clarify an arbitration award, the parties should jointly request that the arbitrator provide additional guidance or that the parties select another arbitrator to review the issue of compliance, whichever may be appropriate.[324]

---

[321]5 U.S.C. 7123(a)(1).
[322]*U.S. Marshals Serv. and Department of Justice v. FLRA*, 708 F.2d 1417 (9th Cir. 1983).
[323]*Overseas Educ. Ass'n v. FLRA*, 824 F.2d 61, 125 LRRM 3330 (D.C. Cir. 1987).
[324]*Headquarters U.S. Army Communications Command and AFGE Local 1662*, 2 FLRA 785 (1980).

Another means of enforcing an arbitration award is, in the appropriate circumstance, for the FLRA to seek judicial enforcement. The FLRA has authority to seek judicial enforcement of its own orders.[325] However, unless exceptions were filed to the original arbitration award and a subsequent FLRA order issued, arbitration awards are not FLRA orders and, therefore, are not subject to the judicial enforcement procedures.[326] The judicial enforcement procedures are available for the unexcepted arbitration award if the injured party files an unfair labor practice challenging the other party's failure to implement the arbitration decision. The FLRA review does not reach the merits of the original arbitration decision, but is limited to determining whether the alleged failure to implement the arbitrator's decision constitutes an unfair labor practice. If the FLRA concludes that an unfair labor practice has occurred and the offending party continues to refuse to comply, then the unfair labor practice order of the FLRA is ripe for the judicial enforcement procedures described above.[327]

Arbitration decisions, for which no exceptions were filed with the FLRA, can reach the judicial enforcement procedure by using the unfair labor practice procedure even when the original arbitration decision could not have been reviewed by the FLRA. For example, as discussed above, the FLRA is without authority to review arbitration decisions involving appealable adverse actions or performance-based actions. Nevertheless, the FLRA can hear the unfair labor practice allegation that such an arbitration decision is not being properly implemented.[328]

Agency Administrative Grievance Procedures

Where no collective bargaining agreement exists, those actions discussed in Chapter 1, "Other Agency Actions," are processed in the agency administrative grievance procedures. Most executive agencies, military departments, and organizational units in the legislative and judicial branches that have positions in the competitive service are required by OPM regulation to establish an agency administrative grievance system[329] which covers—

---

[325]5 U.S.C. 7123(b).

[326]*Headquarters, U.S. Army Communications Command and AFGE Local 1662, supra* note 324.

[327]*Id.*

[328]*Army Adjutant Gen. Publications Center and AFGE Local 2761*, 22 FLRA 200 (1986); *Department of Justice, Bureau of Prisons and AFGE Local 3882, supra* note 315.

[329]5 C.F.R. 771.203. Agencies excluded from coverage are the CIA, FBI, Defense Intelligence Agency, National Security Agency, Nuclear Regulatory Commission, Tennessee Valley Authority, Postal Rate Commission, and the U.S. Postal Service. 5 C.F.R. 771.206.

any matter of concern to the employment of an employee which is subject to the control of agency management, including any matter on which an employee alleges that coercion, reprisal, or retaliation has been practiced against him or her.[330]

Two other actions may be covered by the agency grievance procedure to the extent that the agency provides for such coverage in its own regulations. These two actions are as follows:

1. return of an employee from an initial appointment as a supervisor or manager to a nonsupervisory or nonmanagerial position for failure to complete satisfactorily the probationary period; and
2. a separation action that is not excluded in the 16 excepted actions listed below.

The reference to "excluded" separation actions requires further explanation. An example would be the separation of an excepted service employee who lacks veterans' preference. Such a separation action is not appealable to the MSPB. Thus, it is not excluded or excepted from agency grievance procedures. However, neither is it included in an agency administrative grievance procedure unless the agency specifically provides for it.[331]

The broad coverage of the OPM Agency Grievance regulations is subject to the following list of exceptions:

1. the content of published agency regulation and policy;
2. a decision that is appealable to the MSPB, to the OPM, or to the EEOC;
3. nonselection for promotion from a group of properly ranked and certified candidates;
4. a preliminary warning of notice of an action;
5. the return of an individual from the Senior Executive Service (SES) to the General Schedule during the one-year probationary period or "for less than fully successful executive performance";
6. a reassignment of an SES appointee following the appointee's receipt of an unsatisfactory rating;
7. an action that terminates a temporary promotion within a maximum period of two years and returns the employee to the position from which the employee was temporarily appointed, or reassigns or demotes the employee to a different position that is not at a lower grade or pay than the position from which the employee was temporarily promoted;

---

[330]5 C.F.R. 771.205.
[331]5 C.F.R. 771.206(c)(2).

8. an action that terminates a term promotion at the completion of the project or specified period, or at the end of a rotational assignment in excess of two years but not more than five years, and returns the employee to the position from which he or she was promoted or to a different position of equivalent grade and pay;

9. the substance of the critical elements and performance standards of an employee's position which have been established in accordance with the requirements of 5 U.S.C. 4301–4305 and 5 C.F.R. Part 430;

10. the granting of, or failure to grant, an employee-performance award; or the adoption of, or failure to adopt, an employee suggestion or invention; or the granting of, or failure to grant, an award of the rank of meritorious or distinguished executive;

11. the receipt or failure to receive a performance award or a quality salary increase;

12. a decision to grant or not to grant a general increase, merit increase, or performance award under the Performance Management and Recognition System, or a decision on the granting of or failure to grant cash awards or honorary recognition;

13. the termination of a probationary employee for unsatisfactory performance;

14. the termination of an SES appointee during probation;

15. performance evaluations of members of the SES; and

16. an action taken in accordance with the terms of a formal agreement voluntarily entered into by an employee which either assigns the employee from one geographical location to another or returns an employee from an overseas assignment.[332]

Actual procedural requirements will vary from agency to agency, but minimum regulatory requirements have been established by OPM. The procedure must provide for prompt consideration and reasonable time limits for processing each grievance. There must be a hearing when one is suitable to ascertain the circumstances concerning the grievance. The fact finding must be carried out by a person who has not been involved in the matter being grieved and who does not occupy a position subordinate to any official who is or was involved in the matter being grieved.

The agency regulations must assure the grievant certain rights such as freedom from restraint, interference, coercion, discrimination, or reprisal in presenting a grievance. The grievant has a right to be accom-

---

[332] 5 C.F.R. 771.206(c).

panied and advised by a representative of his or her own choosing. An agency may disallow a representative only when it would result in a conflict of interest or position, a conflict with priority needs of the agency, or an unreasonable cost to the Government. The grievant must be given a reasonable time to present the grievance if the employee is in a duty status, that is, the employee is not suspended, terminated, on leave without pay, or in any other nonduty status. The grievant also has the right to communicate with the servicing personnel office. The grievant's representative must be assured similar rights by the agency regulations such as freedom from restraint and a reasonable amount of official time to present the grievance, if the representative is an agency employee in a duty status.

When a fact-finding process is utilized, agency regulations must require the establishment of a grievance file which is made available to the grievant and his or her representative for comment. Furthermore, when a grievance is put in writing, the agency decision must be in writing with a report of the findings and reasons therein. The agency decision must be made by an official at a level higher than any employee involved in any phase of the grievance, except when the head of the agency has been involved.[333]

The grievant must request relief that is personal to him or to her. Thus, for example, the grievant must request that a certain personnel action taken by the agency against the grievant be canceled (e.g., formal reprimand or suspension of 14 days or less) or that certain action involving the grievant be taken (e.g., grant a training request or a request for reassignment). A proper request for relief may not involve another individual, that is, a request that a supervisor be disciplined for his or her treatment of a grievant in a matter.[334]

---

[333]5 C.F.R. 771.302.
[334]5 C.F.R. 771.303(c).

Employee Relations

II. The Evolving Law

3. Appealable Actions

SANDRA H. SHAPIRO*

This chapter presents the various major types of personnel actions that federal employees can appeal to the Merit Systems Protection Board (MSPB).[1] However, under 5 U.S.C. 7121, the parties may contract to have arbitral review of matters not appealable to the MSPB in cases where a negotiated agreement exists. We will examine what procedures are required for an agency to take these actions and the substantive rights of the employees and agencies.

Adverse Actions

What Constitutes an Adverse Action

Under 5 U.S.C. 7512, an adverse action is defined as a removal, suspension for more than 14 days,[2] reduction in grade,[3] reduction in pay,

---

*This chapter was written by Sandra Shapiro in her private capacity. No official endorsement by the Department of Health and Human Services is intended or should be inferred.

[1] Employees who are covered by collective bargaining agreements may elect to appeal actions under 5 U.S.C. 4303 or 7512 either to MSPB or through the negotiated grievance procedure. 5 U.S.C. 7121(e)(1). Whichever procedure the employee elects, the same substantive law will apply. *Cornelius v. Nutt*, 472 U.S. 648, 119 LRRM 2905, 2906 (1985).

[2] Suspensions for 14 days or less are not appealable actions (see Chapter 1, "Other Agency Actions"). However, certain procedures must be followed when a short suspension is imposed on an employee, including a specific notice of charges, opportunity to respond orally or in writing or both, representation by an attorney, and a final decision. 5 U.S.C. 7501–7504.

[3] Employees who are reduced in grade or pay due to reduction in force or reclassification are entitled to retain their grade for two years, 5 U.S.C. 5362, and to retained pay thereafter, 5 U.S.C. 5363. See 5 C.F.R. Part 536. Reductions in grade and pay under such

or a furlough of 30 days or less. These actions are limited to disciplinary actions for misconduct and do not include disciplinary actions taken for poor performance. They are appealable only by "employees." The term "employee" is defined as an individual (1) who is appointed[4] in the competitive service and has completed a probationary or trial period,[5] or

circumstances cannot be appealed to the MSPB as adverse actions. Rather, they may be appealed only through the appropriate reduction-in-force or classification routes. *Atwell v. MSPB*, 670 F.2d 272 (D.C. Cir. 1981).

[4]Appointments in the federal service are not contractual in nature and an individual may not assume the benefits of a position until actually appointed to it. *United States v. Testan*, 424 F.2d 392 (1976). Appointments usually take place when an authorized individual, usually the personnel officer for the agency, signs a Standard Form 50 (SF-50), or its equivalent, indicating the individual's appointment. *Costner v. United States*, 665 F.2d 1016 (Ct. Cl. 1981); *Goutos v. United States*, 552 F.2d 922 (Ct. Cl. 1976); *Vukonich v. Civil Serv. Comm'n*, 589 F.2d 494 (10th Cir. 1978). Thereafter, the information on the SF-50 will govern the nature of the employment relationship. *Shaw v. United States*, 622 F.2d 520 (Ct. Cl. 1980); *Rhinehart v. SSA*, 4 MSPB 190 (1980). MSPB decisions finding that formal appointment documents are not necessary but that the Board will look to the totality of circumstances to determine whether an individual is an "employee," *Scott v. Department of the Army*, 7 MSPB 741 (1981); *Wenk v. OPM*, 21 MSPR 218 (1984), appear to have been reversed by the recent decision in *Horner v. Acosta*, 803 F.2d 687 (Fed. Cir. 1986), where the court notes that it would require "a significant degree of formality in the appointment process." See also *Watts v. OPM*, 814 F.2d 1576 (Fed. Cir. 1987).

To be a federal employee, an individual must meet all the requirements of 5 U.S.C. 2105. These include an appointment in the civil service, performance of a federal function, and supervision by another federal employee. *Horner v. Acosta, supra; McCarley v. MSPB*, 757 F.2d 280 (Fed. Cir. 1985). If an appointment is revoked before an individual reports for duty, he or she is not an employee and the revocation of the appointment is not reviewable. *Miller v. MSPB*, 794 F.2d 660 (Fed. Cir. 1986); *Hall v. Department of the Army*, 18 MSPR 23 (1983). An individual who erroneously is appointed to a position cannot be removed without adverse action procedures unless (1) the appointment violated an absolute statutory prohibition, or (2) the appointee committed fraud or misrepresentation in obtaining the appointment. *Jakes v. VA*, 793 F.2d 293 (Fed. Cir. 1986); *Bridgeman v. HUD*, 25 MSPR 178 (1984).

Simply being appointed is not sufficient to obtain appeal rights, however, because such rights are not available until completion of a probationary or trial period. *NTEU v. Reagan*, 663 F.2d 239, 108 LRRM 2948 (D.C. Cir. 1981); *Pratte v. NLRB*, 683 F.2d 1041 (7th Cir. 1982).

[5]Unless excepted by OPM or by statute, all civilian positions are in the competitive service. 5 C.F.R 1.2. The first year of an appointment in the competitive service is considered a probationary or trial period during which an adverse action against an employee may not be appealed to the MSPB or to the courts unless the employee makes a nonfrivolous allegation that the adverse action was based on discrimination on the basis of marital status or political affiliation. *Bates v. Department of the Navy*, 6 MSPB 279 (1981); *Poorsina v. MSPB*, 726 F.2d 507 (9th Cir. 1984). See generally *Sampson v. Murray*, 415 U.S. 61 (1974); *Connolly v. United States*, 716 F.2d 882 (Fed. Cir. 1983) (en banc); *Rosano v. United States*, 800 F.2d 1126 (Fed. Cir. 1985). Similarly, removal of a probationary employee is not subject to arbitration. *Immigration and Naturalization Serv. v. FLRA*, 709 F.2d 724, 113 LRRM 3488 (D.C. Cir. 1983). Individiuals with prior government service must serve a new probationary period if they are appointed off a register to a new position. *Marcus v. United States*, 473 F.2d 896 (Ct. Cl. 1973); *Dunard v. Farmers Home Admin.*, 13 MSPB 261 (1983). A probationer who is removed for preemployment reasons has a limited

(2) who is preference eligible[6] in the excepted service and has completed one year of current and continuous service.[7]

To take an adverse action against an employee, an agency must comply with applicable statutory and regulatory requirements.[8] At the outset, it must provide the employee 30 days' advance, written notice of the charges.[9] In computing the 30-day notice period, the day upon which the notice is given is not counted,[10] and the notice period runs through the close of business on the 30th day. If that day is a Sunday or a legal holiday,[11] the notice period expires on the next business day.

The notice of proposed adverse action must explain the charge or charges against the employee and must be specific enough to permit a thorough and informed reply.[12] The employee must be informed of the right to review all of the material relied upon by the agency in taking the action.[13] The action will not be reversed, however, if it mislabels the regulatory provision under which it is proceeding, as long as the notice is

---

right to appeal procedures followed by the employing agency in effecting his or her termination. 5 C.F.R. 315.805–806.

[6]"Preference-eligible employee" is defined at 5 U.S.C. 2108. Generally the term refers to individuals who have served in the armed forces of the United States and were discharged under honorable conditions. It also includes certain wives and mothers of some disabled or deceased veterans. See *Jacaruso v. Department of the Army*, 1 MSPB 360 (1980).

[7]OPM is authorized to exempt some positions from the competitive service, usually on the ground that it is inappropriate to examine for the positions. The largest group of federal employees in the excepted service is attorneys whose positions are included in Schedule A. 5 C.F.R. 213.3101. Confidential and policy-making positions also are excepted from the competitive service and are found in Schedule C. 5 C.F.R. 213.3301. In addition, OPM has provided for certain positions to be in the excepted service when filled by handicapped or mentally retarded individuals, on the ground that such individuals may not be able to establish their ability to do the jobs through normal tests but can establish such ability on the job. 5 C.F.R. 213.3101(t) and (u). Although non-preference-eligible employees in the excepted service are excluded by statute from appealing adverse actions taken against them to the MSPB and, moreover, may not seek judicial review of actions taken against them, *United States v. Fausto*, 56 USLW 4128 (1988); *Harrison v. Bowen*, 815 F.2d 1505 (D.C. Cir. 1987); *Mack v. United States*, 814 F.2d 120 (2d Cir. 1987); *Doe v. Department of Justice*, 753 F.2d 1092 (D.C. Cir. 1985); *Schwartz v. Department of Transp.*, 714 F.2d 1581 (Fed. Cir. 1983); *Smith v. MSPB*, 813 F.2d 1216 (Fed. Cir. 1987), some courts have found such rights based on agency assurances that the individual would serve until he or she gave cause to be removed or other constitutional considerations. *Ashton v. Civiletti*, 613 F.2d 923 (D.C. Cir. 1979).

[8]*Vitarelli v. Seaton*, 359 U.S. 535 (1959).

[9]5 U.S.C. 7513(b)(1).

[10]*Stringer v. United States*, 90 F. Supp. 375 (Ct. Cl. 1950).

[11]*Englehardt v. United States*, 125 Ct. Cl. 603 (1953).

[12]*Burkett v. United States*, 402 F.2d 1002 (Ct. Cl. 1968). In *Brewer v. Postal Serv.*, 647 F.2d 1093 (Ct. Cl. 1981), the court notes that the previous standard of "specifically and in detail" has been reduced to "stating the specific reasons for the proposed action." This, while reducing the detail required, still requires the agency to state the reasons in enough detail for the employee to make an informed reply.

[13]5 C.F.R. 752.404(b)(1); *Forrester v. HHS*, 27 MSPR 450 (1985).

sufficiently specific about the factual nature of the charges to allow the employee to make an informed reply.[14]

To determine whether an adverse action against a particular employee is appropriate, an agency may undertake an investigation. While the investigation is being conducted, the employee is required to cooperate[15] and need not be advised of the nature of the charges being considered.[16] If the employee has reason to believe that, as a result of the investigation, he or she may be subject to criminal charges, disciplinary action may not be brought for failure to cooperate in the investigation unless the employee is advised that any information he or she provides will not be the basis for a criminal action.[17] However, if the employee responds without a grant of immunity, the responses may be used against him or her in the adverse action.[18] If there is no possibility that criminal charges may result from the investigation, the employee may be charged with failure to cooperate.[19] An employee has no right to counsel during the investigation,[20] but members of a bargaining unit are entitled, by statute, to union representation.[21]

An agency may not place an employee on annual leave during the notice period if the employee is ready, willing, and able to work.[22] Moreover, an agency may not suspend an employee during the notice period on the ground that retaining that employee in a duty status may be injurious to fellow workers or to the public. Such action is, itself, an adverse action that may only be taken after the appropriate notice.[23]

---

[14]*Darby v. IRS*, 672 F.2d 197 (D.C. Cir. 1982); *Drew v. Department of the Navy*, 672 F.2d 197 (D.C. Cir. 1982); *Kochanny v. BATF*, 694 F.2d. 698 (Fed.Cir. 1982). However, the employee must be able to make an informed reply. Thus, where the employee is being removed for poor performance, specific examples must be given. *Smith v. Department of the Interior*, 8 MSPB 663 (1981).

[15]*Weston v. HUD*, 724 F.2d 943 (Fed. Cir. 1983).

[16]*Ashford v. Bureau of Prisons*, 6 MSPB 389 (1981).

[17]*Gardner v. Broderick*, 392 U.S. 273 (1968); *Kalkines v. United States*, 473 F.2d 1391 (Ct. Cl. 1973). However, failure to give such immunity is not fatal to an adverse action if the action is not based on the results of the investigative interview. *Anderson v. Postal Serv.*, 8 MSPB 334 (1981).

[18]*Womer v. Hampton*, 496 F.2d 99 (5th Cir. 1974).

[19]*Weston v. HUD*, supra note 15; *Ashford v. Bureau of Prisons*, supra note 16.

[20]*Ashford v. Bureau of Prisons*, supra note 16.

[21]5 U.S.C. 7114(a)(2). However, it is not necessary to notify an employee each time he or she is subject to questioning of the right to have a representative present; such notification need only be provided annually. *O'Kane v. Department of the Air Force*, 23 MSPR 25 (1984); *Sears v. Department of the Navy*, 7 MSPB 290 (1981).

[22]*Hart v. United States*, 284 F.2d 682 (Ct. Cl. 1960); *Taylor v. United States*, 131 Ct. Cl. 387 (1955). This erroneous status during a notice period, however, does not render illegal an otherwise valid removal. *Sirkin v. McAboy*, 182 F. Supp. 679 (E.D. Pa. 1960). *Thomas v. GSA*, 756 F.2d 86 (Fed. Cir. 1985).

[23]OPM's regulation, 5 C.F.R. 752.404(d)(3), allowing for the suspension of an

In some instances, an agency may place an employee on enforced leave. This may occur during the notice period or may occur while the agency awaits the results of a physical or mental examination or an Office of Personnel Management (OPM) ruling on an application for disability retirement. Enforced leave constitutes an appealable suspension if the action is taken for disciplinary motives or to keep the employee away from the workplace.[24] Enforced leave due to the agency belief that retention of the employee on duty would endanger other employees is "disciplinary" and, if it exceeds 14 days, is appealable to the MSPB.[25] If the enforced leave was not for disciplinary reasons, the MSPB will assume jurisdiction if the employee (1) was placed on sick leave without his or her consent, and (2) was ready, willing, and able to work during the period of leave.[26]

An agency may shorten the notice period if there is reasonable cause to believe that an employee against whom an adverse action has been proposed has committed a crime.[27] In addition, an agency may indefinitely suspend an employee pending the resolution of possible criminal misconduct if an indictment has been brought, if there is a nexus (or connection) between the crime the employee is alleged to have committed and the efficiency of the service, and if the penalty of suspension is reasonable.[28]

---

employee during the notice period in these instances was held to be invalid on the ground that, under 5 U.S.C. 7512(a), a suspension for more than 14 days is itself an adverse action requiring notice. *Cuellar v. Postal Serv.*, 8 MSPB 282 (1981). But see new OPM regulation at 5 C.F.R. 752.404(b)(3).

[24]*Thomas v. GSA, supra* note 22; *Passmore v. Department of Transp.*, 31 MSPR 65 (1986); *Lynch v. Department of Justice*, 32 MSPR 33 (1986).

[25]*Mercer v. HHS*, 772 F.2d 856 (Fed. Cir. 1985).

[26]*Mosely v. Department of the Navy*, 4 MSPB 220 (1980), *aff'd*, 229 Ct. Cl. 721 (1981); *Johnson v. Orr*, 747 F.2d 1352, 36 FEP Cases 515 (10th Cir. 1984).

[27]5 U.S.C. 7513(b)(1); *Schapansky v. Department of Transp.*, 735 F.2d 477 (Fed. Cir. 1984). Under 5 C.F.R. 752.404(d), in such circumstances, an agency may require the employee to answer within no less than 7 days and, if necessary, also may place the employee in a nonduty status with pay for up to 10 days.

[28]*Martin v. Customs Serv.*, 10 MSPB 568 (1982). See *Polcover v. Secretary of the Treasury*, 477 F.2d 1223 (D.C. Cir. 1973). In certain limited circumstances short of an indictment, such as an employee's arrest or the fact that an employee is the subject of a criminal investigation, there may be "reasonable cause" to suspend an employee. *Martin v. Customs Serv., supra*. However, solely the existence of complaints and warrants against an employee, absent the development of additional facts does not provide reasonable cause for a suspension. *Dunnington v. Department of Justice*, MSPB No. DA07528610554 (Feb. 2, 1988). An indefinite suspension based upon an employee's indictment must be discontinued when the indictment is dismissed. *Shaffer v. Defense Logistics Agency*, 35 MSPR 664 (1987). There is a split of authority concerning whether an employee who is suspended pending a criminal prosecution and subsequently is acquitted is entitled to back pay. Compare *Wiemers v. MSPB*, 792 F.2d 1113 (Fed. Cir. 1986) and *Janowitz v. United States*, 533 F.2d 538 (Ct. Cl. 1976) with *Brown v. Department of Justice*, 715 F.2d 662 (D.C. Cir. 1983), *Otherson v. Department of Justice*, 728 F.2d 1513 (D.C. Cir. 1984) and *Shaffer v. Defense Logistics Agency, supra*.

After receiving notice of proposed adverse action, an employee has a reasonable time, but not less than seven days, to respond to the notice orally or in writing or both.[29] He or she also has the right to be represented by counsel during this period.[30] Prior to responding, the employee must be granted the opportunity to review all of the material relied upon by the agency in making the charges.[31]

The oral reply has traditionally been considered an extremely significant part of the pretermination procedures. The oral reply must be heard by an official with sufficient rank to make either the final decision or a recommendation to the final decision maker.[32] Although there is no specific statutory or regulatory requirement that there be a dialogue between the oral reply officer and the employee, it is inappropriate to have the oral reply heard by an investigator who is trained only to listen to the reply but not to engage in any discussion with the employee.[33]

The final agency decision may be based upon only those reasons specified in the notice of proposed action.[34] Thus, if an employee is charged with stealing money, he cannot be removed for poor accounting procedures.[35] Improper *ex parte* communications with the agency's offi-

---

[29]5 U.S.C. 7513(b)(2).

[30]5 U.S.C. 7513(b). An agency may disallow as an employee's representative an individual whose representational activities would cause a conflict of interest or position. 5 C.F.R. 752.404(e). A conflict of interest was held to exist where the employee subject to the adverse action supervised employees who were members of the union in which the representative was an official, *Arnstein v. Department of the Army*, 9 MSPB 729 (1982), but not where the accused employee did not supervise members of the bargaining unit. *Sweeney v. Department of the Treasury*, 3 MSPB 321 (1980). While an employee against whom an adverse action is proposed has the right to counsel, *Dyson v. OPM*, 19 MSPR 118 (1984), the employee has the obligation to acquire counsel and is bound by the actions of the counsel whom he or she chooses. *Richards v. Department of the Navy*, 24 MSPR 50 (1984).

[31]5 C.F.R. 752.404(b) and 752.404(c)(1).

[32]*Riccuci v. United States*, 425 F.2d 1252 (Ct. Cl. 1970); *Polcover v. Secretary of the Treasury, supra* note 28. A high level personnel official appropriately heard an oral reply because he was in a position to advise the deciding official on agency personnel policy. *Swindell v. VA*, 10 MSPB 691 (1982). When the second line supervisor who heard the oral reply was replaced by a different second line supervisor who made the actual decision, no harmful error occurred because the first individual made a recommendation to the second individual. *Peterson v. HHS*, 25 MSPR 572 (1985). See also *Monroe v. Department of the Treasury*, 770 F.2d 1044 (Fed. Cir. 1985) where the court held that it was valid for the oral reply officer to provide a written summary of the oral reply to his successor who made the final decision.

[33]*Riccuci v. United States, supra* note 32; *Paterson v. Untied States*, 319 F.2d 882 (Ct. Cl. 1963).

[34]5 C.F.R. 752.404(f).

[35]*Knuckles v. Bolger*, 654 F.2d 25 (8th Cir. 1981). By the same token, charges of particular conduct that do not involve criminal activity cannot result in a final decision removing an individual for criminal activity. Cf. *Fugate v. LeBaube*, 372 F. Supp. 1208 (N.D. Tex. 1974).

cial who makes the final decision can result in overturning a final decision.[36]

If an employee is removed for criminal conduct, acquittal in the criminal action does not necessarily result in reversal of the removal as long as the agency proves its case against the employee before the MSPB.[37] However, an employee who is convicted of a crime cannot relitigate the conduct underlying the conviction before the MSPB.[38]

In taking an adverse action an agency may rely upon a prior disciplinary action if (1) the employee was informed of that action in writing, (2) the employee was provided the opportunity to have the prior action reviewed on its merits by an authority different from the one taking the action, and (3) the action was a matter of record. If these elements are present, a prior disciplinary action will be considered by the MSPB as a factor in the adverse action unless the decision in the prior action was "clearly erroneous," that is, if the action "leaves the Board with the definite and firm conviction that a mistake has been committed."[39] If

---

[36]*Sullivan v. Department of the Navy,* 720 F.2d 1266 (Fed. Cir. 1983); *Camero v. United States,* 375 F.2d 777 (Ct. Cl. 1967). However, other cases indicate that consultations by the deciding official with others are not necessarily improper unless a party with whom a deciding official consults is seeking vengeance. *DiSarno v. Department of Commerce,* 761 F.2d 657 (Fed. Cir. 1985); *Hanley v. GSA,* 829 F.2d 23 (Fed. Cir. 1987) (proposing and deciding official the same person); *Gonzales v. Defense Logistics Agency,* 772 F.2d 887 (Fed. Cir. 1985) (deciding official consulted with her supervisor). See also *Boddie v. Department of the Navy,* 827 F.2d 1578 (Fed. Cir. 1987) (improper for agency to remove proposing official and substitute another proposing official after first proposing official proposed a penalty that agency considered inadequate); *Monroe v. Department of the Treasury,* supra note 32 (not improper for agency counsel to interview appellant's witness prior to hearing). To support an allegation that *ex parte* communication during the decision-making process injured an employee, it must be demonstrated by the employee that (1) a new allegation was considered by the deciding official that the employee was not able to review and respond to, (2) the deciding official was influenced by the new allegation, and (3) the procedural error was harmful. *Appling v. SSA,* 30 MSPR 375 (1986); *Anderson v. Department of State,* 27 MSPR 344 (1985).

[37]*Messersmith v. GSA,* 8 MSPB 496 (1981); *Wiemers v. Department of Justice,* 29 MSPR 9 (1985). In any event, acquittal of a crime does not prevent removal for the same conduct since standard of proof in a civil action is more lenient than "beyond a reasonable doubt" required for criminal conviction. *Finfer v. Caplin,* 344 F.2d 38 (2d Cir. 1965).

[38]*Crofoot v. GPO,* 823 F.2d 495 (Fed. Cir. 1987); *Graybill v. Postal Serv.,* 782 F.2d 1567 (Fed. Cir. 1986); *Chisholm v. Defense Logistics Agency,* 656 F.2d 42 (3d Cir. 1981). An employee also may be collaterally estopped from denying that he is guilty of the crimes for which he was convicted pursuant to an *Alford* plea. (See *North Carolina v. Alford,* 400 U.S. 25, 38 (1970). *Loveland v. Department of the Air Force,* 34 MSPR 484 (1987).

[39]*Bolling v. Department of the Air Force,* 8 MSPB 658 (1981); *Gamble v. VA,* 31 MSPR 649 (1986). The pendency of a grievance pending on the prior disciplinary action should trigger an examination by the Board as to whether the decision in the prior action was clearly erroneous. *Carr v. Department of the Air Force,* 9 MSPB 714 (1982). Existence of prior disciplinary actions can be relied upon even if prior actions were based on charges different in nature from charges in the pending action. *Henson v. Department of the Air Force,* 14 MSPR 401 (1983).

these elements are not present, the agency will be required to prove before the MSPB the underlying charges of the prior disciplinary action if the employee challenges them.[40]

"Efficiency of the Service" Concept

An adverse action may be taken only for "such cause as will promote the efficiency of the service."[41] In addition, it is a prohibited personnel practice for an agency to take an action based on conduct that does not adversely affect the performance of the employee or the performance of others.[42] Thus, the agency must prove that any adverse action for misconduct was taken to promote the efficiency of the service. Among the activities which have been held to constitute appropriate grounds for adverse action are: lying about qualifications on preemployment documents,[43] falsification of other government documents including travel vouchers,[44] threatening or using abusive language to supervisors or others or otherwise disrupting an office,[45] violations of the standards of conduct or actions giving the appearance of impropriety,[46] sexual harassment of

---

[40]*Howard v. Department of the Army,* 6 MSPB 180 (1981). When an employee is notified that the agency intends to rely on prior disciplinary actions and does not challenge that reliance before the MSPB, the prior disciplinary actions should be considered by the Board. *Barbour v. Department of Defense,* 10 MSPB 750 (1982).

[41]5 U.S.C. 7313(a).

[42]5 U.S.C. 2302(b)(10).

[43]*Kissner v. OPM,* 792 F.2d 133 (Fed. Cir. 1986); *Harp v. Department of the Navy,* 791 F.2d 161 (Fed. Cir. 1986); *Rodriguez v. Seamans,* 463 F.2d 837 (D.C. Cir. 1982). To remove an employee for false statements on an application, it must be shown that the statements were made with intent to deceive. *Naekel v. Department of Transp.,* 782 F.2d 975 (Fed. Cir. 1986); *Pichot v. Department of Justice,* 29 MSPR 477 (1986). In determining whether an employee falsified prior employment, OPM investigative records can be probative evidence. *Howard v. OPM,* 31 MSPR 617 (1986).

[44]*Quinton v. Department of Transp.,* 808 F.2d 826 (Fed.Cir. 1986); *DeLong v. Hampton,* 422 F.2d 21 (3d Cir. 1970); *Hutchins v. Department of Justice,* 7 MSPB 475 (1981). Falsification of a travel document can form the basis of a disciplinary action only if it is proven that incorrect information was given with intent to deceive or mislead the agency. *Allen v. Department of the Air Force,* 34 MSPR 314 (1987); *Boers v. Department of the Air Force,* 35 MSPR 341 (1987).

[45]*Tirado v. HUD,* 757 F.2d 265 (Fed. Cir. 1985) (employee can be removed for disrupting office even though he is disturbed if employee is ineligible for disability retirement); *James v. FERC,* 747 F.2d 1581 (Fed. Cir. 1984); *Williams v. VA,* 701 F.2d 764 (8th Cir. 1983); *Roberson v. VA,* 27 MSPR 489 (1985). In *Metz v. Department of the Treasury,* 780 F.2d 1001 (Fed. Cir. 1986), the court held that, to determine whether a threat actually was made, MSPB should consider (1) the speaker's intent, (2) the listener's reactions, (3) the listener's apprehension of harm, and (4) any conditional nature of the statements. See *Carroll v. Department of the Air Force,* 34 MSPR 87 (1987).

[46]*Stanek v. Department of Transp.,* 805 F.2d 1572 (Fed. Cir. 1986); *Ferrone v. Department of Labor,* 797 F.2d 962 (Fed. Cir. 1986); *Lowery v. Richardson,* 390 F. Supp. 356 (W.D. Okla. 1973); *Connett v. Department of the Navy,* 31 MSPR 322 (1986). See *Massa v.*

subordinates,[47] striking,[48] abuse of or failure to properly request leave,[49] gambling on government property,[50] misuse or misappropriation of government property,[51]and insubordination.[52] Under 31 U.S.C. 638a(c)(2), any federal employee who willfully uses a government-owned vehicle for other than official purposes must be suspended for at least 30 days.[53] It must be shown, however, that the misuse was willful which means, "voluntarily and consciously using a government car with knowledge and reckless disregard of whether the use was for other than official purposes."[54]

The requirement that adverse actions be taken only for "such cause as will promote the efficiency of the service" has been interpreted to mean that when the adverse action is based on off-duty conduct, the agency particularly must show a "nexus" or connection between the conduct and the efficiency of the service.[55]

> [A] nexus determination must be based on evidence linking the employee's off duty misconduct with the efficiency of the service or, in "certain egregious circumstances," on a presumption of nexus which may arise from

Department of Defense, 815 F.2d 69 (Fed.Cir. 1987) (to remove employee for accepting a gratuity from government contractor, agency must establish that employee was aware he was accepting such a gratuity).

[47]*SSA v. Carter*, 35 MSPR 466 (1987); *Vakili v. Department of Agric.*, 35 MSPR 534 (1987); *Carosella v. Postal Serv.*, 30 MSPR 199 (1986), aff'd, 816 F.2d 638, 43 FEP Cases 845 (Fed. Cir. 1987); *Marotta v. HHS*, 34 MSPR 252 (1987); *Hillen v. Department of the Army*, 35 MSPR 453 (1987). If an agency charges an employee with a violation of Title VII of the Civil Rights Act, the employee's actions must meet the sexual harassment standards of that Act. However, the conduct need not meet the Title VII standard for sexual harassment if the agency charges the employee with violating the agency's own policy or rule.

[48]*Schapansky v. FAA*, 735 F.2d 477 (Fed. Cir. 1984). See *Korte v. OPM*, 797 F.2d 967 (Fed. Cir. 1985) (permissible for OPM to find an applicant unsuitable for having been on strike). See also *Brown v. Department of Transp.*, 735 F.2d 543 (Fed. Cir. 1984) (nexus between advocating strike and efficiency of the service).

[49]*Davis v. VA*, 792 F.2d 1111 (Fed. Cir. 1986).

[50]*Hunt v. HHS*, 758 F.2d 608 (Fed. Cir. 1985).

[51]*Major v. Department of the Navy*, 31 MSPR 283 (1986) (action for theft of government property requires intent to appropriate property to a use inconsistent with owner's rights and benefits); *Kumferman v. Department of the Navy*, 785 F.2d 286 (Fed.Cir. 1986); *Crofoot v. GPO*, 761 F.2d 661 (Fed. Cir. 1985).

[52]*Bassett v. Department of the Navy*, 34 MSPR 66 (1987). Employees are required to obey agency orders. *Hubble v. Department of the Navy*, 6 MSPR 659 (1981); *McPartland v. Department of Transp.*, 14 MSPR 506 (1983), aff'd, 795 F.2d 1017 (Fed. Cir. 1986).

[53]*Cabral v. HHS*, 7 MSPR 372 (1981).

[54]*Felton v. EEOC*, 820 F.2d 391 (Fed. Cir. 1987); *Cottman v. Department of Labor*, 23 MSPR 688 (1984); *Woody v. GSA*, 6 MSPB 410 (1981). See also *D'Elia v. Department of the Treasury*, 14 MSPR 54 (1982) (stopping at a disco on route from restaurant to hotel not misuse); *Lynch v. Department of Justice*, 32 MSPR 33 (1986) (stopping for prescheduled dental appointment not misuse); *Ford v. HUD*, 450 F. Supp. 559 (N.D. Ill. 1978) (taking car home when needed to use it early next day not misuse); *Harrington v. Department of Transp.*, 14 MSPR 307 (1983); *Doolin v. Department of Justice*, 21 MSPR 563 (1984) (taking car home when supervisor refused permission is misuse).

[55]*Norton v. Macy*, 417 F.2d 1161, 9 FEP Cases 1382 (D.C. Cir. 1969).

the nature and gravity of the misconduct. In the latter situation, the presumption may be overcome by evidence showing an absence of adverse effect on service efficiency, in which case the agency may no longer rely solely on the presumption, but must present evidence to carry its burden of proving nexus.[56]

In establishing the existence of a nexus, an agency need not present proof of a direct effect on the employee's job performance if the employee's conduct is inimical to the agency's mission.[57]

Homicide has been held by all adjudicative bodies to present an "egregious circumstance" under which nexus can be presumed.[58] Although there is some dispute among courts, in most other instances, however, the burden is upon the agency to plead and prove that the efficiency of the service is promoted by the removal.[59]

A common situation requiring a nexus determination involves an action taken for nonpayment of debts. In most instances, such nonpayment has been found to be a matter between the employee and his creditor, and only "inveterate and unrepentant deadbeats were to be disciplined."[60]

Another area raising nexus issues is that of nontraditional sexual behavior. The government may not take action against a homosexual without proving that the individual's sexual activity is a detriment to the

[56]*Merritt v. Department of Justice*, 6 MSPB 493 (1981). In *Merritt*, the MSPB concluded that the passage of 5 U.S.C. 2302(b)(10) reversed the position taken by some courts that the nexus determination was for the agency to make and should not be reversed unless clearly arbitrary and capricious. Rather, the MSPB held that it was required to determine in every case whether the agency had met its burden of proving nexus. The Court of Appeals for the Federal Circuit will affirm the MSPB nexus decision if it is based upon substantial evidence. *Allred v. HHS*, 786 F.2d 1128 (Fed. Cir. 1986).

[57]*Allred v. HHS, supra* note 56; *Wild v. HUD*, 692 F.2d 1129 (7th Cir. 1982); *Morones v. Department of Justice*, 35 MSPR 285 (1987).

[58]*Gueory v. Hampton*, 510 F.2d 1222 (D.C. Cir. 1974). Authorities are not in agreement on whether particularly heinous off-duty conduct, such as sexual molestation of a child, can be grounds for a *per se* nexus. Those holding that a nexus can be presumed in such circumstances include *Hayes v. Department of the Navy*, 727 F.2d 1535 (Fed. Cir. 1984); *Doe v. NSA*, 6 MSPB 467 (1981), *aff'd sub nom. Stalans v. NSA*, 678 F.2d 482 (4th Cir. 1982). Other courts have required the government to prove the nexus between conduct and the efficiency of the service. *D.E. v. Department of the Navy*, 707 F.2d 1049 (9th Cir. 1983); *Bonet v. Postal Serv.*, 661 F.2d 1071 (5th Cir. 1981). It would appear that in the Fifth and Ninth circuits, nexus can never be presumed no matter how heinous the conduct. Even where nexus is presumed, however, the employee can always rebut that nexus by showing that efficiency of the service will not be promoted by his or her removal.

[59]*Crofoot v. GPO, supra* note 51; *Young v. Hampton*, 568 F.2d 1253 (7th Cir. 1977); *Phillips v. Bergland*, 586 F.2d 1007 (4th Cir. 1978); *Gloster v. GSA*, 720 F.2d 700 (D.C. Cir. 1983); *McLeod v. Department of the Army*, 714 F.2d 918 (9th Cir. 1983).

[60]*Norton v. Macy, supra* note 55; *White v. Bloomberg*, 345 F. Supp. 133 (D. Md. 1972); *Vilt v. Marshals Serv.*, 16 MSPR 192 (1983). In *Cornish v. Department of Commerce*, 9 MSPB 611 (1982), the MSPB upheld removal of an employee whose repeated telephone calls from creditors were causing disruption in the office.

efficiency of the service.[61] Furthermore, the government may not punish cohabitation out of wedlock.[62]

In recent years, several cases have arisen on the nexus between conviction for sexual molestation, particularly of children, and the efficiency of the service. The courts have split on whether a nexus can be presumed from such conduct.[63]

Certain types of actions, although occurring off duty have been held to be so closely related to the employee's work as to give rise to a nexus. These include, among others, deliberate misrepresentation by employees of the Internal Revenue Service of their own income,[64] falsification of job applications,[65] violations of agency standards of conduct which create a conflict of interest,[66] and defrauding the government of welfare benefits.[67]

Many cases have arisen on the subject of punishment for the possession or distribution of controlled substances. Even in this instance, the government must prove the nexus between the actions and the efficiency of the service.[68] Finally, in the nexus area, mere conviction of a crime, unless the crime is homicide, is insufficient for a removal action in the absence of proof by the government of a nexus.[69]

---

[61]*SIR v. Hampton*, 63 F.R.D. 399 (N.D. Cal. 1973); *Norton v. Macy, supra* note 55. But see *George v. Department of the Air Force*, 29 MSPR 95 (1985) (off-duty homosexual solicitation constituted sexual harassment which was grounds for removal).

[62]*Mindel v. Civil Serv. Comm'n*, 312 F. Supp. 485 (N.D. Cal. 1970); *Major v. Hampton*, 413 F. Supp. 66 (E.D. La. 1976).

[63]See *supra* note 58. Some other cases on sexual molestation include *Graybill v. Postal Serv.*, 782 F.2d 1567 (Fed. Cir. 1986); *Allred v. HHS, supra* note 56; *Hackney v. Department of Justice*, 23 MSPR 462 (1984).

[64]*Rotolo v. MSPB*, 636 F.2d 6 (1st Cir. 1980); *Monaco v. Department of the Treasury*, 15 MSPR 727 (1983). An employee's failure to pay taxes also may be a ground for disciplinary action. *Eilertson v. Department of the Navy*, 23 MSPR 152 (1984).

[65]See *supra* note 43.

[66]See *supra* note 46.

[67]*Gamble v. Postal Serv.*, 6 MSPB 487 (1981). But see *Gloster v. GSA, supra* note 59.

[68]*Parker v. Postal Serv.*, 819 F.2d 1113 (Fed. Cir. 1987); *Stump v. Department of the Treasury*, 761 F.2d 680 (Fed. Cir. 1985); *Masino v. United States*, 589 F.2d 1043 (Ct. Cl. 1978); *Borsari v. FAA*, 699 F.2d 106 (2d Cir. 1983); *Grebosz v. Civil Serv. Comm'n*, 472 F. Supp. 1081 (S.D.N.Y. 1979); *Young v. Hampton, supra* note 59; *McLeod v. Department of the Army, supra* note 59; *Parker v. Postal Serv.*, 31 MSPR 58 (1986); *Averill v. Department of the Navy*, 30 MSPR 327 (1986). In *Kruger v. Department of Justice*, 32 MSPR 71, 25 GERR 95 (1987), MSPB held that prison guards could be suspended for 60 days for off-duty marijuana smoking because the conduct could "cause the public, and their co-workers, to question whether the drug laws were properly enforced within the correctional facility." The punishment was reduced from removal based on the employee's long-time service, lack of prior disciplinary records, absence of negative publicity, and the agency's failure to prove that the employees were habitual users. See also *Facer v. Department of the Air Force*, 33 MSPR 243, 25 GERR 645 (1987).

[69]*Ahr v. Nelson*, 632 F.2d 148 (S.D. Tex. 1985); *Abrams v. Department of the Navy*, 11 MSPR 143 (1982). But see *Ferris v. Department of the Navy*, 810 F.2d 1121 (Fed. Cir. 1987) (MSPB had no jurisdiction when employee removed as a result of convicting court ordering disqualification from "holding any office . . . with the United States.").

Other Issues

Many factors enter into the appropriateness of an agency's determination to take disciplinary action against an employee. One of these factors is the presence of an alcohol problem. In addition to the fact that alcoholism (and drug abuse) are handicapping conditions within the terms of the Rehabilitation Act of 1973, federal employees are also protected by the Comprehensive Alcohol and Alcoholism Prevention, Treatment and Rehabilitation Act of 1970,[70] which prohibits removal "solely" upon the ground of prior alcoholism, but does not prohibit removal of an employee who cannot function in his or her position,[71] or whose alcoholism or drug abuse constitutes a danger to the public.[72] An agency must offer rehabilitation assistance to an employee with an alcohol problem prior to proposing disciplinary action, even in a case in which the agency was unaware of the nature of the problem.[73] An employee must have a reasonable period of time in which to demonstrate rehabilitation.[74] After such reasonable time, if rehabilitation is not effected, disciplinary action may be taken if otherwise appropriate.[75]

If an agency believes that the reason an employee committed an offense or performed so poorly results from the fact that he or she is mentally disabled, and the employee has at least five years of federal service, but is too handicapped to apply for a disability retirement, the agency is obligated to make application on the employee's behalf.[76] The

---

[70]42 U.S.C. 290dd-1. Comparable provisions for drug abuse are found at 42 U.S.C. 290ee-1.

[71]*Spragg v. Campbell*, 466 F. Supp. 658 (D.S. D. 1979).

[72]*Kulling v. Department of Transp.*, 24 MSPR 56 (1984) (air traffic controller who abuses drugs need not be accommodated because of agency's overriding concern for public safety). But see *Green v. Department of the Air Force*, 31 MSPR 152 (1986) (nurse who was successfully participating in drug rehabilitation program and who was not shown to have been a danger to her patients must be given opportunity to complete program).

[73]*Ruzek v. GSA*, 7 MSPB 307 (1981); *Noe v. Postal Serv.*, 28 MSPR 86 (1985) (employee must be accommodated who raises alcoholism for first time at oral reply); *Corral v. Department of the Navy*, MSPB No. SF07528610409, 25 GERR 647 (1987); *Chaplin v. Department of the Navy*, 35 MSPR 639 (1987) (employee must be given chance to complete rehabilitation program when he accepts agency offer during notice period).

[74]*Keels v. Department of the Navy*, 8 MSPB 385 (1981).

[75]*Washington v. Department of the Navy*, 30 MSPR 323 (1986) ("The requirement upon an agency to reasonably accommodate an employee's alcoholism handicap does not obligate an agency to tolerate indefinitely misconduct stemming from an alcoholic condition."); *Smith v. Postal Serv.*, 13 MSPB 267 (1983); *Holmes v. IRS*, 9 MSPB 547 (1982).

[76]*Mail Handlers v. Postal Serv.*, 657 F. Supp. 295 (D.Colo. 1987); *Anderson v. Morgan*, 263 F.2d 903 (D.C. Cir. 1959); *Lizut v. Department of the Army*, 717 F.2d 1396 (Fed.Cir. 1983) (agency has duty to file if it believes disability is caused by mental disease and not willful misconduct); *Asberry v. Postal Serv.*, 25 MSPR 314 (1984); *Brink v. VA*, 4 MSPB 419 (1980). See OPM regulations at 5 C.F.R. 339.101–304, which put the burden on employees to demonstrate a medical condition and initiate disability retirement.

agency's obligation does not depend upon whether MSPB finds, if an appeal is brought, that the employee was, in fact, disabled but, rather, upon "what reasonable conclusion would have been drawn based upon the facts known to the proper agency officials at the time when a decision had to be made."[77] If the employee is not eligible for disability retirement because he or she has not worked for the requisite five years, but is unable to perform due to a disability, he or she can be removed.[78]

A common source of difficulty arises in disciplinary actions for excessive absence. As a general rule, an absence that has been excused cannot be the basis for a disciplinary action.[79] However, an exception will be made if (1) the absence was unavoidable so that agency approval was immaterial, (2) the absence continued beyond a reasonable time and the employee was warned that adverse action might be initiated unless he or she became available for duty, and (3) the agency shows that the position needed to be filled by an employee available on a regular basis.[80] Proof of unauthorized absences is sufficient cause to discipline.[81]

Generally, requests for sick leave must be approved if accompanied by appropriate documentation.[82] Such request need not be approved, however, if the agency has reason to question the documentation or it can establish that, due to its workload, it requires the services to be performed. In those circumstances, the agency can remove the employee for unreliable attendance.[83]

---

[77]*Steve v. Department of the Air Force*, 13 MSPB 143 (1983).

[78]*Tirado v. HUD*, 757 F.2d 265 (Fed. Cir. 1985). If an employee is removed for physical inability to perform, there must be a clear relationship between the employee's ability to do the job and the efficiency of the service. The agency cannot rely on the existence of a disabling condition and speculation on how it will affect ability to do the job. *Sebald v. Department of the Air Force*, 32 MSPR 164 (1987); *White v. Department of the Army*, 8 MSPR 575 (1982).

[79]*Webb v. Postal Serv.*, 9 MSPB 749 (1982); *Moore v. Defense Logistics Agency*, 670 F. Supp. 800 (N.D. Ill. 1987). However, this does not prevent the agency from requiring the employee to provide medical certification. *Moore v. Defense Logistics Agency, supra*.

[80]*Rabago v. Department of the Army*, 25 MSPR 530 (1985) (removal reversed because agency did not show necessary warning).

[81]*Williams v. Department of the Army*, 24 MSPR 537 (1984).

[82]The agency must specify the documentation it will require in order to grant leave. *Schultz v. Navy*, 810 F.2d 1133 (Fed. Cir. 1987). See also *Morton v. Department of the Navy*, 32 MSPR 104 (1987); *Agnes v. Postal Serv.*, 4 MSPB 173 (1980); *Smith v. Department of Labor*, 25 MSPR 102 (1984). Sick leave must be granted if the employee meets the requirements of 5 C.F.R. 630.401. *Wade v. Department of the Navy*, 829 F.2d 1106 (Fed. Cir. 1987).

[83]*Lawson v. GPO*, 8 MSPB 157 (1981). An agency is not precluded from showing that an employee is of "marginal value" because of "unreliable attendance." *Washington v. Department of the Army*, 813 F.2d 390 (Fed. Cir. 1987); *Cade v. Postal Serv.*, 8 MSPR 717 (1981).

The granting of leave without pay (LWOP) is at the discretion of the agency. However, if an adverse action is based upon a charge of Absence Without Offical Leave (AWOL) due to the denial of LWOP, the circumstances will be reviewed to determine if the denial of LWOP was reasonable.[84] An employer is required to grant an employee's request for a leave of absence for military duty.[85]

An agency is prohibited from taking an action against an employee on a basis which violates his or her constitutional rights.[86] A disciplinary action taken because an employee exercised his or her right to free speech would constitute such a prohibited action. Not all speech is protected, however. Speech is not protected if it is determined that, on balance, the interest of the government in promoting the efficiency of the service outweighs the individiual's private interest in a particular case,[87] the matter is not one of public concern,[88] or the employee's actions were purely self-serving.[89] To establish a claim of reprisal for engaging in a protected activity, the appellant must demonstrate (1) that he or she engaged in the protected activity, (2) that he or she was later treated in an adverse fashion by the agency, (3) that the deciding official had actual or constructive knowledge that he or she engaged in the protected activity, and (4) there is a casual connection between the protected activity and the adverse action.[90]

The courts recently have considered the issue of whether the MSPB can review the denial of a security clearance if that denial results in the loss of a job. The MSPB had earlier held that it had only limited jurisdiction to review whether the agency had afforded minimal due process in denying the clearance. On review, the Supreme Court has held that the MSPB is limited to determining whether in fact the clearance was denied and whether transfer to a nonsensitive position was feasible.[91]

---

[84]*Wells v. HHS*, 29 MSPR 346 (1985); *Holt v. Department of the Navy*, 5 MSPB 453 (1981). Removal for absence without leave may be an appropriate penalty. *Davis v. VA*, 792 F.2d 1111 (Fed. Cir. 1986); *Washington v. Department of the Army, supra* note 83.

[85]*Genus v. Department of the Army*, 35 MSPR 345 (1987).

[86]*Perry v. Sindermann*, 408 U.S. 593 (1972).

[87]*Pickering v. Board of Educ.*, 391 U.S. 563 (1968); *Mings v. Department of Justice*, 813 F.2d 384 (Fed. Cir. 1987).

[88]*Connick v. Myers*, 461 U.S. 138, 1 IER Cases 178 (1983); *Ledeaux v. VA*, 29 MSPR 440 (1985); *Barnes v. Small*, 840 F.2d 972 (D.C. Cir. 1988).

[89]*Fiorillo v. Department of Justice*, 795 F.2d 1544 (Fed. Cir. 1986); *Foster v. Ripley*, 645 F.2d 1142 (D.C. Cir. 1981); *Prescott v. National Inst. of Child Health & Dev.*, 6 MSPB 216 (1981). In some instances, even an employee with no statutory or regulatory appeal rights may acquire the right to a hearing if he or she makes a genuine allegation that First Amendment rights may have been violated. *Perry v. Sindermann, supra* note 86; *Borrell v. USIA*, 682 F.2d 981 (D.C. Cir. 1982).

[90]*Cooney v. Department of the Air Force*, 34 MSPR 183 (1987).

[91]*Department of the Navy v. Egan*, 56 USLW 4150 (1988). See *Hoska v. Department of the Army*, 677 F.2d 131 (D.C. Cir. 1982).

Penalties Assessed

In any particular adverse action, the MSPB may determine that the penalty imposed by an agency was excessive under the circumstances and that a lesser penalty would be appropriate.[92] In judging the appropriateness of a penalty, the MSPB will take into account the so-called *Douglas*[93] factors which include the nature and seriousness of the offense; nature of the job; employee's past disciplinary record; past work record, including length of service; effect of the offense on the employee's ability to perform; consistence of the penalty with that levied on other employees for similar offenses; agency's table of penalties; notoriety of the offense, if any; clarity with which the agency notified the employee of its expectations; potential for rehabilitation; mitigating circumstances; and adequacy of alternative sanctions to deter such actions in the future.

Although the MSPB must consider the factors relevant to each case, it need not list and discuss all of the *Douglas* factors.[94] The penalty should be reviewed by the MSPB to determine whether the agency abused its discretion, but in no event should the presiding official substitute his or her judgment for that of the agency concerning the seriousness of the offense.[95] Rather than "freely substitute its judgment for that of the agency, [the Board] will assure only that managerial judgment has been properly exercised within tolerable limits of reasonableness."[96]

---

[92]*Douglas v. VA*, 6 MSPB 313 (1981). Failure by MSPB to properly consider the appropriateness of a penalty may be grounds for reversal. *Parsons v. Department of the Air Force*, 707 F.2d 1406 (D.C.Cir. 1983).

[93]*Douglas v. VA, supra* note 92.

[94]*Kumferman v. Department of the Navy*, 785 F.2d 286 (Fed.Cir. 1986); *Southers v. VA*, 813 F.2d 1223 (Fed. Cir. 1987); *Nagel v. HHS*, 707 F.2d 1384 (Fed. Cir. 1983). Some examples of penalty considerations include: *Miguel v. Department of the Army*, 727 F.2d 1081 (Fed. Cir. 1984) (removal too harsh for stealing one bar of soap after 24 good years of service); *Dominguez v. Department of the Air Force*, 803 F.2d 680 (Fed.Cir. 1986) (removal not too harsh for beating up supervisor in light of the (1) brutal nature of the conduct, (2) notoriety it received from other employees, and (3) lack of evidence of remorse); *Quinton v. Department of Transp.*, 808 F.2d 826 (Fed.Cir. 1986) (removal not too harsh although only two of seven charges were affirmed when they were the most egregious); *Hagmeyer v. Department of the Treasury*, 757 F.2d 1281 (Fed.Cir. 1985) (removal too harsh when all but one charge was dropped and that was the least egregious); *Gonzales v. Defense Logistics Agency*, 772 F.2d 887 (Fed. Cir. 1985) (removal not too harsh for supervisor with 32 years of service who stole agency property because he had continuous access to valuable materials).

[95]*Stump v. Department of Transp.*, 761 F.2d 680 (Fed. Cir. 1985); *Beard v. GSA*, 801 F.2d 1318 (Fed.Cir. 1986); *Weiss v. Postal Serv.*, 700 F.2d 754 (1st Cir. 1983). An agency need not have considered the appropriateness of alternative penalties, nor need it show that it selected the best penalty, it need show only that the penalty it selected was reasonable. *Thias v. Department of the Air Force*, 32 MSPR 46 (1986); *Martinez v. Department of Defense*, 21 MSPR 556 (1984).

[96]*Brown v. Department of the Treasury*, 34 MSPR 132 (1987).

If an agency has a table of penalties, the courts have held that there is doubt whether an agency can "violate its own regulations." To the extent that a table of penalties is expressed in mandatory language rather than simply providing guidance, an agency is obligated to comply with its table of penalties.[97]

Harmful Error

An agency's decision to take an adverse action against an employee will not be sustained if there was a harmful procedural error made in arriving at the decision.[98] In determining whether a procedural error was "harmful," the burden is on the employee to show that, in the absence of the error, the result reached *might* have been different,[99] either at the level of the agency decision or at the MSPB.[100]

Involuntary Reassignment

An agency may transfer any employee to any place at any time for the good of the service.[101] In the event that an employee refuses to accept a transfer, is disciplined, and appeals to the MSPB, the agency must demonstrate before the Board that its decision to reassign the employee was based on legitimate management reasons. If the employee submits evidence to put into question the legitimacy of the decision to reassign him, the agency must present further evidence to show that the efficiency

---

[97]*Facer v. Department of the Air Force*, 836 F.2d 535 (Fed.Cir. 1988). See *Parsons v. Department of the Air Force, supra* note 92.

[98]5 U.S.C. 7701(c)(2)(A).

[99]*Cornelius v. Nutt*, 472 U.S. 648, 119 LRRM 2905 (1985); *Mercer v. HHS*, 772 F.2d 856 (Fed. Cir. 1985); *Monroe v. Department of the Treasury*, 770 F.2d 1044 (Fed. Cir. 1975). Accord *Harp v. Department of the Navy*, 791 F.2d 161 (Fed. Cir. 1986) (loss of transcript by MSPB not harmful error); *Handy v. Postal Serv.*, 754 F.2d 335 (Fed.Cir. 1985) (violation of procedure prescribed by statute not per se harmful; failure to give oral reply not harmful error since appellant did not show how it might have altered decision); *Clark v. Department of the Army*, 34 MSPR 284 (1987); *Smith v. Postal Serv.*, 789 F.2d 1540 (Fed. Cir. 1986) (late receipt of notice not harmful error since appellant did not indicate he would have said or done anything at predetermination conference which might have altered result); *Miguel v. Department of the Army*, 727 F.2d 1081 (Fed. Cir. 1984) (failure to have union representative present as provided by contract was harmful error since he might have aided appellant in pleading his case); *Miyai v. Department of Transp.*, 32 MSPR 15 (1986) (complete failure to give procedural protections is harmful error); *Boddie v. Department of the Navy*, 827 F.2d 1578 (Fed. Cir. 1987) (substitution of new proposing official for former proposing official due to pressure to propose a harsher penalty is harmful error).

[100]*Harp v. Department of the Navy, supra* note 99.

[101]*Coyne v. Boyett*, 490 F. Supp. 292 (S.D.N.Y. 1980); *Kletschka v. Driver*, 411 F.2d 436 (2d Cir. 1969).

of the service was promoted by the transfer.[102] In the absence of indication that a reassignment was not based on valid management reasons a reassignment is not reviewable by the MSPB, but if a reassignment is connected with another reviewable action, the entire matter becomes reviewable.[103]

It is considered a valid management action for an agency to transfer an employee who is unable to function properly or to get along with fellow employees, although there may be no pressing need for his services at another location.[104] In addition, the Board will not review a transfer simply because the new location is not as desirable or the employee will not be as happy there.[105] However, an agency may not reassign an employee as a sham with the object of either punishment for protected activities,[106] or encouragement to resign.[107] If there are valid management reasons behind the reassignment, however, the employee bears the burden at all times of convincing the reviewing authority that the reasons for the removal were not genuine or were otherwise improper.[108]

Coerced Resignation

In certain limited circumstances, a resignation (or retirement) may constitute an adverse action.[109] This is the case if the resignation is obtained through fraud, coercion, or misrepresentation.[110] A resignation normally is presumed to be voluntary, and the presumption will prevail unless the employee presents sufficient evidence that the resignation was obtained by duress or coercion.[111] In making such a determination, the MSPB applies a three-part test: (1) one side involuntarily accepted the

[102]*Ketterer v. Federal Crop Ins. Corp.*, 2 MSPB 459 (1980).

[103]*Brewer v. American Battle Monuments Comm'n*, 779 F.2d 663 (Fed. Cir. 1985).

[104]*Sexton v. Kennedy*, 523 F.2d 1311 (6th Cir. 1975); *Hernandez v. Alexander*, 607 F.2d 920 (10th Cir. 1979); *Robb v. Railroad Retirement Bd.*, 11 MSPB 103 (1982). This includes being transferred for creating disharmony and discontent in an office by filing a large number of complaints. *Hayden v. Department of the Interior*, 5 MSPB 162 (1981). See *Frazier v. Hall*, 1 MSPB 159 (1979), *aff'd in part and remanded, Frazier v. MSPB*, 472 F.2d 150, 28 FEP 185 (D.C. Cir. 1982) and discussion of prohibited personnel practices.

[105]*Comberiate v. United States*, 203 Ct. Cl. 285 (1973).

[106]*Ketterer v. Federal Crop Ins. Corp.*, supra note 102.

[107]*McClelland v. Andrus*, 606 F.2d 1278 (D.C. Cir. 1979); *Motto v. GSA*, 335 F. Supp. 694 (E.D. La. 1971).

[108]*Bechtel v. OPM*, 10 MSPB 269 (1982).

[109]A resignation is normally considered a voluntary action which cannot be appealed to the MSPB or the courts.

[110]*Burgess v. MSPB*, 758 F.2d 641 (Fed. Cir. 1985); *Dabney v. Freeman*, 358 F.2d 533 (D.C. Cir. 1965); *Gonzales v. Department of the Treasury*, 701 F.2d 36 (5th Cir. 1983).

[111]*Musone v. Department of Agric.*, 31 MSPR 85 (1986); *Myslik v. VA*, 2 MSPB 241 (1980).

terms of the other, (2) circumstances permitted no other alternative, and (3) the circumstances were the result of coercive acts by the opposite party.[112]

If the employee raises factual issues which reasonably put into issue the voluntariness of a resignation, the MSPB must hold a hearing to determine whether the resignation was, in fact, an adverse action taken without proper procedures.[113] In making that determination, the fact that the resigning party was faced with the unpleasant alternative of resigning or being fired does not, in and of itself, make the resignation involuntary.[114] However, when the employee is given no time to consider the matter or to consult with family or attorney,[115] or is told, for example, either to resign or be given no transportation home from the Middle East, that has been considered to be involuntary.[116] A resignation is involuntary if it is due to misinformation or lack of information provided by the agency.[117] A resignation is involuntary if the employee's mental condition is such that he or she lacks the capacity to resign voluntarily. This is true even if the agency is unaware of the employee's mental condition at the time it accepts the resignation.[118] Finally, an employee may withdraw a resignation at any time prior to its effective date unless the agency can show a valid reason, such as having filled the position, for refusing to allow withdrawal and explains that reason to the employee.[119]

---

[112]*Calvert v. Marine Corps*, 32 MSPR 23 (1986).

[113]*Dumas v. MSPB*, 789 F.2d 892 (Fed. Cir. 1986) (to be entitled to a hearing employee need only make a nonfrivolous allegation that resignation was involuntary; he need not prove it); *Burgess v. MSPB*, supra note 110 (case remanded to MSPB for hearing because administrative judge did not inform employee of what she needed to show to obtain a hearing); *Murray v. Defense Mapping Agency*, 1 MSPB 338 (1980).

[114]*Musone v. Department of Agric.*, supra note 111 (fact that employee retired to obtain annuity since he would not have been able to afford an appeal had he stayed and been fired was not coercion); *Hijar v. Department of the Army*, 6 MSPB 121 (1981); *Christie v. United States*, 518 F.2d 584 (Ct. Cl. 1975). See also *Griessenauer v. Department of Energy*, 754 F.2d 361 (Fed. Cir. 1985) (FPM section stating what agencies should do in the event an employee announces his resignation does not give employee any rights).

[115]*Paroczay v. Hodges*, 219 F.Supp. 89 (D.D.C. 1963).

[116]*Wilson v. Schultz*, 475 F.2d 997 (D.D.C. 1973). See also *Covington v. HHS*, 750 F.2d 937 (Fed. Cir. 1984) (retirement involuntary when employee given incorrect information on RIF appeal rights); *Schultz v. Navy*, 810 F.2d 1133 (Fed.Cir. 1987) (resignation involuntary when incapacitated employee was improperly denied sick leave).

[117]*Covington v. HHS*, supra note 116; *Scharf v. Department of the Air Force*, 710 F.2d 1572 (Fed.Cir. 1983). See also *Filliben v. Department of the Army*, 34 MSPR 33 (1987); *Gleaves v. Department of the Navy*, 36 MSPR 554 (1988) (employee entitled to a hearing who was told that if he resigned record would be clean but actual forms stated he resigned in lieu of an adverse action).

[118]*Liebke v. Brown*, 312 F. Supp. 1053 (D. Mass. 1970); *Manzi v. United States*, 198 Ct. Cl. 489 (1972); *Solga v. Department of the Army*, 11 MSPB 257 (1982).

[119]5 C.F.R. 715.202; *Goodman v. United States*, 424 F.2d 914 (D.C. Cir. 1970). Avoidance of an adverse action is not good cause to refuse to accept an employee's with-

Standards of Review

The MSPB is required to review adverse actions to determine whether the agency established the validity of the action by the preponderance of the evidence.[120] On review, the court will set aside an agency action if it is arbitrary, capricious, an abuse of discretion, taken without proper procedures, or unsupported by substantial evidence.[121] The MSPB has no jurisdiction to consider an appeal from an employee who has waived his or her appeal rights through a previous "last chance agreement."[122] Review of MSPB decisions lies in the Court of Appeals for the Federal Circuit.[123]

Performance-Based Actions

Since the effective date of the Civil Service Reform Act, January 11, 1979, actions against federal employees for failure to perform can be taken under different statutory and regulatory procedures than adverse actions. Adverse actions are now defined to include only actions for misconduct.[124]

As the outset, all agencies are required to adopt a performance appraisal system, a "plan," which must provide for periodic appraisals of job performance, encourage employees to participate in the adoption of performance standards, and use the results of performance appraisals as a basis for training, rewarding, reassigning, promoting, reducing in grade, retaining, and removing employees.[125] The agency performance plan

---

drawal of resignation but the hiring or commitment to hire a replacement is such good cause. 5 C.F.R. 715.202. See *McBeen v. Department of the Interior*, 27 MSPR 207 (1985) (refusal to accept withdrawal of resignation because employee was troublesome constitutes improper removal); *Pronechen v. Department of Justice*, 25 MSPR 54 (1984) (refusal to accept withdrawal of resignation when agency had properly refilled position was not improper separation).

[120]5 U.S.C. 7701(c)(1)(B). This includes the determination of whether there was a nexus between the action taken and disciplining the employee to promote the efficiency of the service. *Merritt v. Department of Justice*, 6 MSPB 493 (1981).

[121]5 U.S.C. 7703(c). Actions taken without proper procedures will be overturned if the lack of appropriate procedure created a harmful error. See text accompanying *supra* note 99.

[122]*McCall v. Postal Serv.*, 839 F.2d 664 (Fed. Cir. 1988).

[123]Prior to October 1, 1982, review of MSPB decisions resided in either the Court of Claims or a United States Court of Appeals. 5 U.S.C. 7703(b)(1). Effective October 1, 1982, all review is in the Court of Appeals for the Federal Circuit, Public Law 97-164. The Act applies only to cases initially filed after October 1, 1982.

[124]5 U.S.C. Chapter 43. Of course, performance-based actions can, at the agency's option, be taken under Chapter 75. See discussion, *infra*.

[125]5 U.S.C. 4302.

must be approved by OPM[126] and, in an appeal before the MSPB, the agency must prove that it obtained OPM approval for its performance plan.[127] Performance plans were required by statute to have been in place no later than October 1, 1981.[128]

However, an agency may take action against an employee for poor performance under either 5 U.S.C. Chapter 43 or Chapter 75, the chapters governing disciplinary actions for misconduct.[129] The procedural requirements for taking action under the two chapters are different. For example, if the agency uses the provisions of Chapter 75, it must prove its case by a preponderance of the evidence and must also prove a nexus between the employee's performance and the efficiency of the service. On the other hand, if the agency takes the action under Chapter 43 it need only prove its case by substantial evidence, but it must show that the procedural requirements of that chapter, such as the requirement to afford the employee the opprtunity to improve, are met.[130]

Every performance appraisal system must provide for the establishment of performance standards for a position, identify critical elements of the position, establish methods and procedures to appraise performance against the standards, and make personnel decisions based on that appraisal.[131] Standards are required to be based, to the maximum extent possible, on objective criteria.[132] Although standards cannot always be

---

[126]5 U.S.C. 4304(b)(1) and (3).

[127]*Griffin v. Department of the Army*, 23 MSPR 657 (1984). OPM approval of an agency's performance plan can be proved through submission of agency regulations which so state. *Chennault v. Department of the Army*, 796 F.2d 465 (Fed. Cir. 1986); *Brown v. Department of the Army*, 28 MSPR 648 (1985); *Shorter v. Department of the Army*, 28 MSPR 622 (1985).

[128]5 U.S.C. 4302(b)(2).

[129]*Lovshin v. Department of the Navy*, 767 F.2d 826 (Fed. Cir. 1985), *cert. denied*, 475 U.S. 1111 (1986). *Lovshin* reversed a previously established MSPB position that performance-based actions could only be taken under Chapter 43. *Gende v. Department of Justice*, 23 MSPB 604 (1984). *Gende*, in turn, reversed the position MSPB had earlier taken in *Wells v. Harris*, 1 MSPB 199 (1979). In *Wells*, MSPB had found invalid OPM interim regulations allowing for performance-based actions to be taken under Chapter 43 prior to the establishment of a performance appraisal system on the ground that Congress did not intend the more streamlined procedures of Chapter 43 to be used until the employee had an opportunity to be evaluated under a performance appraisal system meeting the requirements of 5 U.S.C. 4302. If an agency uses Chapter 75 because it does not have an approved performance appraisal system in place, or for any other reason, it must comply strictly with the procedural requirements of that chapter.

[130]*Archuleta v. Department of Agric.*, 34 MSPR 22 (1987); *Fairall v. VA*, 844 F.2d 775 (Fed. Cir. 1987); *Mealy v. Department of the Navy*, 34 MSPR 187 (1987) ("the lack of an improvement period, however, is relevant to the mitigating factor identified in *Douglas v. Veterans Administration* [6 MSPB 313 (1981)] that addresses the extent to which the employee was on notice that his or her performance was deficient").

[131]5 U.S.C. 4302; 5 C.F.R. Part 430.

[132]5 U.S.C. 4301(g)(1).

based upon numerical criteria, to be valid they must be (1) reasonable,[133] (2) sufficient to permit adequate measurement, and (3) adequate to inform employees of what is needed for a satisfactory rating.[134] Words such as "usually" or "most of the time," while not encouraged in performance standards, can comply with the requirement that standards be as objective as possible when they are fleshed out with the supervisor's written instructions, letters, and memoranda.[135]

Critical elements are defined as those components of an employee's job that are of such importance that "performance below the minimum standard established by management requires remedial action."[136] A plan can have any number of critical elements, and each critical element has standards against which performance is measured. A plan usually has five levels of performance consisting of a fully satisfactory level and two levels above and below. All five levels may not necessarily be spelled out but may simply be described as a level above or below a defined level. In any event, however, the standards must be written so that the employee clearly understands what is expected at each level.[137] In drafting standards, it is not necessary that standards for employees having the same job description be identical.[138] Performance standards may consist of more

---

[133]*Rocheleau v. SEC*, 29 MSPR 193 (1985) (requirement that incumbent conduct 30 examinations of investment advisors per year unreasonable since no examiner at any grade had ever done that many and no other examiners had numerical requirements in their performance standards); *Walker v. Department of the Treasury*, 28 MSPR 229 (1985) (error rate set for accounting clerk unrealistic and unreasonable). The MSPB has held that an absolute performance standard (one that provides that one incident of poor performance will result in an unsatisfactory rating) is reasonable only under very limited circumstances. *Callaway v. Department of the Army*, 23 MSPR 592 (1984). See *Fuller v. Department of the Treasury*, 28 MSPR 355 (1985); *Faust v. Smithsonian Inst.*, 29 MSPR 496 (1985); *Komara v. Veterans Admin.*, 28 MSPR 239 (1985) (removal for failure to timely perform a single STAT test improper without showing that such failure is life threatening).

[134]*Stone v. HHS*, 35 MSPR 603 (1987) (standard impermissibly vague); *Adkins v. HUD*, 781 F.2d 891 (Fed.Cir. 1986); *Rogers v. Department of Defense Dependents Schools*, 814 F.2d 1549 (Fed. Cir. 1987). The Court of Appeals for the Federal Circuit has held that it "wholly agrees" with the position taken by the MSPB in *Siegelman v. HUD*, 13 MSPB 27 (1983), that in the case of a professional employee it is not always possible to incorporate specific deadlines and numerical measures into the standards. *Wilson v. HHS*, 770 F.2d 1048 (Fed. Cir. 1985). However, the standards must be sufficiently objective and precise that most professionals will understand what is required of them. In arriving at that understanding the help of the supervisor is crucial. *De Pauw v. UITC*, 782 F.2d 1564 (Fed. Cir. 1986). See *Evans v. Department of the Treasury*, 28 MSPR 366 (1985).

[135]*Wilson v. HHS*, supra note 134; *Baker v. Defense Logistics Agency*, 782 F.2d 1579 (Fed. Cir. 1986); *Alexander v. Department of Commerce*, 30 MSPR 243 (1986); *Mouser v. HHS*, 32 MSPR 543, 25 GERR 454 (1987). However, "an agency may not orally change a written performance standard under the guise of giving content to it." *Williams v. HHS*, 30 MSPR 217 (1986).

[136]5 C.F.R. 430.202(c).

[137]*Stone v. HHS*, supra note 134.

[138]*Wells v. Harris*, supra note 129. However, when there are substantial variations in

than one component and an action for unacceptable performance may be based on components of a standard.[139]

Although the law requires consultation with employees on the adoption of performance standards and critical elements, the final decision on the standards and elements remains a management function.[140] Adoption of a performace appraisal system is not negotiable,[141] nor can an employee appeal solely from the failure of his or her agency to permit participation in the development of standards.[142] Agencies are required to appraise employees regularly, however, an employee has no appeal to the MSPB from his or her appraisal.[143] Only if disciplinary action is taken against an employee for uacceptable performance during the appraisal period may the employee challenge the standard under which the performance was appraised.[144]

Procedures for Taking Action Under Chapter 43

Unacceptable performance is defined as performance that fails to meet established standards in one or more critical elements of the employee's position.[145] The employee must be given 30 days' advance written notice which identifies specific examples of unacceptable performance and the critical elements involved.[146] He or she is entitled to respond orally or in writing or both,[147] to be represented by counsel,[148]

---

what is expected of employees working under the same standards, these variations must be taken into account in appraising performance. *Williams v. Department of the Treasury,* 35 MSPR 432 (1987).

[139]*Shuman v. Department of the Treasury,* 23 MSPR 620 (1984). The agency must show that failure to perform acceptably in one subelement constitutes failure to perform in the element as a whole.

[140]5 U.S.C. 4302(a); 5 C.F.R. 430.203(b).

[141]*NTEU v. FLRA,* 691 F.2d 553, 111 LRRM 2540 (D.C. Cir. 1982).

[142]*Alford v. HEW,* 1 MSPB 305 (1980).

[143]*Marsh v. Department of the Army,* 2 MSPB 143 (1980). An employee may grieve his or her appraisal under the applicable grievance procedure.

[144]*Siegelman v. HUD, supra* note 134.

[145]5 U.S.C. 4301(3). Where an agency has created a five-level evaluation system for each critical element, it must inform employees what level of performance is required to be minimally satisfactory. In addition, performance rating plans cannot extrapolate on a critical element more than one level below the only level for which there is a written standard. *Donaldson v. Department of Labor,* 27 MSPR 293 (1985).

[146]5 U.S.C. 4303(b)(1)(A); *Smith v. Department of the Interior,* 8 MSPB 663 (1981); *Rana v. United States,* 812 F.2d 887 (4th Cir. 1987). The agency must have some methodology for selecting examples of alleged unacceptable performance so that a reasonable person might conclude that performance fell below the critical element's percent standard. *Ryerson v. Department of the Army,* 35 MSPR 123 (1987).

[147]5 U.S.C. 4303(b)(1)(C).

[148]5 U.S.C. 4303(b)(1)(B).

and to a decision which has been concurred in by an employee at a level higher than the employee proposing the action.[149]

Removal or reduction in grade can be based only on performance occurring within one year prior to the date of the notice of proposed action.[150] An employee can be removed or reduced in grade for poor performance only after being given an opportunity to demonstrate acceptable performance,[151] which opportunity has been called "one of the most important substantive rights in the entire Chapter 43 performance appraisal framework."[152] The agency is required to identify for the employee the critical elements for which performance has been unacceptable and to give the employee a reasonable time to demonstrate acceptable performance before a removal is proposed.[153] During that time he or she is expected to receive supervisory assistance to correct deficiencies in performance. Unlike actions taken under Chapter 75, the MSPB has no authority in actions taken under Chapter 43 to mitigate the severity of the penalty chosen by the agency.[154]

Unlike adverse actions, the procedures required for taking performance-based actions also apply to employees in the excepted service.[155] However, the right of appeal to the MSPB and to judicial review is limited to employees in the competitive service who have completed one year of service and to preference eligibles who have completed one year of current and continuous service.[156]

---

[149]5 U.S.C. 4323 (b)(1)(D)(ii). There is no comparable requirement for concurrence by a higher level official in actions taken under Chapter 75.

[150]5 U.S.C. 4303(c)(2). The one-year removal period need not coincide with the regular appraisal period. *Weirauch v. Department of the Army*, 782 F.2d 1560 (Fed. Cir. 1986).

[151]5 U.S.C. 4302(b)(6).

[152]*Boggess v. Department of the Air Force*, 31 MSPR 461 (1986), citing *Sandlund v. GSA*, 23 MSPR 583 (1984).

[153]5 C.F.R. 432.203(b); *Colgan v. Department of the Navy*, 28 MSPR 116 (1985); *Grand v. Department of Transp.*, 24 MSPR 663 (1984). The court will not second-guess MSPB on the adequacy of the opportunity to improve or whether it was "meaningful." *Warren v. Department of the Army*, 804 F.2d 654 (Fed Cir. 1986).

[154]*Lisiecki v. MSPB*, 769 F.2d 1558 (Fed. Cir. 1985), cert. denied, 475 U.S. 1108 (1986). Arbitrators are similarly bound by the restriction against modifying agency penalties in Chapter 43 actions. *Horner v. Bell*, 825 F.2d 391 (Fed. Cir. 1987); *Horner v. Garza*, 832 F.2d 150 (Fed. Cir. 1987).

[155]5 U.S.C. 4301 defines "employee" as an "individual employed in or under an agency." Although provision is made in 5 U.S.C. 4301 for OPM to exclude the excepted service from this chapter, OPM has not done so. The chapter on procedural requirements for removal or reduction in grade does not apply, however, to excepted employees who have not completed one year of current and continuous service, 5 U.S.C. 4303(f)(3), or to probationers in the competitive service, 5 U.S.C. 4303(f)(2). These latter employees are covered by the requirements of the establishment of a performance appraisal system as set forth in 5 U.S.C. 4302.

[156]5 U.S.C. 4303(a)(e); *Harrison v. Bowen*, 815 F.2d 1505 (D.C. Cir. 1987).

Within-Grade Increases

Under 5 U.S.C. 5335, an employee whose work is judged to be at an acceptable level of competence is entitled to periodic step increases. Prior to the establishment of performance appraisal systems, agencies were required to give advance written notice of deficiencies in performance which might result in the withholding of a within-grade increase. However, the regulations were amended in 1981 to reflect the fact that the performance appraisal process would be the mechanism for warning the employee that his or her performance was not at an acceptable level of competence.[157] An employee whose performance in any one critical element is less than satisfactory is considered not to be performing at an acceptable level.[158]

The determination of whether an employee is performing at an acceptable level of competence is based upon the employee's performance during the waiting period for the next step increase which, in turn, varies depending upon the step of the grade the employee occupies and how many years the employee has been in that step. The acceptable level of competence decision must be based on performance during the entire period.[159] The decision to withhold an increase must be supported by the employee's most recent appraisal.[160]

The fact that an employee is not performing at an acceptable level must be communicated in writing. The reasons for the determination, what the employee must do to improve his or her performance, and the employee's right to request reconsideration must be stated.[161] The agency has no obligation to provide the employee with an opportunity to improve before denying a within-grade increase.[162] An employee who has been denied an increase has the right to request reconsideration by filing a written response to the negative determination within 15 days.[163] On reconsideration, an employee may have a representative and has the right

---

[157]5 C.F.R. 531.409.
[158]5 C.F.R. 531.403.
[159]5 C.F.R. 531.409(b). In making the determination, the employer must consider the entire relevant waiting period, not just the bad parts. *Bergman v. HHS*, 4 MSPB 452 (1980); *Hunt v. HHS*, 3 MSPB 507 (1980). However, the agency may place greater weight on the employee's performance during the latter stages of the waiting period. *Mullins v. Department of the Navy*, 31 MSPR 358 (1986); *Lance v. Department of Energy*, 28 MSPR 467 (1985); *Whitehead v. Department of the Navy*, 20 MSPR 8 (1984). Of particular importance is performance during the period in which employee is on notice that performance is not acceptable. *Zaph v. Federal Maritime Comm'n*, 6 MSPB 522 (1981).
[160]5 C.F.R. 531.409(b).
[161]5 C.F.R. 531.409(e).
[162]*Wilson v. Department of Agric.*, 28 MSPR 472 (1985).
[163]5 C.F.R. 531.410.

to review the reconsideration file which must contain all pertinent documents.[164]

If a negative determination is sustained on reconsideration, the employee may appeal to the MSPB.[165] On appeal, the agency must show that (1) the within-grade increase was denied under a performance appraisal system that was approved by OPM,[166] (2) the employee was aware of the relevant performance standards throughout the waiting period,[167] (3) substantial evidence established that the employee's performance was unacceptable,[168] and (4) the denial was reasonable under the circumstances.[169] An agency may grant a within-grade increase at any time after an initial denial but must, at a minimum, review an employee's performance within 52 weeks after a denial regardless of the employee's waiting period.[170]

Standards for MSPB Review

The appropriate standard for MSPB and judicial review of the denial of a within-grade increase has been the matter of some controversy. Under the statute, the MSPB reviews "an action based on unacceptable performance described in section 4303 of this title" to determine whether it is supported by substantial evidence. All other actions must be supported by a preponderance of the evidence. The MSPB has held that although the denial of a within-grade increase is not described in section 4303, it is clearly a performance-based action and should be reviewed to determine if it is based on substantial evidence.[171] This view is shared by the Court of Appeals for the Federal Circuit,[172] but other circuit courts have held that based on the plain words of the statute, denials of within-grade increases must be reviewed to determine whether they are based on a

---

[164]*Id.*

[165]5 C.F.R. 531.410(d). However, an employee who is a member of a bargaining unit covered by a collective bargaining agreement which provides for a grievance procedure must follow the negotiated grievance procedure and cannot appeal to MSPB unless the contract specifically excludes within-grade increase denials. *Moreno v. MSPB*, 728 F.2d 499 (Fed. Cir. 1984); *Espenschied v. MSPB*, 804 F.2d 1233 (Fed. Cir. 1986); *NTEU v. Cornelius*, 617 F. Supp. 365 (D.D.C. 1985).

[166]*Renshaw v. Department of the Army*, 28 MSPR 638 (1985).

[167]If the employee has not been made aware of the specific requirements for acceptable performance, the within-grade determination must be delayed. *Supra* note 160.

[168]*Parker v. Defense Logistics Agency*, 1 MSPB 489 (1980).

[169]*Renshaw v. Department of the Army, supra* note 166.

[170]5 C.F.R. 531.411.

[171]*Parker v. Defense Logistics Agency, supra* note 168.

[172]*Romane v. Defense Contract Audit Agency*, 760 F.2d 1286 (Fed. Cir. 1985).

preponderance of the evidence.[173] Although all appeals from MSPB decisions on within-grade denials are heard by the Court of Appeals for the Federal Circuit, some confusion may occur if the issue arises in a mixed case which is reviewed by a district court sitting in a circuit with a different standard of review.

Reduction in Force

The application of reduction-in-force regulations is required whenever an agency releases a competing employee from his/her competitive level by separation, demotion, furlough for more than 30 days, or reassignment requiring displacement, when the release is required because of lack of work, shortage of funds, reorganization, reclassification due to change in duties, or the exercise of reemployment rights or restoration rights."[174] A downgrading resulting from a reorganization rather than a natural erosion of functions requires the application of reduction-in-force procedures.[175]

In taking a reduction in force, an agency is required by law to consider (1) tenure of employment, (2) whether the employee has veterans preference, (3) length of federal service, and (4) efficiency or performance ratings.[176] Tenure refers to the type of appointment, that is, an indefinite appointment, an appointment for a fixed term, or one for the length of a project. The OPM has promulgated regulations to put into effect these requirements, and any individual who believes that the procedures set

---

[173]*Schramm v. HHS*, 682 F.2d 85 (3d Cir. 1982); *Stankis v. EPA*, 713 F.2d 1181 (5th Cir. 1983); *White v. Department of the Army*, 720 F.2d 209 (D.C. Cir. 1983); *Ommaya v. NIH*, 726 F.2d 827 (D.C. Cir. 1984).

[174]5 C.F.R. 351.201(a)(2). An agency need not fill a vacant position during a reduction in force. *Madsen v. VA*, 754 F.2d 343 (Fed. Cir. 1985). However, if it chooses to do so, and fills the position with an employee who has been released from his or her competitive level, it must do so based on relative retention standing. 5 C.F.R. 351.201(b). This is true unless an employee is assigned to the vacancy at the same grade and pay. *McMurdo v. Department of Agric.*, 24 MSPR 388 (1984).

In determining whether RIF regulations need be applied, a reassignment requiring displacement refers to the displacement of other employees and has no reference to the dislacement of the reassigned employee. *Elmore v. Hampton*, 373 F. Supp. 360 (E.D. Tenn. 1973). Thus an employee's reassignment outside his competitive area to a vacant position that does not require displacing another employee need not be effected under RIF procedures. *Thomas v. United States*, 709 F.2d 48 (Fed. Cir. 1983); *Musone v. Department of Agric.*, 31 MSPR 85 (1986).

[175]*Cramton v. Department of the Treasury*, 9 MSPB 722 (1982); *Parks v. United States*, 147 F. Supp. 261 (Ct. Cl. 1957).

[176]5 U.S.C. 3502.

forth in OPM regulations have not been properly applied to him or to her[177] can appeal to the MSPB.[178]

Retention Registers

Agencies are required to adopt retention registers that classify employees on the basis of their relative retention standing.[179] These registers place employees in groups and subgroups based on the factors noted above. Thus, 5 C.F.R. 351.501 provides "The descending order of retention standing: (1) By groups is group I, group II, and group III; (2) Within each group is subgroup AD, subgroup A, subgroup B; (3) Within each subgroup persons are ranked beginning with the earliest service date." In establishing the service date, employees are entitled to additional service credit for outstanding performance.[180]

Group I consists of career employees[181] who are not serving a probationary period, Group II includes probationers[182] and career-conditional employees, and Group III includes temporary and indefinite employees. Subgroup AD consists of veterans who are at least 30 percent disabled, Subgroup A contains other veterans, and Subgroup B is composed of nonveterans.[183]

---

[177]Unlike adverse actions and performance-based action, employees in the excepted service can appeal reductions in force to the MSPB. 5 C.F.R. 351.901.

[178]An employee who is a member of a bargaining unit which has a collective bargaining agreement that includes a negotiated grievance procedure can only appeal a RIF through the negotiated grievance procedure and can appeal to MSPB only if the collective bargaining agreement excludes RIF appeals. *Bonner v. MSPB*, 781 F.2d 202 (1986).

[179]5 C.F.R. 351.501. Agencies are required to set up a parallel register for the excepted service. 5 C.F.R. 351.502.

[180]Recently revised OPM regulations provide additional service credit for performance. An additional 20 years of service is given for a performance rating of outstanding, 16 additional years of service for a performance rating of exceeds fully satisfactory, and 12 years of additional service is given for a performance rating of fully successful. An employee's entitlement to additional credit is based on the average of the employee's last three performance ratings. An employee who has not received three annual performance ratings is given an assumed rating of fully satisfactory for the missing ratings. 5 C.F.R. 351.504.

In determining whether an agency improperly withheld a performance appraisal so it would not be "of record" at the time of the RIF, the agency must show that "such absence was due to a reasonable exercise of its discretion in accordance with the provisions of its performance appraisal system." *Mazzola v. Department of Labor*, 25 MSPR 682 (1985). This is to ensure that the employee receives all additional credit to which he or she is entitled for performance. See *Haataja v. Department of Labor*, 25 MSPR 594 (1985).

[181]Career employees are employees who have completed three years of service.

[182]The probationary or trial period required for new supervisors or managers, 5 U.S.C. 3321, has no effect on tenure groups.

[183]Preference eligibility for RIF purposes is defined in 5 U.S.C. 3501.

Scope of Competition

In defining the scope of competition in the event of a reduction in force, agencies are required to establish "competitive areas" and "competitive levels." Generally speaking, a competitive area is an organizational and geographic location and includes all the employees within the competitive area so defined.[184] In the face of a challenge to a reduction in force brought before the MSPB, the agency taking the action has the burden of proving that the competitive area was properly established.[185] An agency is not required to expand competitive areas merely to provide competition, even if it results in all of the positions within a given competitive area being abolished.[186]

The agency is also required to establish competitive levels comprising all the positions within a competitive area in the same grade "which are similar enough in duties, qualification requirements, pay schedules, and working conditions so that the incumbent of one position could successfully perform the critical elements of any other position upon entry into it, without any loss of productivity beyond that normally expected in the orientation of any new but fully qualified employee."[187] A separate retention register must be established for each competitive level.[188] Again, the burden before the MSPB is on the agency which must show that the competitive levels were properly established.[189]

---

[184]5 C.F.R. 351.402.

[185]Compton v. Department of Energy, 3 MSPB 522 (1980). See Sadler v. Department of Educ., 27 MSPR 636 (1985) (competitive area not too narrow when it consisted of activity under separate administration within local commuting area); Dancy v. Department of Agric., 26 MSPR 321 (1985). The purpose of competitive areas is to avoid the chaos of governmentwide disruption with every reduction in force. Finch v. United States, 179 Ct. Cl. 1 (1967); Wilmot v. United States, 205 Ct. Cl. 686 (1974). If competitive areas are established in conformance with regulations, normally the courts will not disturb them.

[186]Grier v. HHS, 750 F.2d 944 (Fed. Cir. 1984). The decision whether to expand the competitive area is within the agency's discretion. Ginnodo v. OPM, 760 F.2d 246 (Fed. Cir. 1986).

[187]5 C.F.R. 351.403(a). The MSPB has held that this definition represents no significant change from the definition in the prior regulations. Marcinowsky v. GSA, 35 MSPR 6 (1987).

[188]5 C.F.R. 351.404.

[189]Foster v. Coast Guard, 7 MSPB 707 (1981). Competitive levels are established based on the requirements of the position which the employee occupies and not the qualifications of the particular employee. O'Donnell v. Department of the Army, 11 MSPB 378 (1982). An employee who is on detail remains the official incumbent of his most recent position of record. Bjerke v. Department of Educ., 25 MSPR 310 (1984). Thus, all employees are placed in competitive levels based on the position in which they have been carried on the rolls and paid. Apodaca v. Department of Educ., 19 MSPR 540 (1984); Lester v. Department of Educ., 18 MSPR 63 (1983).

Release From Competitive Level

Employees are selected for release from the competitive levels, which may result in their removal or demotion, in the inverse order of their retention standing.[190] Once an agency has selected an employee for release from his or her competitive level, it must do one of the following: assign the employee, with his or her consent, to a position which will last at least three months; furlough him or her; or separate him or her.[191] An employee has no right of assignment to a vacant position unless the agency decides to fill the vacant position during the reduction in force in which case it must be filled in accordance with reduction-in-force regulations.[192] As a general rule, an agency may not release an employee from a competitive level while retaining employees in that level with lower retention standing.[193] The burden is on the agency to prove that it effected an employee's assignment properly if the employee raises the issue of his or her assignment rights.[194]

To be reassigned to another position during a reduction in force, an employee must meet the qualifications for the position.[195] Thus, he or she must meet any OPM qualification standards for the position, meet any physical qualifications,[196] have any special qualifying skills which OPM formally approved for the position, and be able to perform without undue interruption.[197] For this purpose, the employee has the right to an up-to-date folder setting out his or her qualifications.[198]

---

[190]5 C.F.R. 351.602. In the event of a tie, agencies may adopt any reasonable procedures to break the tie. *Ackelmacker v. Kelly*, 101 F. Supp. 528 (S.D.N.Y. 1951).

[191]5 C.F.R. 351.603. Under recently revised OPM regulations, an employee who displaces another employee, or "bumps" that employee, can only bump a maximum of three grades or grade levels. A 30% disabled veteran can bump five grades or grade levels. 5 C.F.R. 351.701.

[192]*Starling v. HUD*, 757 F.2d 271 (Fed. Cir. 1985).

[193]5 C.F.R. 351.601. For exceptions to this rule, see 5 C.F.R. 351.606 and 351.607.

[194]*Lewellen v. Department of the Air Force*, 25 MSPR 525 (1985).

[195]5 C.F.R. 351.701. An employee can be removed who refuses to accept a position for which he or she is qualified. 5 C.F.R. 351.603; *Ratkus v. GSA*, 11 MSPB 101 (1982). An employee who turns down a proper offer is not entitled to a second offer even if (1) other employees got second offers, and (2) there are other jobs available. *Pettis v. HHS*, 803 F.2d 1176 (Fed. Cir. 1986).

[196]*O'Connor v. Department of the Air Force*, 9 MSPR 400 (1982).

[197]5 C.F.R. 351.701. An employee has the right of assignment to a position held by a lower standing employee if the released employee has the capacity, adaptability, and skills to perform the duties without undue interruption. See Federal Personnel Manual, Chapter 351, § 2–3(a)(1); *Peters v. Department of the Navy*, 5 MSPB 188 (1981); *Porter v. Department of Commerce*, 13 MSPR 177 (1982) (program is not unduly interrupted if optimal quality and quantity can be regained within 90 days); *Rasmussen v. United States*, 543 F.2d 134 (Ct. Cl. 1976); *Narcisse v. Department of Transp.*, 32 MSPR 232 (1987) (not improper for agency not to ask for special exception for marginally qualified employee if it can show it had pressing need for employee immediately capable of performing).

[198]*Coleman v. Department of the Army*, 19 MSPR 358 (1984). An employee has the

Under certain circumstances, "riffed" employees may "retreat." A retreat occurs when another employee is in a position from which the riffed employee was promoted and that other employee is in a lower retention subgroup or has lower retention standing in the same subgroup. The other position must be in the same competitive area.[199]

Procedural Requirements

Employees who are to be separated through reduction in force are entitled to at least 30 days' written notice.[200] Agencies may issue notices stating that a general reduction in force will occur without stating its effect on particular employees. An agency may then follow with a specific notice which cannot take effect for at least 10 days. The notices must state the actions to be taken, their effective date, the competitive area and competitive level of the employees involved, the places where the employees can inspect the regulations and records, any exceptions to retention standing rules, and the right to appeal.[201]

MSPB Review

A reduction in force can only be taken for genuine management reasons and cannot be used as a ruse to avoid an adverse action.[202] If an agency has *bona fide* management reasons for a reorganization, however, the adjudicatory bodies will not review the method by which management reorganizes its business.

Before the Board, the agency must establish a prima facie case that the reduction was undertaken for appropriate reasons. If the employee challenges those reasons, the agency may be required to put on further evidence of the *bona fides* of its management reasons.[203] However, once the agency has established that the reduction-in-force procedures were

---

right to have the folder updated until the date of the RIF. *Quartaro v. Department of Labor,* 23 MSPR 110 (1984). However, the employee has the obligation to place relevant information in the file.

[199]5 C.F.R. 351.701(c). Employees may retreat no more than three grades or grade intervals.

[200]5 C.F.R. 351.801.

[201]5 C.F.R. 351.803.

[202]*Fitzgerald v. Hampton,* 467 F.2d 755 (D.C. Cir. 1972); *Ketterer v. Department of Agric.,* 2 MSPB 459 (1980).

[203]*Losure v. ICC,* 2 MSPB 361 (1980).

invoked for legitimate reasons, the Board will not review the management considerations which lay behind those reasons.[204]

An employee who challenges an otherwise appropriate reduction in force by asserting that the action constitutes a prohibited personnel practice must prove this allegation by the preponderance of the evidence.[205] The MSPB has no authority to review the classifications of the positions of either the displacing or the displaced employee.[206]

In the event the Board finds an error in the agency's procedures, it will examine the record to determine whether correction of that error would have made any difference in the ultimate outcome. If the record is sufficient to determine that the absence of the error would not have made a difference, it will not reverse the action. If the record is incomplete, it will reverse.[207]

Furlough

A furlough is defined as the "placing of an employee in a temporary status without duties and pay because of lack of work or funds or other nondisciplinary reasons.[208] A furlough of 30 days or less is considered an adverse action and must be taken in accordance with adverse action procedures.[209] A furlough of more than 30 days is a reduction in force and subject to those procedures.[210] Placing seasonal employees in nonduty status is neither a reduction in force nor a furlough.[211] In emergency

---

[204]*Griffin v. Department of Agric.*, 2 MSPB 335 (1980); *Bacon v. HUD*, 757 F.2d 265 (Fed. Cir. 1985) (MSPB will not look behind agency choice of RIF to correct workload and skills imbalances which occurred because of budget cutbacks); *Gandola v. Federal Trade Comm'n*, 773 F.2d 308 (Fed. Cir. 1985) (agency could properly use as basis for decision of which jobs to abolish the fact that individuals in certain jobs were more qualified than individuals in other jobs).

[205]*Shockro v. FCC*, 5 MSPB 181 (1981).

[206]*Madsen v. VA*, 754 F.2d 343 (Fed. Cir. 1985). The Board will review classifications only to determine whether two positions were actually different. *Apodaca v. Department of Educ.*, supra note 189.

[207]*Mayo v. Edwards*, 562 F.Supp. 907 (D.D.C. 1983); *Foster v. Coast Guard*, supra note 189; *Butler v. Department of the Interior*, 9 MSPB 305 (1982). But see *Ray v. Department of the Air Force*, 3 MSPB 516 (1980); *Horne v. MSPB*, 684 F.2d 155 (D.C. Cir. 1982).

[208]5 U.S.C. 7511.

[209]5 U.S.C. 7512.

[210]5 C.F.R. 351.201(a). The MSPB has accepted the OPM interpretation that 30 calendar days means 22 workdays whenever the furlough was not to be served on consecutive days. *Clerman v. ICC*, 35 MSPR 190 (1987); *Klimek v. Department of the Army*, 3 MSPB 139 (1980).

[211]*Strickland v. MSPB*, 748 F.2d 681 (Fed. Cir. 1984). OPM could properly interpret furlough to exclude the laying off of seasonal employees. *NTEU v. MSPB*, 743 F.2d 895 (D.C. Cir. 1984).

situations, such as a sudden breakdown of equipment, a furlough may be imposed without advance written notice.[212]

Transfer of Function

A transfer of function occurs when the work of one or more employees is moved from one competitive area to another.[213] An employee who is identified with a function that is so moved is entitled to transfer with that function.[214] If an employee elects not to transfer, the agency has the option of either separating the employee through adverse action proceedings or reassigning him or her through reduction-in-force procedures.[215]

There is no right of appeal from a transfer of function. An employee whose function has been transferred can appeal only if he or she (1) accepts the transfer and undergoes a reduction in grade at the new competitive area, or (2) refuses the transfer and is removed through adverse action procedures or is reduced in grade through a reduction in force.[216] It is not a transfer of function if work is being performed in two competitive areas at the same time and a readjustment is made in the volume at each place; in that case there is a nonappealable transfer of workload.[217]

Finally, employees in Groups I and II who are separated through reduction in force are put on a reeemployement priority list.[218] They then have preference for appointment to all positions in the commuting area (that is, the area in which people live and can reasonably be expected to travel back and forth daily)[219] for which they are qualified and which their former employing agency decides to fill. Employees are placed on the list unless they turn down a position at the same grade and pay as their prior

---

[212]5 C.F.R. 752.404(d)(2); *Horner v. Andrzjewski,* 811 F.2d 571 (Fed. Cir. 1987).

[213]5 C.F.R. 351.301. OPM published revised transfer of function regulations in March 1987.

[214]5 C.F.R. 361.302. See *Certain Former CSA Employees v. HHS,* 762 F.2d 978 (Fed. Cir. 1985); *Menoken v. HHS,* 784 F.2d 365 (Fed Cir. 1986). An employee has no right to transfer with his or her function unless the alternative in the losing competitive area is separation or demotion.

[215]*Baldwin v. United States,* 175 Ct. Cl. 264 (1966); *Colbath v. United States,* 341 F.2d 626 (Ct. Cl. 1965); *Brown v. Department of the Air Force,* 4 MSPB 298 (1980).

[216]*Brown v. Department of the Air Force, supra* note 215.

[217]5 C.F.R. 351.203; *Hayes v. HHS,* 829 F.2d 1092 (Fed. Cir. 1987); *Seidel v. Department of Agric.,* 26 MSPR 605 (1985).

[218]5 C.F.R. 351.1002.

[219]5 C.F.R. 351.203. For a discussion of commuting area, see *Beardmore v. Department of Agric.,* 761 F.2d 677 (Fed. Cir. 1984).

position.[220] They remain on the list for two years or until they accept a position.[221]

Senior Executive Service Actions

The Senior Executive Service (SES) consists of positions in what were formerly Levels 16, 17, and 18 of the General Schedule and Levels IV or V of the Executive Schedule. The incumbent must perform supervisory or managerial functions.[222] After completion of a one-year probationary period, a member of the SES can be removed for misconduct, neglect of duty, or malfeasance.[223] He or she is entitled to 30 days' written notice, a reasonable time to answer orally or in writing or both, representation by an attorney or other individual, and a written decision. A member of the SES who is removed for misconduct is entitled to the procedural protections of 5 U.S.C. 7701.[224] He or she cannot be removed within 120 days after the appointment of his or her most immediate supervisor or the head of the agency.[225]

Agencies are required to establish separate performance appraisal systems for the SES, which must be approved by OPM.[226] The systems must provide for each senior executive one or more fully successful levels, a minimally satisfactory level, and an unsatisfactory level.[227] Performance appraisals are conducted annually, but in the case of a career appointee, may not be made within 120 days after the beginning of a new presidential administration.[228] An SES member receiving an unsatisfactory rating may be transferred or removed from the SES, but a member who

---

[220] 5 C.F.R. 351.1004(c)(2).

[221] 5 C.F.R. 351.1004.

[222] 5 U.S.C. 3132.

[223] 5 U.S.C. 7543; *Foster v. Department of Labor*, 31 MSPR 74 (1986) (due to the far more serious consequences to a career SES employee from a Chapter 75 removal action than one taken under Chapter 43, the Board would "carefully examine the charges . . . in order to determine if the seriousness of the offenses actually warranted the classification placed upon them by the agency."); *Berube v. GSA*, 30 MSPR 581 (1986), *rev'd and remanded*, 820 F.2d 396 (Fed. Cir. 1987). Pursuant to an opinion of OPM, concurred in by the Comptroller General, there is no authority to suspend a member of the SES for less than 14 days.

[224] 5 U.S.C. 7541.

[225] 5 U.S.C. 3592(b).

[226] 5 U.S.C. 4312.

[227] 5 U.S.C. 4314.

[228] 5 U.S.C. 4314(b). Agencies must establish performance review boards to make recommendations to the appropriate authority on the performance of senior executives. 5 U.S.C. 4314.

receives two unsatisfactory ratings in any period of five consecutive years *must* be removed form the SES.[229] An employee who is removed from the SES for less than fully successful performance, is entitled to placement in a position at GS-15 or above of the General Schedule.[230] He or she may request an informal hearing before the MSPB at least 15 days before the removal but the employee is not entitled to the procedural protections of 5 U.S.C. 7701.[231] A member of the SES removed during the probationary period is not entitled to an informal hearing.[232]

In the event of a reduction in force, a senior executive is entitled to a reassignment to a vacant position within his or her agency or, if no such position exists, to placement by OPM in a vacant SES position in another agency for which he or she is qualified, or to be detailed to such a position.[233] A career appointee who, after a reduction in force, is not placed in a new position under these provisions is entitled to appeal to the MSPB concerning (1) whether the reduction in force complied with appropriate procedures, (2) whether OPM took all reasonable steps to place the appointee, and (3) whether the agency decided correctly that the appointee was not qualified to be placed in a position.[234]

Suitability

The Office of Personnel Management is required to investigate applicants for appointment to positions in the competitive service to determine their qualifications and suitability for employment.[235] An individual may not be declared unsuitable for appointment on the basis of conduct, unless that determination promotes the efficiency of the service.[236]In making that determination, OPM must base its findings on whether the conduct reasonably may be expected to interfere with, or to prevent effective performance by the applicant or interfere with the mission of the employing agency. Among the factors which may be considered are misconduct in prior employment, criminal, dishonest,

---

[229]5 U.S.C. 4314(b)(3).
[230]5 U.S.C. 3594(b).
[231]5 U.S.C. 3592(a)(2).
[232]*Gaines v. HUD*, 13 MSPB 131 (1983); *Wynes v. GSA*, 13 MSPB 137 (1983).
[233]5 U.S.C. 3595(b)(3).
[234]5 U.S.C. 3595(c); *Vanderburgh v. HHS*, 15 MSPR 57 (1983).
[235]5 C.F.R. 731.201.
[236]5 C.F.R. 731.202; *SIR v. Hampton*, 63 FRD 399 (N.D. Cal. 1973); *Kirkland v. OPM*, 27 MSPR 199 (1985).

infamous, or notoriously disgraceful conduct;[237] intentional false statements or fraud in examination or appointment; refusal to furnish required testimony to an investigator; habitual excessive use of intoxicating beverages;[238] abuse of narcotics; reasonable doubt as to loyalty;[239] and an unsatisfactory attendance record in a prior position.[240]

For a period of one year after an appointment of an employee who is subject to a suitability determination, OPM may require the employing agency to remove the appointee if he or she is found to be unsuitable.[241] An applicant or employee who is disqualified by OPM may appeal to the MSPB.[242]

Before the MSPB, the applicant has the right to confront and question the source of the information against him or her during a *de novo* hearing.[243] If the applicant prevails, the proper remedy is to order the agency to cancel the unsuitability rating and to return the affected applicant to the eligibility list for employment. The applicant is not entitled to placement in a position or to back pay.[244]

Civil Service Retirement

Decisions of the Office of Personnel Management involving civil service retirement are appealable to the MSPB.[245] Among the issues which the Board has adjudicated, are eligibility for disability retirement,[246] restoration to earning capacity,[247] determination of recovery

---

[237]*Stewart v. OPM*, 7 MSPB 746 (1981). Among the factors to be considered by OPM is whether an applicant with a prior criminal background has been rehabilitated.

[238]A disqualification for habitual use of alcohol can only be taken it it meets the requirements of the Comprehensive Alcohol and Alcoholism Prevention, Treatment and Rehabilitation Act of 1970, see *supra* note 70, as well as the Rehabilitation Act of 1973. Thus each disqualification must, based on its facts, meet the requirements set forth by MSPB in *Ruzek v. GSA*, 7 MSPB 307 (1981); *Mattson v. OPM*, 7 MSPB 639 (1981).

[239]5 C.F.R. 731.202.

[240]*Forbes v. Department of Justice*, MSPB No. AT07318710201 (Feb. 2, 1988). OPM may rely on hearsay in making suitability determinations if the record is internally consistent, contains corroborative testimony, and contains documents corroborated by the testimony.

[241]5 C.F.R. 731.302.

[242]5 C.F.R. 731.401.

[243]*Schaefer v. Department of Justice*, 25 MSPR 277 (1984).

[244]*Schaefer v. Immigration & Naturalization Serv.*, 28 MSPR 566 (1985).

[245]5 U.S.C. 8347(d).

[246]To qualify for disability retirement, an applicant must show inability, due to disease or injury, to render useful and efficient service in the position last occupied and that he or she is not qualified for reassignment to a vacant position at the same grade. 5 U.S.C. 8337(a). "The applicant bears the burden of proving his or her eligibility by the

from disability,[248] eligibility for retirement based on status as a federal employee,[249] eligibility for survivor annuity,[250] entitlement to discontinued service annuity,[251] apportionment of civil service annuity pursuant to a divorce decree,[252] determination of law enforcement officer and firefighter status for purposes of early retirement,[253] and adjudications of agency-filed disability retirement applications.[254]

Restoration Rights After Compensable Injury

Employees receiving disability compensation benefits based on a work-related injury are entitled to certain restoration rights upon recovery.[255] These rights are available only to employees who recover from a work-related disability and not employees recovered from civil service disability retirement which is based on a disability that is not work related.[256] An employee who fully recovers from the compensable injury within one year is entitled to restoration to his or her former position,[257]

---

preponderance of the evidence." *Chavez v. OPM*, 6 MSPB 343 (1981); *Everett v. OPM*, 32 MSPR 197 (1987). On appeal, MSPB is not limited to review of the record before OPM, but must review, *de novo*, all relevant evidence submitted by the parties. *Cook v. OPM*, 31 MSPR 683 (1986). Judicial review is limited to a determination of whether "there has been a substantial departure from important procedural rights, a misconstruction of the governing legislation, or some like error 'going to the heart of the administrative determination.' " 5 U.S.C. 8347(c) bars review of MSPB factual determinations. *Lindahl v. OPM*, 470 U.S. 768 (1985).

[247]*Olds v. OPM*, 34 MSPB 105 (1987); *Blunk v. OPM*, 34 MSPR 267 (1987).

[248]*Prestien v. OPM*, 8 MSPB 698 (1981). On OPM inquiry, a disability retiree must show that he or she is still disabled for useful and efficient service in the position from which he or she retired. OPM can declare a retiree recovered for disability purposes even if that agency erroneously granted disability retirement in the first place. *McMakin v. OPM*, 32 MSPR 294 (1987).

[249]See *Horner v. Acosta*, 803 F.2d 687 (Fed. Cir. 1986).

[250]*Money v. OPM*, 811 F.2d 1474 (Fed. Cir. 1987); *Darsigny v. OPM*, 787 F.2d 1555 (Fed. Cir. 1986); *Cheeseman v. OPM*, 791 F.2d 138 (Fed. Cir. 1986) (widow has burden of proving annuitant received misinformation about electing survivor annuity); *Jones v. OPM*, 31 MSPR 622 (1986).

[251]*Anderson v. OPM*, 10 MSPB 49 (1982); *Paterson v. United States*, 436 F.2d 438 (Ct. Cl. 1971).

[252]*Bray v. OPM*, 9 MSPB 756 (1982); *Hobbs v. OPM*, 485 F. Supp. 456 (M.D. Fla. 1980).

[253]*Morgan v. OPM*, 773 F.2d 282 (Fed. Cir. 1985); *Ryan v. MSPB*, 779 F.2d 669 (Fed. Cir. 1985); *Obremski v. OPM*, 9 MSPB 743 (1982); *Ellis v. United States*, 610 F.2d 760 (Ct. Cl. 1980).

[254]*Daley v. OPM*, 10 MSPB 518 (1982). In an agency-filed disability retirement, the agency has the burden of proving that the employee is disabled.

[255]5 U.S.C. 8151(b).

[256]*Johnson v. MSPB*, 812 F.2d 705 (Fed. Cir. 1987).

[257]5 C.F.R. 353.301. Employees must have been injured in the line of duty. *Enright v. Postal Serv.*, 28 MSPR 414 (1985); *Brooks v. Postal Serv.*, 26 MSPR 217 (1985).

unless the employee was separated for reasons other than disability.[258]
An employee who fully recovers after having received compensation benefits for more than one year is entitled to priority placement in his or her former position or an equivalent one.[259] In addition, agencies are required to make every effort to restore employees who have partially recovered from the medical condition that gave rise to their entitlement to compensation and are able to return to limited duty.[260] Employees who believe that they improperly were denied restoration rights may appeal to the MSPB.[261]

Compliance

Any employee who appeals an agency action to the MSPB and prevails must be returned to the position from which he or she was removed or demoted.[262] An agency does not have the option of waiting to comply with the Board's order until the OPM has made a decision on an agency request to intervene.[263] An employee who believes he or she has not been so returned may request the MSPB to enforce compliance with the decision. "In determining whether an agency has complied with a Board order, the Board must determine whether the agency has placed the employee 'as nearly as possible in the *status quo ante*.'"[264]

If the employee's former position still exists, but the employee is not placed in that position, the agency must show a strong, overriding reason

---

[258]*Miller v. Postal Serv.*, 3 MSPB 418 (1980). The right to restoration also applies to probationary employees. *Roche v. Postal Serv.*, 828 F.2d 1555 (Fed. Cir. 1987); *Rishavy v. Postal Serv.*, 35 MSPR 528 (1987). However, an employee is entitled to restoration when his separation was substantially related to the compensable injury. *Ruppert v. Postal Serv.*, 8 MSPB 256 (1981).

[259]5 C.F.R. 353.307. Priority consideration means that an agency may not fill a competitive position without first giving consideration to an individual on the reemployment priority list. 5 C.F.R. 330.201. Failure to give such consideration is itself appealable to the MSPB. 5 C.F.R. 330.202. Upon failure to employ an individual on the reemployment priority list, an agency is required to show that there were no equivalent jobs at any agency facility for which the individual qualified. *Whitfield v. Postal Serv.*, 5 MSPB 283 (1981); *Raicovich v. Postal Serv.*, 675 F.2d 417 (D.C. Cir. 1982); *Thompson v. Postal Serv.*, 5 MSPB 274 (1981).

[260]5 C.F.R. 353.306; *Montgomery v. Postal Serv.*, 16 MSPR 578 (1983); *Hicks v. Postal Serv.*, 35 MSPR 27 (1987).

[261]5 C.F.R. 353.401.

[262]*Kerr v. National Endowment for the Arts*, 726 F.2d 730 (Fed. Cir. 1984); *Higashi v. Department of the Army*, 26 MSPR 330 (1985); *Sarver v. Department of the Treasury*, 20 MSPR 499 (1984).

[263]*Ferry v. Department of the Navy*, 35 MSPR 12 (1987).

[264]*Mann v. VA*, 29 MSPR 271 (1985).

for not having done so.[265] If an employee is reinstated and that reinstatement is followed immediately by a reassignment or transfer, that action does not satisfy the Board's test for compliance.[266] If an agency meets its burden to justify not placing the reinstated employee in the former position, the position in which the employee is placed must be as nearly as possible at the *status quo ante*.[267]

The MSPB also has authority to examine the merits of petitions for enforcement which allege that the employee was given an inadequate award of back pay.[268] In order to obtain back pay under the Back Pay Act,[269] the employee has the burden of proving that he or she was ready, willing, and able to work at all times during the period between the date of the wrongful removal and subsequent reinstatement.[270] In order to put the employee to the proof, however, the agency must demonstrate that it has some positive evidence that the employee was not ready, willing, or able to work during that period.[271]

[265]*Id.; Cofield v. GPO,* 22 MSPR 392 (1984); *Williams v. HHS,* 32 MSPR 259 (1987) (the fact that agency filled former position is not sufficient justification unless agency can show it would have been more disruptive to reassign the new occupant than the reinstated employee).

[266]*Sarver v. Department of the Treasury,* 26 MSPR 685 (1985).

[267]In determining whether another position satisfies the *status quo ante* test, such factors as a change in supervisory or budgeting responsibilities are significant. *Miller v. Department of the Air Force,* 27 MSPR 593 (1985). See also *Vincent v. Department of Justice,* 32 MSPR 263 (1987) (argument that agency could not trust employee in prior position not adequate since it was rejected by administrative judge in initial action).

[268]The Board will not nullify the method utilized by the agency in calculating the back pay award unless it is shown that the method used was unreasonable or unworkable. *Spezzaferro v. FAA,* 24 MSPR 25 (1984). An agency must recredit all annual leave even if it exceeds the maximum carryover of 240 hours. *Broadnax v. Postal Serv.,* 35 MSPR 219 (1987).

[269]5 U.S.C. 5596.

[270]*Bartel v. FAA,* 24 MSPR 560 (1984); *Piccone v. United States,* 407 F.2d 866 (Ct.Cl. 1969).

[271]*Redding v. Postal Serv.,* 32 MSPR 187 (1987). Overtime earned during the back pay period in excess of that which would have been earned in the desired job would not be offset. *Phelps v. Department of Labor,* 35 MSPR 273 (1987).

4. Prohibited Personnel Practices and the Office of the Special Counsel

KATHRYN A. BLEECKER

The Civil Service Reform Act of 1978 defined 11 prohibited personnel practices, the violation of which can give rise to certain agency
personnel actions being set aside or to disciplinary action being taken
against the agency official who committed the prohibited practice, or
both.[1] The Whistleblower Protection Act of 1989 establishes the Office of
the Special Counsel (OSC) as an independent agency whose primary role
is to protect employees, especially whistleblowers, from prohibited personnel practices.[2] The Special Counsel has authority to investigate and to
seek stays of personnel actions, corrective action, and disciplinary action
for violations of the prohibited personnel practices.[3] The Special Counsel
also has authority to investigate and seek disciplinary action with respect
to allegations of employment discrimination, unlawful political activities,
arbitrary and capricious withholding of information requested under the
Freedom of Information Act, and violations of certain other civil service
laws.[4] The OSC also provides a channel through which federal employees
and applicants can disclose information of official wrongdoing in their
agencies (whistleblowing).[5]

Under the Whistleblower Protection Act of 1989, a current or former
employee or an applicant for employment may also seek a stay of a

---

[1]The prohibited personnel practices are defined at 5 U.S.C. 2302 and are discussed
infra.

[2]Pub. Law 101-12, April 10, 1989, 103 Stat. 16, *et seq.* (1989). The Special Counsel is
appointed by the President, with the advice and consent of the Senate, for a term of 5 years.
5 U.S.C. 1211(b).

[3]5 U.S.C. 1212, 1214–1215.

[4]5 U.S.C. 1216.

[5]5 U.S.C. 1213.

personnel action and corrective action directly from the Merit Systems Protection Board (MSPB) with respect to any personnel action he or she believes was the result of reprisal for whistleblowing. This individual right of action is available if the employee or applicant has sought, but not received, timely assistance from the Special Counsel or may be raised in connection with an otherwise appealable adverse action.[6]

What Is a Prohibited Personnel Practice

Prerequisites

There are certain prerequisites to establishing a prohibited personnel practice violation:

1. A "personnel action" must have been taken or have failed to be taken with regard to an employee or an applicant for employment who is the alleged victim of the prohibited personnel practice.[7] "Personnel action" means:[8]

    a. appointment;
    b. promotion;
    c. an action under 5 U.S.C. Chapter 75 or other disciplinary or corrective action;[9]
    d. detail, transfer, or reassignment;
    e. reinstatement;
    f. restoration;

---

[6]5 U.S.C. 1214(a)(3), 1221.

[7]The MSPB has held that the taking or failing to take a personnel action is not a prerequisite to finding the prohibited personnel practice of discrimination (5 U.S.C. 2302(b)(1)(A)). *Special Counsel v. Russell*, 85 FMSR 5284 (1985), *aff'd*, 87 FMSR 5070 (1987). The only requirement is that the discrimination be related to the authority to take, recommend, or approve a personnel action. The Board noted that a personnel action is required to establish prohibited personnel practices concerning reprisal for whistleblowing and exercising appeal rights (5 U.S.C. 2302(b)(8) and (9)) and violation of civil service laws which implement or directly concern the merit system principles (5 U.S.C. 2302(b)(11)). *Id.* The Board did not address whether a personnel action per se was required under the other prohibited practices, although the wording of those provisions appears to make it unnecessary. *Id.*

[8]5 U.S.C. 2302(a)(2)(A).

[9]Although a probationary employee or a nonveteran Schedule A excepted service employee does not have adverse action appeal rights under 5 U.S.C. Chapter 75, the removal of such an employee may be regarded as a disciplinary or corrective action and subject to protection under 5 U.S.C. 2302. *Harrison v. Bowen*, 815 F.2d 1505, 87 FMSR 7035 (D.C. Cir. 1987). Separation or downgrading by reduction in force is normally not covered unless it is a subterfuge for removal for cause or performance and is taken for one or more of the prohibited reasons.

g. reemployment;

h. a performance evaluation under 5 U.S.C. Chapter 43;

i. a decision concerning pay, benefits, awards, or education or training if the education or training may reasonably be expected to lead to an appointment, promotion, performance evaluation, or other personnel action;

j. any other significant change in duties or responsibilities which is inconsistent with the employee's salary or grade level.

2. The employee affected by the personnel action must be or have been in, or have been an applicant for, a "covered position," which means any position in the competitive service, the executive service, or a career appointee position in the Senior Executive Service (SES). Not covered are confidential and policy-making positions, such as Schedule C or non-career SES positions, and other positions specifically excluded by the President. [10]

3. The challenged personnel action must have taken place in a "covered agency," which includes an executive agency (as defined under 5 U.S.C. 105), the Administrative Office of the U.S. Courts, and the Government Printing Office. Excluded from coverage are government corporations, the General Accounting Office, the Federal Bureau of Investigation, the Central Intelligence Agency, the Defense Intelligence Agency, the National Security Agency, and any other agency excluded by the President because of its foreign intelligence or counterintelligence activities. [11]

4. The alleged prohibited personnel practice must have been taken by an employee who has the authority to take, direct others to take, recommend, or approve a personnel action. [12] This personnel authority is not defined narrowly or technically and a specific delegation of personnel authority is not required. However, there can be no prohibited personnel practice unless the alleged violator had management status or was directed to take the action by others who had management status. [13]

---

[10] 5 U.S.C. 2302(a)(2)(B).

[11] 5 U.S.C. 2302(a)(2)(C). The General Accounting Office has its own parallel system. See 4 C.F.R. Parts 2, 7, 27, and 28. The Department of Justice has adopted regulations which implement the Reform Act's requirement to protect FBI employees from reprisal for whistleblowing. 5 U.S.C. 2303; 28 C.F.R. 0.39c.

[12] 5 U.S.C. 2302(b).

[13]*Lopez v. Veterans Admin.*, 10 MSPB 724, 726, 82 FMSR 5289 (1982).

Elements of Proof[14]

Discrimination

It is a prohibited personnel practice for an employee with personnel authority to discriminate for or against any employee or applicant for employment on the basis of race, color, religion, sex (including Equal Pay Act violations and sexual harassment[15]), national origin, age (over 40), handicapping condition, marital status, or political affiliation.[16] Discrimination of the type covered by EEO procedures of the agencies and the Equal Employment Opportunity Commission are discussed in detail in Chapter 5.

The MSPB applies the same elements of proof as developed under applicable discrimination laws. Either the Special Counsel or the employee must first establish a prima facie case of discrimination. The burden then shifts to the agency, in employee appeals and employee and Special Counsel corrective actions, or to the charged official, in Special Counsel disciplinary actions, to articulate a legitimate nondiscriminatory reason for the challenged action. To prevail, the Special Counsel or the employee must prove that the purported legitimate reason was a pretext for discrimination.[17]

An employee with a discrimination complaint can go through the agency EEO process, go to the MSPB if it is a mixed case involving both allegations of discrimination and an appealable adverse action, or go to the Special Counsel. If a discrimination complaint is filed with the Special Counsel, it should be in addition to, not instead of, filing under the agency EEO procedures in order to preserve the employee's appeal rights to the EEOC, MSPB, or the federal courts. However, the Special Counsel normally defers to the EEO process in discrimination cases to avoid

---

[14]As discussed *infra*, allegations of prohibited personnel practices can be raised by the Special Counsel and by employees during an appeal of an adverse action. The elements of proof required to establish a prohibited personnel practice are the same for both employee appeals and Special Counsel proceedings.

[15]As with the other forms of discrimination, sexual harassment can be found even if there has been no personnel action taken, since the loss of tangible job benefits is not required for a finding of sex discrimination. *Special Counsel v. Russell, supra* note 7. *See Lopez v. Veterans Admin., supra* note 13.

[16]5 U.S.C. 2302(b)(1)(A)–(E). Reprisal for the exercise of rights under Title VII of the Civil Rights Act of 1964 is covered under both subsections 2302(b)(1)(A) and 2302(b)(9). *Robert J. Frazier, Jr.*, 1 MSPB 159, 184–85, 79 FMSR 7006 (1979), *aff'd in part sub nom. Frazier v. MSPB*, 672 F.2d 150, 165, 82 FMSR 7024 (D.C. Cir. 1982). The elements of proof necessary for reprisal allegations are discussed *infra*.

[17]*Taylor v. HUD*, 6 MSPB 157, 81 FMSR 5324 (1981).

duplicative investigations and other proceedings, unless it appears that the process is not being carried out in a reasonably timely manner.[18]

The OSC also has jurisdiction over discrimination based on marital status or political affiliation. These forms of discrimination are not covered by the EEO procedure. Therefore, the Special Counsel's deferral policy does not apply.

To constitute a prohibited personnel practice, the marital status or political affiliation discrimination must be specifically prohibited by a law, rule, or regulation.[19] The prohibited discrimination must affect the employee personally.[20] To establish marital status discrimination, the challenged action must go to the essence of the marital status, be it married, separated, divorced, or single.[21] Discrimination on the basis of political affiliation must relate to partisan politics and the discrimination must be based on affiliation with a political party or candidate.[22]

Soliciting or Considering Recommendations

It is also a prohibited personnel practice to solicit or consider certain oral or written recommendations or statements concerning anyone who requests or is under consideration for a personnel action. The only recommendations or statements that may be considered are those based on the personal knowledge or records of the persons furnishing them and

---

[18]5 C.F.R. 1251.3.

[19]5 U.S.C. 2302(b)(1)(E). Discrimination on the basis of marital status is prohibited under 5 U.S.C. 7202, 7204(b); 5 C.F.R. 7.1, 720.901, and 29 C.F.R. 1613.401. Political affiliation discrimination is prohibited under 5 C.F.R. 4.2, 7.1, 720.901(a) and (b); see also *Branti v. Finkel*, 445 U.S. 507 (1980); *Elrod v. Burns*, 427 U.S. 347 (1976).

[20]*Kukla v. Department of Agric.*, 12 MSPB 107, 108, 82 FMSR 5453 (1982) (no marital status discrimination where employee alleged that his removal was in reprisal for his wife's and mother-in-law's rejection of his supervisor's advances); *Harris v. Department of Justice*, 85 FMSR 5013 (1985).

[21]*Shah v. GSA*, 7 MSPB 460, 81 FMSR 2208 (1981) (allegations that an employee was discriminated against by derogatory comments about being married to a white American concerned race and national origin discrimination and not marital status). See *Pommert v. Department of the Army*, 12 MSPB 275, 276–77, 82 FMSR 5496 (1982) (denial of divorced custodial parent's request to leave work early was not marital status discrimination); *Uriarte v. Department of Agric.*, 6 MSPB 334, 335, 81 FMSR 5346 (1981) (termination based on status as pregnant married woman presented allegation of marital status discrimination as well as a claim under the Pregnancy Discrimination Act); *Craighead v. Department of Agric.*, 6 MSPB 142, 142–43, 81 FMSR 5322 (1981) (prima facie discrimination shown by single employee who was geographically reassigned while married employee was not).

[22]*Harris v. Department of Justice, supra* note 20 (no political affiliation discrimination where employee alleged that agency removed him in order to lessen possible embarrassment and retribution by U.S. senator whose nephew was also being removed). See *Sweeting v. Department of Justice*, 6 MSPB 598, 601, 81 FMSR 5365 (1981) (construing "partisan political reasons" language under 5 C.F.R. 315.806(b)).

must concern an evalution of the employee's or applicant's work performance, ability, aptitude, general qualifications, character, loyalty, or
suitability for employment.[23] This provision was intended to prevent the
use of political influence in obtaining a position or promotion,[24] and
generally relates to statements or recommendations of people outside the
agency, such as senators or representatives.[25] It does not prohibit an
agency official from taking an action against an employee when the official
does not have personal knowledge of the charges or a report concerning
the charges. The official can rely on the recommendations or statements of
another agency official based on that official's personal knowledge or
records.[26]

Coercing Political Activity

An employee with personnel authority is prohibited from coercing
any person to engage in political activity, including providing a political
contribution or service. Such employee also is precluded from taking any
action against an employee or applicant for employment in reprisal for
refusing to engage in political activity.[27] This section was intended to
incorporate the Hatch Act, which prohibits the use of official authority or
influence for the purpose of interfering with or affecting the result of an
election.[28]

Obstructing Competition

It is a prohibited personnel practice to deceive or willfully obstruct
any person's right to compete for employment.[29] There have been very few
cases involving this provision. However, it is apparent that the challenged
conduct must have been deliberate and must involve the right to compete
for employment.[30]

---

[23]5 U.S.C. 2302(b)(2).
[24]*Roane v. HHS*, 8 MSPB 37, 39, 81 FMSR 5489 (1981); *Williamson v. HHS*, 3 MSPB
142, 144, 80 FMSR 5598 (1980).
[25]*Depte v. United States*, 715 F.2d 1481, 1484, 83 FMSR 7059 (Fed. Cir. 1983)
(discussion between deciding offical and impartial agency witness to misconduct charged
against employee is not prohibited under 5 U.S.C. 2302(b)(2)).
[26]*Littlejohn v. Postal Serv.*, 84 FMSR 6120 (1984); *Hammonds v. HHS*, 10 MSPB 193,
193–94, 82 FMSR 5196 (1982); *Fike v. IRS*, 9 MSPB 379, 381–82, 82 FMSR 5077 (1982).
[27]5 U.S.C. 2302(b)(3).
[28]5 U.S.C. 7324(a)(1). The Hatch Act is discussed *infra*.
[29]5 U.S.C. 2302(b)(4).
[30]*Special Counsel v. Hoban*, 84 FMSR 5914 (1984). See *Special Counsel v. Ross*, 87
FMSR 5428 (1987); *In re Exceptions From Competitive Merit Plans (FPM 335)*, 8 MSPB
466, 467–68, 81 FMSR 5557 (1981).

Influencing to Withdraw

An employee with authority to take personnel actions may not influence any person to withdraw from competition for any position for the purpose of improving or injuring another person's prospects for employment.[31] This provision requires the involvement of at least two people, one who is influenced to withdraw and another whose prospects for employment are either improved or injured by the other person's withdrawal.[32] The provision was intended to protect all phases of the hiring process and is not limited to actions affecting applicants.[33]

Granting Preference or Advantage

It is a prohibited personnel practice for an employee with personnel authority to grant any unlawful preference or advantage to an employee or applicant for employment (including defining the scope or manner of competition or the requirements for a position) for the purpose of improving or injuring the prospects of any particular person for employment.[34] The preferential action must not be authorized by any law, rule, or regulation, and must have been taken for the purpose of improving one person's prospects or injuring another's.[35] It is not required that the unauthorized action actually result in an advantage, only that it had that purpose.[36]

Nepotism

A public official cannot appoint, employ, promote, advance, or advocate the same on behalf of a relative, if it involes a position in the agency in which the official is serving or over which the official exercises

---

[31]5 U.S.C. 2302(b)(5).

[32]*Filiberti & Dysthe v. MSPB*, 804 F.2d 1504, 86 FMSR 7097 (9th Cir. 1986). Two related regulations prohibit influencing withdrawal for the purpose of improving or injuring the prospects of *that* applicant for employment. 5 C.F.R. 4.3 and 330.601.

[33]*Filiberti v. MSPB, supra* note 32 at 1509.

[34]5 U.S.C. 2302(b)(6).

[35]*Price v. Department of the Army*, 12 MSPB 319, 321, 82 FMSR 5510 (1982) (no prohibited personnel practice because no evidence that training of employee was for purpose of improving that employee's prospects or injuring appellant's). See also *Special Counsel v. Hoban, supra* note 30 (violation of 5 U.S.C. 2302(b)(6) by official's directing preparation of new, more favorable performance appraisal for employee who was competing for position for purpose of harming another employee's prospects for position); *Baum v. Department of the Treasury*, 13 MSPB 74, 83 FMSR 5026 (1983), *aff'd*, 727 F.2d 1117 (Fed. Cir. 1983); *Wellman v. Department of Commerce*, 9 MSPB 798, 82 FMSR 2017 (1982).

[36]*Special Counsel v. DeFord*, 85 FMSR 5274 (1985).

jurisdiction or control.[37] Advocating means recommending or referring a relative for consideration for appointment, employment, promotion, or advancement to another official who is lower in the chain of command.[38] A violation can be established regardless of whether the official's actions on behalf of a relative are successful.[39]

Reprisal for Whistleblowing

It is unlawful to take or fail to take, or threaten to take or fail to take, a personnel action with respect to an employee or applicant for employment because of any lawful disclosure of information which the employee or applicant reasonably believes evidenced a violation of law, rule, or regulation, gross mismanagement, gross waste of funds, abuse of authority, or substantial and specific danger to public health and safety.[40]

Prior to the Whistleblower Protection Act, to establish prima facie reprisal for whistleblowing under section 2302(b)(8), as well as for the exercise of appeal rights under 2302(b)(9) (discussed below), by the Special Counsel or by an employee in an adverse action appeal, the following elements had to be proved by a preponderance of evidence: (1) that the employee engaged in protected conduct;[41] (2) that the offend-

---

[37]5 U.S.C. 2302(b)(7). "Public official" is defined at 5 U.S.C. 3110(a)(2); "relative" is defined at 5 U.S.C. 3110(a)(3). Nepotism is also prohibited under 5 U.S.C. 3110.

[38]See 5 C.F.R. 310.103(c).

[39]See *Rentz v. Postal Serv.*, 84 FMSR 5043 (1984).

[40]5 U.S.C. 2302(b)(8), as amended by section 4(a) of the Whistleblower Protection Act, 103 Stat. 32. Employees can also claim that their disclosures were protected under the First Amendment. The Board applies the tests developed in cases involving public employee free speech and balances the employee's interest in commenting on matters of public concern against the government's interests in maintaining an efficient and effective work force. See *Ledeaux v. Veterans Admin.*, 85 FMSR 5507 (1985), citing *Pickering v. Board of Educ.*, 391 U.S. 563 (1968); *Osokow v. OPM*, 84 FMSR 6099 (1984). This test is not the same as applied by the Board in whistleblower reprisal cases. It is the employee's reasonable belief, and not the *Pickering* balancing test, which determines whether the disclosure is protected under 5 U.S.C. 2302(b)(8). *Special Counsel v. Department of State (Rohrmann)*, 9 MSPB 14, 15–16, n.4, 82 FMSR 7001 (1982).

[41]To be protected, the disclosure of the information did not specifically have to be prohibited by law or Executive Order. 5 U.S.C. 2302(b)(8)(A). In addition, the employee must have reasonably believed that the disclosed information evidenced a violation of law, rule, or regulation, or other official wrongdoing. The employee's belief could be found reasonable without having to show that the disclosures were correct. *Special Counsel v. Hoban*, supra note 30. But see *Prescott v. National Inst. of Child Health & Dev.*, 6 MSPB 216, 81 FMSR 7042 (1981) (employee's belief not reasonable when employee deliberately distorted information); *Quinton v. Department of Transp.*, 808 F.2d 826, 86 FMSR 7098 (Fed. Cir. 1986) (not protected because there was legal opinion, prepared prior to disclosures and known by employee, that matters disclosed were not illegal). The employee's primary motivation for disclosing the information had to be "the desire to inform the public on matters of public concern, and not personal vindictiveness." *Fiorillo v. Department of Justice*, 795 F.2d 1544, 1550 (Fed. Cir. 1986). But see *Plaskett v. HHS*, 9 MSPB 530, 533,

ing official knew about the disclosure;[42] (3) that a personnel action was taken, or failed to be taken, in retaliation for the disclosure; and (4) that there was a causal connection between the protected activity and the adverse personnel action.[43] Prima facie reprisal was established only if the protected disclosure also was found to have been a significant factor in the decision to take the personnel action.[44] The agency could overcome this by proving by a preponderance of evidence that it had a legitimate management reason for its action.[45]

---

82 FMSR 5095 (1982); *Robert J. Frazier, Jr.*, 1 MSPB 159, 179, 79 FMSR 7006 (1979), *aff'd in part sub nom. Frazier v. MSPB*, 672 F.2d 150, 82 FMSR 7024 (D.C. Cir. 1982) (employee's motive for disclosing information is generally not considered material). In addition, the Board has found that whistleblower protection was not intended to protect dissident employees or to require agencies to tolerate disruptive activities. *Oliver v. HHS*, 87 FMSR 5489 (1987); *Osokow v. OPM*, *supra* note 40; *Prescott v. National Inst. of Child Health & Dev.*, *supra*, 6 MSPB at 221.

[42]The knowledge requirement is satisfied when it is shown that the employee who took or failed to take the personnel action had actual or constructive knowledge of the protected disclosure. *Frazier v. MSPB*, *supra* note 41, 672 F.2d at 166–67. Constructive knowledge means that the official should have known about the disclosure. *Church v. Department of the Army*, 6 MSPB 614, 615, 81 FMSR 2072 (1981).

[43]*Stanek v. Department of Transp.*, 805 F.2d 1572, 86 FMSR 7093 (Fed. Cir. 1986); *Sullivan v. Department of the Navy*, 720 F.2d 1266, 83 FMSR 7071 (Fed. Cir. 1983); *Robert J. Frazier, Jr.*, *supra* note 41, 1 MSPB at 186. Proof of retaliatory intent in most circumstances was inferred from circumstantial evidence. *Id.*; *Bodinus v. Department of the Treasury*, 7 MSPB 385, 387, 81 FMSR 7061 (1981). There are various factors from which causal connection was inferred, including the employer's reaction to the protected activity, the extent to which the disclosures formed the basis of the protected activity, the seriousness of the disclosures, and the time during which the issues raised by the disclosures remained unresolved. *Valerino v. HHS*, 7 MSPB 347, 348, 81 FMSR 5430 (1981).

[44]*Special Counsel v. Department of State (Rohrmann)*, *supra* note 40, 9 MSPB at 20. See also *Gerlach v. Federal Trade Comm'n*, 8 MSPB 599, 603, 81 FMSR 7080 (1981). Under the Reform Act, the Special Counsel or employee was required to prove that reprisal was the "motivating factor" or the "real reason" for the agency's action. *Id.*

[45]See *Stromfeld v. Department of Justice*, 84 FMSR 5526 (1984) (employee appeal); *Special Counsel v. Department of State (Rohrmann)*, *supra* note 40, 9 MSPB at 20 (corrective action). Under the Reform Act, the MSPB applied a different standard for proving reprisal depending on the nature of the proceeding. In employee appeals and Special Counsel corrective actions, if the evidence showed that the personnel action was taken both for legitimate and prohibited reasons, the agency was required to prove by a preponderance of the evidence that it would have taken the same action regardless of whether the protected conduct had occurred. *Id.*; *Gerlach v. Federal Trade Comm'n*, *supra* note 44, 8 MSPB at 605. In Special Counsel disciplinary actions involving dual motivation, the Board found reprisal if the Special Counsel proved that retaliation was a significant factor in the decision, regardless of whether the charged official also had any legitimate reasons for the action. *Special Counsel v. Brown*, 85 FMSR 5280 (1985); *Special Counsel v. Harvey*, 84 FMSR 6044 (1984), *rev'd on other grounds sub nom. Harvey v. MSPB*, 802 F.2d 537, 86 FMSR 7089 (Fed. Cir. 1986). The Court of Appeals for the Federal Circuit questioned, without deciding, the appropriateness of the Board's applying different standards for establishing retaliation in different types of actions. *Id.* at 548 n.5; *Starrett v. MSPB*, 792 F.2d 1246, 1253 n.12, 86 FMSR 7086 (4th Cir. 1986). See also *Special Counsel v. Mongan*, 87 FMSR 5288 (1987).

Under the Whistleblower Protection Act, reprisal will be found if the disclosure was "a contributing factor" in the challenged personnel action.[46] It is likely that the Board will continue to require proof of the four elements discussed above to establish prima facie reprisal for whistleblowing. The Board must order corrective action unless the agency demonstrates by clear and convincing evidence that it would have taken the same personnel action in the absence of the disclosure.[47] The Whistleblower Protection Act was intended to strengthen and improve the protection provided to federal employees and applicants who disclose wrongdoing within the government by making it easier to establish reprisal.[48]

Reprisal for Exercising Appeal Rights

It is a prohibited personnel practice to take or fail to take, or to threaten to take or fail to take, any personnel action against an employee or applicant for employment: (1) because of the exercise of any appeal, complaint, or grievance right granted by law, rule, or regulation; (2) for testifying for or otherwise lawfully assisting any individual in the exercise of any such right; (3) for cooperating with or disclosing information to the Inspector General or the Special Counsel, in accordance with applicable provisions of law; or (4) for refusing to obey an order that would require the individual to violate a law.[49] As revised under the Whistleblower Protection Act, this provision codifies the Board's practice of protecting an employee or applicant who exercises rights under a lawful appeal procedure or who testifies, assists, or otherwise participates in any lawful appeal process.[50] It also extends protection to an employee or applicant who cooperates with or discloses information to the Inspector General and OSC.[51]

---

[46]5 U.S.C. 1214(b)(4)(B)(i) (Special Counsel corrective actions) and 1221(e)(1) (employee actions involving reprisal for whistleblowing).

[47]5 U.S.C. 1214(b)(4)(B)(ii), 1221(e)(2).

[48]Section 2(b) of the Whistleblower Protection Act, 103 Stat. 16; 5 U.S.C. 1201 note.

[49]5 U.S.C. 2302(b)(9), as amended by section 4(b) of the Whistleblower Protection Act, 103 Stat. 32.

[50]See *Bodinus v. Department of the Treasury*, 7 MSPB 385, 81 FMSR 7061 (1981). See also *Special Counsel v. Harvey, supra* note 45 (petitioning the Special Counsel); *McClellan v. Postal Serv.*, 84 FMSR 5106 (1984) (participating in appeal as union steward); *Robert J. Frazier, Jr., supra* note 41, 1 MSPB 159 (filing EEO complaints). The Board found protected an employee's false, but nonmalicious statements made in the course of a grievance proceeding. *Bartel v. FAA*, 12 MSPB 217, 223, 82 FMSR 7052 (1982).

[51]5 U.S.C. 2302(b)(9)(C). Although this appears to duplicate the whistleblower protection under section 2302(b)(8), section 2302(b)(9)(C) could be used to extend protection to an employee or applicant who cooperates with an investigation even though the employee or applicant did not actually make a disclosure.

Prior to the Whistleblower Protection Act, the MSPB required the same elements and applied the same burdens of proof to establish reprisal for exercising appeal rights as it did to establish reprisal for whistleblowing. Thus, to establish prima facie reprisal under this provision, the following elements had to be proved by a preponderance of evidence: (1) that the employee engaged in protected conduct; (2) that the offending official knew about the disclosure; (3) that a personnel action was taken or failed to be taken in retaliation for the disclosure; and (4) that there was a causal connection between the protected activity and the adverse personnel action.[52] Reprisal was established only if the protected conduct also was found to have been a significant factor in the decision to take the personnel action.[53] The agency was required to prove by a preponderance of evidence that it would have taken the same action regardless of the protected activity.[54]

The standards and burdens of proof for establishing reprisal for the exercise of appeal rights were not specifically changed under the Whistleblower Protection Act.[55] Thus, the board should continue to apply its established case law in proceedings involving allegations of reprisal under section 2302(b)(9), including applying the significant factor test and requiring the agency to rebut the showing of reprisal by a preponderance of evidence.

Discrimination Based on Non-Job-Related Conduct

An agency may not discriminate for or against an employee or applicant for employment on the basis of conduct that does not adversely affect the performance of the employee, the applicant, or others. However, an agency is not prohibited from taking into account a criminal conviction in determining suitability or fitness for employment.[56]

This provision primarily applies to situations involving off-duty misconduct. In *Merritt v. Department of Justice*,[57] the MSPB ruled that the

---

[52]See, e.g., *Wildeman v. Department of the Air Force*, 84 FMSR 5823 (1984) (employee appeal); *Special Counsel v. Department of the Army (Mortensen)*, 83 FMSR 7053 (1983) (corrective action); *Special Counsel v. Harvey, supra* note 45 (disciplinary action).
[53]*Gerlach v. Federal Trade Comm'n, supra* note 44, 8 MSPB at 603–04.
[54]*Id.*, 8 MSPB at 605.
[55]Section 1214(b)(4)(A) states that, in actions brought by the Special Counsel, the Board shall order appropriate corrective action if it determines that the Special Counsel has demonstrated that a prohibited personnel practice other than reprisal for whistleblowing under 5 U.S.C. 2302(b)(8), has occurred, exists, or is to be taken.
[56]5 U.S.C. 2302(b)(10).
[57]6 MSPB 493, 81 FMSR 7046 (1981). In *Wild v. HUD*, 692 F.2d 1129, 82 FMSR 7054 (7th Cir. 1982), the court refused to find a violation of 5 U.S.C. 2302(b)(10) where HUD proved that the employee's off-duty misconduct of managing substandard housing directly conflicted with the mission of the agency.

agency must establish a connection between an employee's off-duty misconduct and the efficiency of the service. The Board also stated that in certain egregious circumstances, as determined by the nature and seriousness of the misconduct, it will allow a presumption of a connection or nexus, which can be overcome by showing that there was no adverse effect on the efficiency of the service.[58] If the presumption is rebutted, the agency must prove the actual existence of nexus.[59] These same standards are applied to employee appeals and Special Counsel actions alleging violation of section 2302(b)(10) concerning off-duty misconduct.

Although the Board has implied that reprisal for performance-related conduct could constitute a violation of this provision,[60] the Federal Circuit stated in *Harvey v. MSPB*,[61] that section 2302(b)(10) applies only to conduct that is totally unrelated to job performance. In addition, the Board has indicated that discrimination for certain conduct protected under other prohibited personnel practice provisions may also be covered under this provision.[62] This interpretation has not yet been tested and it is unclear whether it will be allowed by the court.

Violation of Merit System Principles

It is a prohibited personnel practice to take, or fail to take, any other personnel action in violation of a law, rule, or regulation which imple-

---

[58]*Merritt v. Department of Justice, supra* note 57, 6 MSPB at 508. A criminal conviction does not automatically establish nexus.

[59]*Id.* At least two courts refused to apply the presumption of nexus and held that the agency must prove that the employee's action adversely affected his performance of the agency's function. *D.E.v. Department of the Navy*, 707 F.2d 1049 (9th Cir. 1983) (agency proved that employee sexually abused his young daughter but failed to prove that conduct affected his work); *Bonet v. Postal Serv.*, 661 F.2d 1071 (5th Cir. 1981) (employee indicted for indecent conduct with child, but charge was later dismissed). In spite of these decisions, the MSPB continues to apply the presumption in appropriate cases. E.g., *Faint v. Postal Serv.*, 84 FMSR 5719 (1984) (employee accused of assault with deadly weapon); *Williams v. GSA*, 84 FMSR 5723 (1984) (employee accused of sexually assaulting minor).

[60]*Special Counsel v. HUD (Mullin)*, 10 MSPB 331, 82 FMSR 5221 (1982) (while denying Special Counsel's stay request, Board stated that retaliation against HUD employees for participating in foreclosure actions affecting their supervisor could constitute violation of 5 U.S.C. 2302(b)(10)). See also *Special Counsel v. Harvey, supra* note 45.

[61]*Supra* note 45, 802 F.2d at 551. In *Harvey*, the Board had found a violation of 5 U.S.C. 2302(b)(10) because the charged official took a personnel action on the basis of his incorrect belief concerning the employee's conduct. The court found that the focus should be on the nature of the alleged conduct, which in this case was job-related and therefore not covered under 5 U.S.C. 2302(b)(10), and not on whether the conduct actually occurred.

[62]E.g., *Ketchum v. FAA*, 85 FMSR 5318 (1985) (reprisal for testifying at MSPB appeal); *Special Counsel v. Harvey, supra* note 45 (reprisal for whistleblowing). This is signifcant since reprisal allegations could be raised under this subsection even though there is no personnel action, as required under 5 U.S.C. 2302(b)(8) and (9).

ments or directly concerns the merit system principles.[63] Section 2301(b) provides that federal personnel management should be implemented consistent with the merit principles, including the principles that all employees and applicants should receive fair and equitable treatment without discrimination and with proper regard for their privacy and constitutional rights, that the federal work force should be used efficiently and effectively, and that employees should be retained on the basis of the adequacy of their performance. Subsection 2302(b)(11) is a "catchall" intended to prohibit actions that are inconsistent with the merit system principles but do not fall within the other provision of section 2302(b).[64]

The MSPB applies a two-step analysis for establishing violations of this provision: (1) that the action violates a law, rule, or regulation, and

---

[63]5 U.S.C. 2302(b)(11). The merit system principles are enumerated at 5 U.S.C. 2301(b), as follows:

Federal personnel management should be implemented consistent with the following merit system principles:

(1) Recruitment should be from qualified individuals from appropriate sources in an endeavor to achieve a work force from all segments of society, and selection and advancement should be determined solely on the basis of relative ability, knowledge, and skills, after fair and open competition which assures that all receive equal opportunity.

(2) All employees and applicants for employment should receive fair and equitable treatment in all aspects of personnel management without regard to political affiliation, race, color, religion, national origin, sex, marital status, age, or handicapping condition, and with proper regard for their privacy and constitutional rights.

(3) Equal pay should be provided for work of equal value, with appropriate consideration of both national and local rates paid by employers in the private sector, and appropriate incentives and recognition should be provided for excellence in performance.

(4) All employees should maintain high standards of integrity, conduct, and concern for the public interest.

(5) The Federal work force should be used efficiently and effectively.

(6) Employees should be retained on the basis of the adequacy of their performance, inadequate performance should be corrected, and employees should be separated who cannot or will not improve their performance to meet required standards.

(7) Employees should be provided effective education and training in cases in which such education and training would result in better organizational and individual performance.

(8) Employees should be —

(A) protected against arbitrary action, personal favoritism, or coercion for partisan political purposes, and

(B) prohibited from using their official authority or influence for the purpose of interfering with or affecting the result of an election or a nomination for election.

(9) Employees should be protected against reprisal for the lawful disclosure of information which the employees reasonably believe evidences —

(A) a violation of any law, rule, or regulation, or

(B) gross mismanagement, a gross waste of funds, an abuse of authority, or substantial and specific danger to public health or safety.

[64]*Special Counsel v. Harvey, supra* note 45; *Special Counsel v. Sullivan*, 6 MSPB 442, 443, 81 FMSR 7047 (1981).

(2) that the violated law, rule, or regulation implements[65] or directly concerns[66] a merit system principle.[67] In other words, the merit system principles are not self-executing. It is not sufficient to show that the personnel action was taken in violation of one of the principles listed under section 2301(b). There must also be a violation of a law, rule, or regulation related to the principle.

When to Allege a Prohibited Personnel Practice

Employee Proceedings Before the MSPB

Employee Stay Requests

The Whistleblower Protection Act provides that an employee, former employee, or applicant who is seeking corrective action from the Board with respect to reprisal for whistleblowing, or pursuing an adverse action appeal involving reprisal for whistleblowing, may request the Board to order a stay of the involved personnel action.[68] The Board must grant the stay within 10 calendar days (excluding weekends and legal holidays) if it determines that a stay would be appropriate.[69] The Board must allow the agency to comment on the stay request before it is granted.[70] The stay will remain in effect for such time as the Board determines to be appropriate.[71] The Board may modify or dissolve the stay at any time it determines this to be appropriate.[72]

---

[65]"Implement" as used in the provision means "to carry out, accomplish, fulfill or give practical effect to, in the context of a manifest purpose or design to prevent conduct which directly and substantially 'undermines' the merit system principles and the 'integrity' of the merit system" (footnotes omitted). *Wells v. Harris*, 1 MSPB 199, 230, 79 FMSR 7005 (1979).

[66]"Directly concerns" means that the connection between the law, rule, or regulation and the merit principles is clear and plain, not by implication. *Special Counsel v. Harvey, supra* note 45.

[67]*Bodinus v. Department of the Treasury, supra* note 50, 7 MSPB at 389; *Wells v. Harris, supra* note 65, 1 MSPB at 229 n. 71. In *Lovshin v. Department of the Navy*, 767 F.2d 826, 85 FMSR 7038 (Fed. Cir. 1985), *cert. denied*, 475 U.S. 111 (1986), the court stated that it is a violation of 5 U.S.C. 2302(b)(11) to violate any of the merit system principles. It did not specifically address the Board's two-step analysis. According to the Board, the court "did not expressly disagree with the Board's ruling in *Wells* that the merit system principles were not self-executing." *Fairall v. Veterans Admin.*, 87 FMSR 7020 (1987). Thus, the Board continues to apply its analysis.

[68]5 U.S.C. 1221(c)(1) and 1221(i). The opportunity for an employee to seek corrective action and a stay of a personnel action directly from the Board is a new right under the Whistleblower Protection Act.

[69]5 U.S.C. 1221(c)(2).

[70]5 U.S.C. 1221(c)(3)(A).

[71]5 U.S.C. 1221(c)(3)(B).

[72]5 U.S.C. 1221(c)(3)(C).

Employee Corrective Actions

Under the Whistleblower Protection Act, an employee, former employee, or applicant may seek corrective action directly from the Board with respect to any personnel action taken, or proposed to be taken, as a result of reprisal for whistleblowing.[73] The employee, former employee, or applicant must first request the Special Counsel to seek corrective action.[74] The employee may go to the MSPB after the Special Counsel notifies him or her that the investigation has been terminated, but it must be within 60 days of the notification.[75] The employee may also go to the Board if the Special Counsel fails to notify him or her within 120 days that it will seek corrective action on the employee's behalf.[76]

If the employee demonstrates that the disclosure was a contributing factor in the personnel action, the MSPB may order whatever corrective action it determines to be appropriate.[77] The Board will not order corrective action if the agency proves by clear and convincing evidence that it would have taken the same personnel action in the absence of the protected disclosure.[78] The Board is required to issue its final decision on employee corrective actions as soon as practicable.[79] If the employee is the prevailing party and the Board finds that a prohibited personnel practice occurred, the agency is liable to the employee for reasonable attorney's fees and other costs incurred.[80] An employee who is adversely affected or aggrieved by a final order or decision of the Board may appeal to the Court of Appeals for the Federal Circuit.[81] If the employee prevails on the appeal, the agency is liable for the employee's reasonable attorney's fees and other costs, regardless of the basis for the decision.[82]

---

[73]5 U.S.C. 1214(a)(3) and 1221. This right is new under the Whistleblower Protection Act.

[74]*Id.* The employee, former employee, or applicant may seek corrective action directly from the Board before seeking it from the Special Counsel if he or she has the right to appeal directly to the Board under any law, rule, or regulation. 5 U.S.C. 1221(b).

[75]5 U.S.C. 1214(a)(3)(A).

[76]5 U.S.C. 1214(a)(3)(B). If the employee, former employee, or applicant seeks corrective action from the Board, the Special Counsel may continue to seek corrective action personal to the employee only if he or she consents. 5 U.S.C. 1214(a)(4).

[77]5 U.S.C. 1221(e)(1). The fact that the Special Counsel terminated its investigation cannot be considered in these proceedings. 5 U.S.C. 1221(f)(2).

[78]5 U.S.C. 1221(e)(2). These same burdens of proof also apply to an employee adverse action appeal involving allegations of reprisal for whistleblowing. 5 U.S.C. 1221(i).

[79]5 U.S.C. 1221(f)(1).

[80]5 U.S.C. 1221(g)(1).

[81]5 U.S.C. 1221(h). The appeal must be filed within 30 days after the employee receives notice of the Board's final order. 5 U.S.C. 1221(h)(2), 7703.

[82]5 U.S.C. 1221(g)(2).

Employee Adverse Action Appeal

An employee may raise a prohibited personnel practice allegation as an affirmative defense during an adverse action appeal to the MSPB.[83] The Board does not have jurisdiction over a prohibited personnel practice allegation unless it is brought in conjunction with an action that is otherwise appealable to the Board, an employee corrective action involving reprisal for whistleblowing, or an action brought by the Special Counsel.[84] Employee adverse action appeals are discussed in Chapter 3.

In an adverse action appeal, an employee must prove by a preponderance of the evidence that the agency's decision was "based on" a prohibited personnel practice (other than reprisal for whistleblowing), which means that the prohibited personnel practice was the "motivating factor" or the "real reason" for the action.[85] If the employee prevails on this affirmative defense, he or she may be eligible for an award of attorney's fees if the Board finds that the award is warranted in the interest of justice.[86] Attorney's fees are discussed in Chapter 12.

Preference in Receiving Transfers

The Whistleblower Protection Act provides that an agency may give preference to any employee in the same or another Executive agency to transfer to a position of the same status and tenure as the position the employee occupies on the date of the transfer, if the employee is otherwise qualified for the position, is eligible for an appointment to the position, and the MSPB has determined that the employee was the victim of reprisal for whistleblowing.[87] The employee may voluntarily apply for the position.[88] If the selecting official rejects the application, he or she must

---

[83]5 U.S.C. 7701(c)(2)(B).

[84]See *Wren v. Department of the Army*, 2 MSPB 174, 175, 80 FMSR 5042 (1980), *aff'd sub nom. Wren v. MSPB*, 681 F.2d 867 (D.C. Cir. 1982). An employee affected by a prohibited personnel practice which also falls under the negotiated grievance procedure must choose either to raise the allegation under the grievance system or before the MSPB, if the action is otherwise appealable, but not both. 5 U.S.C. 7121(d). Negotiated grievance procedures are discussed in Chapter 2.

[85]5 U.S.C. 7701(c)(2)(B). *Alley v. Veterans Admin.*, 690 F.2d 153, 82 FMSR 7059 (8th Cir. 1982); *Gerlach v. Federal Trade Comm'n*, 8 MSPB 599, 603; 81 FMSR 7080 (1981); *Shockro v. FCC*, 5 MSPB 181, 182, 81 FMSR 5264 (1981).

[86]5 U.S.C. 7701(g)(1).

[87]5 U.S.C. 3352(a). This preference will be provided for no more than one transfer from or within the agency where the employee worked at the time of the Board's finding of reprisal and no later than 18 months after the Board's determination. 5 U.S.C. 3352(e). This preference will not be provided to an employee if a preference eligible employee, as defined at section 2108(3), also applied for the same position. 5 U.S.C. 3352(f).

[88]5 U.S.C. 3352(b).

provide the employee with written notification of the rejection and the reasons for it within 30 days after receiving the application.[89] The employee may ask the head of the agency to review the rejection. This request must be submitted 30 days after receiving notification of the rejection. The agency head must review the matter and provide a written statement of its findings to the employee and the MSPB within 30 days of receiving the request.[90]

Special Counsel Proceedings Before the MSPB

Special Counsel Investigations

The Special Counsel has authority to investigate allegations of prohibited personnel practices made by an employee, former employee, or applicant for employment or on its own initiative.[91] When OSC receives an allegation of any prohibited personnel practice, it must investigate to the extent necessary to determine whether there are reasonable grounds to believe that a prohibited personnel practice has occurred, exists, or is to be taken.[92] Within 15 days after receiving the complaint, OSC must send written notification to the complaining employee that the allegation was received and provide the name of a contact person within OSC.[93] Unless the investigation is terminated, OSC must notify the complainant of the status of the investigation and any action taken by OSC within 90 days of the initial notification and at least every 60 days thereafter.[94]

If the Special Counsel terminates the investigation, it must so notify the complainant in writing and provide a summary of relevant facts, including those facts which do and do not support the allegations, and the reasons for terminating the investigation.[95]

The OSC may not respond to any inquiry or provide information concerning anyone making an allegation of a prohibited personnel practice, except in accordance with the Privacy Act, 5 U.S.C. 552a, or as required by other applicable federal statute.[96] Notwithstanding these exceptions, OSC may not respond to any inquiry concerning the solicita-

---

[89] 5 U.S.C. 3352(c).
[90] 5 U.S.C. 3352(d).
[91] 5 U.S.C. 1212(a)(2) and 1214(a).
[92] 5 U.S.C. 1214(a)(1)(A).
[93] 5 U.S.C. 1214(a)(1)(B).
[94] 5 U.S.C. 1214(a)(1)(C).
[95] 5 U.S.C. 1214(a)(2)(A). The Special Counsel's statement cannot be used as evidence in any judicial or administrative proceeding without the consent of the complainant. 5 U.S.C. 1214(a)(2)(B).
[96] 5 U.S.C. 1212(g)(1).

tion or consideration of any recommendation or statement about a person under consideration for any personnel action as described under section 2302(b)(2), unless it has obtained the consent of that individual or the information requested is necessary for the requesting agency to make a determination concerning an individual's access to information that could affect the national security.[97]

The MSPB has no authority over OSC's investigations or its decision whether to pursue an action.[98] The Whistleblower Protection Act makes OSC an independent agency, thereby severing all administrative and other ties between it and the MSPB.[99]

Stays of Personnel Actions

The Special Counsel is authorized to request any member of the Board to order a stay of any personnel action[100] for a period of 45 days, when there are reasonable grounds to believe that the personnel action was or is to be taken as a result of a prohibited personnel practice.[101] The Board member must grant the stay within three calendar days (excluding weekends and legal holidays) unless he or she determines that, under the facts and circumstances involved, such a stay would not be appropriate.[102] If the Board member does not specifically deny the initial stay request, it is automatically granted on the fourth calendar day (excluding weekends and legal holidays) after the request is made.[103]

The full Board may extend the stay for any period which it considers appropriate.[104] The Board must allow the agency involved the opportunity to comment before granting the extension.[105] A stay may be terminated by the Board at any time provided that, if the termination is on a motion by the Board or the agency, notice and opportunity for a hearing is first provided to the Special Counsel and to the individual for whom the stay has been granted or, if the termination is on motion of the Special Counsel, notice

---

[97]5 U.S.C. 1212(g)(2).

[98]Wren v. MSPB, supra note 84, 681 F.2d at 873; Special Counsel v. Harvey, supra note 45 (decision to pursue investigation or to take action as result of investigation within Special Counsel's discretion); Special Counsel v. HUD (Lesht), 83 FMSR 7027 (1983) (Special Counsel is responsible for its own investigations).

[99]See 5 U.S.C. 1211.

[100]Only a personnel action as defined under 5 U.S.C. 2302(b)(1)(A), can be stayed.

[101]5 U.S.C. 1214(b)(1)(A)(i).

[102]5 U.S.C. 1214(b)(1)(A)(ii) and (iii).

[103]5 U.S.C. 1214(b)(1)(A)(iii).

[104]5 U.S.C. 1214(b)(1)(B).

[105]5 U.S.C. 1214(b)(1)(C). No opportunity is provided for the agency to comment before the Board grants the initial 45-day stay.

and opportunity for a hearing is first provided to the involved individual.[106]

The purpose of a stay is to preserve the status quo while the Special Counsel investigates the alleged prohibited personnel practice and while the Board considers the Special Counsel's request for corrective action or for disciplinary action.[107] It is not necessary to show that the employee would suffer irreparable harm if the personnel action is not stayed.[108] It is obviously preferable to seek a stay prior to the effective date of the personnel action. However, even if the agency has already taken a personnel action, a stay may be granted to restore the employee to his or her position pending the Special Counsel's investigation.[109]

Under the Reform Act, there were three possible stay requests—an initial request for a 15-day stay, a request for a 30-day extension, and a request for an additional extension for an undefined period. The stays had to be requested and issued separately and sequentially, although the Board found that a lapse of time between the stay orders did not preclude it from extending the stay.[110] The Board would deny an initial 15-day stay request if, on its face, "the facts and circumstances involved appear to make a stay request so inherently unreasonable that the granting of a stay would be inappropriate."[111] Where the facts were in dispute as to whether there were reasonable grounds to believe a prohibited personnel practice had been or was to be taken, the Board member interpreted the facts in a manner most favorable to the Special Counsel.[112] When requesting a 30-day extension of the initial stay, the Special Counsel was required to make a somewhat stronger showing of the basis for believing a prohibited

---

[106]5 U.S.C. 1214(b)(1)(D). Under the Reform Act, there was no opportunity for a hearing with respect to a stay request or termination.

[107]*Mildred G. Kass*, 2 MSPB 251, 80 FMSR 7011 (1980); *Manuel Munoz*, 3 MSPB 482, 80 FMSR 5129 (1980). A stay will be granted only for the purpose of allowing completion of OSC's investigation or the Board's corrective or disciplinary action proceeding. See *Mildred G. Kass*, *supra*, at 256.

[108]*Robert J. Frazier, Jr.*, 1 MSPB 2, 6, 79 FMSR 7001 (1979).

[109]*Manuel Munoz*, 4 MSPB 292 (1980). See also *Special Counsel v. Department of the Army (Mortensen)*, 82 FMSR 5051 (1982) (granting stay request involving proposed personnel action). The employee must be retained in or returned to the same position and grade level under the same terms and conditions of employment as existed prior to the challenged personnel action. *Special Counsel v. Department of Labor (Coffield)*, 3 MSPB 46, 80 FMSR 5066 (1980) (agency not allowed to place employee in temporary status during pendency of stay).

[110]*Manuel Munoz*, 4 MSPB 103, 80 FMSR 5162 (1980).

[111]*Mildred G. Kass*, *supra* note 107, 2 MSPB at 260. See also *Robert J. Frazier, Jr.*, *supra* note 108, 1 MSPB at 4 (initial request granted unless facts and circumstances show that request was "so intrinsically or inherently irrational as to be arbitrary or capricious").

[112]*Mildred G. Kass*, *supra* note 107, 2 MSPB at 265. Although the Board gave deference to the Special Counsel's determination of reasonable grounds, it refused to "rubber stamp" a stay request. *Id.* at 260.

personnel practice was involved.[113] The Whistleblower Protection Act combines the 15- and 30-day stay requests established under the Reform Act into one request for a 45-day stay. When reviewing the request, the Board will probably require the stronger showing of grounds for the stay but continue to defer to OSC's interpretation of the facts.

Under the Reform Act, the full Board granted a further extension only if it concurred with the Special Counsel's determination that there were reasonable grounds to believe a prohibited personnel practice was involved and after the agency had an opportunity to comment.[114] The Board will probably continue to apply the same standards developed under the Reform Act when considering OSC's requests for further extensions of the stay.

Corrective Actions

Upon completion of an investigation, if the Special Counsel finds that there are reasonable grounds to believe that a prohibited personnel practice has occurred and that corrective action is required, it must report this determination, together with any findings or recommendations, to the Board, the agency involved, and the Office of Personnel Management (OPM).[115] If, after consulting with the individual subject to the prohibited personnel practice, OSC finds that the agency has corrected the problem, the Special Counsel must file this finding with the Board, along with any written comments the individual might provide.[116] If the agency does not act to correct the practice within a reasonable period of time, the Special Counsel may petition the Board for corrective action.[117]

When the Special Counsel files a corrective action petition, the Board must provide an opportunity for oral or written comments by the Special Counsel, the agency, and OPM.[118] It must also provide an

---

[113]*Id.*, at 253–54, 260; *Special Counsel v. Department of State (Rohrmann)*, 2 MSPB 477, 478 (1980). The purpose of this extension was to give OSC time to complete its investigation. *Id.*

[114]*Mildred G. Kass, supra* note 107, 2 MSPB at 261. According to the Board, an agency's failure to respond to the Special Counsel's request for further extension of the stay raised a strong inference that it did not challenge the conclusions made by the Special Counsel. *Robert J. Tariela*, 1 MSPB 116, 122, 79 FMSR 5007 (1979). However, even if the agency presented convincing evidence to contradict the Special Counsel's conclusions, the Board granted the extension as long as the preponderance of the agency's evidence was not "overwhelmingly disproportionate." *Special Counsel v. Department of the Army (Mortensen)*, 5 MSPB 9, 10, 81 FMSR 5231 (1981).

[115]5 U.S.C. 1214(b)(2)(A). The Special Counsel may also provide its report to the President. *Id.*

[116]5 U.S.C. 1214(b)(2)(C).

[117]5 U.S.C. 1214(b)(2)(B).

[118]5 U.S.C. 1214(b)(3)(A).

opportunity for written comments by the individual who is the subject of the alleged prohibited personnel practice.[119] The Board will order whatever corrective action it considers appropriate if it finds that the Special Counsel has demonstrated that a prohibited personnel practice, other than reprisal for whistleblowing, has occurred, exists, or is to be taken.[120]

In cases involving reprisal for whistleblowing, the Special Counsel must demonstrate that the disclosure was "a contributing factor" in the challenged personnel action.[121] However, the Board will not order corrective action if the agency demonstrates by clear and convincing evidence that it would have taken the same action in the absence of the protected disclosure.[122]

Under the Reform Act, the Special Counsel was required to prove by a preponderance of evidence that a prohibited personnel practice had occurred.[123] The agency could overcome this by presenting preponderant evidence that it did not commit the prohibited personnel practice or, in cases involving reprisal for whistleblowing or for the exercise of appeal rights, that it had a legitimate management reason for its action.[124] The Board will probably continue to impose the preponderance of the evidence standard on the Special Counsel and the agency in proceedings involving

[119]5 U.S.C. 1214(b)(3)(B). Although the Reform Act also did not require that a corrective aciton hearing be held, the Board determined that an evidentiary hearing was appropriate. *Robert J. Frazier, Jr.*, 1 MSPB 159, 176, 79 FMSR 7006 (1979). The court endorsed that determination. *Frazier v. MSPB*, 672 F.2d 150, 164, 82 FMSR 7024 (D.C. Cir. 1982). It is likely that the Board will continue to hold hearings in corrective actions brought by the Special Counsel.

[120]5 U.S.C. 1214(b)(4)(A). Under the Reform Act and presumably also under the Whistleblower Protection Act, the Board may order cancellation or correction of the challenged personnel action. Under appropriate circumstances, the Board may fashion its order to be substantially broader in order to address systemic abuses. In determining the scope of its order, the Board will consider the following factors: the nature of the prohibited personnel practice, its root causes, and the likelihood of future similar abuses. *Robert J. Frazier, Jr., supra* note 119, 1 MSPB at 190-91. The Board has stated, however, that, even if it makes a finding of a technical prohibited personnel practice, it is not automatically compelled to set aside the personnel action or to order any corrective action. *Id.* at 190 n.56.

[121]5 U.S.C. 1214(b)(4)(B)(i). Under the Reform Act, the Board required the Special Counsel to prove that the protected disclosure was a significant factor in the personnel action. *Special Counsel v. Department of State (Rohrmann)*, 9 MSPB 14, 20, 82 FMSR 7001 (1982). The Whistleblower Protection Act of 1988, which was passed by Congress but pocket-vetoed by President Reagan, provided that the Special Counsel had to prove that the disclosure was "a factor" in the personnel action by showing that the official taking the personnel action knew of the disclosure and that the personnel action occurred within a period of time such that a reasonable person could conclude that the disclosure was a factor in the personnel action. This latter requirement was not included in the Whistleblower Protection Act of 1989.

[122]5 U.S.C. 1214(b)(4)(B)(ii).

[123]*Robert J. Frazier, Jr., supra* note 119, 1 MSPB at 178.

[124]*Special Counsel v. Department of State (Rohrmann), supra* note 121, 9 MSPB at 20.

allegations of prohibited personnel practices other that reprisal for whistleblowing. It is unclear whether the Board will require the Special Counsel (or an employee) to establish prima facie reprisal for whistleblowing in corrective actions by a preponderance of evidence or whether it will require a lesser burden of proof to establish that the disclosure was a "contributing factor" in the personnel action. However, as provided under the Whistleblower Protection Act, the agency must rebut this showing with clear and convincing evidence, which is a higher burden of proof than preponderance of the evidence.

Disciplinary Actions

The Special Counsel may file a complaint for disciplinary action, together with a statement of supporting facts, with the Board against a federal employee for committing a prohibited personnel practice or other violation under the Special Counsel's jurisdiction, or for knowing and willful refusal or failure to comply with a Board order.[125] If the case involves an employee in a confidential, policy-making, policy-determining, or policy-advocating position appointed by the President, by and with the consent of the Senate, the Special Counsel must present the complaint, and any response by the employee, to the President for appropriate action.[126] If the case involves members of the uniformed services or individuals employed by any person under contract with an agency to provide goods or services, the Special Counsel may transmit recommendations for disciplinary or other appropriate action to the head of the involved agency.[127] The agency head must respond to OSC within 60 days and report on each OSC recommendation and the action taken or proposed to be taken with respect to each recommendation.[128]

Except as stated above, the Special Counsel is not required to report its findings and recommendations to the agency or to allow the agency to

---

[125]5 U.S.C. 1215(a)(1). The Special Counsel must provide a copy of the complaint and statement of facts to the charged employee. Id. The complaint may be filed only against an employee and not against a former employee. Id. See Special Counsel v. Owens, Smith & Farrow, 10 MSPB 110, 82 FMSR 5178 (1982). Thus, an employee whose alleged prohibited activities are being investigated by the Special Counsel may escape discipline by resigning or retiring before the complaint is filed. However, once the complaint is filed, the Board's jurisdiction has attached and subsequent resignation will not preclude the disciplinary action from proceeding. Id., at 110 n.1. Moreover, the Board can order that the former employee be debarred, which means that the former employee cannot be rehired into the federal government for up to five years. See Special Counsel v. Zimmerman & Pouy, 88 FMSR 7011 (1988).

[126]5 U.S.C. 1215(b).

[127]5 U.S.C. 1215(c)(1).

[128]5 U.S.C. 1215(c)(2).

investigate or take disciplinary action prior to the Special Counsel's filing a complaint with the Board.[129] The agency must obtain the Special Counsel's permission to take disciplinary action against an employee who is under investigation by OSC for the same or related conduct.[130]

An employee against whom a disciplinary action complaint is filed is entitled to: (1) a reasonable time to answer orally and in writing and to furnish supporting documentary evidence; (2) be represented by an attorney; (3) a hearing before the Board or an administrative law judge designated by the Board; (4) have a transcript kept of the hearing; and (5) a written decision with the reasons therefor at the earliest practicable date, including a copy of any final Board order imposing disciplinary action.[131]

The Special Counsel must prove the charges by a preponderance of the evidence.[132] If the Board finds that OSC met its burden, it may impose disciplinary action in the form of removal, reduction in grade, debarment from federal employment for up to five years, suspension, reprimand, or a civil penalty not to exceed $1,000.[133] In determining the appropriate penalty, the Board considers mitigating factors such as the nature and seriousness of the offense, the employee's past work record, his or her length of federal service, the employee's past disciplinary record, and mitigating circumstances surrounding the offense.[134]

---

[129]*Special Counsel v. Filiberti & Dysthe*, 85 FMSR 5407 (1985), *aff'd in part, rev'd and remanded in part sub nom. Filiberti & Dysthe v. MSPB*, 804 F.2d 1504, 86 FMSR 7097 (9th Cir. 1986).

[130]5 U.S.C. 1214(f).

[131]5 U.S.C. 1215(a)(2).

[132]*Special Counsel v. Sullivan*, 6 MSPB 442, 457, 81 FMSR 7047 (1981). This case was decided under the Reform Act. The Whistleblower Protection Act does not specify the burden of proof or revise significantly the substantive provisions concerning OSC disciplinary actions. Compare 5 U.S.C. 1206(g) and 1207 under the Reform Act with 5 U.S.C. 1215 under the Whistleblower Protection Act. The Board will probably continue to apply the burden of proof and other factors from its established case law.

[133]5 U.S.C. 1215(a)(3). In *Special Counsel v. Filiberti & Dysthe*, 85 FMSR 5246 (1985), the charged employee retired prior to the imposition of a 60-day suspension. The Board ordered the agency to withhold the equivalent of 60 days' salary from his accrued leave pay in lieu of the suspension. On appeal, the court of appeals disallowed the penalty, holding that the Board's authority was limited to only those penalties set out under the statute. *Filiberti v. MSPB*, 804 F.2d 1504, 86 FMSR 7097 (9th Cir. 1986). It has not yet been determined whether the Board can impose more than one of the specified penalties. In *Starrett v. MSPB*, 792 F.2d 1246, 1255, 86 FMSR 7086 (4th Cir. 1986), the court stated, in dicta, that the use of the word "or" in 5 U.S.C. 1207 (now section 1215(a)(3)) implies that the penalties are in the alternative and not cumulative. The Board has held, however, that the existence of more than one legal basis for the charged violations, such as a finding of more than one prohibited personnel practice violation, does not justify imposing a greater penalty. *Special Counsel v. Ross*, 87 FMSR 5428 (1987); *Special Counsel v. Mongan*, 87 FMSR 5288 (1987).

[134]*Special Counsel v. Hoban*, 84 FMSR 5914 (1984). Other possible mitigating factors are discussed in *Douglas v. Veterans Admin.*, 5 MSPB 313, 332, 81 FMSR 7037 (1981).

Other Authority of the Special Counsel

Intervention in MSPB Proceedings

The Special Counsel may as a matter of right intervene or otherwise participate in any proceeding before the Board.[135] However, the Special Counsel may not intervene in an action brought by an individual under section 1221 (corrective action involving reprisal for whistleblowing) and section 7701 (employee adverse action appeal) except with the consent of that individual.[136] The OSC has used its intervention authority infrequently.

Prohibited Political Activity—Hatch Act[137]

A federal or District of Columbia employee may not use his or her official authority or influence to interfere with, or affect the result of, an election or take an active part in political management and political campaigns.[138] Examples of what constitutes prohibited political management or political compaigning are set forth in 5 C.F.R. 733.122, and include managing the political campaign of a candidate in a partisan election, being a candidate for elective office in a partisan election, running for, or serving as, an officer of a political party or partisan political club, or soliciting political contributions.[139] The Act applies to employees regardless of whether they are on annual leave or leave without pay.[140]

The Hatch Act prohibits only partisan political activity. This is determined by such factors as whether the employee-candidate, or any other candidate, is running as a candidate for a particular political party or has been endorsed by such a party. Certain other political activities are

---

[135]5 U.S.C. 1212(c)(1).

[136]5 U.S.C. 1212(c)(2).

[137]At the time of this writing, amendments to the Hatch Act are pending before Congress. Readers should be aware that the Act may have changed after this chapter was prepared.

[138]5 U.S.C. 7324.

[139]E.g., *Special Counsel v. Willett*, 84 FMSR 5009 (1984) (Postal Service employee violated Hatch Act even though he was sole candidate for the Republican executive committee and assumed position after primary election); *Special Counsel v. West*, 84 FMSR 5070 (1984) (declaration of candidacy not essential; Hatch Act prohibits any activity directed toward success of partisan political candidate).

[140]*Special Counsel v. Biller*, 87 FMSR 7009 (1987) (Board found that Hatch Act applies to full-time union officials who were on extended leaves of absence for purpose of serving union), *rev'd on other grounds sub nom. Blaylock v. MSPB*, 851 F.2d 1348 (11th Cir. 1988) (court found that publishing articles in union newsletters criticizing incumbent President and urging support of opposition party's candidate does not constitute partisan political activity prohibited by Hatch Act). The Hatch Act also applies to state and local employees covered under 5 U.S.C. 1501–1508, who are on leave of absence. *Minnesota Dep't of Jobs & Training v. MSPB*, 666 F. Supp. 1305, 87 FMSR 7053 (D. Minn. 1987); *Special Counsel v. Daniel*, 83 FMSR 5175 (1983).

expressly permitted under the statute and regulations, such as registering and voting in any election, expressing an opinion as an individual on political subjects and candidates, displaying political pictures, stickers, or buttons, signing political petitions as an individual, and making a financial contribution to a political party or candidate.[141]

The Special Counsel has exclusive authority to investigate and prosecute violations of the Hatch Act.[142] Disciplinary action is initiated by the Special Counsel filing a complaint against the employee with the MSPB.[143] The employee has all the rights provided under section 1215.[144] If the employee fails to respond to the complaint without good cause, the MSPB will find that the charges have been admitted and enter default judgment against the employee.[145]

As in all actions brought by the Special Counsel, he or she has the prosecutorial discretion to withdraw the complaint or to seek its dismissal.[146] The Special Counsel frequently exercises this discretion after settling the case and obtaining the Board's approval of the settlement agreement.[147]

A federal or District of Columbia employee who violates the Hatch Act must be removed unless the Board finds unanimously that removal is not warranted. In this case the Board must order no less than a 30-day suspension without pay.[148] Removal is appropriate when the activity is substantial and the circumstances demonstrate that the employee acted knowingly in disregard of the law.[149] The Board considers relevant

---

[141]See 5 U.S.C. 7324(b), 7326, 7327; 5 C.F.R. 733.111. OPM has determined that employees in certain geographic areas may actively participate in political management and political campaigns in partisan elections involving *only* local offices of the municipality or subdivision. 5 U.S.C. 7327, 5 C.F.R. 733.124(b). The District of Columbia, its residents and employees do not fall within these exemptions. *Joseph v. Civil Service Comm'n*, 554 F.2d 1140, 1154–56 (D.C. Cir. 1977).

[142]*Sims v. District of Columbia*, 6 MSPB 652, 81 FMSR 7050 (1981).

[143]5 U.S.C. 1215, 1216(a)(1).

[144]See "Disciplinary Actions," *supra*. Attorney's fees authorized under 5 U.S.C. 7701(g)(1) are not available to an employee who successfully defends against a Hatch Act prosecution brought by the Special Counsel under 5 U.S.C. 1215 and 1216(a)(1). See *Saldana v. MSPB*, 766 F.2d 514, 85 FMSR 7041 (Fed. Cir. 1985).

[145]*Special Counsel v. Johnson*, 85 FMSR 5123 (1985).

[146]*Special Counsel v. Trujillo*, 84 FMSR 5064 (1984); *Special Counsel v. Dukes*, 81 FMSR 5520 (1981).

[147]A settlement agreement must contain stipulations of fact sufficient to establish a violation of the Hatch Act and contain any relevant mitigating or aggravating factors so that the Board can determine an appropriate penalty. *Special Counsel v. Zanjani*, 84 FMSR 5419 (1984).

[148]5 U.S.C. 1216(c)(1) and 7325. See *Special Counsel v. Childlow*, 84 FMSR 5534 (1984); *Special Counsel v. Morgan*, 83 FMSR 7072 (1983).

[149]*Special Counsel v. Seastruck*, 85 FMSR 5266 (1985); *Special Counsel v. Mahone*, 84 FMSR 5535 (1984); *Special Counsel v. Comito*, 9 MSPB 188, 82 FMSR 5036 (1982). The

mitigating and aggravating factors in determining the appropriate penalty.[150] The employee can appeal the Board's decision to the appropriate U.S. court of appeals.[151]

The Hatch Act also prohibits certain political activity by employees of a state or local agency whose principal employment is in connection with an activity financed in whole or in part by federal loans or grants or if the employee exercises some function in connection with that activity.[152] The Special Counsel is authorized to investigate these matters and to prosecute violations before the MSPB.[153] The proceedings are governed by 5 U.S.C. 1504–1508 and not under section 1215.[154] Judicial review is with the appropriate U.S. district court.[155]

If the Board finds that a violation was committed by a covered state or local employee, it must determine whether removal is warranted.[156] There is no intermediate penalty; if removal is not warranted, no penalty will be imposed.[157] A violation must be "knowing, serious and conspicuous" in order to warrant removal.[158] Once removed, the employee cannot be reappointed within 18 months in the same state to any state or local agency.[159] However, the Board does not have the authority to order a state or local employing agency to remove an employee for violating the Hatch Act or to not reappoint that employee within 18 months. The only recourse is to seek withholding of federal funds from the state or local agency.[160]

---

violation will be found to be knowing if the employee continued the political activity after receiving a warning letter from OSC. *Special Counsel v. Comito, supra.* Active candidacy in a partisan election is considered a serious and conspicuous violation, but may not necessarily result in removal. *Special Counsel v. Sims,* 84 FMSR 5290 (1984).

[150]See *Special Counsel v. Zanjani, supra* note 147. An employee's good faith reliance on the advice of counsel or an agency official that his political activity would not violate the Hatch Act does not negate the violation, but generally will be considered to mitigate against removal. *Special Counsel v. Hayes,* 83 FMSR 5214 (1983); *Special Counsel v. Davis,* 8 MSPB 266, 81 FMSR 5528 (1981).

[151]5 U.S.C. 1215(a)(4) and 7703(b).

[152]5 U.S.C. 1501–1508.

[153]5 U.S.C. 1216(a)(2) and 1504–1505.

[154]5 U.S.C. 1215(a)(5). One significant distinction is that the Board must notify both the charged employee and the employing agency of the Special Counsel's complaint and the agency may participate in the hearing.

[155]5 U.S.C. 1508.

[156]5 U.S.C. 1505(2).

[157]*Special Counsel v. Suso,* 85 FMSR 5150 (1985); *Special Counsel v. Yoho,* 83 FMSR 5136 (1983).

[158]*Special Counsel v. Daniel, supra* note 140.

[159]5 U.S.C. 1506(a)(2).

[160]5 U.S.C. 1506. In *Special Counsel v. Camillieri,* 87 FMSR 5605 (1987), the Board denied the state's request to stay pending appeal the witholding of funds since the state had refused to remove the employee who had been found in violation of the Hatch Act.

The Hatch Act's restrictions on employee political activity have been found constitutional.[161] The Special Counsel provides advisory opinions on whether an employee is subject to the Hatch Act and whether an activity would be in violation of that Act.[162]

The Special Counsel is also authorized to investigate and prosecute certain other prohibited political activity, including coercing political activity or contributions.[163] In addition, a federal employee (other than a presidential appointee approved by the Senate) may not request, receive from, or give to, an employee, member of Congress, or officer of the uniformed service a thing of value for a political purpose. The penalty for this latter activity is removal.[164]

Arbitrary and Capricious Withholding of Information

The Special Counsel is authorized to investigate allegations that an agency has refused to provide information under the Freedom of Information Act (FOIA), if the refusal to provide the record is not based on good-faith reliance on one or more of the statutory exemptions.[165] The Special Counsel can seek corrective action for such violations in the same manner as if a prohibited personnel practice were involved.[166] In addition, the Special Counsel is authorized to investigate, with a view to proposing disciplinary action, situations in which a court has ordered production of an agency record improperly withheld and issued a written finding raising questions as to whether agency personnel acted arbitrarily or capriciously with respect to such withholding.[167]

Activities Prohibited by Civil Service Law

The Special Counsel is also authorized to investigate and pursue disciplinary action with regard to activities prohibited by any civil service law, rule, or regulation, including any activity relating to political intru-

---

[161]*Civil Serv. Comm'n v. Letter Carriers*, 413 U.S. 548 (1973); *Public Workers v. Mitchell*, 330 U.S. 75 (1947) (coverage over federal employees); and *Broadrick v. Oklahoma*, 413 U.S. 601 (1973); *Oklahoma v. Civil Serv. Comm'n*, 330 U.S. 127 (1947) (coverage over certain state and local employees).

[162]See 5 U.S.C. 1212(f), which prohibits the Special Counsel from issuing advisory opinions convering any law, rule, or regulation other than the Hatch Act.

[163]5 U.S.C. 1216(a)(1) and 7321–7322.

[164]5 U.S.C. 7323.

[165]5 U.S.C. 552, 1216(a)(3).

[166]5 U.S.C. 1216(c)(2). This authority was added under the Whistleblower Protection Act.

[167]5 U.S.C. 552(a)(4)(F).

sion in personnel decision making.[168] The Special Counsel can seek corrective action for such violations in the same manner as if a prohibited personnel practice were involved.[169]

The scope of the Special Counsel's authority under this provision is unclear. In *Special Counsel v. Williams*,[170] the Special Counsel brought a disciplinary action complaint against an employee for, among other things, violating OPM's standards of conduct, 5 C.F.R. Part 735, by accepting gifts from subordinates and from a union official. The Board found that the Special Counsel had authority to enforce these regulations.[171] On appeal by OPM, the Court of Appeals for the Federal Circuit overturned the Board's decision, holding that "the Special Counsel does not have authority under section 1206(e)(1)(D) [section 1216(a)(4) under the Whistleblower Protection Act] to bring a general disciplinary action . . . simply because it can be said to be an activity prohibited by *any* civil service law, rule or regulation" (emphasis in original).[172] The court found that the Special Counsel did not have jurisdiction to enforce OPM's standards of conduct but provided little guidance as to what "civil service laws, rules or regulations" OSC can enforce under this provision.[173]

Involvement in Prohibited Discrimination

The Special Counsel is authorized to investigate and pursue corrective and disciplinary action with regard to allegations of prohibited discrimination found by any court or appropriate administrative authority to have occurred in the course of any personnel action.[174] The Special Counsel cannot pursue such allegations if he or she determines that the matter may be resolved more appropriately under an administrative appeals procedure.[175]

---

[168]5 U.S.C. 1216(a)(4).

[169]5 U.S.C. 1216(c)(2). This authority was added under the Whistleblower Protection Act.

[170]85 FMSR 5159 (1985). See also *Special Counsel v. Russell*, 85 FMSR 5284 (1985), *aff'd*, 87 FMSR 5070 (1987).

[171]*Special Counsel v. Williams, supra* note 170.

[172]*Horner v. MSPB*, 815 F.2d 668, 87 FMSR 7021 (Fed. Cir. 1987).

[173]Some guidance may be found in the Board's decision concerning the Special Counsel's authority under this provision: *Special Counsel v. Ross*, 87 FMSR 5428 (1987); *Special Counsel v. Starrett*, 85 FMSR 5269 (1985), *rev'd on other grounds*, 792 F.2d 1246, 86 FMSR 7086 (4th Cir. 1986); *Special Counsel v. Russell*, 87 FMSR 5070 (1987).

[174]5 U.S.C. 1215 and 1216(a)(5) and (c)(2). See *Special Counsel v. Zimmerman & Pouy*, 88 FMSR 7011 (1988). The authority to pursue corrective action was added under the Whistleblower Protection Act.

[175]5 U.S.C. 1216(b).

Whistleblower Reports

In addition to investigating and prosecuting prohibited personnel practices and other civil service law violations, OSC functions as a channel for certain whistleblower allegations.[176] If an employee, former employee, or applicant for employment discloses information which he or she reasonably believes evidences a violation of law, rule, or regulation, gross mismanagement,[177] gross waste of funds,[178] abuse of authority,[179] or substantial and specific danger to public health and safety, the Special Counsel must review the information and, within 15 days of receipt, determine whether there is a substantial likelihood that the information discloses a violation of any law, rule, or regulation, or other misconduct.[180] If OSC makes a positive determination[181] and if the information was obtained from an employee, former employee, or applicant for employment in the agency which the information concerns or from an employee who obtained the information in connection with the performance of his or her duties and responsibilities,[182] OSC must promptly

---

[176]These provisions do not authorize disclosure of information which is specifically prohibited from disclosure by any other provision of law or is required by Executive Order to be kept secret in the interest of national defense or foreign affairs. 5 U.S.C. 1213(i). If the disclosure involves foreign-intelligence or counterintelligence information, the Special Counsel must transmit it to the National Security Advisor, the House Permanent Select Committee on Intelligence, and the Senate Select Committee on Intelligence. 5 U.S.C 1213(j).

[177]Mismanagement is defined as "wrongful or arbitrary and capricious actions that may have an adverse effect on the efficient accomplishment of the agency mission." 5 C.F.R. 1250.3(e). The word "gross" was added before "mismanagement" under the Whistleblower Protection Act.

[178]Gross waste of funds means "unnecessary expenditure of substantial sums of money, or a series of instances of unnecessary expenditures of smaller amounts." 5 C.F.R. 1250.3(d).

[179]Abuse of authority is defined as "arbitrary or capricious exercise of power by a Federal official or employee that adversely affects the rights of any person or that results in personal gain or advantage to himself or to preferred other persons." 5 C.F.R. 1250.3(f).

[180]5 U.S.C. 1213(a) and (b).

[181]If OSC determines that the information does not demonstrate a substantial likelihood of violation of a law, rule, or regulation, gross mismanagement, gross waste of funds, or substantial and specific danger to public health or safety, it may transmit the information to the agency, but only with the consent of the complainant. 5 U.S.C. 1213(g)(2). The agency head must inform OSC in writing, within a reasonable time, of what action has been or will be taken with respect to the allegations. *Id.* The Special Counsel must inform the complainant of the agency's report. *Id.*

[182]If the information is from an individual who does not meet these requirements, OSC may transmit the information to the agency head, who must inform OSC in writing, within a reasonable time, of what action has been or will be taken with respect to the allegations. 5 U.S.C. 1213(g)(1). The Special Counsel must inform the complainant of the agency's report. *Id.* If OSC does not transmit the information to the agency, it must return it to the complainant. *Id.*

transmit the information to the appropriate agency head. OSC must require the agency to conduct an investigation and to submit a written report to OSC within 60 days summarizing the findings. [183]

The report must be signed by the head of the agency and must include: (1) a summary of the information obtained from OSC; (2) a description of the agency's investigation; (3) a summary of any evidence obtained; (4) a listing of any violation or apparent violation of any law, rule, or regulation; and (5) a description of any action taken or planned as a result of the investigation, such as changes in the agency's rules, regulations, or practices; restoration of any aggrieved employee; disciplinary action against any employee; and referral to the Attorney General of any evidence of a criminal violation. [184] Except in the case of a criminal violation, OSC must transmit a copy of the report to the complainant, who may submit comments about the report to OSC within 15 days of receipt. [185] The OSC must transmit the agency's report, the complainant's comments, and any comments or recommendations by the Special Counsel to the President, the congressional committees with jurisdiction over the agency, and the Comptroller General. [186]

If the Special Counsel does not transmit the information to the agency head, the Special Counsel must return the information to the complainant and inform him or her why the disclosure may not be further acted on and what other offices are available for receiving disclosures. [187] The identity of the complainant may not be disclosed by the Special Counsel without the individual's consent unless the Special Counsel determines that it is necessary because of imminent danger to public health or safety, or imminent violation of any criminal law. [188]

Review of OPM Rules and Regulations

The Special Counsel may file a complaint with the Board concerning an OPM rule or regulation if the Special Counsel determines that the

---

[183] 5 U.S.C. 1213(c). The agency can respond within a longer period of time only with the written consent of OSC. 5 U.S.C. 1213(c)(1)(B).

[184] 5 U.S.C. 1213(d). The Special Counsel must review the report to determine whether it contains all the required information and whether the findings appear to be reasonable. 5 U.S.C. 1213(e)(2). If the report contains evidence of a criminal violation, it must be transmitted to the Attorney General and the agency must inform OPM and the Office of Management and Budget (OMB) of the referral. 5 U.S.C. 1213(f). A report containing such evidence may not be sent to the complainant. *Id.*

[185] 5 U.S.C. 1213(e)(1).

[186] 5 U.S.C. 1213(e)(3). If the Special Counsel does not receive a report from an agency head, this must be reported to the President, the appropriate congressional committee, and the Comptroller General. 5 U.S.C. 1213(e)(4).

[187] 5 U.S.C. 1213(g)(3).

[188] 5 U.S.C. 1213(h).

provision would on its face or as implemented require the commission of a prohibited personnel practice as defined by section 2302(b).[189] The Board may also review OPM regulations on its own motion or upon petition by any interested person, although the Board has sole discretion whether to hear such petition.[190] The OPM and any agency implementing the challenged rule or regulation may participate in the proceeding.[191]

A rule or regulation "would require" commission of a prohibited personnel practice if it is reasonably foreseeable that this would result.[192] If the MSPB finds a rule or regulation invalid on its face or as implemented, it must order the agency to cease compliance with it or to correct the invalid implementation.[193]

Rights and Responsibilities During Special Counsel Investigations

Rule 5.4 of the Civil Service Rules requires agencies to make available any records relating to a matter being investigated by OSC and to make their employees available to provide testimony. Employees and applicants are required to provide to OSC all requested information, testimony, documents, and material, unless disclosure is otherwise prohibited by law or regulation.[194] Testimony may be secured under oath or affirmation.[195] The Special Counsel is authorized to issue a subpoena requiring attendance and testimony of witnesses and production of records and to order the taking of depositions and responses to interrogatories.[196] An OSC subpoena may be enforced by the Board in the appropriate U.S. district court.[197]

There is no general right of an employee or other witness to have a representative present during an OSC investigative interview unless the witness is compelled to appear and give testimony under subpoena. It has been OSC policy, however, to permit an employee to be accompanied by

[189]5 U.S.C. 1212(a)(4).
[190]5 U.S.C. 1204(a)(4) and (f)(1).
[191]5 U.S.C. 1204(f)(3)(A).
[192]*Wells v. Harris*, 1 MSPB 199, 233, 79 FMSR 7005 (1979). See *NTEU v. Devine*, 9 MSPB 448, 82 FMSR 7007 (1982); *In re Exceptions from Competitive Merit Plans (FPM 335)*, 8 MSPB 466, 81 FMSR 5557 (1981).
[193]5 U.S.C. 1204(f)(3)(C).
[194]5 C.F.R. 5.4. See also 5 U.S.C. 1204(e)(1)(B).
[195]5 U.S.C. 1204(b).
[196]5 U.S.C. 1212(b)(2). Although the Special Counsel has independent subpoena authority, that authority ends when an adjudicative proceeding is initiated before the Board. *Special Counsel v. Sullivan*, 4 MSPB 126, 127–28, 80 FMSR 5164 (1980).
[197]5 U.S.C. 1212(b)(3).

an attorney or other representative as long as the representative is not also a witness or potential witness in the case, or otherwise has a conflict. The OSC will allow the witness to be represented by an agency attorney so long as the attorney personally represents the witness and is not present solely on behalf of the agency.[198] The agency itself is not entitled to representation during a Special Counsel investigation. Of course, once the Special Counsel has completed an investigation and has filed a complaint for disciplinary action, the charged employee is entitled to representation, as well as the other rights under 5 U.S.C. 1215.

Discovery in proceedings brought by the Special Counsel are governed by MSPB regulations.[199] An employee during an adverse action appeal under 5 U.S.C. 7701, may obtain discovery of certain portions of Special Counsel investigative files. In *In re Subpoena Addressed to the Office of the Special Counsel*,[200] the Board held that "documents prepared by and for the Special Counsel in an investigation into allegations of prohibited personnel practices . . . were prepared 'in anticipation of litigation,' inasmuch as that route constitutes the only means available for enforcement by the Special Counsel." Thus, the documents are covered by the work product privilege and are not subject to discovery. In addition, the Court of Appeals for the District of Columbia held that OSC witness affidavits and the interview notes of an OSC attorney were protected from disclosure under the Freedom of Information Act and the Privacy Act.[201]

If the Special Counsel files a corrective action complaint, the affected employee is not a party to the action, although he or she will probably be called as a witness by the Special Counsel. Under the Whistleblower Protection Act, an employee is allowed to provide written comments to the MSPB in connection with an OSC corrective action.[202] An employee can seek to intervene in a Special Counsel corrective action

---

[198]The Board has refused to enjoin agency counsel from representing both the agency and an employee witness during an OSC investigation stating that the Special Counsel can obtain relief through enforcement of a subpoena in U.S. district court. *Special Counsel v. HUD (Lesht)*, 83 FMSR 7027 (1983).

[199]See 5 C.F.R. 1201.71–1201.75. There is no discovery during stay proceedings. *Special Counsel v. Department of Commerce (Beyer)*, 85 FMSR 7002 (1985).

[200]83 FMSR 5425 (1983). See also *In re Subpoena Addressed to the Special Counsel*, 84 FMSR 5293 (1984), *aff'd sub nom. Martin v. Office of the Special Counsel*, 819 F.2d 1181, 87 FMSR 7042 (Fed. Cir. 1987).

[201]*In re Subpoena Addressed to the Special Counsel*, supra note 200, 819 F.2d at 1188. The court found the documents protected from disclosure under FOIA, 5 U.S.C. 552(b)(5), which exempts from release "inter-agency or intra-agency memorandums or letters which would not be available by law to a party other than an agency in litigation with the agency" and under the Privacy Act, 5 U.S.C. 552a(d)(5), which exempts documents prepared in anticipation of litigation, which the court found to include actions before the MSPB. *Id.*

[202]5 U.S.C. 1214(b)(3)(B).

proceeding and, if allowed by the Board, will be accorded all the rights of a full party, including possible entitlement to attorney's fees.[203]

If the employee intervenes in a proceeding brought by the Special Counsel, the Board may apply collateral estoppel in any subsequent proceeding involving that employee. This means that the Board will not allow any additional evidence concerning any issue which was decided in the Special Counsel proceeding and will apply its findings from that proceeding as long as the issues are identical, the issue was actually litigated in the prior action, and determination of the prior issue was necessary to the resulting judgment.[204] However, the Board may refrain from applying collateral estoppel even if all the prerequisites are met if it determines that injustice would result or considerations of public policy would be compromised.[205]

Generally, Special Counsel corrective and disciplinary actions are heard by an administrative law judge, who issues a recommended decision. The decision becomes final unless either party files exceptions within 35 days of the date of service of the recommended decision.[206] In reviewing the recommended decision, the Board may accept or reject, in whole or in part, the findings of fact and conclusions of law made by the administrative law judge.[207]

There is no administrative appeal following a Board decision on a Special Counsel stay petition, corrective action request, or disciplinary action complaint. The Board will reconsider its decision only upon a showing of clear and material legal error, generally involving conflicts between the holding and controlling precedent or statute, or new evidence.[208]

The Special Counsel cannot appeal MSPB decisions to the courts.[209]

---

[203]See *Frazier v. MSPB*, 672 F.2d 150, 82 FMSR 7024 (D.C. Cir. 1982).

[204]*Chisholm v. Defense Logistics Agency*, 3 MSPB 273, 80 FMSR 7022 (1980), *aff'd*, 656 F.2d 42, 81 FMSR 7078 (3d Cir. 1981).

[205]*Payer v. Department of the Army*, 84 FMSR 5179 (1984). In *Mortensen v. Department of the Army*, 85 FMSR 5219 (1985), the Board refused to apply collateral estoppel against an employee in her appeal of her removal with regard to findings made in a Special Counsel corrective action concerning the same removal action. The Board stated that applying collateral estoppel would compromise the purpose and policy behind employee appeals to provide the opportunity to rebut charges personally and to have a full and fair consideration of the case. In *Mortensen*, the employee had not intervened in the Special Counsel's corrective action proceeding. The Board noted that had the employee intervened, collateral estoppel would have applied since the employee would have been a full participant in the earlier proceeding. The Board held that since the agency had been a party in the corrective action, it was estopped from relitigating in the appeal any issues which had been decided against it in the corrective action.

[206]5 C.F.R. 1201.129.

[207]*Starrett v. MSPB*, 792 F.2d 1246, 1254, 86 FMSR 7086 (4th Cir. 1986).

[208]*Special Counsel v. Sullivan*, 7 MSPB 239, 241, 81 FMSR 7057 (1981).

[209]The Whistleblower Protection Act of 1988, which was vetoed by President Reagan,

An employee who is adversely affected by an MSPB corrective action decision may appeal the decision to the Court of Appeals for the Federal Circuit.[210] An employee subject to a Board order imposing disciplinary action may appeal to the appropriate U.S. court of appeals.[211] The court reviews the Board's decision to determine whether it is supported by substantial evidence.[212]

With the exception of allegations of reprisal for whistleblowing, there is no private right of action to enforce the prohibited personnel practice provisions.[213] This means that an employee cannot file an appeal with the Board or file a complaint in court alleging prohibited personnel practices other than reprisal for whistleblowing. An employee's only recourse for alleging a prohibited personnel practice in a matter not involving whistleblower reprisal or not otherwise appealable to the Board or in the court is to bring it to the attention of the Special Counsel. If the Special Counsel decides not to pursue the matter, the employee can appeal to the court. However, the court's review of the Special Counsel's determinations is very limited. The Special Counsel's authority to seek a stay is purely discretionary; there is no statutory provision for review.[214] The court will review OSC's decision not to investigate or to bring actions before the MSPB only to ensure that OSC met the minimum statutory requirements to inquire into employee allegations to the extent necessary to determine if the allegations are meritorious and to provide a brief statement of the reasons for terminating an investigation.[215] The court will not otherwise second-guess OSC determinations.

---

provided that the Special Counsel could appeal MSPB corrective action decisions to the Court of Appeals for the Federal Circuit. It also provided that the Special Counsel could represent itself in court, rather than being represented by the MSPB or the U.S. Attorney. Neither of these provisions was included in the 1989 Act.

[210]5 U.S.C. 1214(c). The appeal is governed by section 7703(b)(1). Under the Reform Act, only those employees who intervened in a corrective action could appeal the Board's decision to the court. See Frazier v. MSPB, supra note 203, 672 F.2d at 158–59. Frazier was heard by the D.C. Circuit Court because, at that time, 5 U.S.C. 7703 provided that a petition to review a final order of the Board must be filed in the Court of Claims or an appropriate U.S. court of appeals. The law was amended in 1982 to require filing in the Federal Circuit. Pub. L. 97-164, 96 Stat. 45 (1982).

[211]5 U.S.C. 1215(a)(4) and 7703(b).

[212]Harvey v. MSPB, 802 F.2d 537, 543, 86 FMSR 7089 (Fed. Cir. 1986) (substantial evidence means the amount of relevant evidence that a reasonable mind might accept as adequate to support conclusions).

[213]Borrell v. ICA, 682 F.2d 981 (D.C. Cir. 1982); Cutts v. Fowler, 692 F.2d 138, 34 FEP Cases 698 (D.C. Cir. 1982); Moss v. Department of Justice, 537 F. Supp. 281, 87 FMSR 7028 (S.D. Ohio 1987).

[214]Gilley v. United States, 649 F.2d 449, 453 (6th Cir. 1981).

[215]Borrell v. ICA, supra note 213, at 988, citing Wren v. MSPB, 681 F.2d 867, 872 (D.C. Cir. 1982).

5. Equal Employment Opportunity

MICHAEL J. RISELLI

Title VII of the Civil Rights Act

Coverage

Title VII of the Civil Rights Act of 1964[1] was amended in 1972 to apply to federal civilian employment.[2] With limited exceptions, it is the exclusive protection for all federal employees and all applicants for employment against employment-related discrimination based on race, sex (includes sexual harassment), national origin, color, or religion.[3] Among its provisions is a requirement for agency affirmative action programs to correct historic discrimination.[4] By affirmative action is meant focused and intensified recruitment and training of women and minorities, and development of career programs, to overcome the linger-

---

[1]42 U.S.C. 2000e et seq.

[2]42 U.S.C. 2000e-16. The Act does not apply to the uniformed services. Johnson v. Alexander, 572 F.2d 1219, 16 FEP Cases 894 (8th Cir.), cert. denied, 439 U.S. 986, 18 FEP Cases 965 (1978); Taylor v. Jones, 653 F.2d 1193, 28 FEP Cases 1024 (8th Cir. 1981). But see Hill v. Berkman, 635 F. Supp. 1228, 40 FEP Cases 1444 (E.D.N.Y. 1986) (holding that Title VII is exclusive judicial remedy for claims of sex discrimination brought by member of uniformed military).

[3]Brown v. GSA, 425 U.S. 820, 12 FEP Cases 1361 (1976); Kizas v. Webster, 707 F.2d 524, 31 FEP Cases 905 (D.C. Cir. 1983), cert. denied, 464 U.S. 1042, 33 FEP Cases 1084 (1984). However, Title VII does not preempt independent bases for suits by federal employees, e.g., where a claim under the Constitution, another federal statute, or state law could not be remedied under Title VII. See, e.g., Ethnic Employees of the Library of Congress v. Boorstin, 751 F.2d 1405, 36 FEP Cases 1216 (D.C. Cir. 1985); Rochon v. FBI, 691 F. Supp. 1548, 47 FEP Cases 872 (D.D.C. 1988); Langster v. Schweiker, 565 F. Supp. 407, 36 FEP Cases 1623 (N.D. Ill. 1983); Stewart v. Thomas, 538 F. Supp. 891, 30 FEP Cases 1609 (D.D.C. 1982).

[4]42 U.S.C. 2000e-16(b).

ing effects of past discrimination by the Federal Government. The Act also prohibits reprisal or retaliation for civil rights activity.[5]

Enforcement

The Equal Employment Opportunity Commission (EEOC) administers the federal employee EEO program under authority established by Presidential Reorganization Plan No. 1 of 1978.[6] The EEOC regulations[7] provide federal employees with a comprehensive scheme for administrative complaint processing within each federal executive branch agency (see Chapter 2). The complainant must exhaust administrative remedies, after which a full trial on the merits may be conducted in a federal district court.[8] The trial is held before a judge with no jury,[9] with appeal to the appropriate U.S. court of appeals.

Definitions of Discrimination

Disparate Treatment

There are three broad definitions of discrimination that have developed under Title VII: disparate treatment, disparate impact, and reprisal. Disparate treatment is discrimination that results when people are treated differently because of their race, sex, national origin, color, or religion.[10] At issue is the conduct of others. For that reason, the courts have required a showing of intent as an element of proof.[11] Statistics alone are generally considered insufficient but may be used to support proof of constructive

---

[5]42 U.S.C. 2000e-3. See *Judge v. Marsh*, 649 F. Supp. 770, 42 FEP Cases 1003 (D.D.C. 1986); *Neely v. Blumenthal*, 458 F. Supp. 945 (D.D.C. 1978).

[6]43 FED. REG. 1980 (1978), 92 Stat. 3781.

[7]29 C.F.R. Part 1613. The EEOC regulations were substantially revised in 1987. See 52 FED. REG. 41920 (1987).

[8]*Chandler v. Roudebush*, 425 U.S. 840, 12 FEP Cases 1368 (1976) (referred to in the case law as *de novo* judicial review). In a trial *de novo* of a federal employee discrimination claim, the administrative record may be admitted subject to the Federal Rules of Evidence for whatever weight the trial judge wishes to accord it. *Hackley v. Roudebush*, 520 F.2d 208 (D.C. Cir. 1985).

[9]*Robinson v. Lorillard Corp.*, 444 F.2d 791, 3 FEP Cases 653 (4th Cir.), *cert. denied*, 404 U.S. 1006 (1971); *Johnson v. Georgia Highway Express*, 417 F.2d 1122, 2 FEP Cases 231 (5th Cir. 1969); *Giles v. EEOC*, 520 F. Supp. 1198, 27 FEP Cases 1757 (E.D. Mo. 1981).

[10]*Texas Dep't of Community Affairs v. Burdine*, 450 U.S. 248, 25 FEP Cases 113 (1981).

[11]*Id.* at 256. See also *Teamsters v. United States*, 431 U.S. 324, 335 n.15, 14 FEP Cases 1514 (1977).

intent in disparate treatment cases.[12] Except in instances where clear, actual intent is shown, proof is made through circumstantial or comparative evidence.[13] A typical disparate treatment case is one in which the complainant alleges that the selecting official denied the complainant a promotion because of race[14] or sex.[15]

Disparate Impact

A disparate impact case is one in which discrimination is alleged to have resulted from the manner in which the system was operated.[16] It is not the conduct or motivation of a particular employer at issue but, rather, the system in which employment decisions are made.[17] Statistics alone may support a disparate impact case and intent is not an element of proof.[18] A typical disparate impact case is one in which the complainant alleges that the criteria routinely applied in the selection process are discriminatory because, when applied, they have an adverse impact on one group of employees.[19]

Reprisal

The third definition is reprisal or retaliation by an employer against employees and applicants who oppose alleged violation of Title VII, or

---

[12]*McDonnell Douglas Corp. v. Green*, 411 U.S. 792, 5 FEP Cases 965 (1973), *on remand*, 390 F. Supp. 501, 10 FEP Cases 161 (E.D. Mo. 1975), *aff'd*, 528 F.2d 1102, 12 FEP Cases 161 (8th Cir. 1976); *Teamsters v. United States, supra* note 11. See also *Furnco Constr. Corp. v. Waters*, 438 U.S. 567, 17 FEP Cases 1062 (1978) on use of statistics for employer rebuttal. "Constructive intent" is a legal doctrine that recognizes that intent to take action can be inferred from the circumstances surrounding the action. For example, one might infer that a manager who regularly and invariably awards males higher performance evaluations than females over a period of years intends to discriminate against women. The inference that the employer intended to discriminate is constructed from the circumstances. An example of proof of "actual intent" would be testimony that the manager spoke of his or her intention to evaluate women lower than men.

[13]*McDonnell Douglas Corp. v. Green, supra* note 12; *Slack v. Havens*, 522 F.2d 1091, 11 FEP Cases 27 (9th Cir. 1975); *Gates v. Georgia-Pacific Corp.*, 326 F. Supp. 397, 2 FEP Cases 978 (D. Or. 1970), *aff'd*, 492 F.2d 292, 7 FEP Cases 416 (9th Cir. 1974).

[14]*Lanphear v. Prokop*, 703 F.2d 1311, 31 FEP Cases 671 (D.C. Cir. 1983).

[15]*Trout v. Lehman*, 702 F.2d 1094, 31 FEP 286 (D.C. Cir. 1983).

[16]*Watson v. Fort Worth Bank & Trust*, 487 U.S. ___, 47 FEP Cases 102 (1988); *Teamsters v. United States, supra* note 11; *Albemarle Paper Co. v. Moody*, 422 U.S. 405, 10 FEP Cases 1181 (1975); *Griggs v. Duke Power Co.*, 401 U.S. 424, 3 FEP Cases 175 (1971).

[17]*Watson v. Fort Worth Bank & Trust, supra* note 16; *Griggs v. Duke Power Co., supra* note 16; *Dothard v. Rawlinson*, 433 U.S. 321, 15 FEP Cases 10 (1977); *Teamsters v. United States, supra* note 11; *Albemarle Paper Co. v. Moody, supra* note 16.

[18]*Watson v. Fort Worth Bank & Trust, supra* note 16; *Dothard v. Rawlinson, supra* note 17; *Teamsters v. United States, supra* note 11; *Albemarle Paper Co. v. Moody, supra* note 16.

[19]*Griggs v. Duke Power Co., supra* note 16.

who participate in the EEO process and/or other civil rights activity.[20] An employee who alleges reprisal must demonstrate that he or she engaged in some protected activity and was subjected to a negative action in an employment context.[21] A causal connection must be shown between the employee's participation in the protected activity and the negative employment action affecting him or her.[22] Motive or intent of the employer is at issue.[23] Consequently, the employee must demonstrate that the employer knew of the employee's protected activity and that his actions were motivated by the employee's activity.[24] Most courts, however, are willing to draw an inference that a causal connection exists between a negative employment action and protected activity when the negative practice follows the protected activity closely in time.[25]

Protection from reprisal does not extend to all employee activities. For example, repeatedly filing complaints,[26] taking illegal actions against the employer, leaving the work site, failing or refusing to perform assigned duties, refusing to follow a supervisor's orders, engaging in excessively hostile or disruptive behavior, or spending an inordinate amount of time on administrative discrimination complaints instead of assigned tasks have been held to go beyond reasonable employee EEO activities.[27] In general, civil rights activity is protected by Title VII, but the Act was not meant to protect an employee from the consequences of poor performance or misconduct.

Continuing Discrimination Theory

The courts have addressed the question of the lingering effects of discriminatory policies or practices by recognizing that past discrimination

[20]42 U.S.C. 2000e-3. See *supra* note 5. But see *McDonnell Douglas Corp. v. Green*, *supra* note 12, on the limits of employee protection under 42 U.S.C. 2000e-3.

[21]*Miller v. Williams*, 590 F.2d 317, 20 FEP Cases 809 (9th Cir. 1979); *Blizard v. Fielding*, 454 F. Supp. 318, 17 FEP Cases 1556 (D. Mass. 1978), *aff'd sub nom. Blizard v. Frechette*, 601 F.2d 1217, 20 FEP Cases 102 (1st Cir. 1979); *Novotny v. Great Am. Fed. Sav. & Loan Ass'n*, 584 F.2d 1235, 17 FEP Cases 1252 (3d Cir. 1978), *rev'd on other grounds*, 442 U.S. 366, 19 FEP Cases 1482 (1979).

[22]See cases cited *supra* note 21; *Brown v. Biglin*, 454 F. Supp. 394, 22 FEP Cases 228 (E.D. Pa. 1978).

[23]*Miller v. Williams*, *supra* note 21; *Aguirre v. Chula Vista Sanitary Serv.*, 542 F.2d 779, 13 FEP Cases 1436 (9th Cir. 1976); *Downey v. A.H. Belo Corp.*, 402 F. Supp. 1368, 14 FEP Cases 395 (N.D. Tex. 1975); *Brown v. Biglin*, *supra* note 22.

[24]*Judge v. Marsh*, *supra* note 5.

[25]*Brown v. Biglin*, *supra* note 22.

[26]*Hernandez v. Alexander*, 607 F.2d 920, 22 FEP Cases 1268 (10th Cir. 1979).

[27]*McDonnell Douglas Corp. v. Green*, *supra* note 12; *Garrett v. Mobil Oil Corp.*, 531 F.2d 892, 12 FEP Cases 397 (8th Cir.), *cert. denied*, 429 U.S. 848, 13 FEP Cases 963 (1976); *Blizard v. Fielding*, *supra* note 21; *Brown v. Biglin*, *supra* note 22; *Hochstadt v. Worcester Found. for Experimental Biology*, 545 F.2d 222, 13 FEP Cases 804 (1st Cir. 1976); *Brown v. Ralston Purina Co.*, 557 F.2d 570, 15 FEP Cases 362 (6th Cir. 1977).

may have present effects and that a pattern or practice of discrimination may result in continuing discrimination over a long period of time. Consequently, there is a line of cases dealing with the present effects of past discrimination[28] and another dealing with continuing discriminatory patterns and practices.[29] The latter line of cases, however, represents a variation on the disparate treatment and impact definitions of discrimination and is used primarily to overcome timeliness requirements for filing a complaint. For example, if an employee were continuously kept in a leave without pay (LWOP) status against his or her will for more than 30 days, he or she would be able to overcome the usual 30-day time limit to initiate the administrative complaint process by showing that the challenged LWOP status was continuing in nature. (Time requirements for EEO complaint processing are discussed in Chapter 2.)

Sexual Harassment

While it has been generally recognized for some time that proven sexual harassment in the workplace, including the Federal Government, is prohibited,[30] it was not until 1986 that the Supreme Court expressly ruled in the case of *Meritor Savings Bank v. Vinson*[31] that sexual harassment gives rise to a cause of action under Title VII.

Sexual harassment has been defined as "deliberate or repeated unsolicited verbal comments, gestures or physical conduct of a sexual nature which are unwelcome."[32]

---

[28]*United Airlines v. Evans*, 431 U.S. 553, 14 FEP Cases 1510 (1977).

[29]*Teamsters v. United States*, supra note 11; *Hazelwood School Dist. v. United States*, 433 U.S. 299, 15 FEP Cases 1 (1979); *Dothard v. Rawlinson*, supra note 17; *Jones v. Lee Way Motor Freight*, 431 F.2d 245, 2 FEP Cases 895 (10th Cir. 1970), cert. denied, 401 U.S. 954, 3 FEP Cases 193 (1971). See also *Ste. Marie v. Eastern R.R. Ass'n*, 650 F.2d 395, 29 FEP Cases 167 (2d Cir. 1981).

[30]See, e.g., *Downes v. FAA*, 775 F.2d 288, 39 FEP Cases 70 (Fed. Cir. 1985); *McKinney v. Dole*, 765 F.2d 1129, 38 FEP Cases 364 (D.C. Cir. 1985); *Katz v. Dole*, 709 F.2d 251, 31 FEP Cases 1521 (4th Cir. 1983); *Henson v. City of Dundee*, 682 F.2d 897, 29 FEP Cases 787 (11th Cir. 1982); *Bundy v. Jackson*, 641 F.2d 934, 24 FEP Cases 1155 (D.C. Cir. 1981); *Barnes v. Costle*, 561 F.2d 983, 15 FEP Cases 345 (D.C. Cir. 1977); *Garber v. Saxon Prods.*, 552 F.2d 1032, 15 FEP Cases 344 (4th Cir. 1977) (per curiam).

[31]477 U.S. 57, 40 FEP Cases 1822 (1986).

[32]U.S. Merit Systems Protection Board, Office of Merit Review and Studies, *Sexual Harassment in the Federal Workplace: Is it a Problem?* G-3-G-4 (1981). See also 29 C.F.R. 1604.11(a), which defines sexual harassment as follows:
Unwelcome sexual advances, requests for sexual favors, and other verbal or physical conduct of a sexual nature constitute sexual harassment when (1) submission to such conduct is made either explicitly or implicitly a term or condition of an individual's employment, (2) submission to or rejection of such conduct by an individual is used as the basis for employment decisions affecting such individual, or (3) such conduct has the purpose or effect of unreasonably interfering with an individual's work performance or creating an intimidating, hostile, or offensive working environment.

Generally, two categories of sexual harassment cases have emerged from the legal experience: (1) *quid pro quo* claims and (2) abusive environment claims. *Quid pro quo* sexual harassment "is harassment that forces an employee to choose between acceding to sexual demands or forfeiting job benefits, continued employment, or promotion."[33] A typical example of such a claim is one in which a female employee is harassed or denied an employment benefit after rejecting an unwelcome sexual advance.[34] On the other hand, "abusive environment" cases generally involve claims

> challenging the persistent subjection of female employees to an intimidating, hostile, or offensive working environment. The conclusion that such harassment violates Title VII is premised on the argument that an employer who permits a hostile working environment discriminates against women in the "conditions" of employment. The employment-related detriment that results from such an environment may be less obvious than the injury caused by *quid pro quo* harassment, but it is not necessarily less serious. An abusive environment harms the employee psychologically. . . .
>
> An abusive environment claim, unlike a *quid pro quo* claim, does not revolve around the denial of a specific employment benefit. . . .[35]

In the typical abusive environment case, the employer is found to have created, or condoned, a substantially discriminatory work environment, regardless of whether the complaining employee lost any tangible job benefits or pay as a result of the discrimination.[36]

In the federal sector, proven sexual harassment of a serious nature can subject offending employees to severe disciplinary action.[37] However, proof of an occasional, isolated, or trivial remark of a sexual nature will not establish a sexual harassment claim.[38] Indeed, sexual harassment claims are often difficult to prove by virtue of their nature,[39] and they often

---

[33]Note, *Sexual Harassment Claims of Abusive Work Environment Under Title VII*, 97 HARV. L. REV. 1449, 1454 (1984) (hereinafter referred to as *Sexual Harassment Claims*).

[34]*Barnes v. Costle, supra* note 30.

[35]*Sexual Harassment Claims, supra* note 33, at 1455 (footnotes omitted).

[36]*Bundy v. Jackson, supra* note 30; *Katz v. Dole, supra* note 30. See also *Broderick v. Ruder*, 685 F. Supp. 1269, 46 FEP Cases 1272 (D.D.C. 1988) (court held that SEC employee was sexually harassed by exposure to sexual remarks and other actions by supervisors which created discriminatory atmosphere in the workplace).

[37]See, e.g., *Carosella v. Postal Serv.*, 30 MSPR 199 (1986), *aff'd*, 816 F.2d 638, 43 FEP Cases 845 (Fed. Cir. 1987) (removal); *Botkin v. Department of the Interior*, 22 MSPR 326 (1984) (same); *Snipes v. Postal Serv.*, 6 MSPR 1 (1981), *aff'd*, 677 F.2d 375, 30 FEP Cases 1257 (4th Cir. 1982) (same); *Jackson v. Veterans Admin.*, 30 MSPR 24 (1986) (demotion to nonsupervisory position); *Thiesen v. Veterans Admin.*, 31 MSPR 288 (1986) (30-day suspension); *Special Counsel v. Russell*, 32 MSPR 115 (1987) (3-year debarment of SES employee from returning to federal employment at higher than GS-13 level).

[38]*Downes v. FAA, supra* note 30.

[39]*Grubka v. Department of the Treasury*, 858 F.2d 1570 (Fed. Cir. 1988); *Flores v. Department of Labor*, 13 MSPR 281 (1981); *Walls v. Postal Serv.*, 10 MSPR 274 (1982).

turn on close credibility determinations.[40] Ordinarily, federal employees claiming sexual harassment are limited to pursuing their claims under Title VII.[41] However, at least one recent court decision suggests that federal employees may not be immune from certain state tort actions based on sexual harassment claims (see Chapter 6 for detailed discussion of supervisory liability).[42]

Types of EEO Action Available

A Title VII case may be an individual complaint, a consolidated complaint, or a class action complaint.[43] An individual complaint is filed by one person seeking remedy for himself. Several of these may be consolidated for consideration in the same complaint process. A class action complaint is filed by one or more individuals representing a larger number of persons similarly situated.

Although the courts have recognized the principle that discrimination by its nature is discrimination against a larger class of people,[44] class actions per se may proceed under Title VII only where the requirements of Rule 23 of the Federal Rules of Civil Procedure have been met.[45] Under Rule 23, the complainant(s) seeking court certification as a class must demonstrate that (1) the number of others properly included in the class is too great to make consideration of their individual complaints practicable, (2) there are questions of law or fact common to the class, (3) the claims or defenses are typical of the claims or defenses of the class, and (4) the parties bringing the action are prepared and able to represent the interests of all class members adequately and fairly. These four requirements are commonly called numerosity, commonality, typicality, and adequacy of representation.

Title VII class actions proceed under section 23(b)(2) of Rule 23, which provides no advance notice to individual class members as to their inclusion in the class and provides no opportunity to opt into or opt out of the class before the class certification.[46] The courts have been increas-

---

[40]*Hillen v. Department of the Army*, 35 MSPR 453 (1987).
[41]*Brown v. GSA*, 425 U.S. 820, 12 FEP Cases 1361 (1976).
[42]*Owens v. United States*, 822 F.2d 408, 44 FEP Cases 247 (3d Cir. 1987), *after remand sub. nom. Owens v. Turnage*, 681 F. Supp. 1095, 46 FEP Cases 528 (D.N.J. 1988) (state-tort claim based on unwelcome sexual remarks not dismissed as remarks held not to be within "outer perimeter" of defendant-supervisor's official duties).
[43]*East Tex. Motor Freight Sys. v. Rodriguez*, 431 U.S. 395, 14 FEP Cases 1505 (1977).
[44]*Hall v. Werthan Bag Corp.*, 251 F. Supp. 184, 1 FEP Cases 120 (M.D. Tenn. 1966).
[45]*General Tel. Co. of the Sw. v. Falcon*, 457 U.S. 147, 28 FEP Cases 1745 (1982).
[46]*Elliott v. Weinberger*, 564 F.2d 1219 (9th Cir.), *aff'd in part and rev'd in part on other grounds*, 441 U.S. 682 (1977).

ingly cautious about class certification, in part because inclusion in a class has a *res judicata* effect on all class members.[47] (See Chapter 2 for a discussion of the administrative procedure with respect to class actions.)

Allocation of Burden of Proof

In a Title VII complaint, the rules governing the burdens of proof, persuasion, and going forward, and the standards and methods of proof, are applicable to both the administrative process and *de novo* (fresh) review in the federal district courts.

The burdens of proof and persuasion are always with the complainant. He or she must prove discrimination by a preponderance of the evidence.[48] The burden of going forward shifts. Initially the burden is with the complainant. He or she must demonstrate facts sufficient to raise the inference of discrimination, that is, to establish a prima facie case of discrimination. The burden then shifts to the employer to articulate a legitimate nondiscriminatory reason for the action(s) taken against the complainant. At this stage it is not required that the reason given be proven or even that it be, in fact, the real reason behind the action. It is left to the complainant to rebut the employer's reason by showing it to be pretextual, that is, bearing no relation to the real reason for the employer's action.[49]

Employee's Prima Facie Case

Establishing a prima facie case varies among the three types of cases.

In a typical disparate treatment case, a prima facie case is established if the complainant can demonstrate that he or she (1) belongs to a protected class under Title VII; (2) applied for, or would otherwise have been considered for, an employment opportunity or benefit for which the

---

[47]*Id. Res judicata* is a legal doctrine that means that "the matter has been adjudicated." The doctrine is raised to prevent relitigation of the same facts and issues decided in an earlier proceeding. Where a class action is certified and relief granted, any subsequent action based on the same facts and issues by a member of the class will be dismissed by the application of the doctrine.

[48]*Watson v. Fort Worth Bank & Trust*, 487 U.S. ___, 47 FEP Cases 102 (1988); *Postal Serv. Bd. of Governors v. Aikens*, 460 U.S. 711, 31 FEP Cases 609 (1983); *McDonnell Douglas Corp. v. Green*, 411 U.S. 792, 5 FEP Cases 965 (1973), *on remand*, 390 F. Supp. 501 (E.D. Mo. 1975), *aff'd*, 528 F.2d 1102 (8th Cir. 1976); *Texas Dep't of Community Affairs v. Burdine*, 450 U.S. 248, 25 FEP Cases 113 (1981); *Furnco Constr. Corp. v. Waters*, 438 U.S. 567, 17 FEP Cases 1062 (1978); *Board of Trustees of Keene State C. v. Sweeney*, 439 U.S. 24, 18 FEP Cases 520 (1978).

[49]*Id.*

employer was seeking someone; and (3) was rejected despite proper qualifications, and that, after the rejection, the employer sought others possessed of the complainant's qualifications for the employment opportunity or benefit.[50] These general standards have been applied with appropriate variations in cases addressing application for employment, promotion, and other employment benefits and opportunities, in cases dealing with each of the types of discrimination covered by Title VII. The standards are meant to be flexible and may vary slightly from case to case.[51]

In a disparate impact case, the prima facie case is usually established by statistical proofs.[52] Without going into an elaborate discussion of technical and complicated mathematical formulae, there are generally three types of statistical proofs used: demographic, concentration, and comparative.

Demographic statistical analysis is a comparison of the racial or sexual composition of the employer's work force, or a relevant portion thereof, with the relevant labor market composition from which the employer's workers are drawn. Demographic analysis presents a static picture. It is like a photograph of the labor force inside and outside the place of employment as it appears at the time the picture is taken. The usefulness of the statistics will depend on the number of positions, employees, or other pertinent facts. If too few employees or jobs are involved or if too few women or minorities in the local labor force are qualified, no significant statistical conclusions may be drawn.[53] Conversely, the larger the statistical universe and the greater the numerical disparity shown, the stronger the inference that can be drawn.

Demographic comparisons are useful only if the segment of the employer's work force at issue is compared against a relevant, available labor force.[54] Comparison of an employer's clerical staff, for example, against the nationwide prevalence of race, sex, or national origin in the general population is an irrelevant comparison. The chances are that the employer recruits locally, not nationally, to fill clerical positions. Nationwide statistics are relevant when the employer recruits nationwide; when the employer recruits locally, the relevant base for comparison will usually be

[50]*McDonnell Douglas Corp. v. Green, supra* note 48.

[51]*Id.; Ste. Marie v. Eastern R.R. Ass'n*, 650 F.2d 395, 29 FEP Cases 167 (2d Cir. 1981); *Furnco Constr. Corp. v. Waters, supra* note 48.

[52]*Watson v. Fort Worth Bank & Trust, supra* note 48.

[53]*Eubanks v. Pickens-Bond Constr. Co.*, 635 F.2d 1341, 24 FEP Cases 897 (8th Cir. 1980).

[54]*Ste. Marie v. Eastern R.R. Ass'n, supra* note 51; *EEOC v. Radiator Specialty Co.*, 610 F.2d 178, 21 FEP Cases 351 (4th Cir. 1979); *Davis v. Califano*, 613 F.2d 957, 21 FEP Cases 272 (D.C. Cir. 1979).

162   EMPLOYEE RELATIONS

the local recruiting (labor market) area defined by the Bureau of Census Standard Metropolitan Statistical Areas (SMSAs) and, in some instances, by the Bureau of Labor Statistics.

In addition to the relevant geographical statistical area, a sound statistical analysis will account for the availability of necessary job skills. Clerical work requires skills that differ from the skills necessary to perform mechanical or electrical work. Lastly, relevant demographic comparison will account for the fact that not everyone in the general population is available to work. Thus, children, aliens, and institutionalized persons are usually included in general population figures, but they are not available to work. Whenever demographic statistical analysis is used, care must be taken to make relevant comparisons or a prima facie case will not be established.[55]

Concentration statistical analysis is a method used to show where minorities and females may be found within the work force. Concentration analysis is also a static picture analysis. Useful comparison requires that the elements of the employer's organization that are compared to each other be essentially similar to each other. For example, a comparison of the numerical composition of the legal staff of an agency with that of the personnel office would reveal nothing statistically significant. But a comparison of two branches of a division each staffed with workers of essentially similar job responsibilities, positions, required credentials, and pay levels, would be useful.

The most commonly occurring concentration is that in which members of the complainant's class are lumped or concentrated in the lower level positions in the branches examined. In many courts, that showing alone would be insufficient to establish a prima facie case. Indeed, such a showing, depending upon the nature of the qualifications required, may demonstrate effective EEO hiring practices. For example, it has only been fairly recently that minority engineers have been available in measurably significant numbers. Assuming all engineers enter the employer's work force at basically the same level and individuals progress through the system at normal rates, concentration at the lower levels within the work force will disappear over time and a completely integrated work force will result.

---

[55]Wards Cove Packing Co. v. Atonio, 57 USLW 4583, 49 FEP Cases 1519 (1989). Hazelwood School Dist. v. United States, 433 U.S. 299, 15 FEP Cases 1 (1979); New York City Transit Auth. v. Beazer, 440 U.S. 568, 19 FEP Cases 149 (1979); Eubanks v. Pickens-Bond Constr. Co., supra note 53; Ste. Marie v. Eastern R.R. Ass'n, supra note 51. See also Schmid v. Frosch, 680 F.2d 248, 29 FEP Cases 163 (D.C. Cir. 1982); Copeland v. Donovan, 29 FEP Cases 119 (D.D.C. 1981); EEOC v. Radiator Specialty Co., supra note 54; Davis v. Califano, supra note 54.

Another kind of concentration picture may present itself by the use of concentration analysis that would be sufficient to establish a prima facie case. If the complainant can demonstrate that one segment of the employer's work force is disproportionately composed of members of the complainant's class in comparison to another segment of the work force engaged in essentially the same work, requiring essentially the same qualifications, and possessing similar positions and pay levels, most courts will draw the inference of discrimination and find the complainant's proofs sufficient to establish a prima facie case.

Comparative statistical analysis is a comparison of the rate at which one group of employees is able to take advantage of employment opportunities or benefits when compared with that of another group of employees. This type of statistical analysis is usually the least likely analysis to be used because it is more difficult. Comparative statistical analysis is not a static picture but one taken over time. For that reason historical data are required. The discovery process and the mathematical difficulties in applying the analysis increase its cost to the complainant, but it is also the surest way in many cases to establish a strong prima facie case. In the first example of concentration statistical analysis discussed above, the complainant's class was concentrated in the lower levels. It was noted that such a showing alone would usually be insufficient to establish a prima facie case. But using the same example, if the complainant demonstrates that advancement has continued over the years at a slower rate for the complainant's group resulting in the concentration of those in the complainant's class in the lower levels, he or she has established a prima facie case. This is true even though questions may remain about such matters as the integrity of the sample, choice of the particular employee group, and relative individual employee skills and abilities.

Employer's Rebuttal

The employer may be able to demonstrate that the complainant's statistical methods or proofs are insufficient or inaccurate and thereby prevent the complainant from making out a prima facie case. Practically speaking, this usually occurs through objections to the statistics offered or to the statistical methods used by the complainant to establish a prima facie case.

Once the complainant has established a prima facie case, the burden of going forward shifts to the employer.[56] The tests applied to meet that

---

[56]*Watson v. Fort Worth Bank & Trust, supra* note 48; *Postal Serv. Bd. of Governors v. Aikens, supra* note 48; *McDonnell Douglas Corp. v. Green, supra* note 48; *Texas Dep't of Community Affairs v. Burdine, supra* note 48; *Furnco Constr. Corp. v. Waters, supra* note 48.

burden vary with the types of discrimination alleged, the actions complained of, and the definition of discrimination applied.

Where disparate treatment is alleged, the employer must meet the articulation test, that is, the employer must articulate a legitimate nondiscriminatory reason for his or her actions.[57]

Where policies and practices, neutral on their face, operate with disproportionate impact on one group when compared with another, the employer must demonstrate that (1) the policy or practice at issue is essential to the safe and efficient operation of the business or completion of agency mission, and (2) no alternative less discriminatory policy or practice was available. This is referred to as the business necessity test.[58] Because both parts of the test must be met, it is a difficult test for the employer to meet.

Where policies are discriminatory on their face and relate to the qualifications necessary to perform the job, the courts apply the bona fide occupational qualification (BFOQ) test.[59] The BFOQ test compels the employer to show that the required qualifications are directly job-related. It applies only in cases challenging qualifications to do a job and only in cases based on sex, national origin, and religion. Race is not listed as a BFOQ under Title VII. Examples of policies that would survive the BFOQ test include a policy that males be employed to portray male characters on television and females to portray female characters, a policy that all waiters in a Japanese restaurant be Japanese, and a policy that only Catholic priests be engaged to celebrate the Mass. Examples of policies that would likely not survive would include those that denied employment to males as flight attendants, that required only Hispanics, but all Hispanics, to take a literacy test prior to employment, or that directed that no Buddhist would be hired to teach philosophy.

A number of cases have examined policies and practices meant to protect one group of employees but not others. Protective policies and practices may or may not be neutral on their face. For example, a policy that no female employee may work after normal working hours unless accompanied by a male employee seeks to protect female employees from whatever dangers might lurk after normal working hours. A policy that re-

[57]Id.

[58]Griggs v. Duke Power Co., 401 U.S. 424, 3 FEP Cases 175 (1971). See also Robinson v. Lorillard Corp., 444 F.2d 791, 3 FEP Cases 653 (4th Cir.), cert. denied, 404 U.S. 1006 (1971).

[59]Diaz v. Pan Am. World Airways, 442 F.2d 385, 3 FEP Cases 337 (5th Cir.), cert. denied, 404 U.S. 950, 3 FEP Cases 337 (1971); Dothard v. Rawlinson, 433 U.S. 321, 15 FEP Cases 10 (1977); Weeks v. Southern Bell Tel. & Tel. Co., 408 F.2d 228, 1 FEP Cases 656 (5th Cir. 1969).

quires all construction workers to weigh at least 180 pounds and be at least 6 feet tall seeks to protect the safety of the workers. In the first example the policy is discriminatory on its face. In the second the policy is neutral on its face. Different standards and proofs would apply depending on the type of policy examined.

In the case of the female employees who must find a male to stay after normal working hours in order to stay themselves, the policy does not apply to males. Female employees could be denied overtime or discouraged from assuming career-enhancing responsibility. Furthermore, the policy is based on the stereotypical notion that all females need the protection of males, any males. Where such a policy can be reduced to a stereotypical notion for which exceptions can be found, it is not likely to survive judicial scrutiny.[60] In the example above, the robust black-belt female karate expert is as much an exception to the stereotype as is the male who is perennially having sand kicked in his face at the beach. Who would protect whom if together they were attacked in the late hours after work?

In the second example above, weight and height requirements would undoubtedly exclude a disproportionate number of females. A great number of men could meet such qualifications. Where a disproportionate adverse impact on one sex results from the policy in operation, the employer must be able to show a clear job-relatedness to support it.

Another standard is applied in certain religion cases, that is, the reasonable accommodation test. This test requires the employer to show that a reasonable effort was made to accommodate the employee's practice of his or her religious beliefs.[61] Cases in which this test is applied most frequently arise from employee observance of religious holidays and from overtime assignment. The standard the employer must meet is that a reasonable effort was made to accommodate the employee's practice of his or her beliefs without inconvenience to other employees, or without creating undue hardship to the business or endangering the completion of the agency's mission.[62] Arbitrarily changing a work schedule at the last minute to accommodate one employee will most likely inconvenience other employees who have a reasonable expectation of some advance

---

[60]*Id.*; *Phillips v. Martin Marietta Corp.*, 400 U.S. 542, 3 FEP Cases 40 (1971); *Sprogis v. United Air Lines*, 444 F.2d 1194, 3 FEP Cases 621 (7th Cir.), *cert. denied*, 404 U.S. 991, 4 FEP Cases 37 (1971).

[61]*Trans World Airlines v. Hardison*, 432 U.S. 63, 14 FEP Cases 1697 (1977).

[62]*Id.* Of course, if the religious animus is the basis of a disparate treatment claim, the normal disparate treatment methods of proof will be applied. See e.g., *Stoller v. Marsh*, 682 F.2d 971, 29 FEP Cases 85 (D.C. Cir. 1982), *cert. denied*, 460 U.S. 1037, 31 FEP Cases 368 (1983).

notice of schedule changes. Locating another employee willing to make a schedule change, or expressing a willingness to make a schedule change should the employee requesting it find another employee willing to change shifts, would undoubtedly be considered reasonable efforts to accommodate an employee's practice of religious beliefs. The closer the request to alter work schedules is to the date the work is to be performed, the less the burden on the employer to take measures to accommodate the request.

The question of what constitutes a religion for the purpose of applying the reasonable accommodation test is a difficult one. Most courts avoid the question because the statute defines religion broadly to include all aspects of religious observance and practice, as well as beliefs.[63] Because the definition is so broad, employers are ordinarily well-advised to attempt reasonable accommodation when an employee requests it and exercise caution in questioning the nature of the employee's beliefs.[64]

Finally, a number of cases have addressed the standards to be applied in the area of testing. When an employer administers a test in order to determine whether an individual will be entitled to a job or to a benefit of employment, and a disproportionate adverse impact on one race, sex, national origin, color, or religion results, the employer must show that the test has been validated for job-relatedness.[65] The term "test" is applied broadly to include any examination or measuring device, not just a paper-and-pencil test.[66] Where an employee is requested to provide information that, in turn, will be used to determine the employee's eligibility or qualifications for employment or employment benefits, an examination results. Consequently, interviews are subject to judicial scrutiny under the testing standards just as are the civil service examinations administered by the Office of Personnel Management (OPM). The criteria used to grade an employee on examinations are subject to one of three types of validation—criterion-related, content, and construct

---

[63]42 U.S.C. 2000e(j). At least one court has held that this broad definition of protected religious beliefs includes the freedom not to believe. *Young v. Southwestern Sav. & Loan Ass'n*, 509 F.2d 140, 10 FEP Cases 522 (5th Cir. 1975) (atheist).

[64]Generally, the employer has no duty to accommodate until an employee establishes a sincere religious belief. *Young v. Southwestern Sav. & Loan Ass'n, supra* note 63. See also *Hansard v. Johns-Manville Prods. Corp.*, 5 FEP Cases 707 (E.D. Tex. 1973) *bona fide* sincerity of beliefs not demonstrated); *McGinnis v. Postal Serv.*, 512 F. Supp. 517, 24 FEP Cases 999 (N.D. Cal. 1980) (*bona fide* sincerity of beliefs demonstrated).

[65]*Griggs v. Duke Power Co.*, *supra* note 58. See also *Washington v. Davis*, 426 U.S. 229, 12 FEP Cases 1415 (1976) (decided on Fifth Amendment grounds).

[66]*Griggs v. Duke Power Co.*, *supra* note 58; *Albemarle Paper Co. v. Moody*, 422 U.S. 405, 10 FEP Cases 1181 (1975). See also Uniform Guidelines on Employee Selection Procedures, 29 C.F.R. Part 1607.

validation.[67] These three types of validation are methods by which an examination can be measured for its job-relatedness. They vary in their application depending upon the nature of the examination and the criteria used.

Employee's Opportunity to Demonstrate Pretext

Once the agency has met its burden by the appropriate standard discussed above, the burden of proceeding falls again on the complainant. At this stage he or she has the opportunity to demonstrate that the employer agency's reasons are pretextual, that is, that the reasons given were not in fact the reasons for the action at the time the agency took it.[68]

Determining the Remedy

Before an appropriate remedy is granted to a complainant who has successfully met the burden of proof on the issue of discrimination, the employer has the opportunity to demonstrate that had discrimination not occurred the result would have been the same. The test that is applied is called the "but for" test, and, stated another way, asks whether the complainant would have had an employment benefit but for the discrimination suffered.[69] To avoid liability, the employer must meet the "but for" test by clear and convincing evidence.[70]

---

[67]See *Albemarle Paper Co. v. Moody, supra* note 66; *Bridgeport Guardians v. Bridgeport Civil Serv. Comm'n,* 482 F.2d 1333, 5 FEP Cases 1344 (2d Cir. 1973), *cert. denied,* 421 U.S. 991, 10 FEP Cases 912 (1975); *Carter v. Gallagher,* 452 F.2d 315, 3 FEP Cases 900 (8th Cir. 1971), *cert. denied,* 406 U.S. 950, 4 FEP Cases 771 (1972). The Uniform Guidelines on Employee Selection Procedures, Appendix A, FPM Supplement 271-1, August 31, 1979, provides the following definitions:

In criterion-related validity, a selection procedure is justified by a statistical relationship between scores on the test or other selection procedure and measures of job performance. In content validity, a selection procedure is justified by showing that it representatively samples significant parts of the job, such as a typing test for a typist. Construct validity involves identifying the psychological trait (the construct) which underlies successful performance on the job and then devising a selection procedure to measure the presence and degree of the construct. An example would be a test of "leadership ability."

[68]*Watson v. Fort Worth Bank & Trust, supra* note 48; *Postal Serv. Bd. of Governors v. Aikens, supra* note 48; *McDonnell Douglas Corp. v. Green, supra* note 48; *Texas Dep't of Community Affairs v. Burdine, supra* note 48.

[69]*Day v. Mathews,* 530 F.2d 1083, 12 FEP Cases 1131 (D.C. Cir. 1976). But see *Price Waterhouse v. Hopkins,* _____ U.S. _____, 49 FEP Cases 954 (1989) (Supreme Court held that "but for" test could be met by preponderance of the evidence instead of by clear and convincing evidence).

[70]*Id.* See also 29 C.F.R. 1613.271(c)(1).

Named plaintiffs and unnamed class members in a class action may be handled differently in determining the appropriate remedies. Furthermore, the courts vary as to the method for determining remedies in a class action. Some have applied formulas for distribution of monetary awards; others have created subclasses or have required that individual claims be filed at the remedy stage.[71] Consequently, in a class action the employer may not be given the opportunity to meet the "but for" test.

A successful complainant is entitled to a remedy to make him or her whole.[72] Title VII provides relief of an equitable nature.[73] Legal remedies are not available. The make-whole remedy is intended to put the employee in the employment circumstances he or she would have been in had no discrimination occurred.[74]

In addition, the doctrine of sovereign immunity requires that any remedy against the Federal Government must be based on an explicit statutory waiver of sovereign immunity.[75] Sovereign immunity is a legal doctrine that holds the sovereign—the Federal Government—immune from lawsuit against it. To recover against the Federal Government, the government must waive its own immunity from suit. The government waives its immunity through a statute specifically allowing for an action and for specific remedies against itself. If the government is sued but has not waived its sovereign immunity, the suit must be dismissed. The government has waived sovereign immunity for certain specific remedies against itself under Title VII. As a result, remedies available under Title VII against federal agencies vary from those available against private employers.

Remedies Available

Remedies available to federal employees against the government under Title VII include back pay, retroactive personnel actions (e.g.,

---

[71]*McKenzie v. Sawyer*, 684 F.2d 62, 29 FEP Cases 633 (D.C. Cir. 1982); *Pettway v. American Cast Iron Pipe Co.*, 494 F.2d 211, 7 FEP 1115 (5th Cir. 1974); *Stewart v. General Motors Corp.*, 542 F.2d 445, 13 FEP Cases 1035 (7th Cir. 1976), *cert. denied*, 433 U.S. 919, 15 FEP 31, *reh'g denied*, 434 U.S. 881 (1977); *Eisen v. Carlisle & Jacquelin*, 417 U.S. 156, 9 FEP Cases 1302 (1974); *Johnson v. Goodyear Tire & Rubber Co.*, 491 F.2d 1364, 7 FEP Cases 627 (5th Cir. 1974).

[72]*Albemarle Paper Co. v. Moody, supra* note 66; *Johnson v. Goodyear Tire & Rubber Co., supra* note 71; *Day v. Mathews, supra* note 69.

[73]*Curtis v. Loether*, 415 U.S. 189 (1974); *Albemarle Paper Co. v. Moody, supra* note 66; *Robinson v. Lorillard Corp., supra* note 58; *Pearson v. Western Elec. Co.*, 542 F.2d 1150, 13 FEP Cases 1202 (10th Cir. 1976).

[74]*Albemarle Paper Co. v. Moody, supra* note 66.

[75]*Richerson v. Jones*, 551 F.2d 918, 14 FEP Cases 1348 (3d Cir. 1977); *Wilson v. Califano*, 473 F. Supp. 1350, 20 FEP Cases 1024 (D. Colo. 1979). See also *Lehman v. Nakshian*, 453 U.S. 156, 26 FEP Cases 65 (1981).

retroactive promotion), expungement or correction of records, injunctive relief (e.g., enjoining the agency against continued use of a particular policy or practice), attorney's fees, and costs[76] (see Chapter 12). In class actions, injunctive relief may include a quota order for future personnel determinations when warranted.[77]

Remedies Not Available

Remedies generally not available to federal employees under Title VII include an amount based on inflation, recovery of expert witness fees, compensatory damages (e.g., damages for pain and suffering, mental anguish, loss of consortium), or punitive damages.[78] Until very recently, interest on back pay was not available; however, the EEOC has ruled that interest is now available in federal sector cases.[79] Ordinarily, courts will not order the government to take disciplinary action against offending officials or to apologize to the successful complainant.[80]

Although the Supreme Court has held that Title VII is the exclusive remedy for federal employees against the government for discrimination based on race, sex, national origin, color, or religion,[81] the Court has not specifically addressed the issue of the availability of damages against a management official in his or her individual capacity in the context of a discrimination case. As noted above, however, the possibility for individual liability exists where a complainant can demonstrate that the remedies afforded under Title VII are insufficient to make the complainant whole or if there is an independent basis for action exclusive of Title VII.[82] Usually, federal officials enjoy at least a qualified official

---

[76]42 U.S.C. 2000e-5(g); 29 C.F.R. 1613.271; *Albemarle Paper Co. v. Moody, supra* note 66.

[77]*Bridgeport Guardians v. Bridgeport Civil Serv. Comm'n, supra* note 67; *Carter v. Gallagher, supra* note 67; *McKenzie v. Sawyer, supra* note 71.

[78]*Richerson v. Jones, supra* note 75; *Wilson v. Califano, supra* note 75.

[79]*James W. Thompkins, Jr. v. William L. Ball, III, Secretary of the Navy*, EEOC Nos. 05890432 and 01872684 (June 14, 1989). The EEOC held that the 1987 amendments to the Back Pay Act of 1966, see 5 U.S.C. 5596 (b)(2)(A), provide authority to award interest on back pay under section 717 of Title VII notwithstanding the Supreme Court's prior decision in *Shaw v. Library of Congress*, 478 U.S. 310, 41 FEP Cases 85 (1986). See also Loeffler v. Frank, 486 U.S. 549, 46 FEP Cases 1659 (1988) (Postal Service held liable for interest on back pay awards under Title VII as private enterprise and, therefore, not exempt from "no-interest" rule under doctrine of sovereign immunity).

[80]The decision to discipline a federal employee is usually left to the sole discretion of the employing agency. *Giesler v. MSPB*, 686 F.2d 844, 849 (10th Cir. 1978). See also *Bundy v. Jackson*, 641 F.2d 934, 24 FEP Cases 1155 (D.C. Cir. 1981), where the court suggested, but did not order, that an agency head should consider taking appropriate disciplinary action against an employee found guilty of sexual harassment. *Id.*, at 947.

[81]*Brown v. GSA*, 425 U.S. 820, 12 FEP Cases 1361 (1976).

[82]See *supra* note 3.

immunity in such actions.[83] However, recent judicial activity has resulted in significant erosion of the general rule that federal officials are usually immune from suit in discrimination-related cases.[84] The proper party in a Title VII action is the head of the executive department, agency, or unit.[85] Neither the United States nor an individual in his or her individual capacity is a proper party. Suits against individuals must proceed under some other theory (i.e., as a constitutional tort, common law or state-tort, and/or other federal statutory claim). (See Chapter 6 for a more detailed discussion.)

The Age Discrimination in Employment Act

Coverage

The Age Discrimination in Employment Act (ADEA) of 1967, as amended in 1974 and 1978,[86] prohibits discrimination on the basis of age in federal employment.[87] It applies to individuals who are at least 40 years of age.[88] Reprisal and retaliation against an employee for exercising his or her rights under the Act are also prohibited.[89]

Allocation of Burden of Proof

The ADEA prohibits discrimination based on age except where age can be shown to be a BFOQ reasonably necessary to the operation of the agency's business.[90] An employer is not prohibited from basing employ-

---

[83]*Harlow v. Fitzgerald*, 457 U.S. 800 (1982).

[84]*Westfall v. Erwin*, 484 U.S. 292, 56 USLW 4087 (1988) (see Chapter 6); *Owens v. United States*, 822 F.2d 408, 44 FEP Cases 247 (3d Cir. 1987), *after remand sub nom. Owens v. Turnage*, 681 F. Supp. 1095, 46 FEP Cases 528 (D.N.J. 1988).

[85]42 U.S.C. 2000e-16(c). *Bey v. Bolger*, 540 F. Supp. 910, 32 FEP Cases 1652 (E.D. Pa. 1982); *Stephenson v. Simon*, 427 F. Supp. 467, 18 FEP Cases 732 (D.D.C. 1976).

[86]29 U.S.C. 621–634.

[87]29 U.S.C. 633a.

[88]29 U.S.C. 631(b).

[89]29 U.S.C. 623(d).

[90]29 U.S.C. 623(b). The BFOQ exception has been narrowly construed by the courts. *Orzel v. City of Wauwatosa Fire Dep't*, 697 F.2d 743, 30 FEP Cases 1070 (7th Cir.), *cert. denied.* 464 U.S. 992, 33 FEP Cases 440 (1983); *Smallwood v. United Air Lines*, 661 F.2d 303, 26 FEP Cases 1376 (4th Cir. 1981), *cert. denied*, 456 U.S. 1007, 28 FEP 1656 (1982).

ment actions on reasonable factors other than age.[91] The occupational qualification test applied in age cases encompasses aspects of the business necessity test discussed more fully under Title VII above. The test prohibits discrimination based on stereotypical notions. An employer can meet the requirements of the test by demonstrating that a reasonable, factual basis for the age limitation exists. The burden can be met by demonstrating that substantially all persons over a particular age could not safely and efficiently perform the job, or that some persons over a particular age possess traits unascertainable any other way than through knowledge of age.[92] For example, the employer may be able to demonstrate that the incidence of heart attacks increases dramatically in individuals over the age of 45 and that a heart attack on the job could endanger the safety of others. Decreased sensory perception and senility are examples of debilitating effects of age which may be impracticable or impossible to determine by individual examinations.

Generally, the courts have adopted the same shifting burden analysis and standards of proof as in Title VII cases discussed above.[93] A number of courts have placed an additional burden on the employee to demonstrate by a preponderance of the evidence that age was a determining factor in the employment action.[94] In these jurisdictions, age need not be the sole factor, but it must be a determining one. That is, a complainant

---

[91]See, e.g., *Moore v. Sears, Roebuck and Co.*, 683 F.2d 1321, 29 FEP Cases 931 (11th Cir. 1982); *Anderson v. Savage Laboratories*, 675 F.2d 1221, 28 FEP Cases 1473 (11th Cir. 1982); *Houghton v. McDonnell Douglas Corp.*, 553 F.2d 561, 14 FEP Cases 1594 (8th Cir.), *cert. denied*, 434 U.S. 966, 16 FEP Cases 146 (1977); *Aritt v. Grisell*, 567 F.2d 1267, 17 FEP Cases 753 (4th Cir. 1977); *Usery v. Tamiami Trail Tours*, 531 F.2d 224, 12 FEP Cases 1233 (5th Cir. 1976); *Hodgson v. Greyhound Lines*, 499 F.2d 859, 7 FEP Cases 817 (7th Cir. 1974), *cert. denied*, 419 U.S. 1122, 9 FEP Cases 58 (1975).

[92]*Schwager v. Sun Oil Co.*, 591 F.2d 58, 19 FEP Cases 872 (10th Cir. 1979); *Hughes v. Black Hills Power & Light Co.*, 585 F.2d 918, 18 FEP Cases 1368 (8th Cir. 1978); *Houghton v. McDonnell Douglas Corp.*, *supra* note 91; *Usery v. Tamiami Trail Tours*, *supra* note 91; *Hodgson v. Greyhound Lines*, *supra* note 91.

[93]See, e.g., *Garner v. Boorstin*, 690 F.2d 1034, 29 FEP Cases 1765 (D.C. Cir. 1982); *Allison v. Western Union Tel. Co.*, 680 F.2d 1318, 29 FEP Cases 393 (11th Cir. 1982); *Goodman v. Heublein, Inc.*, 645 F.2d 127, 25 FEP Cases 645 (2d Cir. 1981); *Laugesen v. Anaconda Co.*, 510 F.2d 307, 10 FEP Cases 567 (9th Cir.), *cert. denied*, 422 U.S. 1045 (1975); *Loeb v. Textron, Inc.*, 600 F.2d 1003, 20 FEP Cases 29 (1st Cir. 1979); *Jackson v. Sears, Roebuck & Co.*, 648 F.2d 225, 25 FEP 1684 (5th Cir. 1981). See also *Lindsey v. Southwestern Bell Tel. Co.*, 546 F.2d 1123, 15 FEP Cases 138 (5th Cir. 1977).

[94]*Pena v. Brattleboro Retreat*, 702 F.2d 322, 31 FEP Cases 198 (2d Cir. 1983); *Cuddy v. Carmen*, 694 F.2d 853, 30 FEP Cases 600 (D.C. Cir. 1982); *Cancellier v. Federated Dep't Stores*, 672 F.2d 1312, 28 FEP Cases 115 (9th Cir.), *cert. denied*, 459 U.S. 859, 31 FEP Cases 704 (1982); *Loeb v. Textron, Inc.*, *supra* note 93; *Spagnuolo v. Whirlpool Corp.*, 641 F.2d 1109, 25 FEP Cases 376 (4th Cir.), *cert. denied*, 454 U.S. 860, 26 FEP Cases 1688 (1981).

must show that "but for" the employer's motive to discriminate against him or her because of age, the complainant would not have suffered the action. The employer's action will be overturned only where the employer was motivated by the complainant's age as a determining factor in taking the employment action.[95] The key element of proof in an age case is motive based on age considerations. The courts usually will not question the employer's business judgment.

The ADEA was not meant to prohibit employment decisions based on factors that sometimes accompany advancing age, such as declining health or diminished vigor and competence. Consequently, employment policies and practices that discriminate on the basis of age will survive judicial scrutiny where the employer can demonstrate that after a certain age the debilitating effects of age impair some employees' ability to perform the job safely and efficiently, and there is no reasonable way to distinguish between those who cannot perform, because of the effects of advancing age, and those who can.[96]

Any federal agency policy that uses age as a factor must be approved by the EEOC before it may be used by the agency.[97] Responsibility for enforcement of the ADEA, originally vested in the Civil Service Commission, was transferred to the EEOC by Presidential Reorganization Plan No. 1 of 1978.[98]

Exhaustion of Administrative Remedies

An ADEA complainant may file a complaint in the administrative process or may file a notice of intent to sue in federal district court with the EEOC.[99] If the complainant elects to file an administrative complaint, he or she must exhaust those administrative remedies before taking the action to court.[100] If the complainant elects to file a notice of intent to sue, he or she must do so within 180 days of the action giving rise to the complaint and must wait not less than 30 days before filing suit in court.[101] The 30-day rule is intended to provide some time for the EEOC to notify the agency and to allow it to attempt resolution. There is a split in authority

[95]Id.
[96]Houghton v. McDonnell Douglas Corp, supra note 91; Arritt v. Grisell, supra note 91; Loeb v. Textron, Inc., supra note 93.
[97]29 U.S.C. 633a(b).
[98]43 FED. REG. 19807 (1978). See also 29 C.F.R. 1613.501(c).
[99]29 U.S.C. 633a(d).
[100]Purtill v. Harris, 658 F.2d 134, 26 FEP Cases 940 (3d Cir. 1981), cert. denied, 462 U.S. 1131, 31 FEP Cases 1850 (1983).
[101]29 U.S.C. 633a(d). Romain v. Shear, 799 F.2d 1416, 43 FEP Cases 264 (9th Cir. 1986), cert. denied, 481 U.S. 1050, 43 FEP 1896 (1987).

over whether the notice requirement is an absolute jurisdictional pre-requisite to filing a civil action.[102]

Determining the Remedy

Remedies Available

If the complainant is successful, the Act provides for appropriate legal and equitable remedies, including reinstatement, promotion, back pay, and injunctive relief.[103] Damages for unpaid wages and overtime are also available. Attorney's fees are payable to the prevailing complainant for judicial processing,[104] but not for administrative procedures[105] (see Chapter 12).

Remedies Not Available

Compensatory and punitive damages are not recoverable.[106] Examples include reimbursement for medical or psychiatric fees, damages for pain and suffering or loss of consortium, and damages to penalize the employer. Liquidated damages (i.e., a specific amount of damages to be recovered as a penalty) are available against a private sector employer for a "willful" violation of the Act.[107] Under the Act, liquidated damages which, in effect, double the employee's actual monetary loss, are recoverable where a willful violation has occurred.[108] The Act contains no specific provision, however, for liquidated damages against the Federal Government, and it has generally been held that no liquidated damages

---

[102]Compare *Ray v. Nimmo*, 704 F.2d 1480, 31 FEP 1310 (11th Cir. 1983) (notice requirement held subject to equitable modification and not absolute jurisdictional requirement) with *Hinton v. Solomon*, 475 F. Supp. 105, 20 FEP 1211 (D.D.C. 1979) (notice requirement held jurisdictional in nature).

[103]29 U.S.C. 626(b) and 633a(c).

[104]*Krodel v. Young*, 576 F. Supp. 390, 33 FEP Cases 701 (D.D.C. 1983).

[105]*Palmer v. GSA*, 787 F.2d 300, 40 FEP Cases 630 (8th Cir. 1986); *Kennedy v. Whitehurst*, 690 F.2d 951, 29 FEP Cases 1373 (D.C. Cir. 1982). See also 5 U.S.C. 504; *Muth v. Marsh*, 525 F. Supp. 604, 27 FEP Cases 262 (D.D.C. 1981).

[106]*Pfeiffer v. Essex Wire Corp.*, 682 F.2d 684, 29 FEP Cases 420 (7th Cir.), *cert. denied*, 459 U.S. 1039, 30 FEP Cases 440 (1982) (compensatory and punitive damages not allowed under ADEA); but see *Hassan v. Delta Orthopedic Medical Group*, 476 F. Supp. 1063, 20 FEP Cases 1813 (E.D. Cal. 1979) (compensatory damages allowed); *Wise v. Olan Mills, Inc.*, 485 F. Supp. 542, 22 FEP Cases 595 (D. Colo. 1980) (punitive damages allowed). See also *Vazquez v. Eastern Air Lines*, 579 F.2d 107, 17 FEP Cases 1116 (1st Cir. 1978); *Murphy v. American Motor Sales Corp.*, 570 F.2d 1226, 17 FEP Cases 180 (5th Cir. 1978); *Carter v. Marshall*, 457 F. Supp. 38, 17 FEP Cases 1182 (D.D.C. 1978).

[107]29 U.S.C. 626(b).

[108]*Trans World Airlines v. Thurston*, 465 U.S. 111, 36 FEP Cases 977 (1985).

are available under the doctrine of sovereign immunity.[109] Finally, a court generally will not order the agency to discipline other employees or to apologize.[110]

Types of Action Available in Court

Once the complainant files in court, the case proceeds to a *de novo* trial.[111] In contrast to employees in the private sector, the federal employee is not entitled to a jury trial in an ADEA action.[112] Class actions by federal employees are generally available under the ADEA, subject to the requirements of Rule 23 of the Federal Rules of Civil Procedure. (See the discussion of class actions in "Title VII of the Civil Rights Act," *supra*.)[113]

The Rehabilitation Act

Coverage

The Rehabilitation Act of 1973, as amended in 1978, prohibits, among other things, discrimination based on handicapping conditions. The Act requires "reasonable accommodation" in employment practices for handicapped persons, provision of physical access to worksites, and affirmative action measures.[114] (For a discussion of affirmative action, see the opening paragraph of "Title VII of the Civil Rights Act," *supra*.)

As this book goes to press, the United States Congress is considering proposed legislation that would greatly expand the rights of disabled persons. On September 7, 1989, the U.S. Senate passed S. 933, which provides disabled persons, including people suffering from AIDS, with the same protections against discrimination in employment, accommodations, and services that currently apply to minorities, women, and the

---

[109]*Chambers v. Weinberger*, 591 F. Supp. 1554, 35 FEP Cases 1294 (D. Ga. 1984); *Wilkes v. Postal Serv.*, 548 F. Supp. 642, 30 FEP Cases 20 (N.D. Ill. 1982); *Muth v. Marsh*, *supra* note 105.

[110]See *supra* note 80.

[111]*Nabors v. United States*, 568 F.2d 657 (9th Cir. 1978).

[112]*Lehman v. Nakshian*, *supra* note 75.

[113]*Moysey v. Andrus*, 481 F. Supp. 850, 21 FEP Cases 836 (D.D.C. 1979); *Carter v. Marshall*, *supra* note 106; *Espelding v. Thornhill*, 13 EPD ¶ 11,463 (E.D. Mich. 1976).

[114]29 U.S.C. 791 *et seq.*; *School Bd. of Nassau County, Atlanta v. Arline*, 480 U.S. 273, 43 FEP Cases 81 (1987). The purpose behind the Act is to require federal agencies to take "affirmative efforts" to help individuals overcome disabilities caused by handicap. *Southeastern Community C. v. Davis*, 442 U.S. 397, 410 (1979); *Guinn v. Bolger*, 598 F. Supp. 196, 200 n.6, 36 FEP Cases 506 (D.D.C. 1984).

elderly. Therefore, care should be taken to thoroughly research the applicability of any new legislation when dealing with handicap discrimination issues.

Definitions of Discrimination

A handicapped individual under the Act is one who (1) has a physical or mental impairment that substantially limits one or more of that person's major life activities, (2) has a record of such an impairment, or (3) is regarded as having such an impairment.[115] Alcohol and drug dependency are considered handicapping conditions.[116] So, too, are contagious diseases such as tuberculosis.[117] Chronic gambling is not a handicapping condition.[118] A major life activity has been defined by the EEOC as a function, such as caring for one's self, performing manual tasks, walking, seeing, hearing, speaking, breathing, learning, and working.[119] Physical or mental impairment means (1) any physiological disorder or condition, cosmetic disfigurement, or anatomical loss affecting one or more of the following body systems: neurologic, musculoskeletal, reproductive, digestive, genito-urinary, hemic and lymphatic, skin, and endocrine; or (2) any mental or psychological disorder, such as mental retardation, organic brain syndrome, emotional or mental illness, and specific learning disabilities.[120]

Allocation of Burden of Proof

A federal agency is required to make reasonable accommodation to the known physical or mental limitations of a qualified handicapped employee[121] unless the agency can demonstrate that the accommodation would pose an undue hardship on the operation of its program.[122]

When raising a claim of handicap discrimination, an employee must first establish a prima facie case of discrimination. While the necessary elements may vary from case to case depending on the particular facts,[123] they generally include (1) a showing that the employee is a "handicapped

---

[115]29 C.F.R. 1613.702(a).
[116]*Ruzek v. GSA*, 7 MSPR 437 (1981) (alcoholism); *Kulling v. FAA*, 24 MSPR 56 (1984) (drug abuse). See also 43 Op. Att'y Gen. No. 12 (1977).
[117]*School Bd. of Nassau County, Atlanta v. Arline, supra* note 114.
[118]*Johnson v. Postal Serv.*, 12 MSPR 580 (1982).
[119]29 C.F.R. 1613.702(c). *Ahr v. Department of Justice*, 23 MSPR 238 (1984).
[120]29 C.F.R. 1613.702(b).
[121]29 C.F.R. 1613.702(f).
[122]29 C.F.R. 1613.704(a).
[123]*Stalkfeet v. Postal Serv.*, 6 MSPR 637, 647 (1981).

person" and that the action complained of was caused by the handicap; and (2) to the extent possible, articulation of a "reasonable accommodation" under which the employee believes that he or she can perform the essential duties of his or her position or of a vacant position to which he or she could be reassigned.[124]

Once the employee establishes a prima facie case, the agency has the burden of showing that the action at issue was caused by a legitimate, nondiscriminatory reason. Generally, the agency will try to do this by showing that the action was not based on the employee's handicap[125] or by showing that the employee is not a "qualified handicapped person."[126] The agency may also attempt to show that, even if the employee is a qualified handicapped person, the accommodation(s) requested by the employee would impose an undue hardship on the operation of its program.[127] In this context, reasonable accommodation includes actions such as reassignment to a vacant position,[128] job restructuring, acquisition of equipment or other devices, and other similar actions.[129] Factors to be considered in determining whether a proposed accommodation would impose an undue hardship on the operation of an agency's program include (1) the overall size of the agency's program with respect to the number of employees, number and type of facilities, and size of budget; (2) the type of agency operation, including the composition and structure of the agency's work force; and (3) the nature and cost of the accommodation.[130] If an agency fails to assert that a requested accommodation will cause undue hardship

[124]*Savage v. Department of the Navy*, 36 MSPR 148, 151–52 (1988).

[125]See, e.g., *Richardson v. Postal Serv.*, 613 F. Supp. 1213, 40 FEP Cases 703 (D.D.C. 1985); *Conti v. Department of the Army*, 34 MSPR 272 (1987); *Myers v. Department of the Air Force*, 28 MSPR 479 (1985); *Miller v. HHS*, 23 MSPR 128 (1984), *aff'd*, 770 F.2d 182 (Fed. Cir. 1985).

[126]*Savage v. Department of the Navy, supra* note 124 at 153.

[127]29 C.F.R. 1613.704(a).

[128]*Ignacio v. Postal Serv.*, 30 MSPR 471 (1986). But see *Carter v. Tisch*, 822 F.2d 465, 44 FEP Cases 385 (4th Cir. 1987); *Davis v. Postal Serv.*, 675 F. Supp. 225 (M.D. Pa. 1987); *Hoffman v. Department of the Army*, No. 85-C-6045 (E.D. Ill., Mar. 24, 1987); *Dancy v. Kline*, 639 F. Supp. 1076, 40 FEP Cases 1099 (N.D. Ill. 1986); *Carty v. Carlin*, 623 F. Supp. 1181, 39 FEP Cases 1217 (D. Md. 1985); *Jasany v. Postal Serv.*, 33 FEP 1115 (N.D. Ohio 1983), *aff'd on other grounds*, 755 F.2d 1244, 37 FEP Cases 210 (6th Cir. 1985). See also *Ellis v. Postal Serv.*, 37 MSPR 503 (1988) (reaffirming *Ignacio* Special Panel decision notwithstanding court decisions to the contrary regarding whether reassignment is reasonable accommodation under Rehabilitation Act).

[129]29 C.F.R. 1613.704(b). See, e.g., *Treadwell v. Alexander*, 707 F.2d 473, 32 FEP Cases 62 (11th Cir. 1983) (job restructuring); *Mantolete v. Bolger*, 767 F.2d 1416, 38 FEP Cases 1081 (9th Cir. 1985) (modification of equipment); *Board of Educ. v. Rowley*, 458 U.S. 176 (1982) (readers and interpreters).

[130]29 C.F.R. 1613.704(c). See also *Prewitt v. Postal Serv.*, 662 F.2d 292, 27 FEP Cases 1043 (5th Cir. 1981); *Dexler v. Tisch*, 43 FEP Cases 1662 (D. Conn. 1987); *Mackay v. Postal Serv.*, 607 F. Supp. 271 (E.D. Pa. 1985).

and, instead, argues that it has adequately accommodated the employee in other ways, it runs the risk of not meeting its burden of proof on this element of its case.[131]

Finally, if the agency meets its burden of establishing a legitimate reason for its action, the employee is given the opportunity to show that the agency's stated reason for failing to accommodate the appellant's handicap is pretextual.[132]

Alcohol or Drug Dependency

Generally, alcohol and drug abuse claims by federal employees are raised under the auspices of the Rehabilitation Act.[133] Where an employee's handicap is alcohol or drug dependency, agencies are usually required to refer the employee to an assistance program before taking disciplinary action against the employee when the agency knew or should have known of the employee's condition.[134] This obligation does not attach where the agency can demonstrate that it was unaware of the employee's handicap.[135] Also, the Merit Systems Protection Board (MSPB) has recently ruled that an agency is not under a duty to accommodate an alcoholic or drug addict who engages in certain acts of misconduct that renders that person not a "qualified handicapped employee."[136] The Board has defined such misconduct as that "which, by its very nature,

---

[131]*Lynch v. Department of Educ.*, 37 MSPR 12 (1988), *on remand sub nom. Lynch v. Bennett from* 665 F. Supp. 62 (D.D.C. 1987).

[132]*Savage v. Department of the Navy, supra* note 124, at 155.

[133]Alcohol and drug abuse claims may also be raised under the Comprehensive Alcohol Abuse and Alcoholism Prevention, Treatment, and Rehabilitation Act, 42 U.S.C. 290dd-1 and the Drug Abuse Prevention, Treatment, and Rehabilitation Act, 42 U.S.C. 290ee-1. Among other things, these Acts provide that no person may be denied or deprived of federal employment solely on the grounds of prior alcohol or drug abuse unless the position is in the CIA, FBI, or is designated sensitive. 42 U.S.C. 290dd-1(b)(1) and (2) and 290ee-1(b)(1) and (2). Also, neither Act prohibits the dismissal of a civilian employee from federal employment who cannot properly function in his or her job because of alcohol or drug abuse. 42 U.S.C. 290dd-1(c) and 290ee-1(c). However, even if an employee's position is designated sensitive, he or she is not precluded from raising a handicap discrimination claim based on alcohol or drug abuse under the Rehabilitation Act because that act does not exempt sensitive positions from coverage. See, e.g., *Dougherty v. Department of the Treasury*, 35 MSPR 381 (1983); *Marren v. Department of Justice*, 29 MSPR 118 (1985); *Velie v. Department of the Treasury*, 26 MSPR 376 (1975). But see *Hougens v. Postal Serv.*, 38 MSPR 135 (1988) (reversing *Marren* and *Velie*).

[134]*Ruzek v. GSA, supra* note 116. See also 5 C.F.R. Part 792.

[135]See, e.g., *McGilberry v. Defense Mapping Agency*, 18 MSPR 560 (1984) (alcoholism); *Ritter v. Postal Serv.*, 37 MSPR 334 (1988) (AIDS).

[136]*Hougens v. Postal Serv., supra* note 133. At this writing, the *Hougens* decision has not been reviewed by the EEOC or the courts. Therefore, care should be taken to research the status of the decision for precedent reliance purposes.

strikes at the core of the job or the agency's mission, or is so egregious or notorious that an employee's ability to perform his duties or to represent the agency is hampered."[137] However, it has been held that an agency is put on notice of an alcohol dependency problem even if the employee first raises the problem as a defense to a proposed notice of adverse action.[138]

In the typical situation, once the agency is on notice of the employee's handicapping condition,[139] it is required to give the employee a "firm choice" between rehabilitation and discipline in order to reasonably accommodate the employee.[140] Generally, the agency is only required to provide one such opportunity for rehabilitation.[141] If the employee refuses the offer of assistance or fails to follow through, the agency has met its accommodation burden and may discipline the employee.[142] However, once the employee begins rehabilitation efforts, the agency must allow the employee reasonable time to complete a rehabilitation program.[143] This is true even if an agency offers an employee more than one opportunity to participate in a program.[144] The agency does not satisfy its reasonable accommodation obligation by imposing a less severe form of disciplinary action in lieu of offering the employee rehabilitation assistance.[145] Only after reasonable accommodation efforts have been made, which is usually determined on a case-by-case basis, may the agency then discipline the employee. Even then, the agency may not be able to rely on prior dependency-related misconduct to enhance the penalty imposed.[146]

---

[137]*Id.*, at 144. Cf. *Kruger v. Department of Justice*, 32 MSPR 71 (1987).

[138]*Noe v. Postal Serv.*, 28 MSPR 1986 (1985). See also *Deskins v. Department of the Navy*, 29 MSPR 276 (1985); *Swafford v. TVA*, 18 MSPR 481 (1983).

[139]As a practical matter, it appears that the employee must present sufficient medical evidence verifying the existence of a drug or alcohol dependency at the time of the misconduct in question. *McCaffrey v. Postal Serv.*, 36 MSPR 224 (1988). See also *Campbell v. Defense Logistics Agency*, 37 MSPR 691 (1988); *Brinkley v. Veterans Admin.*, 37 MSPR 682 (1988).

[140]*Whitlock v. Donovan*, 598 F. Supp. 126, 36 FEP Cases 425 (D.D.C. 1984), *aff'd sub nom. Whitlock v. Brock*, 790 F.2d 964, 45 FEP Cases 520 (D.C. Cir. 1986).

[141]*Brann v. Postal Serv.*, 25 MSPR 83 (1988).

[142]*Stewart v. Veterans Admin.*, 19 MSPR 147 (1984); *Hairston v. Department of the Treasury*, 16 MSPR 40 (1983).

[143]*Rison v. Department of the Navy*, 23 MSPR 118 (1984); *Lundy v. Department of the Navy*, 11 MSPR 469 (1982); *Keels v. Department of Labor*, 7 MSPR 499 (1981); *Felten v. Department of Labor*, 7 MSPR 499 (1981).

[144]*Chaplin v. Department of the Navy*, 35 MSPR 39 (1987); *Haskins v. FAA*, 21 MSPR 507 (1984).

[145]*Friel v. Department of the Navy*, 29 MSPR 216 (1985). But see *Hougens v. Postal Serv.*, *supra* note 133 (reversing *Friel*).

[146]*Walker v. Weinberger*, 600 F. Supp. 757 (D.D.C. 1985).

Relationship to Title VII

The Rehabilitation Act was amended in 1978 to apply Title VII procedures and remedies to federal employees aggrieved by handicap discrimination in employment.[147] (For a discussion of Title VII rights and remedies see discussion in preceding sections, *supra*. For a discussion of Title VII administrative procedures see Chapter 2.)

Exhaustion of Administrative Remedies and Types of Action Available in Court

Exhaustion of administrative remedies is required before an aggrieved party may pursue a case in federal district court.[148] Once in federal court, the complainant is entitled to a trial *de novo* without a jury.[149]

The Equal Pay Act

Coverage

The Equal Pay Act of 1963, as amended in 1974,[150] prohibits paying males and females in any establishment[151] in which they work a different wage for "equal work," that is, work that requires equal skill, effort, and responsibility and that is performed under similar working conditions.[152] Congressionally mandated job classification systems, seniority systems, and merit systems like those applicable to federal employees are specifi-

---

[147]29 U.S.C. 794a(a)(1).

[148]*Anderson v. Block*, 807 F.2d 145, 42 FEP Cases 982 (8th Cir. 1986); *Prewitt v. Postal Serv.*, *supra* note 130; *Counts v. Postal Serv.*, 631 F.2d 46, 24 FEP Cases 677 (5th Cir. 1980); *Ryan v. FDIC*, 565 F.2d 762 (D.C. Cir. 1977); *Mackay v. Postal Serv.*, *supra* note 130.

[149]29 U.S.C. 794a.

[150]29 U.S.C. 206(d). The 1974 amendments to the Fair Labor Standards Act extended coverage of the Equal Pay Act to federal agencies and employees. See Pub. L. 93-259, 88 Stat. 55 (Apr. 8, 1974); 29 U.S.C. 203(d).

[151]In the federal sector the appropriate "establishment" for job comparison purposes has been held to be the entire federal civil service. *Grumbine v. United States*, 586 F. Supp. 1144, 34 FEP Cases 847 (D.D.C. 1984).

[152]"Equal" work does not require that the jobs be identical, but only that they must be "substantially equal." *Schultz v. Wheaton Glass Co.*, 421 F.2d 259, 9 FEP Cases 502 (3d Cir.), *cert. denied*, 398 U.S. 905, 9 FEP Cases 1408 (1970); *Thompson v. Sawyer*, 678 F.2d 257, 28 FEP Cases 1614 (D.C. Cir. 1982).

cally excepted.[153] Also excepted are those pay schemes supported by a "bona fide business necessity," that is, systems that measure earnings by quantity or quality of production, or where the differences in pay are based on any factor other than sex.[154] The Act applies only to differing pay between workers of different sexes.[155]

The Equal Pay Act was enacted as an amendment to the Fair Labor Standards Act (FLSA) of 1938, as amended.[156] Consequently, the enforcement of the Equal Pay Act provisions is governed by applicable provisions of the FLSA as interpreted by the Department of Labor.[157] Presidential Reorganization Plan No. 1 of 1978 transferred enforcement responsibilities from the then Civil Service Commission (now OPM) to the EEOC.[158]

The Act was intended to counter what Congress and the Supreme Court have called the "ancient but outmoded belief that a man, because of his role in society, should be paid more than a woman even though his duties are the same."[159] Higher-paid employees' wages may not be reduced, however, to remedy an existing unlawful differential.[160]

Relationship to Title VII

The Act addresses "equal work," not comparable work or work of comparable value. Theories of comparable work and work of comparable value may find support in the sex provision of Title VII,[161] but are insufficient to meet the equal work standard of the Equal Pay Act.[162] Actions may be brought under both Title VII and the Equal Pay Act where

---

[153]29 U.S.C. 206(d)(1)(i) and (ii). See, e.g., Classification Act of 1949, as amended, 5 U.S.C. 5101 et seq. Note, however, that, even under the Classification Act, Congress mandated that "the principle of equal pay for substantially equal work will be followed." 5 U.S.C. 5101(1)(A). See also Grumbine v. United States, supra note 151, for a discussion of the relationship between the Classification Act and the Equal Pay Act.

[154]29 U.S.C. 206(d)(1)(iii) and (iv). See, e.g., Hodgson v. Robert Hall Clothes, 473 F.2d 589, 11 FEP Cases 1271 (3d Cir.), cert. denied, 414 U.S. 866, 11 FEP Cases 1310 (1973); Shultz v. First Victoria Nat'l Bank, 420 F.2d 648, 9 FEP Cases 496 (5th Cir. 1969).

[155]29 U.S.C. 206(d)(1).

[156]29 U.S.C. 201 et seq.

[157]29 C.F.R. Part 1620.

[158]43 FED. REG. 19807 (1978), 92 Stat. 3781.

[159]S. REP. No. 176, 88th Cong., 1st Sess., 1 (1963); Corning Glass Works v. Brennan, 417 U.S. 188 (1974).

[160]29 U.S.C. 206(d)(1).

[161]County of Washington, Or. v. Gunther, 452 U.S. 161, 25 FEP Cases 1521 (1981). See also State, County & Mun. Employees v. Washington, 578 F. Supp. 846, 33 FEP Cases 808 (W.D. Wash. 1983), rev'd, 770 F.2d 1401, 38 FEP Cases 1353 (9th Cir. 1985), reh'g denied, 813 F.2d 1034 (9th Cir. 1987).

[162]Id.

unlawful pay differences between males and females are alleged.[163] Aggrieved parties are well-advised to pursue a timely remedy under both laws. Where Title VII may allow a comparable work or comparable value theory, the Equal Pay Act provides liquidated damages where the violation of the Act has been willful.[164] (For a discussion of liquidated damages see "The Age Discrimination in Employment Act: Remedies Not Available," *supra*).

Standards Applied

Equal Work Standard

The equal work standard does not require that the jobs at issue be identical, just substantially equal.[165] The controlling factor in an Equal Pay Act analysis is an overall comparison of job content, that is, the actual duties performed, not job classification or title.[166]

Equal Skill Standard

The equal skill standard requires substantially equal skills actually and regularly performed in the jobs compared. Examples of skill factors include experience, training, education, and ability.[167]

Equal Effort Standard

The equal effort standard includes such factors as physical and mental exertion.[168] The effort expended to perform the jobs compared must be substantially equal and must be actually and regularly expended. Where the ultimate degree of effort expended is substantially equal, it may not matter that two jobs call for expenditure of effort of different

---

[163]*County of Washington, Or. v. Gunther, supra* note 161; *Northwest Airlines v. Transport Workers*, 451 U.S. 77, 25 FEP Cases 737 (1981); *Thompson v. Sawyer, supra* note 152; *Laffey v. Northwest Airlines*, 567 F.2d 429, 13 FEP Cases 1068 (D.C. Cir. 1976), *cert. denied*, 434 U.S. 1086, 16 FEP Cases 998 (1978).

[164]29 U.S.C. 216(b) and (c). *Pearce v. Wichita County, City of Wichita Falls, Tex., Hosp. Bd.*, 590 F.2d 128, 19 FEP Cases 339 (5th Cir. 1979).

[165]See *supra* note 152.

[166]*Orahood v. Trustees of the Univ. of Ark.*, 645 F.2d 651, 25 FEP Cases 1739 (8th Cir. 1981); *EEOC v. Universal Underwriters Ins. Co.*, 653 F.2d 1243, 26 FEP Cases 775 (8th Cir. 1981); *Pearce v. Wichita County, City of Wichita Falls, Tex., Hosp. Bd., supra* note 164.

[167]29 U.S.C. 1620.15; *Pearce v. Wichita County, City of Wichita Falls, Tex., Hosp. Bd., supra* note 164.

[168]29 C.F.R. 1620.16; *Brennan v. Sterling Seal Co.*, 363 F. Supp. 1230 (W.D. Pa. 1973); *Hodgson v. Oil City Hosp.*, 363 F. Supp. 419, 9 FEP Cases 802 (W.D. Pa. 1973).

kinds.[169] Additional tasks alone, unless they consume significant employee time, will not justify a pay differential.[170]

Equal Responsibility Standard

The equal responsibility standard involves factors including the degree of accountability required in the performance of the job.[171] Different duties may carry different weight or degrees of priority. The responsibility examined is that which is actually and regularly performed.[172]

Similar Working Conditions Standard

Finally, the similar working conditions standard requires examination of the physical surroundings and hazards.[173] It does not include such things as shift or time of day worked. Surroundings and hazards include such things as toxic fumes or chemicals regularly encountered by the worker, and physical hazards regularly encountered.[174] The frequency of exposure and potential severity of injuries suffered are also elements considered.[175]

Allocation of Burden of Proof

The initial burden in an Equal Pay Act case is on the complainant to meet the factors discussed above. Once met, a prima facie case is established and the burden shifts to the defendant employer to justify the pay differential by demonstrating that it falls within one of four statutory exceptions—a seniority system, a merit system, a system that sets wages by referencing quantity or quality of production, or any system based on any factor other than the sex of the workers.[176]

---

[169]*Usery v. Columbia Univ.*, 568 F.2d 953, 15 FEP Cases 1333 (2d Cir. 1977).

[170]*Brennan v. Prince William Hosp. Corp.*, 503 F.2d 282, 9 FEP Cases 979 (4th Cir.), *cert. denied*, 420 U.S. 972 (1974); *Brennan v. South Davis Community Hosp.*, 538 F.2d 859, 13 FEP Cases 258 (10th Cir. 1976); *Peltier v. City of Fargo*, 533 F.2d 374, 12 FEP Cases 945 (8th Cir. 1976); *Brennan v. Sterling Seal Co.*, *supra* note 168; *Usery v. Columbia Univ.*, *supra* note 169.

[171]29 C.F.R. 1620.17; *Pearce v. Wichita County, City of Wichita Falls, Tex., Hosp. Bd.*, *supra* note 164.

[172]*Laffey v. Northwest Airlines*, *supra* note 163.

[173]29 C.F.R. 1620.18; *Laffey v. Northwest Airlines*, *supra* note 163; *Corning Glass Works v. Brennan*, *supra* note 159.

[174]*Id.*

[175]*Corning Glass Works v. Brennan*, *supra* note 159.

[176]29 U.S.C. 206(d)(1); *Morgado v. Birmingham-Jefferson County Civil Defense Corps*, 706 F.2d 1184, 32 FEP Cases 12, *reh'g denied*, 715 F.2d 580 (11th Cir. 1983), *cert. denied*, 464 U.S. 1045, 33 FEP Cases 1084 (1984); *Strecker v. Grand Forks County Social Serv. Bd.*, 640 F.2d 96, 24 FEP Cases 1019 (8th Cir. 1980); *Laffey v. Northwest Airlines*, *supra* note 163; *Pearce v. Wichita County, City of Wichita Falls, Tex., Hosp. Bd.*, *supra* note 164.

Determining the Remedy

Remedies include promotion, back pay, liquidated damages, and attorney's fees.[177] (See Chapter 12.) However, a two-year statute of limitations applies to the recovery of unpaid wages, except that an action arising out of a willful violation of the Act may be commenced within three years after the cause of action accrues.[178] Liquidated damages are available in an amount equal to the back pay awarded where there is a finding of "bad faith" against the employer.[179] (For a discussion of liquidated damages, see "The Age Discrimination in Employment Act: Remedies Not Available," *supra*.)

Exhaustion of Administrative Remedies and Types of Action Available in Court

There is no requirement that a federal employee exhaust administrative remedies before filing an action in court under the Equal Pay Act.[180] However, an employee may pursue an administrative Equal Pay Act claim with the EEOC. (See Chapter 2.) Whether or not the administrative process is followed, a court action for relief under the Act must be filed within the appropriate statute of limitations period, that is, within two years of when a cause of action accrues for nonwillful violation and within three years for willful violations. Plaintiffs suing under the Equal Pay Act, including federal employees, are entitled to a jury trial.[181] Class actions may also be brought under the Act.[182] However, such an action under the Act allows potential class members to "opt in" and is governed by the provision of the FLSA.[183] Therefore, Equal Pay Act class action procedures differ somewhat from those applicable to a traditional Title VII class action and Rule 23 of the Federal Rules of Civil Procedure (discussed in the section concerning Title VII, *supra*, and in Chapter 2).

---

[177]29 U.S.C. 216(b).

[178]29 U.S.C. 255; 29 C.F.R. 1620.33. For statute of limitations purposes, a cause of action accrues each payday that an employee is paid in a manner that violates the Act. *Hall v. Ledex, Inc.*, 669 F.2d 397, 30 FEP Cases 82 (6th Cir. 1982). However, the "continuing violation" theory does not operate where employment terminates or the alleged unlawful pay practice ceases. *Jenkins v. Home Ins. Co.*, 635 F.2d 310, 24 FEP Cases 990 (4th Cir. 1980).

[179]29 U.S.C. 216(b); 29 C.F.R. 1620.33. See also *Laffey v. Northwest Airlines, supra* note 163; *Pearce v. Wichita County, City of Wichita Falls, Tex., Hosp. Bd., supra* note 164.

[180]29 U.S.C. 204(b).

[181]*Carter v. Marshall*, 17 FEP Cases 1186 (D.D.C. 1978).

[182]29 U.S.C. 216(b); *Schmidt v. Fuller Brush Co.*, 527 F.2d 532, 22 WH Cases 629 (8th Cir. 1975).

[183]*Id.*

Other Protections Against Discrimination

There are other protections against discrimination in federal employment. The Office of Personnel Management has promulgated regulations prohibiting discrimination based upon race, political, or religious discrimination and marital status.[184] In addition, the prohibited personnel practices section of the Civil Service Reform Act of 1978 incorporates prohibitions against discrimination of all kinds.[185] The Special Counsel of the MSPB has authority to investigate and prosecute prohibited personnel practice complaints based on discrimination, including the prosecution of disciplinary actions against supervisory and nonsupervisory employees[186] that can result in removal, reduction in grade, debarment from federal employment for a period not to exceed five years, suspension, reprimand, or the assessment of a civil penalty not to exceed $1,000.[187] (See Chapter 4 for detailed discussion of Prohibited Personnel Practices.)

---

[184]5 C.F.R. 4.2 and 315.806 (dealing with probationary status termination); FEDERAL PERSONNEL MANUAL, Chapter 713, Subchapters 4-1 and 4-2.

[185]5 U.S.C. 2302(b)(1)(A)–(E).

[186]5 U.S.C. 1206; 5 C.F.R. Parts 1251 and 1254. See, e.g., *Special Counsel v. Zimmerman & Pouy*, 36 MSPR 274 (1988) (religious discrimination); *Special Counsel v. Russell*, 32 MSPR 115 (1987) (sexual harassment).

[187]5 U.S.C. 1207(b).

6. Supervisory Liability

R. JOHN SEIBERT*

The vast majority of adverse federal personnel actions pit the employee against his or her employing agency. Disputes are normally resolved in the context of administrative proceedings. If the employee prevails, he or she may retain a current position, advance to a new one, and, where appropriate, secure back pay. In each case, the relief is provided by the employing agency. The employee's supervisor is not required to make any personal monetary contribution.

Under certain circumstances, however, the federal employee may sue his supervisor directly for money damages. If the employee prevails, the court will enter judgment against the supervisor personally. Where the supervisor's employing agency has no arrangement for reimbursing the supervisor in such instances, the supervisor must pay the money judgment from personal assets.

Employee suits against supervisors for money damages are relatively common. The vast majority, however, never reach the trial stage.[1] The courts have recognized several broad defenses to such suits that typically result in their dismissal before trial.

The willingness of courts to regularly dismiss personal damage suits against supervisors is based on both pragmatic and statutory considerations. A government whose employees, including supervisors, face daily

---

*This chapter was written by R. John Seibert in his private capacity. No official support or endorsement by the Department of Justice is intended or should be inferred.

[1]Few plaintiffs, in fact, who have sued federal employees in tort for damages have succeeded in recovering monetary awards. See Euler, *Personal Liability of Military Personnel for Actions Taken in the Course of Duty*, 133 MIL. L. REV. 137 (1986) (between 1971 and 1986, in excess of 12,000 common law and constitutional tort suits were filed against both supervisory and nonsupervisory federal personnel of which only 32 resulted in verdicts against the individual defendants).

threat of personal suit for carrying out job-related duties would fast become an inefficient one and seriously cripple the effective administration of public affairs. Additionally, the need for personal damage recovery against supervisors may be unnecessary where Congress has legislated alternate effective means of statutory relief such as reinstatement and back pay for wrongful supervisory action.

Notwithstanding the existence of important considerations militating against employees recovering money damages directly from their supervisors, such relief has been recognized in limited circumstances. To understand those circumstances, this chapter examines the types of supervisory conduct that will justify a personal damage action by employees, as well as the types of defenses that may block recovery.

Grounds for Suing a Supervisor

Federal supervisors may be sued in a court of law by their employees for invading some legal right of the employee. Such actions are known as tort suits. They are civil in nature and run against the supervisor in his individual capacity. The federal employee bringing the lawsuit is said to be the plaintiff and the supervisor the defendant. Normally, the employee will ask for monetary damages to compensate him or her for the civil injury allegedly committed by the supervisor.[2]

There are two categories of civil injuries or torts upon which an employee can elect to sue: common law torts and constitutional torts. Common law torts are civil injuries that have evolved from our common law legal system. In the federal employment context they most often include libel and slander, assault and battery, and intentional infliction of emotional distress. Specific examples are discussed later in this chapter.

Constitutional torts are of more recent vintage. First recognized by the Supreme Court in 1971,[3] they encompass injuries resulting from a supervisor's violation of an employee's federal constitutional right. Rights sued upon typically include due process, freedom from discrimination, freedom of speech, and constitutional privacy rights.[4]

---

[2]The employee may also ask for injunctive or declaratory relief. For example, the employee might request a court order enjoining the supervisor from physically touching the employee.

[3]*Bivens v. Six Unknown Named Agents of Fed. Bureau of Narcotics*, 403 U.S. 388 (1971).

[4]Paralleling constitutional torts as a basis for federal supervisory liability are actions brought under the Civil Rights Act, 42 U.S.C. 1983 and 1985(3). These sections permit suit for fewer types of constitutional wrongdoing than constitutional torts. Section 1983, for example, requires that the federal supervisor conspire to violate civil rights with one acting

Limitations to Supervisory Liability

Recognizing that not all federal personnel, including federal supervisors, are guilty of the allegedly tortious conduct charged against them, and further recognizing that the threat of such suits may impede the effective discharge of duty, the Supreme Court has erected several barriers that a plaintiff must overcome in order to test the merits of his or her damage action. A federal employee must demonstrate, for example, that Congress has not created an adequate alternate forum for remedying the supervisor's alleged wrongdoing. Where a comprehensive and elaborate remedial system exists for resolving an employee's grievance against a supervisor, such as the Civil Service Reform Act (CSRA) of 1978[5] or Title VII of the Civil Rights Act,[6] the federal employee may not sue his supervisor on a constitutional tort theory.[7]

If, however, no alternate comprehensive remedy exists, the employee still must confront and overcome one or more statutory or judicially created immunity defenses available to the federal supervisor. Federal personnel, including supervisory staff, sued for common law torts are accorded an absolute statutory immunity for performing actions that fall within the scope of their official duties.[8] A federal supervisor sued for libel and slander because of statements made in a written employee

---

under color of state law. See generally *Freier v. New York Life Ins. Co.*, 679 F.2d 780, 783 (9th Cir. 1982); *Zernial v. United States*, 714 F.2d 431, 435 (5th Cir. 1983). 42 U.S.C. 1985(3) has been limited by the Supreme Court to actions based on racial or ethnic discriminatory conduct. *Carpenters Local 610 v. Scott*, 463 U.S. 825, 113 LRRM 3145 (1983); *Gibson v. United States*, 781 F.2d 1334, 1341 (9th Cir. 1986); *Schultz v. Sundberg*, 759 F.2d 714, 718 (9th Cir. 1985); *Harrison v. Kvat Food Mgmt.*, 766 F.2d 155, 157, 160–63 (4th Cir. 1985); *Wilhelm v. Continential Title Co.*, 720 F.2d 1173, 1175–77, 33 FEP Cases 385 (10th Cir. 1983), *cert. denied*, 465 U.S. 1104, 34 FEP Cases 416 (1984). Successful litigation of a 42 U.S.C. 1983 or 1985(3) suit, however, may result in entitlement to attorney's fees under 42 U.S.C. 1986. Judicially recognized constitutional tort actions against federal employees have no comparable attorney's fees provision. Although Civil Rights Act suits against federal supervisors for monetary damages are beyond the scope of this chapter, many of the judicially recognized immunities from liability accorded federal personnel in constitutional tort actions, that are discussed here, apply as well to Civil Rights Act cases. *Davis v. Scherer*, 468 U.S. 183, 194 n.12 (1984).

[5]Pub. L. No. 95-454, 92 Stat. 1111 (codified as amended in various sections of 5 U.S.C.)

[6]42 U.S.C. 2000e *et seq.*

[7]*Bush v. Lucas*, 462 U.S. 367 (1983); *Brown v. GSA*, 425 U.S. 820 (1976).

[8]Federal Employees Liability Reform and Tort Compensation Act of 1988, Pub. L. No. 100-694, amending 28 U.S.C. 2679 to immunize federal employees against common law tort liability arising from activities performed within the scope of their employment. In such situations, the Act makes the United States the exclusive defendant for monetary recovery pursuant to the provisions of the Federal Tort Claims Act, 28 U.S.C. 1346(b), 2671, *et seq.*

evaluation will be given absolute statutory immunity resulting in the likely dismissal of the employee's suit.[9]

Federal personnel, including supervisors, sued for allegedly violating a plaintiff's constitutional rights generally receive only a qualified immunity to the extent that their challenged actions do not violate clearly established constitutional standards.[10] This immunity is determined by reference to objective factors such as the state of the law at the time of the alleged conduct. Supervisor's subjective good-faith belief in the constitutionality of their conduct normally is not considered.[11]

Successfully suing federal supervisors for money damages has been made deliberately difficult by the Supreme Court and Congress in recognition of the likelihood that broader liability exposure would seriously undermine the effective discharge of federal duty,[12] and because, in certain instances, Congress has determined that alternate forms of redress offer more suitable remedies.[13]

The remainder of this chapter examines more closely the grounds for such suits; the types of alternate remedies that may act to preclude them; and the immunities available to federal supervisors, including the procedural steps for their invocation.

Common Law Liability

Federal supervisory personnel sued for common law torts are typically sued for the kinds of activities that could generate a personal damage action between any two private individuals. Most often, however, when employees proceed with a common law tort action against super-

---

[9]Even prior to Congress' creation in 1988 of absolute statutory immunity for common law torts arising from conduct by a federal employee within the scope of his employment, see *supra* note 8, a federal supervisor likely would have been accorded absolute judicial immunity for this type of supervisory conduct. See, e.g., *Bradley v. Computer Sciences Corp.*, 643 F.2d 1029 (4th Cir. 1981), relying on *Barr v. Matteo*, 360 U.S. 564 (1958).

[10]*Harlow v. Fitzgerald*, 457 U.S. 800 (1982).

[11]Federal personnel sued for violating constitutional rights receive absolute immunity only when they perform special functions where the public interest, as determined by reference to the common law and our constitutional heritage and structure, demands a full exemption from liability. Examples of such special functions include those undertaken by judges, *Stump v. Sparkman*, 435 U.S. 349 (1978); prosecutors, *Imbler v. Pachtman*, 424 U.S. 409 (1975); and the President of the United States, but not his aides, *Nixon v. Fitzgerald*, 457 U.S. 731 (1982); *Harlow v. Fitzgerald*, *supra* note 10.

[12]*Westfall v. Erwin*, 484 U.S. 292, 56 USLW 4087, 4088 (1988); *Harlow v. Fitzgerald*, *supra* note 10, at 813–15; *Gregoire v. Biddle*, 177 F.2d 579, 581 (2d Cir. 1949), *cert. denied*, 339 U.S. 949 (1950).

[13]*Schweiker v. Chilicky*, 56 USLW 4767 (1988).

visors it will be for one of three varieties of tort noted earlier, that is, libel and slander, assault and battery, or intentional infliction of emotional distress.[14]

Libel and Slander

Libel and slander suits typically arise when supervisors make critical remarks about subordinates, often in the context of performance evaluations or adverse personnel practices. In *Barr v. Matteo*,[15] for example, the soon-to-become acting director of a federal office issued a press release announcing that his first act as acting director would be the suspension of two employees for sanctioning a plan providing a cash payment to agency employees for accumulated annual leave. The press release characterized the conduct as violative of the spirit of a pertinent congressional enactment. The two employees sued the acting director for libel and slander alleging that the publication and content of the press release were actuated by malice.

Assault and Battery

Assault and battery actions often arise as the consequence of emotional exchanges between a supervisor and a subordinate. They are typified by claims of physical touching, known as battery, or threats of personal harm, known as assault. In *McKinney v. Whitfield*,[16] a budget supervisor with the Federal Aviation Administration (FAA) allegedly used physical force to restrain an employee while he was discussing her proposed furlough. The plaintiff-subordinate alleged that her supervisor had pushed an office chair into her leg in order to prevent her exit and then held her arm in a tight, twisting fashion causing abrasions and swelling.[17]

---

[14]Supervisors also may be sued for negligent conduct that is alleged to have proximately caused a subordinate's physical injuries. See *Westfall v. Erwin, supra* note 12 (suit by Army civilian warehouseman against three supervisors for improperly and negligently storing bags of soda ash whose contents were inhaled by plaintiff causing serious injury).
[15]*Supra* note 9; as discussed *infra*, the acting director was accorded an absolute judicially created immunity from liability.
[16]736 F.2d 766 (D.C. Cir. 1984).
[17]See also *Araujo v. Welch*, 742 F.2d 802 (3d Cir. 1984) (suit for common law assault, battery, and intentional infliction of emotional distress by Equal Employment Opportunity officer against her male supervisor for allegedly poking her in the chest and threatening her employment with federal government); *Dretar v. Smith*, 752 F.2d 1015 (5th Cir. 1985) (action for common law assault and battery by Interior Department employee against her supervisor for allegedly pushing her out of his office and slamming door behind her causing door handle to strike plaintiff).

Intentional Infliction of Emotional Distress

A category of common law tort actions related to assault and battery cases are those alleging the intentional infliction of emotional distress. These generally involve a supervisor's threats to terminate a subordinate's employment that are motivated by an intention to upset or harass the employee.[18]

Immunity From Common Law Tort Suits

General Rule—Absolute Immunity

Despite the seeming ease with which federal employees could bring suit against supervisors for any of the foregoing types of common law tort, especially that based on the intentional infliction of emotional distress, the Supreme Court and lower courts had generally accorded federal personnel, including supervisors, an absolute immunity from such actions.[19] The general rule evolving from these cases had held that federal officials and employees sued for common law torts received absolute immunity from liability insofar as the subject conduct was related to the performance of discretionary duties falling within the outer perimeter of the supervisor's official responsibilities.[20]

This immunity was based on the pragmatic recognition that a government whose officers and employees faced daily threat of suit for carrying out job-related duties fast became a severely inefficient one.[21]

---

[18]See, e.g., *Araujo v. Welch, supra* note 17; *Palermo v. Rorex*, 806 F.2d 1266 (5th Cir.), *cert. denied*, 56 USLW 3243 (1988) (suit by wife of deceased IRS employee against deceased's supervisors for intentionally inflicting emotional distress on husband through wrongfully initiating disciplinary proceedings against him that allegedly caused him to commit suicide); *Bradley v. Computer Sciences Corp., supra* note 9 (suit against supervisor for allegedly preparing unsatisfactory performance evaluation in order to harass subordinate).

[19]While the scope of this chapter is limited to discussing the personal liability of federal supervisors as a consequence of federal personnel practices, the supervisor, like any federal employee, may be liable at common law for tortious conduct he or she allegedly commits against private citizens, as opposed to federal employees. See, e.g., *Johnson v. Pettibone Corp.*, 755 F.2d 1484 (11th Cir. 1985) (wrongful death action against TVA employees for electrocution of construction worker); *Wyler v. United States*, 725 F.2d 156 (2d Cir. 1983) (common law claim for tortious search and seizure); *Johnson v. Busly*, 704 F.2d 419 (8th Cir. 1983) (suit against employees of Farmers Home Administration for willful and malicious denial of loan); *Evans v. Wright*, 582 F.2d 20 (5th Cir. 1978) (tortious inference with right to contract); *Expeditions Unlimited Aquatic Enters. v. Smithsonian Inst.*, 566 F.2d 298 (D.C. Cir. 1977) (en banc), *cert. denied*, 438 U.S. 915 (1978) (libel action against museum official for writing letter critical of plaintiff's professional capabilities).

[20]*Westfall v. Erwin, supra* note 12; *Barr v. Matteo, supra* note 9, at 575.

[21]The modern doctrine of absolute immunity for common law torts has its genesis in

In *Barr v. Matteo*,[22] for example, the federal supervisor was held to have been acting within the outer perimeter of his duties when issuing the press release that formed the basis of his subordinates' libel and slander action. Accordingly, the Supreme Court recognized an absolute immunity from liability for him. Similarly, the Court of Appeals for the Fifth Circuit recognized absolute immunity for federal supervisors alleged to have initiated disciplinary proceedings for the purpose of intentionally inflicting mental and emotional distress on a subordinate.[23] The court of appeals held that the act of initiating disciplinary proceedings was conduct clearly within the scope of the supervisor's duties. Under *Barr*, plaintiff's allegations of malice were irrelevant to the availability of absolute immunity.[24]

Creation of Statutory Immunity

Westfall v. Erwin

In 1988, the Supreme Court revisited the law of absolute immunity in *Westfall v. Erwin*,[25] and, in the process, potentially narrowed the degree of protection afforded federal supervisors by the immunity. The Court sustained an Eighth Circuit ruling reversing a lower court's grant of absolute immunity accorded federal supervisors. The plaintiff was a

---

the Supreme Court's decision in *Spalding v. Vilas*, 161 U.S. 483 (1896), where an attorney representing postmasters seeking certain salary readjustments brought a libel action against the Postmaster General for advising his clients that they no longer required the attorney's services to secure the relief they sought. In holding that the Postmaster General was immune from suit, irrespective of whether he acted with malice, the Supreme Court noted that withholding immunity "would seriously cripple the proper and effective administration of public affairs as entrusted to the executive branch of government." *Id.*, at 498.

For earlier rulings recognizing immunity from liability in damages for injuries caused by a federal employee's official actions, see *Crowell v. McFadon*, 12 U.S. (8 Cranch) 94 (1814); *Otis v. Watkins*, 13 U.S. (9 Cranch) 339 (1815); *Osborn v. United States Bank*, 22 U.S. (9 Wheat.) 738 (1824); *Kendall v. Stokes*, 44 U.S. (3 How.) 87 (1845); *In re Neagle*, 135 U.S. 1, 75 (1890) (federal officer who does an act authorized by federal law that was "no more than what was necessary and proper for him to do, *cannot* be guilty of a crime under [state] law").

[22]*Supra* note 9, at 574.

[23]*Palermo v. Rorex, supra* note 18, at 1272.

[24]Absolute immunity for common law tort liability also has been accorded under *Barr* for a supervisor alleged to have intimidated a subordinate into believing he would be harmed if he left the supervisor's office, *Wallen v. Domm*, 700 F.2d 124 (4th Cir. 1983); for a supervisor alleged to have defrauded the subordinate out of disability benefits, *Oyler v. National Guard Ass'n*, 743 F.2d 545 (7th Cir. 1984); and for a supervisor alleged to have prepared an unsatisfactory performance evaluation in order to harass the subordinate, *Bradley v. Computer Sciences Corp., supra* note 9. Conversely, subordinates have been accorded absolute immunity in a suit by a supervisor alleging that the subordinates defamed him by falsely accusing him of incompetency, *Strothman v. Gefreh*, 739 F.2d 515 (10th Cir. 1984).

[25]484 U.S. 292, 56 USLW 4087 (1988).

federal civilian employee working as a warehouseman who allegedly suffered chemical burns when he inhaled soda ash dust that had spilled from its bag. Plaintiff sued his supervisors in common law tort for negligence, alleging that they should have warned him of the bag's presence and danger.

The district court granted the supervisor's motion to dismiss on grounds of absolute immunity after finding that the alleged tort was committed while the supervisors were acting within the scope of their employment. The district court held that "any federal employee is entitled to absolute immunity for ordinary torts committed within the scope of their jobs."[26]

In affirming the Eighth Circuit's reversal of the trial court for failing to consider whether the challenged conduct was discretionary, in addition to being within the scope of the supervisors' duties, the Supreme Court reasserted the importance of the discretionary function component of the absolute immunity doctrine as set forth in *Barr*. The Court reasoned that the purpose of official immunity, which is to promote effective government by alleviating the fear of vexatious lawsuits, would not be furthered if the tortious conduct were nondiscretionary in character.[27] The Court observed that "[i]t is only when officials exercise decisionmaking discretion that potential liability may shackle 'the fearless, vigorous, and effective administration of policies of government.'"[28]

The Court did not address in *Westfall* whether the alleged tortious failure to advise plaintiff of the soda ash bags was discretionary conduct. Significantly, however, the Court rejected the government's argument that the discretionary component of absolute immunity is satisfied as long as the official exercises "minimal discretion."[29] The Court eschewed the argument because, if accepted, it would all but eliminate the discretionary component of absolute immunity since "virtually all official acts involve some modicum of choice."[30]

Westfall was significant in its emphasis on the discretionary function component. For many years following *Barr*, the emphasis in evaluating absolute immunity defenses had been placed on the scope of authority component, with little attention given to whether challenged conduct was ministerial or discretionary. This greatly facilitated securing dismissal on absolute immunity grounds. The Court's renewed emphasis on requiring

---

[26]*Id.*, 56 USLW at 4088; accord *General Elec. Co. v. United States*, 813 F.2d 1273, 1276–77 (4th Cir. 1987); *Poolman v. Nelson*, 802 F.2d 304, 307 (8th Cir. 1986).
[27]56 USLW at 4088.
[28]*Id.*
[29]*Id.*, at 4089.
[30]*Id.*

the federal defendant to prove the existence of discretionary conduct presented the plaintiff with a potentially important avenue for resisting absolute immunity defenses insofar as he could establish that the challenged conduct involved, at best, only a "modicum of choice."

Congress' Response

In response to *Westfall*, Congress statutorily eliminated the holding's discretionary conduct test by amending the Federal Tort Claims Act to make the United States the exclusive defendant in common law tort suits against federal employees irrespective of whether the conduct giving rise to the lawsuit was discretionary.[31] Under the legislation, the United States would become the exclusive defendant in such suits so long as the challenged conduct was undertaken by the federal employee within the scope of his employment. Thus, where an employee brings a personal damage action against his supervisor on a common law tort theory, as in the case of libel and slander, and the Attorney General certifies that the supervisor was acting within the scope of his employment, the new legislation mandates that the United States be substituted as the exclusive defendant in the action.

The legislation removes an employee's previous ability to sue his supervisor directly for alleged common law torts if the Attorney General certifies that the supervisor was acting within the scope of his employment. Where, however, the Attorney General declines to make the certification, a direct action against the supervisor remains.[32]

The 1988 amendments both enhance and diminish an employee's earlier recourse against a tortious supervisor. In the event the employee prevails on his action against the newly substituted United States, a deep pocket exists to satisfy any monetary judgment. The amendments, however, require that the employee pursue his tort claim against the United States under the provisions of the Federal Tort Claims Act.[33] The Act excepts certain categories of conduct from recovery.[34] Among these are claims arising out of assault, battery, libel, and slander.[35] Since the discretionary conduct requirement of *Westfall* is no longer germane to triggering the provisions of the Federal Employees Liability Reform Act, an

---

[31]Federal Employees Liability Reform and Tort Compensation Act of 1988, Pub. L. No. 100-694, amending 28 U.S.C. 2679.

[32]In such a case, and where the court denies the supervisor's petition to find that he was acting within the scope of employment, a supervisor's ability to claim absolute immunity as a defense to the action is effectively lost. See *infra* note 38.

[33]28 U.S.C. 2671 *et seq*.

[34]28 U.S.C. 2680.

[35]28 U.S.C. 2680(h).

employee may well forfeit the possibility of recovering money damages for the nondiscretionary assault or slander of a supervisor so long as the supervisor's conduct was undertaken within the scope of his employment.[36]

Assault and Battery

The enactment of the Federal Employees Liability Reform Act likely will reduce significantly an employee's ability to maintain any type of common law tort action directly against his supervisor. It should be expected that in most cases the Attorney General will certify that the supervisor was acting within the scope of employment thus requiring that the United States be substituted as the exclusive defendant.

Common law tort suits based on allegations of assault and battery, however, may present fact situations sufficiently egregious that the Attorney General will decline to certify that the supervisor was acting within the scope of employment.[37] In such situations, the supervisor may petition the court to find that he or she was, in fact, within the scope of employment.[38] The supervisor's task, however, may be a difficult one. Prior to enactment of the Federal Employees Liability Reform Act, as well as the Supreme Court's decision in *Westfall v. Erwin*,[39] there had been a growing reluctance in some circuits to accept the argument that supervisory conduct rising to the level of assault and battery could ever be conduct within the outer perimeter of a supervisor's duty.

The Court of Appeals for the District of Columbia Circuit concluded in *McKinney v. Whitfield*[40] that an FAA budget supervisor was acting

---

[36]Following substitution of the United States in cases brought on claims of a supervisor's alleged assault and battery, the government may move to dismiss arguing that the claims are barred by the assault and battery exception to the Federal Tort Claims Act, 28 U.S.C. 2680(h). The Supreme Court, however, has yet to expressly rule on whether this section bars such claims where the assault and battery is alleged to arise from the government's negligent hiring, training, or supervision of the offending supervisor. *Sheridan v. United States*, 487 U.S. ___, 56 USLW 4761 (1988). Compare *United States v. Shearer*, 473 U.S. 52 (1985) (plurality concludes 2680(h) does bar such actions).

[37]In such situations, the supervisor is given the statutory right to seek judicial review of the Attorney General's declination to certify. 28 U.S.C. 2679(d)(3), as amended.

[38]Where the Attorney General has declined to certify that the supervisor was acting within the scope of employment, the supervisor may petition the court to find that he was so acting. 28 U.S.C. 2679(d)(3), as amended. If he prevails, the United States is substituted as a defendant. If the supervisor fails to convince the trial court that he was acting within the scope of employment, he may, in theory, attempt to argue entitlement to absolute immunity. In practice, however, the court's refusal to find that the supervisor was acting within the scope of employment will effectively preclude any reliance by the supervisor on absolute immunity which is available only where a defendant is found to have acted within the scope of employment.

[39]484 U.S. 292, 56 USLW 4087 (1988).

[40]736 F.2d 766, 769–70 (D.C. Cir. 1984).

outside the scope of his authorized duties when he allegedly pushed an office chair into his subordinate's leg in order to prevent her from leaving his office during a discussion concerning her furlough. The court of appeals reasoned that the outer perimeter test was not met because federal personnel regulations did not sanction the use of physical force by desk supervisors. The Third Circuit reached a similar result in *Araujo v. Welch*,[41] holding that an EEO officer was not absolutely immune from a common law tort based on assault and battery because, if true, the allegation that he poked his subordinate in her chest, would constitute conduct outside the scope of his employment.

The suggestion in *Whitfield* and *Araujo* that *Barr* absolute immunity fails to apply any time a supervisor's battery is alleged was rejected by the Fifth Circuit in *Dretar v. Smith*,[42] where a supervisor was sued for slamming his office door behind plaintiff causing some injury to her back. The court held that *Barr* would provide absolute immunity from a common law tort suit alleging assault and battery except in cases where the supervisor's battery causes severe injuries "grossly disproportionate" to the need for action under the circumstances, and the battery is motivated by malice. The court explained that the "slight battery" sustained by the plaintiff was a "price that we must pay to free our public officials from the fear of defending vindictive and ill-founded damage suits."[43]

While these assault cases turned, in large measure, on the scope of authority component of absolute immunity, those decisions siding with the supervisor must now be reassessed in light of *Westfall*. In short, the court must examine whether exercise of the challenged supervisory conduct comprises more than a "modicum of choice."[44] If it does not, the supervisor's efforts to convince the court that his or her challenged conduct was within the scope of employment will likely fail.[45]

Constitutional Tort Liability

For 75 years after *Spalding v. Vilas*,[46] damage actions against federal officers in their individual capacities were relatively rare for the

[41]742 F.2d 802, 806 (3d Cir. 1984).
[42]752 F.2d 1015, 1017 (5th Cir. 1985); accord *Palermo v. Rorex*, 806 F.2d 1266, 1272 (5th Cir.), *cert. denied*, 56 USLW 3243 (1988).
[43]752 F.2d at 1017.
[44]*Westfall v. Erwin, supra* note 39, 56 USLW at 4089.
[45]As noted in *supra* note 38, a supervisor will only be required to make this showing when the Attorney General has declined to certify that the supervisor was acting within scope. 28 U.S.C. 2679(d)(3), as amended.
[46]161 U.S. 483 (1896).

obvious reason that such suits normally took the form of common law tort actions for which the officers enjoyed an absolute immunity. This insulation from personal liability was dramatically altered by the Supreme Court in 1971, with its ruling in *Bivens v. Six Unknown Named Agents*[47] holding that federal officials could be sued for violations of certain constitutional rights. The Court reasoned that where a federal official's conduct had violated another's constitutional rights, and no common law tort theory existed to remedy the injury, the aggrieved party should be given a separate cause for recovery on the violation of the constitutional right alone.[48]

Bivens, itself, only addressed the question of remedy and provided no guidance as to what, if any, immunity might protect an official from a constitutional tort action.[49] Given the favored position that federal constitutional guarantees have in our law, lower courts tended to reject the argument that federal officers sued in constitutional tort should be accorded the same absolute immunity available to them in the face of common law tort suits.[50] Instead, they developed a qualified immunity requiring the federal defendant to show both a good-faith belief in the lawfulness of his challenged conduct and an objective demonstration that this belief was a reasonable one.[51]

The Supreme Court agreed with this approach in 1978, with its decision in *Butz v. Economou*.[52] The Court held that qualified immunity would be the general rule for constitutional tort actions, although some officials performing special functions still would be protected by absolute immunity in the face of constitutional tort suits, such as federal judges and prosecutors. Further refinement of these principles came with the Court's opinion four years later in *Harlow v. Fitzgerald*,[53] where the Court modified the qualified immunity test by eliminating the subjective, good-faith component in favor of retaining only the objective reasonable standard.

---

[47]403 U.S. 388, 397 (1971).
[48]*Id.*, at 394–95.
[49]*Id.*, at 397–98.
[50]*Black v. United States*, 534 F.2d 524 (2d Cir. 1976); *States Marine Lines v. Shultz*, 498 F.2d 1146 (4th Cir. 1974); *Mark v. Groff*, 521 F.2d 1376 (9th Cir. 1975); *G.M. Leasing Corp. v. United States*, 560 F.2d 1011 (10th Cir. 1977); *Apton v. Wilson*, 506 F.2d 83 (D.C. Cir. 1974).
[51]*States Marine Lines v. Shultz, supra* note 50, at 1158–59; *Apton v. Wilson, supra* note 50, at 90–95; *Mark v. Groff, supra* note 50, at 1379–80.
[52]438 U.S. 478 (1978).
[53]457 U.S. 800 (1982).

Bivens and the Federal Supervisor

Bivens v. Six Unknown Named Agents[54] involved Fourth Amendment violations against federal law enforcement officers by a private citizen. Although the Supreme Court did not address the applicability of its remedy to violations of other constitutional rights, lower courts began expanding *Bivens* to other portions of the Bill of Rights.[55] Subsequent Supreme Court decisions viewed with approval the application of *Bivens* to rights beyond the Fourth Amendment.[56]

For the federal supervisor, *Bivens* has meant potential constitutional tort liability for a variety of personnel actions with principal emphasis on those implicating freedom of speech guaranteed by the First Amendment, equal protection and due process secured by the Fifth Amendment, and privacy interests protected by the Ninth Amendment.

First Amendment Bivens *Actions*

First Amendment *Bivens* actions brought by federal employees against supervisors customarily arise as a consequence of disciplinary actions occasioned by an employee's unauthorized public statements about agency affairs. The employee will argue that the disciplinary action was undertaken in retaliation for the employee's whistleblowing protected by the First Amendment.[57] In *Bush v. Lucas*,[58] for example, a National Aeronautics and Space Administration (NASA) engineer was disciplined for giving television interviews that were highly critical of his agency. After successfully pursuing available administrative remedies under the CSRA, which resulted in reinstatement and back pay, the engineer

---

[54]*Supra* note 47.

[55]*States Marine Lines v. Shultz, supra* note 50, at 1156–57 (*Bivens* extended to Fifth Amendment claims); accord *Apton v. Wilson, supra* note 50, at 93; *Paton v. LaPrade*, 524 F.2d 862, 870 (3d Cir. 1975) (*Bivens* extended to First Amendment).

[56]*Davis v. Passman*, 442 U.S. 228 (1979) (*Bivens* extended to Fifth Amendment claims); *Carlson v. Green*, 446 U.S. 14 (1980) (*Bivens* extended to Eighth Amendment claims).

[57]Employee speech pertaining to internal agency matters in which the public would normally not have an interest, generally does not enjoy the same level of protection as more familiar forms of public speech. The Supreme Court has developed a balancing test for assessing the character of employee speech in order to evaluate the propriety of agency limitations on it. See *Connick v. Myers*, 461 U.S. 138 (1983); *Mt. Healthy City School Dist. Bd. of Educ. v. Doyle*, 429 U.S. 274 (1977); *Perry v. Sindermann*, 408 U.S. 593 (1972); *Pickering v. Board of Educ.*, 391 U.S. 563 (1968).

[58]462 U.S. 367 (1983).

initiated a *Bivens* action for alleged First Amendment violations against the director of the NASA center employing the plaintiff.[59]

First Amendment *Bivens* actions have also been brought against supervisors for refusing to rehire an employee because of union activities,[60] allegedly taking adverse action against an employee for representing a fellow employee in a grievance matter,[61] and terminating an employee for allegedly having a romantic relationship with an administrative law judge.[62]

Fifth Amendment Bivens *Actions*

Fifth Amendment *Bivens* actions typically are brought on the basis of discrimination or the deprivation of due process. As discussed in the following section, the viability of sex, race, or age discrimination suits against executive branch supervisors based on a Fifth Amendment *Bivens* theory largely has been voided by the Supreme Court's decision in *Bush v. Lucas*[63] insofar as adequate alternative statutory remedies are available to the subordinate. Where such remedies are unavailable, Fifth Amendment discrimination actions under *Bivens* may be pursued, as in the case of sex discrimination complaints against members of the legislative or judicial branches,[64] or discrimination of a type not covered by statutory remedies.[65]

Fifth Amendment *Bivens* actions based on due process violations customarily challenge alleged procedural deficiencies in personnel actions.[66] Examples include suits charging the failure to accord plaintiff a

---

[59]Similarly, in *Nixon v. Fitzgerald*, 457 U.S. 731 (1982) and *Harlow v. Fitzgerald*, *supra* note 53, a civilian management analyst with the Department of the Air Force initiated a First Amendment *Bivens* action against the President and his aides for allegedly conspiring to have him discharged in retaliation for his congressional testimony critical of cost-overruns incurred by the Air Force in the development of an aircraft.

[60]*Gaj v. Postal Serv.*, 800 F.2d 64 (3d Cir. 1986).

[61]*McCollum v. Bolger*, 794 F.2d 602 (11th Cir. 1986).

[62]*Germane v. Heckler*, 804 F.2d 366, 369 (7th Cir. 1986); compare *Kotarski v. Cooper*, 799 F.2d 1342 (9th Cir.), *judgment vacated* 56 USLW 3879 (1938), *rev'd on other grounds*, 866 F.2d 311 (9th Cir. 1989), where similar allegations were presented as a deprivation of Ninth Amendment privacy rights.

[63]*Supra* note 58.

[64]*Davis v. Passman, supra* note 56 (Fifth Amendment *Bivens* action by congressional employee against her employing congressman on grounds of sex discrimination).

[65]*Kotarski v. Cooper, supra* note 62, 799 F.2d at 1345 (Navy civilian employee brings Fifth Amendment *Bivens* action as consequence of his demotion allegedly motivated, *inter alia*, by discriminatory bias against his personal sexual life style).

[66]Less frequently, Fifth Amendment *Bivens* actions are based on the alleged deprivation of property interests in either existing or prospective employment situations. *Kizas v. Webster*, 707 F.2d 524, 31 FEP Cases 905 (D.C. Cir. 1983), *cert. denied*, 464 U.S. 1042, 35 FEP Cases 1084 (1984) (FBI clerks alleged unconstitutional taking of vested right to special preference in selection for position of special agent).

hearing in a termination proceeding,[67] the termination of a temporary promotion,[68] and the involuntary reassignment of a plaintiff with no change in pay.[69] Fifth Amendment due process actions may also be predicated upon conduct ancillary to an adverse personnel proceeding such as a supervisor's alleged dissemination of defamatory statements regarding plaintiff during a termination proceeding.[70] Each of these liability suits challenges a supervisor's alleged failure to accord a plaintiff the perceived procedural notices, rights, and remedies allegedly needed to avert the aggrieved event.

Miscellaneous Bivens Actions

In addition to First and Fifth amendment *Bivens* actions against federal supervisors, employees have pursued constitutional tort actions against their superiors under the Fourth,[71] Eighth,[72] and Ninth amendments.[73]

Bush-Carlson Limitation on Bivens

The Supreme Court accepted plaintiff's contention in *Bivens* that personal liability should flow from constitutional violations, in part, because plaintiff was without an alternate adequate remedy.[74] Additionally, the Court noted that the case involved "no special factors counselling hesitation in the absence of affirmative action by Congress,"[75] thereby suggesting that congressional action of some sort could restrict the availability of a constitutional tort action. The Court reiterated this notion nine years later in *Carlson v. Green*.[76] The Court added, in *Carlson*, that a

---

[67]*Broussard v. Postal Serv.*, 674 F.2d 1103 (5th Cir. 1982).
[68]*Pinar v. Dole*, 747 F.2d 899 (4th Cir.), *cert. denied*, 471 U.S. 1016 (1985).
[69]*Broadway v. Block*, 694 F.2d 979 (5th Cir. 1982).
[70]*Doe v. Department of Justice*, 753 F.2d 1092 (D.C. Cir. 1985).
[71]*Schowengerdt v. General Dynamics Corp.*, 823 F.2d 1328 (9th Cir. 1987) (Fourth Amendment *Bivens* claim based on nonconsensual search of employee's desk).
[72]*Palermo v. Rorex*, 806 F.2d 1266, 1271–72 (5th Cir.), *cert. denied*, 56 USLW 3243 (1988) (Eighth Amendment claim rejected in employee disciplinary context because Amendment is limited to only criminal actions following conviction).
[73]*Kotarski v. Cooper, supra* note 62 (alleged retaliatory demotion for living out of wedlock with woman friend claimed to violate plaintiff's Ninth Amendment privacy rights).
[74]In *Bivens*, the plaintiff alleged that federal agents had arrested him and searched his home without a warrant or probable cause resulting in his humiliation, embarrassment, and mental suffering. He claimed damages on the theory that the alleged violation of his Fourth Amendment rights, occasioned by the arrest and search, provided an independent basis for relief. Under the circumstances of the case, equitable relief was not sufficiently remedial. As noted by Justice Harlan, concurring in the judgment, for "people in Bivens' shoes, it is damages or nothing." 403 U.S. 388, 410 (1971).
[75]*Id.*, at 396.
[76]*Supra* note 56, at 18–19.

Bivens action could be defeated, as well, where Congress has provided an alternate and exclusive statutory remedy. [77]

Carlson took on particular importance for the federal supervisor three years later in 1983, when the Supreme Court ruled in *Bush v. Lucas*[78] that the CSRA presented "special factors counselling hesitation" earlier referred to in *Bivens* and *Carlson*. Although Congress had not directed expressly that the CSRA should be a federal employee's exclusive remedy for vindicating adverse personnel actions implicating the denial of constitutional rights, the Supreme Court found that it evinced such a high level of congressional intent to regulate closely federal employment, that it justified precluding *Bivens* actions for conduct reviewable under the Act. [79] In short, the Act provided federal employees with an elaborate remedial system to redress alleged constitutional wrongdoing, something unavailable to the plaintiff in *Bivens*.

The Supreme Court in *Bush* did not reach the question of whether *Bivens* actions remained available in the case of personnel actions not embraced by the CSRA. As the Court noted, "[n]ot all personnel actions are covered by the Act."[80] There is no provision, for example, to appeal either suspensions for 14 days or less,[81] or adverse actions against probationary employees. [82]

In 1988, the Supreme Court revisited this area in *Schweiker v. Chilicky*.[83] At issue was whether a comprehensive remedial scheme Congress had devised for allowing applicants to appeal the denial of Social Security disability benefits precluded disappointed applicants from suing government officials under *Bivens* for the alleged unconstitutional denial of benefits. The Court held against the applicants. Relying on its analysis in *Bush*, the Court noted that "[t]he absence of statutory relief for a constitutional violation, for example, does not by any means necessarily imply that courts should award money damages against the officers responsible for the violation."[84] Additionally, it urged "appropriate judicial deference to indications that congressional inaction [in creating a monetary remedy for constitutional violations] has not been inadvertent."[85]

---

[77]*Id.*, at 19.
[78]*Supra* note 58, at 388–89.
[79]*Id.*, at 385, 388–89.
[80]*Id.*, at 385 n.28.
[81]5 U.S.C. 7503 (1982 ed.).
[82]5 U.S.C. 7511 (1982 ed.).
[83]56 USLW 4767 (1988).
[84]*Id.*, at 4769.
[85]*Id.*, at 4770.

Application of *Bush-Carlson*

Lower courts have applied *Bush* and *Carlson* to deny *Bivens* actions against federal supervisors for a variety of personnel practices regulated by statutes in addition to the CSRA, including those related to allegations of race discrimination,[86] and age discrimination.[87] At least two circuits have also relied upon *Carlson* and *Bush* to defeat *Bivens* actions where collective bargaining agreements provided the federal employee with an adequate means for redressing alleged constitutional injuries by supervisors.[88]

The circuits initially split, however, over the application of *Carlson* and *Bush* to personnel practices that Congress has elected to exclude from statutory regulation. Prior to the Supreme Court's decision in *Chilicky*, the Ninth Circuit had ruled, for example, that in the case of alleged First Amendment violations on the part of a supervisor, the CSRA did not preclude a *Bivens* action by a probationary subordinate because of the limited nature of remedies afforded by the Act to probationary personnel.[89] The majority opinion of a divided panel explained that under *Bush*, a congressional enactment must provide a "meaningful remedy" for the alleged constitutional conduct in order to preempt a *Bivens* action.[90] The majority held that in the case of alleged prohibited personnel practices lodged by probationary employees, the CSRA, including the remedial provisions of the Merit Systems Protection Board and the Special Counsel, allowed for the application of too much discretion by reviewing personnel to be a meaningful remedy.[91] The dissent, however, concluded that it is the existence of a comprehensive congressional scheme for dealing with prohibited personnel practices that "counsels hesitation" under *Bush* and not the nature of a specific remedy in a given case.[92]

The District of Columbia, Seventh, and Eighth circuits reached conclusions similar to that of the majority in *Kotarski*,[93] while the Fourth,

---

[86]*Daly-Murphy v. Winston*, 820 F.2d 1470 (9th Cir. 1987); *Heaney v. Veterans Admin.*, 756 F.2d 1215 (5th Cir. 1985) (Title VII of Civil Rights Act precludes *Bivens* actions against federal supervisors for alleged racial discrimination).

[87]*Ellis v. Postal Serv.*, 784 F.2d 835 (7th Cir. 1986) (holding that Age Discrimination in Employment Act, 29 U.S.C. 621, *et seq.*, precludes *Bivens* remedy against federal supervisors for alleged age discrimination).

[88]*McCollum v. Bolger*, 794 F.2d 602 (11th Cir. 1986) (postal union collective bargaining agreement affords sufficient protection to preclude *Bivens* remedy); accord *Harding v. Postal Serv.*, 802 F.2d 766 (4th Cir. 1986).

[89]*Kotarski v. Cooper*, 799 F.2d 1342, 1348–49 (9th Cir. 1988).

[90]*Id.*

[91]*Id.*

[92]*Id.*, at 1351.

[93]*Williams v. Internal Revenue Serv.*, 745 F.2d 702 (D.C. Cir. 1984) (*per curiam*); *Doe v. Department of Justice*, 753 F.2d 1092, 1118 n.2 (D.C. Cir. 1985) (Wald, J., dissenting)

Fifth, and Tenth circuits sided with the dissenting opinion's analysis.[94] The Supreme Court's subsequent ruling in *Chilicky*, however, resulted in the Ninth, District of Columbia, and Eighth circuits abandoning the majority's approach in *Kotarski*.[95] *Chilicky* reaffirmed the principle that a comprehensive legislative scheme to remedy a constitutional wrongdoing, such as the CSRA, can preempt a *Bivens* action even if there is no provision to recover monetary damages for constitutional wrongdoing.

In reversing an earlier ruling favoring the creation of a *Bivens* remedy by subordinates alleging promotion discrimination, the Eighth Circuit noted in *McIntosh v. Turner*,[96] that *Chilicky* creates "a sort of presumption against judicial recognition of direct *[Bivens]* actions for violations of the Constitution by federal officials or employees." The District of Columbia Circuit reached a similar conclusion in *Spagnola v. Mathis*[97] where it concluded that in light of *Chilicky*,

> courts must withhold their power to fashion damages remedies when Congress has put in place a comprehensive system to administer public rights, has "not inadvertently" omitted damages remedies for certain claimants, and has not plainly expressed an intention that the courts preserve *Bivens* remedies.

Circuit court interpretation of *Chilicky* would thus appear to have greatly diminished a supervisor's *Bivens* liability where a disgruntled subordinate enjoys at least some sort of remedial opportunity under the CSRA, no matter how small or nonmonetary.[98]

Immunity From Constitutional Tort Liability

In light of the preeminent position held by the Constitution in our federal legal system, courts generally have declined to accord federal

---

(*Bush* should not apply to *Bivens* action by former Department of Justice attorney against her supervisors because she is member of excepted civil service and, thus, not entitled to all remedies of CSRA); *Egger v. Phillips*, 710 F.2d 292, 297–98 (7th Cir.) (en banc), *cert. denied*, 464 U.S. 918 (1983) (exemption of FBI agents from civil service regulations permits *Bivens* action); *McIntosh v. Weinberger*, 810 F.2d 1411, 45 FEP 398 (8th Cir. 1987).

[94]*Pinar v. Dole*, 747 F.2d 899, 907–09 (4th Cir.), *cert. denied*, 471 U.S. 1016 (1985) (*Bush* precludes *Bivens* action to challenge temporary promotion allegedly terminated by employee's whistleblowing); *Carroll v. United States*, 721 F.2d 155 (5th Cir.), *cert. denied*, 467 U.S. 1241 (1984) (*Bush* denies *Bivens* action for reinstatement and back pay where administrative remedy is available only for reinstatement but not back pay); *Heaney v. Veterans Admin.*, supra note 86; *Franks v. Nimmo*, 796 F.2d 1230 (10th Cir. 1986).

[95]*Kotarski v. Cooper*, 866 F.2d 311 (9th Cir. 1989); *Spagnola v. Mathis*, 859 F.2d 223 (D.C. Cir. 1988); *McIntosh v. Turner*, 861 F.2d 524 (8th Cir. 1988).

[96]*McIntosh v. Turner*, supra note 95, at 526.

[97]859 F.2d at 228; accord, *Kotarski v. Cooper*, supra note 95.

[98]This would include, for example, the limited right of petitioning the Office of Special Counsel of the Merit Systems Protection Board for corrective action. *McIntosh v. Turner*, supra note 95, at 526.

personnel absolute immunity from constitutional tort liability under *Bivens*. Absolute immunity, in fact, has been limited to rare instances in which the responsibilities of a federal official or employee are sufficiently special and important that the public interest demands complete protection even in the face of alleged constitutional wrongdoing.

In all other situations, federal employees are accorded a lesser degree of protection from constitutional tort liability known as qualified immunity. Despite its less encompassing shield, it has proven a significant barrier to aggrieved plaintiffs, including federal employees pursuing *Bivens* actions against their supervisors.

Absolute Immunity

The question of whether absolute immunity is available to protect a federal officer from charges of constitutional wrongdoing, turns on whether his duties encompass "special functions" so essential to the conduct of government that a serious erosion in government efficiency would result without absolute immunity.[99] Guidance in resolving this question typically is drawn from the Constitution, common law, and federal statutes.[100]

Under this "special function" analysis, absolute immunity from constitutional tort liability has been accorded federal officials and employees responsible for initiating, pursuing, and adjudicating criminal and administrative prosecutions, including judges and prosecutors.[101] The immunity is available only insofar as the judge or prosecutor is engaging in an adjudicative or prosecutive task.[102] Where a judge,

---

[99]*Butz v. Economou*, 438 U.S. 478, 508 (1978).

[100]*Nixon v. Fitzgerald*, 457 U.S. 731, 747–48 (1982); *Harlow v. Fitzgerald*, 457 U.S. 800, 813 n.20 (1982).

[101]*Stump v. Sparkman*, 435 U.S. 349, 356–57 (1978) (judges absolutely immune except when acting in "clear absence of all jurisdiction"); *Imbler v. Pachtman*, 424 U.S. 409, 431 (1975) (prosecutor absolutely immune for conduct during trial); *Gray v. Bell*, 712 F.2d 490, 502–03 (D.C. Cir. 1983) (absolute immunity for prosecutorial conduct in connection with grand jury proceedings); *Taylor v. Kavanagh*, 640 F.2d 450, 453 (2d Cir. 1981) (absolute immunity accorded in connection with plea bargaining process); but see *Forsyth v. Kleindienst*, 599 F.2d 1203, 1215 (3d Cir.), *cert. denied sub nom. Mitchell v. Forsyth*, 453 U.S. 913 (1981) (absolute immunity for prosecutors does not extend to securing evidence unnecessary to decision to initiate prosecution).

Absolute immunity has been accorded, as well, in connection with administrative adjudicative and prosecutive functions of the Executive Branch. *Butz v. Economou*, 438 U.S. 478, 511–17 (1978). See also *Jayvee Brand, Inc. v. United States*, 721 F.2d 385, 395 n.8 (D.C. Cir. 1983) (suggesting that members of regulatory commissions are protected by quasi-judicial absolute immunity when they adjudicate set of facts under a statutory standard).

[102]*Stump v. Sparkman, supra* note 101; *Forsyth v. Kleindienst, supra* note 101.

however, is charged by a subordinate with constitutional wrongdoing in the performance of a supervisory personnel function, the Supreme Court has held that absolute immunity is not available to protect the judge.[103] A similar result is to be expected in the case of prosecutors. In both cases, no special functions justifying absolute immunity are implicated or jeopardized by the threat of liability in the discharge of internal personnel matters.[104]

Where, however, a supervisor is charged with the administration of a critically sensitive program, absolute immunity may be available to preclude *Bivens* actions by subordinates in extreme cases where the threat of such actions could have a dangerously delibitating effect on the program.[105] As a general matter, however, federal supervisors sued by subordinates under *Bivens* will not be accorded absolute immunity from liability.

Qualified Immunity

In the absence of absolute immunity, federal supervisors, like virtually all federal officers and employees, are accorded a qualified immunity from suit based on a *Bivens* claim.[106] Prior to 1982, the immunity required satisfying a two-part test. The first portion, known as the subjective standard, required a federal defendant to demonstrate that he believed in good faith that his challenged conduct did not violate the plaintiff's clearly established constitutional rights.[107] The second portion of the qualified immunity test, known as the objective standard, required a demonstration that the belief was reasonable, which is to say that the

---

[103]*Forrester v. White*, 484 U.S. 219, 45 FEP Cases 1112 (1988) (state judge not entitled to absolute immunity for demoting and discharging probation officer under his authority); accord *Guercio v. Brody*, 814 F.2d 1115 (6th Cir.), *cert. denied*, 56 USLW 3482 (1988) (absolute immunity not available to federal judge for firing secretary because of alleged whistleblowing); *McMillan v. Svetanoff*, 793 F.2d 149, 40 FEP Cases 1737 (7th Cir.), *cert. denied*, 43 FEP Cases 80 (1986) (state court judge not shielded by absolute judicial immunity for firing his court reporter).

[104]See, e.g., *Davis v. Passman*, 442 U.S. 228 (1979), where the Supreme Court held that absolute speech or debate immunity was unavailable to protect a congressman from liability in the case of sex discrimination charges by a former staff member.

[105]*Tigue v. Swaim*, 585 F.2d 909, 914 (8th Cir. 1978) (special functions justify absolute immunity in light of plaintiff's position to control launch of nuclear weapons); see also *Lawrence v. Acree*, 665 F.2d 1319, 1327 (D.C. Cir. 1981) (strong governmental interest in frank assessments of employee work performance justifies absolute immunity from 42 U.S.C. 1985(3) actions).

[106]As noted earlier, the question of immunity for federal supervisors sued in *Bivens* actions need never be reached if adequate, alternate statutory remedies exist of the kind recognized in *Bush* and *Chilicky*.

[107]*Butz v. Economou*, 438 U.S. 478, 506–07 (1978).

contested conduct did not violate clearly established constitutional rights of which a reasonable person knew or should have known.[108] As framed, the subjective standard turned on issues of fact while the objective standard constituted a question of law.

The qualified immunity test was significantly altered by the Supreme Court in 1982, when it discarded the subjective, or good-faith, portion of the test. Reacting to the difficulties encountered by federal defendants trying quickly to terminate distracting *Bivens* actions on motions for summary judgment, the Supreme Court in *Harlow v. Fitzgerald*[109] sought to streamline qualified immunity by discarding the subjective standard. No longer would federal personnel have to demonstrate whether they held a good-faith belief in the lawfulness of their conduct. Instead, to secure qualified immunity from a constitutional tort action, federal defendants need only demonstrate that as a matter of law their challenged discretionary conduct did not violate any clearly established constitutional rights of which a reasonable person would have known.[110] The Supreme Court reasoned that reliance on an objective reasonableness standard, as measured by reference to clearly established law at the time of the challenged conduct, should avoid the need to adjudicate factual issues that often delay the early termination of a lawsuit.[111] Emphasizing the nonfactual orientation of its amended qualified immunity standard, the *Harlow* Court additionally ruled that litigation discovery should not be allowed until the threshold immunity question is resolved.[112]

For federal personnel, including federal supervisors, qualified immunity under *Harlow* has meant a significant increase in protection from *Bivens* liability. Federal defendants need only show that their conduct did not violate clearly established constitutional principles. The federal defendant sued for constitutional violations does not lose qualified immunity merely because his or her conduct violated some statutory or administrative provision.[113] Additionally, a court's inquiry is normally limited to objective considerations in light of *Harlow's* seeming rejection of any inquiry into the defendant's state of mind.[114]

Courts are still developing guidance on what is meant by the phrase "clearly established" as used to modify constitutional rights. The Supreme Court has noted that for a constitutional right to be clearly

[108]*Id.*; see also *Procunier v. Navarette*, 434 U.S. 555, 562 (1978).
[109]457 U.S. 800, 818 (1982).
[110]*Id.*
[111]*Id.*
[112]*Id.*
[113]*Davis v. Scherer*, 468 U.S. 183, 195–96 (1984).
[114]457 U.S. 800, 819 (1982).

established, "the right must be sufficiently clear that a reasonable official would understand that what he is doing violates that right."[115] This is not to say, however, that an official action is protected by qualified immunity "unless the very action in question has been held unlawful."[116] Rather, in light of preexisting law, "the unlawfulness must be apparent."[117] Where, however, the constitutional question is sufficiently difficult that judges themselves disagree, it would seem far easier for the federal defendant to demonstrate the absence of any clearly established constitutional right.[118] As long as there is a "legitimate question" about the constitutionality of particular conduct, "it cannot be said that [such conduct] violates clearly established law."[119]

Yet for federal supervisors, the exclusively objective nature of *Harlow* qualified immunity may be overstated. This is especially the case where the existence of a constitutional injury turns on the supervisor's state of mind as in the case of intentional sex or race discrimination. Such discrimination, by its nature, is conduct of intent whose outcome is motivated by constitutionally impermissible standards. In the context of a sex discrimination suit against a county judge, the Eighth Circuit has ruled that *Harlow* qualified immunity is unavailable because the right to be free from invidious discrimination on the basis of sex is a clearly established constitutional right.[120] However, at least one circuit has held that in cases involving a claim of unconstitutional motive, plaintiffs must present in their complaint nonconclusory allegations of evidence of such intent in order to proceed to discovery on the claim.[121]

For the federal supervisor, the issue of whether *Harlow* qualified immunity is available to preclude suits alleging intentional race or sex discrimination normally will not arise. The existence of adequate alter-

---

[115]*Anderson v. Creighton*, 97 L.Ed. 523, 531 (1987).

[116]*Id.*

[117]*Id.*; *People of Three Mile Island v. Nuclear Regulatory Comm'rs*, 747 F.2d 139, 148 (3d Cir. 1984). Accord *Zweibon v. Mitchell*, 720 F.2d 162, 173 (D.C. Cir. 1983).

[118]*Harris v. Young*, 718 F.2d 620, 624 (4th Cir. 1983) ("It would not be fair to hold a[n] . . . official liable for not fulfilling 'clearly established' obligations when a federal Circuit Court of Appeals was unable to unanimously decide the same issue"). See also *McSurely v. McClellan*, 753 F.2d 88, 100 (D.C. Cir. 1985); *Zweibon v. Mitchell*, 720 F.2d 162, 169 (D.C. Cir. 1983).

[119]*Mitchell v. Forsyth*, 472 U.S. 511, 535 n.12 (1985).

[120]*Goodwin v. St. Louis County Circuit Court*, 729 F.2d 541, 546, 34 FEP Cases 347 (8th Cir. 1984); see also *Stathos v. Bowden*, 728 F.2d 15, 19–20, 34 FEP Cases 142 (1st Cir. 1984) (in suit alleging discriminatory purpose, a separate jury instruction on qualified immunity would be "superfluous").

[121]*Hobson v. Wilson*, 737 F.2d 1, 29 (D.C. Cir. 1984) (evidentiary allegations of intent "need not be extensive, but they will have to be sufficiently precise to put defendants on notice of the nature of the claim and enable them to prepare a response and, where appropriate, a summary judgment motion on qualified immunity grounds").

nate statutory remedies, such as the CSRA or Title VII of the Civil Rights Act, will intervene to preclude *Bivens* liability under *Carlson* and *Bush*.[122] Only in cases where such statutory remedies are unavailable might the issue of the immunity's availability be present in *Bivens* actions against federal supervisors.[123] In such cases, the Supreme Court has indicated that "discovery should be tailored specifically to the question" of a defendant's qualified immunity.[124]

Presenting the Immunity Defense

Immunity Motion

Absolute and qualified immunities are affirmative defenses that must be pleaded or the defenses are waived.[125] Once the immunities are pleaded, the circuits differ as to which party bears the burden of persuasion.[126]

The immunities are customarily presented in the context of threshold motions to dismiss or for summary judgment prior to the filing of a responsive pleading.[127] Because the immunity doctrines are designed to protect federal personnel not only from liability but also from the burdens of litigation, the Supreme Court has ruled that discovery should not be permitted until the threshold immunity defenses have been decided.[128]

In preparing a dispositive motion raising immunity defenses, consideration should be given to requesting dismissal on the separate ground that the complaint fails to plead its claims of tortious wrongdoing with sufficient specificity. Unlike the more general notice pleading require-

---

[122]See discussion *supra*, on *Bush-Carlson* limitations to *Bivens* liability.

[123]As noted *supra*, the Supreme Court's ruling in *Schweiker v. Chilicky*, 56 USLW 4767 (1988), may narrow even further this category of cases.

[124]*Anderson v. Creighton*, 97 L.Ed. 523, 535 (1987).

[125]*Gomez v. Toledo*, 446 U.S. 635, 640 (1980) (burden of pleading qualified immunity rests with defendant); But see *Adams v. Gunnell*, 729 F.2d 362, 371 (5th Cir. 1984) (qualified immunity might not be waived if not pleaded where plaintiff is not prejudiced). See also *Hartley v. Fine*, 780 F.2d 1383, 1387 (8th Cir. 1985) (absolute immunity characterized as affirmative defense); accord *Espanola Way Corp. v. Meyerson*, 690 F.2d 827, 829 (11th Cir. 1982).

[126]See *Saldana v. Garza*, 684 F.2d 1159, 1163 n.14 (5th Cir. 1982), and cases there cited.

[127]In order to toll the time established by Rule 12(a), Federal Rules of Civil Procedure, for answering the complaint, a Rule 12(b) motion to dismiss must be filed. Filing only a motion for summary judgment under Rule 56(b) will not toll Rule 12(a) answering requirements. Frequently, immunity defenses are presented in a jointly filed motion to dismiss or, alternatively, for summary judgment.

[128]*Harlow v. Fitzgerald*, *supra* note 109; *Mitchell v. Forsyth*, 472 U.S. 511, 526 (1985).

ments permitted under Rule 8(a) of the Federal Rules of Civil Procedure, claims seeking to hold government employees personally liable in common law or constitutional tort law must present specific allegations of their personal involvement or responsibility.[129] Allegations of common law or constitutional wrongdoing presented in conclusory terms or pitched upon broad allegations of conspiracy will frequently not withstand a motion to dismiss.[130]

As a corollary principle, courts have recognized that a complaint may not state a claim against a supervisory official for a subordinate's misconduct by relying on the doctrine of *respondeat superior*.[131] Instead, a plaintiff must affirmatively allege personal conduct by the supervisor leading to the alleged tortious conduct as, for example, a failure to establish prior procedures for training or supervision resulting in the alleged injury.[132]

Assuming that the complaint adequately presents allegations of wrongdoing with sufficient specificity, the claims should be categorized into common law and constitutional tort claims. Care should be exercised in analyzing constitutional claims to see if they state nothing more than a common law tort. It is not uncommon for a plaintiff to plead a common law tort under the rubric of a *Bivens* action in order to deny the federal defendant the benefit of an absolute immunity defense.[133]

In the event an immunity defense is presented in the context of a summary judgment motion supported by extrinsic evidence, a plaintiff may request discovery to repudiate factual contentions raised in the motion.[134] The Supreme Court's injunction on discovery pending resolution of the immunity defense should be noted.[135] Additionally, several circuits have indicated or suggested that a plaintiff must be prepared to

---

[129]*Elliott v. Perez*, 751 F.2d 1472, 1479 & n.20 (5th Cir. 1985); *Doutit v. Jones*, 641 F.2d 345, 346 (5th Cir. 1981); *Hobson v. Wilson*, 737 F.2d 1, 29–31 (D.C. Cir. 1984); *Ostrer v. Aronwald*, 567 F.2d 553 (2d Cir. 1977).

[130]*Id.*

[131]See, e.g., *Lojuk v. Quandt*, 706 F.2d 1456, 1468 (6th Cir. 1983); *Beard v. O'Neal*, 728 F.2d 894, 900 (7th Cir.), *cert. denied*, 469 U.S. 825 (1984) (FBI agent not liable for acts of informant because agent was not "personally responsible").

[132]*McClelland v. Facteau*, 610 F.2d 693, 696 (10th Cir. 1979).

[133]The Supreme Court has cautioned against this practice. *Paul v. Davis*, 424 U.S. 693 (1976); see also *Beard v. Mitchell*, 604 F.2d 485, 495 (7th Cir. 1979) (*Bivens* claim for violation of substantive due process was actually common law tort claim for wrongful death); *Arnold v. IBM*, 637 F.2d 1350, 1355 (9th Cir. 1981).

[134]Rule 56(f) of the Federal Rules of Civil Procedure permits a party opposing a summary judgment motion to resist on the ground that he or she lacks sufficient facts, absent discovery, to adequately resist the motion.

[135]*Harlow v. Fitzgerald*, 457 U.S. 800, 818 (1982); *Mitchell v. Forsyth*, *supra* note 128.

present a prima facie case of the defendant's wrongdoing before commencing suit.[136]

Immunity Appeal

Denials of motions raising an immunity defense are immediately appealable as final orders under 28 U.S.C. 1291. Such is the case with respect to the denial of motions based on either absolute immunity,[137] or qualified immunity.[138] This result is a recognition that posttrial appeals leave a district court's adverse immunity ruling effectively unreviewable since the federal defendant will have been denied the right to avoid trial, a right that the immunity is designed to confer.[139]

A court of appeals has jurisdiction to consider an immunity appeal even where the district court holds that disputed issues of fact preclude resolution of the issue on a motion for summary judgment.[140] It is less certain that reviewing courts have jurisdiction where the district court allows discovery to go forward without ruling on a pending immunity motion. The federal defendant may consider arguing that such delay constitutes a de facto denial of the motion.[141]

---

[136]*Krohn v. United States*, 742 F.2d 24, 31–32 (1st Cir. 1984); *Miller v. Solem*, 728 F.2d 1020, 1025 n.1 (8th Cir. 1984); *Elliott v. Perez*, 751 F.2d 1472, 1479–82 (5th Cir. 1985); *Capeoman v. Reed*, 754 F.2d 1512 (9th Cir. 1985); *Backlund v. Barnhart*, 778 F.2d 1386, 1389 (9th Cir. 1985) (plaintiff must show "that the particular facts of his case support a claim of clearly established rights").

[137]*Nixon v. Fitzgerald*, 457 U.S. 731, 741–43 (1982).

[138]*Mitchell v. Forsyth*, 472 U.S. 511, 526–27 (1985).

[139]*Id.*

[140]*Id.*

[141]See generally, *San Filippo v. U.S. Trust Co. of New York*, 737 F.2d 246 (2d Cir. 1984) ("both the denial of summary judgment [asserting a claim of absolute immunity] and the order requiring defendants to be deposed are properly before this court under the 'collateral order' doctrine").

Labor Relations

7. Representation and Elections

ROBERT T. SIMMELKJAER

The Federal Service Labor-Management Relations Statute (Title VII of the Civil Service Reform Act of 1978) replaced Executive Order 11491 and its predecessors, Executive Orders 10988 and 10987. Title VII codified and prescribed the labor-management relations rights and obligations of agencies and labor organizations in the federal service.

Available data indicate that as of January 31, 1987, 2,052,924 federal nonpostal employees were covered by the Civil Service Reform Act (CSRA) of which 62 percent (1,266,129) were represented by exclusive labor organizations. Although the number of bargaining units in the Federal Government continues to decline from the peak of 3,608 reported in 1975, attributable mainly to consolidations, the 62 percent union representation figure is an all-time high. Of the employees exclusively represented by a union in 1987, 53 percent (1,208,718) were covered by collective bargaining agreements.[1]

The relative standing of the major federal unions with respect to their representation growth or decline in a period following enactment of CSRA is summarized as follows:[2]

---

[1]Office of Personnel Management, *Union Recognition in the Federal Government Statistical Summary: Summary Reports Within Agencies* (Jan. 1987).

[2]*Id.*, Office of Personnel Management, *Analysis of Data and Report on Union Recognition in the Federal Service*, FPM BULL. (June 24, 1982). The percentages shown in the table are based on total federal service, nonpostal, employment figures which include employees excluded from union coverage under 5 U.S.C. 71. These percentages, therefore, are not indicative of the proportion of union representation among *eligible* federal employees, nor of union *membership*, for which no record is maintained by OPM (emphasis and footnote from *supra*, note 1, at 17).

213

Employees Covered by Exclusive Recognitions by Union

Union	1981	Recognition Units	1987	Recognition Units
American Federation of Government Employees (AFGE)	692,225	1,093	685,368	1,026
National Federation of Federal Employees (NFFE)	136,323	423	151,652	381
National Treasury Employees Union (NTEU)	106,747	28	121,774	45
National Association of Government Employees (NAGE)	75,635	232	68,826	221
Metal Trades Council (MTC)	65,628	49	66,920	46
International Association of Machinists & Aerospace Workers (IAM)	35,596	88	32,532	80
Total	1,112,154	1,913	1,127,072	1,799

The labor relations provisions of the CSRA are administered by the Federal Labor Relations Authority (FLRA). Included among the powers and the duties delegated to the FLRA in section 7105 are (1) to supervise or conduct representation elections to accord exclusive recognition of labor organizations (section 7111); and (2) to determine the appropriate bargaining units (section 7112).

Representation Petitions

The Act gives employees the right to form, join, or assist a labor organization or to refrain from such activities. These rights may be exercised by permitting labor organizations or employees to file a petition to select, decertify, or amend a unit of recognition.

Seven types of petitions are permitted by employees of the federal government, labor organizations, and federal agencies:

1. Exclusive Recognition (RO) cases—petitions for exclusive recognition;
2. Decertification (DR) cases—petitions for decertification of a representative;
3. Agency Representation (RA) cases—agency petitions seeking clarifications of representation matters;
4. Amendment of Certification/Recognition (AC) cases—petitions seeking amendment of recognition or certification;
5. Clarification of Unit (CU) cases—petitions seeking clarification of an existing unit;

6. Dues Allotment (DA) cases—petitions seeking determination of eligibility for dues allotments;

7. Unit Consolidation (UC) cases—petitions for unit consolidation.[3]

Exclusive Recognition (RO Petition)

Typically, a labor organization seeking recognition and the right to represent the employees would petition the FLRA for exclusive recognition. Pursuant to sections 7111 and 7112 of the Statute, an agency shall accord exclusive recognition to a labor organization if the organization has been selected as the representative in a secret ballot election by a majority of the employees in an appropriate unit who cast valid ballots in the election.[4]

Thus, the first step for a labor organization seeking recognition as the exclusive representative under the Act is to file a petition with the Authority alleging that 30 percent of the employees in the appropriate unit support the union (section 7111(b)). Where such a "showing of interest" has been made, the Authority shall investigate the petition, ascertain whether a representation question exists, and conduct a representation hearing. Where the findings of the hearing indicate a representation issue exists, the Authority conducts an election by secret ballot and certifies the results thereof. A labor organization certified as the exclusive representative is required to represent all the employees in the unit and negotiate a collective bargaining agreement on their behalf.

Decertification Petition (DR Petition)

In an appropriate unit for which there is an existing exclusive representative, a petition can be filed by any person alleging that 30 percent of the employees in the unit claim that the exclusive representative is no longer the representative of the majority of employees.[5]

Agency Representation Petition (RA Petition)

An agency or activity may file an RA petition for an election to determine whether a labor organization should cease to be the exclusive

---

[3]*Seventh Annual Report of the Federal Labor Relations Authority and the Federal Service Impasses Panel*, FY 1985, at 12.

[4]Federal Service Labor-Management Relations Statute, Title VII of the Civil Service Reform Act of 1978, (5 U.S.C. 7101–7135), Subchapter II—Rights and Duties of Agencies and Labor Organizations.

[5]*Id.*

representative. A good-faith agency doubt, based upon objective evidence, that the labor organization no longer represents a majority of the employees or that the composition of the unit has changed so that the current unit is not appropriate is a prerequisite.

Clarification of Unit or Amendment of Certification/Recognition (CU and AC Petitions)

A petition can be filed by an agency or labor organization seeking clarification of, or an amendment to, a certification or recognition previously issued. A clarification petition would be appropriate where there is uncertainty about the status of an employee with respect to the bargaining unit or in cases where reorganization has altered the scope of the unit. An amendment of certification would be sought to effect nonsubstantive, technical changes such as a new name for one of the bargaining parties.

In a case brought by the American Federation of Government Employees (AFGE), the union's filing of an AC petition to exclude temporary employees was considered by the Authority despite procedural deficiencies. According to the FLRA, an AC petition is intended to accommodate a nominal change of an activity or an exclusive representative whereas a CU petition is the appropriate mechanism to resolve the bargaining unit status of temporary employees. "A CU petition is intended to clarify, consistent with the parties' intent, the unit inclusions or exclusions after the basic question of representation has been resolved."[6]

Dues Allotment (DA Petition)

Where there is no exclusive representative in an appropriate unit, a labor organization that alleges it represents 10 percent of the employees in the unrepresented unit can petition the Authority to obtain certification of eligibility for dues allotment. Following investigation and upon certification, the agency would be required to negotiate with the labor organization solely concerning the deduction of dues until such time as an exclusive representative was selected.[7]

Unit Consolidation (UC Petition)

Two or more units which are in an agency and for which a labor organization is the exclusive representative may, upon petition by the

---

[6]*Department of the Treasury and AFGE*, 32 FLRA 508 (1988).
[7]Federal Service Labor-Management Relations Statute, *supra* note 4.

labor organization or the agency, be consolidated with or without an election into a single larger unit if the Authority considers the larger unit to be appropriate. An election is unnecessary if both the labor organization and the agency agree, provided 30 percent of the employees in the proposed consolidated unit do not petition the Authority for an election. An election is required if requested by 30 percent of the employees, the labor organization, or the agency.

National Consultation Rights

Under the CSRA, federal agencies may give either exclusive recognition or national consultation rights under section 7113 to unions which meet the appropriate requirements. The granting of national consultation rights indicates that the union is the substantial representative (10 percent or 3,500) of the civilian employees in the specified federal agency and no labor organization has been granted exclusive recognition on an agency basis. This recognition entitles the union so recognized to "be informed of any substantive changes in conditions of employment proposed by the agency" and an opportunity to present its views prior to agency final action.

For example, in *General Service Administration and AFGE*,[8] the Authority found the GSA in violation of the national consultation rights provision when it distributed a memorandum addressing paid parking by GSA employees without notifying the union and providing it with an opportunity to state its views prior to finalizing changes in a substantive employment condition.[9]

Intervention

A labor organization that has been designated by 10 percent of the employees as their representative, has submitted a valid copy of a current or expired collective bargaining agreement, or has submitted other evidence indicating exclusive representation of the employees involved may seek intervention and, if successful, may be placed on the ballot for any election held pursuant to the petition (section 7111(c)).[10] The employees

---

[8]6 FLRA 430 (1981).

[9]*Union Recognition in the Federal Government, supra* note 1, Table E, p. 26, lists unions granted governmentwide consultation rights by granting agency (e.g., OPM, OMB, EEOC, and GSA) and the dates granted.

[10]Federal Service Labor-Management Relations Statute, *supra* note 4.

may select the petitioning labor organization, the intervening labor organization, or no labor organization, affording them considerable latitude in exercising their representational rights.

Procedure

The FLRA has delegated to the General Counsel the responsibility for the processing of representation cases in the regional offices.[11] When representation petitions are filed in the regional offices, investigations are conducted to determine the proper disposition of the case. Initially, disposition of representation cases can result in approval of a consent election agreement, the issuance of a notice of hearing, the issuance of a decision and order, the withdrawal of a petition, or the dismissal of the petition.

A consent election is ordered when the labor organization and agency agree on the unit proposed and sign a contract to this effect with the regional director following his or her preliminary review. The election is conducted to determine whether a majority of the employees desires to be represented by the labor organization which filed the petition. Where the petition is contested by the agency, an intervenor labor organization, or another union alleging representation of the proposed unit, a formal investigative hearing is conducted to resolve disputes (e.g., scope of the unit, employee eligibility, accretion to another unit). The entire record of the hearing is reviewed by the regional director who subsequently drafts a decision and order.

The Authority's delegation of representation decisions to regional directors precludes review of such decisions absent compelling reasons— that is, either clearly erroneous or deemed to have prejudicially affected the rights of any party. Mere disagreement with the regional director's findings will not suffice (section 2422.17, FLRA Rules and Regulations). Subsequent FLRA decisions have reinforced its reluctance, except on narrow grounds, to reverse the representation determination of a regional director. Finally, representation decisions are not appealable to the courts.

---

[11]The General Counsel, who is appointed by the President, with the advice and consent of the Senate, for a term of five years, has direct authority over and responsibility for the employees of the General Counsel including employees in the regional offices of the FLRA.

In *Bureau of Indian Affairs*,[12] the actions of a hearing officer provided the grounds for an Agency application for review of a regional
director's decision. Among the Agency's (activity) contentions were:
substantial questions of law and/or policy with respect to the community of
interest standard, including conflict of interest; hearing officer rulings and
conduct which were deemed prejudicial, specifically, interruption of
management's case; and a regional director's decision which was clearly
erroneous based upon the foregoing. The FLRA found no compelling
reason to grant the Agency's application for review. The hearing officer's
rulings were deemed a matter within the broad discretion afforded and no
evidence was found to support the contention that the rulings interfered
with the presentation of all relevant facts.

During its initial fiscal period, January 1 to September 30, 1979, the
regional offices of the FLRA processed 457 new cases, including
198 petitions for exclusive recognition, 10 decertification petitions,
18 petitions for clarification of a matter relating to representation, 99 petitions for unit clarification, 50 petitions for amendment of certification,
21 unit consolidation petitions, and 11 petitions for determination of
eligibility for dues allotment.[13] During the same period, the FLRA
supervised 123 elections for exclusive recognition. Since October 1983
the number of applications for review in representation cases filed with the
Authority has declined because the decision-making responsibility was
delegated to the Authority's regional directors.[14] To illustrate, there were
27 representation cases pending at the start of FY 1985—a reduction of
59 from the previous year—and only 5 at the end of FY 1985.[15]

Elections

Where representation elections are held they can be of four types:
exclusive recognition (RO), decertification (DR), agency petition (RA),
and unit consolidation (UC).

---

[12]*Bureau of Indian Affairs and National Federation of Federal Employees, Council of
BIA Locals*, 29 FLRA 935 (1987). See also *Department of the Navy, Pearl Harbor Naval
Shipyard Restaurant Sys., Pearl Harbor, Haw. and Service Employees Int'l Union,
Local 556, AFL-ClO*, 28 FLRA 172 (1987).

[13]*First Annual Report of the Federal Labor Relations Authority and Federal Service
Impasses Panel*, FY 1979.

[14]Under regulations issued in October 1983 (48 FED REG. 40, 189 *et seq.*) which
delegated the responsibility for the initial decision on all representation matters to the
Authority's regional directors, the Authority will review a regional director's decision "only
if it appears that a compelling reason exists therefore," 5 C.F.R. 2422.17(c). For example,
mere disagreement with the regional director's findings which were not clearly erroneous
have not been reviewed. *Letterman Army Medical Center*, 15 FLRA 241 (1984).

[15]*Seventh Annual Report, FLRA, supra* note 3.

These elections conducted pursuant to the respective representation petitions ensure employee freedom of choice, subject to specific limitations (which advance the equally important objective of labor relations stability). The CSRA in balancing these respective interests has imported, in large part, from the National Labor Relations Act and National Labor Relations Board (NLRB) decisions statutory restrictions on elections which for specific periods maintain continuity in the existing labor-management relationship.

These restrictions on elections, referred to as "bars," are as follows:

Election Bar

An election bar exists when a valid election has been held under section 7111(b) within 12 calendar months.

Certification Bar

A certification bar exists when the FLRA has certified a labor organization as the exclusive representative of employees in the appropriate unit within the previous 12 calendar months, unless a signed and dated agreement covering the claimed unit is effective.

Contract Bar

A contract bar exists where there is a collective bargaining agreement between an agency and an exclusive representative (excluding the labor organization petitioning for exclusive recognition). However, an exception to the contract bar exists when (1) the collective bargaining agreement has been in effect for more than three years, or (2) the petition for exclusive recognition is filed not more than 105 days and not less than 60 days before the expiration date of the collective bargaining agreement—the so-called "open period" (section 7111(f)(3)(A)(B)). Where a collective bargaining agreement exists, a labor organization may submit a petition challenging the incumbent union during the 45-day open period, following the expiration of the agreement, or in the absence of a renewed agreement, or where the parties have improperly extended the agreement to preclude a challenge (5 C.F.R. 2422.3(f)).

The Authority has established rules governing voting eligibility, runoff elections, if no choice receives a majority, and criteria for exclusive recognition. The absence of a 30 percent showing of interest or the presence of a lawful, written collective bargaining agreement between the agency and an exclusive representative can preclude exclusive recognition for the petitioning union. Again, if the Authority has conducted a valid election within the preceding 12 calendar months resulting in the election and certification of a labor organization as exclusive representative, potential union successors are barred.

In a number of cases, the Authority has had to decide whether collective bargaining agreements stood as a bar to representation elections under the Statute. In *Department of the Army, Concord Recruiting Command*,[16] the Authority ruled that a labor contract ambiguous as to its effective date and duration did not bar an election. Also, when an agency head's eventual approval of an agreement occurred after the filing of a representation petition, the FLRA held that the agreement did not bar an election based on the petition.[17] In a similar case, the Authority held that an expired collective bargaining agreement did not bar a decertification election, even though the activity and the union had agreed to extend the agreement pending renegotiation. The Authority contended that there was no final agreement of fixed duration in existence when the decertification petition was filed.[18] Moreover, in *Department of Health and Human Services, Philadelphia Regional Office, Region III*,[19] "the Authority determined that a document initialed by the parties which did not conform to the parties' agreed upon method for effectuating a final negotiated agreement did not constitute a written collective bargaining agreement within the meaning of section 7111(f)(3) so as to bar a rival labor organization's petition."

Under certain circumstances, a constituent local union may file a petition for exclusive recognition of the unit during the contract bar period provided evidence is produced of a schism between itself and the international union or federation. In such cases, the Authority has found that a negotiated agreement does not act as a bar to a representation petition. For example, in *Department of the Navy, Pearl Harbor Naval Shipyard Restaurant System*,[20] the FLRA held the existence of a schism to depend on two conditions derived from decisions of the NLRB in the private sector, namely: (1) a basic intraunion conflict over fundamental policy questions within the highest level of an international union or federation; and (2) a conflict that causes employees in the local unit to take action, based on the conflict itself, which creates such confusion in the bargaining relationship that stability can only be restored through an election.

---

[16]14 FLRA 73 (1984).
[17]*National Park Serv., Harper's Ferry, W. Va.*, 15 FLRA 786 (1984).
[18]*Corpus Christi, Army Depot*, 16 FLRA 281 (1984).
[19]12 FLRA 167 (1983).
[20]*Supra* note 12.

In addition, the regional director cited private sector law which holds that no schism is found where the continuity of the bargaining relationship remains unbroken despite the fact that a union changes affiliation from one international or federation to another.

Objections to Elections

It has been established that parties to an election may be bound by their informal agreements regarding the status of certain employees. Thus, in *Federal Trade Commission*[21] the FLRA dismissed a clarification of a unit petition because the status of the employees covered by the petition had been settled by the parties and the regional director in the process of resolving challenged ballots in a previous case.

In a case of potential significance, the Court of Appeals for the Fifth Circuit reversed the Authority's decision in *Immigration & Naturalization Service*.[22] While holding that it lacked jurisdiction to review the Authority's order setting aside an election based upon AFGE objections, the court nevertheless disagreed with the FLRA conclusion that the agency was required to continue certain practices on uniforms and checkpoints while a representation election was pending. According to the court, since the practices involved matters about which the agency could not bargain (section 7106(b)(1)), once the agreement expired, the agency was free to discontinue the practice.

With respect to objections to election, the Authority has found that preelection statements contained in leaflets and distributed by competing unions do not necessarily provide ground for setting aside an election especially where ample time to respond was available.[23]

The affirmative duty of management to maintain a position of neutrality in any representation election campaign has been often reiterated by the Authority. "Where management deviates from its posture of neutrality and thereby interferes with the free and untrammeled expression of the employees choice in the election, such election will be set aside and a new election ordered."[24]

Unit Determination

Following the filing of a representation petition in accordance with section 7111(b), the regional director for the region in which the petition

---

[21]15 FLRA 247 (1984).
[22]9 FLRA 253 (1982).
[23]*Department of the Navy, Naval Air Rework Facility, Norfolk, Va.*, 12 FLRA 15 (1983).
[24]*Department of the Air Force and NFFE, Local 1958*, 5 FLRA 492 (1981).

was filed must conduct an investigation to determine whether the proposed unit is appropriate for the purposes of collective bargaining. The regional director's investigation not only applies the criteria for determining appropriateness contained in section 7112(a)(1) but also ensures that the unit does not contain excluded categories of employees identified in sections 7112(b)(1)–7112(b)(7).

Excluded Categories of Employees

Managers and Supervisors

In various representation cases, the Authority has examined, interpreted, and applied the exclusions from an appropriate unit contained in section 7112(b). With limited exceptions,[25] management officials and supervisors cannot be included in a bargaining unit of employees (sections 7103(a)(10) and 7103(a)(11)). Expanding upon the definition of a management official in 7103(a)(11) as "an individual employed by an agency in a position the duties and responsibilities of which require or authorize the individual to formulate, determine or influence the policies of the agency," the FLRA included in a lead case[26] those who engaged in the following activities:

1. creating, establishing, or prescribing general principles, plans, or courses of action for an agency;
2. deciding or settling upon general principles, plans, or courses of action for an agency; or
3. bringing about or obtaining a result as to the adoption of general principles, plans, or courses of action for an agency.

This definition, as interpreted, has been applied to determine whether specific individuals or the incumbents of specific positions should be excluded from the bargaining unit.

The FLRA has distinguished highly trained employees with significant responsibilities from those employees with actual management authority or control over agency operations. In a number of cases, the Authority found that professional employees who assisted in implementing agency policy but did not shape the policy were not management

---

[25] 5 U.S.C. 7135(a), continuation of existing laws, recognitions, agreements, and procedures permits inclusion of management officials or supervisors historically represented by labor organizations.

[26] *Department of the Navy, Automatic Data Processing Selection Office*, 7 FLRA 172 (1981).

officials.[27] However, an employee is likely to be deemed a management official if he or she has signatory authority to bind the government to formal contracts or agreements or is primarily responsible for managing an entire agency program.[28] From another perspective, the Authority has held that "an agency's determination that an employee is a management official for purposes of merit pay has no bearing on the employee's inclusion or exclusion from a unit of recognition."[29]

Supervisors are similarly excluded from coverage under the Act. As defined in section 7103(a)(10), Chapter 71:

> (10) "supervisor" means an individual employed by an agency having authority in the interest of the agency to hire, direct, assign, promote, reward, transfer, furlough, layoff, recall, suspend, discipline, or remove employees, to adjust their grievances or to effectively recommend such action, if the exercise of the authority is not merely routine or clerical in nature but requires the consistent exercise of independent judgment, except that, with respect to any unit which includes firefighters or nurses, the term "supervisor" includes only those individuals who devote a preponderance of their employment time to exercising such authority;

In three early decisions on this issue of supervisor exclusion, the Authority reinforced the "preponderance of their employment time test" to exclude or include certain classifications of firefighters and nurses.[30] Subsequently, in a *Department of the Navy* case,[31] the Authority further interpreted and applied the definition of supervisor to individuals who happen to be in units with firefighters or nurses. While all supervisors must be excluded from appropriate units of employees under section 7112(b)(1), nurses and firefighters may be excluded as supervisors only if they devote a "preponderance of their employment time" to exercising supervisory authority. Also excluded were those individuals employed by an agency whose "duties involve the exercise of any indicia of supervisory authority and which are not merely routine or clerical in nature but require the consistent exercise of independent judgment," regardless of whether they meet the "preponderance of time test" which

---

[27]See *Hanscom AFB*, 14 FLRA 266 (1984); *Georgia Nat'l Guard*, 14 FLRA 187 (1984); *Department of Agric.*, *Tick Eradication Program*, 15 FLRA 250 (1984); *HUD Boston, Mass.*, 16 FLRA 38 (1984).

[28]*1947th Admin. Support Group, Washington, D.C.*, *U.S. Air Force*, 14 FLRA 220 (1984), cited in *1(4)* LAB. LAW, Fall 1985.

[29]*Department of Energy, Fed. Energy Regulatory Comm'n and AFGE, Local 421*, 22 FLRA 3 (1986) which reaffirmed position in *Interpretation and Guidance*, 4 FLRA 754 (1981), cited in *Committee Reports Issue*, 3(3) LAB. LAW., Summer 1987.

[30]*Department of the Navy, Naval Educ. & Training Center*, 3 FLRA 324; *Veterans Admin. Hosp.*, 4 FLRA 122 (1980); *Veterans Admin. Medical Center*, 4 FLRA 229 (1980).

[31]*Department of the Navy, Naval Undersea Warfare Eng'g Station, Keyport, Wash.*, 7 FLRA 526 (1981).

REPRESENTATION AND ELECTIONS 225

applies *only* to firefighters and nurses and not to individuals in units with them.

The Authority has consistently held that individuals who use independent judgment to assign and direct work, discipline employees, or adjust grievances are supervisors.[32] Conversely, those who have no role in hiring, no authority to promote, or whose authority to discipline is limited to making recommendations to a superior have not been considered supervisors.

An exception to the manager and supervisor exclusion set forth in section 7112(b)(1) exists under section 7135(a)(2) where the Statute permits the renewal, continuation, or initial according of recognition for units of supervisors or management officials historically represented by labor organizations in the private sector and which held exclusive recognition when the Statute was enacted.

Confidential Employees

In *Red River Army Depot*,[33] the Authority first addressed the confidential employee exclusions under the Statute. In excluding one employee from the unit as having a "confidential" position and including another, the Authority relied on the definition contained in section 7103(a)(13) which states "confidential employee means an employee who acts in a confidential capacity with respect to an individual who formulates or effectuates management policies in the field of labor-management relations."

Other Exclusions

In subsequent decisions, the Authority further found under section 7112(b)(4) grounds for excluding from a collective bargaining unit: (1) federal mediators because such employees are engaged in administering the provisions of the Statute, specifically via the Federal Mediation and Conciliation Service established in section 7119(a);[34] (2) individuals engaged in security work which directly affects the national security under 7112(b)(6);[35] (3) employees engaged in operations, repair, and maintenance of cryptographic equipment under 7103(b);[36] and (4) the secretary

---

[32]*Georgia Nat'l Guard, supra* note 27; *Veterans Admin. Medical Center, Lyons, N.J.,* 14 FLRA 46 (1984).
[33]2 FLRA 658 (1979).
[34]*FMCS, Region 7, San Francisco, Cal.*, 3 FLRA 137 (Apr. 25, 1980).
[35]*Department of Energy, Oak Ridge Operations*, 4 FLRA 644 (1980).
[36]*Department of Naval Telecommunications Center, Ward Circle*, 6 FLRA 498 (1981).

to a manager who dealt with the union on a daily basis and who belonged to several management committees that discussed union proposals deemed confidential.[37]

Employees engaged in federal personnel work in other than a purely clerical capacity are also excluded from appropriate bargaining units (section 7112(b)(3)). In this connection the Authority has found: (1) civilian recruiters involved in the recruitment of Army Reserve personnel not to be engaged in personnel work other than in a purely clerical capacity;[38] (2) Office of Personnel Management (OPM) employees who are not involved in doing OPM's internal personnel work, but rather work related to its mission of delivering personnel assistance to other agencies may be included;[39] and (3) four collateral duty Equal Employment Opportunity (EEO) counselors not excludable from the collective bargaining unit because they were not assigned to the personnel office and received only technical guidance and review from the chief EEO counselor.[40]

Both professional and nonprofessional employees may not be included in an appropriate unit unless a majority of the professional employees vote for inclusion in the unit (section 7112(b)(5)). Finally, the Authority has excluded from coverage under section 7112(b)(7) those employees the agency contended would be performing internal audit functions.[41]

Appropriate Bargaining Unit

Criteria

The Authority as per section 7112(a)(1) "shall determine any unit to be an appropriate unit only if the determination will ensure a clear and identifiable community of interest among the employees in the unit and will promote effective dealings with, and efficiency of the operations of the agency involved." With respect to whether a petitioned-for unit is appropriate under the Statute for the purpose of exclusive recognition, the Authority has held that to be found appropriate, a proposed unit must meet all three unit criteria and that a failure to satisfy one of the criteria must

---

[37]*Environmental Protection Agency, Region IX*, 16 FLRA 273 (1984).
[38]*Army Dist. Recruiting Command, Philadelphia*, 12 FLRA 409 (1983).
[39]*Office of Personnel Management*, 5 FLRA 238 (1981).
[40]*832nd Combat Support Group, Luke AFB Ariz. and AFGE, Local 1547*, 23 FLRA 768 (1986). This case is distinguished from the holding in *Department of the Air Force and AFGE, Local 1617*, 3 FLRA 208 (1980), in which FLRA found that the base's full-time EEO counselors were involved in federal personnel work and were thus excludable.
[41]*Department of Labor, Office of Inspector Gen.*, 7 FLRA 834 (1982).

result in a finding that the unit sought is inappropriate. Applying this standard, the Authority has dismissed representation petitions where the employees in the unit sought did not share a clear and identifiable community of interest.[42]

To determine the "community of interest" among employees and thereby implement the community of interest standard, the Authority has developed several factors—derived from those evolved at the NLRB— namely whether: (1) the employees share a common mission and duties, (2) there is interaction or interchange among the employees, (3) the employees are subject to the same personnel policies and practices, (4) the employees share common supervision, (5) the employees have experienced a similar collective bargaining history, and (6) the employees work in geographical proximity to one another.

The degree of interchange among employees, the extent to which they interact on a continuous basis or function in integrated operations can constitute the determining factor in a community of interest decision. In *International Federation of Professional and Technical Engineers, Local 3*,[43] the Authority concluded that the significant interchange among the petitioned-for employees consuming from 30 to 40 percent of their time at other duty locations did not meet the community of interest criteria since this interchange was also shared with other activity employees not included in the proposed unit. Thus, the Authority denied the petition on grounds that the interchange alone was an insufficient distinguishing factor to find a community of interest.

In contrast, the Authority found a reorganization which abolished an administrative unit and caused the employees therein to no longer share a community of interest with the employees in the remaining unit since the former "are now part of a new separate activity; are under separate supervision and authority; and have little or no contact, interchange or transfer with the other employees represented. . . ."[44]

Common supervision, or the lack thereof, is often an integral aspect of the community of interest. Those employees who are commonly supervised will typically be subject to the same personnel and labor relations policies, interact on a regular basis, and share a common mission and duties.

Geographical proximity, generally a secondary criterion, tends to corroborate rather than determine unit appropriateness. In *National*

---

[42]See *Department of the Navy, Navy Publications and Printing Serv. Branch Office, Vallejo, Cal.*, 10 FLRA 659 (1982).

[43]7 FLRA 626 (1982).

[44]*Department of Labor and National Council of Field Labor Locals, AFGE, AFL-CIO*, 23 FLRA 464 (1986).

Marine Fisheries Service, Southeast Fisheries Center and AFGE, Local 2875,[45] a common location was insufficient evidence for finding of a community of interest absent other shared terms and conditions of employment. In addition, the history of collective bargaining between the parties can be a pivotal factor especially in cases involving the proposed severance of a unit.

Finally, the Authority may consider the extent to which employees in the proposed unit have organized. However, this criterion, which is not controlling, precludes Authority determination of unit appropriateness based solely upon union organizing success or lack of success among the employees.

It should be noted that in consolidating units under section 7112(d), the same factors used to determine appropriate single units are applied such as: (1) degree of commonality and the integration of the mission and function of the components involved, (2) employee distribution throughout the organization, (3) geographical components, (4) similarity of occupational activities of employees in the proposed unit, and (5) the scope of personnel and labor functions.[46] For example, in *U.S. Army Training & Doctrine Command,*[47] the Authority found that the petitioning labor organization had failed to satisfy the community of interest criterion because it had not included within the proposed consolidated unit all the units at one location that were party to a multiunit agreement.

Reorganization within the agency or activity can generate unit determination petitions; however, the same criteria are applied to ascertain appropriateness. A reorganization where the formal restructuring of a particular program transformed it into an independent component of the agency did not warrant a separate unit since the employees continued to work at the same location and perform the same primary job functions.[48]

Excerpts from two pertinent cases illustrate the Authority's application and interpretation of the threefold unit determination criteria and related factors. First, in dismissing a petition, the FLRA concluded:

> that the unit which the Petitioner seeks to represent is not appropriate for the purpose of exclusive recognition under section 7112(a) of the Statute as it does not encompass employees who share a clear and identifiable community of interest separate and distinct from other employees of the

---

[45]3 FLRA 498 (1980).
[46]*Air Force Logistics Command, Wright Patterson AFB, Ohio,* 7 FLRA 210 (1981); *Department of the Navy, Marine Corps,* 8 FLRA 15 (1982).
[47]11 FLRA 105 (1983).
[48]*Department of Labor and National Council of Field Labor Locals,* 23 FLRA 464 (1986). Also involved herein was the application of 5 U.S.C. 7135(a)(1) on continued recognition of a unit found appropriate under Executive Order 11491, as amended.

Activity, and it will not promote effective dealings and efficiency of the operations of the agency. Thus, employees who would be included in, and employees who would be excluded from, the unit sought perform the same functions, possess essentially the same job classifications, skills and qualifications, are engaged in common and integrated work projects, and enjoy common supervision and working conditions. Hence, there is no clear and identifiable community of interest among the employees in the proposed unit, separate and distinct from those employees who would be excluded. . . . Under these circumstances, the Authority finds that the unit sought would not promote effective dealings and efficiency of the operations of the agency.[49]

Second, in finding a unit appropriate for the purpose of exclusive recognition, the Authority found:

that all the employees sought enjoy a common mission, common supervision, inter-related duties, training and general working conditions, are subject to uniform personnel and labor relations policies, and share a clear and identifiable community of interest. Further, in view of the overall mission of the Activity, the demand that all the employees GS and WG alike, work closely together to accomplish that mission within strict time frames, the Authority finds that the unit sought by the Petitioner and Intervenor would promote effective dealings and efficiency of operations. It is therefore found that the unit sought by the Petitioner and Intervenor is appropriate for purposes of collective bargaining.[50]

To gain approval as an appropriate unit, the proposed unit, as indicated, must present a separate and distinct community of interest which would promote efficiency of operations and effective agency dealings. In fulfilling these criteria, the proposed unit must avoid fragmentation into numerous units, which tends to result in increased expenditures related to contract administration.

The commonality of personnel policies and procedures are accorded significant weight in determining community of interest in that these operations have direct impact on employees, establishing uniformity in their terms and conditions of employment. Interestingly, although employees may have similar day-to-day working conditions, those hired for a specific period of time with no reasonable expectation of continued employment do not share a community of interest with "permanent employees."[51]

[49]*National Marine Fisheries Serv., Se. Fisheries Center and AFGE, supra* note 45.
[50]*Trident Refit Facility, Bangor, Me., and International Ass'n of Machinists & Aerospace Workers, Dist. Local 282,* 5 FLRA 606 (1981).
[51]*National Ocean Survey, National Oceanic & Atmospheric Admin. and Radio Officers Union, United Tel. Workers, AFL-CIO,* 6 FLRA 257 (1981).

Accretion

An accretion is the incorporation of a group of employees into an existing, usually larger, collective bargaining unit. Accretions can result from the reorganization of an agency or the creation of new positions, departments, or activities. A clarification of unit (CU) petition is the means utilized to determine if new or reorganized employees have been accreted to an existing collective bargaining unit.

Community of interest, among other factors, has been utilized by the Authority in adjudicating the accretion of bargaining units to other bargaining units. Thus accretion to a nationwide consolidated unit of certain agency employees in the Panama Canal Area was approved.[52] On a smaller scale, a reorganization of employees who were "organizationally and operationally integrated and thus accreted to the bargaining unit" extant was sanctioned because the resulting unit shared, for example, a clear and identifiable community of interest.[53] The Authority has also distinguished reorganization where bargaining units were administratively transferred and no functional integration with the receiving unit occurred such as in *GSA, National Capital Region*[54] from the functional integration which constituted accretion in *Defense Contract Administrative Service Region, St. Louis*,[55] where an accretion was found in the consolidation of two naval supply depots.

---

[52]*Federal Aviation Admin., Southern Region, Balboa Canal Area, Airway Facilities Branch*, 3 FLRA 708 (1980).
[53]*Defense Contract Admin. Servs. Region, St. Louis, Mo. and AFGE, AFL-CIO and NAGE, Local R14-56, Neosho, Mo.*, 5 FLRA 281 (1981).
[54]5 FLRA 285 (1981).
[55]*Supra* note 53.

8. Unfair Labor Practices

DAVID L. FEDER

Section 7116 of Title 5 of the United States Code prescribes certain conduct by agencies or unions as unfair labor practices.[1] The Federal Labor Relations Authority administers these provisions (see Chapter 2, "Processing an Unfair Labor Practice Charge"). Conduct constituting unfair labor practices can be organized into 10 major categories discussed below, based on the type of statutory right violated: (1) interference with protected union activities, (2) discrimination in retaliation for engaging in protected union activities, (3) provision by an agency of customary and routine facilities for a union's use, (4) bargaining violations, (5) duty to furnish information, (6) representation violations by agencies, (7) official time violations by agencies, (8) violations concerning the voluntary withholding of dues, (9) breaches of the duty of fair representation by unions, and (10) illegal strikes and picketing by unions. The principles discussed in this chapter are derived from decisions by the Authority and by U.S. courts of appeal.[2]

---

[1]The Authority's procedures for filing and investigating unfair labor practice charges and the prosecuting and settling of unfair labor practice complaints are set forth in 5 C.F.R. Part 2423 (1988). For a discussion of the role of the General Counsel of the Authority, the administrative law judges, and the Authority in processing unfair labor practice charges, see Chapter 2, "Processing an Unfair Labor Practice Charge." The various agency and union unfair labor practices are set forth in Chapter 1. See also *Labor-Management Relations, Civil Service Reforms and EEO in the Federal Government*, Federal Bar Association, Committee on Public Sector Labor Relations of the Council on Labor Law and Labor Relations, May 1980, 84–117.

[2]5 U.S.C. 7123(a) provides that any person aggrieved by any final unfair labor practice order of the Authority may seek judicial review of the Authority order in the U.S. circuit court in the circuit in which the person resides or transacts business or in the Court of Appeals for the District of Columbia Circuit. The Authority may seek enforcement of its unfair labor practice orders in any appropriate U.S. court of appeals. Authority decisions

Interference With Protected Activities[3]

Agency Interference With Union Activities

Section 7102 of the Statute affords all employees "the right to form, join or assist any labor organization, or to refrain from any such activity, freely and without fear of penalty or reprisal, and each employee shall be protected in the exercise of such right." It is an unfair labor practice for an agency representative to make threatening statements, implied threats, or engage in surveillance, interrogation, or other conduct which tends to interfere with, restrain, or coerce any employee covered by the Statute[4] in the exercise of any right guaranteed by section 7102.

It is a violation of section 7116(a)(1) for an agency to issue a letter of reprimand to an employee for statements made at a grievance meeting which are related to the grievant's expressed concerns that the grievant's supervisor had been discriminating against him or her. For example, a

---

cited herein which have been enforced, reversed, or modified by a U.S. court of appeals will be noted.

The U.S. courts of appeal will not disturb the Authority's interpretation and application of the Statute unless it is found to be arbitrary, capricious, an abuse of discretion, or otherwise not in accordance with law. 5 U.S.C. 7123(c), 5 U.S.C. 7106. The Supreme Court in *FLRA v. Department of the Army, Aberdeen Proving Ground*, 127 LRRM 3137 (1988) has described the standard of review of Authority decisions as follows:

Although "reviewing courts should uphold reasonable and defensible constructions of an agency's enabling Act . . . they must not 'rubber-stamp . . . administrative decisions that they deem inconsistent with a statutory mandate or that frustrate the congressional policy underlying a statute.'" *Bureau of Alcohol, Tobacco & Firearms v. FLRA*, 464 U.S. 89, 97 (1983), quoting *NLRB v. Brown*, 380 U.S. 278, 291-292 (1965).

The Supreme Court in *Bureau of Alcohol, Tobacco, & Firearms v. FLRA*, 464 U.S. 89, 97, 114 LRRM 3393 (1983), also stated that "the Authority is entitled to considerable deference when it exercises its 'special function of applying the general provisions of the Act to the complexities' of federal labor relations."

[3]This conduct is violative of 5 U.S.C. 7116(a)(1) or 7116(b)(1).

[4]For purposes of the Federal Service Labor-Management Relations Statute, the term "employee" is defined at 5 U.S.C. 7103(a)(2) as an individual—

(A) employed in an agency; or

(B) whose employment in an agency has ceased because of any unfair labor practice under section 7116 of this title and who has not obtained any other regular and substantially equivalent employment, as determined under regulations prescribed by the Federal Labor Relations Authority; but does not include—

    (i) an alien or noncitizen of the United States who occupies a position outside the United States;

    (ii) a member of the uniformed services;

    (iii) a supervisor or management official;

    (iv) an officer or employee in the Foreign Service of the United States employed in the Department of State, the Agency for International Development, or the International Communication Agency; or

    (v) any person who participates in a strike in violation of section 7311 of this title.

union president had called the supervisor "racist, sexist and ageist" during a grievance meeting. Although the Authority did not condone such "indelicate and intemperate language" for the conduct of labor-management relations, the Authority held that under the circumstances, none of the statements constituted " 'flagrant misconduct' beyond the ambit of protected activity" and thus found an agency violation of section 7116(a)(1). The Authority ordered the agency to cease and desist from unlawful conduct, to post an appropriate notice, to remove or expunge from its files any reference to the reprimand given to the union president, and to acknowledge the removal in writing.[5]

Similarly, it is an unfair labor practice for an agency to threaten employees that it will impose a reduction in force if the employees continue to file grievances or unfair labor practice charges.[6] Such statements were found by the Authority to have an "obvious restraining effect" and to "manifestly interfere with the right of employees to invoke the negotiated grievance procedure."[7]

The Authority has found that the legitimate conduct of an employee representative in seeking to publicize, through contacts with the media, issues having a direct bearing upon the working conditions of unit employees is protected.[8] The Authority also has held that section 7102 encompasses an employee's right, in the absence of special circumstances, to wear union insignia at the workplace.[9] An exclusive representative has the right to distribute handbills publicizing a union's position with respect to matters affecting unit employees' conditions of employment, even though such handbilling would have occurred on an overseas military base.[10]

Whether or not a particular statement directed to an employee constitutes interference, restraint, or coercion depends upon whether the employee could reasonably have drawn a coercive inference from the statement.[11] The intent of the employer is not determinative. It should be noted, however, that section 7116(e) allows an agency supervisor to

---

[5]*Department of Housing and Urban Development, San Francisco Area Office, San Francisco, Cal.*, 4 FLRA 460 (1980).
[6]*Army & Air Force Exch. Serv. (AAFES), Fort Carson, Colo.*, 6 FLRA 607 (1981).
[7]*Id.*, at 613.
[8]*Bureau of Prisons, Fed. Correctional Inst., Danbury, Conn.*, 17 FLRA 696 (1985).
[9]*Immigration & Naturalization Serv., Port of Entry, San Ysidro, Cal.*, 25 FLRA 447 (1987); *Immigration & Naturalization Serv., Port of Entry, San Ysidro, Cal.*, 25 FLRA 490 (1987).
[10]*Department of the Air Force, 3d Combat Support Group, Clark Air Base, Republic of the Philippines*, 29 FLRA 1044 (1987).
[11]*Federal Mediation & Conciliation Serv.*, 9 FLRA 199 (1982); *Customs Serv., Region IV, Miami, Fla.*, 19 FLRA 956 (1985).

express his or her personal view, argument, or opinion if such statement contains no threat of reprisal, force, or promise of benefit and is not made under coercive conditions.[12]

Protected activity under section 7102 must be on behalf of a labor organization. Unlike private sector labor law, the Statute does not protect concerted employee activity unrelated to supporting a union.[13] Supervisors are not protected when engaged in certain activities for which protection is provided. However, the Authority, under some circumstances, will view discipline taken against a supervisor to have a chilling effect on the exercise by employees of protected rights. Under these circumstances, the discipline of the supervisor is found to interfere with, restrain, or coerce the employees in the exercise of their rights in violation of section 7116(a)(1).[14] In addition, conduct by an employee may exceed the realm of protected activity and thus be deemed flagrant misconduct unprotected by the Statute.[15] For example, the Authority has found that racial epithets and the disparagement of a manager based upon racial stereotyping in a union newspaper article is clearly inexcusable, and has no place in the Federal Service Labor-Management Relations program. The Authority thus found that a written reprimand of the union representative for the contents of the article was not an unfair labor practice.[16]

An agency does not violate the Statute when it attempts to act in accordance with the "conflict of interest" provision of section 7120(e).[17] The Authority found no violation when an agency, with no evidence of antiunion motivation, terminated an employee as an EEO counselor because the employee was also a union representative.[18]

In a section 7116(a)(1) case involving internal security, the Authority found that an employee-union representative's action in taking photographs of a possible contract violation of safety standards was protected activity. Nonetheless the activity's subsequent conduct of keeping the employee under surveillance by security guards for almost two hours pending

[12]*Oklahoma City Air Logistics Center (AFLC), Tinker AFB, Okla.*, 6 FLRA 159 (1981); *Army & Air Force Exch. Serv. (AAFES), Ft. Carson, Colo.*, 9 FLRA 620 (1982).

[13]*Internal Revenue Serv., Andover Serv. Center, Andover, Mass.*, 13 FLRA 481 (1983).

[14]*Department of the Navy, Portsmouth Naval Shipyard, Portsmouth, N.H.*, 16 FLRA 93 (1984).

[15]*Department of the Air Force, Ogden Air Logistics Center, Hill AFB, Utah*, 25 FLRA 342 (1987).

[16]*Veterans Admin., Washington, D.C. and Veterans Admin. Medical Center, Cincinnati, Ohio*, 26 FLRA 114 (1987).

[17]5 U.S.C. 7120(e) provides that the Statute "does not authorize particpation in the management of a labor organization or acting as a representative of a labor organization . . . by an employee if the participation or activity would result in a conflict or apparent conflict of interest or would otherwise be incompatible with law or the official duties of the employees."

[18]*Harry S. Truman Memorial Veterans Hosp., Columbia, Mo.*, 8 FLRA 42 (1982).

an investigation of the matter was held not to be unreasonable and thus was found not to be contrary to section 7116(a)(1), due to the agency's sole motivation of maintaining the security of the base. [19]

The section 7102 right to file an unfair labor practice charge also encompasses the right of an employee to gather information in support of the charge and to conduct an investigation on an employee's own time to support a grievance, or in contemplation of filing a grievance. [20]

The Authority has also concluded that certain safeguards are necessary to protect employee rights under section 7102 when they are interviewed by management in preparation for a third-party proceeding (e.g., an arbitration or unfair labor practice hearing). Thus, management must (1) inform the employee of the purpose of the questioning, assure that there will be no reprisal for a refusal to participate, and obtain that participation voluntarily; (2) not conduct the questioning in a coercive context; and (3) not exceed the scope of the legitimate purpose of the inquiry or otherwise interfere with the employee's protected rights. [21] The failure to give the above warnings, however, is not per se a violation of the Statute. Rather, the Authority will examine all the circumstances to determine whether the conditions in which interviews occur are coercive instead of simply determining whether these precautionary safeguards were stated. [22]

During an election campaign, management must remain neutral. [23] A question concerning representation exists when a determination is pending regarding which labor organization should represent certain employees. During this time, management must not violate its duty of neutrality. The Authority has found that an agency violated its duty to remain neutral during an election campaign by dealing on conditions of unit employees with representatives of a rival union. [24]

Distribution of Union Literature and Solicitation of Membership

The Authority has consistently held that the right guaranteed employees under section 7102 of the Statute encompasses the right to

[19]*Defense Property Disposal Region, Ogden, Utah, and Defense Property Disposal Office (DPDO), Camp Pendleton, Oceanside, Cal.*, 24 FLRA 653 (1986).

[20]*Bureau of Prisons, Fed. Correctional Inst., Butner, N.C.*, 18 FLRA 831 (1985).

[21]*Internal Revenue Serv. and Brookhaven Serv. Center*, 9 FLRA 930 (1982).

[22]*Department of the Air Force, F.E. Warren AFB, Cheyenne, Wyo.*, 31 FLRA 541 (1988).

[23]Agency management is precluded from conducting "vote no" preelection campaigns under the Statute. Agencies are to remain neutral in connection with representation elections. However, nonthreatening personal statements by agency management are protected under 5 U.S.C. 7116(e). See *supra* note 12.

[24]*Department of the Army, Headquarters, Washington, D.C. and U.S. Army Field Artillery Center and Fort Sill, Fort Sill, Okla.*, 29 FLRA 1110 (1987).

distribute union literature in nonwork areas during nonwork time.[25] The Authority also has determined that the right of employees to engage in solicitation of membership on behalf of a labor organization during nonwork time is protected.[26] This right may even extend to solicitation in work areas, absent any disruption of the activity's operations or other unusual circumstances.[27] Section 7102 has been extended by the Authority to afford employees the same right to engage in solicitation and distribution of literature on behalf of candidates for union office as they would have if they were acting on behalf of representation by a labor organization generally.[28] Governmentwide regulations promulgated by the General Services Administration also have been found to violate section 7116(a)(1) when they were applied in a manner that interfered with an employee's statutory right to distribute literature.[29]

The Authority has not yet determined whether a union representative who is not an employee of a given agency may have an unrestricted right of access to that agency's facilities in the absence of agreed-upon procedures.[30] In determining whether a ban on the distribution or posting of union literature violates the Statute, the Authority must determine whether the matter alleged is protected under section 7116(a)(1) or whether it involves the interpretation of a contractual right, such as the posting of union literature on bulletin boards.[31]

Union Interference With Employees' Rights

Unions also have been found to interfere with an employee's section 7102 rights to form, join, or assist any labor organization, or to refrain from any such activity, freely and without fear of penalty or reprisal. The Authority found a violation of section 7116(b)(1) by a union which disciplined and discriminated against an employee for giving testimony in an Authority proceeding.[32] The Authority concluded that the right guaran-

---

[25]*General Servs. Admin.*, 9 FLRA 213 (1982); *Internal Revenue Serv., N. Atl. Serv. Center, Andover, Mass.*, 7 FLRA 596 (1982).
[26]*Oklahoma City Air Logistics Center (AFLC), Tinker AFB, Okla.*, supra note 12.
[27]*Social Sec. Admin.*, 13 FLRA 409 (1983).
[28]*Social Sec. Admin., Se. Program Serv. Center*, 21 FLRA 748 (1986).
[29]*General Servs. Admin.*, 29 FLRA 684 (1987).
[30]*Army & Air Force Exch. Serv. (AAFES), Lowry AFB Exch.*, Lowry, Colo., 13 FLRA 310 (1983); *Department of Defense Dependents Schools, Mediterranean Region, Naples Am. High School, Naples, Italy*, 21 FLRA 849 (1986).
[31]*Department of the Air Force, 31st Combat Support Group, Homestead AFB*, 13 FLRA 239 (1983).
[32]*NTEU and NTEU, Chapter 53 (Internal Revenue Serv. and Brooklyn Dist. Office)*, 6 FLRA 218 (1981).

teed to employees under section 7102 "is sufficiently broad to include within its scope the right of an employee to appear as a witness in an Authority proceeding to which a union is a party and to give testimony supporting or opposing the union's interest in that proceeding."[33]

An exclusive representative is a labor organization certified by the Authority as the sole representative of employees in an appropriate unit pursuant to a secret ballot election among the employees conducted by the Authority. A labor organization that has been accorded exclusive recognition is entitled to act for, and negotiate collective bargaining agreements covering, all employees in the unit. An exclusive representative may not expel a member for filing, and urging other employees to file, unfair labor practices against the exclusive representative.[34] Similarly, a union was found to have violated the Statute when it threatened to discipline a union member for filing unfair labor practice charges against the agency. The employees' charges involved the agency's alleged interference with the employee's attempt to assist a rival labor organization.[35] The Authority also found that the union's action could reasonably tend to have a "restraining or chilling" effect on other members who might similarly wish to exercise their right to support a labor organization. A union's section 7116(c) right to discipline its members pursuant to the procedures contained in its constitution or bylaws must be exercised in a manner consistent with the Statute. To threaten to discipline a member for the exercise of a section 7102 right is inconsistent with that section and beyond the legitimate right of a union to regulate its internal affairs. On the other hand, an employee who is a union official may be removed from union office for being disloyal to the union. The Authority found that a union did not violate section 7116(b)(1) by removing a union official from office since the real reason for the removal was the union steward's attempt to bring in a rival union.[36]

Discrimination in Retaliation for Union Activity[37]

Discrimination in an employee's condition of employment in retaliation for an employee's exercise of protected section 7102 rights

---

[33]Id., at 218.
[34]NAGE, Local R5-66 and James A. Confer, Jr., 17 FLRA 796 (1985).
[35]AFGE, AFL-CIO and Edward Hanlon, 29 FLRA 1359 (1987).
[36]AFGE, Local 1920, AFL-CIO and Department of the Army, Headquarters, III Corps and Fort Hood, Fort Hood, Tex., 16 FLRA 464 (1984).
[37]Conduct encompassed under this heading is violative of 5 U.S.C. 7116(a)(1) and (2).

constitutes an unfair labor practice. Such retaliation might take the form of a written reprimand, failure to promote, transfer, or suspension for less than 14 days.[38] In determining whether an employee has been subjected to such retaliation, the Authority has abandoned the "in part" test used under Executive Order 11491, as amended.[39] Rather, in situations where consideration of an employee's participation in activities protected by the Statute played a part in a management decision affecting that employee, the test is as follows:[40]

> [T]he burden is on the General Counsel to make a *prima facie* showing that the employee had engaged in protected activity and that this conduct was a motivating factor in agency management's decision. . . . Once this is established, the agency must show by a preponderance of the evidence that it would have reached the same decision as to the [action taken against the employee] even in the absence of protected activity.

This test is commonly referred to as the "but for" test, that is, but for the protected union activity, the action involving the employee would not have been taken.

The Authority has applied this same but for test in cases alleging violations of section 7116(a)(4) regarding discrimination in a condition of employment based on an employee's participation in filing unfair labor practice charges with the Authority and giving information in connection with those charges.[41] Thus, even though union activity may be a consideration in a personnel action, absent satisfaction of the but for test, the Authority will not find consideration of union activity to be an independent violation of section 7116(a)(1).[42]

An individual must be an employee in order to be protected by conduct violative of section 7116(a)(2). A former employee has been found to be an "employee" within the meaning of section 7103(a)(2) for

---

[38]Back pay orders are available under the Back Pay Act (5 U.S.C. 5596(b)). However, a removal, suspension for more than 14 days, reduction in grade or pay, and furlough of 30 days or less in retaliation for an employee's exercise of a protected statutory right may not be raised as an unfair labor practice since such adverse actions are covered by 5 U.S.C. 7512 and thus only may be raised before the MSPB. Accordingly, 5 U.S.C. 7116(d) precludes the Authority from asserting jurisdiction over such issues. See Chapter 2.

[39]Under Executive Order 11491, as amended, it was a violation of §19(a)(1) and (2) of the Executive Order where a legitimate basis for the management action existed but union considerations also were shown to have played a part in the action. See *Directorate of Supply Operations, Defense Logistics Agency, Headquarters*, 2 FLRA 937 (1980).

[40]*Internal Revenue Serv.*, 6 FLRA 96 (1981).

[41]*Department of the Navy, Navy Resale Sys., Field Support Office, Commissary Store Group, Norfolk, Va.*, 16 FLRA 257 (1984).

[42]*Army Military Traffic Mgmt. Command, E. Area, Bayonne, N.J.*, 16 FLRA 881 (1984).

purposes of the protection afforded by the unfair labor practice rules in section 7116(a)(2).[43]

Section 7116(a)(2) precludes discrimination in conditions of employment based on an employee's unit status as well as on an employee's exercise of protected section 7102 rights. It is a violation of section 7116(a)(2) when an agency excludes employees from using the agency's administrative grievance procedure regarding matters not covered by the grievance/arbitration procedure in their collective bargaining agreement.[44]

The Authority also has recognized that irreconcilable conflicts may arise between management's right to insist on the performance of a job that cannot be deferred and an employee's right to engage in protected representational activities. When such conflicts arise, management must be free to assign the employee, without loss of pay, to other duties that will not impair any essential function of the agency. Management must, however, permit the employee to perform those other duties and also to engage in protected union activity. The burden is on management to establish that such a transfer of assignment was warranted.[45] The Authority routinely requires the unlawful conduct to be rescinded and the employee restored to the status quo and to be made whole to remedy section 7116(a)(2) violations.[46]

Agency Provision of Customary and Routine Facilities to Unions[47]

It is an unfair labor practice for an agency to sponsor, control, or otherwise assist any labor organization. An agency may, upon request, however, furnish a labor organization with customary and routine services and facilities if the services and facilities also are furnished on an impartial basis to other labor organizations having equivalent status.[48] Thus, if an agency grants a union's request for such services or facilities

[43]Social Sec. Admin., Baltimore, Md. and Wilkes-Barre Data Operations Center, 17 FLRA 435 (1985).
[44]Portsmouth Naval Shipyard and Department of the Navy, Washington, D.C., 23 FLRA 475 (1986).
[45]Department of the Navy, Norfolk Naval Shipyard, Portsmouth, Va., 15 FLRA 867 (1984); Social Sec. Admin., Baltimore, Md., 18 FLRA 55 (1985).
[46]Department of the Navy, Norfolk Naval Shipyard, Portsmouth, Va., supra note 45; Long Beach Naval Shipyard, Long Beach, Cal. and Long Beach Naval Station, Long Beach, Cal., 25 FLRA 1002 (1987).
[47]Conduct encompassed under this topic is violative of 5 U.S.C. 7116(a)(1) and (3).
[48]Labor organizations which are parties to a pending representation proceeding are deemed to be in equivalent status.

during a representation proceeding, the agency must, upon request, provide such services or facilities to another union having equivalent status, that is, a union that is a party to the representation proceeding. The Authority, however, has found no compelling indication in the plain language or legislative history of section 7116(a)(3) that requires an agency to furnish a labor organization that has achieved equivalent status with an incumbent union in a representation proceeding with the exact same services and facilities obtained by the incumbent union through collective bargaining before the proceeding. Rather, the Authority has found it reasonable to expect that an incumbent labor organization will have acquired some advantages in agency services and facilities over a rival union through collective bargaining, and that the Statute does not require an agency to equalize their positions upon request of the rival.[49]

Section 7120(e) prohibits management officials from participation in the management of a labor organization or acting as a representative of a labor organization.[50] Conduct inconsistent with this prohibition violates section 7116(a)(3). Contrary to the Authority's interpretation, the Court of Appeals for the District of Columbia Circuit has concluded that section 7120(e) does not preclude supervisors from voting in internal union elections.[51] Thus, the court found that Congress did not intend to deny supervisors one of the most successful vestiges of union membership, the right to cast a vote in the election of their union officials.

Bargaining Violations[52]

Unilateral Changes in Negotiable Conditions of Employment

It is an unfair labor practice for an agency to fail to give adequate notice to the exclusive representative of a change in a condition of employment. An agency is also obligated to bargain in good faith, upon request, prior to the implementation of a change.

Congress has found that labor organizations and collective bargaining in the civil service are in the public interest.[53] The Statute requires an agency to accord exclusive recognition to a union selected as the repre-

---

[49]*Department of the Army, Army Air Defense Center, and Fort Bliss, Fort Bliss, Tex.*, 29 FLRA 362 (1987), *reconsideration denied*, 31 FLRA 904 (1988).

[50]See *supra* note 17.

[51]*AFGE, Local 2513, AFL-CIO v. FLRA*, 834 F.2d 174, 126 LRRM 3217 (D.C. Cir. 1987), *rev'g sub nom. Department of Labor*, 20 FLRA 296 (1985).

[52]Conduct encompassed under this heading is violative of 5 U.S.C. 7116(a)(1) and (5) or 5 U.S.C. 7116(b)(5).

[53]5 U.S.C. 7101(a).

sentative by a majority of employees in an appropriate bargaining unit casting valid ballots in a secret ballot election.[54] After a union is accorded exclusive recognition status, the agency and the union have a statutory duty to meet and to negotiate in good faith for the purpose of arriving at a collective bargaining agreement.[55] This duty to bargain in good faith extends to conditions of employment affecting all employees in the bargaining unit.[56] The Authority has held that "the collective bargaining relationship envisaged by the Statute requires that each party have the ability to function as an equal partner within the relationship" and "that each party should therefore deal with the other with the directness and dignity appropriate to partners on an equal footing."[57] Thus, an exclusive representative must be given advance notice of any proposed changes in conditions of employment affecting union employees so as to afford the union an opportunity to request to bargain over such change.[58]

The statutory duty to bargain extends only to conditions of employment. The Authority has established two factors which determine whether a matter proposed for negotiations involves a condition of employment of bargaining unit employees: (1) whether the matter proposed pertains to bargaining unit employees, and (2) the nature and extent of the effect of the matter proposed on working conditions of those employees.[59] Thus, in the context of unfair labor practice proceedings, the Authority has found housing for "geographical bachelors,"[60] base privileges for off-base employees in situations where such privileges were necessary to ensure employees adequate living conditions,[61] employee breakroom conve-

---

[54]5 U.S.C. 7111(a).

[55]5 U.S.C. 7114(a)(4).

[56]"Conditions of employment" encompass personnel policies, practices, and matters, whether established by rule, regulation, or otherwise, which affect working conditions. Excluded, however, from the definition of conditions of employment are policies, practices, and matters: (1) relating to political activities prohibited under 5 U.S.C. 7321 *et seq.*; (2) relating to the classification of any position; or (3) to the extent such matters are specifically provided for by federal statute.

A condition of employment is negotiable if the subject matter (or proposal) sought to be negotiated is not inconsistent with any federal law, governmentwide rule or regulation, agency rule or regulation for which a compelling need exists, or statutory management right. See Chapter 9 for a discussion of Authority negotiability decisions and the scope of bargaining under the Statute.

[57]*Air Force, Air Force Logistics Command, Aerospace Guidance & Metrology Center, Newark, Ohio*, 4 FLRA 512 (1982), *enforcement denied, Air Force v. FLRA*, 681 F.2d 466, 110 LRRM 2809 (6th Cir. 1982).

[58]Cf. *Department of the Air Force, Air Force Sys. Command, Elec. Sys. Div., Hanscom AFB, Mass.*, 5 FLRA 637 (1981).

[59]*Antilles Consol. Educ. Ass'n and Antilles Consol. School Sys.*, 22 FLRA 235 (1986).

[60]*Department of the Army, Dugway Proving Ground, Dugway, Utah*, 23 FLRA 578 (1986).

[61]*Department of the Air Force, Eielson AFB, Alaska*, 23 FLRA 605 (1986); *Department of the Army, Fort Greely, Alaska*, 23 FLRA 858 (1986).

niences,[62] and EEO settlement procedures[63] to constitute conditions of employment. It has found procedures for the temporary filing of supervisory positions,[64] annual agency picnics,[65] and exchange privileges for off-base employees which are not necessary to enable employees to sustain adequate living standards[66] not to constitute conditions of employment.

The mutual obligation to bargain as articulated in the Statute exists only at the level of the agency where the union is recognized as the exclusive representative. Accordingly, the Authority has held that once a labor organization is certified as the new exclusive representative for a consolidated unit, a new bargaining obligation is created in lieu of that which existed regarding smaller units now included in the consolidated one.[67] Thus, absent agreement, an agency is under no obligation to bargain with a local union regarding changes in conditions of employment after a consolidation in which the level of recognition exists at the national rather than local level.[68]

At the level of exclusive recognition an agency subdivision does not violate the Statute when it admittedly refuses to bargain over a negotiable condition of employment in those instances where it had no choice but to ministerially follow the dictates of higher level agency management.[69] The Authority has further found, however, that where agency management at a level above exclusive recognition directs the immediate implementation of a policy that alters an established condition of employment at the level of exclusive recognition, agency management at the higher level violates sections 7116(a)(1) and (5) of the Statute.[70]

While a question concerning representation is pending, a unilateral change in an existing condition of employment which was not "required consistent with a necessary functioning of the agency" is a violation of sec-

---

[62]*Internal Revenue Serv., Washington, D.C. and Internal Revenue Serv., Hartford Dist. Office,* 27 FLRA 322 (1987).

[63]*Social Sec. Admin.,* 26 FLRA 865 (1987).

[64]*Veterans Admin. and Veterans Admin. Medical Center, Lyons, N.J.,* 24 FLRA 505 (1986).

[65]*U.S. Army Adjutant Gen. Publication Center, St. Louis, Mo.,* 24 FLRA 695 (1986), rev'd, No. 87-1099 (D.C. Cir. 1989).

[66]*Department of the Army, Fort Buchanan, San Juan, P.R.,* 24 FLRA 971 (1986).

[67]*Social Sec. Admin.,* 6 FLRA 202 (1981).

[68]*Social Sec. Admin., Mid-America Program Serv. Center, Kansas City, Mo.,* 10 FLRA 15 (1982). See also *Social Sec. Admin.,* 10 FLRA 77 (1982).

[69]*Department of the Interior, Water & Power Resources Serv., Grand Coulee Project, Grand Coulee, Wash.,* 9 FLRA 385 (1982). Cf. *Veterans Admin. Cent. Office, Veterans Admin. Medical Center, Long Beach,* 9 FLRA 325 (1982).

[70]*Social Sec. Admin., Region VI and Social Sec. Admin., Galveston, Tex., Dist.,* 10 FLRA 26 (1982); *Social Sec. Admin., Office of Program Operations & Field Operations, Sutter Dist. Office, San Francisco, Cal.,* 5 FLRA 504 (1981).

tions 7116(a)(1) and (5). This is so notwithstanding an exclusive representative's failure to request bargaining after being given timely notice of the proposed change.[71]

Upon the expiration of a collective bargaining agreement, established personnel policies, practices, and matters affecting working conditions continue, to the maximum extent possible, following the expiration of each agreement, in the absence of either an express agreement to the contrary or the modification of those conditions of employment in a manner consistent with the Statute.[72] Where management elects to negotiate concerning a permissive matter covered by section 7106(b)(1), or the parties agree to a matter outside the required scope of bargaining under the Statute, and the parties reach agreement, either party retains the right to unilaterally terminate the practice embodied in such a provision upon expiration of that negotiated agreement.[73] Thus, either party may reassert its right not to negotiate with regard to the "permissive" subject of bargaining in question once the applicable agreement has expired.

The Authority has found that the public interest is served when an agency and two or more unions exclusively representing separate units of the agency's employees voluntarily enter into a multiunit bargaining arrangement for negotiating over conditions of employment affecting employees in their respective units.[74] When a party to such a multiunit or multiemployer bargaining arrangement wishes to withdraw from that arrangement, the withdrawal must be effected in a timely manner, that is, prior to the commencement of multiunit negotiations over the conditions of employment at issue. In the absence of a timely withdrawal, and after negotiations have begun, withdrawal may occur only where there is mutual consent by the affected parties, or where unusual circumstances exist.

Where the decision to make a change was itself negotiable, the question is whether the statutory obligation to notify and negotiate with the exclusive representative concerning the change was fulfilled. The extent of impact of the unilateral change in conditions of employment on the unit employees is not the issue.[75] The latter inquiry is appropriate only when the bargaining obligation of management with respect to the action taken

---

[71]*Immigration & Naturalization Serv.*, 9 FLRA 253 (1982), *rev'd on other grounds*, 727 F.2d 481, 115 LRRM 3499 (5th Cir. 1986).

[72]*Nuclear Regulatory Comm'n*, 6 FLRA 18 (1981).

[73]*Federal Aviation Admin., Nw. Mountain Region, Seattle, Wash.*, 14 FLRA 644 (1984).

[74]*Immigration & Naturalization Serv.*, 16 FLRA 80 (1984).

[75]*Social Sec. Admin., Baltimore, Md.*, 19 FLRA 1085 (1985); *Army Reserve Components Personnel & Admin. Center, St. Louis, Mo.*, 19 FLRA 290 (1985).

is limited to procedures and appropriate agreements pursuant to sections 7106(b)(2) and (3).

It is an unfair labor practice for a party to insist to impasse at the bargaining table over the inclusion of a permissive subject of bargaining in a collective bargaining agreement, for example, a proposal to establish prefiling conditions for an unfair labor practice charge when such filing conditions are inconsistent with the section 7118 right to file charges directly with the Authority. [76]

The Authority concluded that issues relating to whether a compelling need exists for an agency regulation to bar negotiations on proposals inconsistent with the agency regulation may be raised and decided in an unfair labor practice proceeding when the agency raises compelling need as an affirmative defense. [77] The Authority's rationale was adopted by the Court of Appeals for the District of Columbia Circuit but rejected by the Fourth Circuit. [78] On April 8, 1988, the Supreme Court agreed with the Fourth Circuit and reversed the Authority, concluding that where a matter is covered by an agency regulation, no duty to bargain arises until the Authority, in a negotiability proceeding, has first determined that no compelling need justifies adherence to the rule or regulation. [79]

Midterm Bargaining

After reversal by the District of Columbia Circuit, [80] the Authority agreed with the court's rationale, and consonant with case law in the private sector, found that the duty to bargain in good faith imposed by the Statute requires an agency to bargain during the term of a collective bargaining agreement on negotiable union proposals concerning matters not contained in the agreement unless the union has waived its right to bargain about the subject matter involved. [81] A waiver of bargaining rights may be established by express agreement or bargaining history. Further, a waiver must be clear and unmistakable. The Authority will render such deter-

---

[76]*Department of Agric., Food Safety & Inspection Serv.*, 22 FLRA 586 (1986).

[77]*Defense Logistics Agency, Cameron Station, Va.*, 12 FLRA 412 (1983), *aff'd*, 754 F.2d 1003, 118 LRRM 2829 (D.C. Cir. 1985); *Department of the Army, Aberdeen Proving Ground*, 21 FLRA 814 (1986).

[78]*Army Eng'r Center and Fort Belvoir*, 13 FLRA 707 (1984), *rev'd*, 762 F.2d 409, 119 LRRM 2854, *reh'g denied* (4th Cir. 1985). The Authority's Supplemental Decision and Order in that case, *Army Eng'r Center and Fort Belvoir*, 19 FLRA 746 (1985), accepted the Fourth Circuit opinion "as the law of the case. . . ."

[79]*FLRA v. Department of the Army, Aberdeen Proving Ground*, 127 LRRM 3137 (1988).

[80]*NTEU v. FLRA*, 810 F.2d 295, 124 LRRM 2489 (D.C. Cir. 1987), *rev'g sub nom. Internal Revenue Serv.*, 17 FLRA 731 (1985).

[81]*Internal Revenue Serv.*, 29 FLRA 162 (1987).

minations on a case-by-case basis. Thus, a union may, by express agreement, contractually agree to waive its right to initiate midterm bargaining
in general by a "zipper clause," that is, a clause intended to waive the
obligation to bargain during the term of the agreement on matters not
contained in the agreement. Or, a union may waive its right to initiate bargaining over a particular subject matter. The Authority will examine the
wording of contract provisions as well as the other relevant provisions of
the contract, bargaining history, and past practice to determine whether
the contract provision constitutes a clear and unmistakable waiver of the
union's right to initiate bargaining.

A clear and unmistakable waiver as evidenced by bargaining history
must concern subject matters discussed in contract negotiations but not
specifically covered in the resulting contract. On a case-by-case analysis
of the facts and circumstances, a waiver will be found where the subject
matter of the proposal offered by the union during midterm negotiations
was fully discussed and explored by the parties at the bargaining table.
The proposals need not be identical for a waiver to exist; rather the
determinative factor is whether the subject matter of the proposals offered
during contract and midterm negotiations is the same. If the union's midterm proposals are not negotiable, however, there is no duty to negotiate
midcontract.[82] Further, the duty to bargain midcontract extends to impact
and implementation negotiable proposals as well as to substantively
negotiable proposals.[83]

Impact and Implementation Bargaining

Although agency management is not required to negotiate over the
exercise of management rights, it is required to give adequate notice to the
union of anticipated changes in working conditions and, upon request, to
bargain in good faith over the procedures which management officials will
observe in exercising any management right and over appropriate arrangements for employees who are adversely affected by the exercise of any
management right. This is commonly referred to as impact and implementation bargaining.[84] Failure either to give adequate notice of the impend-
ing change involving the exercise of a management right, or to bargain in
good faith over procedures or appropriate arrangements for employees
who are adversely affected, is an unfair labor practice. Thus, even if the
change proposed by the agency involves a nonnegotiable management

---

[82]*General Servs. Admin.*, 29 FLRA 197 (1987).
[83]*Internal Revenue Serv., Dist. Office Unit*, 29 FLRA 268 (1987).
[84]5 U.S.C. 7106(b)(1) and (2).

right,[85] the agency must give proper notice and afford the union an opportunity to negotiate over the procedures which management officials will observe in implementing the management right and over appropriate arrangements for employees adversely affected by the exercise of such right.[86]

To determine whether a change in conditions of employment requires bargaining over negotiable impact and implementation proposals, the impact must be more than *de minimis*. The Authority has reassessed and modified its *de minimis* standards and now places principal emphasis on such general areas of consideration as the nature and extent of the effect or reasonably forseeable effect of the change on condition of employment of bargaining unit employees.[87] Equitable considerations are also taken into account in balancing the various interests while the number of employees involved is no longer a controlling consideration, but rather is applied primarily to expand, rather than limit, the number of situations where bargaining will be required. The parties' bargaining history will be subject to similar limited application while the size of the bargaining unit will no longer be considered by the Authority in applying its *de minimis* standard.

The Authority, under certain circumstances, will order *status quo ante* remedies in impact and implementation bargaining cases. The Authority has established certain criteria to determine whether the failure and refusal to bargain over the procedures to be observed in implementing certain changes and the impact that those changes have on the adversely affected employees require a *status quo ante* remedy.[88] These are:

1. whether, and when, notice was given to the union by the agency concerning the action or change decided upon;
2. whether, and when, the union requested bargaining on the procedures to be observed by the agency in implementing such action or change and/or concerning appropriate arrangements for employees adversely affected by each action or change;
3. the willfulness of the agency's conduct in failing to discharge its bargaining obligations under the Statute;
4. the nature and extent of the impact experienced by adversely affected employees; and

---

[85]See discussion in Chapter 7.

[86]See the Authority's negotiability determination in *NAGE, Local R14-87 and Kansas Army Nat'l Guard*, 21 FLRA 24 (1986) for a discussion of the negotiability of appropriate arrangements under 5 U.S.C. 7106(b)(3).

[87]*Social Sec. Admin.*, 24 FLRA 403 (1986).

[88]*Federal Correctional Inst.*, 8 FLRA 604 (1982). A *status quo ante* remedy orders the activity or union which has committed the unfair labor practice to return to the practice which was in effect prior to the unlawful change.

5. whether, and to what degree, a *status quo ante* remedy would disrupt or impair the efficiency and effectiveness of the agency's operations.

Back pay also may be an appropriate remedy in cases of a refusal to bargain over "impact and implementation." When it is established that employees were affected by a refusal to bargain violation, and that the agency action giving rise to the violation resulted in a withdrawal or reduction in the pay, allowances, or differentials of employees, the Authority will find that such violation warrants a remedy of back pay.[89] Thus, except as otherwise agreed by the parties, an agency must provide back pay to any employee who suffered a withdrawal or reduction in pay differential because of the unilateral change to the extent that bargaining in compliance with the Authority's order over such change eliminates or reduces the loss of pay differentials caused by the unlawful unilateral change. The Authority, however, remains reluctant to order retroactive remedial action to remedy impact and implementation bargaining violations.[90] Rather, the Authority finds that such retroactive remedies impair the flexibility of the Federal Service Impasses Panel to execute its statutory function should the parties ultimately bargain to impasse over the change and file a request for Panel assistance. Thus, absent a *status quo ante* remedy or the award of back pay when warranted, the Authority will order prospective bargaining rather than a retroactive application of any agreement reached by the parties.

Past Practice

It is an unfair labor practice to change a past practice involving a condition of employment without notice to the exclusive representative and fulfillment of the bargaining obligation.[91] A change in a past practice may trigger a bargaining obligation if management had knowledge of, or condoned, the past practice for an extensive period of time.[92] The Authority also has held, however, that there is no obligation to negotiate over a decision to change a past practice when the change was made to conform with the requirements of law and regulation.[93] The duty to bargain over

---

[89]*Federal Aviation Admin., Washington, D.C.*, 27 FLRA 230 (1987). See Chapter 12 for a discussion of the Back Pay Act.

[90]*Environmental Protection Agency*, 21 FLRA 786 (1986).

[91]*Immigration & Naturalization Serv., Washington, D.C.*, 31 FLRA 145 (1988).

[92]*Internal Revenue Serv., Washington, D.C., and Internal Revenue Serv., Hartford Dist. Office, Hartford, Conn.*, 27 FLRA 322 (1987).

[93]*Department of the Interior, Geological Survey, Conservation Div., Gulf of Mex. Region, Metairie, La.*, 9 FLRA 543 (1982).

the impact and implementation of the decision to change such an illegal past practice, however, remains. Thus, while management may be required to correct an unlawful practice once discovered, there is nonetheless an obligation to give notice of the change and, upon request, bargain, to the extent consonant with law and regulation, concerning the impact and/or implementation of the required change.

Bad-Faith Bargaining

A refusal to bargain in good faith is an unfair labor practice. Once a proposal has been established as negotiable through the existing processes of the Statute (see Chapter 9), it is a violation of sections 7116(a)(1) and (5) for an agency to refuse to negotiate in good faith on that proposal, or on a proposal without material differences.[94] Thus, once the negotiability of a proposal is established by Authority precedent, it is a refusal to bargain in good faith to maintain that a substantially similar proposal is not negotiable.[95]

It is clear that each party is required to deal with the other with the directness and dignity appropriate to partners on an equal footing. Factors such as unilaterally setting the dates for negotiations (which should have been subject to mutual agreement), imposing deadlines on the submission of proposals, limiting a union's caucus time during negotiations, and refusing to return to the bargaining table on a matter after negotiations were disbanded are indicative of bad-faith bargaining.[96]

A union is not required to file a negotiability appeal after its proposals have been deemed nonnegotiable by an agency. Rather, a union has a right to submit alternate proposals and to continue bargaining in good faith.[97] Further, absent agreement between the parties, the Statute does not require that a union present specific, substantive, written proposals in advance of negotiations. Such an agency request is in the nature of a proposed ground rule itself, and thus is a negotiable matter between the parties.[98]

Rejection of a Collective Bargaining Agreement

The Authority has determined that it will not police violations of collective bargaining agreements. Such disputes more appropriately

---

[94]*Department of the Air Force, Air Force Academy,* 6 FLRA 548 (1981), *aff'd sub nom. Air Force Academy v. FLRA,* 717 F.2d 1314, 114 LRRM 2525 (11th Cir. 1983).

[95]*Department of Agric. and Department of Agric., Agricultural Mktg. Serv., Livestock Div., Washington, D.C.,* 29 FLRA 940 (1987).

[96]*Social Sec. Admin.,* 18 FLRA 511 (1985).

[97]*Internal Revenue Serv.,* 9 FLRA 178 (1982).

[98]*Environmental Protection Agency,* 16 FLRA 602 (1984).

should be resolved through the parties' negotiated grievance and arbitration provisions. Thus, the Authority will find a violation of the duty to bargain in good faith only where the activity's conduct constitutes a patent and flagrant breach of the contract rather than an arguable interpretation of the contract. This violation amounts, in effect, to a unilateral rejection of a term or terms of the collective bargaining agreement.[99]

Bypassing the Union

An agency's direct communication with bargaining unit employees, rather than the exclusive representative, concerning conditions of employment, in an attempt to undermine the status of, or denigrate, the exclusive representative, is an unfair labor practice.[100] Section 7114(a)(1) provides that a labor organization that has been accorded exclusive recognition is the exclusive representative of the employees in the unit it represents and is entitled to act for, and negotiate collective bargaining agreements covering, all employees in the unit. Nevertheless, the Authority has held that not all direct communications between management and employees are prohibited. Thus, communications with employees which are intended as information gathering, which are reasonably understood to be for such purposes, and which are done in a manner that in no way threatens, or promises, benefits to employees or otherwise undermines the union, will not be found to be unlawful direct dealings in violation of sections 7116(a)(1) and (5).[101] As part of its overall management responsibility to conduct operations in an effective and efficient manner, an agency may question employees directly, provided it does not attempt to negotiate directly concerning matters properly bargainable with its employees' exclusive representative.[102] The Authority held that management must have the latitude to gather information, including opinions, from unit employees to ensure the efficiency and effectiveness of its operations. This approach has been affirmed by the District of Columbia Circuit.[103]

An agency does not violate the Statute by meeting directly with a bargaining unit employee and negotiating an informal adjustment of the em-

[99]*Social Sec. Admin., Baltimore, Md.*, 18 FLRA 855 (1985).
[100]*Social Sec. Admin., Baltimore, Md.*, 9 FLRA 909 (1982).
[101]*Kaiserslautern Am. High School, Department of Defense Dependents Schools, Germany N. Region*, 9 FLRA 184 (1982).
[102]*Internal Revenue Serv., Dist., Region, Nat'l Office Units*, 19 FLRA 353 (1985).
[103]*NTEU v. FLRA*, 826 F.2d 114, 126 LRRM 2157 (D.C. Cir. 1987). See *Internal Revenue Serv., Washington, D.C. and Internal Revenue Serv., Indianapolis, Ind., Dist. Office*, 31 FLRA 832 (1988), for a discussion of the factors the Authority will analyze to determine if polling of employees is an unlawful bypass.

ployee's EEO complaint.[104] Since any employee is entitled to elect or pursue a complaint of discrimination under the regulations of the EEOC, an unfair labor practice cannot be found based solely on an agency's conduct in resolving an EEO complaint pursuant to the regulations of the EEOC. Although the exclusive representative has no right to participate in the informal adjustment of an EEO complaint where a bargaining unit employee has elected to pursue the complaint of discrimination under the EEOC regulatory process, the exclusive representative nonetheless may have a role if the settlement affects the bargaining unit. Thus, if the adjustment of an EEO complaint results in a change of unit employees' conditions of employment, the agency would have an obligation, under the Statute, to give prompt notice of that change to the exclusive representative of the unit employees. The agency must then provide the union with an opportunity to bargain to the extent required by the Statute. An exclusive representative's right to bargain upon receiving notice of an EEO complaint settlement, however, cannot conflict with, or overturn, the substance of a settlement.

Agency Duty to Furnish Information to Unions

It is an unfair labor practice to refuse to furnish the exclusive representative, on request, data which are normally maintained by the agency in the regular course of business and are reasonably available and necessary for the exclusive representative to fulfill its representational obligations, including the processing of grievances under a negotiated contract. Data are not disclosable, however, if disclosure is prohibited by law or if the data constitute guidance, advice, counsel, or training relating to collective bargaining for management representatives.[105]

Data requested by a union which are necessary and relevant to carry out effectively its statutory representational obligation in processing an employee grievance is encompassed within the duty to furnish data.[106]

The union's right to receive relevant and necessary data is derived from section 7114(b)(4) and not section 7114(a)(1).[107] Noting particularly that the obligation to furnish data is an integral part of an agency's duty to negotiate in good faith under section 7114(b)(4), the Authority has

---

[104]*Government Printing Office*, 23 FLRA 35 (1986).

[105]5 U.S.C. 7114(b)(4). Conduct inconsistent with the duty to furnish data under 5 U.S.C. 7114(b)(4) is violative of 5 U.S.C. 7116(a)(1), (5), and (8).

[106]*Department of Health and Human Servs., Region IV, Health Care Fin. Admin.*, 21 FLRA 431 (1986).

[107]*Veterans Admin. Regional Office, Denver, Colo.*, 7 FLRA 629 (1982).

concluded that it would further congressional intent to require an agency to furnish the data, subject to the limitations set in section 7114(b)(4), without cost to the exclusive representative.[108]

The obligation to furnish information is not fulfilled merely by allowing a union to look at information.[109] Rather, relevant information must be furnished.

The Authority has rejected the position that all information involving bargaining unit employees is presumptively relevant.[110] Section 7114(b)(4) requires that the information requested be reasonably available and necessary and that a union's bare assertion that it needs data to process a grievance does not automatically oblige the agency to supply the data. Rather, the duty to supply data under section 7114(b)(4) turns upon the nature of the request and the circumstances in each particular case. In circumstances where the need for requested information is not apparent from the circumstances and the union fails to reveal why it is seeking the information despite management's reasonable request for clarification to make an informed judgment as to whether or to what extent the information sought was necessary for collective bargaining purposes, the Authority has not found a refusal to furnish the information an unfair labor practice.[111]

An agency cannot provide information that does not exist. However, the fact that specific information sought does not exist does not relieve an agency of its obligation to reply to a union's request. Section 7114(b)(4) has been interpreted so as to require an agency to reply to a request for information from an exclusive representative even if the response is that the information sought does not exist.[112] Finding that such a reply is necessary for full and proper discussion, understanding, and negotiation of subjects within the scope of collective bargaining within the meaning of section 7114(b)(4)(B), the Authority has ruled that an agency's refusal or neglect to reply, even if such information does not exist, is an unfair labor practice violative of sections 7116(a)(1), (5), and (8).

Information concerning nonunit employees, for example, supervisors and management officials, is not excluded from the scope of sec-

---

[108]*Veterans Admin. Regional Office, Denver, Colo.*, 10 FLRA 453 (1982).

[109]*Veterans Admin., Washington, D.C. and Veterans Admin. Regional Office, Buffalo, N.Y.*, 28 FLRA 260 (1987); *Department of Agric., Animal & Plant Health Inspection Serv., Plant Protection & Quarantine*, 26 FLRA 630 (1987).

[110]*Social Sec. Admin. and Social Sec. Admin. Field Operations, N.Y. Region*, 21 FLRA 517 (1986).

[111]*Social Sec. Admin. and Social Sec. Admin., Field Operations, N.Y. Region*, 21 FLRA 253 (1986), *rev'd sub nom. AFGE, AFL-CIO v. FLRA*, 811 F.2d 709, 124 LRRM 2705 (D.C. Cir. 1987).

[112]*Naval Supply Center, San Diego, Cal.*, 26 FLRA 324 (1987).

tion 7114(b)(4). Rather, the Authority will review the information requested to determine if the data are necessary to enable the union to fulfill its representational responsibilities. After a remand by the District of Columbia Circuit, the Authority has found information concerning the discipline of management officials and supervisors for making false statements necessary to aid a union in establishing whether a unit employee was being treated differently for the same or similar misconduct.[113]

The section 7114(b)(4) duty to furnish information does not extend, however, to the representation of employees in agency regulatory proceedings, such as before OPM, MSPB, or the EEOC.[114] However, the Authority has found the duty to disclose to encompass promotion packages required to evaluate grievances over nonselection of a unit employee to a nonunit position.[115] To process such grievances, the union is required to make a comparative assessment of the various evaluations involved in the merit promotion action involved.

The resolution of grievability questions cognizable under law is for an arbitrator under the parties' negotiated agreement to determine, unless the parties agree otherwise. Thus, the existence of a threshold question regarding the arbitrability of a grievance does not of itself relieve an agency of its obligation to furnish otherwise necessary information pursuant to section 7114(b)(4).[116] However, in situations where the Authority has held that the underlying matter cannot, as a matter of law, go to an arbitrator, there ordinarily would be no duty to furnish such information.[117] There is nothing in the language of section 7114(b) or the legislative history which implies that Congress intended a union's right to data under the provision to be dependent on whether the data are reasonably available from an alternative source.[118]

Although information that would enable a union to process an employee grievance effectively is encompassed under the duty to furnish relevant information, witnesses' statements taken by an agency in preparation for an arbitration proceeding are not included. In contrast to

---

[113]Department of Defense Dependents Schools, Washington, D.C. and Department of Defense Dependents Schools, Germany Region, 28 FLRA 202 (1987). See North Germany Area Council, Overseas Educ. Ass'n v. FLRA, 805 F.2d 1044, 123 LRRM 3141 (D.C. Cir. 1986), rev'g and remanding sub nom. Department of Defense Dependents Schools, Washington, D.C. and Department of Defense Dependents Schools, Germany Region, 19 FLRA 790 (1985).

[114]Library of Congress, 19 FLRA 267 (1985).

[115]Internal Revenue Serv., Nat'l Office, 21 FLRA 646 (1986).

[116]Internal Revenue Serv., Washington, D.C. and Internal Revenue Serv., Omaha Dist., Omaha, Neb., 25 FLRA 181 (1987).

[117]Director of Admin., Headquarters, Air Force, 17 FLRA 372 (1985).

[118]Army Reserve Components Personnel & Admin. Center, St. Louis, Mo., 26 FLRA 19 (1987).

statements taken during the investigation prior to the taking of such action, these prehearing statements are not necessary for the union's understanding of the basis for an employee's removal, for processing the grievance concerning the removal, or for representing the employee effectively at the arbitration hearing.[119]

An agency has the right to engage in internal discussion and deliberation prior to making decisions under the management rights sections of the Statute (section 7106). The right of management to engage in open discussions among themselves is an essential part of making decisions and taking actions. Thus, the Authority has found that release of the recommendations of one management official to another concerning the exercise of a management right is prohibited by section 7106 and disclosure of the details of those recommendations is thus prohibited by law within the meaning of section 7114(b)(4).[120] Release of this disputed information in the Authority's opinion, would give the union access to management's internal decision-making processes.[121] The District of Columbia Circuit, however, has rejected this interpretation of the Statute.[122] The matter is currently pending on remand before the Authority for analysis of the section 7114(b)(4)(C) exemption.

Information which is otherwise necessary but whose disclosure is prohibited by law is outside the scope of section 7114(b)(4). Application of this provision encompasses the interpretation of statutes other than the Federal Service Labor-Management Relations Statute. The Privacy Act is one such law which generally prohibits the disclosure of personal information about federal employees without their consent. Exception (b)(2) of the Privacy Act, however, provides that the prohibition against disclosure is not applicable if disclosure of the information is required under the Freedom of Information Act (FOIA). Exemption (b)(6) of the FOIA pertinently provides that information contained in personnel files may be withheld if disclosure of the information would constitute a "clearly unwarranted invasion of personal privacy." Thus, the Authority is often called upon to determine whether requested information falls within FOIA Exemption (b)(6), and must strike a balance between an individual's right to privacy and the public interest in having the information disclosed. In striking this balance in section 7114(b)(4) information cases, the Authority considers the congressional findings in section 7101 that collective bargaining is in the public interest, and that the release of information

---

[119]*Id.*, at 28.
[120]*NLRB*, 26 FLRA 108 (1987).
[121]*National Park Serv., Nat'l Capitol Region*, 26 FLRA 441 (1987).
[122]*NLRB v. FLRA and Police Ass'n of the District of Columbia v. FLRA*, 127 LRRM 3145 (D.C. Cir. 1988).

necessary for a union to perform its statutory representational functions promotes important public interests.[123]

One area which has been the subject of considerable litigation involves the release of names and home addresses of bargaining unit employees to exclusive representatives. After reversal by the Second Circuit,[124] the Authority concluded that the release of the names and home addresses of bargaining unit employees to the exclusive representatives of those employees is not prohibited by law (the Privacy Act), is necessary for unions to fulfill their duties under the Statute, and meets all the other requirements established by section 7114(b)(4).[125] The release of the information is generally required regardless what other alternative means of communication may be available. Four U.S. circuit courts have agreed with the Authority's approach while one has modified it by allowing employees to request their employer not to release such information.[126] Numerous cases are currently pending before the District of Columbia Circuit.[127]

Representational Violations by Agency Management[128]

Formal Agency-Employee Discussions

Failure to provide an exclusive representative with notice giving it an opportunity to be represented at a *formal* discussion between one or more representatives of an agency and one or more bargaining unit employees concerning a grievance, personnel policy or practices, or other general condition of employment, constitutes an unfair labor practice.[129] A formal discussion within the meaning of section 7114(a)(2)(A) exists if there is: (1) a discussion, (2) which is formal, (3) between one or more representa-

---

[123]*Army & Air Force Exch. Serv. (AAFES), Fort Carson, Colo.*, 25 FLRA 1060 (1987).

[124]*AFGE, Local 1760, AFL-CIO v. FLRA*, 786 F.2d 554, 122 LRRM 2137 (2d Cir. 1986), *rev'g sub nom. Social Sec. Admin., Ne. Program Serv. Center*, 19 FLRA 913 (1985).

[125]*Farmers Home Admin. Fin. Office, St. Louis, Mo.*, 23 FLRA 788 (1986).

[126]*Social Sec. Admin. v. FLRA*, 833 F.2d 1129, 126 LRRM 3235 (4th Cir. 1987); *Department of the Air Force, Scott AFB v. FLRA*, 838 F.2d 229, 127 LRRM 2710 (7th Cir. 1988); *Department of Agric. and the Farmers Home Admin. Fin. Office, St. Louis, Mo. v. FLRA*, 836 F.2d 1139, 127 LRRM 2360 (8th Cir. 1988); *Department of the Navy and Philadelphia Naval Shipyard v. FLRA*, 840 F.2d 1131, 127 LRRM 3010 (3d Cir. 1988).

[127]As this book went to press, the D.C. Circuit ruled that the Privacy Act precludes disclosure of unit employees' names and home addresses under §7114(b)(4). *FLRA v. Department of the Treasury*, 884 F.2d 1446, 132 LRRM 2464 (D.C. Cir. 1989). Petition for certiorari is currently pending before the Supreme Court.

[128]Conduct inconsistent with this representational right is violative of 5 U.S.C. 7116(a)(1) and (8).

[129]5 U.S.C. 7114(a)(2)(A).

tives of the agency and one or more employees in the unit or their representatives, (4) concerning any grievance or personnel policies or other general condition of employment.[130]

The Authority uses the following criteria in determining whether or not a discussion was formal in nature: (1) whether the individual who held the discussion is merely a first level supervisor or is higher in the management hierarchy, (2) whether any other management representatives attended, (3) where the individual meetings took place (i.e., in the supervisor's office, at each employee's desk, or elsewhere), (4) how long the meetings lasted, (5) how the meetings were called (i.e., with formal, advance, written notice or more spontaneously and informally), (6) whether a formal agenda was established for the meeting, (7) whether each employee's attendance was mandatory, and (8) the manner in which the meetings were conducted (i.e., whether the employee's identity and comments were noted or transcribed).[131]

The Authority has found meetings to be formal discussions where management representatives called meetings with employees in which attendance was mandatory and an agenda had been established by management to discuss a number of matters involving general conditions of employment or specific changes in job duties.[132] Meetings concerning a grievance filed by a unit employee under a negotiated grievance procedure, which were structured in accordance with the specific requirements of the grievance procedure and included meeting records made and given to the employee, also have been considered to be formal discussions.[133]

In 1985 the Authority concluded that "actual representation" (the presence of any union representative) at a formal discussion is sufficient to demonstrate compliance with the requirement of section 7114(a)(2)(A) that such an exclusive representative "be given an opportunity to be represented."[134] The Authority has reexamined this area of precedent and has determined it does not effectuate the intent of section 7114(a)(2)(A). Thus, prior notice to the exclusive representative is necessary to enable

---

[130]Bureau of Gov't Fin. Operations, Headquarters, 15 FLRA 423 (1984), rev'd on other grounds sub nom. NTEU v. FLRA, 704 F.2d 1181, 120 LRRM 2807 (D.C. Cir. 1985).

[131]Social Sec. Admin., Bureau of Field Operations, San Francisco, Cal., 10 FLRA 115 (1982); Social Sec. Admin. and Social Sec. Admin. Field Operations, Region II, 29 FLRA 1205 (1987).

[132]Social Sec. Admin., Office of Program Operations, Field Operations, San Francisco Region, 10 FLRA 172 (1982). See also 5 U.S.C. 7121(b)(3)(B) which assures the exclusive representative the right to be present during the grievance proceeding even though an employee has the right to present a grievance on the employee's own behalf.

[133]General Servs. Admin. Region 8, Denver, Colo., 19 FLRA 20 (1985).

[134]Veterans Admin. Medical Center, Muskogee, Okla., 19 FLRA 1054 (1985).

the union to choose its own representative.[135] Otherwise, if "actual representation" is sufficient to meet the requirement of section 7114(a)(2)(A), the choice of a union representative might be made not by the union, but rather by chance or by the agency.

Of course, a requirement that a union receive formal prior notice where the record reflects that the union has received actual notice would interject needless formality into the process. Thus, where the record does not establish that a union was given formal prior notice of a formal discussion, the record will be examined to determine if a union representative received actual notice and if so, whether that receipt was sufficient to establish that the union had an opportunity to be represented at the formal discussion, including the opportunity to designate a representative of its own choosing.[136]

The Authority also has recently returned to its original precedent in determining that the term "grievance" in section 7114(a)(2)(A) can encompass a statutory appeal.[137] However, if there is a conflict between rights under section 7114(a)(2)(A) and those under other statutes establishing statutory appeals, the Authority will consider that conflict in determining whether section 7114(a)(2)(A) has been violated.

The Authority also has concluded that Congress intended the term "discussion" to be synonymous with "meeting."[138] Thus, where agency management decides to hold a meeting with unit employees concerning grievances, personnel policies or practices, or other general conditions of employment, section 7114(a)(2)(A) requires management to give the employees' representative adequate notice of, and an opportunity to be present at, the meeting even if the meeting was called to make a statement or announcement rather than to engender dialogue.

Formal discussions also may occur in the context of interviews of unit employees by agency representatives in preparation for a third-party proceeding, such as an arbitration or unfair labor practice hearings. The exclusive representative's right under section 7114(a)(2)(A) is independent of an employee's right under section 7102 and thus may be violated even if the interview is voluntary and not coercive.[139]

---

[135]*Department of the Air Force, Sacramento, ALC, McClellan AFB, Cal.*, 29 FLRA 594 (1987).

[136]*Id.*, at 606.

[137]*Bureau of Prisons, Federal Correctional Inst., Ray Brook, N.Y.*, 29 FLRA 584 (1987).

[138]*Department of Defense, Nat'l Guard Bureau, Tex. Adjutant Gen's. Dep't, 149th TAC Fighter Group (ANG)(TAC), Kelly AFB*, 15 FLRA 529 (1984).

[139]*Supra* note 135.

It also is an unfair labor practice for an agency to prevent a union representative from speaking at a formal discussion.[140] Discussion means more than merely a right to be present. It also means the union representative has a right to comment, speak, and make statements. A union representative, however, is not entitled to take charge of or disrupt a meeting, and comments by a union representative must be governed by a rule of reasonableness. This requires respect for orderly procedures and that the union representative's comments be related to the subject matter addressed by the agency representative at the meeting.

Employee Examination in Connection With an Investigation

Section 7114(a)(2)(B) of the Statute provides that an exclusive representative of an appropriate unit in an agency shall be given the opportunity to be represented when a unit employee is being examined by a representative of the agency in connection with an investigation, if the employee reasonably believes that the examination may result in disciplinary action and requests union representation.[141] There is no requirement that agency representatives advise the employee of this right. However, each agency must annually inform its employees of this right to representation.[142] Thus, the right to representation is triggered when there is: (1) an examination in connection with an investigation, (2) of an employee in the unit, (3) by a representative of the agency, which (4) the employee may reasonably expect to result in disciplinary action, and (5) at which the employee requests representation.

An employee must request union representation to trigger the right to representation. An employee's request must be sufficient to put the employer on notice of the employee's desire for representation. Thus, an employee's mention of a need to see a union representative was found sufficient to put the activity on notice that the employee had an interest in representation, especially since the employee stated at the same time that he did not want to write anything that could be used against him by management.[143]

In determining whether an employee has a reasonable belief that discipline will result from the examination, an objective, as opposed to a

---

[140]*Nuclear Regulatory Comm'n*, 21 FLRA 765 (1986).
[141]This conduct is violative of 5 U.S.C. 7116(a)(1) and (8).
[142]5 U.S.C. 7114(a)(3).
[143]*Bureau of Prisons, Metro. Correctional Center, New York, N.Y.*, 27 FLRA 874 (1987).

subjective, test is used.[144] Thus, the Authority has rejected considering an employee's subjective feelings and opted instead for an approach whereby, under all the circumstances of the case, objective standards are considered in assessing whether an employee reasonably believes that discipline might result from the interview.

The meeting at issue must constitute an examination in connection with an investigation. Counseling sessions during which employees are made aware of performance deficiencies without the solicitation of additional information are considered remedial rather than investigatory in nature and thus are not encompassed within the section 7114(a)(2)(B) right to representation.[145] A meeting held to inform an employee of a previously reached decision likewise is not an examination in connection with an investigation encompassed under the right to representation.[146]

Once an employee makes a valid request for union representation, the burden shifts to the employer to: (1) grant the request, (2) discontinue the interview, or (3) offer the employee the choice between continuing the interview unaccompanied by a union representative or having no interview at all.[147]

It is an unfair labor practice to take disciplinary action against an employee for the employee's failure to obey an order to participate in an examination in connection with an investigation, when an employee's request for union representation has been denied.[148] It has not been determined, however, whether an employee is required to be granted time to confer with the union representative prior to the meeting.[149]

Section 7114(a)(2)(B) also applies to a request by an employee for union representation for an examination by an agency representative in connection with a criminal investigation.[150] However, agencies are permitted to engage in unannounced surveillance of allegedly dishonest employees as an investigative technique without first notifying the employee and providing an opportunity to request representation. These surveillance activities are not encompassed within the right to union repre-

---

[144]*Internal Revenue Serv., Washington, D.C. and Internal Revenue Serv., Hartford Dist. Office*, 4 FLRA 237 (1980), *aff'd sub nom. Internal Revenue Serv. v. FLRA*, 671 F.2d 560, 110 LRRM 2153 (D.C. Cir. 1982).

[145]*Internal Revenue Serv., Detroit, Mich.*, 5 FLRA 421 (1981); *Internal Revenue Serv.*, 8 FLRA 324 (1982); *Department of the Air Force, 2750th Air Base Wing Headquarters, Air Force Logistics Command, Wright Patterson AFB, Ohio*, 10 FLRA 97 (1982).

[146]*Department of the Navy, Portsmouth Naval Shipyard*, 7 FLRA 766 (1982).

[147]*Supra* note 143.

[148]*Id.*, at 881.

[149]*Department of the Navy, Norfolk Naval Base, Norfolk, Va.*, 14 FLRA 731 (1984).

[150]*Internal Revenue Serv., Jacksonville Dist. and Internal Revenue Serv., Se. Regional Office of Inspection*, 23 FLRA 876 (1986).

sentation for investigatory interviews. Thus, unannounced monitoring of an employee's conversation by agency management does not constitute an "examination" within the meaning of section 7114(a)(2)(B).[151]

The Authority has recognized management's need, under certain circumstances, to place reasonable limitations on the exclusive representative's participation during an examination of an employee, to prevent an adversary confrontation with that representative and to achieve the objective of the examination.[152] However, management cannot go beyond what is reasonably necessary under the specific circumstances of the case since the right to representation includes the right to take an active part in the defense of the employee.[153]

Although an agency may not be the employer of an individual who is subject to an examination, once a nonemploying agency becomes aware of the employee's statutory right to union representation in the interview, it cannot interfere with that right. Thus an entity of an agency not in the same chain of command as the entity at the level of exclusive recognition, violates section 7116 by unlawfully interfering with the rights of employees other than its own when it examines an employee and denies a request for representation under section 7114(a)(2)(B).[154]

Official Time Violations by Agency Management

Time, Travel, and Per Diem During Negotiation of a Collective Bargaining Agreement

Refusal to grant official paid time to a representative of an exclusive representative who would otherwise be in a work or paid leave status, while engaged in the negotiation or renegotiation of a collective bargaining agreement or in midterm bargaining, is an unfair labor practice.[155] Section 7131(a) provides that any employee representing an exclusive representative in the negotiation of a collective bargaining agreement shall be

---

[151]*Bureau of Alcohol, Tobacco & Firearms, Se. Regional Office, Atlanta, Ga.*, 24 FLRA 521 (1986).

[152]*Norfolk Naval Shipyard*, 9 FLRA 458 (1982).

[153]*Customs Serv., Region VII, Los Angeles, Cal.*, 5 FLRA 297 (1981); *Federal Aviation Admin., St. Louis Tower, Bridgeton, Mo.*, 6 FLRA 678 (1981).

[154]*Department of Defense, Defense Criminal Investigative Serv., Defense Logistics Agency and Defense Contract Admin. Servs. Region, N.Y.*, 28 FLRA 1145 (1987).

[155]Conduct encompassed under this heading is violative of 5 U.S.C. 7116(a)(1) and (8).

authorized official time for such purposes, including attendance at impasse proceedings.[156]

An employee also is on official paid time when traveling during duty hours to participate in activities for which the employee will be on official time under section 7131(a).[157] The negotiation of ground rules is also encompassed within the entitlement to official time since it involves the bilateral participation of the parties and is part of the good-faith negotiating process leading to agreement.[158]

The Authority initially determined that employees who are on official time under section 7131 while representing an exclusive representative in the negotiation of a collective bargaining agreement are entitled to payments from agencies for their travel and per diem expenses.[159] However, the Supreme Court rejected the Authority's interpretation requiring the automatic payment of travel expenses and per diem.[160] The Court found that while section 7131(a) provided for official time, the Statute did not require payment for travel expenses and per diem. The Authority thereafter in a negotiability determination concluded that proposals seeking the payment of travel expenses and per diem for union representatives on official time under section 7131(a) or (d)[161] constitute a condition of employment within an agency's administrative discretion, and are therefore, not inconsistent with law or governmentwide regulation.[162] The District of Columbia Circuit has affirmed the Authority's finding that the payment of travel expenses and per diem to union representatives on official time under sections 7131(a) and (d) is a negotiable matter.[163]

Section 7131(a) provides further that the number of employees representing the union for whom official time is authorized shall not exceed the number of individuals designated as representing the agency for such purposes. Further, the "official time entitlement under section 7131(a) accrues only to a representative of an exclusive representa-

[156]*Internal Revenue Serv., Washington, D.C., Indianapolis, Ind., and Dallas, Tex., Dists.*, 10 FLRA 210 (1982).

[157]*Department of the Treasury, Bureau of the Pub. Debt*, 17 FLRA 1045 (1985).

[158]*Department of Defense Dependents Schools*, 14 FLRA 191 (1984).

[159]*Interpretation & Guidance*, 2 FLRA 264 (1979).

[160]*Bureau of Alcohol, Tobacco & Firearms v. FLRA*, 464 U.S. 89, 114 LRRM 3393 (1983).

[161]5 U.S.C. 7131(d) provides for the negotiation of reasonable and necessary official time for representational purposes other than negotiation or renegotiation of a collective bargaining agreement or cooperation in impasse procedures encompassed within 5 U.S.C. 7131(a). This negotiable official time also is subject to the 5 U.S.C. 7131(b) ban on use of official time for the conduct of internal union affairs, including solicitation of membership.

[162]*NTEU and Department of the Treasury, Customs Serv.*, 21 FLRA 6 (1986).

[163]*Customs Serv. v. FLRA*, 127 LRRM 2378 (D.C. Cir. 1988).

tive who is a member of the bargaining unit to which the right to negotiate the bargaining agreement applies."[164]

The Authority initially determined that section 7131(a) does not apply to the negotiation of a local agreement which supplements a national master agreement.[165] Rather, the issue of whether official time is to be granted during the negotiation of supplemental agreements is a matter negotiable under section 7131(d). Based on a reversal of this position by the District of Columbia Circuit,[166] the Authority reexamined the issue and concluded that the official time provisions of section 7131(a) encompass the negotiation of local agreements supplementing master agreements. These local negotiations must be authorized by the parties at the level of exclusive recognition.[167] Any unit employee representing the union at local supplemental negotiations is entitled to official time regardless of whether the employee is stationed at the location which is the subject of local negotiations.[168]

Under section 7131(d), official time for representational activities is a negotiable matter.[169] An exclusive representative also may negotiate official time to prepare for midterm negotiations over changes in conditions of employment,[170] or for impasse proceedings.[171] There is no obligation, however, for an agency to negotiate with a union concerning authorization of official time for one of its employees to represent the union in a different collective bargaining unit engaged in collective bargaining.[172]

Management can deny official time for representational functions, including negotiations, to a representative of the exclusive representative if it can establish that the use of official time will interfere with the accomplishment of the agency's work.[173] Thus, an exclusive representa-

[164]*Department of the Air Force, 2750th Air Base Wing Headquarters, Air Force Logistics Command, Wright Patterson AFB, Ohio*, 7 FLRA 738 (1982); *Department of the Army, 94th Army Reserve Command, Hanscom AFB, Mass.*, 8 FLRA 83 (1982).
[165]*Interpretation & Guidance*, 7 FLRA 682 (1982).
[166]*AFGE, AFL-CIO v. FLRA*, 750 F.2d 143, 118 LRRM 2021 (D.C. Cir. 1984).
[167]*Department of the Air Force, Headquarters, Air Force Logistics Command, Wright Patterson AFB, Ohio*, 19 FLRA 169 (1985).
[168]*Veterans Admin. Cent. Office, Washington, D.C. and VA Medical Center, Cincinnati, Ohio*, 23 FLRA 512 (1986).
[169]*NAGE, SEIU, AFL-CIO and Veterans Admin. Medical Center, Brockton/W. Roxbury, Mass.*, 23 FLRA 542 (1986).
[170]*Harry S. Truman Memorial Veterans Hosp., Columbia, Mo.*, 17 FLRA 408 (1985).
[171]*NLRB, Washington, D.C.*, 6 FLRA 213 (1981).
[172]*Naval Space Surveillance Sys., Dahlgren, Va.*, 12 FLRA 731 (1983), *aff'd sub nom. AFGE, Local 2096 v. FLRA*, 738 F.2d 633, 116 LRRM 3400 (4th Cir. 1984).
[173]*Department of the Navy, Norfolk Naval Shipyard, Portsmouth, Va.*, 15 FLRA 867 (1984).

tive cannot claim that it is entitled to the allocation of official time to a particular employee without regard to management's needs and requirements regarding the performance of assigned work.[174]

Time, Travel, and Per Diem for Participation in Processing an Unfair Labor Practice Charge

It is an unfair labor practice to refuse official time and to refuse to pay travel expenses and per diem to an employee who is processing an unfair labor practice charge upon a determination by the Authority's regional director that the participation is necessary. Section 7131(c) empowers the Authority to determine whether employees participating in proceedings before it shall be authorized official time, which encompasses payment of travel expenses and per diem. This statutory requirement has been implemented by the Authority in section 2429.13 of its regulations. It provides, in part, for the participation on official time, including transportation and per diem, by any employee in any phase of any proceeding before the Authority which encompasses preparation for a formal hearing in an unfair labor practice proceeding if deemed necessary "by the Authority, General Counsel, . . . or other agent of the Authority designated by the Authority. . . ."[175] Regional office Authority agents have been deemed to come within the definition of "other agent[s] of the Authority designated by the Authority" and thus have been held to be authorized to require that an employee participate in preparation for formal hearings in unfair labor practice proceedings.[176] The Authority has specifically rejected a "reasonableness test" with regard to a regional director's authority to determine whether an employee is necessary for participation in pre-unfair labor practice hearing proceedings.[177]

While payment of per diem and travel expenses is a negotiable matter under section 7131(a), whether term, supplemental, or midcontract, and for representational activities under section 7131(d), these expenses are an entitlement when an employee is required to participate in an unfair labor practice hearing pursuant to section 7131(c) as interpreted in section 2429.13 of the Authority's regulations.[178] In addition,

---

[174]*Federal R.R. Admin.*, 21 FLRA 508 (1986).
[175]*Norfolk Navy Shipyard, Portsmouth, Va.*, 5 FLRA 788 (1981).
[176]*Bureau of Alcohol, Tobacco & Firearms*, 10 FLRA 10 (1982); *Social Sec. Admin., Great Lakes Program Serv. Center*, 10 FLRA 510 (1982).
[177]*Bureau of Alcohol, Tobacco & Firearms*, 13 FLRA 558 (1983).
[178]*Department of the Air Force, Headquarters, Air Force Logistics Command, Wright Patterson AFB, Ohio*, 24 FLRA 187 (1986). As this book went to press, the D.C. Circuit reversed this decision and, at 131 LRRM 2864, ruled that §7131(c) does not require the payment of per diem and travel expenses.

federal employees required to participate in unfair labor practice proceedings are entitled to official time and payment of travel and per diem expenses even though their employing agency is not a party to the proceeding.[179]

Once the participation of an employee has been deemed necessary by the Authority in any phase of any proceeding before the Authority, the agency has no discretion to determine whether or not an employee should be on official time. An agency thus has been found to interfere with the protected rights of employees in violation of section 7116(a)(1) when it imposed the condition that employees whose participation had been deemed necessary either had to wear the appropriate military work uniform of the National Guard in order to receive official time or had to participate at the hearing in an annual leave status.[180]

Dues Allotments

Failure to honor an employee's revocation of dues authorization as provided for in section 7115(a) constitutes an unfair labor practice. Violations may be committed by both labor organizations and agencies.[181] Section 7115(a) states that an agency which has received from an employee in an appropriate unit a written assignment authorizing deductions for the payment of regular and periodic union dues from the employee's pay must honor the assignment and make an appropriate allotment. These allotments are made at no cost to the exclusive representative or the employee. Employee dues allotments must be implemented in a timely manner.[182] It is an unfair labor practice to refuse to honor properly authorized dues allotments and/or to terminate dues allotments prematurely.[183] In such cases, the agency is ordered to reimburse the union for all dues revocations effectuated in a manner inconsistent with section 7115(a). The deduction of dues terminates when the agreement between the agency and the exclusive representative involved ceases to be applicable to the employee, when the employee is suspended or expelled from membership in the union,[184] or when the employee revokes the dues authorization

---

[179]*AFLC, McClellan AFB, Cal.*, 24 FLRA 274 (1986).
[180]*162d Tactical Fighter Group, Ariz. Air Nat'l Guard, Tucson, Ariz.*, 21 FLRA 715 (1986). Cf. *Department of the Navy, Norfolk Naval Station*, 22 FLRA 338 (1986).
[181]This conduct is violative of 5 U.S.C. 7116(a)(1) and (8) and/or 7116(b)(1) and (8).
[182]*Department of Health and Human Servs.*, 12 FLRA 250 (1983).
[183]*Department of Labor*, 7 FLRA 688 (1982); *Department of the Navy, Naval Underwater Sys. Center, Newport, R.I.*, 16 FLRA 1124 (1984).
[184]5 U.S.C. 7115(b).

during the "open period."[185] Thus, when an employee has been promoted to a supervisory position, the employee is outside the bargaining unit, and the collective bargaining agreement "ceases to be applicable to the employee." Accordingly, the employee's allotment must terminate pursuant to section 7115(a).[186]

The Authority initially determined that management does not violate sections 7116(a)(1) and (8) by recovering from subsequent dues allotments the overpayment of dues.[187] The Second and Fifth circuits disagreed with the Authority's interpretation and found that recouping overpayments of union dues previously remitted by the agency to the union by deducting such overpayments from subsequent remittances was an unfair labor practice. The Authority continued, however, to disagree with the two circuit courts, concluding that an agency's recoupment of dues erroneously paid to an exclusive representative constitutes the correction of an administrative error in compliance with the terms of the Statute.[188] Thereafter, the District of Columbia Circuit agreed with the two previous circuit courts and again rejected the Authority rationale.[189]

Subsequent to the District of Columbia Circuit reversal, the Authority abandoned its previous decisions and followed the reasoning and conclusions of the three U.S. courts of appeals.[190] Thus, section 7115 imposes an absolute duty on agencies to honor the current assignments of unit employees by remitting regular and periodic dues deducted from their accrued salaries to their exclusive representatives. Recoupment of prior erroneous payments from a subsequent remittance of dues is violative of sections 7116(a)(1) and (8).[191]

---

[185]Interpretation & Guidance, 1 FLRA 183 (1979); Army, Army Materiel Dev. & Readiness Command, Warren, Mich., 7 FLRA 194 (1981). An employee's dues authorization is irrevocable for a one-year period. After each year of dues deductions, an employee must be afforded an opportunity in which to revoke dues authorization if the employee chooses. The parties may define through negotiations the yearly intervals. Department of the Navy, Portsmouth Naval Shipyard, Portsmouth, N.H., 19 FLRA 586 (1985).

[186]Internal Revenue Serv., Fresno Serv. Center, Cal., 7 FLRA 371 (1981), rev'd on other grounds sub nom. Internal Revenue Serv., Fresno Serv. Center, Fresno, Cal. v. FLRA, 706 F.2d 1019, 113 LRRM 3006 (9th Cir. 1983).

[187]Department of the Air Force, 3480th Air Base Group, Goodfellow AFB, Tex., 9 FLRA 394 (1982).

[188]Department of the Air Force, Headquarters, AFLC, Wright Patterson AFB, Ohio, 23 FLRA 376 (1986). See AFGE, AFL-CIO, Local 2612 v. FLRA, 739 F.2d 87, 116 LRRM 3171 (2d Cir. 1984); AFGE, AFL-CIO, Local 1816 v. FLRA, 715 F.2d 224, 114 LRRM 2529 (5th Cir. 1983).

[189]AFGE, Council 214, AFL-CIO v. FLRA, 835 F.2d 1458, 127 LRRM 2141 (D.C. Cir. 1987), rev'g sub nom. Department of the Air Force, Headquarters, AFLC, Wright Patterson AFB, Ohio, 23 FLRA 376 (1986).

[190]Lowry AFB, Denver, Colo., 31 FLRA 793 (1988).

[191]As a remedy, the agency will be ordered to reimburse the union the amount of dues

Duty of Fair Representation[192]

It is an unfair labor practice for an exclusive representative to fail to represent all bargaining unit employees without discrimination and without regard to union membership.[193] When union membership is not a factor, the standard for determining whether an exclusive representative has breached its duty of fair representation under section 7114(a)(1) is whether the union deliberately and unjustifiably treated one or more bargaining unit employees differently from other employees in the unit.[194] Thus, the union's actions must be more than mere negligence or ineptitude. Rather, the union must have acted arbitrarily or in bad faith, and the action must have resulted in disparate or discriminatory treatment of a bargaining unit employee.[195]

The Authority initially concluded that the duty of fair representation is not restricted to proceedings under the sole control of the exclusive representative.[196] Rather, the Authority found that when an exclusive representative decides to represent unit employees in any matter affecting their conditions of employment, it has the duty, under section 7114, to represent all unit employees, and may not discriminate with regard to that representation on the basis of union membership.[197] The Authority held that a union violated its duty of fair representation when it supplied attorneys only to members to help in representational efforts, such as appeals to the MSPB.[198]

After rejection of this theory by the District of Columbia Circuit, the Authority reexamined the scope of the duty of fair representation under the Statute.[199] In agreement with the Distict of Columbia Circuit, the Au-

---

it would have received from the pay of employees but did not receive as a result of the unlawful withholding of such monies in order to recoup a prior erroneous payment. The Authority expressed no view on what other actions, if any, an agency may take to recover amounts claimed to have been improperly remitted previously as dues to an exclusive representative.

[192]This conduct is violative of 5 U.S.C. 7116(b)(1) and (8).

[193]5 U.S.C. 7114(a)(1).

[194]*NFFE, Local 1453 and Kenneth A. Crawford*, 23 FLRA 686 (1986).

[195]Cf. *IAM & AW, Local 39, AFL-CIO and Roy G. Evans*, 24 FLRA 352 (1986) *and AFGE, Local 1857, AFL-CIO and John M. Neill*, 28 FLRA 677 (1987) *with NFFE, Washington, D.C. and Henry M. Thompson*, 24 FLRA 320 (1986).

[196]*NTEU (Customs Serv.)*, 10 FLRA 519 (1982), *enf'd sub nom. NTEU v. FLRA*, 721 F.2d 1402, 114 LRRM 3440 (D.C. Cir. 1983).

[197]*AFGE, AFL-CIO (Social Sec. Admin.)*, 17 FLRA 446 (1985), *decision and order on remand*, 30 FLRA 35 (1987).

[198]*AFGE, AFL-CIO, Local 916 (Department of the Air Force, Oklahoma City Air Force Logistics Center, Tinker AFB, Okla)*, 18 FLRA 5 (1985), *rev'd sub nom. AFGE, Local 916 v. FLRA*, 812 F.2d 1326, 124 LRRM 3220 (10th Cir. 1987).

[199]*NTEU v. FLRA*, 800 F.2d 1165, 123 LRRM 2129 (D.C. Cir. 1986), *rev'd sub nom. NTEU and NTEU, Chapter 121 (Bureau of Alcohol, Tobacco & Firearms)*, 16 FLRA 717 (1984).

thority concluded that section 7114(a) is intended by Congress to incorporate the private sector duty of fair representation. Thus, the Authority will analyze a union's responsibilities under section 7114(a) in the context of whether or not the union's representational activities on behalf of employees are grounded in the union's authority to act as exclusive representative.[200] Where the union is acting as the exclusive representative of its members, the Authority continues to require that the union's activities be undertaken without discrimination and without regard to union membership under section 7114(a)(1). The Authority, however, will not extend the statutory obligation to situations where the union is not acting as the exclusive representative nor will the Authority continue to decide cases based on whether or not the union's activities relate to conditions of employment of unit employees. Accordingly, a union may discriminate on the basis of membership in those representational activities not grounded in the union's authority to act as exclusive representative, such as when a proceeding was not in the sole control of the union by virtue of its certification as the exclusive representative.[201]

The Authority has remedied violations of the duty of fair representation by ordering unions to make employees whole should an agency fail to permit the filing of a late grievance concerning an employee's suspension and should the agency fail to pay an employee lost overtime.[202] These make-whole remedies are required since agencies are not parties in duty of fair representation cases. The Supreme Court has held there is no federal district court jurisdiction over federal sector duty of fair representation claims.[203] Rather, Congress vested exclusive enforcement authority over the duty of fair representation in the Authority and its General Counsel.

Strikes and Picketing

A union's call or participation in a strike, work stoppage, slowdown, or picketing (if such picketing interferes with the agency's operation) of an agency in a labor-management dispute, and a union's failure to condemn such activity by failing to take action to prevent or stop such unlawful activity, is an unfair labor practice.[204] Section 7120(f) provides that, in

---

[200]*Fort Bragg Ass'n of Educators, National Educ. Ass'n, Fort Bragg, N.C. (Fort Bragg Dep't of Defense Dependents Schools, Fort Bragg, N.C.)*, 28 FLRA 908 (1987).
[201]*AFGE, AFL-CIO (Social Sec. Admin.)*, 30 FLRA 35 (1987).
[202]*AFGE, Local 1857, AFL-CIO and John M. Neill*, 28 FLRA 677 (1987).
[203]*Karahalios v. NFFE, Local 1263*, 130 LRRM 2737 (1989).
[204]Such conduct is violative of 5 U.S.C. 7116(b)(1) and (7).

the case of any labor organization which by omission or commission has willfully and intentionally violated section 7116(b)(7) with regard to any strike, work stoppage, or slowdown, the Authority shall, upon an appropriate finding of such violation, (1) revoke the exclusive recognition status of the labor organization, which shall then immediately cease to be legally entitled and obligated to represent employees in the unit; or (2) take any other appropriate disciplinary action.

The only Authority decision issued concerning alleged unlawful strike activity involved the Professional Air Traffic Controllers Organization (PATCO), wherein the Authority determined the PATCO willfully and intentionally violated sections 7116(b)(7)(A) and (B).[205] Accordingly, the Authority revoked PATCO's status as the representative of the employees in a nationwide bargaining unit of air traffic control specialists in the Federal Aviation Administration and ordered that PATCO no longer be considered a labor organization within the meaning of section 7103(a)(4).[206]

With respect to picketing, the language and legislative history of section 7116(b)(7) makes it clear that Congress rejected the "reasonably threatens to interfere" part of the standard under the predecessor Executive Order and instead requires actual "interference" for picketing to be an unfair labor practice under the Statute.[207] In determining whether the inconvenience or disturbance to a particular agency's operations resulting from the picketing constitutes an unfair labor practice, the Authority will examine the picketing in each case, examining such factors as the government interest involved, the sensitivity of the function and its purpose, the location of the picketed operation, the duration of the picketing, and the number and conduct of the pickets. An operation of high sensitivity, such as one involving national security or the critical functions related to health or safety, could justify a relatively high degree of restraint of even First Amendment-related activities such as picketing. In these situations, even a relatively brief and minor disruption could in some circumstances justify a finding of unlawful interference. On the other hand, in an operation involving a relatively lower degree of sensitivity, the same picketing activities might not be found to be unlawful interference.

[205]*PATCO, affiliated with MEBA, AFL-CIO (FAA, Department of Transp.)*, 7 FLRA 34 (1981), enf'd sub nom. *PATCO v. FLRA*, 685 F.2d 547, 110 LRRM 2676 (D.C. Cir. 1982).

[206]Each member of the Authority issued a separate opinion as did the three judges of the District of Columbia Circuit when affirming the decertification and disestablishment of PATCO.

[207]*AFGE, Local 2369, AFL-CIO (Social Sec. Admin., N.Y. Regional Office)*, 22 FLRA 63 (1986).

9. Negotiability in Federal Labor-Management Agreements

STUART R. HORN*

The Federal Service Labor-Management Relations Statute prescribes a duty to bargain matters directly affecting the conditions of employment of bargaining unit employees, to the extent consistent with applicable laws, governmentwide rules or regulations, or internal regulations for which an agency has "compelling need."[1] Disagreements on what is consistent with law, governmentwide rules or regulations, or internal regulations with compelling need may be appealed by the unions to the Federal Labor Relations Authority (FLRA).

Appealing a Negotiability Issue

Procedural Considerations

If an agency involved in collective bargaining alleges that a particular union proposal is inconsistent with federal law, governmentwide regulations, or internal regulations for which the agency has a compelling need and is, therefore, outside the statutorily defined scope of the duty to bargain, it raises a "negotiability issue." The union may appeal that allegation directly to the FLRA[2] and the Authority will consider such an appeal in accordance with the rules set forth in 5 C.F.R. Part 2424.

---

*This chapter was written by Stuart R. Horn in his private capacity without official support from, or endorsement by, the Federal Labor Relations Authority.

[1] 5 U.S.C. 7103(a)(12), 7114, and 7117(a) are read in conjunction to establish this definition. *Antilles Consol. Educ. Ass'n and Antilles Consol. School Sys.*, 22 FLRA 235, 236 (1986).

[2] 5 U.S.C. 7117(b) and (c).

NEGOTIABILITY IN FEDERAL LABOR-MANAGEMENT AGREEMENTS   269

A negotiability appeal should be solely concerned with whether a particular proposal, as worded, is within the scope of bargaining prescribed by the Statute. If the Authority finds that a disputed proposal is within the scope of mandatory bargaining, it issues a bargaining order. If it finds that the proposal is outside the scope of bargaining, it dismisses the appeal.[3]

A negotiability appeal may not concern matters involving the parties' conduct such as when, why, whether, with whom, or how bargaining is—or is not—being accomplished. Disputes over matters of conduct may not be resolved under the negotiability appeal procedures. Other forums exist for their resolution.[4]

Who May Appeal

Only a union which is a party to the negotiations may appeal an agency allegation of nonnegotiability.[5] An agency may not file a petition for review of a union's claim that the agency's proposal is nonnegotiable.[6]

Conditions for FLRA Review

A union has 15 days to file an appeal after it has been served by the agency with an allegation that the scope of the duty to bargain does not extend to the matter proposed by the union.[7] To start the time limit on the union's appeal[8] the agency must put its allegation *in writing* and serve it on the union within 10 days of the union's *written request* to the agency.[9] The union's failure to file an appeal within 15 days of having been served a procedurally correct agency allegation of nonnegotiability will bar any

---

[3]Unfair labor practice remedies for breaches of the bargaining obligation are not available in a negotiability dispute. *Decision on Petition for Amendment of Rules,* 23 FLRA 405 (1986), *aff'd sub nom. National Labor Relations Board Union v. FLRA,* 834 F.2d 191 (D.C. Cir. 1987).

[4]Conversely, a pure negotiability issue cannot be resolved under the unfair labor practice procedures, see 5 C.F.R. 2423.5 (1987), and interest arbitrators are not authorized to make negotiability rulings although they can impose disputed proposals which they find are within the scope of bargaining by applying existing Authority case law. *Commander, Carswell AFB, Tex. and AFGE, Local 1364,* 31 FLRA 620, 621–22 (1988).

[5]5 C.F.R. 2424.2.

[6]5 C.F.R. 2424.2. *Veterans Admin. Medical Center, Salisbury, N.C. and AFGE, Local 1738,* 2 FLRA 404 (1980).

[7]Service may be accomplished by certified mail or in person. The date of service is the day when the allegation is deposited in the U.S. mail or is delivered in person. 5 C.F.R. 2429.27.

[8]See *AFGE, Local 3385 and Federal Home Loan Bank Bd. Dist. 7, Chicago, Ill.,* 7 FLRA 398 (1981).

[9]5 C.F.R. 2424.3.

appeal of that allegation. The 15-day time limit for union appeals is a jurisdictional requirement which may not be extended or waived by the Authority.[10]

The union does not have to file an appeal of an agency allegation not in accordance with established procedure in order to protect its rights. For example, if an agency serves an allegation of nonnegotiability on a union without the union's having requested one, the union does not need to file an appeal within 15 days to protect its rights. The union can subsequently request, and be entitled to receive, an allegation concerning the same proposal.[11] However, if a union waives the protection of the rules and files an appeal from an unrequested allegation, the appeal must be filed within the 15-day period, as if the allegation had been requested.[12] If a union requests an allegation in writing but the agency does not respond within 10 days of receipt the union may appeal to the FLRA without an allegation.[13]

The timely disapproval of provisions in a locally negotiated agreement by an agency head is treated by the Authority as an allegation of nonnegotiability made on request of the union. The union must file a petition for review within 15 days of service of the disapproval or lose the right to appeal.[14]

Grounds for Appealing

A union may appeal because it disagrees with the agency's allegation that the disputed proposal is inconsistent with a federal law, government-wide rule or regulation, or the agency's own, internal regulation.[15]

If the agency alleges that its own regulation bars negotiations, the union may appeal because it believes that the regulation violates applicable law or the regulation of a controlling authority outside the agency.[16]

---

[10] C.F.R. 2429.23(d).

[11] *Production, Maintenance, and Pub. Employees, Local No. 1276 and Defense Logistics Agency, Defense Depot Tracy, Tracy, Cal.*, 9 FLRA 919 (1982).

[12] *Id.*

[13] 5 C.F.R. 2424.3.

[14] *Id.* The Statute provides in 5 U.S.C. 7114(c)(1) that negotiated agreements are subject to approval by the head of the agency. An untimely disapproval by the agency head does not raise negotiability issues. The local agreement goes into effect, including the disputed provisions; the negotiability dispute is rendered moot. The validity of those provisions under applicable law, rule, or regulation can be raised in subsequent grievance arbitration or unfair labor practice proceedings seeking to enforce them. *NTEU, Chapter 52 and Internal Revenue Serv., Austin Dist.*, 23 FLRA 720 (1986).

[15] 5 C.F.R. 2424.1(a) and (b).

[16] 5 C.F.R. 2424.1(b)(1).

However, the union need not attack the underlying validity of the regulation to establish that it does not bar negotiations on the union's proposal. Rather, the union may contest the regulation's validity only as a bar to negotiations, on grounds that it was not issued at the requisite organizational level of the agency (i.e., agency headquarters or a primary national subdivision), or that the union has achieved an extent of recognition in the agency which precludes assertion of the regulation (i.e., an appropriate unit including not less than a majority of the employees to whom the regulation applies).[17]

The most frequent basis for challenging an agency regulation is that the regulation does not meet the compelling need standards prescribed in the Authority's rules. The rules state that there is a compelling need when the agency demonstrates that its regulation (1) is essential to accomplishing the mission or functions of the agency or primary national subdivision in a manner consistent with an effective and efficient government, (2) is necessary to maintain basic merit principles, or (3) implements a non-discretionary mandate of controlling outside authority.[18]

Documentation

The pleadings in a negotiability case are (1) the union's petition for review, (2) the agency's statement of position, and (3) the union's response. The petition is required to initiate an appeal. The other pleadings are optional. However, a party loses the opportunity to make its case before the Authority if it fails to file a complete statement of position as permitted, as discussed below. While the union's petition for review need not set forth all the union's arguments in support of negotiability, it must provide enough information to put the agency on notice of the nature of the appeal.

A petition must include at a minimum the exact wording of the proposal(s) which the agency has alleged to be nonnegotiable, and a statement as to the intended meaning of that wording, including (1) an explanation of any uncommon terms used; (2) a description of the intended application of the proposal; (3) a copy of the agency allegation of nonnegotiability and any other documentary material which the union considers relevant, such as copies of agency regulations; and (4) notifica-

---

[17]5 C.F.R. 2424.1(b)(2); 5 U.S.C. 7117(a)(3).
[18]5 U.S.C. 7117(b). 5 C.F.R. 2424.11 sets forth illustrative criteria for determining whether there is a compelling need for an agency regulation to bar negotiations on a conflicting proposal.

tion of any pending related unfair labor practice charges.[19] If a related unfair labor practice charge is pending before the General Counsel of the Authority, the union must elect which appeal it wants the Authority to process first.[20]

The agency's statement of position must be filed within 30 days after receipt by the agency head of a copy of the petition for review. At this point, the agency may withdraw, in whole or part, the allegation that a proposal is outside the scope of the duty to bargain. It should (1) state the agency's full position on the remaining matters in dispute, including all procedural and substantive arguments; (2) cite evidence relied on; (3) provide a copy of internal regulations; and (4) explain the agency's understanding of the proposal's meaning and application in a manner comparable to that required of the union in the petition for review.[21]

The union's response must be filed within 15 days after receipt of an agency's statement of position. It may withdraw the appeal of all or part of the agency's allegation. It should provide a full and detailed statement of the union's position on all procedural and substantive matters which the union wishes the Authority to consider in reaching its decision.[22]

Scope of Mandatory Bargaining

Conditions of Employment

Conditions of employment are personnel policies, practices, and matters affecting working conditions (whether established by rule, regulation, or otherwise), except for situations relating to (1) prohibited political activities, (2) the classification of a position, or (3) conditions specifically provided for by federal statute.[23]

The Authority considers two factors in deciding whether a proposal concerns a condition of employment: (1) whether the proposal pertains to bargaining unit employees, and (2) the nature and effect of the proposal on their working conditions.[24] For the Authority to find that a proposal concerns a condition of employment, the record must establish that it

---

[19]5 C.F.R. 2424.4. The rule states that an incomplete petition for review may be dismissed or accorded a lower processing priority.

[20]5 C.F.R. 2424.5.

[21]5 C.F.R. 2424.6.

[22]5 C.F.R. 2424.7.

[23]5 U.S.C. 7103(a)(14).

[24]*Antilles Consol. Educ. Ass'n and Antilles Consol. School Sys.*, 22 FLRA 235, 237 (1986).

focuses on bargaining unit employees (or positions)[25] and directly affects their work situation or employment relationship.[26]

Bars to Negotiation

Applicable laws, rules, or regulations which bar negotiations on conflicting bargaining proposals are federal laws,[27] governmentwide rules or regulations,[28] and internal agency regulations for which there is a compelling need.[29]

Laws, Rules, and Regulations

The phrase "governmentwide rules or regulations" is not limited to directives promulgated under the Administrative Procedures Act.[30] Under the Statute, the phrase refers to any regulations and official declarations of policy which apply to the federal civilian work force as a whole and are binding on the federal agencies and officials to which they apply.[31] Thus, where the Authority has determined that a provision of the

---

[25]See, e.g., *NFFE, Local 1451 and Naval Training Center, Orlando, Fla.*, 3 FLRA 87 (1980), *aff'd sub nom. NFFE v. FLRA*, 652 F.2d 191 (D.C. Cir. 1981) (proposal requiring management to designate a certain number of representatives to negotiations is not a condition of employment). See also *Antilles Consol. Educ. Ass'n and Antilles Consol. School Sys.*, *supra* note 24, at 242-43 for a listing of Authority decisions finding proposals to be outside the duty to bargain because of the "impact on individuals or parties outside the bargaining unit." Note that the reasoning underlying these decisions was overturned in *AFGE, Local 32 v. FLRA*, 853 F.2d 986 (D.C. Cir. 1988). On remand from the court, FLRA stated that it will no longer examine the effect of a proposal on nonunit employees or positions. Rather, it will follow the private sector rule that a proposal affecting nonunit employees is within the duty to bargain as long as it "vitally affects" working conditions of employees in the bargaining unit. *AFGE, Local 32 and OPM*, 33 FLRA 335, 338 (1988).

[26]Proposals concerning the involvement of employees in nonwork activities while off duty are not bargainable conditions of employment unless there is a direct nexus to working conditions. Compare *AFGE, Local 2094 and Veterans Admin. Medical Center, New York, N.Y.*, 22 FLRA 710 (1986) (Proposal 3), *aff'd sub nom. AFGE, Local 2094 v. FLRA*, 833 F.2d 1037 (D.C. Cir. 1987) (use of agency's recreational facilities concerned employee's nonwork activities when off duty and therefore did not relate to conditions of employment) with *NFFE, Local 1363 and Headquarters, Army Garrison, Yongsan, Korea*, 4 FLRA 139 (1980), *aff'd sub nom. Department of Defense v. FLRA*, 685 F.2d 641 (D.C. Cir. 1982) (agent's "ration control" policy was related to its duty to maintain standards of health and decency and therefore concerned conditions of employment).

[27]5 U.S.C. 7117(a)(1).

[28]*Id.*

[29]5 U.S.C. 7117(a)(2) and (3).

[30]See *AFGE, Local 2782 v. FLRA*, 803 F.2d 737, 741–42 (D.C. Cir. 1986).

[31]*NTEU, Chapter 6 and Internal Revenue Serv., New Orleans Dist.*, 3 FLRA 747, 754 (1980). The legislative history of the Statute clearly indicates that this was the intent of Congress. The House-Senate Conference Committee stated as follows:

The conferees specifically intend, however, that the term "rules or regulations" be

Federal Personnel Manual (FPM) is binding, it has found that the provision constitutes a rule or regulation within the meaning of the Statute which will bar negotiations on conflicting proposals.[32] On the other hand, where the FPM provisions were determined to be merely guidance which agency officials may at their discretion decide not to follow, the Authority has found that the provisions cannot bar negotiations.[33]

Compelling Need

A compelling need exists for an agency's regulation, which is not a governmentwide regulation, when the agency demonstrates that the regulation meets one of the criteria established by the Authority to judge whether the regulation is essential.[34] The compelling need provisions of the Statute ensure that otherwise negotiable matters are barred from negotiation only if the agency demonstrates and justifies an overriding need that the regulatory policy be applied uniformly throughout the agency. To sustain a claim that a compelling need exists, an agency must (1) identify a specific agencywide regulation, (2) show a conflict between the regulation and the proposal, and (3) demonstrate a compelling need for the regulation under the criteria in the Authority's regulations.[35]

Management Rights

The management rights reserved by the Statute are, of course, provisions of federal law which bar the negotiation of conflicting proposals, for the most part. The right of management to take the actions enumerated in the Statute must be exercised in accordance with all applicable laws and regulations.[36] The exercise of these management rights, furthermore, as distinct from all other matters committed by law to management action, are "subject to" rather extensive negotiations over "procedures" and "appropriate arrangements."

An agency's duty to bargain over matters involving its management rights includes the *procedures* which management officials must follow in

---

interpreted as including official declarations of policy of an agency which are binding on the officials and agencies to which they apply.
H. REP. No. 95-7112, 95th Cong., 2d Sess. 158 (1978).
[32]E.g., *NFFE, Local 1497 and Department of the Air Force, Lowry AFB, Colo.*, 9 FLRA 151, 154–55 (1982) (FPM Chapter 511).
[33]See, e.g., *NTEU and Customs Serv.*, 21 FLRA 6, 9 n.3 (1986), *aff'd sub nom. Department of the Treasury v. FLRA*, 836 F.2d 1381 (D.C. Cir. 1988).
[34]5 C.F.R. 2424.11.
[35]*AFGE, Local 1923 and HHS, Office of the Secretary, Office of the Gen. Counsel, Social Sec. Div.*, 21 FLRA 178, 180 (1986).
[36]5 U.S.C. 7106.

exercising the reserved rights.[37] The Authority determines whether a union proposal concerns a negotiable procedure by asking whether implementation of the proposal would *directly interfere* with management's reserved rights.[38] If the Authority finds that the proposal would not prescribe the substance of management's prerogatives, it concerns a negotiable procedure.[39]

An agency's duty to bargain over matters involving management rights also includes *appropriate arrangements* for employees who are adversely affected by the exercise of those rights by management officials.[40] The Authority applies a two-part test to determine whether a union proposal constitutes an appropriate arrangement for adversely affected employees. First, it asks whether the proposal is intended to be an "arrangement" for such employees. If so, the Authority proceeds and weighs the competing practical needs of employees and managers to determine whether the proposed arrangement *excessively interferes* with management's reserved rights.[41] If the proposal would not "impinge upon management's prerogatives to an excessive degree,"[42] it is "appropriate" and therefore negotiable.[43]

Permissive Bargaining

Some matters are outside the scope of the *duty* to bargain because they do not have the requisite nexus to the working conditions of bargain-

---

[37]5 U.S.C. 7106(b)(2).

[38]*AFGE and Air Force Logistics Command, Wright Patterson AFB, Ohio*, 2 FLRA 603, 613 (1980), *aff'd sub nom. Department of Defense v. FLRA*, 659 F.2d 1140 (D.C. Cir. 1981), *cert. denied*, 455 U.S. 945 (1982).

[39]E.g., *New York State Nurses Ass'n and Veterans Admin. Bronx Medical Center*, 30 FLRA 706 (1987) (Proposal 6); *AFGE, Local 85 and Veterans Admin. Medical Center, Leavenworth, Kan.*, 30 FLRA 400 (1987) (Proposal 3).

[40]5 U.S.C. 7106(b)(3).

[41]*NAGE, Local R14-87 and Kansas Army Nat'l Guard*, 21 FLRA 24 (1986).

[42]*AFGE v. FLRA*, 702 F.2d 1183, 1188 (D.C. Cir. 1983).

[43]The Court in *AFGE, Local 1923 v. FLRA*, 819 F.2d 306 (D.C. Cir. 1987) succinctly summarized the distinction between the "direct" and "excessive" interference tests, as follows:

Although the distinction between these two tests may not be immediately apparent, it is nonetheless real. Excessive interference is something more than direct interference: implementation of a proposal may interfere directly with managerial prerogatives, yet the interference may not be excessive. The determination whether an interference with managerial prerogatives is excessive depends primarily on the extent to which the interference hampers the ability of an agency to perform its core functions—to get its work done in an efficient and effective way. Thus, if implementation of a proposal will directly interfere with substantive managerial rights, but will not significantly hamper the ability of an agency to get its job done, the proposal is not negotiable as a procedure, but is negotiable (assuming the threshold test described above is met) as an appropriate arrangement. [Citation omitted.]

ing unit employees.[44] The Authority has stated that the Statute *permits* parties to bargain over such matters to the extent consistent with applicable law, rules, or regulations.[45]

Additionally, various matters may be bargained under the Statute only if the agency involved in negotiations chooses to do so. First, the management-rights clause in the Statute specifically provides for negotiating "at the election of the agency" concerning (1) various aspect of the agency's staffing pattern—the "numbers, types, and grades of employees or positions assigned to any organizational subdivision, work project, or tour of duty"; and (2) the "technology, methods, and means of performing work."[46] Second, any matter that is inconsistent with an internal agency regulation for which a compelling need exists may be bargained if the agency waives, or grants an exception to, its regulation.[47]

If an agency negotiator executes an agreement that includes permissive provisions, those provisions cannot be disapproved by the agency head under the statutory review procedures.[48] The provisions must be approved since they are in accordance with "the provisions of this chapter and any other applicable law, rule, or regulation (unless the agency has granted an exception to the provision)."[49]

Selected Issues and the Law

Contracting Out

Contracting out work performed by bargaining unit employees to private organizations or individuals results in the loss of bargaining unit positions and the release of employees. Therefore, matters relating to such contracting out directly affect the "conditions of employment" of bargaining unit employees[50] normally appealable to the Authority. But, since the Statute reserves to management the right to "make determinations with

---

[44]See *supra* note 26.
[45]See *AFGE, Local 32 and OPM*, 22 FLRA 478, 483 (1986), *remanded on other grounds sub nom. AFGE, Local 32 v. FLRA*, 853 F.2d 986 (D.C. Cir. 1988) ("competitive areas" within agency for reduction-in-force purposes).
[46]5 U.S.C. 7106(b)(1).
[47]See 5 U.S.C. 7114(c)(2).
[48]5 U.S.C. 7114(c).
[49]*Supra* note 47.
[50]*State, County & Mun. Employees, Local 3097 and Department of Justice*, 31 FLRA 322, 323–32 (1988), *petition for review filed sub nom. Department of Justice, Justice Mgmt. Div. v. FLRA*, No. 88-1316 (D.C. Cir. Apr. 22, 1988).

respect to contracting out,"[51] bargaining over proposals that substantively limit the exercise of management rights in this respect is precluded.[52]

As in other instances covered by section 7106, however, management's right to contract out is subject to the obligation to negotiate over procedures and appropriate arrangements.[53] This obligation encompasses the procedures management will follow in making determinations with respect to contracting out, not merely the "impact and implementation" of a decision to contract out.[54] A proposal that simply restates management's existing obligation to comply with requirements in applicable laws and regulations concerning contracting out constitutes a negotiable procedure—one which does not prescribe the substance of management's right—under section 7106(b)(2). Management's right to contract out is limited by the laws and regulations, not by the proposal.[55] Similarly, a proposal requiring management to provide the union with (1) notice of its intention to solicit bids for contract work that could result in a reduction-in-force or transfer or abolition of function affecting employees in the bargaining unit, (2) a full explanation of the reasons for the action, and (3) sufficient opportunity to respond in writing, constitutes a negotiable procedure.[56] A proposal concerned with minimizing the effect of a decision to contract out on bargaining unit employees may be negotiable as an appropriate arrangement for employees adversely affected by management's exercise of its reserved right,[57] unless the proposal excessively interferes with the right.[58]

Pay and Money-Related Fringe Benefits

The negotiability of pay and money-related fringe benefits under the Statute is too unsettled to permit looking very far into the future. While a

---

[51]5 U.S.C. 7106(a)(2)(B).

[52]E.g., *AFGE, Local 1923 and Health Care Fin. Admin., Baltimore, Md.*, 17 FLRA 661 (1985).

[53]See *supra* notes 37–43 and accompanying text.

[54]*State, County & Mun. Employees, Local 3097 and Department of Justice, supra* note 50, at 340–42.

[55]*Id.* See also *AFGE, National Council of EEO Locals and EEOC*, 10 FLRA 3 (1982), enforced sub nom. *EEOC v. FLRA*, 744 F.2d 842 (D.C. Cir. 1984), *cert. dismissed*, 54 USLW 4408 (1986) (per curiam) (Proposal 1); contra *HHS v. FLRA*, 822 F.2d 430 (4th Cir. 1987), *reh'g denied*, No. 86-2619 (4th Cir. 1988) (en banc). The Supreme Court has been asked to resolve the split in the circuits over whether matters relating to the exercise of management's contracting-out authority are grievable. *Internal Revenue Serv. v. FLRA*, 862 F.2d 880 (D.C. Cir. 1988) *petition for cert. filed*, 58 USLW 3009 (1989).

[56]*AFGE, National Council of EEOC Locals and EEOC, supra* note 55, at 5–6.

[57]*Machinists, Local 2424 and Department of the Army, Aberdeen Proving Ground, Md.*, 8 FLRA 679, 682 (1982).

[58]*See supra* notes 40–42.

majority of the Authority held in a lead decision in 1986 that Congress did not intend to exclude those matters categorically from the duty to bargain,[59] subsequent developments cast doubt on whether that decision will stand.[60]

In line with the present state of the law, matters of pay and most money-related fringe benefits are not within the duty to bargain for most federal employees. Those matters have been determined to be "specifically provided for" by law and, therefore, excluded from the definition of "conditions of employment" subject to the duty to bargain under section 7103(a)(14). Furthermore, since the matters are provided for by law, proposals to modify them are inconsistent with the law and, therefore, nonnegotiable under section 7117(a).[61]

However, for a small minority of federal employees, pay and fringe benefits are not specifically set by law but are left, to some extent, to agency discretion. For these employees, the Authority has held proposals concerning wage-related matters to be negotiable if they are otherwise consistent with applicable law and regulations.[62] In finding the proposals to be negotiable, the Authority has ruled that they do not necessarily (1) directly determine the conditions of employment of nonunit employ-

---

[59]*AFGE, Local 1897 and Eglin AFB, Fla.*, 24 FLRA 377 (1986) (Chairman Calhoun dissenting), *appeal filed sub nom. Department of the Air Force, Eglin AFB v. FLRA*, No. 87-8073 (11th Cir. Feb. 2, 1987), *appeal withdrawn* (May 26, 1987).

[60]First, there has been a change in the membership of the Authority. Second, more than 30 Authority decisions finding pay and fringe benefit proposals negotiable based on *AFGE and Eglin AFB, supra* note 59, were appealed to various circuits of the U.S. court of appeals. At this writing, many of the appeals which were not withdrawn still are pending. Some of those which have been decided have reversed the Authority decisions. For example, *Department of the Navy, Military Sealift Command v. FLRA*, 836 F.2d 1409 (3d Cir. 1988) (proposals relating to pay of vessel crew employees is nonnegotiable—5 U.S.C. 5348 vests discretion in Secretary of the Navy to set wages "as nearly as is consistent with the public interest in accordance with prevailing rates and practices," and this section cannot be harmonized with collective bargaining); *Department of the Treasury, Bureau of Engraving & Printing v. FLRA*, 833 F.2d 1341 (D.C. Cir. 1988) (proposal to align wage rates with those paid the craft at the Government Printing Office is nonnegotiable based on rationale of *Military Sealift Command, supra*; *Ft. Knox Dependent Schools v. FLRA*, 895 F.2d 1179 (6th Cir. 1989).
In some cases, the Authority's decision that pay is negotiable was enforced. For example, *West Point Elementary School Teachers Ass'n v. FLRA*, 855 F.2d 936 (2d Cir. 1988); *Ft. Stewart Schools v. FLRA*, 860 F.2d 396 (11th Cir. 1988), *petition for cert. filed*, 57 USLW 3025 (1989).

[61]E.g., *AFGE, Council of Fed. Grain Inspection Locals and Department of Agric., Fed. Grain Inspection Serv., Washington, D.C.*, 3 FLRA 529 (1980), *aff'd sub nom. AFGE v. FLRA*, 653 F.2d 669 (D.C. Cir. 1981).

[62]E.g., *AFGE and Eglin AFB, supra* note 59; *Fort Bragg Unit of N.C. Ass'n of Educators, NEA and Fort Bragg Dependents Schools, Fort Bragg, N.C.*, 12 FLRA 519 (1983). In the year following *Eglin AFB*, the Authority issued more than 30 decisions finding pay and fringe benefit proposals to be negotiable.

ees,[63] or (2) directly interfere with management's right to establish its budget under section 7106(a)(1).[64] Furthermore, the Authority has examined the relationship between some of the proposals and agency regulations for which a compelling need[65] was claimed to exist.[66]

Official Time for Union Representatives

Official time means paid duty time used for various labor relations purposes under section 7131 of the Statute. Section 7131(d) authorizes the negotiation of the quantity of official time to be available to employees during any given period of time. It authorizes any quantity which the parties "agree to be reasonable, necessary, and in the public interest."[67]

Examples of labor relations purposes for which official time may be negotiated are: (1) contract negotiation;[68] (2) preparation of counterproposals and related duties during negotiations;[69] (3) preparation for negotiations and other union-management "interface" activities;[70] (4) preparation for impasse proceedings;[71] (5) union participation with management in activities concerning the performance evaluation system;[72] (6) performance of duties by a union official to expedite griev-

---

[63]E.g., AFGE and Eglin AFB, supra note 59, at 384–86 (proposal did not "prescribe what the Agency would pay towards the cost of nonbargaining unit employee benefits or even that it make lesser contributions as opposed to using other means to finance its increased costs with respect to bargaining unit employee benefits.").

[64]E.g., Id., at 386. Under the test applied by the Authority, a proposal does not interfere with management's right to determine its budget unless: (1) it requires a particular program or operation to be included in the budget, (2) it directly determines the specific amount which must be allocated to that program, or (3) the agency substantially demonstrates that the proposal would result in significant and unavoidable costs which are not offset by compensating benefits.

[65]See supra note 34.

[66]E.g., AFGE and Eglin AFB, supra note 59, at 387–89.

[67]5 U.S.C. 7131 (d). Military Entrance Processing Station, Los Angeles, Cal. and AFGE, Local 2866, 25 FLRA 685, 688 (1987).

[68]AFGE, Council 214 and Department of the Air Force, AFLC, Wright Patterson AFB, Ohio, 21 FLRA 575, 578 (1986), relying on AFGE and EPA, 15 FLRA 461 (1984) (Proposal 2, seeking official time for a greater number of union negotiators than the number designated by management, held negotiable).

[69]AFGE, National EPA Council and EPA, 21 FLRA 635 (1986).

[70]AFGE, Local 1692 and Headquarters, 323d Flying Training Wing (ATC), Mather AFB, Cal., 3 FLRA 304 (1980).

[71]AFGE, Local 225 and Army Armament Research and Dev. Command, Dover, N.J., 4 FLRA 148 (1980).

[72]AFGE, Local 3804 and Federal Deposit Insurance Corp., Chicago Region, Ill., 7 FLRA 217, 232 (1981).

ances;[73] and (7) union-sponsored training for bargaining unit employees, stewards, and union officers.[74]

The major limitation on labor relations activities for which official time may be negotiated is that activities relating to the internal business of a labor union must be performed in a nonduty status.[75] These are activities that relate to the union as an organization and pertain to its operation, such as union business meetings and other similar and associated activities related solely to the institutional structure of the union.[76]

Thus, a proposal to allow employees to distribute union insurance literature while on official time was held to be nonnegotiable. The Authority found that since union membership was necessary to participate in the health plan described in the brochure, the distribution of the brochure constituted a solicitation of membership.[77] In contrast, a proposal to allow a union official to distribute "Chapter announcement cards" annually to bargaining unit employees on official time was held to be negotiable. The cards provided employees information about the union and invited the employees to provide certain information about themselves to the union. The Authority found that the cards were not an overt plea for membership and that, by advising employees of the union's status as exclusive representative, distributing the cards aided in implementing the labor-management relationship.[78]

In regard to proposals to negotiate a particular quantity of official time, or when official time may be used, earlier decisions of the Authority applied a test of whether the use of official time would interfere with the accomplishment of the agency's work. That test is no longer followed. In 1987, the Authority reexamined the relationship between management's right to assign work under section 7106(a)(2)(B) and the authorization to negotiate official time for representational purposes under section 7131(d). The Authority stated that an agency's generalized concern to carry out its mission and the reserved right to assign work do not render

---

[73]*NAGE and Veterans Admin. Medical Center, Brockton/W. Roxbury, Mass.*, 23 FLRA 542 (1986).

[74]*NFFE, Local 951 and Department of the Interior, Bureau of Reclamation*, 3 FLRA 883 (1980).

[75]5 U.S.C. 7131(b). The section specifies that the internal business of a labor organization includes "the solicitation of membership, elections of labor organization officials, and collection of dues."

[76]*AFGE, Local 2823 and Veterans Admin. Regional Office, Cleveland, Ohio*, 2 FLRA 4 (1979).

[77]*NTEU and Department of Energy*, 19 FLRA 224, 225–26 (1985).

[78]*NTEU and Department of the Treasury, Internal Revenue Serv.*, 6 FLRA 508, 518–20 (1981).

the quantity of official time available to employees nonnegotiable. It cited a decision of the Court of Appeals for the District of Columbia Circuit:[79]

> Section 7131(d) "carves out an exception" to management's right to assign work; otherwise, that right "would preclude any negotiation of official time provisions, since official time always affects an agency's ability to assign work." [Citation omitted.]

In other words, in authorizing the negotiation of official time Congress contemplated some encroachment on management's rights to assign work and determine its staffing patterns. Thus, absent an emergency or other special circumstances, the use of official time under section 7131(d)—its quantity, allocation, and scheduling—is negotiable.[80]

Travel and Per Diem

Proposals seeking payment by an agency of the travel expenses and per diem allowances incurred by employees using official time in the conduct of labor-management relations activities are negotiable. In the lead case, the Authority found such a proposal concerned a condition of employment that is within the agency's discretion and is not inconsistent with law or regulation.[81]

On appeal, the Court of Appeals for the District of Columbia Circuit upheld the Authority. It stated that it agreed with the Authority "that to the extent the travel expense reimbursement is discretionary, a proposal that the discretion shall always be exercised in favor of the employees must be bargained about."[82] The court concluded that "the Authority correctly decided that there is a large measure of discretion in the determination of an agency's convenience and the government's primary interest, and that the Agency here must bargain as to its exercise of that discretion."[83]

---

[79]*Military Entrance Processing Station, Los Angeles, Cal.,* supra note 67, quoting *AFGE, Council of Locals No. 214 v. FLRA,* 798 F.2d 1525, 1530–31 (D.C. Cir. 1986) (reversing and remanding Authority decision that proposal requiring agency to permit certain employees to devote 100% of their on-duty time to representing union was nonnegotiable).

[80]*AFGE, Local 2354 and Department of the Air Force, Headquarters, 90th Combat Support Group, F.E. Warren AFB, Wyo.,* 30 FLRA 1130, 1131–35 (1988) (holding negotiable proposals requiring agency to automatically—with certain work-related exceptions—grant requests by employees to meet with union representative and by union officers to be released on official time to engage in representational activity).

[81]*NTEU and Customs Serv.,* 21 FLRA 6 (1986).

[82]*Customs Serv. v. FLRA,* 836 F.2d 1381, 1387 (D.C. Cir. 1988).

[83]*Id.,* at 1390.

Joint Labor-Management Committees

The negotiability of a particular proposal concerning the establishment of a joint committee, union participation on an established committee, or some other, similar, form of union participation in the implementation of agency functions, is not simply determined. Under the Authority's decisions, the negotiability of the proposal will turn on matters such as whether the committee (1) involves the exercise of a management right, and (2) has the power to take action, or has a role limited to advising or recommending action.

In two decisions the Authority held negotiable proposals providing for the creation of committees to review and make recommendations or comments concerning agency programs. It ruled that the proposals were procedures under section 7106(b)(2). Under such proposals management retains its discretion to accept or reject the recommendations. Therefore, the proposals did not involve the union in the substance of the agency's decision making or affect the agency's right to make the final decision.[84] However, proposals seeking to create committees authorized to take actions with respect to powers and authority granted to management by statute, executive order, or governmentwide regulations, are nonnegotiable.[85]

Similarly, the Authority has held that proposals that make the union party to the management decision-making process, thereby giving the union access to the discussions and deliberations concerning management decisions, are nonnegotiable.[86] The Authority takes the position that union involvement to *any* extent in such management deliberations directly and substantively interferes with management rights under section 7106.[87]

In contrast, the Authority has held proposals for union participation in the planning and administration of particular agency functions that did

---

[84]*NTEU and Customs Serv., Region VIII, San Francisco, Cal.*, 2 FLRA 254 (1979) (section 3, last sentence); *AFGE, Local 3804 and Federal Deposit Insurance Corp., Chicago Region, Ill.*, 7 FLRA 217 (1981) (Proposal 6).

[85]E.g., *NTEU and Department of the Treasury, Bureau of Gov't Fin. Operations*, 21 FLRA 652 (1986).

[86]E.g., *NFFE, Local 1001 and Vandenburg AFB, Cal.*, 15 FLRA 804, 809–12 (1984) (proposals for union representation on panels convened to select from among candidates for appointments under parties' negotiated upward mobility and merit promotion plans); *NFFE, Local 1431 and Veterans Admin. Medical Center, East Orange, N.J.*, 9 FLRA 998 (1982) (proposal for union representation on management committee making recommendations concerning agency staffing).

[87]*NFFE, Local 1167 and Headquarters, 31st Combat Support Group (TAC), Homestead AFB, Fla.*, 6 FLRA 574 (1981) (proposal for union representatives to be "present" at management meetings concerning contracting out).

not affect management rights to be negotiable.[88] The participation of union representatives on a joint committee concerning conditions of employment does not necessarily conflict with management's right to assign work under section 7106(a)(2)(B).[89] The Authority has found, however, that an impermissible interference with the right to assign work arises where (1) the duties of the committee concern the performance of officially prescribed duties,[90] or (2) the proposed role of the union participant conflicts with the official duties assigned to management officials.[91]

---

[88]*NFFE, Local 1579 and Veterans Admin. Regional Office, Louisville, Ky.*, 12 FLRA 600 (1983) (proposal for union representation on committee to plan, stimulate interest in, and evaluate suggestion program); *NFFE, Local 541 and Veterans Admin. Hosp., Long Beach, Cal.*, 12 FLRA 270 (1983) (proposal for joint committee to design, develop, and administer incentive awards program).

[89]*NFFE, Local 541 and Veterans Admin. Hosp., Long Beach, Cal.*, supra note 88, at 274–75.

[90]See *id*.

[91]*NAGE, Local R14-87 and Kansas Army Nat'l Guard*, 19 FLRA 381 (1985) (proposal to alternate chairmanship of joint safety committees where committees had been established by regulations and duties had been assigned to particular management officials).

10. Collective Bargaining and Impasses

ROBERT T. SIMMELKJAER*

Duty to Bargain

The federal employee labor-management relations program which evolved under executive orders commencing with Executive Order 10988 culminated with the Civil Service Reform Act (CSRA) in 1978. The CSRA provides guidance for conducting labor contract negotiations and delineates procedures for resolving impasses that occur during the bargaining process. For example,

> The CSRA placed into the law the rights and obligations of the parties to a collective bargaining relationship and established independent third parties to resolve disputes. In addition, the act established reserved management rights which paralleled current practice, authorized an expanded coverage for grievance arbitration, provided specific remedial authority and subpoena power and spelled out in greater detail the obligation to bargain in good faith.[1]

The duty of agency and labor organization representatives to negotiate in good faith is set forth in section 7114(b). This duty includes several obligations as follows:

1. to approach negotiations with a sincere resolve to reach a collective bargaining agreement;

*The comments and suggestions of Howard W. Solomon, former Executive Director of FSIP, are gratefully acknowledged. The assistance of Sharon Edwards who provided word processing and editing skills and Marjorie Archie, Columbia University, School of Law Library, who provided research support are similarly acknowledged.
[1]*Report to the Chairman, Subcommittee on Investigations.* Committee on the Post Office and Civil Service, *Labor Contract Negotiations Under the Civil Service Reform Act of 1978*, General Accounting Office, May 3, 1984.

2. to be represented at the negotiations by duly authorized representatives prepared to discuss and negotiate on any condition of employment;
3. to meet at reasonable times and convenient places as frequently as may be necessary, and to avoid delays;
4. in the case of the agency to furnish to the exclusive representative . . . upon request . . . data maintained within the normal course of business and not prohibited by law.[2]

Under section 7114(c) agreements reached between representatives of the parties are subject to the approval of the agency head within 30 days provided it does not contravene applicable law, rule, or regulation, or an exception has been granted to the agency. If the agency head does not approve or disapprove the agreement within 30 days, it becomes binding on the parties thereto.

Given this background, cognizance should be taken of the unique setting in which federal sector labor negotiations occur. Unlike the private sector, the parties are limited in their scope of bargaining. With economic issues, namely, wages and fringe benefits, largely determined by law,[3] and the absence of traditional bargaining incentives such as the agency shop or the bargaining leverage provided by the lockout or the right to strike, the parties devote a significant portion of their time to negotiability and procedural issues.[4] On the one hand, the unions attempt to expand

---

[2]Federal Service Labor-Management Relations Statute (Title VII of the Civil Service Reform Act of 1978) (5 U.S.C. §§ 7101–7135), Section 7114. Representation Rights and Duties.

[3]As with prior executive orders, federal employees are prohibited under CSRA from bargaining over wages, basic hours of work, and employee benefits as these are largely determined by congressional enactment specifically, Pay and Allowances at 5 U.S.C. subpart Chapters 51–59. Case law is emerging that may establish exceptions to the general rule that wages if covered by statute are not negotiable (i.e., *Fort Stewart Schools v. FLRA*, 860 F.2d 396 (9th Cir. 1988). See Chapter 9.
  5. Pay for Employees of Particular Agencies
  a. General Rule
    Pay for federal employees is set by General Schedule pay rates at 5 USC 5532. These rates apply to agencies and employees defined by 5 USC 5102. A proposal to set or adjust pay is nonnegotiable. Matters expressly provided for by federal statute are expressly excluded from the definition of conditions of employment in section 7103(a)(14)(C), and are therefore not within the scope of bargaining relative to conditions of employment of unit employees. *NTEU and Pension Benefit Guaranty Corp.*, . . . , 9 FLRA 692 (1982). To the extent that compensation is not specifically provided for by statute but is a matter of discretion of the agency, it is a condition of employment and therefore negotiable. Should matters of cost be of concern to the agency, those considerations may be presented to FSIP if there is a failure to reach an agreement. *Ft. Bragg Unit, North Carolina Ass'n of Educators and Ft. Bragg Dependents Schools, Fort Bragg, N.C.*, . . . , 12 FLRA 519 (1983).

[4]*Labor Contract Negotiations Under the Civil Service Reform Act of 1978, supra* note 1.

the menu of negotiable issues affecting the terms and conditions of employment, while on the other, agency management attempts to limit the scope of issues over which it is compelled to bargain.

Duty to bargain issues encompass the various phases of the collective bargaining process in the federal sector (i.e., ground rules, term, mid-term/impact, and implementation) as well as involve certain obligations of the parties in the bargaining process such as bargaining in good faith. Issues affecting the duty to bargain generally arise in the context of an unfair labor practice charge. This subject is addressed in Chapter 8.

Negotiability

The scope of negotiations initially set forth in section 7117 and subsequently clarified in case law includes required or mandatory, permissive, and prohibited or illegal subjects of bargaining.

As in the private sector, the federal agency and the exclusively recognized union must periodically negotiate in good faith over mandatory subjects of collective bargaining, including working conditions, certain personnel policies, and "appropriate arrangements" for employees adversely affected by the impact of management policies. The parties are also allowed to bargain over subjects that are permissible. However, the refusal of either party is sufficient to foreclose negotiation on such matters. Permissible subjects include: (1) numbers, types, and grades of employees or positions assigned to any organizational unit, work project, or tour of duty; and (2) technology of the workplace and methods and means of performing work.[5] Prohibited subjects include wages, matters specifically provided by statute, and matters covered by management rights (section 7106). An extensive discussion of the scope of negotiations in the federal sector appears in Chapter 9.

Resolution of Collective Bargaining Impasses

The majority of federal sector labor contracts are voluntarily negotiated and settled by the parties without outside assistance. A significant portion, however, annually require third-party intervention which can be required at any level of the negotiations process. Provision for assistance in the resolution of negotiation impasses has been made in section 7119 of the Federal Service Labor-Management Relations Statute.

---

[5]*Id.*

Federal Mediation and Conciliation Service

Given the statutory prohibition of the right to strike, if agreement cannot be reached, the parties can avail themselves of mediation from the Federal Mediation and Concilation Service (FMCS). The FMCS is the federal agency established in 1947 by the Taft-Hartley Act to promote labor-management peace, better labor-management relations, and thus to minimize commercial interrruptions caused by labor disputes. Although the FMCS is required to assist the parties in resolving negotiation impasses, the Service is authorized to determine under what circumstances and in what manner it will provide such assistance. Its service is provided without cost.

The FMCS becomes involved in 300 to 400 federal cases per year, which in Fiscal Year (FY) 1988 represented approximately 5 percent of the total caseload of about 7,500.[6] Since the parties to a labor-management agreement in the federal service should file a notice (Form 53) with the FMCS if agreement is not reached 30 days in advance of a contract termination or reopening date, the agency can often monitor the negotiations process and receive early warnings of possible bargaining problems. Form 53, available in the national office, located in Washington, D.C., may also be used to inform the FMCS when the parties are entering into initial negotiations.[7]

The FMCS assists the parties in resolving impasses by assigning federal mediators or commissioners. Dispatched from two regional offices each with five district offices and seventy-five field offices, these federal mediators (approximately 200) use mediation and conflict resolution techniques to facilitate voluntary settlement between the parties.[8] Although each case presents a unique amalgam of issues and positions, mediation procedures that enable the parties to convey their priorities to an impartial third party have proven to be highly effective. Prioritizing the issues, negotiating separately with the parties, and trading off demands are some of the methods experienced mediators have employed to initiate bargaining (i.e., ground rules) to resolve a particular issue (i.e., midterm or impact/implementation bargaining) or to effect a final contract settlement.

---

[6]Testimony of Jack W. Johnson, Executive Director, FMCS House Committee on Post Office and Civil Service, Subcommittee on Civil Service, June, 1988.

[7]Form 53 is currently being revised to conform with recent FMCS reorganization. Form 53 is found at 29 C.F.R. 1425.2.

[8]The Western Regional Office is located in San Francisco. The Eastern Regional Office is located in Atlanta. The assistance of Theodore Chaskelson, Attorney Advisor, FMCS, is acknowledged for this section.

Federal Service Impasses Panel

Those issues that remain at impasse after FMCS assistance (143 cases in 1987) may be referred to the Federal Service Impasses Panel (FSIP). The FSIP, as an entity within the Federal Labor Relations Authority, has authority under section 7119 of the CSRA to recommend procedures, such as arbitration, for the resolution of an impasse. It also provides direct assistance to the parties through fact-finding, written submission, or other methods it deems appropriate. The negotiating parties may request FSIP to approve a procedure for binding arbitration of the impasse, or the FSIP may use its discretion to take whatever action is necessary to resolve the impasse.[9]

The Federal Service Impasses Panel consists of at least six presidentially appointed members and one chairperson.[10] The chairperson and other members of the panel, who reside in different parts of the country, serve on a part-time basis. The FSIP office is located in Washington, D.C. In addition to its authority under the Statute, the FSIP has jurisdiction to resolve disputes under the Federal Employees Flexible and Compressed Work Schedules Act of 1982. Labor-management disputes involving the Panama Canal Commission and other U.S. government agencies located in the former Canal Zone are also within the panel's jurisdiction pursuant to the Panama Canal Act of 1979, 22 U.S.C. 3701. Finally, the panel's staff supports the Foreign Service Impasse Disputes Panel in resolving negotiation disputes arising under the Foreign Service Act of 1980.

The panel may take whatever action it deems necessary to resolve an impasse:

> Such final action, typically an arbitration award or a *Decision and Order* of the Panel itself, is binding on the parties during the term of their agreement unless they agree otherwise. In the event the parties adopt a procedure for using a private arbitrator, the procedure must be approved by the Panel.[11]

The parties need not request the panel's assistance in resolving a negotiation impasse; however, either party (or the parties jointly) has the right to request such assistance. As is the case with other rights under the Statute, this right can be waived jointly by the parties provided such

[9]FLRA Form 14 2118.

[10]The current members of the panel are: Chairman, Roy M. Brewer; Executive Director, Linda A. Lafferty; Professor Jean T. McKelvey; N. Victor Goodman; Professor Daniel H. Kruger; Susan S. Robfogel; and Thomas A. Farr; John Van de Water.

[11]*Federal Service Impasses Panel, FY 86 Annual Report*, Mar. 10, 1987.

waiver is "clear and unmistakable" as described in *Nuclear Regulatory Commission and NTEU*.[12]

The broad authority given to the panel under the Statute enables it to use the various dispute resolution techniques: mediation, fact-finding, written submissions, and arbitration by panel members as well as by private arbitrators. Although the procedure employed depends upon the circumstances of the dispute, the panel's selection is always influenced by its ultimate objective of reaching an expeditious settlement.

Equally important from the panel's perspective is the use of the process best suited to facilitate a voluntary settlement between the negotiating parties. In this regard, unpredictability is a major asset at the panel's disposal which it uses to encourage voluntary settlement. Not knowing which impasse resolution procedure will be ultimately selected by the panel encourages many parties to increase their informal settlement efforts. Overreliance on FSIP services is also discouraged by the practice of sending the parties back to the bargaining table when the panel concludes that negotiation and mediation efforts have not been exhausted. A third approach to expeditious and voluntary settlement is the FSIP policy of urging the parties to select the procedure themselves to resolve the dispute.[13]

In FY 1986, the panel received 143 requests for assistance (a 7.5 percent increase over the prior fiscal year) of which 136 were filed under the Statute; the balance were filed pursuant to the Federal Employees Flexible and Compressed Work Schedules Act of 1982.[14] No cases were received under the Foreign Service Act of 1980 or under the Panama Canal Act of 1979. Approximately 59 percent of the cases for panel assistance involved midterm negotiations and the remainder involved end-of-contract or term bargaining. As previously noted, many of the midterm disputes concern the impact and implementation of agency management decisions. Other requests involved "substantive negotiations under reopener provisions or proposed changes in conditions of employment."[15]

In FY 1986, 42 percent of all cases submitted to the FSIP were voluntarily withdrawn. One-half of these withdrawals were submitted

---

[12]8 FLRA 715 (1982). The parties need not request the panel's assistance in resolving a negotiation impasse, either party (or the parties jointly) has the right to request such assistance. As is the case with other rights under the Statute, this right can be waived provided such waiver is "clear and unmistakable." *Id.*, at 716.

[13]*Supra* note 11.

[14]*Id.*

[15]*Id.*

following settlements reached as a result of assistance by the panel members or staff. "The settlements took place at various stages of the Panel's procedures including the initial investigation, during an informal conference, in the course of written submissions, and, in two cases, during 'med-arb' sessions conducted by a member of the Panel or its staff."[16]

The panel declined to assert jurisdiction in 22 percent of its case dispositions, the substantial majority of which involved threshold questions concerning the obligation of the parties, usually the employer, to bargain and the balance involving matters in which the parties had not exhausted voluntary efforts to settle the dispute.[17] In such cases the parties were encouraged to resume face-to-face bargaining or request FMCS assistance in the event their counterpart was unresponsive.

The panel closed 15 percent of its cases by issuing Decisions and Orders largely based on written submissions from the parties. In other cases, the report of a panel member following an informal conference with the parties led to settlement.

Arbitration Opinion and Decisions either by members of the panel serving as arbitrators using med-arb proceedings or by outside arbitrators using either conventional arbitration or med-arb procedures at the recommendation or direction of the panel closed the balance of the cases.

From the broad authority accorded FSIP in resolving negotiation impasses have emerged several procedures used in varying combinations to achieve a desired result. These procedures are discussed below.

Resumption of Negotiations

This procedure is ordered when the panel concludes that the parties have not exhausted voluntary efforts to reach settlement and further bargaining may resolve the dispute or reduce the number of issues on the table. The decision to order further negotiations is usually accompanied by the panel's refusal to assert jurisdiction, without prejudice to the right of either party to resubmit its request for assistance. In *Library of Congress*,[18] the panel's investigation revealed there had been only five short bargaining sessions. Thus the panel declined to assert jurisdiction.

---

[16]*Id.*
[17]*Id.*
[18]Case No. 85 FSIP 16 (1985). Since the Panel declined to assert jurisdiction, the case was not issued in a Panel Release and therefore was not assigned a Panel Release number.

Another variation on this procedure is for the panel to decide the merits of some issues and remand others to the parties for further negotiations.[19]

Resumption of Negotiations With Mediation Assistance

The panel may opt for a referral to the FMCS when it decides the parties have not fully used the mediation services. The FSIP may, in other cases, provide the mediation assistance of a staff member which can lead to settlement during an informal meeting. In a dispute over an employer-initiated change in compensatory time accrual, the parties reached a voluntary agreement with panel staff assistance, obviating further panel intervention.[20] In a Department of the Navy case, the panel directed the parties to meet with the chairman who, in an informal conference for resolving all outstanding issues, facilitated voluntary agreement.[21]

Resolution of Negotiability (Duty to Bargain) Issues

The panel may decide to decline jurisdiction when a party (usually the employer) alleges it has no obligation to bargain with respect to a proposal. In such cases the parties are referred to the FLRA for a scope of negotiations decision. If a duty to bargain is found, further negotiation may resolve the impasse. If these negotiations are unsuccessful, FSIP services again can be requested. When the panel asserts jurisdiction at the request of a party, it may assign a member of the panel to serve as mediator or fact finder. If the impasse is not resolved, it may appoint a panel member as interest arbitrator, encourage parties to voluntarily submit their dispute to binding interest arbitration, or impose interest arbitration on the parties. The effect of an arbitration award depends on the method selected and the conduct of the parties, particularly the agency head.

Finally, "where a claim of non-negotiability appears to be frivolous, the Panel will not permit it to block the handling of an impasse."[22] In multiple-issue cases, the panel can resolve issues where negotiability has not been invoked and refer the others to the parties for submission to the FLRA.

---

[19]*A Guide to the Dispute Resolution Procedures Used by the Federal Service Impasses Panel.*
[20]*Department of the Navy, Naval Underwater Sys. Command,* Case No. 86 FSIP 72 (1986). Case not issued in a Panel Release.
[21]*Department of the Navy, Naval Weapons Station,* Case No. 85 FSIP 13 (1985). Case not issued in a Panel Release.
[22]*Supra* note 19, at 3.

Fact Finding Followed by Recommendations

The fact-finding hearing is a formal procedure conducted by the panel's designated representative to establish a complete record of the issues in a dispute and the respective positions of the parties regarding them. Each party has an opportunity to call witnesses and present evidence and arguments in support of its position. The fact finder issues a report summarizing the evidence and arguments, concluding with recommendations he or she contends may resolve the dispute.[23]

Following issuance of the fact finder's recommendations or recommendations for settlement issued by the panel after review of the fact finder's report, the parties have 30 days in which to reach an agreement before the panel takes further action.

Fact Finding Followed by a Decision and Order

Such further action may take the form of a Decision and Order after fact finding has been completed. A Decision and Order is final and binding, equivalent to interest arbitration, occasionally without the rationale accompanying these arbitration awards.

An issue concerning merit promotion was at impasse in *New Jersey Department of Defense.*[24] Following the employer's rejection of the fact finder's recommendation for settlement, the panel, rather than making its own settlement recommendation, issued a Decision and Order directing the parties to adopt the recommendation of the fact finder.

Decision and Order Following Written Submissions

Relying on the written submissions as the basis for its determinations saves the panel time and expense and expedites resolution of issues. The process is described as follows:

> Typically, the parties exchange written statements of positions, with supporting evidence and argument. Then they may be given the opportunity to revise their proposals prior to exchanging rebuttal briefs. The Panel will consider the written material and may thereafter make recommendations for settlement or issue a binding decision for resolution of the dispute. If recommendations do not result in a settlement, a binding decision is likely to follow.[25]

---

[23]*A Guide to Hearing Procedures of the Federal Service Impasses Panel* provides a description of the fact-finding hearing process.
[24]84 FSIP 79 (1985), Panel Release No. 231.
[25]*Supra* note 19, at 3.

For example, in *Department of Energy, Western Area Power Administration*,[26] the panel, after considering the parties' written statements addressing the panel's jurisdiction over the dispute (specifically, the agency's contention that advisory rather than binding arbitration was the parties' agreed-upon dispute resolution procedure), determined that the impasse should be resolved on the merits pursuant to supplementary statements of positions from the parties. As the impasse resolution procedure, the panel issued a Decision and Order adopting the union's proposal to provide that the arbitrator's decision be final and binding, barring the timely filing of exceptions under section 7122 of the Statute.

Outside Arbitration

The Statute permits the parties to submit their negotiation dispute to an independent arbitrator, provided the procedure has been approved by the panel as per section 7119(b). When the parties submit a joint request for the resolution of an impasse through private arbitration, the panel will normally approve it, with the expenses of the arbitration shared equally. The panel has recommended, and occasionally ordered, the use of private arbitration enabling the parties to select the arbitrator of their choice. A joint request for outside binding arbitration as well as additional indications of the need for the arbitration format are prerequisites of panel approval.[27] With a national jurisdiction, seven part-time members, and a limited staff, the panel will occasionally direct the parties to use private arbitration.

Final-Offer Selection

Final-offer selection, also known as "last best offer" and final-offer arbitration, has been used by the panel after receipt of either a fact finder's report or the parties' written submissions. In this procedure, the panel informs the parties that it will select either party's package of proposals, in its entirety or on an issue-by-issue basis, as the method of resolving the impasse. The parties' desire to prevail creates an incentive to submit final offers which are reasonable and has the additional effect of narrowing the gap between the proposals.

The parties are given advance notice of the final-offer proceeding, including the deadline for submission of proposals and the extent to which

---

[26]*Department of Energy, W. Area Power Admin., Golden Colorado and Gov. Coordinating Council*, Case No. 84 FSIP 29 (1984), Panel Relase No. 229.
[27]*Internal Revenue Serv.*, Case No. 86 FSIP 36 (1986). Case not issued in a Panel Release.

"final offers" can be changed. Here again, voluntary settlement may obviate the procedure. In one case, following written submissions concerning matters of health and safety, smoking in the workplace, and location of equipment, the panel issued a Decision and Order in which it adopted the employer's final offer.[28]

Med-Arb

Med-Arb is the term used for mediation followed, where necessary, by binding arbitration. It can be described as the "carrot and stick" approach. It is conducted either through a sole med-arb designee or a tripartite panel on which the union and employer have a representative. The parties' knowledge that the alternative to unsuccessful mediation is binding arbitration enhances the informal settlement of outstanding issues. This procedure often leads to a resolution during the mediation phase without the mediator having to conduct a formal arbitration hearing or issue an arbitration award. The neutral must possess both mediation skills which facilitate the parties' reaching their own settlement as well as arbitrators' decision-making skills should mediation prove partially or totally unsuccessful. A typical outcome ensued in *Army Armament Munitions*[29] when the parties, failing to agree on eight articles, engaged in med-arb with the FSIP's executive director. They reached voluntary settlement during mediation, avoiding the risks of arbitration.

Finally, similarities exist between the FSIP and the FMCS in that both provide mediation services and both organizations can become involved at any level of the negotiations process and occasionally at two levels simultaneously. For example, in one case negotiations over the implementation of a drug-testing program became entwined with a union ground rules negotiation proposal—resulting in deferral of the former matter to the courts. By deferring to the courts on the drug-testing issue, the panel was able to continue its efforts to resolve the remaining negotiation disputes.[30]

Flexible and Compressed Work Schedules

The panel was granted jurisdiction (during FY 1982) under the Federal Employees Flexible and Compressed Work Schedules Act of

---

[28]*Department of Health and Human Servs., Health Care Fin. Admin.*, 84 FSIP 92 (1985), Panel Release No. 231.
[29]*Army Armament Munitions & Chem. Command*, Case No. 85 FSIP 5 (1985). See also *Federal Trade Comm'n*, Case No. 83 FSIP 65 (1984). Neither of these cases was issued in a Panel Release.
[30]*Department of the Army, Ft. Bragg and AFGE, Local 1770*, 86 FSIP No. 114 (1986), Panel Release No. 249.

1982 to resolve impasses between federal agencies and unions represent-ing federal employees arising from agency determinations (1) not to establish a flexible or compressed work schedule, or (2) to terminate such a schedule. The 1982 Act requires the panel to take final action in favor of the agency's determination if it finds evidence that the flexible or com-pressed schedule has caused or is likely to cause an adverse agency impact as defined in 5 U.S.C. 6131(b).

During FY 1986, for example, the panel considered alternative work schedules under the Act. In *Department of the Air Force and AFGE*[31] the employer met its burden of showing a likely adverse impact, "by demon-strating that a previous experiment of a four day, ten hour work schedule had adversely affected aircraft maintenance and repair operations." In *Department of the Treasury and NTEU*,[32] the union's attempt to reinstitute employee flexibility in their 5-4-9 schedule was not approved by the panel. Instead it supported the employer in favoring conformity with the larger group of employees. The union proposal was accepted in *HHS and AFGE*,[33] establishing flexible starting times from 7:00 to 9:30 a.m., core time from 9:30 a.m. to 3:00 p.m., and departure after eight hours of work.

In other cases, the parties either reached voluntary settlement or the panel declined to assert jurisdiction. In *Department of Agriculture and AFGE*,[34] the panel did not address the merits of the dispute, and instead ordered the parties to resume bargaining for 30 days with the assistance of FMCS. This was the only case in FY 1986 in which the panel made a substantive determination on the issue of smoking, continuing its restrictive position.

Of the seven requests for assistance filed pursuant to the Compressed Work Schedules Act in FY 1986, six were closed by the panel: two cases by Decisions and Orders and four after withdrawal requests were granted. In other cases, the parties either reached voluntary settlement or the panel declined to assert jurisdiction.

Compliance With Panel Decisions and Orders

The FLRA has concluded that, pursuant to the provisions of section 7114(c), agency heads are empowered to review all provisions of collec-

[31]*Department of the Air Force, Williams AFB and AFGE*, 86 FSIP No. 3 (1986) (Panel Release No. 241). See also *Department of Energy* (1985), Panel Release No. 239.
[32]85 FSIP No. 133 (1986), Panel Release No. 241.
[33]*Department of Health & Human Servs. and AFGE*, 86 FSIP No. 96 (1986), Panel Release No. 250.
[34]85 FSIP No. 104 (1986), Panel Release No. 242.

tive bargaining agreements, including those mandated by the FSIP, to assure conformity with the provisions of the Statute as well as other applicable laws, rules, and regulations. Having established in a series of decisions that procedures of the panel are part of the collective bargaining process and that any agreement, mandated or otherwise, is part of the collective bargaining agreement, the Authority has further held that an agency head can review a Decision and Order of the panel for legal sufficiency.[35]

There are two procedures available under the Statute whereby review of an agency head's disapproval of a panel-imposed provision in an agreement can be obtained, namely, the expedited procedure for review of negotiability issues under section 7117 and Part 2424 of the Authority's Rules and Regulations, and the unfair labor practice procedures set forth in section 7118 and Part 2423 of the Authority's Rules and Regulations. An agency head's disapproval of a provision in a negotiated agreement is an allegation of nonnegotiability for purposes of appeal to the Authority. Thus, a union may choose to file a negotiability appeal under section 7117 upon an agency head's disapproval of any panel-imposed provision of an agreement.

In recent years, the Authority has found an agency in violation of the Statute when an agency head disapproved or failed to implement a panel order. The Department of the Treasury[36] was found in noncompliance when it did not implement a panel order to reimburse union negotiators for travel and per diem expenses. Concluding that the order was consistent with applicable law, rule, and regulation, the FLRA further held that, while the mere act by an agency head of reviewing a panel-imposed provision under section 7114(c) is not an unfair labor practice, "an agency head's disapproval of a Panel-ordered collective bargaining agreement provision may be challenged either through a negotiability appeal under section 7117(c) or an unfair labor practice charge. . . ."[37] And the fact the agency may have requested FSIP assistance does not prevent the union from filing a petition for review of the negotiability of employer proposals by the FLRA.[38]

The union may challenge an agency head's refusal to approve a provision of a collective bargaining agreement imposed by a final order of

---

[35]*Interpretation and Guidance*, 15 FLRA 564 (1984). See also *Electrical Workers (IBEW), AFL-CIO, Local 121 and Department of the Treasury, Bureau of Engraving & Printing, Washington, D.C.*, 10 FLRA 198 (1982). See also AFGE, *Locals 225, 1504, & 3723, AFL-CIO v. FLRA*, 712, F.2d 640, 646, n.24 (D.C. Cir. 1983).
[36]22 FLRA 821 (1986).
[37]*Id.*
[38]*Patent & Trademark Office*, 21 FLRA 580 (1986).

the panel by filing an unfair labor practice charge alleging that such conduct violated the Statute. A finding that the panel order was not contrary to the Statute, law, rule, or regulation would constitute a refusal "to cooperate in . . . impasse decisions" in violation of sections 7116(a)(1) and (6). On the other hand, the FLRA or ultimately the courts may find that the agency head's refusal to implement a panel order was lawful.

The FLRA decisions have held that it is an unfair labor practice for an employer to refuse to implement a panel order concerning medical examinations,[39] hours of work, travel, temporary duty, grooming standards,[40] and the wearing of military uniforms.[41] An employer also can violate the unfair labor practice provisions by refusing to implement a panel order concerning the grievance procedure.[42] Similarly, where a labor organization refused to sign an agreement containing wording from a panel decision, a violation was found.[43] Noncompliance with the panel decision does not *ipso facto* constitute a refusal to bargain under sections 7116(a)(5) and (b)(5) but is reviewable under sections 7116(a)(6) and 7116(b)(6)—the provisions specifically applicable to the FSIP.[44] Refusal to comply with panel procedures such as written submissions and fact finding[45] can constitute an unfair labor practice.

Conditions for Invoking FSIP Services

Thus far, the Authority has denied the FSIP's request for a general policy statement detailing the circumstances in which an agency is obligated to maintain the status quo with respect to changes in personnel policies, practices, and working conditions. In the Authority's view such a request is too broad to be answered in a general ruling since resolution of issues concerning unilateral changes in working conditions during bilateral negotiations or mediation of a labor agreement requires evaluation of the facts in each case.[46] For example, in *Customs Service and NTEU*,[47] the Authority found lawful the agency's implementation of the union's last proposal six days after the parties had reached impasse concerning

---

[39]*Army Corps of Eng'rs*, 16 FLRA 456 (1984).
[40]*Indiana Air Nat'l Guard*, 17 FLRA 23 (Ind.) (1985).
[41]*Puerto Rico Air Nat'l Guard*, 15 FLRA 482 (1984); *Maine Air Nat'l Guard*, 15 FLRA 485 (1984); *Division of Military & Naval Affairs*, N.Y., 15 FLRA 288 (1984).
[42]*National Aeronautics & Space Admin.*, 12 FLRA 480 (1983).
[43]*AFGE, Local 3732 and Merchant Marine Academy*, 16 FLRA 318 (1984).
[44]*Minnesota Army Nat'l Guard*, 16 FLRA 561 (1984).
[45]*Internal Revenue Serv.*, 16 FLRA 904 (1984).
[46]*Federal Serv. Impasses Panel*, 31 FLRA 1294 (1988).
[47]16 FLRA 198 (1984).

overtime assignments, despite the union's imminent intent to file with the panel for assistance. The union's failure to file its request immediately and instead waiting "until afternoon of the following day" was deemed sufficient to dismiss its unfair labor practice charge under section 7116(a)(6).

Interest Arbitration and Negotiability

The panel is not empowered to make an independent negotiability determination since these are matters reserved to the Authority under section 7117(c).[48] However, the panel may assert jurisdiction on the basis of existing precedent in the duty-to-bargain area.[49]

The Authority has consistently held that negotiability disputes between an agency and an exclusive representative under section 7117(c) must be resolved by the Authority pursuant to section 7105(a)(2)(E). Thus, an interest arbitrator acting at the direction of the panel would possess no greater authority to resolve such duty-to-bargain issues than that conferred upon the panel. The FLRA has modified its prior position reserving resolution of duty-to-bargain issues to the Authority rather than to the panel or to an interest arbitrator selected by the parties or assigned by the panel.[50] Its current view is to permit the panel or an arbitrator to apply existing Authority precedent to resolve negotiation impasses. Where either the union or the agency files exceptions to an award under section 7122(a), the Authority uses a four-tier test to determine whether the arbitrator resolved a negotiability issue: (1) was the duty-to-bargain issue substantively identical to one previously addressed by the Authority? (2) were the parties' contentions similar to those addressed by the Authority in previous cases? (3) did the arbitrator apply relevant Authority case law and other precedent? and (4) do other considerations lead one to conclude that the arbitrator correctly or incorrectly considered the duty-to-bargain issue?[51]

If the arbitrator has correctly applied the existing case law, the Authority will resolve the exceptions on their merits and sustain the award. Where the agency raises duty-to-bargain issues and the arbitrator does not resolve these issues on the basis of existing Authority case law, the Authority will strike the disputed provisions and modify the award accordingly.[52]

---

[48]*Interpretation and Guidance*, 11 FLRA 626 (1983).
[49]*Veterans Admin. and AFGE*, 26 FLRA 264 (1987).
[50]*Social Sec. Admin. and AFGE*, 25 FLRA 238 (1987).
[51]*Commander Carswell AFB and AFGE*, 31 FLRA 620 (1988).
[52]*Immigration & Naturalization Serv. and AFGE*, 31 FLRA 1123 (1988).

Challenging Panel Orders and Interest Arbitration Awards

Formerly a party electing to challenge an interest arbitration award of either a panel member or an outside arbitrator filed exceptions under section 7122(a). When a party failed to avail itself of this procedure within the alloted time period, the award became final and binding and the agency was required to take such actions as were required by the award. The rationale for this approach was set forth in *Colorado River Storage Project* as follows: "To allow a party which has not filed exceptions to an award to defend its failure to implement that award in a subsequent unfair labor practice proceeding on grounds that should have been raised as exceptions to the award under section 7122(a) . . . would frustrate the Congressional intent with respect to finality of arbitration awards."[53]

In *Colorado River Storage Project* the FLRA reaffirmed its earlier decisions that the exceptions procedures in section 7122(a) were the means by which an arbitration award was challenged. This section was held applicable not only where the arbitrator was a private individual selected by the parties but also where the arbitrator was designated by the panel. Subsequently, the FLRA held that the arbitration award of a designated panel member was not a final action of the panel under section 7119, but rather an arbitration award reviewable under section 7122(a).[54]

This position was subsequently reinforced in a case distinguishing the interest arbitration award of a panel member designated as arbitrator from a final panel decision under section 7119. The FLRA found the arbitrator's "Opinion and Decision was an interest arbitration award," despite its issuance as a FSIP decision, and not a "final action of the Panel within the meaning of section 7119(c)(5)(c) of the Statute." Therefore, it was reviewable only under section 7122.[55]

In a related case, the Authority further held that "a failure to comply with a final and binding interest arbitration award which resulted from the Panel's granting of the parties' request to resolve their dispute through the use of interest arbitration was not only inconsistent with the requirements of section 7122(b) and therefore a violation of section 7116(a)(1) and (8) of the Statute, but also constituted a failure to cooperate with impasse procedures and decisions in violation of section 7116(a)(1) and (6) of the Statute."[56]

---

[53]*Colorado River Storage Project*, 21 FLRA 86 (1986).
[54]*Edwards AFB*, 21 FLRA 445 (1986).
[55]*Veterans Admin. and AFGE, National Council of Veterans Admin. Locals*, 23 FLRA 661 (1986).
[56]*Air Force, Wright Patterson AFB, Ohio and AFGE*, 15 FLRA 151 (1984).

In *Department of Defense Dependents Schools*,[57] the FLRA considered for the first time whether section 7114(c) authorized agency heads to review provisions included in an agreement by the award of an interest arbitrator designated by the panel. The FLRA concluded that interest arbitration awards were not subject to agency head review under section 7114(c) nor subject to collateral attack in unfair labor practice proceedings under section 7116 but rather the agency head had to file exceptions under section 7122(a) as was the case with private arbitration awards. In addition, where the agency head was not authorized to review and disapprove provisions imposed by an interest arbitration award, the agency head's action did not serve as an allegation of nonnegotiability permitting appeals under section 7117(c).

Reversing the FLRA decision, the Fourth Circuit held that an interest arbitrator designated by the Impasses Panel has no greater authority than that possessed by the panel itself.[58] The court rejected the FLRA determination that the Impasses Panel by delegating its duty to a single panel member could foreclose the agency head view which was available when the full panel acted to end an impasse. Referring to section 7119 statutory provisions for resolving negotiation impasses, the court analyzed the two alternatives available to parties reaching an impasse: agreement to binding arbitration under section 7119(b)(2) if approved by the Impasses Panel, or requesting the Impasses Panel to consider the matter under section 7119(b)(1).

If the parties select arbitration, either party dissatisfied with the award may seek FLRA review under section 7122. The standard for setting aside the award is that it is contrary to any law, rule, or regulation or on other grounds like those applied by federal courts in private sector arbitration. An award issued pursuant to the parties' mutual agreement to final and binding arbitration is not subject to agency head review under section 7114(c). Also, the Authority's decision reviewing such an award is not subject to judicial review under section 7123 unless the Authority's order involved an unfair labor practice under section 7118.

If either party requests panel assistance under section 7119(b)(1), the panel has a two-step process for resolution: First, it may seek the parties' voluntary resolution, section 7119(c)(5)(A), either by recommending procedures for resolution or by assisting the parties through mediation or fact finding. Second, if voluntary procedures do not resolve the impasse, the panel can, under section 7119(c)(5)(B)(iii), end the impasse unilaterally, including the imposition of contract terms, by taking

[57]27 FLRA 586 (1987).
[58]*Department of Defense Dependents Schools v. FLRA*, 852 F.2d 779 (4th Cir. 1988).

"whatever action is necessary and not inconsistent with this chapter. . . ."

In other words, by agreeing to binding arbitration, an agency head forfeits the right of agency head review under section 7114(c) and of ordinary judicial review of an FLRA decision. If, however, the award has been imposed by the panel on the parties, the agency head does not forfeit any statutory rights. Under section 7119(c)(5)(C), the panel's action constitutes "final action," is binding, and is reviewable under section 7123(a). Thus, at the point of impasse the agency head must not only judge which alternative may resolve the impasse but also must recognize the consequences should unacceptable contract provisions be imposed.

The Fifth Circuit reiterated the Fourth Circuit's reasoning in *Panama Canal Commission v. FLRA*.[59] On appeal was whether an interest arbitration award issued by a designee of the panel was reviewable only by filing exceptions under section 7122(a). The agency head, rejecting a provision which addressed matters deemed nonnegotiable, sought review under section 7114(c). The union pursuant to section 7105(a)(2)(E) filed a negotiability appeal with the FLRA, citing section 7122(a) as the exclusive means for reviewing an arbitration award. In reversing the FLRA decision, the court held that "arbitration is binding under the statutory scheme if, and only if, both parties agree to adopt a procedure for binding arbitration of the negotiation impasse. . . ."

The need to establish the fact of agency head agreement to binding interest arbitration rather than the means of that agreement was reinforced in a Department of Agriculture case.[60] Consistent with the *DODDS* decision, the court found the agency head had forfeited his right to approve or disapprove contract provisions by agreeing to accept binding arbitration of the impasse.

Finally, the Fourth Circuit recently clarified its prior decision in *Department of Defense Dependents Schools v. FLRA* in a case involving the same parties. The court extended the "designee" mentioned in section 7119(c)(5)(A) to include not only panel members designated to serve as interest arbitrators, but also private arbitrators ordered to resolve an impasse. In distinguishing voluntary binding arbitration agreed to by the parties under section 7119(b)(2) from nonvoluntary arbitration imposed by the panel under section 7119(b)(1), the court held only the former is exempt from agency head review.[61]

---

[59]867 F.2d 905, 130 LRRM 2930 (5th Cir. 1989).
[60]*Department of Agriculture v. FLRA*, 879 F.2d 655 (9th Cir. 1989).
[61]*Department of Defense, Office of Dependents Schools v. FLRA*, 879 F.2d 1220 (4th Cir. 1989).

11. Arbitration of Grievances in the Federal Sector

JEROME P. HARDIMAN

As of January 1989, there were 1,269,552 federal employees in 2,266 bargaining units represented by unions. Of the 2,266 bargaining units, 1,982 (87 percent) were covered by collective bargaining agreements.[1] Under the Federal Service Labor-Management Relations Statute (the Statute),[2] every collective bargaining agreement must contain a negotiated grievance procedure for the settlement of grievances and every grievance procedure must provide for binding arbitration as the last step in the process.[3] In addition, except for certain matters (discussed under "Election of Remedies," *infra*), the negotiated grievance procedure is the exclusive procedure available to employees in the bargaining unit for resolving grievances within its coverage.[4] This means that all employees in a bargaining unit represented by a union, both union members and nonmembers, must use the negotiated procedures to resolve any grievances concerning matters covered by the collective bargaining agreement. Arbitrators therefore play a special role in resolving disputes in the federal sector.

The Statute also requires that a negotiated grievance procedure must be fair and simple and provide for the expeditious processing of griev-

---

[1]U.S. Office of Personnel Management Biennial Statistical Report: The Status of Union Representation of Federal Employees Under 5 U.S.C. Chapter 71 as of January 1989 (Sept. 1989).

[2]Title VII of the Civil Service Reform Act of 1978, 5 U.S.C. 7101–7135 (1982, and Supp. III, 1985).

[3]5 U.S.C. 7121(a)(1) and 7121(b)(3)(C). See also *Marshals Serv. v. FLRA*, 708 F.2d 1417, 1419 (9th Cir. 1983) (5 U.S.C. 7121 recognizes the "centrality of arbitration" under the Statute).

[4]5 U.S.C. 7121(a)(1).

ances.[5] Perhaps more significantly, the Statute attempts to strike a balance between the sometimes competing or conflicting interests of a union in representing all the employees in a unit and representing individual aggrieved employees in the presentation and processing of grievances. The Statute provides that a negotiated grievance procedure must assure a union, the exclusive representative of all the employees in a bargaining unit, the right to present and process grievances on its own behalf or on behalf of any employee in the unit.[6] At the same time, the Statute assures the right of an employee to present a grievance on his or her own behalf. If an employee elects to argue his or her own grievance and not rely on union representation, the union is entitled to be present during the grievance proceeding.[7] If the employee wants to be represented by someone other than a union representative, the employee has to have the approval of the union, because only the employee or a person designated by the union is entitled to present and process grievances under a negotiated grievance procedure.[8]

The records of the Office of Personnel Management's Labor Agreement Information Retrieval Service (LAIRS) indicate that the majority of grievances that proceed to arbitration are filed by or on behalf of individual employees. Grievances also may be filed by a union or agency to protect institutional rights under law or a collective bargaining agreement. For example, unions have filed grievances to protect alleged rights to determine the number of union representatives to attend training,[9] and to preclude an agency labor relations officer from attending a meeting at the first step of a negotiated grievance procedure.[10]

With regard to agency grievances, the Federal Labor Relations Authority (FLRA) has held that the Statute mandates that agencies must have access to negotiated grievance and arbitration procedures.[11] Agencies have exercised this right on numerous occasions, filing grievances concerning, among others, union compliance with an agreement on the appointment and number of union stewards,[12] union compliance with an

---

[5] U.S.C. 7121(b)(1) and (2).
[6] U.S.C. 7121(b)(3)(A).
[7] U.S.C. 7121(b)(3)(B).
[8] U.S.C. 7114(a)(5). See also *Sheet Metal Workers, Local 97, Philadelphia Metal Trades Council and Robert Cosden*, 7 FLRA 799 (1982).
[9] *Norfolk Naval Shipyard, Portsmouth, Va. and Tidewater, Va., Federal Employees Metal Trades Council*, 10 FLRA 53 (1982).
[10] *AFGE, Local 1178 and Army Quartermaster Center*, 12 FLRA 598 (1983).
[11] *Laborers, Local 1267 and Defense Logistics Agency, Defense Depot, Tracy, Cal.*, 14 FLRA 686 (1984) (Proposals 8 and 9).
[12] *Headquarters, Ft. Sam Houston and AFGE, Local 2154*, 15 FLRA 974 (1984).

agreement on the level at which collective bargaining was required,[13] alleged improper union advice to employees about a management survey,[14] and alleged malicious statements about management published in a union newsletter.[15]

Only the parties to an agreement, and not an aggrieved employee, may invoke arbitration.[16] Thus, a union has a right to screen employee grievances and to determine whether a particular grievance should be processed to arbitration. However, while a union has considerable discretion in deciding whether an employee's grievance has merit and whether to invoke arbitration, the union also has a duty to represent all bargaining unit employees fairly and must not exercise its discretion in a discriminatory or bad-faith manner.[17] In that regard, a union violates its duty of fair representation if it conditions representation of a unit employee on whether the employee is a member of the union.

Since a party to an agreement has a right to invoke arbitration under the negotiated grievance procedures, the other party may not prevent arbitration by refusing to participate in the process. *Ex parte* arbitration proceedings are not prohibited under the Statute. Thus, a party may proceed alone to arbitration, and, moreover, a refusal to participate in an arbitration proceeding may constitute an unfair labor practice.[18] A party therefore acts at considerable risk by failing or refusing to participate in arbitration.[19]

---

[13]*DOD Dependents Schools and Overseas Educ. Ass'n*, 12 FLRA 52 (1983).

[14]*San Antonio Air Logistics Center, Kelly AFB, Tex. and AFGE, Local 1617*, 6 FLRA 412 and 6 FLRA 419 (1981).

[15]*Navy Exch., Naval Station, San Diego, Cal. and AFGE, Interdepartmental Local 3723*, 6 FLRA 408 (1981).

[16]5 U.S.C. 7121(b)(3)(C).

[17]E.g., *AFGE, Local 3529 and Jerry Cyncynatus*, 31 FLRA 1208 (1988); *AFGE, Local 916 and Air Force Logistics Command, Tinker AFB, Oklahoma City, Okla.*, 28 FLRA 989 (1987); *Federal Employees Metal Trades Council, Iron Workers, Local 745 and Portsmouth Naval Shipyard*, Portsmouth, N.H., 12 FLRA 276 (1983); *Overseas Educ. Ass'n and DOD Dependents Schools*, 11 FLRA 377 (1983); *Tidewater, Va., Federal Employees Metal Trades Council and Machinists Local 441*, 8 FLRA 217 (1982). See also *Ft. Bragg Ass'n of Educators, NEA and Ft. Bragg DOD Dependents Schools*, Fort Bragg, N.C., 28 FLRA 908 (1987) (in which FLRA concluded that duty of fair representation of unions in federal sector is same as duty of unions in private sector); *AFGE, Local 1857 and John M. Neill*, 28 FLRA 677 (1987); *NFFE, Local 1453 and Kenneth A. Crawford*, 23 FLRA 686 (1986).

[18]*Warner Robins Air Logistics Center, Warner Robins, Ga. and AFGE, Local 987*, 24 FLRA 968 (1986); *Health Care Fin. Admin. and AFGE, Local 1923*, 22 FLRA 437 (1986); *AFGE, Local 2782 and Department of Commerce, Bureau of the Census*, 21 FLRA 339 (1986); *Department of Labor, Employment Standards Admin., Wage & Hour Div.*, Washington, D.C. and AFGE, Local 12, 10 FLRA 316, 320–21 (1982).

[19]*Id.*; see also *Army & Air Force Exch. Serv., Fort Hood, Tex. and AFGE, Local 1920*, 32 FLRA 124 (1988); *AFGE and Social Sec. Admin.*, 25 FLRA 173 (1987); *Social Sec. Admin. and AFGE*, 24 FLRA 91, 93 (1986); *Social Sec. Admin. and AFGE*, 24 FLRA 6 (1986).

We do not know how many grievances have been filed under negotiated grievance procedures or precisely how many of those grievances proceeded to arbitration since January 11, 1979, the effective date of the Statute. However, according to LAIRS' records, approximately 6,981 arbitration awards were issued between January 1979 and the end of December 1988, that is, the number of awards reported to LAIRS during the 10-year period are as follows: 1979 (602), 1980 (790), 1981 (787), 1982 (731), 1983 (890), 1984 (772), 1985 (615), 1986 (595), 1987 (634), and 1988 (partial reports as of January 1989 of 565 awards). Assuming that the awards reported accurately reflect the total number of arbitrations during the period, the data indicate that the trend in the number of federal sector grievance arbitration cases, which was on the upswing in the early 1980s and reached a high of 890 cases in 1983, has declined to an average of approximately 600 cases a year.

Selection of an Arbitrator

The Statute does not address the matter of selecting an arbitrator. Agency and union parties may utilize any method they agree upon. Some parties have permanent umpires, while others use arbitrators on a rotational basis from a panel they previously selected. Other parties select arbitrators on an ad hoc basis from lists furnished by the Federal Mediation and Conciliation Service or the American Arbitration Association.

Conduct of the Hearing

It is well established in the federal sector that an arbitrator has considerable latitude in the conduct of the hearing and the fact that an arbitrator conducts the hearing in a manner which one of the parties finds objectionable will not provide any basis for finding the arbitrator's award deficient under the Statute.[20]

There are no fixed rules of procedure or rules of evidence governing arbitration proceedings. Such rules are for the parties and arbitrator to determine. Thus, for example, there is no fixed order in which the parties must present their respective sides in a dispute. While the party that filed the grievance may be expected to proceed first, the arbitrator has the discretion to vary that procedure where the nature of the case, such as a

---

[20]*Social Sec. Admin. and AFGE, Local 547*, 24 FLRA 959 (1986); *Oklahoma Air Logistics Center, Tinker AFB, Okla. and AFGE, Local 916*, 30 FLRA 20 (1987); *AFGE, Local 2610 and VA Medical & Regional Office Center, Togus, Me.*, 30 FLRA 1153 (1988).

disciplinary action case, requires a variation in the interest of fairness and expedience. The determination of the order of presentation should, therefore, be made based on how the facts in the case can best be developed. Where one party possesses the basic facts and materials and the other party's case is essentially one of rebuttal, the arbitrator may require the party with the basic facts to proceed first.[21]

In any event, liberal admission of testimony and evidence is the customary practice in arbitration proceedings and both sides should be afforded a full and fair opportunity to present their positions.

Arbitrability

One of the first issues in an arbitration proceeding may be whether the grievance is arbitrable. All arbitrability questions not resolved by the parties at preliminary stages of the negotiated grievance procedure may be submitted to arbitration for resolution.[22] Arbitrability questions may raise a number of substantive and procedural considerations for the participants and the arbitrator.

Scope of the Grievance Procedures

As a general proposition, grievance procedures negotiated under the Statute are broad in scope. One reason is that Congress defined "grievance" in very broad terms. Congress did not confine grievances to alleged violations of a collective bargaining agreement. Grievances may also encompass alleged violations, misinterpretations, or misapplications of law or regulation affecting conditions of employment. Indeed, employee grievances may cover "any complaint . . . concerning any matter related to the employment of the employee . . . ."[23] In addition, Congress

---

[21]Elkouri & Elkouri, How Arbitration Works, 4th ed. (BNA Books, 1985) 266–67; Haughton, *Running the Hearing*, in Zack, ed., Arbitration in Practice (ILR Press, 1984).

[22]*Interpretation and Guidance*, 2 FLRA 273, 278 n.7 (1979).

[23]5 U.S.C. 7103(a)(9). *Bureau of Indian Affairs and NFFE, Local 243*, 25 FLRA 902 (1987); *AFGE, Local 1513 and Naval Air Station, Whidbey Island*, 26 FLRA 289 (1987); *Social Sec. Admin., Mid-American Program Serv. Center and AFGE, Local 1336*, 26 FLRA 292 (1987); *Veterans Admin. Medical Center, Omaha, Neb. and AFGE, Local 2270*, 26 FLRA 371 (1987); *GSA and AFGE, Nat'l Council 236*, 27 FLRA 3 (1987); *USIA and AFGE, Local 1812*, 32 FLRA 739 (1988).

provided that negotiated grievance procedures will cover all matters except those expressly excluded by the parties or by law.[24]

Exclusions

Exclusions in section 7121(c) prohibit an employee from grieving: (1) actions taken against him or her for prohibited political activities; (2) retirement, life and health insurance; (3) suspensions and removals for national security reasons; (4) examination, certification, and appointment; and (5) classification of any position which does not result in the reduction in grade or pay of an employee. The 7121(c) exclusion raised most frequently in arbitration cases is section 7121(c)(5), which deals with job classification. That provision is discussed below in connection with consideration of grievances concerning promotions. In section 5366(b), Congress also excluded from the grievance procedure certain matters relating to grade and pay retention benefits of employees after a change in position or reclassification.[25] (See Chapter 2, note 236.)

A few other matters have been excluded from coverage of negotiated grievance and arbitration procedures as a result of federal court decisions: (1) separation of probationary employees;[26] (2) discipline of professional employees in the Veterans Administration's Department of Medicine and Surgery for ineptitude, inefficiency, or misconduct;[27] and (3) discipline of National Guard technicians.[28] Other exclusions were under congressional and judicial consideration at the end of 1988.[29] The FLRA has

---

[24]5 U.S.C. 7121(a)(2) and 7121(c)(1)–(5). The provisions reflect the intent of Congress that: "All matters that under the provisions of law could be submitted to the grievance procedures shall in fact be within the scope of any grievance procedure negotiated by the parties unless the parties agree as part of the collective bargaining process that certain matters shall not be covered by the grievance procedures." Joint Explanatory Statement of the Committee on Conference, H.R. REP. No. 95-1717, 95th Cong., 2d Sess. 157 (1978), 1978 U.S. CODE CONG. & ADMIN. NEWS 2723, 2891.

[25]*Veterans Admin. Medical Center and AFGE, Local 1843*, 16 FLRA 869 (1984).

[26]*Immigration & Naturalization Serv. v. FLRA*, 709 F.2d 724 (D.C. Cir. 1983).

[27]*Veterans Admin. Medical Center, Minneapolis v. FLRA*, 705 F.2d 953 (8th Cir. 1983); *Veterans Admin. Medical Center, Northport v. FLRA*, 732 F.2d 1128 (2d Cir. 1984).

[28]E.g., *Nebraska, Military Dep't v. FLRA*, 705 F.2d 945 (8th Cir. 1983).

[29]Two federal courts of appeal carved out significant and controversial exclusions in 1988. In *Colorado Nurses Ass'n v. FLRA*, No. 87-1242 (D.C. Cir. 1988), the District of Columbia Circuit decided that all working conditions of the VA's Department of Medicine and Surgery professional employees were excluded from coverage of negotiated grievance procedures unless the VA elected to bargain on including them. That decision was the subject of congressional attention at the close of the 100th Congress in October 1988 and was identified for early further action at the beginning of the 101st Congress in 1989.

In *HHS v. FLRA*, Nos. 87-1595 and 87-1832 (7th Cir. 1988), the court decided that

determined that minor disciplinary actions against National Park Police employees are within the exclusive jurisdiction of the Secretary of the Interior under law and that such actions, therefore, are not grievable or arbitrable under negotiated grievance procedures.[30] An arbitrator must dismiss any grievance that is excluded by law.

Election of Remedies

Matters that are otherwise grievable and arbitrable may be precluded from consideration under negotiated grievance procedures by operation of three election-of-remedy provisions of the Statute, sections 7116(d), 7121(d), and 7121(e). These provisions are designed to prevent relitigation of a dispute after the aggrieved party has made a choice of procedures in which to raise the matter.

Section 7116(d) provides that when, in the discretion of an aggrieved party, an issue has been raised under unfair labor practice procedures, that issue may not be raised later as a grievance. For example, where an unfair labor practice charge concerning an employee's reassignment was filed by the union on behalf of the employee, the employee was precluded from subsequently filing a grievance concerning the same matter.[31]

Section 7121(d) provides that when an employee is affected by a "prohibited personnel practice" under 5 U.S.C. 2302(b)(1) and the employee raised the "matter" earlier under applicable statutory appeals procedures, the matter may not be raised later as a grievance under negotiated grievance procedures.[32] (See also Chapter 2.) The FLRA has determined that the term "matter" as used in section 7121(d) refers not to the issue of discrimination but, rather, to the personnel action involved.[33] The FLRA has also concluded that a grievance filed in accordance with a negotiated grievance procedure raising the matter of alleged discrimination under the Civil Rights Act of 1964 is only precluded or barred by the

---

employees in the excepted service who did not have veterans preference were barred from using arbitration to contest adverse employment decisions taken under either Chapter 43 or Chapter 75 of the Civil Service Reform Act. The reach of that decision remained unclear at the end of 1988, because the issue was pending and awaiting decision in the District of Columbia Circuit in two cases, *Department of the Treasury, Office of Chief Counsel v. FLRA*, No. 88-1159 and *Customs Serv. v. FLRA*, No. 88-1308, and in the 9th Circuit in two other cases, *HHS Region IX v. FLRA*, Nos. 88-7192 and 88-7236.

[30]*Police Ass'n of the D.C. and National Park Serv., U.S. Park Police*, 18 FLRA 348 (1985).

[31]*Immigration and Naturalization Serv. and AFGE, Local 2724*, 20 FLRA 743 (1985).

[32]*AFGE, Local 3230 and EEOC*, 22 FLRA 448 (1986).

[33]*Marshals Serv. and International Council of U.S. Marshals Serv. Locals, AFGE*, 23 FLRA 564 (1986).

grievant having earlier raised the same matter by the timely filing of a formal EEO complaint under the complaint procedures promulgated by the Equal Employment Opportunity Commission (EEOC). Consultation with an agency EEO counselor pursuant to precomplaint procedures does not preclude the subsequent filing of such a grievance.[34]

Section 7121(e) provides that matters covered under 5 U.S.C. 4303 (reductions in grade and removals for alleged unacceptable performance) and 5 U.S.C. 7512 (removals, suspensions for more than 14 days, reductions in grade or pay, and furloughs for 30 days or less) which are also covered by a negotiated grievance procedure may, in the discretion of the aggrieved employee, be raised under statutory appeals procedures or the negotiated procedures, but not both. (The same option exists with respect to similar actions taken under other personnel systems against employees covered by the Statute.) An employee may appeal an action under sections 4303 or 7512 to the Merit Systems Protection Board (MSPB) or file a grievance under negotiated grievance procedures if the parties to the agreement have not excluded the matter from coverage. An employee is deemed to have exercised the option at the time the employee timely files a notice of appeal with MSPB or timely files a grievance in writing in accordance with the negotiated procedures, whichever event occurs first.

Thus, under the Statute, any matter that is not specifically excluded from the coverage of negotiated grievance procedures as a matter of law or by the parties in their collective bargaining agreement, or that is not precluded from consideration under grievance procedures because of the earlier election of an alternative remedy, is grievable and arbitrable. As stated above, any questions that arise concerning the arbitrability of a matter are to be resolved in the first instance under negotiated grievance and arbitration procedures. If a dispute reaches arbitration, such questions may be resolved by the arbitrator hearing the case, subject, of course, to review by the FLRA or the Court of Appeals for the Federal Circuit, as discussed more fully below and in Chapter 3.

An arbitrator's decision on whether a grievance complies with the procedural requirements of a negotiated grievance procedure, such as timeliness, is virtually unreviewable. Exceptions that disagree with an arbitrator's procedural arbitrability rulings provide no basis for finding an award deficient under the Statute and such exceptions are uniformly denied by the FLRA.[35]

---

[34]*Marshals Serv. and International Council of U.S. Marshals Serv. Locals, AFGE*, 23 FLRA 414 (1986).

[35]E.g., *Oklahoma City Air Logistics Center, Tinker AFB, Okla. and AFGE, Local 916*, 30 FLRA 1151 (1988).

Common Issues Before the Federal Sector Arbitrator

Preliminary Considerations

A paramount preliminary consideration is that arbitration in the federal sector operates within a framework of laws, rules, and regulations affecting and governing personnel policies, practices, and the working conditions of employees. Consideration of relevant laws and regulations therefore is always within the scope of an arbitrator's authority and responsibility in the federal sector.[36] While arbitrators have considerable latitude in fashioning appropriate remedies in federal sector grievance arbitration,[37] their awards must be consistent with governing law and regulation.

The laws most frequently cited in arbitration proceedings are the management rights provisions of section 7106(a) of the Statute and the Back Pay Act (5 U.S.C. 5596).

Section 7106(a) provides that "nothing" in the Statute shall "affect the authority" of an agency to exercise the rights enumerated in that section. Based on that statutory language, one of the fundamental principles established by the FLRA in its decisions in arbitration cases is that an arbitration award may not improperly deny an agency the authority to exercise its rights under that section or result in substitution of the arbitrator's judgment for that of the agency in the exercise of those rights.[38] Most arbitration cases obviously involve review of management judgment and actions in exercising section 7106(a) rights and arbitrators frequently direct modification or reversal of those actions. However, that fact alone does not render the arbitrators' awards deficient. One reason is that section 7106 also provides that management's exercise of its rights must be in accordance with applicable laws. Another reason is that management's rights under 7106(a) are subject to sections 7106(b)(2) and (3). Section 7106(b)(2) permits negotiation of procedures which management officials will follow in exercising their rights. Section 7106(b)(3) permits negotiation of "appropriate arrangements" for employees who are adversely affected by management's exercise of its rights. Therefore, an award that simply enforces a negotiable procedure or appropriate arrangement in a collective bargaining agreement is not contrary to sec-

---

[36]See, e.g., *Air Force Logistics Command and AFGE, Council 214*, 32 FLRA 261, 266 (1988); *Panama Canal Comm'n and Masters, Mates & Pilots*, 27 FLRA 907, 910–11 (1987).

[37]*Veterans Admin. Hosp., Newington, Conn. and NAGE, Local R1-109*, 5 FLRA 64 (1981); *HUD and AFGE, Local 3412*, 24 FLRA 442 (1986).

[38]*NTEU and Customs Serv.*, 17 FLRA 38, 39 (1985); *Customs Serv., Laredo, Tex. and NTEU, Chapter 145*, 17 FLRA 68, 69 (1985).

tion 7106(a).[39] For a more detailed discussion of section 7106, see Chapter 9.

The regulations most frequently cited are the Civil Service rules and regulations promulgated by the Office of Personnel Management (OPM) in the Code of Federal Regulations and in mandatory requirements of the Federal Personnel Manual (FPM). Advice and guidance provided by OPM in the FPM chapters or in FPM letters and bulletins, and the advisory opinions of OPM officials, are considered by the FLRA to be just that—advice, guidance, and opinion—and not rules or regulations. They are entitled to consideration but are not binding on agencies or arbitrators.[40] In addition, arbitrators and practitioners should note that once a collective bargaining agreement becomes effective, any subsequently issued regulations, with the exception of governmentwide regulations issued under 5 U.S.C. 2302 (relating to prohibited personnel practices) cannot nullify the terms of the agreement.[41] With that limited exception, the agreement provision must control in any dispute with any subsequently issued regulation, including new provisions of the FPM.

Between 1979 and 1988, the only arbitration awards found by the FLRA to be contrary to regulations were those in conflict with governmentwide regulations. No award was found deficient based on possible conflict with an agencywide or lower level regulation. This indicates that while awards must conform with governmentwide regulations, arbitrators have more discretion in the interpretation and acceptance or rejection of regulations which are not governmentwide in scope.

A review of FLRA and Federal Circuit case law on some of the issues in arbitration cases may be helpful in understanding the legal boundaries of arbitrating grievances in the federal sector. The issues discussed in this chapter include: (1) assignment of work, (2) promotions, (3) performance-based actions under 5 U.S.C. 4303 and adverse actions under 5 U.S.C. 7512, (4) less severe disciplinary actions (suspensions for less than 14 days and written reprimands), (5) performance evaluation, (6) contracting out, (7) official time, travel, and per diem for union representatives, (8) environmental differential pay, (9) claims for back pay, and (10) requests for attorney's fees in grievance proceedings.

Assignment of Work

Section 7106(a)(2)(B) of the Statute reserves to management officials the right to assign work, which includes the right to determine who will do

[39]*PATCO and Federal Aviation Admin.*, 5 FLRA 763, 768–69 (1981).
[40]*AFGE, Local 1568 and HUD*, 21 FLRA 781 (1986).
[41]*International Plate Printers and Bureau of Engraving & Printing*, 25 FLRA 113, 115 (1987); *NTEU and Customs Serv.*, 9 FLRA 983, 985 (1982).

the work and who will not. For example, in a case where the arbitrator's award precluded management from assigning particular duties to the position descriptions of certain employees, the FLRA set aside the award because it interfered with management's section 7106(a)(2)(B) right to assign work.[42] In another case, where management excused certain employees from performing a number of duties and the arbitrator's award directed management to assign the work to those employees and precluded continuation of management's practice, the FLRA set aside the award as contrary to section 7106(a)(2)(B).[43] Likewise, arbitration awards that would preclude management from assigning work normally performed by bargaining unit employees to nonbargaining unit personnel, such as military personnel or supervisors, have been found to be contrary to section 7106(a)(2)(B).[44]

In contrast, an award that directed management to restore certain duties to an employee, based on a determination that the duties were improperly removed from the employee in a disciplinary action that was not for just cause, was not contrary to section 7106(a)(2)(B).[45]

The right to assign work also includes the right to determine when work will be done. For example, the FLRA has found that the assignment of training during duty hours of employees constitutes an exercise of management's right to assign work and an award that interfered with management's training of certain employees was contrary to section 7106(a)(2)(B).[46]

Also encompassed within the right to assign work is the authority to establish the qualifications and skills needed to perform the work involved and to decide whether a particular employee meets those qualifications.[47] However, when management has determined that a number of employees are equally qualified to perform the work, a procedure by which the employees will be selected is negotiable under 7106(b)(2) and, if agreement is reached, it is enforceable through arbitration.[48]

---

[42]*Carswell AFB and AFGE, Local 1364*, 19 FLRA 386 (1985).

[43]*Veterans Admin. Hosp., Lebanon, Pa. and AFGE, Local 1966*, 11 FLRA 193 (1983).

[44]*172d Infantry Brigade, Ft. Richardson, Alaska and AFGE, Locals 1712, 1834, & 1949*, 19 FLRA 542 (1985); *Marine Corps Logistics Base, Albany, Ga. and AFGE, Local 2317*, 19 FLRA 544 (1985); *Southwestern Power Admin. and Electrical Workers (IBEW), Local 1002*, 22 FLRA 475 (1986).

[45]*Portsmouth Naval Shipyard and Federal Employees Metal Trades Council*, 5 FLRA 230 (1981).

[46]*Veterans Admin. Medical Center, Lebanon, Pa. and AFGE, Local 1966*, 19 FLRA 392 (1985).

[47]*Laborers, Local 1276 and Veterans Admin. Nat'l Cemetery Office, San Francisco, Cal.*, 9 FLRA 703, 706 (1982).

[48]*NTEU and Customs Serv.*, 18 FLRA 780 (1985).

For example, in a case where management determined that both permanent and temporary employees were qualified to perform the work, the arbitrator's interpretation and application of a provision in the parties' collective bargaining agreement to give the permanent employees first preference for assignment simply enforced a negotiable procedure and did not improperly interfere with management's right to assign the work under section 7106(a)(2)(B).[49]

However, in other cases where the arbitrators found, contrary to management determinations, that the grievants had the skills necessary to perform the work involved and ordered that the grievants be assigned the work, the FLRA concluded that the awards were not merely enforcing negotiable procedures but, rather, improperly interfered with management's right under section 7106(a)(2)(B).[50]

As stated previously, an arbitrator also may enforce an appropriate arrangement negotiated by the parties in a collective bargaining agreement pursuant to section 7106(b)(3). The FLRA has held, consistent with its decisions in negotiability cases, that the propriety of an arbitrator's enforcement of an appropriate arrangement for employees adversely affected by management's exercise of a section 7106(a) right depends upon whether the award excessively interferes with the right.[51] For example, where an arbitrator found that employees who came in direct contact with toxic chemicals were entitled to personal cleanup time for health and safety reasons before eating lunch, the FLRA found that the award enforced an appropriate arrangement for employees adversely affected by unclean and potentially hazardous conditions inherent in their work and did not violate management's right to assign work.[52]

Promotions

Review of the decisions of the FLRA in promotion disputes indicates that the disputes that reach arbitrators may be divided into questions concerning (1) employee entitlement to permanent promotion, (2) entitlement to temporary promotion, and (3) whether the underlying grievance is

---

[49]*National Marine Fisheries Serv., Ne. Region, NOAA, Gloucester, Mass. and Masters, Mates & Pilots, Boston, Mass.*, 22 FLRA 443 (1986).

[50]*U.S. Naval Ordnance Station and Machinists, Local Lodge 830*, 23 FLRA 671 (1986).

[51]*NAGE, Local R14-87 and Kansas Army Nat'l Guard*, 21 FLRA 24 (1986).

[52]*Washington Plate Printers Union, Local No. 2, IPDEU and Bureau of Engraving & Printing*, 31 FLRA 1250 (1988).

precluded by section 7121(c)(5) of the Statute, which precludes most grievances concerning the classification of positions.

Permanent Promotions

Promotion actions involve the exercise of management's right to select employees under section 7106(a)(2)(C) of the Statute. Management's right to make selections for promotion under section 7106(a)(2)(C) may be constrained, and an agency ordered to select a particular employee for promotion, only if the arbitrator finds that the employee was affected by an improper agency action that directly resulted in the failure of the employee to be promoted.[53] For example, where the arbitrator found that the agency violated the parties' collective bargaining agreement by failing to notify the grievant that she was entitled to priority consideration for a vacancy and, based on a reconstruction of what the selecting official would have done if the grievant had been informed and had applied for the vacancy, determined that the grievant would have been promoted, the arbitrator's award of a permanent promotion did not violate section 7106(a)(2)(C).[54] In contrast, an award of a permanent promotion based solely on a finding that the grievant was entitled to priority consideration was set aside by the FLRA as contrary to section 7106(a)(2)(C).[55] Likewise, an award ordering a permanent promotion based solely on the employee's seniority was set aside by the FLRA for the same reason.[56]

In the typical promotion case that reaches the FLRA, the arbitrator finds that applicable promotion procedures were not followed and a grievant was denied proper consideration as a result. In these cases, the arbitrator can order the selection action to be rerun. However, the arbitrator generally cannot order the position vacated in advance of the corrective action. Under FPM Chapter 335, any incumbent employee is entitled to be retained in the position pending corrective action unless it is specifically determined that the incumbent could not originally have been selected had proper procedures been followed.[57]

---

[53]Veterans Admin. Medical & Regional Office Center, San Juan, P.R. and AFGE, Local 2408, 21 FLRA 418 (1986); U.S. Naval Ordnance Station, Louisville, Ky. and Machinists Local Lodge 830, 22 FLRA 382 (1986).

[54]AFGE, Local 1923 and Health Care Fin. Admin., 33 FLRA 88 (1988).

[55]Department of Transp., Office of the Secretary and AFGE, Local 3313, 17 FLRA 54 (1985). See also AFGE, Local 12 and Department of Labor, 15 FLRA 543 (1984) (FLRA found that grievant's "probable expectation" of promotion and agency's violation of parties' agreement did not provide sufficient basis for arbitrator's award of retroactive promotion and back pay.)

[56]Army & Air Force Exch. Serv., Ft. Knox Exch., Ft. Knox, Ky. and AFGE, Local 2302, 8 FLRA 256 (1982).

[57]State, County & Mun. Employees, Local 2478 and Commission on Civil Rights, 26 FLRA 158, 161 (1987).

Where the arbitrator finds that there was a failure to process a promotion action in a timely manner, the Back Pay Act provides an arbitrator authority to award a retroactive promotion and back pay only if the delay occurred after the action was approved by a duly authorized official.[58]

Promotion disputes frequently involve the question of an employee's entitlement to promotion under a career ladder policy. The FLRA has held that a decision to promote an employee to the next higher grade in a career ladder position does not constitute a selection action under section 7106(a)(2)(C) but merely implements a prior decision to select the employee for appointment to the position.[59]

Arbitrators and practitioners should be aware that management's 7106(a)(2)(C) right includes the right to make selections from "any appropriate source." Thus, an award that limits management to using a particular source for promotions would be contrary to that provision of the Statute. For example, an award ordering management to make a selection from a register of best qualified candidates was set aside by the FLRA as contrary to section 7106(a)(2)(C) because it precluded management from filling the position from other appropriate sources.[60]

Temporary Promotions

In the typical case, an employee's grievance alleges that he or she was temporarily detailed to or performed the duties of a higher graded position for an extended period of time and is entitled to a temporary promotion and back pay. An arbitrator can award a temporary promotion and back pay in such cases. However, there must be a provision in the parties' collective bargaining agreement or in an agency regulation mandating a temporary promotion in the circumstances involved in order for the award to be authorized under law.[61] In addition, the grievant must meet minimum qualification standards for the position,[62] and the promotion must not otherwise be precluded by law or regulation.[63]

---

[58]*EEOC and AFGE, Local 3504*, 18 FLRA 312 (1985).

[59]*NTEU, Chapter 72 and Internal Revenue Serv., Austin Serv. Center*, 11 FLRA 271 (1983) (Proposal 2); *AFGE, Local 17 and Veterans Admin. Cent. Office*, 24 FLRA 424, 425–26 (1986).

[60]*Army Training Center, Ft. Benning, Ga. and AFGE, Local 54*, 12 FLRA 161 (1983).

[61]*Social Sec. Admin. and AFGE, Local 1923*, 20 FLRA 684 (1985).

[62]*Headquarters, XVIII Airborne Corps and Fort Bragg and AFGE, Local 1770*, 18 FLRA 481 (1985).

[63]*Immigration & Naturalizaton Serv. and Immigration & Naturalization Serv. Council, AFGE, Local 2805*, 15 FLRA 862 (1984).

Section 7121(c)(5)

When the substance of a grievance concerns the accuracy of the classification of an employee's position, the grievance is barred by section 7121(c)(5).[64]

A key word in promotion cases in relation to 7121(c)(5) is "temporary." If the claim is for a temporary promotion, section 7121(c)(5) is usually not applicable.[65] However, if the claim is for a noncompetitive, permanent promotion, then there may be a 7121(c)(5) problem. For example, where a GS-5 grievant sought, and the arbitrator awarded, a permanent, noncompetitive promotion to GS-6, even though the agency had determined that the GS-6 grade level could not be supported as a matter of classification, the FLRA held that both the grievance and the award concerned the classification of a position within the meaning of section 7121(c)(5).[66] In another case, where the substance of the grievance concerned the grade level of the duties assigned to and performed by the grievant, the FLRA held that the grievance was precluded by section 7121(c)(5).[67] However, where the grievance only raised an issue of whether the grievant was entitled to a career ladder promotion, the FLRA found that the grievance did not concern the classification of the position.[68]

Grievances involving position descriptions are often claimed to be precluded by section 7121(c)(5) because they allegedly concern position classification. The FLRA has held that a grievance concerning the accuracy of a position description (PD), for example, a grievance alleging that duties regularly assigned to and performed by the grievant are not reflected in his or her PD, is not a grievance concerning classification within the meaning of section 7121(c)(5).[69] Therefore, an arbitrator can consider such a grievance and order an agency to issue the employee an accurate PD. It should be noted that in fashioning an award the arbitrator

---

[64]E.g., *Federal Aviation Admin., Tampa, Fla. and Federal Aviation Science & Technological Ass'n/NAGE*, 8 FLRA 532, 534–35 (1982).

[65]E.g., *New Cumberland Army Depot and AFGE, Local 2004*, 21 FLRA 968, 969–70 (1986); But see *Social Sec. Admin. and AFGE, Local 1923*, 31 FLRA 933 (1988) (arbitrator directed agency to reclassify grievants' positions at higher grade for period they allegedly performed high-graded duties).

[66]*EEOC Memphis Dist. Office and AFGE, National Council of EEO Locals No. 216*, 18 FLRA 88 (1985).

[67]*Veterans Admin. Medical Center, Tampa, Fla. and AFGE, Local 547*, 19 FLRA 1177 (1985).

[68]*Department of Labor and AFGE, Local 12*, 24 FLRA 435 (1986).

[69]*Federal Aviation Admin., Tampa, Fla. and Federal Aviation Science & Technological Ass'n/NAGE*, supra note 64.

cannot order the agency to process and issue a PD that does not reflect the employee's current duties.[70]

However, when the essential nature of the grievance goes beyond the accuracy of the contents of the PD and is integrally related to the accuracy of the classification of the grievant's position (i.e., the title, series, and grade of the duties assigned to and performed by the grievant) then the grievance concerns classification and is precluded by section 7121(c)(5).[71]

Adverse Actions Under 5 U.S.C. 7512 and Performance-Based Actions Under 5 U.S.C. 4303

For a detailed discussion of actions under 5 U.S.C. 7512 and 4303, see Chapter 3, Appealable Actions. For purposes of this chapter, it is sufficient to be aware that if a bargaining unit employee elects to grieve a 7512 or 4303 action rather than appealing to the MSPB and the dispute proceeds to arbitration (noting again that the employee's union would have to invoke arbitration because the employee does not have a right to do so), the arbitrator is faced with certain requirements.

The foremost requirement is that the arbitrator must apply the same statutory standards of proof that would have been applied if the matter had been appealed to the MSPB.[72] Thus, the decision of the agency in a section 4303 action based on unacceptable performance must be sustained by the arbitrator if the action is supported by "substantial evidence," and an agency decision in a section 7512 adverse action must be sustained if supported by a "preponderance of the evidence."

That requirement is balanced by a statutory constraint. An agency's decision may not be sustained by an arbitrator if "harmful error" is shown in the application of the agency's procedures in arriving at the decision, if the decision is shown to be based on any prohibited personnel practice set forth in 5 U.S.C. 2302(b), or if the decision is shown not to be in accordance with law.[73]

In addition to being bound by statutory standards of review, as defined by the MSPB, arbitrators must apply judicially approved princi-

---

[70]AFGE, Local 41 and HHS, Office of the Secretary, 8 FLRA 98 (1982).

[71]Overseas Educ. Ass'n and DOD Dependents Schools, 15 FLRA 358 (1984); Veterans Admin. Medical Center, Tampa, Fla. and AFGE, Local 547, supra note 67.

[72]5 U.S.C. 7121(e)(2) and 7701(c)(1). See, e.g., Cornelius v. Nutt, 472 U.S. 648 (1985); DePauw v. International Trade Comm'n, 782 F.2d 1564 (Fed. Cir. 1986), cert. denied, 107 S.Ct. 69 (1986).

[73]5 U.S.C. 7701(c)(2).

ples established by MSPB in its decisions.[74] Therefore, arbitrators should review relevant decisions of the MSPB and the Court of Appeals for the Federal Circuit in resolving challenges to 7512 and 4303 actions. This is particularly important in considering the appropriateness of penalties and mitigation.

For example, in adverse actions under section 7512, the agency must demonstrate that the penalty imposed "promotes the efficiency of the Service." MSPB reviews adverse action penalties under an abuse of discretion standard. MSPB considers whether the penalty bears some relationship to the offense and the employment relationship and whether it is significantly greater than penalties in similar cases in the same agency. In that regard, MSPB has enumerated a number of factors that should be considered by an agency in selecting a penalty.[75] In reviewing the appropriateness of the selected penalty, arbitrators, like MSPB, should determine whether the agency considered the factors relevant to the case and whether the agency chose a reasonable penalty. Arbitrators may mitigate penalties in adverse action cases.[76]

In reviewing actions under section 4303, that is, removals or demotions for unacceptable performance, arbitrators should be aware that the requirements and elements of such an action are different from those established for section 7512 actions. The requirements and elements of a section 4303 case have been discussed by the MSPB and the Federal Circuit,[77] and should be applied in deciding such cases.

It is especially important for arbitrators to be aware that the Federal Circuit has held that MSPB is not empowered to modify an agency's penalty in a section 4303 case.[78] That court subsequently also reversed an arbitrator's reduction of a 4303 demotion action to a reassignment, ruling that if MSPB did not have the authority to modify the agency's penalty, "it follows that an arbitrator similarly cannot modify an agency penalty imposed in a chapter 43 proceeding."[79] Consequently, in contrast to adverse actions under section 7512, mitigation is precluded in arbitration of section 4303 actions.

While arbitrators are required to apply the statutory standards, as defined by MSPB, and by other judicially approved substantive principles

---

[74]*Horner v. Bell*, 825 F.2d 391 (Fed. Cir. 1987).
[75]*Douglas v. Veterans Admin.*, 5 MSPR 280 (1981).
[76]*AFGE, Local 2718 v. Immigration & Naturalization Serv.*, 768 F.2d 348, 351 (Fed. Cir. 1985).
[77]*Lovshin v. Department of the Navy*, 767 F.2d 826 (Fed. Cir. 1985); *Martin v. Federal Aviation Admin.*, 795 F.2d 995 (Fed. Cir. 1986).
[78]*Lisiecki v. MSPB*, 769 F.2d 1538 (Fed. Cir. 1985), *cert. denied*, 106 S.Ct. 1514 (1986).
[79]*Horner v. Bell, supra* note 74.

established by the Board in deciding 4303 and 7512 cases, arbitrators are not required to reach results identical to MSPB decisions in all similar factual situations. Thus, arbitrators do not have to conduct an exhaustive examination of MSPB case law to assure that their determinations will be the same in the case closest on the facts.[80] Arbitrators are required to apply the prescribed standards and principles but properly may reach different results in deciding similar cases.[81]

Other Disciplinary Actions

Other disciplinary actions, which are not as severe as the 5 U.S.C. 7512 adverse actions discussed above and which frequently are subject to arbitration, are suspensions for less than 14 days and written reprimands. The issue in these cases typically is whether the discipline was in accord with collective bargaining agreement requirements that discipline must be for "just cause" or "for reasons that promote the efficiency of the Federal Service." Such agreement provisions are considered to be appropriate arrangements for employees adversely affected by management's exercise of its right to discipline under section 7106(a)(2)(A). Thus, an arbitrator can set aside or reduce a penalty upon a determination on the merits that the action was not for just cause and such an award does not violate management's right to discipline.[82]

Arbitrators have considerably more latitude in deciding grievances concerning the less severe disciplinary actions than they do in section 7512 adverse actions. First, the MSPB's standard for review (preponderence of the evidence) does not apply to review of suspensions of 14 days or less or to actions of less severity, such as written reprimands. The FLRA has made it clear that an arbitrator is required to apply the standard only in arbitration of the more serious actions enumerated in

---

[80]*Devine v. Pastore*, 732 F.2d 213 (D.C. Cir. 1984).

[81]*Id.; Horner v. Hardy*, 831 F.2d 391 (Fed. Cir. 1987); *Devine v. Duff*, 737 F.2d 1031 (Fed. Cir. 1984); *Devine v. NTEU*, 737 F.2d 1031 (Fed. Cir. 1984); *Devine v. Sutermeister*, 724 F.2d 1558 (Fed. Cir. 1983).

[82]E.g., *Portsmouth Naval Shipyard and Federal Employees Metal Trades Council*, 5 FLRA 230 (1981); *AFGE, Local 2004 and New Cumberland Army Depot*, 27 FLRA 387 (1987). See also *Social Sec. Admin. and AFGE, Local 1923*, 32 FLRA 765 (1988) (FLRA, applying *Paperworkers v. Misco, Inc.*, 484 U.S. 29, 126 LRRM 3113 (1987) and *W.R. Grace & Co. v. Rubber Workers Local 759*, 461 U.S. 757, 31 FEP Cases 1409 (1983), determined that arbitrator's admission of settlement agreement into evidence and mitigation of grievant's suspension based on that settlement was not contrary to public policy). But see *Panama Canal Comm'n and Masters, Mates, & Pilots*, 33 FLRA 15 (1988) (FLRA determined that arbitrator's award setting aside grievant's suspension was contrary to law because arbitrator misapplied decision of Supreme Court in *Rankin v. McPhearson*, 55 USLW 5019 (1987)).

section 7512. Consistent with decisions of the federal courts in the private sector, the FLRA has uniformly held that unless a specific standard of proof or review is required by the parties, arbitrators may establish whatever standard they deem appropriate in review of the less severe actions.[83] The FLRA has likewise held that the "harmful error rule," which pertains to procedural requirements in disciplinary actions, only applies to the more serious actions under section 7512.[84]

A word of caution is in order with respect to an arbitrator's interpretation and application of agreement provisions in disciplinary cases. For example, if an arbitrator sustains the discipline of an employee for conduct committed while the employee was engaged in activity protected by the Statute, such as serving as a union representative, and the FLRA finds that the conduct did not exceed the bounds of the Statute's protection, the award will be set aside as contrary to the Statute.[85] In addition, the FLRA has indicated that an award interpreting procedural requirements of an agreement in a way that would prevent management from investigating alleged misconduct or from proposing an action is contrary to management's 7106(a)(2)(A) right to discipline.[86] In contrast, in a case where the arbitrator found that the agency's delay in imposing discipline was contrary to the parties' agreement and agency regulations, concluded that the discipline was not for just cause, and ordered the agency to rescind the action, the FLRA ruled that the award was not contrary to section 7106(a)(2)(A).[87]

Performance Evaluation

One of the most troublesome and frequently contested issues under the Statute has been the proper role of negotiated grievance procedures

---

[83]E.g., *AFGE, Local 1760* and *Social Sec. Admin., Ne. Program Serv. Center*, 22 FLRA 195 (1986). See also *Department of Educ., Div. of Civil Rights, Atlanta, Ga. and AFGE, Local 3887*, 17 FLRA 997 (1985) (FLRA determined that neither 5 U.S.C. 7701(c), which governs MSPB appellate procedures, nor 5 U.S.C. 7121(e)(2) require arbitrator to apply any particular standard of proof in grievance over denial of within-grade increase and, therefore, that arbitrator did not err in applying preponderance of evidence standard in the case).

[84]*Customs Serv. and NTEU*, 22 FLRA 607 (1986); *Warner Robins Air Logistics Center, Warner Robins, Ga. and AFGE, Local 987*, 24 FLRA 968 (1986).

[85]E.g., *Harry S. Truman Memorial Veterans Hosp., Columbia, Mo. and AFGE, Local 3399*, 14 FLRA 103 (1984); *Overseas Fed'n of Teachers and DOD Dependents Schools, Mediterranean Region*, 21 FLRA 757 (1986).

[86]*NFFE, Local 615 and National Park Serv., Sequoia & Kings Canyon Nat'l Parks*, 17 FLRA 318 (1985), aff'd sub nom. *NFFE, Local 615 v. FLRA*, 801 F.2d 477 (D.C. Cir. 1986).

[87]*NAGE Sec. Guard, Local R4-19, Portsmouth, Va. and Norfolk Naval Shipyard*, 26 FLRA 192 (1987).

and arbitration in resolving employee complaints concerning performance requirements and appraisals. The FLRA case law governing grievances and arbitration in this area changed significantly in 1987 and 1988. Based upon a reexamination of the relevant provisions of the Statute, the legislative history, and prior decisions, the FLRA reversed a number of its earlier holdings which had limited the arbitrability of grievances and the authority of arbitrators.[88]

The identification of critical elements in employee positions and establishment of performance standards for those elements represents an exercise of management's right to direct employees under section 7106(a)(2)(A) of the Statute and its right to assign work under section 7106(a)(2)(B). Previously, the FLRA had construed those provisions as precluding grievances which challenged critical elements and performance standards. An employee had to wait until he or she was adversely affected by application of the elements and standards in an appraisal, and could then only contest the appraisal. Furthermore, the FLRA had ruled that in resolving such a grievance an arbitrator could not substitute his or her judgment for that of management concerning the appropriateness of the elements and standards. Moreover, the arbitrator could not conduct an independent evaluation of the employee's performance and could direct an agency to raise an employee's rating in very limited circumstances, essentially only if management's own appraisal of the performance warranted a higher rating under the established standards. Those holdings have been substantially modified or reversed by the FLRA.

Under current FLRA case law, an employee may now utilize negotiated grievance procedures to challenge the legality of performance elements and standards, unless the parties have excluded such matters from the scope of their negotiated grievance procedures. Therefore, absent an exclusion in the agreement, a grievance alleging that management violated applicable law or regulation when it established an employee's performance elements and standards is grievable and arbitrable. Moreover, an employee may file such a grievance as soon as the elements and standards are established. The employee does not have to wait until he or she receives a performance appraisal.

---

[88]*Newark Air Force Station and AFGE, Local 2221*, 30 FLRA 616 (1987); *Social Sec. Admin. and AFGE*, 30 FLRA 1156 (1988); *Veterans Admin. and AFGE, Local 1228*, 31 FLRA 1271 (1988); *Social Sec. Admin. and AFGE*, 31 FLRA 1277 (1988); *HUD and AFGE, Local 476*, 32 FLRA 196 (1988). See also *Rogers v. DOD Dependents Schools*, 814 F.2d 1549 (Fed. Cir. 1984) (court held that employee in an arbitration proceeding on a 5 U.S.C. 4303 action is entitled to challenge legality of performance standards and arbitrator must resolve issue).

In deciding the merits of such a grievance, however, an arbitrator may examine the performance elements and standards established by management only to determine whether they comply with applicable legal and regulatory requirements. If the arbitrator finds that elements or standards do not comply with applicable requirements, the arbitrator may direct the agency to establish elements or standards that comply with those requirements. An arbitrator still may not determine the content of the elements and standards, and may not alter them or establish new ones. Further, an arbitrator may not impose requirements on an agency beyond those mandated by applicable law and regulation.

Moreover, an arbitrator's award addressing whether an employee's performance elements and standards comply with applicable law and regulation must be consistent with relevant MSPB and Federal Circuit case law. As with other disputes, the FLRA expects parties to present relevant decisions and other authorities and materials to the arbitrator to assist in the resolution of the matter.

Disputes relating to the application of performance elements and standards continue to be grievable and arbitrable. An employee who believes that he or she has been adversely affected by the application of those elements and standards in a performance appraisal may grieve the appraisal and an arbitrator may resolve the grievance. An arbitrator may sustain such a grievance upon finding that management did not apply the established performance elements and standards or that management applied them in violation of law, regulation, or a properly negotiated provision of the parties' collective bargaining agreement.

If the arbitrator makes such a finding, the arbitrator may cancel the defective rating or appraisal. Furthermore, under current FLRA case law, when the arbitrator is able to determine on the basis of the record in the case what the rating of the grievant's work product or performance would have been under the established elements and standards, if they had been applied or if the violation of law, regulation, or agreement had not occurred, the arbitrator may direct the agency to grant the grievant that rating.

However, an arbitrator may not raise an employee's performance rating based only on a finding that management violated a collective bargaining agreement or the spirit and intent of a regulation. Without a finding of what the employee's rating would have been if the violation had not occurred, the award of a higher rating would be contrary to section 7106(a)(2)(A) and (B).[89]

---

[89]*Army Transp. Center, Ft. Eustis, Va. and NAGE, Local R4-106*, 33 FLRA 391 (1988).

If the record does not enable the arbitrator to determine what the grievant's rating would have been if he or she had been evaluated properly, the arbitrator should direct that the grievant's work product or performance be reevaluated by management in accordance with the applicable requirements.

Contracting Out

The case law governing the arbitration of contracting-out disputes is not completely settled.

Section 7106(a)(2)(B) reserves to management officials the right to "make determinations with respect to contracting out." Since 1982, the FLRA has maintained, as with other management rights, that an agency's exercise of this right is grievable and arbitrable, unless the parties to a collective bargaining agreement have excluded the matter from coverage of their negotiated grievance procedures. Thus, the FLRA has consistently held that under a broad scope grievance procedure, a grievance claiming that a contracting-out action fails to comply with applicable procurement law and regulation is grievable and arbitrable.[90] In a landmark 1982 decision, the FLRA found negotiable a union proposal that in contracting-out activities the agency would comply with the requirements of procurement law and Office of Management and Budget (OMB) Circular A-76, the governmentwide authoritiative source in contracting-out decisions. The FLRA was upheld by the Court of Appeals for the District of Columbia Circuit and, after oral argument on the matter, the Supreme Court dismissed the agency's petition for certiorari as having been "improvidently granted."[91]

The FLRA subsequently reaffirmed its view on the subject in a number of other cases.[92] Furthermore, the FLRA specifically adhered to its initial determination while noting that its opinion had been rejected by the Court of Appeals for the Ninth Circuit. The Ninth Circuit found that management's exercise of its right to contract out was not subject to

[90]E.g., AFGE, Nat'l Council of EEO Locals and EEOC, 10 FLRA 3 (1982), enforced sub nom. EEOC v. FLRA, 744 F.2d 842 (D.C. Cir. 1984), cert. dismissed, 54 USLW 4408 (1986) (per curiam); Fitzsimons Army Medical Center and AFGE, Local 2214, 16 FLRA 355 (1984); State, County & Mun. Employees, Local 3097 and Department of Justice, 31 FLRA 322 (1988); AFGE, Local 2052 and Federal Correctional Inst., Petersburg, Va., 31 FLRA 529 (1988).
[91]AFGE Nat'l Council of EEO Locals and EEOC, supra note 90.
[92]E.g., Army Communications Command, Fort McClellan and AFGE, Local 1941, 23 FLRA 184 (1986); NFFE, Local 1374 and Pacific Missile Test Center, 24 FLRA 84 (1986).

arbitral review.[93] Similarly, the Fourth Circuit, in a 6 to 5 en banc decision, denied enforcement of an FLRA determination finding negotiable a provision that would obligate management to make its contracting-out decisions in accordance with applicable law and regulation.[94] The ruling of the entire Fourth Circuit also reversed an earlier 2 to 1 decision of a panel of its own judges in the case. At the end of 1988, the District of Columbia Circuit reaffirmed its earlier decision and upheld the FLRA's position.[95] In doing so, the District of Columbia Circuit expressly rejected an agency argument that section 7106(a)(2)(B) should be read to preclude grievances concerning contracting out. The sharp split in circuit court decisions on the issue of the grievability of contracting-out disputes awaits eventual resolution by the Supreme Court or Congress.

The FLRA has also addressed the authority of arbitrators in resolving grievances concerning contracting-out actions.[96] It is apparent from a reading of the FLRA's decisions on this issue that the remedial authority of arbitrators is limited in a number of significant respects.

First, an arbitrator is without authority to review an agency decision in the procurement process concerning any matter reserved to agency discretion. An arbitrator is also without authority to order cancellation of a procurement action.

Further, while an arbitrator may order an agency to reconstruct a disputed procurement action, the arbitrator may do so only if he or she is able to find: (1) the agency violated mandatory and nondiscretionary provisions of applicable procurement law or regulation, (2) the provisions contain specific standards which allow objective analysis, and (3) the agency's failure to comply with those requirements materially affected the final procurement action and harmed bargaining unit employees.

Moreover, even if an arbitrator is able to order reconstruction of a contracting-out action under those stringent standards, the agency, upon reconstruction in accordance with the applicable provisions of law or regulation, may determine whether the decision to contract out is still justified. Even if the decision can no longer be justified under the results of the reconstruction, the agency may determine whether considerations

---

[93]*Defense Language Inst., Presidio of Monterey, Cal. v. FLRA*, 767 F.2d 1398 (9th Cir. 1985).

[94]*AFGE, Local 1923 and HHS*, 22 FLRA 1071 (1986), *enforced sub nom. HHS v. FLRA*, 882 F.2d 430 (4th Cir. 1987), *rev'd*, No. 86-2619 (4th Cir. Apr. 19, 1988) (en banc).

[95]*Internal Revenue Serv. v. FLRA*, No. 87-1439 (D.C. Cir. Dec. 2, 1988).

[96]E.g., Headquarters, 97th Combat Support Group (SAC), *Blytheville AFB, Ark. and AFGE, Local 2840*, 22 FLRA 656 (1986); *Health Care Fin. Admin. and AFGE, Local 1923*, 30 FLRA 1282 (1988). See also James, *Arbitrating Contracting Out Decisions, What Next?*, GRIEVANCE ARBITRATION IN THE FEDERAL SERVICE (Federal Personnel Management Inst., 1987).

of cost, performance, or disruption of operations override the option of canceling the procurement action and may take whatever action it deems appropriate.

Thus, while the FLRA and the District of Columbia Circuit have determined that there is a right to challenge contracting-out decisions under negotiated grievance procedures, the right is one with a limited remedy.

Official Time, Travel, and Per Diem

Section 7131 authorizes official time (sometimes referred to as "paid time") for employees in certain circumstances. Section 7131(a) authorizes official time for employees representing a union in negotiation of a collective bargaining agreement. Section 7131(d)(1) authorizes official time for employees representing a union in other labor-management relations activities covered by the Statute. Section 7131(d)(2) authorizes official time for bargaining unit employees "in connection with any other matter" covered by the Statute, which has been interpreted to include time for an employee to prepare and present a grievance[97] and time required to testify at an arbitration hearing.[98] Employees are authorized official time under sections 7131(d)(1) and (2) in any amount the agency and the union involved "agree to be reasonable, necessary, and in the public interest."

The entitlement of employees to official time under sections 7131(d)(1) and (2), and to related travel and per diem expenses, has been the subject of considerable litigation and grievance arbitration since 1979. A number of principles governing the arbitration of employee claims for official time, travel, and per diem expenses under section 7131(d) can be identified from the FLRA's decisions.

One key principle is that the Statute provides a remedy when official time under section 7131(d) is wrongfully denied by an agency. Where an arbitrator finds that official time for covered activities authorized by section 7131(d) and a provision of a collective bargaining agreement was wrongfully denied and the covered activities are performed on the employee's off-duty time or annual leave, the employee is entitled to be paid at the appropriate straight time rate for the amount of off-duty time that should have been official time, or to have any annual leave restored.[99]

---

[97]*Federal Correctional Inst., Seagoville, Tex. and AFGE, Council of Prison Locals, Local 1637*, 22 FLRA 56 (1986); *Social Sec. Admin. and AFGE*, 22 FLRA 154 (1986).

[98]*Wright Patterson AFB, Ohio, 2750th Air Base Wing and AFGE, Local 1138*, 23 FLRA 390 (1986).

[99]E.g., *Social Sec. Admin. and AFGE*, 26 FLRA 12, 13–15 (1987), *request for reconsideration denied*, 26 FLRA 781 (1987).

In such cases, the arbitrator may not remedy the wrongful denial of official time by awarding overtime pay or compensatory time off,[100] or administrative leave,[101] or official time for use sometime in the future.[102] There is no requirement that the employee otherwise would have been in a duty status when performing the covered task. The essential requirements of section 7131(d) are that the official time be reasonable, necessary, and in the public interest.

The FLRA has also held that section 7131(d) carves out an exception to management's rights under section 7106(a)(2) and that official time under the section does not violate management's rights to assign work or to assign and direct employees.[103]

On the matter of special uses of official time, the FLRA has held that union representatives may use such time to attend Society of Federal Labor Relations Professionals (SFLRP) training seminars and union-sponsored labor-management relations training.[104] However, 10 months to attend Harvard University to obtain a master's degree in public administration was not an appropriate use of official time under section 7131.[105] Official time is also not authorized for an employee to attend SFLRP executive board and other meetings concerning the business of that organization.[106] Official time is not authorized under section 7131 to assist a former employee in an unemployment compensation hearing,[107] or to assist another employee in a private matter with the local police.[108] Nor does section 7131 permit official time to attend union meetings concerning internal union business.[109] However, to the extent that union meetings concern labor-management relations matters under the Statute and do not pertain to the conduct of internal union business, official time is appropriate under section 7131.[110]

---

[100]*AFGE and Social Sec. Admin.*, 21 FLRA 69, 71–73 (1986); *AFGE and Social Sec. Admin.*, 25 FLRA 173, 174 (1987), *request for reconsideration denied*, 25 FLRA 477 (1987).

[101]*Social Sec. Admin. and AFGE, Local 3231*, 19 FLRA 932 (1985); *AFGE, Local 1164 and Social Sec. Admin., Boston Region*, 19 FLRA 936 (1985).

[102]*Headquarters, Oklahoma City Air Logistics Center, Tinker AFB, and AFGE, Local 916*, 19 FLRA 890 (1985).

[103]*Social Sec. Admin. and AFGE*, 27 FLRA 391, 396 (1987).

[104]*Id.; Social Sec. Admin. and AFGE*, 25 FLRA 479, 483–84 (1987), *motions for reconsideration denied*, 27 FLRA 114 (1987).

[105]*Social Sec. Admin. and AFGE*, 27 FLRA 114, 117 (1987).

[106]*Supra* note 103.

[107]*Id.*, at 392–93.

[108]*National Archives & Records Admin. and AFGE, Council 236, Local 2928*, 24 FLRA 245 (1986).

[109]*Military Dep't of Ark., Office of the Adjutant Gen., Arkansas Nat'l Guard and NFFE, Local 1671*, 23 FLRA 114 (1986).

[110]*Id.; supra* note 103, at 394.

With regard to travel and per diem, an arbitrator can enforce a provision in a collective bargaining agreement requiring the payment of travel and per diem expenses attendant to representational activities performed on official time. However, the arbitrator must allow the agency to determine the appropriateness of the amount claimed under the Federal Travel Regulations.[111]

Environmental Differential Pay

Environmental differential pay (EDP) claims are governed by Federal Personnel Manual (FPM) Supplement 532-1. Appendix J of that regulation lists a number of hazardous or unusually severe working conditions or situations for which EDP is authorized, for example, high work, cold work, dirty work, work with toxic chemicals or poisons, and work involving exposure to airborne asbestos fibers. EDP ranging up to 100 percent of an employee's base pay is authorized for work performed under the various conditions listed.

The conditions listed provide a basis against which particular work situations must be measured in determining whether an environmental differential is payable. Specific work situations for which EDP is payable under FPM Supplement 532-1, Appendix J, are left to local determination, including collective bargaining and arbitration.[112]

Therefore, arbitrators may decide whether work performed by employees warrants payment of EDP and exceptions which constitute nothing more than disagreement with an arbitrator's findings of fact, reasoning, and conclusions or interpretation of an EDP provision in a collective bargaining agreement will be denied by the FLRA as providing no basis for setting aside an arbitrator's EDP award.[113]

However, an arbitrator's authority in EDP disputes is not without limitations. For example, in a case where the arbitrator found that the

---

[111]*NTEU, Chapter 224 and Social Sec. Admin. Office of Hearings & Appeals*, 21 FLRA 384 (1986); *Social Sec. Admin. and AFGE*, 21 FLRA 392 (1986); *General Services Admin. Region 8 and AFGE, Council 236*, 21 FLRA 405 (1986); *Social Sec. Admin. and AFGE*, 22 FLRA 154, 155–56 (1986).

[112]*E.g., Veterans Admin. Medical Center, Fort Howard and AFGE, Local 2146*, 5 FLRA 250 (1981); *Naval Weapons Station, Yorktown, Va. and NAGE, Local R4-1*, 6 FLRA 275 (1981); *AFGE, Local 1857 and Sacramento Air Logistics Center, McClellan AFB, Cal.*, 9 FLRA 922 (1982); *AFGE, Local 2943 and Loring AFB, Me.*, 10 FLRA 57 (1982); *Norfolk Naval Shipyard, Portsmouth, Va. and Tidewater, Va.*, Federal Employees Metal Trades Council, 10 FLRA 413 (1982). See also Reischl, *Arbitration of Federal Sector Environmental Differential Pay Disputes*, GRIEVANCE ARBITRATION IN THE FEDERAL SERVICE (Federal Personnel Management Inst., 1987).

[113]*Id.*

grievant was not entitled to EDP under the FPM criteria, but nevertheless awarded the grievant EDP because another employee was receiving such pay, the FLRA ruled that the award was contrary to the Back Pay Act and the FPM.[114]

Back Pay

Arbitrators in the federal sector frequently have to consider claims for back pay. The Back Pay Act (5 U.S.C. 5596), governs that remedy. (For a detailed discussion of claims under the Back Pay Act see Chapter 12.) For purposes of this chapter, it is sufficient to know that the FLRA has held that before awarding back pay an arbitrator must determine: (1) that the aggrieved employee was affected by an unjust or unwarranted personnel action, which can include a violation of a collective bargaining agreement; (2) that the personnel action directly resulted in the withdrawal or reduction of the grievant's pay, allowances, or differentials; and (3) that but for such action, the grievant otherwise would not have suffered the loss, that is, the grievant would have received the compensation in dispute.[115] To illustrate the application of those criteria by the FLRA, two examples may be helpful.

In one case, the FLRA set aside an award of retroactive overtime pay where the arbitrator only found that the agency had violated the parties' agreement by failing to correct an imbalance in overtime assignments among employees over a particular period. The FLRA ruled that the award was contrary to the Back Pay Act because the arbitrator did not find that the agency should have assigned the grievant any particular overtime work or that but for the agency's violation of the agreement, the grievant would have performed specific overtime assignments and received overtime pay.[116]

In the second example, a dispute over whether the agency's suspension of the grievant was for just cause, the FLRA upheld the arbitrator's award of back pay. The FLRA found that the arbitrator's determination that the suspension was unsupported by the evidence constituted the

---

[114]*Puget Sound Naval Shipyard and Bremerton MTC*, 33 FLRA 56 (1988).

[115]*Naval Air Rework Facility, Norfolk, Va. and Machinists Local Lodge 39*, 21 FLRA 410 (1986); *New Cumberland Army Depot and AFGE, Local 2004*, 21 FLRA 968, 970–71 (1986); *AFGE, Local 17 and Veterans Admin. Cent. Office*, 24 FLRA 424, 426–27 (1986); *Overseas Fed'n of Teachers Dependents Schools and DOD Mediterranean Region*, 26 FLRA 362 (1987); *Department of Labor, OIPA and AFGE, Local 12*, 26 FLRA 368 (1987); *Veterans Admin., Winston-Salem, N.C., and AFGE, Local 2880*, 27 FLRA 44 (1987).

[116]*Navy Public Works Center, Norfolk, Va. and Tidewater, Va., Federal Employees Metal Trades Council*, 33 FLRA 592 (1988).

necessary finding that the discipline was an unwarranted or unjustified personnel action within the meaning of the Back Pay Act. The FLRA further ruled that the arbitrator's order that the grievant be reimbursed for pay lost during the period of the suspension constituted the requisite finding that but for the suspension, the grievant would not have suffered a loss of pay.[117]

There are two other points arbitrators and practitioners should note here. First, the Back Pay Act does not preclude an arbitrator from denying back pay in mitigating a penalty in a disciplinary case.[118] For example, where an arbitrator finds that a grievant was guilty of some misconduct but that a suspension penalty was too severe, the arbitrator may rescind all or part of the suspension without back pay.[119] Second, practitioners and arbitrators should be aware that the Back Pay Act was amended on December 22, 1987, to provide for the payment of interest on awards of back pay.[120]

Attorney's Fees

For a detailed discussion of the law governing attorney's fees, see Chapter 12. For purposes of this chapter, it is sufficient to know that an arbitrator can award attorney's fees only when back pay is granted. The FLRA has identified four basic requirements for an award of attorney's fees. First, the award of fees must be in conjunction with a legal award of back pay to an employee on the correction of an unjustified or unwarranted personnel action as described above. Second, the fees must be reasonable and related to the personnel action. Third, the award must be in accordance with the standards established under 5 U.S.C. 7701(g). Section 7701(g)(1), which applies to all cases except those of discrimination, requires that the employee be the "prevailing party" and that payment of the fees be "in the interest of justice." Section 7701(g)(2), which applies to cases in which discrimination is found, requires only that the employee be the "prevailing party." Fourth, and finally, there must be a "fully articulated, reasoned decision" setting forth the arbitrator's specific findings on each pertinent statutory requirement, including the basis upon

---

[117]*AFGE, Local 1915 and William Jennings Bryan Dorn Veterans Admin. Hosp., Columbia, S.C.*, 32 FLRA 1223, 1226 (1988).

[118]*AFGE, Local 2718 v. Immigration & Naturalization Serv.*, 768 F.2d 348, 351 (Fed. Cir. 1985).

[119]*Headquarters, San Antonio Air Logistics Center, Kelly AFB and AFGE, Local 1617*, 32 FLRA 513 (1988).

[120]Continuing Appropriations Act of 1988, Pub. L. No. 100-202, 1988 U.S. CODE CONG. & ADMIN. NEWS (101 Stat.) 1329-1, 1329-428–1329-429.

which the reasonableness of the amount was determined when fees are awarded. The arbitrator must decide the attorney's fee issue based on the record and results in the underlying grievance arbitration proceeding.[121]

The FLRA has determined that the method to be used in computing fees for attorneys in private practice is the so called "lodestar" method, that is, multiplying the number of hours reasonably expended on the dispute by a reasonable hourly rate. The applicant for the fees has the burden of establishing any entitlement to an award of fees.[122] Where the attorney is an employee of the union, fees to be reimbursed generally are computed on the basis of actual cost plus reasonable union overhead expenses.[123]

In the absence of a time limit established by the parties for filing a request for attorney's fees with the arbitrator, a request for fees may be filed within a reasonable period of time after an award is issued or becomes final and binding, and the arbitrator must decide the request. For example, in a case where the parties did not prescribe a time limit, a request for fees filed with the arbitrator within 25 days after the award became final and binding was found to be timely by the FLRA.[124]

Review of Awards

FLRA Role

The FLRA in the federal sector performs the role that federal district courts perform in the private sector in reviewing arbitration awards under

---

[121]*Army Aviation Sys. Command and NFFE, Local 405*, 22 FLRA 379 (1986); *Bureau of Prisons, Washington, D.C. and Federal Correctional Inst., Ray Brook, N.Y.*, 32 FLRA 20 (1988), petition for review filed sub nom. *AFGE, Local 3882 v. FLRA*, No. 88-1375 (D.C. Cir. May 24, 1988); *Federal Aviation Admin., National Aviation Facilities Experimental Center and NFFE, Local 1340*, 32 FLRA 750 (1988); *Department of the Air Force, Headquarters, 832d Combat Support Group DPCE, Luke AFB, Ariz. and AFGE, Local 1547*, 32 FLRA 1084 (1988). See also *NAGE, Local R4-106 and Langley AFB, Va.*, 32 FLRA 1159, 1165 (1988) (FLRA held that arbitrator's denial of request for attorney's fees also must be supported by "fully articulated and reasoned decision").

[122]E.g., *Department of the Air Force, Headquarters, 832d Combat Support Group DPCE, supra* note 121, at 1100.

[123]*HHS, Health Care Fin. Admin., Region IV, Atlanta, Ga. and NTEU, Chapter 210*, 21 FLRA 910 (1986); *Internal Revenue Serv., Baltimore Dist. Office and NTEU, Chapter 62*, 21 FLRA 918 (1986); *Customs Serv. and NTEU, Chapter 136*, 21 FLRA 932 (1986). But see *DOD Dependents Schools, Pac. Region and Overseas Educ. Ass'n, Pac. Region*, 32 FLRA 757 (1988) (attorney employed by union may be awarded fees at prevailing market rate if fees are paid directly to attorney and if attorney is not required to reimburse union for more than union's actual costs in providing legal representation).

[124]*Philadelphia Naval Shipyard and Philadelphia Metal Trades Council*, 32 FLRA 417 (1988). See also *NAGE, Local R4-106 and Langley AFB, Va.*, 32 FLRA 1159, 1164 (1988).

section 301 of the Labor-Management Relations Act. Section 7105(a)(2)(H) of the Federal Service Labor-Management Relations Statute provides that the FLRA is to resolve exceptions to arbitration awards in accordance with section 7122. Although Congress provided for FLRA review of awards, Congress at the same time made it clear that the scope of that review should be very limited. The Conference Report that accompanied the bill eventually signed into law provides: "The Authority will be authorized to review the award of an arbitrator on very narrow grounds similar to the scope of judicial review of an arbitrator's award in the private sector."[125] The FLRA may modify or set aside an award only when it is deficient on one of the specific grounds set forth in section 7122(a).

Who May Request Review

Section 7122(a) first provides that: "Either party to arbitration . . . may file . . . an exception to any arbitrator's award." As pointed out earlier, under the Statute only the union or the agency, the parties to a collective bargaining agreement, may invoke the arbitration provision of a negotiated grievance procedure.[126] It follows that the union and the agency will be the parties in the arbitration proceeding and only they are entitled to file exceptions to an award with the FLRA. The FLRA has uniformly denied exceptions filed by grievants on the basis that they were not "a party" in the proceedings.[127]

Section 7122(a) further states that an exception may be filed to any award "other than an award relating to a matter described in section 7121(f)" of the Statute, that is, matters covered by 5 U.S.C. 4303 and 5 U.S.C. 7512. As previously explained, these matters can be taken either to the MSPB or to arbitration under negotiated grievance procedures. (See discussion of 5 U.S.C. 4303 and 7512 actions *supra* and in Chapters 2 and 3.)

Jurisdiction

If an employee opts for the negotiated grievance procedure to contest a 5 U.S.C. 4303 or 7512 action, any resulting arbitration award, including an award on related issues, is not subject to review by the FLRA.

---

[125]S. REP. No. 95-1272, 95th Cong., 2d Sess. 153 (1978).
[126]5 U.S.C. 7121(b)(3).
[127]E.g., *Army Fin. & Accounting Office, Ft. Benjamin Harrison, Ind. and AFGE, Local 1411*, 4 FLRA 365 (1981).

Instead section 7121(f) provides that judical review of such an award is available under the same conditions as it would be had the matter been decided by MSPB. That is, such arbitration awards are appealable directly to the Court of Appeals for the Federal Circuit.[128]

Practitioners should note that the FLRA has determined that it has subject matter jurisdiction over exceptions to arbitration awards involving adverse actions against excepted service employees who do not have veterans preference eligibility and, therefore, do not enjoy a right of appeal to MSPB.[129] The FLRA has also determined that it has jurisdiction to review the merits of the termination of temporary employees for unacceptable performance, because such terminations are not section 4303 actions and because temporaries are not covered by other personnel systems within the meaning of 5 U.S.C. 7121(f).[130]

Grounds for FLRA Review

Section 7122(a) describes the narrow grounds for FLRA review of arbitration awards, that is, the FLRA will review an award to determine whether it is deficient: "(1) because it is contrary to any law, rule, or regulation; or (2) on other grounds similar to those applied by Federal courts in private sector labor-management relations."

Despite the limited grounds for appeal and the statutory provision for "binding" arbitration as the last step of negotiated grievance procedures, exceptions to 1,667 awards were filed with the FLRA between January 1979 and the end of December 1988. Comparing the number of exceptions filed with the number of awards issued during the period (approximately 6,981) indicates that approximately 24 percent of the awards issued in federal sector arbitration cases are appealed to the FLRA. Of those 1,667 exceptions, approximately 60 percent were filed by unions, 39 percent by agencies, and 1 percent by individual employees.

---

[128]*DOD Dependents Schools Pac. Region and Overseas Educ. Ass'n*, 16 FLRA 34 (1984) (5 U.S.C. 4303 matter); *Veterans Admin. Medical Center, Kansas City, Mo. and AFGE*, 23 FLRA 323 (1986) (5 U.S.C. 7512 matter); See also *Veterans Admin. Medical Center, Hines, Ill. and Illinois Nurses Ass'n, Hines Local Unit*, 20 FLRA 510 (1985) (supplemental award of attorney's fees); *NTEU, Chapter 49 and Internal Revenue Serv., Indianapolis Dist.*, 23 FLRA 420 (1986) (ruling on motion for pehearing discovery); *Bureau of Prisons and AFGE, Local 1741*, 23 FLRA 802 (1986) (determination on procedural arbitrability issue); *Army Armament Research, Dev. & Eng'g Center, Dover, N.J. and NFFE, Local 1437*, 24 FLRA 837 (1986) (interpretation and application of a settlement agreement).

[129]*Social Sec. Admin. and AFGE*, 32 FLRA 79 (1988).

[130]*Small Business Admin. and AFGE, Local 2532*, 33 FLRA 28 (1988).

We do not know how many section 7122(a)(1) or 7122(a)(2) allegations were raised in those cases. We do know, however, that of 1,516 arbitration cases decided by the FLRA during the 10-year period, the FLRA denied the exceptions on the merits in 918 (60.6 percent), dismissed or otherwise disposed of the exceptions on procedural grounds in 312 (20.5 percent), and set aside or modified the awards in 286 (18.9 percent).[131] Of the awards set aside or modified by the FLRA, approximately 95 percent were found to be deficient on section 7122(a)(1) grounds, that is, contrary to law, rule, or regulation. The remainder, only about 5 percent, were found to be deficient on section 7122(a)(2) grounds..

Section 7122(a)(1)

Section 7122(a)(1) grounds have been discussed above in the examples of FLRA decisions on common federal sector arbitration issues.

Section 7122(a)(2)

The FLRA recognizes five grounds for review under section 7122(a)(2), commonly referred to as the private sector grounds.

1. *Arbitrator Failed to Conduct a Fair Hearing.* As previously stated, the FLRA has held that an arbitrator has considerable latitude in the conduct of a hearing. Therefore, the fact that an arbitrator conducts a hearing in a matter which one party finds objectionable will not support an allegation that the arbitrator denied that party a fair hearing.[132]

An arbitrator's refusal to hear relevant and material evidence may constitute a denial of a fair hearing. But the FLRA and the courts have long recognized that liberal admission of testimony and evidence is the customary practice in arbitration. Therefore, the FLRA has denied virtually all exceptions claiming that the party was denied a fair hearing because the arbitrator admitted and considered certain testimony or evidence.[133] Exceptions which merely assert but do not not establish that the arbitrator improperly refused to consider certain evidence also have

[131]Department of Defense, OASD (Force Management and Personnel) Annual Memorandum Report: Decisions of the Federal Labor Relations Authority on Exceptions to Arbitration Awards Filed under 5 U.S.C. 7122(a)((Jan. 1989).
[132]*Social Sec. Admin. and AFGE, Local 547*, 24 FLRA 959 (1986).
[133]*National Border Patrol Council and National Immigration & Naturalization Serv. Council*, 3 FLRA 400, 404 (1980).

been denied.[134] Arguments that the arbitrator failed to give appropriate weight to particular evidence or testimony have been found to constitute nothing more than disagreement with the arbitrator's evaluation of evidence or testimony and to provide no basis for finding an award deficient.[135] Similarly, unsubstantiated allegations that an arbitrator was biased have been denied.[136]

2. *Award Is Incomplete, Ambiguous, or Contradictory Making Implementation of the Award Impossible*. The FLRA has indicated that in order to find an award deficient on this ground, there must be a showing that the award is so unclear or uncertain in its meaning and effect that it cannot be implemented.[137]

3. *Arbitrator Exceeded His or Her Authority*. The FLRA has held that an arbitrator exceeds his or her authority if the arbitrator resolves an issue that was not submitted by the parties for resolution.[138] However, the FLRA, like the federal courts, will accord an arbitrator's interpretation of a submission agreement and formulation of the issues to be decided the same substantial deference accorded an arbitrator's interpretation and application of a collective bargaining agreement.[139]

The FLRA has also determined that an arbitrator exceeds his or her authority by extending an award to cover employees outside the bargaining unit,[140] or by ordering an agency to take an action that is beyond the authority of the agency.[141] An arbitrator may also exceed his or her authority by extending an award to cover employees who did not file grievances or whose union representative did not file grievances on their behalf.[142] However, the FLRA has also indicated that when a dispute

---

[134]*Social Sec. Admin. and AFGE, Local 547, supra* note 132; *Warner Robins Air Logistics Center, Warner Robins, Ga. and AFGE, Local 987*, 24 FLRA 968 (1986); *Norfolk Naval Shipyard, Portsmouth, Va. and Tidewater, Va., Federal Employees Metal Trades Council*, 26 FLRA 799 (1987); *Health Care Fin. Admin. and AFGE, Local 1923*, 26 FLRA 860 (1987).

[135]*International Trade Comm'n and AFGE, Local 2211*, 13 FLRA 440 (1983).

[136]*Army Corps of Eng'rs, New Orleans Dist. and NFFE, Local 1124*, 13 FLRA 70 (1983); *Social Sec. Admin. and AFGE, Local 547, supra* note 132.

[137]*Delaware Nat'l Guard, Wilmington, Del. and Association of Civilian Technicians, Del. Chapter*, 5 FLRA 50 (1981).

[138]*Veterans Admin. and AFGE, Local 2798*, 24 FLRA 447 (1986).

[139]*HUD and AFGE, Local 3412*, 24 FLRA 442 (1986); *Department of Educ. and AFGE, Local 3893, National Council of Dep't of Educ. Locals, Council 252*, 22 FLRA 961 (1986); *Air Force Logistics Command, Tinker AFB and AFGE, Local 916*, 26 FLRA 783 (1987).

[140]*Bureau of Indian Affairs and NFFE, Local 243*, 25 FLRA 902 (1987).

[141]*Immigration & Naturalization Serv. and AFGE, Local 1917*, 20 FLRA 391 (1985); *Veterans Admin. Medical Center, Leavenworth, Kan. and AFGE, Local 85*, 24 FLRA 902 (1986).

[142]*National Center for Toxicological Research, Jefferson, Ark. and AFGE, Local 3393*, 20 FLRA 692 (1985).

concerns a management practice generally applicable to the entire bargaining unit, the arbitrator's authority is quite broad and relief which encompasses similarly situated unit employees may be appropriate.[143]

A number of exceptions filed with the FLRA have asserted that the arbitrator exceeded his or her authority by acting in a dispute, at the request of only one of the parties, after having rendered a final award. Parties have argued that under the common law doctrine of *functus officio*, the authority of the arbitrator ended when his or her function in the dispute was completed by issuance of the award. However, under FLRA case law, the authority of an arbitrator is not always immediately terminated on issuance of an award.

The FLRA has held that an arbitrator properly may retain authority in a dispute for certain limited purposes after an award has been rendered. An arbitrator has the authority to retain jurisdiction to resolve questions regarding the interpretation and implementation of an award and to correct or clarify an award in some circumstances, even at the request of only one of the parties, and to decide requests for attorney's fees.[144]

However, in correcting or clarifying an award, the arbitrator must not violate the policy against redetermining the merits of an issue already decided. The FLRA has held that an arbitrator is without authority to reopen and reconsider a dispute and issue a new award without a joint request from the parties for such action, and that a failure of the parties to inform the arbitrator of applicable law during the proceeding does not confer jurisdiction on the arbitrator to reopen the case and change the award.[145] Further, in one protracted dispute that spanned a period of more than five years, the FLRA found that the arbitrator was without authority to decide his continuing jurisdiction in the matter.[146]

4. *Award Is Based on a Mistake of Fact.* The FLRA will find an award deficient if the central fact underlying the arbitrator's award is erroneous and, in effect, is such a gross mistake of fact that a different

---

[143]*Air Force Space Div., Los Angeles Air Force Station, Cal. and AFGE, Local 2429*, 24 FLRA 516 (1986).

[144]*Audie L. Murphy Veterans Admin. Hosp., San Antonio, Tex. and AFGE, Local 3511*, 15 FLRA 276 (1984); *Corps of Eng'rs, Army Eng'r Dist., New Orleans, La. and NFFE, Local 1124*, 17 FLRA 315, 316 (1985); *Customs Serv. and NTEU*, 20 FLRA 450 (1985); *AFGE, Local 1923 and Health Care Fin. Admin.*, 33 FLRA 88, 93 (1988); *Philadelphia Naval Shipyard and Philadelphia Metal Trades Council*, supra note 124. See also *NAGE, Local R4-106 and Langley AFB, Va.*, 32 FLRA 1159, 1165 (1988).

[145]*Overseas Fed'n of Teachers and DOD Dependents Schools, Mediterranean Region*, 32 FLRA 410, 415 (1988).

[146]*AFGE and Social Sec. Admin.*, 29 FLRA 1568 (1987). See also *Social Sec. Admin. and AFGE, National Council of Social Sec. Admin. Field Operations Locals, Council 220*, 33 FLRA 743 (1988) (FLRA held that arbitrator did not exceed his authority in framing and resolving the issue FLRA directed to be resolved in *AFGE and Social Sec. Admin.*, supra).

result would have been reached if the error had not occurred. It must be shown that the alleged mistake concerned a fact that was objectively ascertainable, central to the result of the award, and indisputably erroneous and that, but for the arbitrator's mistake, the arbitrator would have reached a different result.[147] Given this stringent standard, it is not surprising that except for certain extraordinary cases, no arbitration awards have been found deficient based on this ground. Two cases will illustrate its limited application.

In one case, the grievance alleged a violation of a local collective bargaining agreement. The arbitrator denied the grievance based on a finding that the local agreement had been superseded by a multiunit agreement. However, the multiunit agreement clearly and unequivocally excluded the local bargaining unit. The FLRA found that the arbitrator's award was deficient because the central finding of fact underlying the award was erroneous and that, but for the arbitrator's mistake, a different result would have been reached.[148]

In another case, the arbitrator found that a requirement in the parties' 1979 agreement was applicable to a personnel selection action in 1978. Because the agreement was not in effect at the time of the selection action, the arbitrator's central finding was indisputably erroneous. Because it was equally clear that but for the arbitrator's error a different result would have been reached, the award was set aside.[149]

It should be emphasized that the FLRA has found that virtually all contentions that an award is based on a mistake of fact (a "nonfact") actually constituted nothing more than a disagreement with the factual findings of the arbitrator. The FLRA has consistently held that mere disagreement with the arbitrator's findings and assessment of the facts in a case does not provide a basis for finding an award deficient under the Statute.[150]

5. *Award Does Not Draw Its Essence From the Collective Bargaining Agreement.* In recognizing this ground, the FLRA explained that the test has been variously described by federal courts as: (1) an award which cannot in any rational way be derived from the agreement; (2) an award that is so unfounded in reason or fact, so unconnected with the workings

---

[147]*Army Missile Materiel Readiness Command and AFGE, Local 1858*, 2 FLRA 432, 438–39 (1980).

[148]*Headquarters, San Antonio Air Logistics Center, Kelly AFB, Tex. and AFGE, Local 1617*, 6 FLRA 292 (1981).

[149]*Army Missile Command, Redstone Arsenal, Ala. and AFGE, Local 1858*, 18 FLRA 374 (1985).

[150]*Social Sec. Admin. and AFGE, Local 547*, 24 FLRA 959, 962 (1986); *Navy Pub. Works Center and Machinists*, 27 FLRA 156 (1987).

and purposes of the agreement, as to manifest an infidelity to the obligation of the arbitrator; (3) an award that evidences a manifest disregard of
the agreement; or (4) an award that on its face does not represent a
plausible interpretaton of the agreement.[151] Again, given this stringent
test, it is not surprising that except for a few extraordinary cases, all such
exceptions have been denied.

In one case, the dispute involved official time for labor relations
activities for which the parties' agreement provided only two options. As
part of his award the arbitrator fashioned a third option not provided by the
agreement. The FLRA found the award deficient as manifesting a disregard of the agreement.[152] In another case the FLRA found the award
deficient in failing to draw its essence from the parties' agreement because
the arbitrator held that the agency's decision on an incentive award was
subject to grievance and arbitration. The arbitrator's determination was in
manifest disregard of the agreement, which expressly excluded incentive
awards from coverage of the negotiated grievance procedure.[153]

Here again, it is important to point out that the great majority of the
many exceptions contending that the award does not draw its essence from
the parties' agreement have been denied by the FLRA. As to most of these
exceptions, it was clear that the appealing party was actually disagreeing
with the arbitrator's interpretation and application of the agreement or was
disagreeing with the arbitrator's reasoning and conclusions. It is well
established under decisions of the FLRA that the arbitrator's interpretation of a collective bargaining agreement and the arbitrator's reasoning
and conclusions are not subject to challenge. Such disagreement provides
no basis on which to find an award deficient under the Statute.[154]

In considering whether to file exceptions to an award with the FLRA,
practitioners should be aware that there is little likelihood of success on
the merits based on the private sector grounds for review described above.
As previously stated, of the awards set aside or modified by the FLRA
since 1979, only about 5 percent were set aside or modified on those
grounds. The great majority of such exceptions are denied by the FLRA.

---

[151]*Army Missile Materiel Readiness Command and AFGE, Local 1858,* supra
note 147, at 437–38; *General Services Admin. Region 8 and AFGE, Council 236,* 21 FLRA
405, 406 (1986).

[152]*Overseas Educ. Ass'n and DOD Dependents Schools,* 4 FLRA 98, 101–3 (1980).

[153]*AFGE, Local 547 and Tampa Veterans Admin. Hosp.,* 19 FLRA 725 (1985).

[154]*Warner Robins Air Logistics Center, Robins AFB, Warner Robins, Ga. and AFGE,
Local 987,* 25 FLRA 969 (1987); *AFGE, Nat'l Council of Social Sec. Admin. Field
Operations Locals and Social Sec. Admin.,* 26 FLRA 670, 671–72 (1987); *Panama Canal
Comm'n and Masters, Mates, & Pilots, Panama Canal Pilots Branch,* 26 FLRA 958 (1987);
Pension Benefit Guaranty Corp. and NTEU, Chapter 211, 32 FLRA 141 (1988).

Compliance With Arbitration Awards

If no exception to an award is filed with the FLRA within 30 days beginning on the date the award is served on the parties by the arbitrator, the award becomes final and binding for compliance purposes. [155] Parties are required to take the action ordered by such a final and binding award. [156] When exceptions to an award are denied by the FLRA, the award also becomes final and binding and parties must comply. Enforcement of arbitration awards is obtained through unfair labor practice case procedures. [157] (See Chapter 8.) Failure or refusal to comply with a final and binding award constitutes an unfair labor practice and a party may not attack or attempt to relitigate the award in an enforcement proceeding. [158]

Judicial Review of FLRA Arbitration Decisions

In contrast to most other final decisions of the FLRA, a decision of the FLRA in the typical grievance arbitration case is not subject to judicial review. Under the Statute, the decision of the FLRA is final unless the decision actually involves adjudication of a statutory unfair labor practice issue. Decisions resolving such issues may be appealed to an appropriate federal court of appeals. [159] Of course, a federal court may review an FLRA decision for alleged violations of the Constitution, [160] or to determine whether the FLRA acted in excess of its statutory jurisdiction. [161]

As to appeal rights in cases involving allegations of unlawful discrimination, see Chapter 5.

---

[155] 5 U.S.C. 7122(b).

[156] *Id.*; See also *Department of the Air Force v. FLRA*, 775 F.2d 727 (6th Cir. 1985).

[157] E.g., *Marshals Serv. and AFGE, Int'l Council of Marshals Serv. Locals*, 13 FLRA 351 (1983).

[158] E.g., *Bureau of Prisons v. FLRA*, 792 F.2d 25 (2d Cir. 1986); *Marshals Serv. v. FLRA*, 778 F.2d 1432 (9th Cir. 1985).

[159] 5 U.S.C. 7123(b); see also *AFGE, Local 1923 v. FLRA*, 675 F.2d 612 (4th Cir. 1982); *Marshals Serv. v. FLRA*, 708 F.2d 1417 (9th Cir. 1983); *Tonetti v. FLRA*, 776 F.2d 929 (11th Cir. 1985).

[160] *Griffith v. FLRA*, 842 F.2d 487 (D.C. Cir. 1988).

[161] *Leedom v. Kyne*, 358 U.S. 184, 43 LRRM 2222 (1958).

Remedies

12. Attorney's Fees in the Litigation of Federal Personnel Disputes

CARL D. MOORE

Prior to enactment of the Civil Service Reform Act (CSRA) on January 11, 1979, it was generally accepted that attorney's fees were not available in the administrative resolution of federal sector employment disputes. Even when a dispute reached federal court, attorney's fees could be awarded only in cases involving equal employment opportunity violations.

The CSRA contains two separate provisions for awarding attorney's fees: one (5 U.S.C. 7701(g)) applies to proceedings before the Merit Systems Protection Board (MSPB) and the second (5 U.S.C. 5596(b)(1)) is an amendment to the Back Pay Act, which provides for the payment of attorney's fees in a wide range of administrative proceedings.[1]

A year later, on April 9, 1980, the Equal Employment Opportunity Commission (EEOC) issued regulations extending coverage of the attorney's fee provision of Title VII of the Civil Rights Act to agency and EEOC decisions in the EEO complaint procedure.[2] Shortly thereafter, Congress passed the Equal Access to Justice Act, which provides standards for the award of attorney's fees against the federal government for cases in court and for certain administrative proceedings.[3] It became

---

[1]The MSPB construes the Savings Provision as meaning that administrative proceedings existed in all cases where employees received notice of proposed personnel actions before, but had their cases decided by the MSPB after, the effective date of the Reform Act., *Kyle v. ICC*, 609 F.2d 540, 542–43 (D.C. Cir. 1980). See also *Wilson v. Turnage*, 791 F.2d 131, 86 FMSR 7046 (Fed. Cir. 1986), *cert. denied*, 479 U.S. 988 (1986); *Thomas v. GSA*, 756 F.2d 86, 85 FMSR 7013 (Fed. Cir. 1985).

[2]29 C.F.R. Part 1613.271(c); 45 FED. REG. 24132 (Apr. 9, 1980).

[3]Title II of Pub. L. No. 96-481, 94 Stat. 2325 (1980).

effective on October 1, 1981. There are, therefore, four separate laws and implementing regulations applicable to the granting of attorney's fees in federal government personnel actions.

An award of attorney's fees requires the resolution of two general issues: "entitlement" and "reasonable amount." The former involves a determination as to whether an award of fees should be made. The factors to be considered in determining entitlement vary depending upon which of the laws is being used as a basis for the claim. Once it has been decided that an employee is entitled to such reimbursement, the latter issue is addressed to establish what amount is "reasonable" for the services rendered in the particular case. The basic criteria for establishing a reasonable fee are, with limited exceptions, the same for each of the four laws.

Entitlement

Entitlement Under the Back Pay Act

To qualify for attorney's fees under the Back Pay Act, the employee must receive a back pay award. If the employee wins such an award, then the entitlement provisions of 5 U.S.C. 7701(g) (discussed below under "Entitlement Before the Merit Systems Protection Board"), must be referred to in order to determine whether the employee should receive an award of attorney's fees.

The Back Pay Act amendment of the CSRA provides that when an "appropriate authority" determines that an employee has been affected by an "unjustified or unwarranted personnel action which has resulted in the withdrawal or reduction of all or part of the pay, allowances or differentials of the employee," the employee is entitled to back pay and, in certain circumstances, to attorney's fees.[4] Each of these terms requires a definition. An "appropriate authority" is defined as a court; the Comptroller General; the Office of Personnel Management; a grievance board established by section 692 of the Foreign Service Act; the head of an agency or an agency official to whom corrective action authority is delegated; an arbitrator selected to decide cases under Chapter 71 of Title 5, United States Code; the Federal Labor Relations Authority; the Merit Systems Protection Board; and the Equal Employment Opportunity Commission.[5]

---

[4]The Back Pay Act amendment, 5 U.S.C. 5596(b).
[5]26 C.F.R. 550.803(d).

An "unjustified or unwarranted personnel action" is defined as follows:

> an act of commission or an act of omission (i.e., failure to take an action or confer a benefit) that an appropriate authority subsequently determines on the basis of substantive or procedural defects, to have been unjustified or unwarranted under applicable law, Executive Order, rule, regulation, or mandatory personnel policy established by an agency, or through a collective bargaining agreement. Such actions include personnel actions and pay actions (alone or in combination).[6]

Application of this definition is not difficult in the review of agency "acts of commission" (e.g., suspensions, demotions, terminations, reductions in force). Such acts of commission result in a loss of pay. If the agency errs in taking such an action, then the employee qualifies for back pay under the Back Pay Act.[7]

A case involving alleged "acts of omission" is more complicated. The concept is that by failing to act, the agency denies money to an employee, money to which the employee has a right. It most often involves an allegation that a substantive or procedural error resulted in a failure to promote the employee. Except when a statute (e.g., Title VII of the Civil Rights Act) or a regulation specifically provides for retroactive promotion and back pay, the courts have invariably denied relief when the claim was that the employee was improperly denied a promotion. The theory behind these court cases is "that one is not entitled to the benefit of a position until he has been duly appointed to it."[8] Therefore, lacking a proper appointment, such a grievant has no claim.

The Comptroller General and the Federal Labor Relations Authority (FLRA) have held, however, that although an employee has no vested right to a promotion at any specific time, an agency, through a collective bargaining agreement or an agency regulation, may limit its discretion so that, under specific circumstances, it becomes mandatory to make a promotion on an ascertainable date.[9] For example, in one case, a negotiated agreement provided that employees assigned to a higher grade for 30 consecutive workdays were to be temporarily promoted and paid the

---

[6]*Id.*

[7]*Ainsworth v. United States*, 399 F.2d 176 (Ct. Cl. 1968).

[8]*United States v. Testan*, 424 U.S. 392 (1976); *Goutos v. United States*, 552 F.2d 922 (Ct. Cl. 1976); *Peter v. United States*, 534 F.2d 232 (Ct. Cl. 1975); *Keim v. United States*, 177 U.S. 290 (1900).

[9]*National Council of OEO Locals*, 54 Comp. Gen. 403 (1974); *Barbara N. Copeland*, 54 Comp. Gen. 538 (1974); *Department of the Treasury*, 55 Comp. Gen. 42 (1975); *Reconsideration of Turner-Caldwell*, 56 Comp. Gen. 427 (1977); *Roy F. Ross*, 57 Comp. Gen. 536 (1978); *Veterans Admin. Hosp. and AFGE, Local 2201*, 4 FLRA 419 (1980).

higher rate for the remainder of the temporary promotion. Certain employees were given the duties of a higher grade for more than 30 days but were not formally "detailed" to the higher grade level. The arbitrator found that the contract provision required that such employees be temporarily promoted, and he awarded temporary promotions with back pay. The Comptroller General upheld the arbitrator's decision.[10]

Once it is established that an act of commission or omission occurred and that such act was substantively or procedurally defective, as described above, the appropriate authority must next decide whether there was a causal relationship between the action and the monetary loss. Prior to passage of the CSRA, it was consistently held that "the remedies under the Back Pay Act are not available unless it is also established that, but for the wrongful action, the withdrawal of pay, allowances, or differentials would not have occurred."[11] This interpretation was also reflected in the civil service regulations[12] and resulted in reversal of some arbitrator back pay awards.[13]

---

[10]*Roy F. Ross, supra* note 9. In another case, a promotion was approved by the appropriate authorizing official, but, due to a clerical error, the effective date was delayed. It was held that retroactive promotion and back pay were appropriate since the omission was a "nondiscretionary act." *Barbara N. Copeland, supra* note 9. Likewise, where the arbitrator found, however, that the grievant "wound have been promoted" if the agency had not violated the procedures and where the agency did not dispute that finding, retroactive promotion and back pay were appropriate. *Russel D. Mikel*, 54 Comp. Gen. 435, 440 (1974). See also *NLRB*, 54 Comp. Gen. 312 (1974). The Comptroller General has, however, distinguished that circumstance from the one in which a clerical error delays the approval of a promotion by the appropriate authorizing official, "unless his exercise of disapproval authority is otherwise constrained by statute, administrative policy or regulation." *John Cahill*, 58 Comp. Gen. 59, 61 (1978).

[11]*Mare Island Naval Shipyard*, 55 Comp. Gen. 629, 633 (1976); *Department of Labor*, 54 Comp. Gen. 760 (1975).

[12]The former regulation, 5 C.F.R. 550.803(a), which was effective prior to enactment of the Civil Service Reform Act's Back Pay Act amendment, reads as follows:

An unjustified or unwarranted personnel action can only be corrected under the provisions of section 5596 of title 5, United States Code, if it is found by appropriate authority that the withdrawal, reduction, or denial of all or part of the pay, allowances, or differential due an employee was the clear and direct result of, and would not have occurred, *but for* the unjustified or unwarranted personnel action. (Emphasis added.)

[13]For example, in one case, management changed the work schedule and required some employees to work on Saturday and Sunday rather than Thursday and Friday. The arbitrator found that the change was made without prior consultation with the union, which was required in the agreement between the parties. Therefore, he awarded overtime pay for Saturday and Sunday and directed that Thursday and Friday be recorded as administrative leave. In overturning that decision, the Comptroller General stated, "Failure-to-consult actions, in the absence of a requirement that the agency carry out the advice received as a result of the consultation, are not likely to result in the necessary 'but for' relationship between the wrongful act and the harm to the individual employee for which the Back Pay Act is the appropriate remedy." *Mare Island Naval Shipyard, supra* note 11. In remanding this case, the Comptroller General noted that it could have been raised as an unfair labor practice. *Id.*, at 634.

Although the civil service regulations and the Comptroller General rulings that were in effect prior to the CSRA required that the appropriate authority make the "but for" finding, they provided no rule as to which party carried the burden of proof.[14] The new regulations, which implement the Back Pay Act amendment, continue the policy of requiring that the appropriate authority find that the wrongful action resulted in a monetary loss without specifying which party bears the but for burden of proof.

The regulations from the Office of Personnel Management (OPM) seem to suggest that appropriate authorities have considerable flexibility in applying the but for standard. The OPM explained, in issuing the implementing regulations, that it was "inappropriate for the back pay regulations to attempt to specify which party bears the burden of proof for determining whether an employee is entitled to back pay."[15] In discussing this burden of proof issue, OPM stated that depending upon the nature of the case, an appropriate authority may require either the grievant or the agency or both to document their position.[16] In any case, regardless of where the burden of proof is placed, the appropriate authority, in awarding back pay, must find that but for the wrongful action, the employee would not have suffered the monetary loss.[17]

In the event that the appropriate authority does not award back pay, attorney's fees may not be awarded under the Back Pay Act amendment.[18] Thus, even when the appropriate authority determines that a reprimand or reassignment was unjustified or unwarranted, an award of attorney's fees is not appropriate, because such actions do not involve a withdrawal or reduction of pay, allowances, or differentials.

When the appropriate authority determines that the employee is entitled to back pay, it is necessary to refer to the "standards" under 5 U.S.C. 7701(g).[19] Furthermore, the standards of 7701(g) are to be applied in awarding attorney's fees regardless of the forum—in grievance arbitration that results in back pay, in a back pay determination by the Comptroller General, or any OPM determination that results in back pay.[20] The standards of 7701(g) are the "prevailing party" and "interest of

---

[14]*Department of Labor, supra* note 11, at 763.
[15]45 FED. REG. 58273 (1981).
[16]*Id.*
[17]*Veterans Admin. Hosp. and AFGE, Local 2201, supra* note 9.
[18]*Department of Defense Dependents Schools and Overseas Educ. Ass'n,* 3 FLRA 259 (1980); *Audie Murphy Veterans Admin. Hosp. and AFGE, Local 3511,* 16 FLRA 1079 (1984).
[19]5 U.S.C. 5596(b)(1)(A)(ii).
[20]Although the Back Pay Act provision for attorney's fees has been subject to different interpretations, it appears that the best interpretation is that the standards of 5 U.S.C. 7701(g) apply regardless of the administrative forum. *Wells v. Harris,* 2 MSPB 572 (1980);

justice" concepts discussed below ("Entitlement Before the Merit Systems Protection Board").[21] Thus, to award attorney's fees in any forum under the Back Pay Act amendment, the parties and the "appropriate authority" must follow MSPB decisions regarding attorney's fees.[22]

Entitlement Issues in Grievance Arbitration

As noted above, an arbitrator selected to decide a case in the negotiated grievance procedure is an "appropriate authority" for purposes of awarding fees under the Back Pay Act. Such fee awards are then subject to review by the FLRA.[23] In reviewing fee awards by arbitrators, the FLRA has confirmed that there must be an award of back pay[24] and that the precedent of the MSPB regarding the interest of justice criterion must be used to guide the decision.[25] However, the FLRA also noted that cases arise in grievance arbitration and in unfair labor practice litigation that are different in nature from the issues that the MSPB adjudicates. Thus, in addition to the MSPB's *Allen*[26] categories, which define the interest of justice criterion, the FLRA added: "disregard of prevailing law, regulation, or negotiated agreement provision."[27] Like the MSPB, the FLRA has made it clear that decisions on attorney's fees must be predicated upon a "fully articulated, reasoned decision setting forth the specific findings supporting the determination on each pertinent statutory requirement."[28]

Sims v. Department of the Navy, 711 F.2d 1578, 83 FMSR 7039 (Fed. Cir. 1983). One early court decision interpreted this provision to mean that attorney's fees are not available in administrative proceedings other than unfair labor practice and grievance arbitration proceedings. *Payne v. Panama Canal Co.*, 607 F.2d 155 (5th Cir. 1979). Another early decision held that attorney's fees are available in various administrative proceedings, but that the "standards" of 5 U.S.C. 7701(g) apply to unfair labor practice and grievance arbitration proceedings and the "prevailing standards" apply in all other administrative proceedings. *Crowley v. Muskie*, 496 F. Supp. 360 (D.D.C. 1980), *rev'd sub nom. Crowley v. Schultz*, 704 F.2d 1269 (D.C. Cir. 1983).

[21]The MSPB has ruled that the standard for awarding fees under 5 U.S.C. 7701(g)(1) and under the Back Pay Act are the same. *Mitchum v. TVA*, 86 FMSR 5035 (MSPB 1986). See also *Devine v. NTEU*, 805 F.2d 384, 387 (Fed. Cir. 1986), *cert. denied*, 56 USLW 3242 (1987).

[22]CONG. REC. at S14295 (Aug. 24, 1978); Conference Committee Markup Session, at 50 (Sept. 27, 1978) ("[The compromise] would allow the appropriate authority, FLRA or the arbitrator or whoever in any grievance decision, to award fees in conformity with the standards to be applied in MSPB cases").

[23]*Audie L. Murphy Veterans Admin. Hosp. and AFGE, Local 3511*, supra note 18.

[24]*Department of Defense Dependents Schools and Overseas Educ. Ass'n*, supra note 18.

[25]*Naval Air Dev. Center and AFGE, Local 1928*, 21 FLRA 131 (1986).

[26]*Allen v. Postal Serv.*, 2 MSPB 582, 80 FMSR 7015 (1980).

[27]*Naval Air. Dev. Center and AFGE, Local 1928*, supra note 25.

[28]*Electrical Workers (IBEW) and Army Support Command, Haw.*, 14 FLRA 680, 684 (1984).

Thus, the decision must address the unjustified or unwarranted personnel action, the withdrawal of pay, allowances, or differentials with resulting back pay, and the standards of section 7701(g), including the prevailing party and, in nondiscrimination cases, the interest of justice criteria and, of course, all fee awards must discuss the reasonableness of the requested fees.

Entitlement Before the Merit Systems Protection Board

Before considering the entitlement issues that arise in attorney's fee cases before the MSPB, a variety of procedural matters must be given attention.

Preliminary Issues

Timeliness. A request for attorney's fees must be made within 10 days of the "final date of a decision" in favor of the appellant.[29] This requirement may be waived on a showing of good cause.[30] The Board may grant a waiver of this time limit using the same factors used to determine whether to waive other regulatory time limits.[31] These factors include the length of the delay in filing for fees, whether the appellant was notified of the time limit or was otherwise aware of it, the existence of circumstances beyond the control of the appellant that affected his or her ability to comply with the time limit, the degree to which negligence was shown by the appellant, circumstances showing excusable neglect, a showing of unavoidable casualty or misfortune, and the extent of the prejudice to the agency resulting from the waiver.[32]

---

[29]5 C.F.R. 1201.37(a)(2).

[30]5 C.F.R. 1201.12.

[31]*Small v. Department of the Navy*, 6 MSPB 312, 81 FMSR 5344 (1981).

[32]*Alonzo v. Department of the Air Force*, 4 MSPB 262, 264, 80 FMSR 7032 (1980); *Pfaehler v. MSPB*, 783 F.2d 187, 86 FMSR 7012 (Fed. Cir. 1986) (pro se employee seeking fees for attorney who occasionally assisted her was granted waiver where she was unaware of deadline and was misled by FPM Bulletin 550-42 that lacked reference to deadline); *Kerr v. National Endowment for the Arts*, 13 MSPB 39, 83 FMSR 5014 (1983), *aff'd*, 726 F.2d 730, 84 FMSR 7001 (Fed. Cir. 1984) (no waiver where attorney's reason was that he was "too busy"); *Taylor v. Department of the Army*, 86 FMSR 5027 (MSPB 1986) (although delay in filing motion for attorney's fees was short, and although agency evidently was not prejudiced by delay, these circumstances do not provide sufficient basis on which to waive regulatory time limit for filing such motions); *McDermott v. District of Columbia*, 84 FMSR 5373 (MSPB 1984) (attorney has an affirmative duty to be familiar with regulatory time limit); *Naviello v. OPM*, 83 FMSR 1341 (MSPB 1983) (attorney's failure to familiarize himself with Board regulations does not amount to showing of good cause for waiving regulatory time limit); *Hennelly v. Department of Transp.*, 85 FMSR 5128 (MSPB 1985) (time limit waived on showing that appellant did not receive Board's decision until nine days after issuance).

Supplemental Applications. The Board's regulation at 5 C.F.R. 1201.37(a)(2) does not specifically provide for supplements or amendments to requests for attorney's fees filed in a timely manner. The regulation only provides for timely submission of a request for fees and of an agency response. Nevertheless, the Board's practice is to accept supplemental attorney's fee requests and supporting evidence for legal services performed in the case either subsequent to, or prior to, the submission of the original fee motion.[33] However, an amended attorney's fee request must relate back to a prior timely filed original fee request.[34] An opportunity to supplement or amend ordinarily has been denied only upon (1) a showing by the agency that such supplementation or amendment would substantially prejudice its right to oppose the fee request, or (2) a finding by the administrative judge[35] that acceptance of the supplemental or amended request for fees would unduly delay the proceedings.[36]

Attorney-Client Relationship. The law provides that attorney's fees must have been "incurred." Attorney's fees are "incurred" when (1) an attorney-client relationship exists, and (2) counsel has rendered legal services on behalf of the appellant in a case before the MSPB.[37] For example, though an employee does not pay the fee of a union attorney who is representing the employee, the lawyer's fee is still "incurred" by the employee for purposes of attorney's fee awards.

Fee awards are only available to individuals licensed to practice law.[38] Attorneys who work for the federal government are allowed to represent other federal government employees, who are the subject of

---

[33]*Brito v. GPO*, 86 FMSR 5275 (MSPB 1986) (attorney "inadvertently" omitted certain services from his original fee request and Board allowed him to later supplement fee request to include such services); *Broadnax v. Postal Serv.*, 85 FMSR 5358 (MSPB 1985); *May v. Department of Transp.*, 85 FMSR 5319 (MSPB 1985); *Logan v. HUD*, 84 FMSR 5821 (MSPB 1984).

[34]*Brito v. GPO, supra* note 33, at p. 429.

[35]Effective May 8, 1986, the Board changed the working title of its hearing officers from presiding official to administrative judge. *Ledeaux v. Veterans Admin.*, 86 FMSR 5334, n.2 (MSPB 1986).

[36]*Brito v. GPO, supra* note 33, at p. 428.

[37]5 U.S.C. 7701(g)(1). *O'Donnell v. Department of the Interior*, 80 FMSR 7016, 2 MSPB 604 (1980).

[38]*Horton v. Postal Serv.*, 7 MSPB 138, 81 FMSR 5396 (1981); *Langenbach v. Postal Serv.*, 82 FMSR 4322 (MSPB 1982). In *Langenbach* the employee designated nonattorneys as his representatives in the MSPB proceeding. However, he retained an attorney to prepare the Petition for Review. The attorney charged $450.00 for his services and the employee had already paid $250.00 when the motion for fees was filed. This further evidenced an attorney-client relationship. Therefore, although the employee did not designate the attorney as his representative in accordance with 5 C.F.R. 1201.31, the MSPB found under the circumstances of this case that the requisite attorney-client relationship existed. However, no such relationship existed with the nonattorney representatives.

personnel administrative proceedings, but must serve "without compensation."[39] One such attorney argued that this provision did not prohibit the MSPB from awarding "costs" connected with a case to the prevailing party. The MSPB concluded that an award of costs alone is not authorized by section 7701(g)(1).[40]

It is appropriate to award a reasonable amount for the services of a paralegal as part of the attorney's fee award, but the paralegal must be an employee of the attorney in order to satisfy the attorney-client relationship.[41]

Attorney Work Outside the MSPB Process. Generally, the Board has not excluded from a representing attorney's compensable time hours reasonably spent outside the Board proceeding but in furtherance of the same goal.[42] Under the test adopted by the Board, the administrative judge will examine (1) whether the claimed portion of work done in the other proceeding is reasonable under the Board's standard set forth in *Kling*,[43] and (2) whether the work done in the other proceeding, or some discrete portion of it, significantly contributed to the success of the subsequent Board proceeding and eliminated the need for work that otherwise would have been required in connection with the Board proceeding.[44] Thus, for example, the MSPB awarded attorney's fees for work done on an unsuccessful EEO complaint made before the agency and which was filed prior to the Board appeal, when the complaint arose from the common core of facts which were the basis of the Board appeal, the appellant prevailed on the MSPB appeal, and attorney's fees were warranted in the interest of justice.[45]

Likewise, when an employee consults with an attorney about a case, but does not subsequently hire that attorney to take the case, any fees for that consultation are reimbursable.[46] When the Board has denied fees for

---

[39]18 U.S.C. 205. *Wallace v. Department of the Treasury*, 12 MSPB 263, 82 FMSR 5492 (1982).

[40]*Wallace v. Department of the Treasury, supra* note 39.

[41]*Mitchell v. HHS*, 84 FMSR 7005 (MSPB 1984); *Harris v. Department of Agric.*, 86 FMSR 5239 (MSPB 1986).

[42]*Blumenson v. Department of the Treasury*, 86 FMSR 5161 (MSPB 1986), citing *Webb v. County Bd. of Educ. of Dyer, Tenn.*, 471 U.S. 234, 37 FEP Cases 785 (1985). See also *Nadolney v. EPA*, 86 FMSR 5152 (MSPB 1986).

[43]*Kling v. Department of Justice*, 2 MSPB 620, 80 FMSR 7018 (1980).

[44]*Blumenson v. Department of the Treasury, supra* note 42, citing *Webb v. County Bd. of Educ. of Dyer, Tenn., supra* note 42. See also *Nadolney v. EPA, supra* note 42.

[45]*Young v. Department of the Air Force*, 86 FMSR 5007 (MSPB 1986). Fees were awarded where the employee was represented by an attorney during the preappeal stage, that is, the defense presented directly to the agency. *Brown v. Coast Guard*, 85 FMSR 5362 (MSPB 1985).

[46]*Johnson v. Department of the Interior*, 84 FMSR 5933, at p. 1288 (MSPB 1984).

hours spent outside a Board proceeding, it has been when those hours were spent pursuing a claim unrelated to the merits of the agency action which is the subject of the Board appeal.[47]

   Actions in Which Fees Are Available. Attorney's fees, of course, may be paid by the MSPB under section 7701(g) of the CSRA when incurred in prosecuting an appeal of an agency action before the MSPB.[48] Likewise, the MSPB may award fees for work done on a case prior to the agency issuing a final decision on its proposed action.[49] When private counsel is allowed to intervene in Special Counsel corrective action proceedings, fees may be awarded for private counsel's work on the case.[50] The MSPB may also award fees incurred in a judicial appeal from an MSPB decision.[51] Other circumstances in which fees may be awarded include (1) unsuccessful actions against administrative law judges,[52] (2) enforcement proceedings in which the agency fails to implement an MSPB decision,[53] (3) enforcement proceedings even where no fees were awarded in the initial appeal,[54] (4) compensation for work on a fee request,[55] (5) compensation for work on defending an appeal of an award of fees,[56] and (6) retirement appeals.[57] Finally, fees may be awarded in

---

[47]*Young v. Department of the Air Force, supra* note 45. See *Lizut v. Department of the Army,* 85 FMSR 5250 (MSPB 1985) (fees denied to appellant in pursuing his claim concerning agency's promotion and early optional retirement decisions, which were completely separate from and unrelated to merits of his removal appeal); *King v. Postal Serv.,* 84 FMSR 3307 (MSPB 1984) (fees for time spent in unemployment compensation hearing not compensable since this proceeding was in no way connected with or necessary to successful prosecution of appeal); *Mannon v. Department of the Army,* 86 FMSR 5323 (MSPB 1986) (no fee award for unrelated EEO complaint and unemployment compensation hearing).

[48]*Allen v. Postal Serv.,* 2 MSPB 582, 80 FMSR 7015 (1980).

[49]*McBride v. Department of Agric.,* 4 MSPB 17 (1980) (prerequisites to such an award are that MSPB have jurisdiction over appeal and that services were rendered in connection with appealable agency action). Reaffirmed in *Brown v. Coast Guard, supra* note 45.

[50]*Frazier v. MSPB,* 672 F.2d 150, 28 FEP Cases 185 (D.C. Cir. 1982). See also *Keely v. MSPB,* 760 F.2d 246, 85 FMSR 7027 (Fed. Cir. 1985).

[51]*Lizut v. Department of the Army, supra* note 47; *Lassiter v. Department of the Navy,* 86 FMSR 5041 (MSPB 1986); *Mitchum v. TVA,* 86 FMSR 5035 (MSPB 1986).

[52]*Social Sec. Admin. v. Goodman,* 85 FMSR 5278 (MSPB 1985).

[53]*Alfaro v. FAA,* 85 FMSR 5078 (MSPB 1985).

[54]*Tri v. SEC,* 85 FMSR 5227 (MSPB 1985).

[55]*LaMorge v. Department of Agric.,* 6 MSPB 125, 81 FMSR 5320 (1981).

[56]*Morgan v. Department of the Air Force,* 11 MSPB 501, 82 FMSR 5399 (1982); *Grace v. OPM,* 86 FMSR 5020 (MSPB 1986).

[57]Attorney's fees may be awarded by the MSPB in disability and in nondisability retirement cases. *Stephens v. OPM,* 87 FMSR 5220, n.6 (MSPB 1987). See also *Simmons v. MSPB,* 768 F.2d 323, 85 FMSR 7048 (Fed. Cir. 1985). In the subsequent remand of this case, the MSPB set forth the standards for determining whether an attorney's fee is warranted in the interest of justice in retirement-related appeals. *Simmons v. OPM,* 86 FMSR 5326 (MSPB 1986). It is important to note that after *Simmons* the MSPB made further distinctions in the "interest of justice" determination in retirement cases. *Kent v.*

one case before the MSPB for work done on another, but factually related MSPB proceeding.[58]

Actions in Which Fees Are Not Available. The MSPB has no authority to award attorney's fees under section 7701(g) unless there is a clear connection between that section and the section covering the underlying action.[59] Thus, the MSPB has no authority to award fees where the appellant succeeded in a civil action on a nonselection for a promotion which was not appealable to the MSPB.[60] Attorney time spent in an unemployment compensation hearing is not compensable since it was in no way connected with, or necessary to, the successful prosecution of the appeal.[61] It has been held that fees are not available for disciplinary actions brought by the Special Counsel under 5 U.S.C. 1206(g).[62] The specific case involved a prosecution for prohibited political activity. However, the basis for the ruling was that all disciplinary actions by the Special Counsel are not sufficiently connected to section 7701(g) to allow a fee award.[63]

Entitlement Criteria—General

The two provisions for awarding attorney's fees by the MSPB are found at 5 U.S.C. 7701(g). Subsection (1) of this section applies to cases that *do not* involve a finding of prohibited discrimination. Subsection (2) applies to cases that *do* involve a finding of discrimination. In a subsection (1) case, the appellant must be the "prevailing party" and the award

---

OPM, 87 FMSR 5266 (MSPB 1987). See also *Bronger v. OPM*, 740 F.2d 1552 (Fed. Cir. 1984); *Obremski v. OPM*, 86 FMSR 5325 (MSPB 1986) (attorney's fees available in retirement cases brought by law enforcement officer); *Leppelman v. OPM*, 85 FMSR 5449 (MSPB 1985) (attorney's fees available in survivor annuity cases).

[58]*Nadolney v. EPA*, *supra* note 42 (where within-grade salary increase (WIG) denial was appealed separately from subsequent removal action and both actions were based upon "common core of facts," successful employee could recover fees in WIG denial case for all work done on removal action also).

[59]*Brown v. Coast Guard, supra* note 45, at n.9.

[60]*Morley v. Defense Logistics Agency*, 83 FMSR 5150 (MSPB 1983).

[61]*King v. Postal Serv.*, 20 MSPR 467 (1984).

[62]*Saldana v. MSPB*, 766 F.2d 514, 85 FMSR 7041 (Fed. Cir. 1985).

[63]On the other hand, the Comptroller General has ruled that agencies have the authority to use appropriated funds to provide a supervisor with representation in an administrative hearing if the supervisor performed the conduct in issue within the scope of the supervisor's employment. *International Trade Comm'n*, 61 Comp. Gen. 515, 516 (1982). Subsequent to that decision, the Comptroller General determined that when a supervisor acquired private counsel and successfully defended against a Special Counsel disciplinary action, the agency, at its discretion and using applicable legal standards to establish a reasonable fee, could reimburse the supervisor for reasonable attorney's fees from the agency's appropriated funds. Jeannette E. Nichols, CG Dec. B-229052 (Oct. 28, 1987).

of attorney's fees must be "in the interest of justice." In a subsection (2) case, the attorney's fee standards prescribed under the Civil Rights Act (42 U.S.C. 2000e-5(k)) are controlling. Thus, in a subsection (2) case, the appellant need only be the "prevailing party" to be entitled to reasonable attorney's fees.

"Prevailing Party" Criterion

The "prevailing party" criterion, common to both subsection (1) and subsection (2) cases, has statutory, administrative, and judicial precedent.[64] Although there are some distinctions between subsection (1) and (2) cases, it is worth noting that the MSPB has ruled that prevailing party has the same meaning in both types of cases.[65] With this in mind, we will cite here principles that have been established by the MSPB in non-EEO cases and by the courts in Title VII litigation.

Generally, an appellant who obtains all, or a significant part, of the relief sought is the prevailing party.[66] A party need not prevail on all issues as long as the party prevails on a significant, separable claim on the merits.[67] Likewise, when a case involves separable issues and some are successful and some are not, only the work on the successful claims is reimbursable.[68] The courts look to the substance of the litigation to determine whether an applicant has substantially prevailed, and not merely to the technical disposition of the case or motion.[69] Thus, for

---

[64]*Albemarle Paper Co. v. Moody*, 422 U.S. 405, 10 FEP Cases 1181 (1975); *Hodnick v. FMCS*, 4 MSPB 431, 80 FMSR 7034 (1980).

[65]*Hodnick v. FMCS, supra* note 64, 4 MSPB at 434-435 (1980).

[66]*Id.*, at 435; *Texas State Teachers Ass'n v. Garland School Dist.*, 49 FEP 465 (1989); *Carpenter v. Bureau of Alcohol, Tobacco & Firearms*, 5 MSPB 423, 81 FMSR 7038 (1981); see also *Newman v. Piggie Park Enters.*, 390 U.S. 400 (1968).

[67]*Van Hoomissen v. Xerox Corp.*, 503 F.2d 1131, 8 FEP Cases 725 (9th Cir. 1974); *Hanrahan v. Hampton*, 446 U.S. 754 (1980); *Grubbs v. Butz*, 548 F.2d 973, 13 FEP Cases 245 (D.C. Cir. 1976); *Parker v. Matthews*, 411 F. Supp. 1059, 13 FEP Cases 595 (D.D.C. 1976), *aff'd sub nom. Parker v. Califano*, 561 F.2d 320, 18 FEP Cases 391 (D.C. Cir. 1977); *Bradley v. Richmond School Bd.*, 416 U.S. 696 (1974).

[68]*Devine v. Sutermeister*, 733 F.2d 892, 898–99, 84 FLRR 1-8053 (Fed. Cir. 1984). The union prevailed on the merits of an appeal. However, the court found that issues regarding timeliness and a rehearing were sufficiently separable from the merits of the case and the court denied fees to the union for its unsuccessful work on those issues.

[69]*Devine v. Sutermeister, supra* note 68, 733 F.2d at 898; *Austin v. Department of Commerce*, 742 F.2d 1417, 84 FMSR 7044 (Fed. Cir. 1984). In *Devine v. Sutermeister*, the union filed a motion to dismiss which OPM successfully opposed. However, the union prevailed on the merits and sought fees. OPM argued that fees were not appropriate for work done on the unsuccessful motion to dismiss. Disagreeing with OPM, the court said, "A court should look to the substance of the litigation to determine whether an applicant has *substantially* prevailed in its position, and not merely the technical disposition of the case or motion." *Id.*, at 898.

In *Koch v. Department of Commerce*, 84 FMSR 7004 (MSPB 1984) the agency

example, an employee, whose challenge to a removal action results in a reduction of the penalty to a suspension, is a "prevailing party."[70] However, if the relief secured by the employee is of a *de minimis* nature, fees may be denied.[71] Similarly, if the relief obtained is no more than "a favorable judicial statement of the law in the course of litigation that results in judgment against the [employee]," then the employee is not a prevailing party.[72] When the employee obtains relief on a significant claim, but does not obtain all relief requested, or does not obtain relief on all claims raised, the employee is a prevailing party. However, "results obtained" can be an important factor in determining the reasonableness of the fee amount, which is discussed here after the entitlement issues.[73]

A fee award may be appropriate where the party has prevailed on an interim order which was central to his or her case[74] or where an interlocutory appeal is sufficiently significant and discrete to be treated as a separate unit.[75] However, merely prevailing on a procedural issue

---

challenged the entire basis for the fee award. The award was substantially upheld by the administrative judge, but appellant's request for deposition costs was denied. The agency argued to the Board that appellant's time spent on the request for deposition costs should be excluded from the award. The Board concluded that this issue was not distinct in all respects from the successful claims. Nor was appellant's success in this appeal and on his motion for fees so limited as to require a reduction in the award because the appellant did not prevail on the issue.

[70]*Sterner v. Department of the Army*, 711 F.2d 1563, 83 FMSR 7038 (Fed. Cir. 1983) ("Whether a party prevails is not a question of merit or justice, but a practical test designed to determine as an initial matter who is eligible for attorney's fees"); *Depte v. Veterans Admin.*, 84 FMSR 5340 (MSPB 1984); *Froehlich v. Department of the Treasury*, 84 FMSR 5479 (MSPB 1984); *Boese v. Department of the Air Force*, 784 F.2d 388, 86 FMSR 7019 (Fed. Cir. 1986).

[71]*Mortensen v. Callaway*, 672 F.2d 822, 29 FEP Cases 111 (10th Cir. 1982). Before the MSPB, the *de minimis* nature of the victory may be considered under the aegis of the interest of justice prerequisite. *Sterner v. Dept. of the Army, supra* note 70. See also *Carpenter v. Bureau of Alcohol, Tobacco and Firearms, supra* note 66 (employee was not prevailing party when, prior to hearing, a reduction in grade from GS-13, step 4 to GS-12, step 1 was changed through settlement to reduction to GS-12, step 10).

[72]*Hewitt v. Helms*, 482 U.S. 755, 44 FEP Cases 15 (1987).

[73]*Hensley v. Eckerhart*, 461 U.S. 424, 31 FEP Cases 1169 (1983).

[74]*Parker v. Matthews, supra* note 67, 411 F. Supp. at 1064.

[75]*Van Hoomissen v. Xerox Corp., supra* note 67, 503 F.2d at 1133. In *Davis v. Bolger*, 512 F. Supp. 61 (D.D.C. 1981), plaintiff did not demonstrate unlawful discrimination in the denial of promotion. However, the court found that the defendant-agency had erected an unnecessary and harmful obstacle in the path of plaintiff's pursuing discrimination claims, contrary to the policies underlying Title VII. The court found that "the practice of differentially compensating plaintiffs and defendant's witnesses [i.e., the former had to use annual leave or leave without pay while the latter were granted administrative leave] in Title VII cases impedes the effectuation of the antidiscrimination policies embodied in [Title VII]." For that reason, the court ordered that plaintiff and his witnesses be paid for their court attendance. In the view of the court, "there can be no doubt but that plaintiff has prevailed on a claim rooted in the antidiscriminatory mandate of Title VII." At footnote 6

or evidentiary ruling does not normally satisfy the prevailing party criterion.[76]

The appellant must be able to show that the relief gained was a result of the institution of the action.[77] An employee who receives at least some relief on the merits of his or her claim can be said to have prevailed. This can occur even outside a formal judgment as long as it is related to the employee's act of bringing the appeal or lawsuit. For example, a lawsuit sometimes brings voluntary corrective action that affords all or some of the relief sought by the employee's appeal or lawsuit. In such circumstances, the employee is the prevailing party.[78]

"Interest of Justice" Criterion

Subsection (1) of section 7701(g) provides that the payment of attorney's fees may be required of an agency when it is determined that the employee is the prevailing party and that "payment by the agency is warranted in the interest of justice, including any case in which a prohibited personnel practice was engaged in by the agency or any case in which the agency's action was clearly without merit."[79] Having considered the prevailing party issue, we turn to the interest of justice requirement.

---

the court distinguished this holding from a similar case as follows:

This is clearly distinguishable from *Grubbs v. Butz* 548 F.2d 973 (D.C. Cir. 1976), where the plaintiff had only prevailed on an interlocutory procedural issue, and where the court stated that, "[f]or all we now know, the defendants in this case may be entirely blameless." *Grubbs v. Butz, supra*, 548 F.2d at 976. In the present case, it has already been determined that defendant is not blameless but has acted contrary to the mandate of Title VII.

[76]*Hanrahan v. Hampton, supra* note 67, at 757 ("It seems clearly to have been the intent of Congress to permit such an interlocutory award only to a party who has established his entitlement to some relief on the merits of his claim."). See also *Austin v. Department of Commerce, supra* note 69 (success in motion to remand to MSPB for further evidence did not make petitions "prevailing parties").

[77]*Young v. MSPB*, 776 F.2d 1027, 85 FMSR 7084 (Fed. Cir. 1985); *Boyett v. Customs Serv.*, 83 FMSR 5035 (MSPB 1983). In both of these cases, the relief granted the employee was as a result of proceedings in another forum rather than before the MSPB. However, if the relief granted is not a result of the institution of the appeal, then an award of attorney's fees is not appropriate. *Boyett v. Customs Serv., supra*. See also Judith Jones, *Administrative Law: Recovery of Attorney's Fees by Prevailing Plaintiffs in Title VII Actions*, 33 OKLA. L. REV., 98–107 (1980); Ann Berkovitz, *A Summary of Issues Involving Attorney's Fees in Civil Rights Cases*, 13 CLEARINGHOUSE REV., 282, 283–84 (1979).

[78]*Hewitt v. Helms, supra* note 72.

[79]5 U.S.C. 7701(g)(1).

The interest of justice standard is not coextensive with the prevailing party requirement.[80] In other words, not all parties who prevail are entitled to attorney's fees.

Awarding attorney's fees is discretionary. Where one or more of the interest of justice criteria are met, attorney's fees "normally" will be awarded. "Conversely," the MSPB has ruled, "that discretion permits the Board to deny fees where such circumstances are present."[81]

Motions for fee awards should be evaluated "from the vantage point of the original administrative judge."[82] This means that an administrative judge's addendum decision on a motion for fees must not be inconsistent with the findings in the initial decision, because those are the controlling findings. In other words, the decision on attorney's fees cannot recast the findings of fact. The findings of fact in the initial decision must support the decision to grant or deny fees.[83] It also means that when the administrative judge, who issued the initial decision, is not available to hear the motion for attorney's fees, the subsequent administrative judge, who hears the motion for fees, may not review the record and characterize the findings differently. The new administrative judge is bound by the findings of the initial decision.[84]

Finally, the fee decisions of the Board and its administrative judge must demonstrate that the various relevant factors were weighed in reaching the decision. For example, the Board will reverse administrative judges who fail to state explicitly the basis for their conclusion that the interest of justice criterion is, or is not, met. The Federal Circuit, furthermore, has rejected the concept that certain circumstances are

---

[80]The administrative judge had improperly ruled that any time the employee prevails, the agency case is "clearly without merit," thereby requiring the payment of fees. In rejecting this conclusion, the MSPB noted that the interest of justice standard is something more than just being the prevailing party and that the concept would have to be developed on a case-by-case basis. *Allen v. Postal Serv.*, 2 MSPB 582, 587, 592, 80 FMSR 7015 (1980).

[81]*Id.*, at 591.

[82]*Yorkshire v. MSPB*, 746 F.2d 1454, 1458, 84 FMSR 7050 (Fed. Cir. 1984); *Mitchum v. TVA*, 86 FMSR 5035 (MSPB 1986).

[83]*Everly v. National Transp. Safety Bd.*, 84 FMSR 5837 (MSPB 1984). See also *Gustin v. Department of Transp.*, 85 FMSR 5314 (MSPB 1985); *May v. Department of Transp.*, 85 FMSR 5319 (MSPB 1985); *Weaver v. Department of the Army*, 85 FMSR 5207 (MSPB 1985); *Wise v. TVA*, 84 FMSR 5971 (MSPB 1984); *Trachy v. Defense Communications Agency*, 84 FMSR 6091 (MSPB 1984).

[84]*Id.*, in *Boese v. Department of the Air Force*, supra note 70, the court relied solely on the administrative judge's decision and rejected the idea of using "[t]he informal remark about Boese (by the judge at the criminal trial) . . . to detract from the MSPB findings and decision." *Id.*, at n.4.

always by definition beyond the interest of justice criterion.[85] Neither the fact that a case turned primarily on the basis of credibility determinations nor the fact that a case was "factually close" automatically excludes the prevailing appellant from a fee award that is in the interest of justice. The court concluded that there was "no warrant" in the law, in the legislative history, or in decisions of the court "for such dogmatic *per se* pronouncements."[86] Rather, the role of credibility determinations and the closeness of the evidence are merely factors in determining whether a fee award would be in the interest of justice.

"Interest of Justice" Defined

The lead case from the MSPB, in which the interest of justice concept is discussed, is *Allen v. Postal Service*.[87] In *Allen*, the MSPB described five categories illustrative of the interest of justice concept. As the MSPB noted in *Allen*, the statutory examples of cases involving prohibited personnel practices or agency actions "clearly without merit" do not exhaust the circumstances in which an award of fees may not be warranted, for the statute plainly authorizes such awards in cases "including"—but not limited to—those examples.[88]

The MSPB then engaged in a lengthy discussion of this concept's legislative history. At the end of the discussion, the Board listed the following five circumstances, emphasizing that this list was "not exhaustive, but illustrative":

1. where the agency engaged in a "prohibited personnel practice";
2. where the agency's action was "clearly without merit," or was "wholly unfounded," or the employee is "substantially innocent" of the charges brought by the agency;
3. where the agency initiated the action against the employee in "bad faith," including:
   a. where the agency's action was brought to "harass" the employee;
   b. where the agency's action was brought to "exert improper pressure on the employee to act in certain ways";

---

[85]*Thomson v. MSPB*, 772 F.2d 879, 85 FMSR 7069 (Fed. Cir. 1985). See also *Boese v. Department of the Air Force, supra* note 70, at n.3.
[86]*Thomson v. MSPB, supra* note 85, at 881.
[87]2 MSPB 582, 80 FMSR 7015 (1980).
[88]*Id.*, at 587.

4. where the agency committed a "gross procedural error" which "prolonged the proceeding" or "severely prejudiced" the employee;

5. where the agency "knew or should have known that it would not prevail on the merits" when it brought the proceeding.

With the exception of the first category, prohibited personnel practices, the reader should not approach the remaining four *Allen* categories as separate and distinct.[89] For example, category 2 uses the phrase "clearly without merit," which is also the statutory phrase that theoretically encompasses the last four categories. Thus, when the Board concludes that in a given circumstance the agency action is clearly without merit, we may not always know whether the statutory term or the category 2 term is being invoked. Furthermore, the Board has not been consistently precise in its use of the descriptive phrases. For example, fees have routinely been found proper when the agency action was contrary to clearly established legal or regulatory principles. The Board has concluded (1) that such agency action was "clearly without merit" and "wholly unfounded,"[90] (2) that it constituted "gross procedural error,"[91] or (3) that the agency "knew or should have known" it would not prevail.[92] Part of the reason for this apparent lack of precision is that the Board never intended these categories to be conclusive or to represent fixed definitions. From the outset, they were labeled "directional markers toward the interest of justice."[93]

Nevertheless, there are discernible categories within the interest of justice concept and it is useful to summarize the case law in this regard.

Category 2 and Category 5 Distinguished

One important trend in the effort to distinguish between the last four *Allen* categories is noteworthy. The Board, following the lead of the Federal Circuit, has repeatedly distinguished between category 2 and category 5. Category 5 is used in evaluating events that led to the agency

---

[89]*Id.*, at 593. Of all the terms used in these examples, one has a very specific definition, which is discussed further in Chapter 4. "Prohibited personnel practices" are abuses of the personnel system that are so egregious Congress specifically listed them in the Civil Service Reform Act. 5 U.S.C. 2302(b). See Chapter 4.

[90]*Emelio v. Postal Serv.*, 85 FMSR 5190 (MSPB 1985).

[91]*Gibson-Meyers v. Veterans Admin.*, 11 MSPB 604, 82 FMSR 5419 (1982).

[92]*Brown v. Department of Defense*, 11 MSPB 1, 82 FMSR 5310 (1982); *Rossebo v. Department of Commerce*, 85 FMSR 5099 (MSPB 1985); *Everly v. National Transp. Safety Bd.*, *supra* note 83 (agency clearly errs with respect to RIF assignment rights).

[93]*Allen v. Postal Serv.*, *supra* note 87, at 593.

action. Category 2 is used in evaluating the results of the case before the Board.[94]

To use the court's words, "Category 5 requires a sensitive evaluation of the agency's original action, i.e., whether the agency 'knew or should have known' that it would not prevail on the appeal."[95] The focus is on the period when the agency was taking the action and the issue is whether the agency possessed trustworthy, admissible evidence or whether the agency was negligent in its conduct of the investigation.[96] The employee "must show that the agency, by making a reasonable inquiry, should have ascertained at the outset that its action was without merit, but nevertheless persisted in its action, and thus, unnecessarily subjected appellant to the substantial burden and expense of litigation."[97]

---

[94]In Kent v. OPM, 87 FMSR 5266 (MSPB 1987), the MSPB defined the requirements for categories 2 and 5 in a disability retirement case somewhat differently from all other appealable actions. In a disability retirement case, the MSPB review focuses on evidence the employee presented to OPM rather than on any agency investigation. Thus, the MSPB considers (1) whether the appellant was misled by OPM to his detriment or whether OPM's initial decision was insufficient under the kind of evidence needed to prevail on reconsideration; (2) the extent to which the reversal was based on evidence that the appellant did not present to OPM, but that nevertheless was readily available to OPM; and (3) the extent to which the appellant produced evidence that was so compelling that reasonable minds could not differ as to his or her eligibility for an annuity and OPM's continued refusal to approve a disability retirement annuity for the appellant prolonged the adjudication. When a fee award is warranted on the basis of OPM's continued, improper refusal to approve an annuity, the award is limited to those fees incurred after OPM has been made aware of the dispositive evidence.

[95]Yorkshire v. MSPB, 746 F.2d 1454, 84 FMSR 7050 (Fed. Cir. 1984); Thomson v. MSPB, supra note 85; Wise v. MSPB, 780 F.2d 997, 85 FMSR 7092 (Fed. Cir. 1985).

[96]O'Donnell v. Department of the Interior, 2 MSPB 604, 608, 80 FMSR 7016 (1980); Stout v. Postal Serv., 3 MSPB 440, 80 FMSR 5124 (1980) (notice of proposed demotion did not specify how appellant was responsible for alleged deficiencies in his unit and his written response refuted charges on same basis as administrative judge found for appellant); Hayes v. Department of the Air Force, 83 FMSR 5054 (MSPB 1983) (proposing official conducting investigation ignored numerous crucial and credible witnesses who corroborated appellant's story and all witnesses except those who supported agency's charges were dismissed summarily); Hockman v. American Battle Monuments Comm'n, 84 FMSR 5735 (MSPB 1984) (prudent inquiries by agency would have revealed that termination action was based on unreasonable actions by supervisor); Steger v. Defense Investigative Serv., 717 F.2d 1402, 83 FMSR 7076 (D.C. Cir. 1983) (appellant presented affidavits that contradicted evidence in notice of proposed removal, but without further investigation deciding official terminated appellant's employment). In Stegar the Board originally denied fees. The court reversed and remanded and the Board awarded fees. See 84 FMSR 5143 (MSPB 1984). In Simmons v. OPM, 86 FMSR 5326 (MSPB 1986), OPM unreasonably denied an application for a disability retirement annuity based upon a subjective statement by a supervisor and in the face of uncontroverted medical evidence. Thus, the agency knew or should have known that it could not prevail on the merits.

[97]Hanson v. Department of Transp., 84 FMSR 5838 (MSPB 1984); Cicero v. Postal Serv., 4 MSPB 145, 80 FMSR 5166 (MSPB 1980) (had deciding official properly considered appellant's response in light of vague and ambiguous evidence supporting the charges, he should have known that demotion could not be sustained); Erdman v. Department of Labor,

However, even when it is determined that a particular charge should not have been brought by the agency, this does not establish that the agency action as a whole was inappropriate.[98] Other charges, though not warranting the agency's adverse action, may have been sufficient to establish that the employee was not "substantially innocent" of the charges. The substantially innocent standard is part of category 2, which "refers to the result of the case in the Board, not to the evidence and information available prior to the hearing."[99] Category 2 requires a finding that the agency's action was "clearly without merit" or was "wholly unfounded" or that the employee is substantially innocent of the charges brought by the agency. At least four observations are important with regard to category 2.

First, category 2 is not punitive. The other *Allen* categories require a finding that the agency, either in taking the action or in defending the action before the Board, violated the law (category 1—prohibited personnel practice), acted with malice or in bad faith (category 3), committed gross procedural error (category 4), or acted with negligence (category 5—"knew or should have known"). However, the court observed that category 2 represents "an effort to minimize the burden an unsubstantiated accusation places upon innocent employees" without regard to the degree of fault or lack of fault on the part of the agency.[100]

Second, the employee must do more than merely defeat the agency's case. To reach the conclusion that defeating the agency's case means that the employee is substantially innocent would make the prevailing party concept and category 2 synonymous. They clearly are not.[101] Thus, when

---

6 MSPB 54, 81 FMSR 2514 (1981) (deciding official ignored evidence that employee was actually on approved leave rather than absent without leave); *Brooks v. Department of Transp.*, 84 FMSR 6107 (MSPB 1984) (employee told deciding official that he was not on strike and that he had not been advised of cancellation of his leave, a circumstance that a proper inquiry could have readily verified).

However, to benefit from this standard the employee is required to "communicate all the facts to the deciding official which would lead the deciding official to rule against" the adverse action. In referring to an employee who deliberately withheld such important facts from the deciding official, the Federal Circuit court said, "Such an individual brings the consequences of the agency's legal proceedings upon himself and is in no way an innocent victim who is entitled to the award of attorney fees in the 'interest of justice.'" *Wise v. MSPB, supra* note 95. The court said that the "substantially innocent" standard is not satisfied by an individual such as petitioner who (1) knows that he is substantially innocent of the charges brought against him, (2) can prove his substantial innocence, and (3) deliberately does not communicate all the facts to the deciding official. . . ." Id., at 1000.

[98]*McMonagle v. Bureau of Alcohol, Tobacco & Firearms*, 85 FMSR 1098 (MSPB 1985).

[99]*Yorkshire v. MSPB, supra* note 95, at 1457.

[100]*Id.*, citing *Sterner v. Department of the Army*, 711 F.2d 1563, 1570, 83 FMSR 7038 (Fed. Cir. 1983).

[101]See *supra* note 80.

the administrative judge finds that the agency's evidence "was not credible and should be given no weight" or is "entitled to little weight," then it is appropriate to conclude that the prevailing appellant also satisfied category 2, that is, was substantially innocent of the charges brought against him or her.[102] Likewise, when the agency has presented no probative testimonial evidence and the agency's evidence fails even to establish a prima facie case, then the agency's action is clearly without merit or wholly unfounded and the employee is substantially innocent of the charges.[103] However, fees have been denied when the "agency's proof before the administrative judge [was not] so woefully inadequate or incredible as to justify a finding that appellant met the substantially innocent criterion for awarding fees."[104]

Third, when a number of charges form the basis for the agency action, the appellant must prevail on substantially all of the charges to be found substantially innocent.[105] In the words of the Federal Circuit, substantial "connotes innocence of the more important and greater part of

---

[102]*Yorkshire v. MSPB*, supra note 95, at 1458. See also *Ledeaux v. Veterans Admin.*, 86 FMSR 5334 (MSPB 1986). In *Ledeaux*, appellant was removed for making "false, slanderous and defamatory statements against his acting supervisor." The administrative judge found appellant's statements to be false. However, intent is a crucial element of the falsification charge and the agency "did not prove . . . intent to make false statements." Furthermore, the administrative judge found "not a scintilla of evidence" to support the "defamatory" and "slanderous" portion of the charges. Thus, appellant was "substantially innocent" of the charges.

[103]*Brown v. Department of Labor*, 86 FMSR 5006 (MSPB 1986).

[104]*Benavides v. Department of the Treasury*, 85 FMSR 1983 (MSPB 1985). See also *Lewis v. Department of the Navy*, 674 F.2d 714, 716, 82 FMSR 7043 (8th Cir. 1982) in which the administrative judge eventually ruled in appellant's favor, but also found that the agency's charges were not "clearly without merit."

[105]*Id*. In *Boese v. Department of the Air Force*, 784 F.2d 388, 86 FMSR 7019 (Fed. Cir. 1986) the major charges were dismissed and only a minor charge was sustained. However, the administrative judge found that the case on the major charges was "close." Therefore, the court held that the administrative judge's decision "may perhaps not show that the [major] charges were '*clearly* without merit' or '*wholly* unfounded' (emphasis [by court]), but the decision does show, at the least, that Boese was 'substantially innocent' . . . of those charges. . . . Insofar as the qualification 'substantial' (in the criterion of 'substantial innocence') connotes innocence of the more important and greater part of the original charges, the prerequisite is also fulfilled here." In *Mannon v. Department of the Army*, 86 FMSR 5323 (MSPB 1986), three of five charges were not sustained, including the charge that was the primary reason for the removal action. The administrative judge ruled the employee was "substantially innocent." The agency argued that he was not substantially innocent since two of its charges were, in fact, sustained. Citing *Weaver v. Department of the Navy*, 2 MSPB 297, 80 FMSR 7012, aff'd, 669 F.2d 613 (9th Cir. 1982), the Board characterized the agency arguments as "mere disagreement with the findings of the presiding official. . . which do not warrant full review of the record by the Board." *Ledeaux v. Veterans Admin.*, supra note 102, at n.2.

the original charges."[106] Thus, fees were denied to an employee who confessed to two of five charges against him and successfully defended the remaining three. Though he ultimately prevailed on the three contested charges, he was not substantially innocent because he had confessed to some wrongdoing.[107] In such cases, "the administrative judge should examine *the degree of fault* on the employee's part and the existence of any reasonable basis for the agency's action."[108]

Finally, the Board has refused to view an agency's filing a frivolous appeal of an administrative judge's decision as a basis for awarding fees to the prevailing party. It did so because of the chilling effect such a policy might have on the filing of meritorious appeals.[109] However, since that decision, the Federal Circuit has held that, "notwithstanding the merits of the agency's initial action, . . . an award of attorney's fees is proper where the agency brings an appeal that is clearly without merit."[110]

Personnel Action That Violates Law, Regulation, or Judicial Precedent

An agency action that ignores legal precedent usually satisfies the interest of justice criterion.[111] The agency's failure to present sufficient

---

[106]*Van Fossen v. MSPB*, 788 F.2d 748, 86 FMSR 7031 (Fed. Cir. 1986) (employee was guilty of charges, but it was "purely technical violation of an agency regulation" and, thus, employee was "substantially innocent.").

[107]See also *Sterner v. Department of the Army*, 711 F.2d 1563, 1567–68, 83 FMSR 7038 (Fed. Cir. 1983).

[108]*Yorkshire v. MSPB*, *supra* note 95, at n.9 (emphasis in original), quoting with approval language of the Board in *Allen v. Postal Serv.*, 2 MSPB 582, n.35, 80 FMSR 7015 (1980).

[109]*Batchelder v. Department of the Treasury*, 82 FMSR 5484 (MSPB 1982).

[110]*Keely v. MSPB*, 760 F.2d 246, 85 FMSR 7027 (Fed. Cir. 1985).

[111]*Emelio v. Postal Serv.*, 85 FMSR 5190 (MSPB 1985) (refusing to reemploy appellant because of absence during period of recovery from work-related injury violates Board precedent and is "clearly without merit"); *Everly v. National Transp. Safety Bd.*, 84 FMSR 5837 (MSPB 1984) (agency's case denying appellant assignment rights in a RIF was "based upon a misinterpretation of 5 CFR. . . ."); *Brown v. Department of Defense*, *supra* note 92 (agency's "classification actions [downgrading employees] were improper because the clear mandate of 20 U.S.C. 902 was not followed."); *Nealen v. Department of the Treasury*, 84 FMSR 6039 (MSPB 1984) (supervisor tells employee to get off agency premises because "he was no longer a Federal employee" and then agency removes employee for being AWOL); *Rossebo v. Department of Commerce*, *supra* note 92 (agency's argument that appellant was not due rights of 5 U.S.C. 7513(b) because he was not appointed pursuant to 5 U.S.C. 2105(a) is not consistent with existing case law); *Jarze v. Department of the Air Force*, 4 MSPB 247, 80 FMSR 5181 (1980) (conduct that led to removal action was result of mental illness and FPM requires that disability retirement be pursued, thus agency removal action "was initiated in disregard of prevailing law and federal policy"); *Morgan v. Department of the Air Force*, 11 MSPB 501, 82 FMSR 5399 (1982) (to downgrade appellant

evidence to show that it removed appellant under an OPM-approved performance appraisal system led the Board to conclude that the agency's action was "clearly without merit."[112] Likewise, an agency, while carrying out a reduction in force, failed to make reasonable inquiries before finding appellant was not qualified for a particular position. As a result, the agency denied the employee appropriate assignment rights in connection with the reduction in force. This led to a finding that the agency "knew or should have known that it could not prevail" on the merits of its action. Thus, an award of attorney's fees was warranted.[113] Cases to the contrary seem to turn on whether the agency action, though in violation of a law, regulation, or judicial precedent, was clearly without merit, wholly unfounded, or taken in bad faith.[114]

Negligent Presentation of a Case

The Board has also placed agencies on notice that lack of preparation or negligent presentation of a case by the agency representative can justify an award of attorney's fees. In *Trowell*,[115] the administrative judge found that the agency representative's "apparent unfamiliarity with prosecuting an appeal amounted to negligence." He continued, "This negligence existed to such a degree as to unconscionably taint the entire proceeding."

in order to promote successful complainant improper and not based upon promoting "efficiency of the service"); *Koch v. Department of Commerce*, 84 FMSR 7004 (MSPB 1984) (agency denied employee appropriate assignment rights in RIF); *Gibson-Meyers v. Veterans Admin., supra* note 91 (agency's refusal without reason to allow appellant to withdraw her resignation in order to avoid adverse action procedures violated C.F.R.); *Cox v. International Trade Comm'n*, 83 FMSR 5138 (MSPB 1983) (had agency read applicable statute and regulations, it would have known that its interpretation was clearly erroneous); *Keely v. MSPB, supra* note 110 (agency failed to research *Powell v. Department of the Treasury*, 8 MSPB 21 (1981)). *Yencho v. Department of Transp.*, 84 FMSR 5016 (MSPB 1984) (using adverse action procedures to suspend employee with medical problem, agency knew or should have known it would not prevail since it cited disciplinary cause of action without any showing of misconduct); *Barson v. Department of Transp.*, 84 FMSR 5677 (MSPB 1984) (indefinite suspension during notice period imposed contrary to established case law means agency knew or should have known it would not prevail as to indefinite suspension and fact that subsequent removal was sustained does not relieve agency of its duty to avoid illegal suspensions); *Froehlich v. Department of the Treasury*, 84 FMSR 5479 (MSPB 1984) (holding similar to *Barson, supra*).
    [112]*Harris v. Department of Agric.*, 86 FMSR 5239 (MSPB 1986); *West v. Department of the Treasury*, 86 FMSR 5235 (MSPB 1986).
    [113]*Koch v. Department of Commerce, supra* note 111.
    [114]*Anderson v. HHS*, 25 MSPR 33 (1984) (though agency could not prove competitive area was properly defined, fees were denied because it could not be said that RIF was clearly improper, wholly without merit, or taken in bad faith, and it was not readily apparent that agency should have known it would not prevail; *Johnson v. Department of the Interior*, 84 FMSR 5933 (MSPB 1984).
    [115]*Trowell v. Postal Serv.*, 3 MSPB 117, 80 FMSR 5085 (1980).

Based upon this finding, the Board concluded that the "agency knew or should have known that it would not prevail on the merits when it brought the proceeding." In another case, the Board held that even though the underlying action may have been proper, negligent presentation of the case at the hearing warrants fees in the interest of justice.[116] Where the agency in another forum has lost on the essential merits of the case that is before the MSPB, then the agency knew or should have known it would also lose before the MSPB.[117] Likewise, where the agency knew or should have known that its alleged new evidence was not new and, therefore, that it would lose on appeal, fees are warranted.[118]

Agency Prevails in Initial Decision

Being successful in the initial decision is no guarantee that the agency will not ultimately be liable for the appellant's attorney's fees. In one case, the agency action was upheld by the administrative judge only to be reversed by the Board. Following the Board's favorable decision, the employee requested an award of attorney's fees from the administrative judge. The administrative judge denied the request for attorney's fees because the case was "one of first impression," the issue was part of an evolving area of law, and the agency had prevailed in the initial decision. The Board reversed. Since the agency's actions were found to be improper in every material aspect as alleged by the appellant, the agency's actions were clearly without merit. Furthermore, the Board noted, the decision was based upon long-established regulatory language and upon a court decision that preceded the agency's action by more than two years. The Board noted specifically that prevailing on the merits before the administrative judge is not a sufficient basis for finding that an award of fees is not warranted after the Board has subsequently reversed the administrative judge's decision on the merits.[119]

Gross Procedural Error

An award of fees on the basis of "gross procedural error" requires a determination that the error amounted to more than a simple "harmful

---

[116]Compton v. Department of Energy, 9 MSPB 91, 82 FMSR 5016 (1982).

[117]An employee grieved an unacceptable performance rating and subsequently appealed to MSPB when the rating was used as the basis for a demotion action. Prior to the MSPB hearing, the grievance hearing examiner recommended that the employee receive a higher rating. Since the agency did not produce any probative evidence at the MSPB hearing that it had not presented to the grievance hearing examiner, the administrative judge concluded that the agency knew or should have known that it would not prevail on the merits of the demotion. Thus, attorney's fees were allowed. Blumenson v. HHS, 86 FMSR 5161 (MSPB 1986).

[118]Keely v. MSPB, supra note 110, at 249.

[119]Phillips v. Department of Transp., 86 FMSR 5114 (MSPB 1986).

procedural error."[120] Failure by the agency to consider alternative penalties does not by itself, constitute gross procedural error.[121]

Personal Malice in Taking the Agency Action

The employee is entitled to attorney's fees when "ill will or negligence" on the part of agency officials "tainted the action" to an "unconscionable" degree.[122] However, a recommending official's simple malice or ill will short of malice [which] played 'a part in the agency's action . . . did not by itself fulfill the interest of justice standard.'"[123]

Settlements and the "Interest of Justice"

Like most other waivers of a statutory right, the waiver of attorney's fees will not be inferred by the MSPB from general language in a settlement agreement. For the agency to successfully argue that an employee waived the right to seek attorney's fees, there must be express language to that effect in the settlement agreement.[124] When a settlement agreement does not clearly resolve the attorney's fee issue or when the agency cancels the action prior to any hearing on the matter, the burden of establishing entitlement to an attorney's fee award under 5 U.S.C. 7701(g)(1) rests with the appellant. Although the burden is especially difficult to meet in a case where appellant has had no opportunity to develop evidence at a hearing, the burden must be met.[125] Thus, when there has been no hearing on the merits, it may be necessary for the administrative judge to convene a hearing on the fee motion.[126]

Entitlement Under Title VII of the Civil Rights Act

General

To be entitled to attorney's fees under Title VII of the Civil Rights Act of 1964, the employee must be the prevailing party.[127] The "prevailing party" concept is discussed above under "Entitlement Before the

---

[120]*Lampack v. Postal Serv.*, 86 FMSR 5024 (MSPB 1986).
[121]*Id.* See also *Tri v. SEC*, 85 FMSR 5227 (MSPB 1985).
[122]*O'Donnell v. Department of the Interior*, 2 MSPB 604, 607, 80 FMSR 7016 (1980).
[123]*Kling v. Department of Justice*, 2 MSPB 620, 623, 80 FMSR 7018 (1980).
[124]*Franks v. Department of the Treasury*, 12 MSPB 154, 82 FMSR 5465 (1982).
[125]*Ingram v. Veterans Admin.*, 86 FMSR 5025 (MSPB 1986); *Kemper v. HUD*, 81 FMSR 5573, 8 MSPB 567 (1981); *Nelson v. Defense Mapping Agency*, 81 FMSR 5312, 6 MSPB 71 (1981); *Miller v. Department of Justice*, 85 FMSR 5380 (MSPB 1985).
[126]*Payne v. Department of the Interior*, 86 FMSR 5021 (MSPB 1986).
[127]42 U.S.C. 2000e-16.

ATTORNEY'S FEES IN LITIGATION OF FEDERAL PERSONNEL DISPUTES   365

Merit Systems Protection Board." The Title VII standard applies to court decisions as well as administrative determinations by an agency, the MSPB, or the EEOC, in which there is a finding of discrimination based upon race, color, religion, sex, or national origin or where there is a finding of retaliation for exercising EEO rights.[128] Since the Rehabilitation Act was amended in 1978 to apply Title VII rights, procedures, and remedies to federal employees, a finding of handicap discrimination would also create an entitlement to attorney's fees.[129] The one form of prohibited discrimination for which attorney's fees are not available under Title VII is age discrimination.[130] However, fees may still be recovered in age discrimination cases using the Equal Access to Justice Act or possibly by using the Back Pay Act.[131]

---

[128]29 C.F.R. 1613.271; 5 U.S.C. 7701(g)(2). Authority for the payment of attorney's fees involving sex discrimination under the Equal Pay Act appears at 29 U.S.C. 216(b). At least one court has held that bridge awards or interim attorney's fees are available in Title VII actions against the federal government. *Brown v. Marsh*, 707 F. Supp. 21, 89 FEOR 5026 (D.D.C. 1989).

[129]29 U.S.C. 794a(a)(1).

[130]The Age Discrimination in Employment Act (ADEA) is part of the Fair Labor Standards Act (FLSA). However, when Congress amended the ADEA to include employees of the federal government, it did not make all the provisions of the FLSA available to federal employees. *Lehman v. Nakshian*, 453 U.S. 156, 26 FEP Cases 65 (1981) (federal employee in age discrimination suit is not entitled to jury trial in action against federal government under amendments that apply ADEA to federal employees). *Muth v. Marsh*, 525 F. Supp. 604, 27 FEP Cases 262 (D.D.C. 1981) and *Nunes-Correia v. Haig*, 543 F. Supp. 812 (D.D.C. 1982) apply the *Nakshian* principle to deny attorney's fees under the ADEA in an action by an employee against the federal government. However, some courts have awarded fees to federal employees for work done in the judicial process. *Sterling v. Lehman*, 574 F. Supp. 415, 417, 40 FEP Cases 707 (N.D. Cal. 1983); *Krodel v. Young*, 576 F. Supp. 393, 395, 33 FEP Cases 701 (D.D.C. 1983); *Defries v. Haarhues*, 488 F. Supp. 1037, 1045, 25 FEP Cases 393 (C.D. Ill. 1980); *Smith v. OPM*, 778 F.2d 258, 264, 39 FEP Cases 1851 (5th Cir. 1985); *Johnson v. Lehman*, 679 F.2d 918, 919, 28 FEP Cases 1485 (D.C. Cir. 1982).

[131]In both *Muth v. Marsh, supra* note 130, and *Nunes-Correia v. Haig, supra* note 130, the courts recognized the applicability of the Equal Access to Justice Act (EAJA) in age discrimination cases tried in federal court. However, the EAJA cannot be used to recover fees for an attorney's services in the administrative proceeding of an age discrimination complaint (see "Entitlement Under The Equal Access to Justice Act, Administrative Proceedings," *infra*). Nevertheless, it does appear that attorney's fees would be recoverable in an age discrimination case in either the administrative process or in court using the Back Pay Act. Though we can find no case in which this approach has been argued, the theory may be summarized as follows. The Back Pay Act refers one to the standards of 5 U.S.C. 7701(g). That section provides for the payment of fees to prevailing parties when the agency has committed a prohibited personnel practice. Prohibited personnel practices include a violation of the ADEA. See 5 U.S.C. 2302(b)(1). Various administrative authorities and federal courts are authorized to make fee awards under the Back Pay Act (see "Entitlement Under the Back Pay Act," *supra*). Therefore, there appears to be a basis for paying attorney's fees in both administrative and judicial proceedings in age discrimination cases whenever the relief ordered involves back pay.

Fees in the Administrative Complaint Process

The EEOC regulation provides that attorney's fees may be awarded as a result of a resolution of the complaint at any point in the EEO complaint process. If the complaint is resolved, but the attorney's fee issue (entitlement or reasonable amount or both) cannot be resolved, the attorney's fees issue may be carried to the agency head for determination, to the EEOC for review of the agency decision, or to the federal district court as any other disputed EEO issue. [132] Attorney's fees are payable only for services rendered after the formal complaint has been filed and after the employee has notified the agency that he or she is represented by an attorney. [133] Fees are also allowable "for a reasonable period of time prior to the notification of representation for any services performed in reaching a determination to represent the complainant." [134]

Entitlement Under the Equal Access to Justice Act

The Equal Access to Justice Act (EAJA) of 1980 provides for the award of attorney's fees against the Federal Government in certain proceedings. One provision of the Act deals with the award of fees in administrative proceedings and two provisions deal with the award of fees in judicial proceedings. [135] As enacted, [136] a three-year "sunset" applied to part of the law. [137] On August 5, 1985, the Act was reauthorized making permanent those provisions which were originally enacted as a three-year experiment. [138]

Timely Filing

The party seeking fees under the EAJA must submit an application for fees within 30 days of final judgment. [139] When a case is settled and the fee award is not part of the settlement, the time limit would begin to run

---

[132] 29 C.F.R. 1613.217.
[133] 29 C.F.R. 1613.271(c)(1)(iv).
[134] 29 C.F.R. 1613.271(c)(1)(iv).
[135] 5 U.S.C. 504 and 28 U.S.C. 2412, respectively.
[136] Title II of Pub. L. No. 96-481, 94 Stat. 2325 (1980) became effective on October 1, 1981.
[137] The "sunset" applied to 28 U.S.C. 2412(d) and 5 U.S.C. 504.
[138] Pub. L. No. 99-80, 99 Stat. 183 (1985).
[139] 28 U.S.C. 2412(d)(1)(B). "Final judgment" is defined as "a judgment that is final and not appealable and including an order of settlement." 28 U.S.C. 2412(d)(2)(G). This time limit is jurisdictional and cannot be waived. *Monark Boat Co. v. NLRB*, 708 F.2d 1322, 113 LRRM 2896 (8th Cir. 1983). The purpose is to allow the filing of fee applications after a case has been fully appealed. H.R. REP. No. 99-120, 99th Cong., 1st Sess. (1985), at 18.

on the date that the proceeding is dismissed pursuant to the settlement or when the adjudicative officer approves the settlement.[140]

Administrative Proceedings

Regarding administrative proceedings, the provision requires a federal agency, which conducts an "adversary adjudication," to award attorney's fees and other expenses to a party prevailing against the agency. However, the definition of adversary adjudication excludes "a matter subject to subsequent trial of the law and the facts de novo in a court."[141] Thus, the administrative complaint process for EEO cases is not an adversary adjudication under this definition.[142] Since the EAJA definition of "adversary adjudication" excludes cases involving "tenure of an employee," the Federal Circuit has held that the EAJA does not apply to MSPB proceedings that involve the issue of tenure.[143] It has also been held that arbitration hearings do not constitute adversary adjudication under the EAJA. Therefore, an arbitrator may not award fees under the EAJA.[144] While unfair labor practice proceedings are an adversary

---

[140]H.R. REP. No. 99-120, at 18, n.26, supplemented by H.R. REP. No. 99-120, Part 2, 99th Cong., 1st Sess. (1985), at 6. The footnote continues as follows:

It should also be noted that in some cases a "settlement" does not necessarily produce an "order" but rather a dismissal with consent. The court should avoid an overly technical construction of these terms. This section should not be used as a trap for the unwary resulting in the unwarranted denial of fees.

If the Government does not appeal an adverse decision, the thirty-day period would begin to run upon expiration of the time for filing the notice of appeal of a petition for certiorari. Thus, appealable orders include all discretionary appeals and include writs of certiorari. When the Government dismisses an appeal, the date of dismissal commences the thirty-day period. In a case remanded by a court of appeals for entry of judgment, the thirty days would commence on expiration of the time for appealing the judgment on remand.

Upon denial of a petition for certiorari, the thirty-day period would begin when the time to seek rehearing expires. For Supreme Court cases heard on the merits, the expiration of the time for seeking rehearing will begin the thirty-day period in any case which is not remanded for entry of judgment. A similar analysis applies in direct appeal cases.

Fee petitions may be filed before a "final judgment." If the court determines that an award of interim fees is inappropriate, the petition should be treated as if it were filed during the thirty-day period following the final decision. The overly technical approach in *Auke Bay Concerned Citizens' Advisory Council v. Marsh*, 755 F.2d 717 (9th Cir. 1985) should be avoided.

[141]5 U.S.C. 554(a)(1) and (2).

[142]*Muth v. Marsh, supra* note 130, at 609 n.45 (court specifically held that attorney's fees were not available for administrative processing of claims of discrimination because administrative proceedings did not constitute "adversary adjudication").

[143]*Gavette v. OPM*, 808 F.2d 1456 (Fed. Cir. 1987).

[144]*Army Corps. of Eng'rs and NFFE, Local 639*, 17 FLRA 424, 85 FLRR 1-1067 (1985).

adjudication for purposes of the EAJA, a union must be the "responding party" in order to recover fees from the General Counsel of the FLRA.[145] It, therefore, appears that the only administrative proceedings in federal personnel litigation that meet the adversary adjudication criteria are unfair labor practice proceedings. In such cases, fees are available only if the successful responding party is a union.[146]

The entitlement standards applied in administrative proceedings for awarding fees under the EAJA are the same as those applied by the courts under the EAJA. Therefore, a discussion of these entitlement standards appears in the next section.

Judicial Proceedings

The Equal Access to Justice Act changed existing law regarding attorney's fees in judicial proceedings in two ways. First, it allows courts to award fees to a prevailing party in any civil act brought by or against the Federal Government where the common law or the express provision of a statute would permit an award of attorney's fees against any other party.[147] The principal common law grounds for attorney's fees are the "bad-faith" and "common-fund" theories. Under the bad-faith theory, a court may award attorney's fees where a party has acted in bad faith, vexatiously, wantonly, or for oppressive reasons. The common fund (or "common benefit") theory allows an award to a party whose successful legal action has created or preserved a fund of money or obtained a benefit for others as well as for the successful party. The fees may be obtained from the fund or from other parties, who are to enjoy the benefits of the litigation.[148] This section of the EAJA is rarely relied upon since the bad-faith theory is more stringent than the "substantially justified" theory in the next section of the EAJA and since it is generally accepted that the common fund theory is

---

[145]*Internal Revenue Serv., Dist., Region, & Nat'l Office Units and NTEU*, 16 FLRA 904, 84 FLRR 1-1794 (1984).

[146]The FLRA has concluded that the attorney's fee provisions of the EAJA were available only to a respondent, other than the United States, who prevailed against the General Counsel of FLRA in an unfair labor practice proceeding. The union, as the charging party, was not entitled to an award of fees from the charged party under the EAJA. The ALJ also declined to make such an award under the Authority's remedial powers due to the ambiguities in the union proposals which management wrongly declared nonnegotiable. *Internal Revenue Serv., Dist., Region, & Nat'l Office Units and NTEU*, *supra* note 145.

[147]28 U.S.C. 2412(b). Though seldom used for the reasons discussed in the text, one advantage to proceeding under this provision is that the $75 cap on fees does not apply to fee awards under this provision.

[148]H.R. REP. No. 96-1418, 96th Cong., 2d Sess. (1980), at 8.

not applicable when fees are sought from the government rather than from a common fund.[149]

Thus, our focus here is on the second provision in the EAJA for judicial awards of fees against the government. Under the second provision, courts are authorized to award fees to "prevailing parties" against the Federal Government in civil actions unless the court finds (1) that the position of the Federal Government was substantially justified, or (2) that special circumstances make an award unjust.[150] Since the prevailing party concept under the EAJA appears to be the same as under Title VII of the Civil Rights Act and under section 7701(g) of Title 5, the above discussion of prevailing party applies to the EAJA as well.[151]

Like section 7701(g)(1), the EAJA is not an automatic fee-shifting device in cases in which the claimant prevails against the government. However, where section 7701(g)(1) requires that the employee prove that an award of fees is warranted "in the interest of justice," the EAJA places the burden on the Federal Government to prove that an award of fees is not appropriate. The government may meet its burden by proving either that the position of the United States was "substantially justified" or by proving that "special circumstances make an award unjust."

We examine first the concept that the position of the United States was substantially justified.[152] In evaluating the position of the United States, the court is to examine both the position taken during the litigation as well as to the agency's act or failure to act, which was the basis of the civil action.[153] Whether the position of the United States was substantially justified is to be determined on the basis of the record, which is made in the civil action itself.[154] The Federal Circuit has ruled that the "substantial justification" standard is more stringent than "mere reasonableness."[155] That circuit also "requires that the Government show that it

---

[149]*McQuiston v. Marsh*, 707 F.2d 1082 (9th Cir. 1983); *Holbrook v. Pitt*, 748 F.2d 1168 (7th Cir. 1984); *Jordan v. Heckler*, 744 F.2d 1397 (10th Cir. 1984); *Grace v. Burger*, 763 F.2d 457 (D.C. Cir. 1985).

[150]28 U.S.C. 2412(d).

[151]H.R. REP. No. 96-1418, 96th Cong., 2d Sess. (1980), reprinted in 1980 U.S. CODE CONG. & ADMIN. NEWS 4984, 4990; *Austin v. Department of Commerce*, 742 F.2d 1417, 84 FMSR 7044 (Fed. Cir. 1984).

[152]For a discussion of "substantially justified" see also *Alspach v. District Director of Internal Revenue Serv.*, 527 F. Supp. 225 (D. Md. 1981); *Globe v. United States*, 553 F. Supp. 7 (D.D.C. 1982); *Berman v. Schweiker*, 531 F. Supp. 1149 (N.D. Ill. 1982).

[153]28 U.S.C. 2412(d)(2)(D). The 1985 amendments to the EAJA make it clear that Congress rejected the cases defining the "position of the United States" as being limited to the litigation position only.

[154]28 U.S.C. 2412(d)(1)(B).

[155]*Schunemeyer v. United States*, 776 F.2d 329 (Fed. Cir. 1985).

was *clearly* reasonable in asserting its position. . . ."[156] Thus, that circuit views the interest of justice standard of section 7701(g) as "a more difficult standard" than the substantial evidence standard.[157] However, the full Court of Appeals for the Eighth Circuit reversed a panel decision that held that a liberal reading of the EAJA was more reflective of congressional intent. The full court concluded that the EAJA should be narrowly interpreted.[158] Fees have been awarded under the EAJA when the FLRA General Counsel's complaint against a union was dismissed for lack of jurisdiction. The position of the General Counsel was "not substantially justified because it [was] not reasonable in the law."[159]

Attorney's fees are not to be paid to prevailing parties under the EAJA where "special circumstances make an award unjust."[160] The principal purpose of this limitation is to insure that the government is not deterred from advancing new legal theories.[161] Nevertheless, in advancing even "novel" theories, the government may still be liable for fees if the government's position is contrary to the "great weight of statutory, regulatory and judicial authority."[162]

Entitlement to Fee Awards to the Government

The prior discussion involves fee awards from the government to a successful employee or applicant for employment. However, in certain limited circumstances, the government can recover certain monetary awards from unsuccessful litigants. The Federal Circuit put the parties on notice in 1982 that in future cases that were deemed to be frivolous employee appeals, the employee-appellant and counsel could be assessed damages and costs in accordance with Rule 38 of the Federal Rules of Appellate Procedure.[163] Since that time, the Federal Circuit has made

---

[156]*Gavette v. OPM*, 785 F.2d 1576, 1579 (Fed. Cir. 1986) (emphasis in original).
[157]*Id.*, at 1576; *Keely v. MSPB*, 793 F.2d 1273, 86 FMSR 7058 (Fed. Cir. 1986).
[158]*Premachandra v. Mitts*, 753 F.2d 635 (8th Cir. 1985) (en banc).
[159]*AFGE, Local 495, Veterans Admin. Medical Center, Tucson, Ariz. and Linda S. Moore*, Case No. 8-CO-20006-2, 22 GERR 929 (FLRA, ALJ 1984).
[160]For a discussion of "special circumstances" see also *Matthews v. United States*, 526 F. Supp. 993 (M.D. Ga. 1981); *Metropolitan Nat'l Bank of Farmington v. United States*, 49 AFTR 2d (P.H.) 82-1090 (E.D. Mich. 1982).
[161]S. REP. No. 96-253, 96th Cong., 1st Sess., at 7, states in pertinent part as follows: "This "safety valve" helps to insure that the government is not deterred from advancing in good faith the novel but credible extensions and interpretation of the law that often underlie vigorous enforcement efforts. It also gives the court discretion to deny awards where equitable considerations dictate an award should not be made.
[162]*Devine v. Sutermeister*, 733 F.2d 892, 84 FLRR 1-8053 (Fed. Cir. 1984).
[163]*Asberry v. Postal Serv.*, 692 F.2d 1378, 82 FMSR 7051 (Fed. Cir. 1982).

awards to the government ranging from $100 to $84,000.[164] On the other hand, the MSPB refuses to award fees to the government as a sanction for frivolous appeals by employees because it would be inconsistent with the intention of Congress to grant a right of appeal and to protect employees from reprisal for their exercise of that right.[165]

Reasonable Amount

After the agency, arbitrator, MSPB, EEOC, FLRA, federal court, or other authority determines that an employee is entitled to attorney's fees, the final issue is determining how much should be paid in reimbursement. Determining the proper amount involves essentially the same criteria, regardless of which of the four fee-shifting statutes is being used with three exceptions.

Variations Among the Statutes

The first exception is that section 7701(g)(1) does not provide for the payment of "costs" while costs are available under Title VII of the Civil Rights Act and the Equal Access to Justice Act.[166] The costs that are not recoverable under section 7701(g)(1) are "taxable costs" as that term is defined under 28 U.S.C. 1920. Taxable costs include stenographers, printing, and marshal's fees.[167] Also included among taxable costs are those for expert witnesses, transcripts, depositions, subpoenas, and duplicating expenses.[168] While taxable costs are not reimbursable under section 7701(g)(1), certain limited "out-of-pocket expenses" are included

---

[164]*Moir v. Department of the Treasury*, 754 F.2d 341, 85 FMSR 7005 (Fed. Cir. 1985) (attempting to reinstate an appeal made "frivolous" by obvious untimeliness); *Griessenauer v. Department of Energy*, 754 F.2d 361, 85 FMSR 7007 (Fed. Cir. 1985) (utter lack of any merit to petitioner's arguments); *Toepfer v. Federal Aviation Admin.*, 792 F.2d 1102, 86 FMSR 7049 (Fed. Cir. 1986); *Amodeo v. Federal Aviation Admin.*, 788 F.2d 1549 (Fed. Cir. 1986), *cert. denied*, 479 U.S. 849 (1986) (court awarded agency attorney's fees of $5,000 against petitioner's counsel for pursuing 10 cases involving issues court had already clearly resolved). See also *Harris v. Marsh*, 679 F. Supp. 1204 (E.D.N.C. 1987) in which court awarded $84,000 to government as sanctions and fees against plaintiffs and their lawyers for bringing a suit that was a senseless waste of taxpayer dollars and limited court time.

[165]*Lewis v. Department of the Army*, 86 FMSR 5311 (MSPB 1986); *Acker v. GSA*, 83 FMSR 1086 (MSPB 1983).

[166]29 U.S.C. 2000e-5(k) and 2412(a).

[167]*Bennett v. Department of the Navy*, 699 F.2d 1140, 83 FMSR 7009 (Fed. Cir. 1983).

[168]*Koch v. Department of Commerce*, 84 FMSR 7004 (MSPB 1984); *Mitchell v. HHS*, 84 FMSR 7005 (MSPB 1984); *Ste. Marie v. Eastern R.R. Ass'n*, 497 F.Supp. 800 (S.D.N.Y. 1980), *rev'd on other grounds*, 605 F.2d 395 (2d Cir. 1981).

in the definition of reimbursable fees under section 7701(g)(1). These include telephone calls, travel, and postage.[169] Thus, an award of fees under Title VII or the EAJA could properly include out-of-pocket expenses as well as costs such as those for expert witnesses, transcripts, depositions, subpoenas, and necessary duplicating.[170]

The second difference in calculating attorney's fees among these various statutes is that the EAJA has a cap of $75 per hour.[171] A court may award a higher fee if it determines that there has been an increase in the cost of living or that a special factor exists, such as the limited availability of qualified attorneys.[172]

These criteria for increasing an award above $75 per hour are far more limited than the criteria used under other statutes for adjusting a fee upward.[173] At the same time, it must be remembered that this provision of the EAJA does not mean that counsel are automatically entitled to receive $75 per hour. A fee applicant is still only entitled to receive the rate prevailing in the particular community for similar work. Thus, as with any of the other statutes, the moving party still must prove a reasonable hourly rate.

The third difference in the criteria for determining a proper amount for a fee award are the provisions for interest. The 1985 amendments to the EAJA allow an award of postjudgment interest if the United States appeals an award of costs or fees and the original award is affirmed, in whole or in part and the 1987 amendments to the Back Pay Act allow interest on back pay awards.[174] Title VII of the Civil Rights Act and section 7701(g) make no such provision for an award of interest.[175]

---

[169]*Bennett v. Department of the Navy, supra* note 167. Early MSPB cases included "photocopying" expenses in the list of allowable "costs" under 5 U.S.C. 7701(g)(1). *O'Donnell v. Department of the Interior,* 2 MSPB 604, 612 n.66, 80 FMSR 7016 (1980). However, the Federal Circuit subsequently ruled that photocopying expenses were not properly included because they were "costs" under 28 U.S.C. 1920. *Bennett v. Department of the Navy, supra.*

[170]*Ste. Marie v. Eastern R.R. Ass'n, supra* note 168; *Mitchell v. HHS, supra* note 168.

[171]28 U.S.C. 2412(d). As noted in "Entitlement," *supra,* the $75 cap applies only to 5 U.S.C. 2412(d) fee awards. Sec. 2412(b) has no such cap, but the entitlement standards are much more difficult to meet.

[172]28 U.S.C. 2412(d)(2)(A).

[173]*Action on Smoking & Health v. Civil Aeronautics Bd.,* 724 F.2d 211 (D.C. Cir. 1984). See "Adjusting the Lodestar Upward," *infra.*

[174]28 U.S.C. 2412(f). Interest under the EAJA must be paid on the amount affirmed. Interest runs from the date of the award until the day before the mandate of affirmance. The interest rate should be equal to the common issue yield equivalent of 52-week U.S. Treasury bills sold at the auction immediately prior to the date of judgment.

5 U.S.C. 5596(b)(2). Interest under the Back Pay Act is to be computed from the effective date of the unjustified or unwarranted personnel action and ending on a date not more than 30 days before the date on which payment is made.

[175]See, e.g., *Library of Congress v. Shaw,* 478 U.S. 310, 41 FEP Cases 85 (1986), in which the Court ruled that interest on attorney's fees cannot be awarded under Title VII of

"Lodestar" Criteria

With the three exceptions stated above, the various statutes use common concepts to calculate a reasonable amount for the attorney's fee.[176] There are two important lines of federal cases on the subject of calculating a reasonable amount. *Johnson v. Georgia Highway Express*,[177] sets forth in some detail 12 criteria that are to be used in

---

the Civil Rights Act because there is no express waiver of sovereign immunity for such interest awards against the United States. However, the EEOC has taken the position that when back pay is awarded in an EEO case, Back Pay Act amendment, discussed at *supra* note 174, provides a basis for awarding interest. *Thompkins v. Ball*, Request No. 05890432 (EEOC June 14, 1989).

[176]In *Morrow v. Department of the Army*, 11 MSPB 205 (1982), the Board held that the method of computing fees authorized by 5 U.S.C. 7701(g)(2) for discrimination cases would be identical to that used for computation pursuant to 5 U.S.C. 7701(g)(1). See also *Mitchell v. HHS, supra* note 168. Furthermore, an "appropriate authority," who is awarding fees under the Back Pay Act, must follow the precedent established by MSPB and by the courts in their review of MSPB attorney's fees decisions. 5 U.S.C. 5596(b)(1)(A)(ii); CONG. REC., at S14295 (Aug. 24, 1978; and see Carl D. Moore, *Awarding Attorney's Fees in Federal Sector Arbitration*, 37 ARB. J. (4)38 (1982); Bufe and Ferris, *A Second View of Awarding Attorney's Fees in Federal Sector* Arbitration, 38 ARB. J. (1) (1983).

[177]488 F.2d 714, 7 FEP Cases 1 (5th Cir. 1974). The *Johnson* factors were summarized by the Board in *Kling v. Department of Justice*, 2 MSPB 620, 626 n.6, 80 FMSR 7018 (1980) as follows:

1. Time and labor required. Hours claimed must be weighed against the judge's own knowledge and experience of the time required for similar activities. The possibility of duplication of efforts should be scrutinized. Legal work should be distinguished from nonlegal work, which commands a lesser rate.

2. Novelty and difficulty of issues: A case of first impression requires more research, which deserves compensation, but time merely devoted to learning a new field of law is an investment for future cases.

3. Skill requisite to properly perform the legal service. Observation of the attorney's work product, preparation, and ability are important to this factor.

4. The preclusion of other employment due to acceptance of the case, through foreclosure of other business due to conflicts of interest or through inability to use time spent on the client's behalf for other purposes.

5. The customary fee for similar work in the community.

6. Whether there is a fixed or contingent fee.

7. Time limitations imposed by the client or circumstances. Some premium should be recognized for priority work which delays the attorney's other work.

8. Amount involved and result. The amount of damages, for example, may be considered, but is not controlling. The effect of the case on the development of the law, or in benefiting similarly situated persons, should be considered.

9. The experience, reputation, and ability of the attorney. Expertise in a specialized field and demonstrated skill and ability are pertinent.

10. The undesirability of the case. Where an unpopular case has been undertaken that may have an economic impact on the attorney's practice, this factor can be considered.

11. The nature and length of the professional relationship with the client. A lawyer or firm may vary the fee in light of the professional relationship with the client.

12. Awards in similar cases.

evaluating the reasonableness of a fee request. While *Johnson* and its progeny provide very important guidance on the issues to be considered in attorney's fee cases, this line of cases did not provide a practical method for evaluating these various factors. The other line of cases filled this gap by providing a simple formula for the calculation. This second line of cases insists that many of the *Johnson* factors are accounted for by two objective variables: the lawyer's customary hourly billing rate multiplied by the number of hours devoted to the case. This product is the so-called "lodestar" or starting point for fee setting.[178] Most courts now use the lodestar approach for calculating the fee, while using the *Johnson* criteria when it is necessary to analyze the reasonableness of the hours claimed or to analyze the reasonableness of the claimed hourly rate or to analyze a request to adjust the lodestar up or down.[179] Certainly this is the approach taken by the MSPB.[180]

As a practical matter, the petitioner's attorney must submit the fee agreement with the client or a statement of its terms, the number of hours claimed for the case, and specific evidence of the prevailing community rate for similar work.[181] The fee arrangement establishes a rebuttable presumption that it is the maximum reasonable fee that could be awarded in the case.[182] Similar considerations arise when an attorney reduces the

---

[178]*Hensley v. Eckerhart*, 461 U.S. 424, n.9, 31 FEP Cases 1169 (1983). See also *Lindy Bros. Builders v. American Radiator & Standard Sanitary Corp.*, 487 F.2d 161 (3d Cir. 1973). See, e.g., *Northcross v. Board of Educ.*, 611 F.2d 624 (6th Cir. 1979), *cert. denied*, 447 U.S. 911 (1980); *Hughes v. Repko*, 578 F.2d 483 (3d Cir. 1978); *King v. Greenblatt*, 560 F.2d 1024 (1st Cir. 1977), *cert. denied*, 438 U.S. 916 (1978); *NTEU v. Nixon*, 521 F.2d 317 (D.C. Cir. 1975); *Grunin v. International House of Pancakes*, 513 F.2d 114 (8th Cir. 1975), *cert. denied*, 423 U.S. 864 (1976); *City of Detroit v. Grinnell Corp.*, 495 F.2d 448 (2d Cir. 1974).

[179]*Pennsylvania v. Delaware Valley Citizens' Council*, 478 U.S. 546, 54 USLC 5017 (1986); *City of Riverside v. Rivera*, 477 U.S. 561, 41 FEP Cases 65 (1986); *Pennsylvania v. Delaware Valley Citizens' Council*, 483 U.S. 711, 45 FEP Cases 1750 (1987); *Hensley v. Eckerhart*, 461 U.S. 424, 31 FEP Cases 1169 (1983).

[180]*Kling v. Department of Justice*, *supra* note 177.

[181]*Gerlach v. Federal Trade Comm'n*, 84 FMSR 7015 (MSPB 1984); *Mitchell v. HHS*, *supra* note 168. Affidavits from local attorneys must recite "the precise fees that attorneys with similar qualifications have received from fee paying clients in comparable cases" rather than "generalized 'information and belief' affidavits from friendly attorneys." *National Ass'n of Concerned Veterans v. Secretary of Defense*, 675 F.2d 1319, 28 FEP Cases 1134 (D.C. Cir. 1982). With regard to the billing practice of the fee applicant, the court said the attorney "may be required to state the rate at which he actually billed his time in other cases during the period he was performing the services for which he seeks compensation from the defendant." *Id.*, at 1326.

[182]*Lassiter v. Department of the Navy*, 86 FMSR 5041 (MSPB 1986); *O'Donnell v. Department of the Interior*, 2 MSPB 604, 80 FMSR 7016 (1980). *Gerlach v. Federal Trade Comm'n*, *supra* note 181 (amount agreed to between petitioner and counsel is generally presumed by Board to represent maximum reasonable fee which may be awarded); *Ishikawa v. Department of Labor*, 85 FMSR 5055 (MSPB 1985) (counsel may overcome

standard fee in light of the professional relationship with the client. Where an attorney requested $12,829, even though he had only charged the employee's union $6,100 under a reduced-rate formula for a long-term client, the MSPB held that the agreement represented the maximum reasonable fee to be awarded.[183]

The application should also provide information from which the Board can conclude that the attorney has billed sufficient work to establish that the rate reflects a market value for his services.[184] An attorney, who varies rates according to the kind of case he or she is handling, should state the average rate he or she charges in cases similar to the one for which the fee award is sought.[185]

Considerable documentation is needed to support an award of attorney's fees. Courts will substantially discount or refuse to accept a simple list of hours without important specifics such as dates and the nature of the work performed.[186] Where multiple claims are litigated and a party prevails on only some of the claims, most courts require attorneys to delineate in the fee request the amount of work performed on each separate claim.[187]

Where the attorney for the fee applicant is from out-of-town, the community where the case was tried is normally the relevant community for determining the prevailing community rate. However, an out-of-town attorney can be compensated at the higher prevailing rate where he or she customarily practices if it was reasonably necessary for the client to employ nonlocal counsel.[188]

The agency may defeat requested travel expenses for out-of-town counsel by showing that there were local attorneys with the specialized expertise of appellant's chosen representative.[189] However, merely show-

---

presumption by showing that hourly rate of $30 charged by her to appellant was not based upon market place considerations, but upon appellant's reduced ability to pay her normal billing rate, which counsel established to be $75 per hour).

[183]O'Donnell v. Department of the Interior, supra note 182, at 611; Vandiver v. GAO, 7 MSPB 429 (1981).

[184]Mitchell v. HHS, supra note 168.

[185]Id.; Brown v. Department of Commerce, 86 FMSR 5006 (MSPB 1986).

[186]The Supreme Court has stated, "Plaintiffs counsel, of course, is not required to record in great detail how each minute of his time was expended. But at least counsel should identify the general subject matter of his time expenditures." Hensley v. Eckerhart, supra note 179, at n.12, and citing with approval Nadeau v. Helgemoe, 581 F.2d 275 (1st Cir. 1978). See also Hughes v. Repko, supra note 178; Scheriff v. Beck, 452 F. Supp. 1254 (D.Colo. 1978).

[187]King v. Greenblatt, supra note 178; Imprisoned Citizens Union v. Shapp, 473 F.Supp. 1017 (E.D. Pa. 1979); Heigher v. Gatter, 463 F. Supp. 802 (E.D. Pa. 1978).

[188]Id. See also Donnell v. United States, 682 F.2d 240, 251–52 (D.C. Cir. 1982); Avalon Cinema Corp. v. Thompson, 689 F.2d 137, 140–41 (8th Cir. 1982).

[189]Hoover v. Department of the Navy, 86 FMSR 5159 (MSPB 1986).

ing that there were local attorneys who allegedly appear regularly before the MSPB may not be sufficient to carry this burden.[190] Otherwise, travel time is compensable as any other time a lawyer spends on a case.[191] Of course, if the travel time is unnecessary, the time should be subtracted from the total hours claimed.[192] Similarly, if the travel time is reasonable, but the cost of the travel is unnecessarily luxurious, the expenses for travel should be reduced so that they reflect a reasonable amount.[193]

The agency may challenge the reasonableness of the hours claimed and the reasonableness of the hourly rate charged. Due to their superior understanding of the litigation and the desirability of avoiding frequent appellate review of what essentially are factual matters, the administrative judge or district court have discretion in determining the amount of a fee award. However, it is still important that the decision on fees, whether by an arbitrator, administrative judge, district court, or other appropriate authority, "provide a concise but clear explanation of its reasons for the fee award."[194] This is no less true when a party is arguing that the lodestar amount should be increased or decreased.

While the appellant before the MSPB has the burden of proving the elements of the lodestar, the attorney whose request falls short of case law requirements may still receive a fee award. The Board will not deny fees where entitlement has been established "unless the record suggests the hourly rate was unreasonable or the hours claimed were excessive." In such cases, "the fee petition will be subject to disallowance based on the Board's judgment in similar cases before it."[195] Keep in mind, especially as we discuss challenges that the agency may raise to the lodestar calculation, that the petitioner bears the burden of proving the lodestar.

Challenging the Lodestar

The product resulting from the lodestar calculation is not merely a "rough guess" or an "initial approximation of the final award to be made." Rather, it "*is presumed* to be the reasonable fee" to which counsel is entitled.[196] The burden of justifying any deviation from the lodestar rests

---

[190]*Id.*

[191]*Crumbaker v. MSPB*, 781 F.2d 191, 86 FMSR 7002 (Fed. Cir. 1986).

[192]*Id.* See also *Hensley v. Eckerhart*, *supra* note 179.

[193]*Id.*

[194]*Hensley v. Eckerhart*, *supra* note 179, at 437.

[195]*Blumenson v. HHS*, 86 FMSR 5161, p. 266 (MSPB 1986) (administrative judge found that request was "not outrageous" and that he could determine rate based on his own experience even though attorney did not show his billing rate was prevailing rate in community). See also *Crumbaker v. MSPB*, *supra* note 191.

[196]*Pennsylvania v. Delaware Valley Citizens' Council*, *supra* note 179, 54 USLW at 5022 quoting from *Blum v. Stenson*, 465 U.S. 886, 34 FEP Cases 417 (1984).

with the party proposing the deviation.[197] Nevertheless, either party may move to increase or decrease the lodestar due to unusual circumstances. A frequent argument for decreasing the lodestar amount is when the employee receives less than the full requested relief. It is clear that the relationship between the extent of success and the amount of the fee award must be addressed in such circumstances.[198] It is also clear that there is no precise rule or formula for making these determinations.[199] If the claims are distinct, hours spent working on the unsuccessful claims must be excluded. If the claims are related and the employee has won substantial relief, the award of fees should not be reduced "simply because the district court did not adopt each contention raised."[200] However, where the employee achieves only limited success in comparison to the total case, the fee award should be adjusted so that it is reasonable in relation to the results obtained.[201] Finally, it is important to remember that in many employment cases, monetary relief is not the sole measure of the success of the case. Cases that redress important civil and constitutional rights cannot be valued solely in monetary terms. Therefore, it is often inappropriate to require that fees in such cases be proportionate to the monetary relief recovered by the employee.[202]

In evaluating the hours claimed, the agency will want to determine whether any of the hours were duplicative. While the presence of two attorneys during proceedings is not necessarily duplicative, claims for such compensation invite careful scrutiny.[203] The adjudicative officer is in the best position to evaluate the reasonableness of such staffing decisions in terms of the factual or legal complexity of the appeal, the length of the hearing, and the roles of counsel in the case.[204]

Counsel should not necessarily be compensated at the same hourly rate for different types of services.[205] For example, a different rate may be

---

[197]*Lindy Bros. Builders v. American Radiator & Standard Sanitary Corp.*, 540 F.2d 102, 118 (3d Cir. 1976) (en banc). This is the successor to the case cited earlier and is commonly referred to as *Lindy II*. See also *Copeland v. Marshall*, 641 F.2d 880, 892, 23 FEP Cases 967 (D.C. Cir. 1980).

[198]*Hensley v. Eckerhart, supra* note 179, at 438.

[199]*Id.*, at 436.

[200]*Id.*, at 440.

[201]*Id.*

[202]*City of Riverside v. Rivera*, 477 U.S. 561, 41 FEP Cases 65 (1986).

[203]*Hinkle v. Christenson*, 548 F. Supp. 630, 632 (D.D.C. 1982); *Melanson v. Veterans Admin.*, 84 FMSR 5098 (MSPB 1984). In *City of Riverside v. Rivera, supra* note 202, 41 FEP Cases at 69 n.6, the Court approved the award of fees for 197 hours of consultation between co-counsel where the district court specifically found such consultation reasonable under the circumstances of the case.

[204]*New York Ass'n for Retarded Children v. Carey*, 711 F.2d 1136, 1146 (2d Cir. 1983); *Melanson v. Veterans Admin. supra* note 203.

[205]*Pennsylvania v. Delaware Valley Citizens' Council*, 478 U.S. 546, 54 USLW 5017 (1986); *Copeland v. Marshall, supra* note 197.

applicable to trial work versus work outside the trial. Also, counsel may be compensated at paralegal and clerical hourly rates for performing such functions.[206]

While the adjudicator should not automatically accept the hours claimed, to the extent that adequately documented hours are rejected, the adjudicator must indicate some reason for its action. Without adequate explanation for rejecting certain hours, reviewing courts cannot determine whether the adjudicator properly exercised its discretion or made an error of law in its conclusion.[207] In reviewing the requested hours, the adjudicator should weigh the time claimed against the adjudicator's experience and expertise, the experience of counsel, and the complexity of the case.[208] However, mere incantation of such considerations does not relieve the adjudicator from providing a "concise but clear explanation of its reasons."[209]

Adjusting the Lodestar Upward

More often than not, it is the fee applicant who moves to increase the lodestar using some enhancement, bonus, or multiplier theory. The Supreme Court through a series of cases has recently addressed many of the more common enhancement or multiplier issues. In one case, the Court held that the government cannot be liable for interest on an attorney's fee award.[210] Similarly, the Court held that no compensation for the delay in payment of attorney's fees could be paid, because that would amount to nothing more than an attempt to avoid the no-interest rule.[211]

It is presumed that the hourly rate properly compensates the attorney for the quality of work performed. Thus, an upward adjustment is warranted only in the rare case in which the fee applicant offers specific evidence to show that the quality of service "was superior to that one should reasonably expect in light of the hourly rates charged and that the success was 'exceptional.'"[212] Stated another way, in moving for an

---

[206]*Prandini v. National Tea Co.*, 557 F.2d 1015, 16 FEP Cases 963 (3d Cir. 1977); *Johnson v. Georgia Highway Express*, 488 F.2d 714, 7 FEP Cases 1 (5th Cir. 1974).

[207]*Northcross v. Board of Educ.*, 611 F.2d 624, 636–37 (6th Cir. 1979), *cert. denied*, 447 U.S. 911 (1980); *Crumbaker v. MSPB*, *supra* note 191; *Hensley v. Eckerhart*, 461 U.S. 424, 31 FEP Cases 1169 (1983).

[208]*Gabriele v. Southworth*, 712 F.2d 1505, 1507 (1st Cir. 1983); *Crumbaker v. MSPB*, *supra* note 191.

[209]*Crumbaker v. MSPB*, *supra* note 191, citing *Hensley v. Eckerhart*, *supra* note 207.

[210]*Library of Congress v. Shaw*, 478 U.S. 310, 41 FEP Cases 85, 88 (1986). However, see *supra* note 174 for a discussion of the "interest" provision under the EAJA and Back Pay Act.

[211]*Id.*, 41 FEP cases, at 89.

[212]*Blum v. Stenson*, *supra* note 196, at 899.

enhancement for the superior quality of work performed, the applicant must present evidence and the court must make specific findings as to why the lodestar amount was unreasonably low and why the quality of representation was not reflected in the product of the reasonable number of hours times the reasonable hourly rate.[213]

Sometimes counsel will take a case with the agreement that some or all of the fee is contingent upon success. The Supreme Court has held that some enhancement of the fee award is proper to compensate for the risk of nonpayment. The enhancement or "risk premium" can be reflected in the hourly rate that goes into the lodestar calculation, or, if the hourly rate does not include consideration of risk, in an enhancement of the lodestar.[214] In either case, to award such an enhancement or premium, the court must decide whether the applicant's attorneys took the case on a contingent basis, whether they are able to mitigate the risks of nonpayment in any way, and whether other economic risks were aggravated by the contingency of payment. The court then should arrive at an enhancement for risk that parallels, as closely as possible, the premium for contingency that exists in the prevailing market rates.[215] It should be emphasized that this analysis is not aimed at determining the degree of risk associated with winning or losing a particular case. Rather, the issue is the "difference in market treatment of contingent fee cases as a class."[216]

Reasonable Fees for Union Attorneys

There is a generally accepted rule in federal courts that public interest law firms may recover attorney's fees.[217] In such cases, most

---

[213]*Pennsylvania v. Delaware Valley Citizens' Council*, supra note 205, 54 USLW at 5022.

[214]*Pennsylvania v. Delaware Valley Citizens' Council*, 483 U.S. 711, 45 FEP Cases 1750, 1760 (1987) (dissenting opinion) (dissenting opinion joined by concurring opinion on issue of whether a premium for risk of noncompensation actually represented majority opinion on this particular issue). This is a decision subsequent to a 1986 decision by the Supreme Court on fees between the same parties, cited above. Hereinafter, this subsequent decision is cited as *"Delaware Valley Citizens' Council II."* See also *McKenzie v. Kennickell*, No. 88-5155 (D.C. Cir. May 23, 1989).

[215]*Id.*, 45 FEP Cases at 1756.

[216]*Id.*, at 1758. Following this decision, the Federal Circuit issued a decision remanding a case to the MSPB with guidance based upon the *Delaware Valley Citizens Council II* case. *Crumbaker v. MSPB*, 827 F.2d 761, 87 FMSR 7045 (Fed. Cir. 1987). In the subsequent decision, the MSPB accepted two affidavits from attorneys as evidence of the "locality's practice regarding contingency fees." The MSPB granted a fee enhancement of 20%, which was the "minimum enhancement" recited in the affidavits. *Crumbaker v. Department of Labor*, 40 MSPR 71, 79–80 (MSPB 1989).

[217]*Wilderness Soc'y v. Morton*, 495 F.2d 1026 (D.C. Cir. 1974) (en banc), *rev'd on other grounds sub nom. Alyeska Pipeline Serv. Co. v. Wilderness Soc'y*, 421 U.S. 240, 10 FEP

federal courts allow the recovery of "market value" fee awards.[218] A number of courts, however, have distinguished union house counsel from attorneys employed by public interest law firms, limiting the award to union house counsel to actual expenses incurred, rather than the market value of the services rendered. The theory of this approach is that unions, unlike legal aid societies or public interest law firms, have a wide range of interests beyond the legal process. Therefore, to allow a union more than expenses incurred would amount to contributing funds to purposes other than those envisioned by the statutory grant for fee awards and would violate the American Bar Association's Code of Professional Responsibility. Therefore, under this approach, the court would allow "no fee exceeding the expenses incurred by the union."[219]

In contrast, some courts do not differentiate between union attorneys and attorneys who represent public interest law firms.[220] Under this approach, the courts reason that the award of fees to public interest law firms and to union attorneys "effectuates the very same policies."[221] For the most part, these courts were dealing with cases involving violations of the federal discrimination statutes.[222] One court of appeals, however, reviewing a claim for attorney's fees under the Federal Pay Comparability Act, left it to the discretion of the district court to decide whether to adopt the "actual expenses to the union" approach or whether to liken the union to public interest law firms and, therefore, adopt the market value approach.[223]

Cases 826 (1975). See also *Rodriguez v. Taylor*, 569 F.2d 1231, 16 FEP Cases 533 (3d Cir. 1977) (presence of attorney-client relationship suffices to entitle prevailing litigants to receive fee awards); *McManama v. Lukhard*, 464 F. Supp. 38 (W.D. Va 1978); *NAACP v. Bell*, 448 F. Supp. 1164 (D.D.C. 1978); *Mid-Hudson Legal Servs. v. G.&U., Inc.*, 518 F.2d 34 (2d Cir. 1978); *Reynolds v. Abbeyville County School Dist.*, 554 F.2d 638 (4th Cir. 1977).

[218]*Torres v. Sachs*, 538 F.2d 10, 13 (2d Cir. 1976); *Reynolds v. Coomey*, 567 F.2d 1166, 16 FEP Cases 736 (1st Cir. 1978); *Zurcher v. Stanford Daily*, 64 F.R.D. 680 (N.D. Cal. 1974), *aff'd*, 550 F.2d 464 (9th Cir. 1977), *rev'd on other grounds*, 436 U.S. 547 (1978); *Kulkarni v. Nyquist*, 446 F. Supp. 1274 (N.D.N.Y. 1977); *Swann v. Charlotte-Mecklenberg Bd. of Educ.*, 66 F.R.D. 484 (W.D.N.C. 1975).

[219]*Anderson v. Department of the Treasury*, 648 F.2d 1, 3 (D.C. Cir. 1979); *Goodrich v. Department of the Navy*, 733 F.2d 1578 (Fed. Cir. 1984); *Devine v. NTEU*, 805 F.2d 384 (Fed. Cir. 1986), *cert. denied*, 56 USLW 3242 (1987).

[220]*Stephenson v. Simon*, 448 F. Supp. 708, 18 FEP Cases 738 (D.D.C. 1978).

[221]*Id.*, at 709.

[222]*Stephenson v. Simon*, *supra* note 220; see also Note, *Promoting the Vindication of Civil Rights Through the Attorney's Fees Awards Act*, 80 COLUM. L. REV. 346, 365–67 (1980).

[223]*NTEU v. Nixon*, 521 F.2d 317 (D.C. Cir. 1975). Some considerations that have influenced the courts in awarding attorney's fees to public interest firms include the following: Such organizations have limited resources, and counsel for such organizations serve for compensation below that obtainable in the market because they believe the organizations further the public interest. Full fee awards to public interest law firms help finance their work, both in the instant case and in others. *Copeland v. Marshall*, 641 F.2d

In *Powell v. Department of the Treasury*,[224] the MSPB opted to follow the "actual expenses" rule "where the award received by the attorney will be turned over to the union." In *Powell*, the MSPB relied heavily upon two decisions by the Court of Appeals for the District of Columbia.[225] The court of appeals and the MSPB were both influenced by the American Bar Association's Code of Professional Responsibility. According to the court, the Code allows lawyers to work for organizations offering prepaid legal services as long as no profit is derived by the organization from the rendition of legal services. The court also noted that the Code prohibits attorneys from splitting fees with laymen or lay organizations. In this way, the court of appeals and the MSPB distinguished public interest law firms from unions.

The *Powell* decision establishes that if the union attorney employment contract requires him or her to turn over fee awards to the union, then only actual expenses may be awarded. A question left unanswered by the court of appeals decision was whether a union could receive a market value fee award if the fee were paid into a special fund established by the union solely for support of its litigation efforts. The MSPB has since held that such a fund does not qualify the union for market value fee awards.[226] This reasoning has been approved by the Federal Circuit.[227]

On the other hand, at least one court of appeals has specifically rejected the analysis relied upon by the MSPB and the Federal Circuit for denying market rate fees to unions where the union has established a litigation fund.[228] Just as the MSPB and the Federal Circuit have relied upon bar ethics to justify their positions, this court cited a more recent position of the bar, which concluded that the separate litigation fund avoided the ethical problems posed by fee awards to unions.[229]

880, 899, 23 FEP Cases 967 (D.C. Cir. 1980). One court concluded that the legislative history of Title VII indicates that in civil rights cases public interest lawyers should be compensated using the market value approach. *Torres v. Sachs, supra* note 218.

[224]8 MSPB 21 (1981). See also *Wells v. Schweiker*, 12 MSPB 329, 82 FMSR 7053 (1982); *Devine v. NTEU, supra* note 219.

[225]*Anderson v. Department of the Treasury*, 648 F.2d 1 (D.C. Cir. 1979) (per curiam); *NTEU v. Department of the Treasury*, 656 F.2d 848 (D.C. Cir. 1981).

[226]*Wells v. Schweiker, supra* note 224; *Powell v. Department of the Treasury*, 84 FMSR 7003 (MSPB 1984); *Goodrich v. Department of the Navy*, 733 F.2d 1578 (Fed. Cir. 1984).

[227]*Goodrich v. Department of the Navy, supra* note 226; *Devine v. NTEU, supra* note 219.

[228]*Curran v. Department of the Treasury*, 805 F.2d 1406, 1409, (9th Cir. 1986) The Circuit Court for the District of Columbia was the first to suggest that existence of a litigation fund would probably resolve the potential ethical problems created by paying market rates to union attorneys. *NTEU v. Department of the Treasury, supra* note 225, at 849. See also *Jordan v. Department of Justice*, 691 F.2d 514 (D.C. Cir. 1982).

[229]D.C. Bar Committee on Legal Ethics, Opinion 176 (1986), cited in *Curran v. Department of the Treasury, supra* note 228. The opinion states in pertinent part: "It is,

In *Powell*, the MSPB also stated that "where the union is ultimately receiving the fee award for services provided by its salaried attorney, three elements of actual cost should be recognized." These elements are: (1) compensation paid to the attorney for time devoted to the case, (2) out-of-pocket expenses related to the litigation, and (3) overhead.[230] Noting that the third element is the most difficult to determine, that it would be counterproductive to spend considerable time and resources trying to determine that element in every case, and that private practice overhead expenses average 100 percent of a salaried attorney's compensation, the MSPB adopted this 100 percent compensation measure for union attorneys. Therefore, the MSPB held: In the absence of evidence from either appellant or the agency showing that such an allowance of 100 percent of attorney compensation for professional overhead is substantially excessive or insufficient in the particular case, such an overhead allowance may normally be included as an element of actual cost."[231] The same standard (i.e., overhead expenses and the cost of the union attorney's salary) has also been adopted by the Federal Circuit for fees paid under the EAJA.[232]

---

however, clear that no ethical restriction exists . . . where market value fees are placed in a separate fund to be used solely by the union's lawyers to finance legal assistance, even if the umbrella organization receives some indirect benefit from this arrangement. . . . In other words, at least where there is a separate legal assistance fund, fees are not 'shared' with a lay entity, as that term is used in the Code." Opinion 176, at 6.

[230]*Powell v. Department of the Treasury, supra* note 226.
[231]*Id.*
[232]*Devine v. NTEU, supra* note 219.

13. Remedies Available and Not Available in the Federal System

A Synthesis

In the Federal Government remedies that may be asked for, and granted, to correct an alleged injustice are prescribed by law, rule, and regulation. This is true for each of the relevant areas discussed in this book.

When an employee has been subjected to an unjustified or unwarranted personnel action, he or she is entitled to have the action canceled and to be placed as nearly as possible in the *status quo ante* position.[1] The single most comprehensive statutory make-whole remedy for federal employees who have been wrongfully deprived of pay, allowances, or differentials, is the Back Pay Act.[2] The Office of Personnel Management (OPM) administers this law and has issued implementing regulations in the Code of Federal Regulations and in the Federal Personnel Manual.[3] The Act allows an "appropriate authority" to reimburse an employee for lost "pay, allowances or differentials" when it is determined that the employee was affected by an "unjustified or unwarranted personnel action" (see Chapter 12).

Since 1987, when Congress amended the Back Pay Act, interest has been allowed on back pay.[4] It begins to accrue on the effective date of the

---

[1]*Kerr v. National Endowment for the Arts*, 726 F.2d 730 (D.C. Cir. 1984).
[2]5 U.S.C. 5596.
[3]5 C.F.R. 353.401.
[4]Further Continuing Appropriations for Fiscal Year 1988, P.L. 100-202, was enacted on December 22, 1987. It amended the Back Pay Act to allow for the payment of interest on back pay awards on or after December 22, 1987. See also *Naekel v. FAA*, No. 87-3274 (Fed. Cir. June 28, 1988). The implementing regulations are found at 5 C.F.R. 550.801(a), 550.805(f), and 550.806.

383

withdrawal of pay, allowances, and differentials. The rate of interest payable is established by the Secretary of the Treasury.[5]

Circumstances under which the employee may be reimbursed include a wrongful withholding of a within-grade salary increase,[6] wrongful suspension,[7] wrongful reduction in grade, and wrongful termination of employment.[8] Back pay is also available when a pay adjustment is withheld in circumstances in which the agency had no discretion[9] to withhold the promotion,[10] overtime pay,[11] post differential,[12] living quarters allowance,[13] training costs,[14] or other pay adjustments.[15]

---

[5]See the provisions for overpayment rate at 26 U.S.C. 6621(a)(1).

[6]*Canal Zone Gov't Employees*, B-173976 (Comp. Gen. July 11, 1972) (agency withheld salary step increase during presidential wage-price freeze when freeze did not cover salary step increases).

[7]Note, however, that placing an employee on involuntary leave pending OPM approval of a disability retirement is not an unjustified or unwarranted personnel action if action is based upon competent medical evidence and such evidence is not overturned by an appropriate authority. *Isma B. Saloshin*, 63 Comp Gen. 156 (1984) and *Memphis Defense Depot*, B-214631 (Comp. Gen. Aug. 24, 1984).

[8]See Chapter 12.

[9]*Department of Agric.*, B-211784 (Comp. Gen. May 1, 1984) (nondiscretionary policy need not be in writing as long as it is implemented according to established procedures and routinely communicated to affected employees).

[10]*Joseph Pompeo, et al.*, B-186916 (Comp. Gen. Apr. 25, 1977) (agency policy to promote in career ladder once supervisor certifies acceptable level of competence removes agency's discretion to promote once supervisor so certifies and, when administrative error delays promotions, back pay is appropriate). *Donna J. Safreed*, B-216605 (Comp. Gen. Mar. 26, 1985) (where nondiscretionary agency policy dictates that each person who temporarily assumes duties of a given position will receive temporary promotion for higher-graded duties, employee assigned to position is entitled to back pay).

[11]*Gerald Owen*, 54 Comp. Gen. 1071 (1975) (where agency violated negotiated procedure for assigning overtime work, agency had no discretion to award overtime work to others). *Ronald J. Ranieri*, B-207977.2 (Comp. Gen. Aug. 23, 1983) (when employee has been wrongfully discharged, back pay should include overtime based on prior overtime payments or on overtime paid o similar employees who were not removed; there is no requirement for nondiscretionary policy governing assignment of overtime when claim is based on wrongful discharge). See also *Kenneth Clark*, 62 Comp. Gen. 370 (1983).

[12]*Vitarelli v. United States*, 150 Ct. Cl. 59 (1960) (employee's removal from overseas position reversed and back pay properly included post differential even though employee was returned to U.S. at time of removal since he would have received it but for his unjustified removal).

[13]*Urbina v. United States*, 192 Ct. Cl. 875 (1970) (employee's removal from overseas position reversed and back pay properly included living quarters allowance even though employee was returned to U.S. at time of removal since he would have received it but for his unjustified removal).

[14]*James B. Ruch*, B-215626 (Comp. Gen. Jan. 7, 1985) (back pay may include training costs, which employee incurred after his removal and which the agency would have paid for but for his unjustified removal).

[15]*Dyneteria*, 55 Comp. Gen. 97 (1977) as modified by *Billy M. Medaugh*, 57 Comp. Gen. 97 (1977) (where agency regulation specifically provided that request for pay adjustment *must* be initiated on behalf of a General Schedule supervisor of higher paid prevailing rate employees, agency's failure to identify the supervisor for appropriate pay

An unjustified or unwarranted denial of a promotion, however, does not necessarily warrant a remedy under the Back Pay Act. A necessary prerequisite for back pay in a promotion case is that the agency, due to law, regulation, or collective agreement, was bound to promote an employee and failed to do so. If the agency was not bound to do so, then the employee has no right to the salary or other benefits associated with the promotion. Back pay may also be available when some administrative error or oversight delays a decision to promote or reward an employee in some manner. An employee who was simply not promoted due to an unjustified or unwarranted reason is not entitled to back pay if it is subsequently decided by an adjudicating authority that he or she should have been promoted. Salary and other entitlements are payable only to the person properly appointed to the position, and an employee who was not promoted cannot retroactively collect pay and benefits lost by not being appointed initially to the position. An employee who qualifies for back pay may also qualify for an award of attorney's fees (see Chapter 12).

Relief under the Back Pay Act is limited to pay, allowances, or differentials. Other expenses that occur as a result of an unjustified or unwarranted personnel action cannot be recovered. For example, an employee who may have incurred moving expenses because of a personnel action cannot be compensated for these.[16] Punitive damages also are not available.[17]

In computing back pay it must be determined whether the employee was ready, willing, and able to perform the job during the period.[18] Any pay or benefits which the employee would have received must be computed. This includes changes in pay, such as a salary step increase, or shift change and premium pay.[19] In placing the employee in the same position that he or she would have been in but for the wrongful personnel action, certain categories of income the employee received during the period of severance must be deducted from the back pay as he or she is reinstated. These include total earnings from other employment,[20] sever-

---

adjustment constituted a failure to carry out a nondiscretionary regulation).

[16]*David C. Corson*, B-182282 (Comp. Gen. May 28, 1975). See also *Jack M. Haning*, 63 Comp. Gen. 170 (1984).

[17]*J. Lawrence McCarty*, 55 Comp. Gen. 564 (1975).

[18]*Kenneth Clark, supra* note 9.

[19]*Charleston Naval Shipyard*, 55 Comp. Gen. 1311 (1976).

[20]*Bennie L. Moore*, 55 Comp. Gen. 48 (1975); *James J. D'Angelillio*, 48 Comp. Gen. 572 (1969). However, it is important to note that where the employee was earning money from part-time activities prior to the removal or suspension, only the portion of income that results from increased activity during the removal or suspension is subject to offset from back pay. *A. Earnest Fitzgerald*, 53 Comp. Gen. 824 (1974).

ance pay,[21] disability compensation,[22] and lump sum leave payments.[23] But unemployment compensation paid by the state to a federal employee during a period of wrongful removal may not be deducted from back pay due the employee.[24]

When the Merit Systems Protection Board (MSPB) orders an adverse personnel action to be rescinded, it requires that all documents with references to that action be removed from the employee's official personnel file.[25] When the Board determines that an agency has erred in taking a personnel action, it will reverse the action only if the error was a "harmful" one.[26] If the MSPB finds a procedural error, it will reverse the action if the record shows that the error would have made a difference in the final result, or if the record is unclear on that point. If the record shows that the error would have made no difference, the Board will not reverse.[27] The MSPB or arbitrators have the authority to mitigate the penalty imposed by the agency in an adverse action if they believe that such penalty was excessive, but have no such authority in a performance-based action.[28] In the event of termination resulting from the loss of a security clearance, the MSPB cannot review the clearance loss. It is limited to determining whether the clearance was actually denied and that this action caused the loss of job, and whether transfer to a nonsensitive position was feasible.[29]

Relief is also provided for employees in certain cases of erroneous overpayment by the government. Normally, the employee is required to

---

[21]*Charles E. Davis*, 57 Comp. Gen. 464 (1978); *Georgia & Leonie Mallory*, B-209349 (Comp. Gen. Apr. 9, 1984).

[22]*Theodore F. Moran*, B-195213 (Comp. Gen. July 7, 1980). While employee is entitled to the difference between back pay computation and disability payments received, employee may be denied back pay for any period of convalescence when he was not "ready, willing and able" to perform his duties.

[23]The lump sum leave payment is offset against back pay and leave is credited to employee's leave account. *Charles E. Davis*, 57 Comp. Gen. 464 (1978). See also *Janet L. Apple*, B-214659 (Comp. Gen. Feb. 12, 1985).

[24]*Glen Gurwit*, 63 Comp. Gen. 99, 1983; *Ralph V. McDermott*, B-125137 (Comp. Gen. Dec. 7, 1983). Under 5 U.S.C. 8501, et. seq., overpayment of unemployment compensation from the state is to be determined by the state and recovered by the state under that state's unemployment compensation law.

[25]*Labadie v. USPS*, 20 MSPR 28 (1984).

[26]5 U.S.C. 7701(c)(2)(A).

[27]*Douglas v. Veterans Admin.*, 6 MSPB 313 (1981). Failure by MSPB to consider properly appropriateness of a penalty may be grounds for reversal. *Parsons v. Department of the Air Force*, 707 F.2d 1406 (D.C. Cir. 1983).

[28]*Lisiecki v. MSPB*, 769 F.2d 1558 (Fed. Cir. 1985), *cert. denied*, 475 U.S. 1108 (1986). Arbitrators are bound by restriction against modifying agency penalties in Chapter 43 action. *Horner v. Bell*, 825 F.2d 391 (Fed. Cir. 1987); *Horner v. Garza*, 832 F.2d 150 (Fed. Cir. 1987).

[29]*Department of the Navy v. Egan*, 56 USLW 4150 (1988). See *Hoska v. Department of the Army*, 677 F.2d 131 (D.C. Cir. 1982).

pay the excess amount. However, the claim against the employee may be waived by the government. [30] The provision in the law applies to pay and to allowances other than travel, transportation, and relocation allowances. [31] When the claim is for less than $500, the head of the agency exercises the waiver authority. Where the claim is for more than $500, the authority is exercised by the Comptroller General of the United States. [32] As a rule, waiver is granted when collection of the erroneous payment "would be against equity and good conscience and not in the best interest of the United States." [33] There will be no waiver if there are indications of fraud, misrepresentation, fault, or lack of good faith on the part of the employee or any other person having an interest in obtaining the waiver. When the employee should have known that the payments were excessive, he or she will be expected to have set aside the overpayment for its eventual return. [34]

An employee who is restored to his or her job following an improper suspension or removal, may either enroll in the health insurance program as a new employee or may have the original coverage restored, with appropriate adjustments made for contributions and claims for the period in which the employee was improperly suspended or removed. [35] However, if he or she obtained private health insurance during that period, the government will not reimburse the cost of that insurance. [36]

With respect to life insurance, the employee is deemed to have been insured during the period of improper suspension or removal from employment. However, unless death or accidental dismemberment occurred during the period, the ordinary deductions for government life insurance are not withheld from the back pay award. [37]

Certain employee actions, such as whistleblowing, are protected by law. An employee, former employee, or applicant for employment who feels that he or she is being subjected to retaliation may appeal to the Special Counsel for relief. Employees, former employees, or applicants for employment may also seek relief through the Special Counsel for

---

[30] 5 U.S.C. 5584.
[31] *James A. Shultz*, 59 Comp. Gen. 28 (1979).
[32] See generally 4 C.F.R. Parts 91–93.
[33] 5 U.S.C. 5584.
[34] *Philip N. McNany*, B-198770 (Comp. Gen. Nov. 13, 1980). See also *Henry B. Jenkins*, 64 Comp. Gen. 15 (1986).
[35] 5 U.S.C. 8908 and *Pay Policy Statement*, B-180021 (Comp. Gen. Mar. 20, 1975).
[36] *James B. Ruch*, B-215626 (Comp. Gen. Jan. 7, 1985).
[37] 5 U.S.C. 8706(e). See also *Pay Policy Statement, supra* note 35. See also *Neal & Roy*, 64 Comp. Gen. 435 (1985) (when their retirements were reversed by MSPB as coerced, they were entitled to reimbursement for life insurance premiums that had been deducted from their annuities during period of erroneous retirement).

actions committed by management that fall into the category of prohibited personnel practices. The Special Counsel will investigate and may request the MSPB to order corrective action for the employee who is the victim of the prohibited personnel practice and/or disciplinary action (see Chapter 4).

In special cases, employees may also request the stay of a personnel action through the Special Counsel. Such request can be granted only by the MSPB. Where reprisal for whistleblowing is involved, however, the employee may request a stay directly from the MSPB.

Title VII of the Civil Rights Act of 1964 is in itself a remedial law with the sole purpose of providing "make-whole relief" to victims of discrimination based on race, color, religion, sex, or national origin.[38] Remedies are available for applicants for employment as well as employees. Discrimination is also a prohibited personnel practice and may, therefore, be cause for appeal to the Special Counsel (see Chapter 4).

Where discrimination is found, the agency is compelled to offer the applicant the position he or she would have occupied absent discrimination or, if justified, a substantially equivalent position.[39] Prevailing complainants may also receive back pay with interest[40] and attorney's fees (see Chapter 12). They are also entitled to employee benefits which may have been denied—such as training, preferential work assignments, and overtime.[41] Prevailing complainants are not entitled to compensatory or punitive damages.[42]

Federal applicants or employees who can show that they have been discriminated against because of age (40 and over) may be entitled to remedies such as injunctions, judgments compelling employment, reinstatement, promotion, back pay, and reimbursement of unpaid wages and overtime.[43] Attorney's fees and costs are payable to prevailing complainants for judicial processing but not for fees and costs incurred exclusively at the administrative stage. As is the case under Title VII, successful complainants are not entitled to compensatory or punitive damages. They also cannot receive "liquidated" damages for willful violations, which are authorized by the Age Discrimination in Employment Act in suits against private employers.

---

[38]42 U.S.C. 2000e et seq. and 42 U.S.C. 2000e-5(g). See also Albemarle Paper Co. v. Moody, 422 U.S. 405, 10 FEP Cases 1181 (1975).

[39]29 C.F.R. 1613.271(b)(1).

[40]James W. Thompkins v. William L. Ball, III, Secretary of the Navy, EEOC Nos. 05890432 and 01872684 (June 14, 1989).

[41]29 C.F.R. 1613.271(c)(5).

[42]Equal Employment Opportunity Comm'n, 62 Comp. Gen. 239 (1983).

[43]29 U.S.C. 626(b).

Federal applicants or employees who can establish that they have been aggrieved under the Rehabilitation Act, which prohibits discrimination based on handicapping physical or mental impairments, including alcoholism, drug addiction, and contagious diseases, are entitled to the same remedies as successful Title VII complainants.[44] Courts or agencies may take into account the reasonableness of the cost of necessary workplace accommodations and the availability of alternatives or other appropriate relief to achieve an equitable and appropriate remedy.[45]

Remedies provided under the Equal Pay Act include promotion, back pay, liquidated damages, and attorney's fees.[46] A two-year statute of limitations applies to the recovery of unpaid wages. Where a willful violation is involved, an action may be commenced within three years after the cause of action occurred.[47]

An employee who believes that he or she has been wronged by a supervisor, may attempt to sue that supervisor personally for monetary damages or injunctive relief (see Chapter 6). Most often such actions are for money damages over and above whatever lost income or back pay the employee might seek through pursuit of administrative remedies. He or she can sue under a common law or constitutional tort theory.

Successful pursuit of either a constitutional or common law tort action directly against the supervisor will be the exception rather than the rule. The exempt categories of conduct under the Federal Tort Claims Act will more likely than not bar recovery. Courts have held that the Civil Service Reform Act of 1978 and Title VII of the Civil Rights Act provide comprehensive remedial schemes that should operate to preclude an employee from being able to sue a supervisor for alleged constitutional violations covered by these acts.[48] It does not appear to matter how slight an employee's remedy might be under one of these statutes. As long as the employee has some right to request administrative review, a constitutional tort action will likely be barred.[49] An employee's best chances for success in directly seeking damages from a supervisor for wrongful actions would appear to be in situations where the supervisor is sued under a common law tort theory for conduct outside the supervisor's scope of employment. Common law torts of assault and battery or threats of harm would appear to fall within this category.

---

[44]29 U.S.C. 794a(a)(1).

[45]Id. As this book goes to press the U.S. Congress is considering legislation that will greatly expand the rights of the disabled (see Chapter 5, at 174).

[46]29 U.S.C. 216(b).

[47]29 U.S.C. 255; 29 C.F.R. 1620.33(b).

[48]Bush v. Lucas, 462 U.S. 367 (1983); Brown v. GSA, 425 U.S. 820 (1976).

[49]See, e.g., Spagnola v. Mathis, 859 F.2d 223 (D.C. Cir. 1988).

With respect to unfair labor practices, the Federal Labor Relations Authority (FLRA) has broad remedial powers under section 7118(a)(7) of the Statute (see Chapter 8). It may require an agency or labor organization to cease and desist from any unfair labor practice, to renegotiate a collective bargaining agreement, to give retroactive effect to that negotiated agreement, and to reinstate an employee with back pay in accordance with the Back Pay Act. The Authority is further empowered to take "such other action as will carry out the purpose of [the statute]."[50]

Section 7120(f) of the Statute provides a specific remedy in any case where a labor organization has violated section 7116(b)(7) with regard to any strike, work stoppage, or slowdown. In such cases the Authority may revoke the exclusive recognition status of the labor organization, which shall then immediately cease to be legally entitled and obligated to represent employees in the unit, or take any other appropriate disciplinary action.[51]

Where an unfair labor practice has occurred, the Authority issues an order requiring the agency or labor organization at fault to cease and desist from the unlawful conduct and to take certain action to effect the purposes and policies of the Statute. In cases where agency discrimination based on protective union activity is found to be a violation of section 7116(a)(2), the Authority may order the personnel action rescinded and the employee reinstated to former status prior to the unlawful discrimination. In addition, references to the discriminatory action may have to be removed from the employee's personnel file and back pay may be awarded under the Back Pay Act.[52]

In unfair labor practice cases involving unilateral changes in conditions of employment, the Authority will, with rare exceptions, order the unlawful change to be rescinded and the preexisting practice to be

---

[50]In pertinent part, section 7116(a)(7) provides that the Authority shall issue and cause to be served on the agency or labor organization an order—
(A) to cease and desist from any such unfair labor practice in which the agency or labor organization is engaged;
(B) requiring the parties to renegotiate a collective bargaining agreement in accordance with the order of the Authority and requiring that the agreement, as amended, be given retroactive effect;
(C) requiring reinstatement of an employee with backpay in accordance with Section 5596 of this title; or
(D) including any combination of the actions described in subparagraphs (A) through (C) of this paragraph or such other action as will carry out the purpose of this chapter.
[51]See Chapter 8, p. 267 discussing the only situation where the Authority has revoked the status of an exclusive representation due to violation of section 7116(b)(7)(A).
[52]See Chapter 8, pp. 237–239.

reinstated where the change itself was negotiable. [53] In situations where the unilateral change was negotiable only with respect to impact and implementation, the Authority will apply specific criteria to determine whether a return to the *status quo ante* is justified. [54] Back pay may also be an appropriate remedy in cases of refusal to bargain over impact and implementation. [55] The Authority, however, has been reluctant to order retroactive remedial action to remedy impact and implementation bargaining violations. [56]

In "duty to furnish information" cases, the Authority's affirmative order routinely requires the agency to furnish the labor organization the requested information to the extent required to be disclosed under section 7114(b)(4). [57] In violations of section 7131(a) involving official time the agency is required to grant official time to employees who had been unlawfully denied such time and to adjust the employee's leave accordingly. [58] In cases where an agency violates section 7115 by failing to deduct authorized dues, the Authority routinely requires the agency to reimburse the union for the monies it would have received had it not been for the agency's unfair labor practice. [59] In "duty of fair representation" cases, the Authority, on occasion, has ordered unions to make employees whole in situations where an employee was denied an opportunity to grieve an alleged violation of the contract and, as a result, lost money. [60]

---

[53]*Id.*, at 240–245, also *Veterans Admin. W. Los Angeles Medical Center, Los Angeles, Cal.*, 23 FLRA 278 (1986).

[54]See Chapter 8, pp. 245–247.

[55]*Id.*, at 247.

[56]*Id.*, at 247.

[57]*Id.*, at 250–254.

[58]*Id.*, at 259–263.

[59]*Id.*, at 263–264.

[60]*Id.*, at 265–266.

Appendices

1. Text of Relevant Statutes

Table of Statutes

Note on Chapter 12 of Title 5, U.S.C., and the WPA

The Whistleblower Protection Act was enacted just as this book was going into print. Therefore, the Act is not yet codified. As a result, the reader will have to do some cross referencing in order to fully understand the effective provisions. The Act amended the previously existing sections of 5 U.S.C. 1201–1209 by adding and deleting various provisions and by renumbering the sections 1201 through 1206. The Act then added Subchapters II and III to title 5 of the U.S. Code and amended Subchapter IV of Chapter 33 of title 5 and sections 7701, 7703, and other more minor conforming amendments.

* * * * *

WHISTLEBLOWER PROTECTION ACT OF 1989

Public Law 101–12
101st Congress
An Act

To amend title 5, United States Code, to strengthen the protections available to Federal employees against prohibited personnel practices, and for other purposes.

Be it enacted by the Senate and House of Representatives of the United States of America in Congress assembled,

SECTION 1. SHORT TITLE.

This Act may be cited as the "Whistleblower Protection Act of 1989".

SEC. 2. FINDINGS AND PURPOSE.

(a) FINDINGS.—The Congress finds that—

(1) Federal employees who make disclosures described in section 2302(b)(8) of title 5, United States Code, serve the public interest by assisting in the elimination of fraud, waste, abuse, and unnecessary Government expenditures;

(2) protecting employees who disclose Government illegality, waste, and corruption is a major step toward a more effective civil service; and

(3) in passing the Civil Service Reform Act of 1978, Congress established the Office of Special Counsel to protect whistleblowers (those individuals who make disclosures described in such section 2302(b)(8)) from reprisal.

(b) PURPOSE.—The purpose of this Act is to strengthen and improve protection for the rights of Federal employees, to prevent reprisals, and to help eliminate wrongdoing within the Government by—

(1) mandating that employees should not suffer adverse consequences as a result of prohibited personnel practices; and

(2) establishing—
    (A) that the primary role of the Office of Special Counsel is to protect employees, especially whistleblowers, from prohibited personnel practices;
    (B) that the Office of Special Counsel shall act in the interests of employees who seek assistance from the Office of Special Counsel; and
    (C) that while disciplining those who commit prohibited personnel practices may be used as a means by which to help accomplish that goal, the protection of individuals who are the subject of prohibited personnel practices remains the paramount consideration.

SEC. 3. MERIT SYSTEMS PROTECTION BOARD; OFFICE OF SPECIAL COUNSEL; INDIVIDUAL RIGHT OF ACTION.

(a) MERIT SYSTEMS PROTECTION BOARD.—Chapter 12 of title 5, United States Code is amended—
    (1) in section 1201 in the second sentence by striking out "Chairman and";
    (2) in the heading for section 1202 by striking out the comma and inserting in lieu thereof a semicolon;
    (3) in section 1202(b)—
        (A) in the first sentence by striking out "his" and inserting in lieu thereof "the member's"; and
        (B) in the second sentence by striking out "of this title";
    (4) in section 1203(a) in the first sentence by striking out the comma after "time";
    (5) in section 1203(c) by striking out "the Chairman and Vice Chairman" and inserting in lieu thereof "the Chairman and the Vice Chairman";
    (6) by redesignating section 1204 as section 1211(b) and inserting such subsection after section 1211(a) (as added in paragraph (11) of this subsection);
    (7) by redesignating section 1205 as section 1204, and amending such redesignated section—
        (A) by striking out "and Special Counsel", "the Special Counsel," and "of this section" each place such terms appear;
        (B) by striking out "subpena" and "subpenaed" each place such terms appear and inserting in lieu thereof "subpoena" and "subpoenaed", respectively;
        (C) in subsection (a)(4) by striking out "(e)" and inserting in lieu thereof "(f)";
        (D) by amending subsection (b)(2) to read as follows:
"(2) Any member of the Board, any administrative law judge appointed by the Board under section 3105, and any employee of the Board designated by the Board may, with respect to any individual—
    "(A) issue subpoenas requiring the attendance and presentation of testimony of any such individual, and the production of documentary or other evidence from any place in the United States, any territory or possession of the

United States, the Commonwealth of Puerto Rico, or the District of Columbia; and

"(B) order the taking of depositions from, and responses to written interrogatories by, any such individual.";

(E) in subsection (c) in the first sentence—

(i) by striking out "(b)(2) of this section," and inserting in lieu thereof "(b)(2)(A) or section 1214(b), upon application by the Board,"; and

(ii) by striking out "judicial";

(F) by redesignating subsections (d) through (k) as subsections (e) through (l), respectively, and inserting after subsection (c) the following new subsection:

"(d) A subpoena referred to in subsection (b)(2)(A) may, in the case of any individual outside the territorial jurisdiction of any court of the United States, be served in such manner as the Federal Rules of Civil Procedure prescribe for service of a subpoena in a foreign country. To the extent that the courts of the United States can assert jurisdiction over such individual, the United States District Court for the District of Columbia shall have the same jurisdiction to take any action respecting compliance under this subsection by such individual that such court would have if such individual were personally within the jurisdiction of such court.";

(G) in subsection (e) (as redesignated by subparagraph (F) of this paragraph)—

(i) in paragraph (1)—

(I) by redesignating such paragraph as subparagraph (A) of paragraph (1); and

(II) by inserting at the end thereof the following new subparagraph:

"(B)(i) The Merit Systems Protection Board may, during an investigation by the Office of Special Counsel or during the pendency of any proceeding before the Board, issue any order which may be necessary to protect a witness or other individual from harassment, except that an agency (other than the Office of Special Counsel) may not request any such order with regard to an investigation by the Office of Special Counsel from the Board during such investigation.

"(ii) An order issued under this subparagraph may be enforced in the same manner as provided for under paragraph (2) with respect to any order under subsection (a)(2).";

(ii) in paragraph (2)—

(I) by redesignating such paragraph as subparagraph (A) of paragraph (2) and striking out "of this section" in the first sentence therein; and

(II) by inserting at the end thereof the following new subparagraph (B):

"(B) The Board shall prescribe regulations under which any employee who is aggrieved by the failure of any other employee to comply with an order of the Board may petition the Board to exercise its authority under subparagraph (A)."; and

(iii) in paragraph (3) by inserting "of Personnel Management" after "Office";

(H) in subsection (f) (as redesignated by subparagraph (F) of this paragraph)—
    (i) in paragraph (1) in the first sentence by inserting "of the Office of Personnel Management" after "Director", and by striking out "of this title";
    (ii) in paragraph (2)—
        (I) in the first sentence by inserting a comma after "subsection";
        (II) in subparagraph (A) by striking out "of this title"; and
        (III) in subparagraph (B) by striking out "of this title"; and
    (iii) in paragraph (3)—
        (I) in subparagraph (A) by striking out "(A)";
        (II) by striking out subparagraph (B); and
        (III) by redesignating subparagraph (C) and clauses (i) and (ii) therein as paragraph (4) and subparagraphs (A) and (B), respectively; and
    (I) in subsection (j) (as redesignated by subparagraph (F) of this paragraph) in the second sentence by striking out "of this title" after "chapter 33";
(8) by striking out sections 1206 through 1208;
(9) by redesignating section 1209(a) as section 1205, and inserting before such section the following section heading:

"§ 1205. Transmittal of information to Congress";

(10) by redesignating section 1209(b) as section 1206, and inserting before such section the following section heading:

"§ 1206. Annual report";

(11) by inserting after section 1206 (as redesignated in paragraph (10) of this subsection) the following:

"SUBCHAPTER II—OFFICE OF SPECIAL COUNSEL

"§ 1211. Establishment

"(a) There is established the Office of Special Counsel, which shall be headed by the Special Counsel. The Office shall have an official seal which shall be judicially noticed. The Office shall have its principal office in the District of Columbia and shall have field offices in other appropriate locations.";
    (12) by amending section 1211(b) (as redesignated and inserted by paragraph (6) of this subsection)—
        (A) in the first sentence by striking out "of the Merit Systems Protection Board" and "from attorneys";
        (B) by striking the second sentence and inserting in lieu thereof "The Special Counsel shall be an attorney who, by demonstrated ability, background, training, or experience, is especially qualified to carry out the functions of the position. A Special Counsel appointed to fill a vacancy occurring before the end of a term of office of the Special

Counsel's predecessor serves for the remainder of the term."; and
(C) by adding at the end thereof "The Special Counsel may not hold another office or position in the Government of the United States, except as otherwise provided by law or at the direction of the President."; and
(13) inserting after section 1211 the following:

"§ 1212. Powers and functions of the Office of Special Counsel

"(a) The Office of Special Counsel shall—
"(1) in accordance with section 1214(a) and other applicable provisions of this subchapter, protect employees, former employees, and applicants for employment from prohibited personnel practices;
"(2) receive and investigate allegations of prohibited personnel practices, and, where appropriate—
"(A) bring petitions for stays, and petitions for corrective action, under section 1214; and
"(B) file a complaint or make recommendations for disciplinary action under section 1215;
"(3) receive, review, and, where appropriate, forward to the Attorney General or an agency head under section 1213, disclosures of violations of any law, rule, or regulation, or gross mismanagement, a gross waste of funds, an abuse of authority, or a substantial and specific danger to public health or safety;
"(4) review rules and regulations issued by the Director of the Office of Personnel Management in carrying out functions under section 1103 and, where the Special Counsel finds that any such rule or regulation would, on its face or as implemented, require the commission of a prohibited personnel practice, file a written complaint with the Board; and
"(5) investigate and, where appropriate, bring actions concerning allegations of violations of other laws within the jurisdiction of the Office of Special Counsel (as referred to in section 1216).
"(b)(1) The Special Counsel and any employee of the Office of Special Counsel designated by the Special Counsel may administer oaths, examine witnesses, take depositions, and receive evidence.
"(2) The Special Counsel may—
"(A) issue subpoenas; and
"(B) order the taking of depositions and order responses to written interrogatories;
in the same manner as provided under section 1204.
"(3)(A) In the case of contumacy or failure to obey a subpoena issued under paragraph (2)(A), the Special Counsel may apply to the Merit Systems Protection Board to enforce the subpoena in court pursuant to section 1204(c).
"(B) A subpoena under paragraph (2)(A) may, in the case of any individual outside the territorial jurisdiction of any court of the United States, be served in the manner referred to in subsection (d) of section 1204, and the United States District Court for the District

of Columbia may, with respect to any such individual, compel compliance in accordance with such subsection.

"(4) Witnesses (whether appearing voluntarily or under subpoena) shall be paid the same fee and mileage allowances which are paid subpoenaed witnesses in the courts of the United States.

"(c)(1) Except as provided in paragraph (2), the Special Counsel may as a matter of right intervene or otherwise participate in any proceeding before the Merit Systems Protection Board, except that the Special Counsel shall comply with the rules of the Board.

"(2) The Special Counsel may not intervene in an action brought by an individual under section 1221, or in an appeal brought by an individual under section 7701, without the consent of such individual.

"(d)(1) The Special Counsel may appoint the legal, administrative, and support personnel necessary to perform the functions of the Special Counsel.

"(2) Any appointment made under this subsection shall be made in accordance with the provisions of this title, except that such appointment shall not be subject to the approval or supervision of the Office of Personnel Management or the Executive Office of the President (other than approval required under section 3324 or subchapter VIII of chapter 33).

"(e) The Special Counsel may prescribe such regulations as may be necessary to perform the functions of the Special Counsel. Such regulations shall be published in the Federal Register.

"(f) The Special Counsel may not issue any advisory opinion concerning any law, rule, or regulation (other than an advisory opinion concerning chapter 15 or subchapter III of chapter 73).

"(g)(1) The Special Counsel may not respond to any inquiry or provide information concerning any person making an allegation under section 1214(a), except in accordance with the provisions of section 552a of title 5, United States Code, or as required by any other applicable Federal law.

"(2) Notwithstanding the exception under paragraph (1), the Special Counsel may not respond to any inquiry concerning a matter described in subparagraph (A) or (B) of section 2302(b)(2) in connection with a person described in paragraph (1)—

"(A) unless the consent of the individual as to whom the information pertains is obtained in advance; or

"(B) except upon request of an agency which requires such information in order to make a determination concerning an individual's having access to the information unauthorized disclosure of which could be expected to cause exceptionally grave damage to the national security.

"§ 1213. Provisions relating to disclosures of violations of law, gross mismanagement, and certain other matters

"(a) This section applies with respect to—

"(1) any disclosure of information by an employee, former employee, or applicant for employment which the employee, former employee, or applicant reasonably believes evidences—

"(A) a violation of any law, rule, or regulation; or

"(B) gross mismanagement, a gross waste of funds, an abuse of authority, or a substantial and specific danger to public health or safety;
if such disclosure is not specifically prohibited by law and if such information is not specifically required by Executive order to be kept secret in the interest of national defense or the conduct of foreign affairs; and

"(2) any disclosure by an employee, former employee, or applicant for employment to the Special Counsel or to the Inspector General of an agency or another employee designated by the head of the agency to receive such disclosures of information which the employee, former employee, or applicant reasonably believes evidences—

"(A) a violation of any law, rule, or regulation; or

"(B) gross mismanagement, a gross waste of funds, an abuse of authority, or a substantial and specific danger to public health or safety.

"(b) Whenever the Special Counsel receives information of a type described in subsection (a) of this section, the Special Counsel shall review such information and, within 15 days after receiving the information, determine whether there is a substantial likelihood that the information discloses a violation of any law, rule, or regulation, or gross mismanagement, gross waste of funds, abuse of authority, or substantial and specific danger to public health and safety.

"(c)(1) Subject to paragraph (2), if the Special Counsel makes a positive determination under subsection (b) of this section, the Special Counsel shall promptly transmit the information with respect to which the determination was made to the appropriate agency head and require that the agency head—

"(A) conduct an investigation with respect to the information and any related matters transmitted by the Special Counsel to the agency head; and

"(B) submit a written report setting forth the findings of the agency head within 60 days after the date on which the information is transmitted to the agency head or within any longer period of time agreed to in writing by the Special Counsel.

"(2) The Special Counsel may require an agency head to conduct an investigation and submit a written report under paragraph (1) only if the information was transmitted to the Special Counsel by—

"(A) an employee, former employee, or applicant for employment in the agency which the information concerns; or

"(B) an employee who obtained the information in connection with the performance of the employee's duties and responsibilities.

"(d) Any report required under subsection (c) shall be reviewed and signed by the head of the agency and shall include—

"(1) a summary of the information with respect to which the investigation was initiated;

"(2) a description of the conduct of the investigation;

"(3) a summary of any evidence obtained from the investigation;

"(4) a listing of any violation or apparent violation of any law, rule, or regulation; and

"(5) a description of any action taken or planned as a result of the investigation, such as—

"(A) changes in agency rules, regulations, or practices;

"(B) the restoration of any aggrieved employee;

"(C) disciplinary action against any employee; and

"(D) referral to the Attorney General of any evidence of a criminal violation.

"(e)(1) Any such report shall be submitted to the Special Counsel, and the Special Counsel shall transmit a copy to the complainant, except as provided under subsection (f) of this section. The complainant may submit comments to the Special Counsel on the agency report within 15 days of having received a copy of the report.

"(2) Upon receipt of any report of the head of an agency required under subsection (c) of this section, the Special Counsel shall review the report and determine whether—

"(A) the findings of the head of the agency appear reasonable; and

"(B) the report of the agency under subsection (c)(1) of this section contains the information required under subsection (d) of this section.

"(3) The Special Counsel shall transmit any agency report received pursuant to subsection (c) of this section, any comments provided by the complainant pursuant to subsection (e)(1), and any appropriate comments or recommendations by the Special Counsel to the President, the congressional committees with jurisdiction over the agency which the disclosure involves, and the Comptroller General.

"(4) Whenever the Special Counsel does not receive the report of the agency within the time prescribed in subsection (c)(2) of this section, the Special Counsel shall transmit a copy of the information which was transmitted to the agency head to the President, the congressional committees with jurisdiction over the agency which the disclosure involves, and the Comptroller General together with a statement noting the failure of the head of the agency to file the required report.

"(f) In any case in which evidence of a criminal violation obtained by an agency in an investigation under subsection (c) of this section is referred to the Attorney General—

"(1) the report shall not be transmitted to the complainant; and

"(2) the agency shall notify the Office of Personnel Management and the Office of Management and Budget of the referral.

"(g)(1) If the Special Counsel receives information of a type described in subsection (a) from an individual other than an individual described in subparagraph (A) or (B) of subsection (c)(2), the Special Counsel may transmit the information to the head of the agency which the information concerns. The head of such agency shall, within a reasonable time after the information is transmitted, inform the Special Counsel in writing of what action has been or is being taken and when such action shall be completed. The Special Counsel shall inform the individual of the report of the agency head. If the Special Counsel does not transmit the information to the head of the agency, the Special Counsel shall return any documents and other matter provided by the individual who made the disclosure.

"(2) If the Special Counsel receives information of a type described in subsection (a) from an individual described in subparagraph (A) or (B) of subsection (c)(2), but does not make a positive determination under subsection (b), the Special Counsel may transmit the information to the head of the agency which the information concerns, except that the information may not be transmitted to the head of the agency without the consent of the individual. The head of such agency shall, within a reasonable time after the information is transmitted, inform the Special Counsel in writing of what action has been or is being taken and when such action will be completed. The Special Counsel shall inform the individual of the report of the agency head.

"(3) If the Special Counsel does not transmit the information to the head of the agency under paragraph (2), the Special Counsel shall—

"(A) return any documents and other matter provided by the individual who made the disclosure; and

"(B) inform the individual of—

"(i) the reasons why the disclosure may not be further acted on under this chapter; and

"(ii) other offices available for receiving disclosures, should the individual wish to pursue the matter further.

"(h) The identity of any individual who makes a disclosure described in subsection (a) may not be disclosed by the Special Counsel without such individual's consent unless the Special Counsel determines that the disclosure of the individual's identity is necessary because of an imminent danger to public health or safety or imminent violation of any criminal law.

"(i) Except as specifically authorized under this section, the provisions of this section shall not be considered to authorize disclosure of any information by any agency or any person which is—

"(1) specifically prohibited from disclosure by any other provision of law; or

"(2) specifically required by Executive order to be kept secret in the interest of national defense or the conduct of foreign affairs.

"(j) With respect to any disclosure of information described in subsection (a) which involves foreign intelligence or counterintelligence information, if the disclosure is specifically prohibited by law or by Executive order, the Special Counsel shall transmit such information to the National Security Advisor, the Permanent Select Committee on Intelligence of the House of Representatives, and the Select Committee on Intelligence of the Senate.

"§ 1214. Investigation of prohibited personnel practices; corrective action

"(a)(1)(A) The Special Counsel shall receive any allegation of a prohibited personnel practice and shall investigate the allegation to the extent necessary to determine whether there are reasonable grounds to believe that a prohibited personnel practice has occurred, exists, or is to be taken.

"(B) Within 15 days after the date of receiving an allegation of a prohibited personnel practice under paragraph (1), the Special Counsel shall provide written notice to the person who made the allegation that—

"(i) the allegation has been received by the Special Counsel; and

"(ii) shall include the name of a person at the Office of Special Counsel who shall serve as a contact with the person making the allegation.

"(C) Unless an investigation is terminated under paragraph (2), the Special Counsel shall—

"(i) within 90 days after notice is provided under subparagraph (B), notify the person who made the allegation of the status of the investigation and any action taken by the Office of the Special Counsel since the filing of the allegation;

"(ii) notify such person of the status of the investigation and any action taken by the Office of the Special Counsel since the last notice, at least every 60 days after notice is given under clause (i); and

"(iii) notify such person of the status of the investigation and any action taken by the Special Counsel at such time as determined appropriate by the Special Counsel.

"(2)(A) If the Special Counsel terminates any investigation under paragraph (1), the Special Counsel shall prepare and transmit to any person on whose allegation the investigation was initiated a written statement notifying the person of—

"(i) the termination of the investigation;

"(ii) a summary of relevant facts ascertained by the Special Counsel, including the facts that support, and the facts that do not support, the allegations of such person; and

"(iii) the reasons for terminating the investigation.

"(B) A written statement under subparagraph (A) may not be admissible as evidence in any judicial or administrative proceeding, without the consent of the person who received such statement under subparagraph (A).

"(3) Except in a case in which an employee, former employee, or applicant for employment has the right to appeal directly to the Merit Systems Protection Board under any law, rule, or regulation, any such employee, former employee, or applicant shall seek corrective action from the Special Counsel before seeking corrective action from the Board. An employee, former employee, or applicant for employment may seek corrective action from the Board under section 1221, if such employee, former employee, or applicant seeks corrective action for a prohibited personnel practice described in section 2302(b)(8) from the Special Counsel and—

"(A)(i) the Special Counsel notifies such employee, former employee, or applicant that an investigation concerning such employee, former employee, or applicant has been terminated; and "(ii) no more than 60 days have elapsed since notification was provided to such employee, former employee, or applicant for employment that such investigation was terminated; or

"(B) 120 days after seeking corrective action from the Special Counsel, such employee, former employee, or applicant has not been notified by the Special Counsel that the Special Counsel shall seek corrective action on behalf of such employee, former employee, or applicant.

"(4) If an employee, former employee, or applicant seeks a corrective action from the Board under section 1221, pursuant to the provisions of paragraph (3)(B), the Special Counsel may continue to seek corrective action personal to such employee, former employee, or applicant only with the consent of such employee, former employee, or applicant.

"(5) In addition to any authority granted under paragraph (1), the Special Counsel may, in the absence of an allegation, conduct an investigation for the purpose of determining whether there are reasonable grounds to believe that a prohibited personnel practice (or a pattern of prohibited personnel practices) has occurred, exists, or is to be taken.

"(b)(1)(A)(i) The Special Counsel may request any member of the Merit Systems Protection Board to order a stay of any personnel action for 45 days if the Special Counsel determines that there are reasonable grounds to believe that the personnel action was taken, or is to be taken, as a result of a prohibited personnel practice.

"(ii) Any member of the Board requested by the Special Counsel to order a stay under clause (i) shall order such stay unless the member determines that, under the facts and circumstances involved, such a stay would not be appropriate.

"(iii) Unless denied under clause (ii), any stay under this subparagraph shall be granted within 3 calendar days (excluding Saturdays, Sundays, and legal holidays) after the date of the request for the stay by the Special Counsel.

"(B) The Board may extend the period of any stay granted under subparagraph (A) for any period which the Board considers appropriate.

"(C) The Board shall allow any agency which is the subject of a stay to comment to the Board on any extension of stay proposed under subparagraph (B).

"(D) A stay may be terminated by the Board at any time, except that a stay may not be terminated by the Board—

"(i) on its own motion or on the motion of an agency, unless notice and opportunity for oral or written comments are first provided to the Special Counsel and the individual on whose behalf the stay was ordered; or

"(ii) on motion of the Special Counsel, unless notice and opportunity for oral or written comments are first provided to the individual on whose behalf the stay was ordered.

"(2)(A) If, in connection with any investigation, the Special Counsel determines that there are reasonable grounds to believe that a prohibited personnel practice has occurred, exists, or is to be taken which requires corrective action, the Special Counsel shall report the determination together with any findings or recommendations to the Board, the agency involved and to the Office of Personnel Management, and may report such determination, findings and recommendations to the President. The Special Counsel may include in the report recommendations for corrective action to be taken.

"(B) If, after a reasonable period of time, the agency does not act to correct the prohibited personnel practice, the Special Counsel may petition the Board for corrective action.

"(C) If the Special Counsel finds, in consultation with the individual subject to the prohibited personnel practice, that the agency has acted to correct the prohibited personnel practice, the Special Counsel shall file such finding with the Board, together with any written comments which the individual may provide.

"(3) Whenever the Special Counsel petitions the Board for corrective action, the Board shall provide an opportunity for—

"(A) oral or written comments by the Special Counsel, the agency involved, and the Office of Personnel Management; and

"(B) written comments by any individual who alleges to be the subject of the prohibited personnel practice.

"(4)(A) The Board shall order such corrective action as the Board considers appropriate, if the Board determines that the Special Counsel has demonstrated that a prohibited personnel practice, other than one described in section 2302(b)(8), has occurred, exists, or is to be taken.

"(B)(i) Subject to the provisions of clause (ii), in any case involving an alleged prohibited personnel practice as described under section 2302(b)(8), the Board shall order such corrective action as the Board considers appropriate if the Special Counsel has demonstrated that a disclosure described under section 2302(b)(8) was a contributing factor in the personnel action which was taken or is to be taken against the individual.

"(ii) Corrective action under clause (i) may not be ordered if the agency demonstrates by clear and convincing evidence that it would have taken the same personnel action in the absence of such disclosure.

"(c)(1) Judicial review of any final order or decision of the Board under this section may be obtained by any employee, former employee, or applicant for employment adversely affected by such order or decision.

"(2) A petition for review under this subsection shall be filed with such court, and within such time, as provided for under section 7703(b).

"(d)(1) If, in connection with any investigation under this subchapter, the Special Counsel determines that there is reasonable cause to believe that a criminal violation has occurred, the Special Counsel shall report the determination to the Attorney General and to the head of the agency involved, and shall submit a copy of the report to the Director of the Office of Personnel Management and the Director of the Office of Management and Budget.

"(2) In any case in which the Special Counsel determines that there are reasonable grounds to believe that a prohibited personnel

practice has occurred, exists, or is to be taken, the Special Counsel shall proceed with any investigation or proceeding unless—
"(A) the alleged violation has been reported to the Attorney General; and
"(B) the Attorney General is pursuing an investigation, in which case the Special Counsel, after consultation with the Attorney General, has discretion as to whether to proceed.

"(e) If, in connection with any investigation under this subchapter, the Special Counsel determines that there is reasonable cause to believe that any violation of any law, rule, or regulation has occurred other than one referred to in subsection (b) or (d), the Special Counsel shall report such violation to the head of the agency involved. The Special Counsel shall require, within 30 days after the receipt of the report by the agency, a certification by the head of the agency which states—
"(1) that the head of the agency has personally reviewed the report; and
"(2) what action has been or is to be taken, and when the action will be completed.

"(f) During any investigation initiated under this subchapter, no disciplinary action shall be taken against any employee for any alleged prohibited activity under investigation or for any related activity without the approval of the Special Counsel.

"§ 1215. Disciplinary action

"(a)(1) Except as provided in subsection (b), if the Special Counsel determines that disciplinary action should be taken against any employee for having—
"(A) committed a prohibited personnel practice,
"(B) violated the provisions of any law, rule, or regulation, or engaged in any other conduct within the jurisdiction of the Special Counsel as described in section 1216, or
"(C) knowingly and willfully refused or failed to comply with an order of the Merit Systems Protection Board,
the Special Counsel shall prepare a written complaint against the employee containing the Special Counsel's determination, together with a statement of supporting facts, and present the complaint and statement to the employee and the Board, in accordance with this subsection.

"(2) Any employee against whom a complaint has been presented to the Merit Systems Protection Board under paragraph (1) is entitled to—
"(A) a reasonable time to answer orally and in writing, and to furnish affidavits and other documentary evidence in support of the answer;
"(B) be represented by an attorney or other representative;
"(C) a hearing before the Board or an administrative law judge appointed under section 3105 and designated by the Board;
"(D) have a transcript kept of any hearing under subparagraph (C); and

"(E) a written decision and reasons therefor at the earliest practicable date, including a copy of any final order imposing disciplinary action.

"(3) A final order of the Board may impose disciplinary action consisting of removal, reduction in grade, debarment from Federal employment for a period not to exceed 5 years, suspension, reprimand, or an assessment of a civil penalty not to exceed $1,000.

"(4) There may be no administrative appeal from an order of the Board. An employee subject to a final order imposing disciplinary action under this subsection may obtain judicial review of the order by filing a petition therefor with such court, and within such time, as provided for under section 7703(b).

"(5) In the case of any State or local officer or employee under chapter 15, the Board shall consider the case in accordance with the provisions of such chapter.

"(b) In the case of an employee in a confidential, policy-making, policy-determining, or policy-advocating position appointed by the President, by and with the advice and consent of the Senate (other than an individual in the Foreign Service of the United States), the complaint and statement referred to in subsection (a)(1), together with any response of the employee, shall be presented to the President for appropriate action in lieu of being presented under subsection (a).

"(c)(1) In the case of members of the uniformed services and individuals employed by any person under contract with an agency to provide goods or services, the Special Counsel may transmit recommendations for disciplinary or other appropriate action (including the evidence on which such recommendations are based) to the head of the agency concerned.

"(2) In any case in which the Special Counsel transmits recommendations to an agency head under paragraph (1), the agency head shall, within 60 days after receiving such recommendations, transmit a report to the Special Counsel on each recommendation and the action taken, or proposed to be taken, with respect to each such recommendation.

"§ 1216. Other matters within the jurisdiction of the Office of Special Counsel

"(a) In addition to the authority otherwise provided in this chapter, the Special Counsel shall, except as provided in subsection (b), conduct an investigation of any allegation concerning—

"(1) political activity prohibited under subchapter III of chapter 73, relating to political activities by Federal employees;

"(2) political activity prohibited under chapter 15, relating to political activities by certain State and local officers and employees;

"(3) arbitrary or capricious withholding of information prohibited under section 552, except that the Special Counsel shall make no investigation of any withholding of foreign intelligence or counterintelligence information the disclosure of which is specifically prohibited by law or by Executive order;

"(4) activities prohibited by any civil service law, rule, or regulation, including any activity relating to political intrusion in personnel decisionmaking; and

"(5) involvement by any employee in any prohibited discrimination found by any court or appropriate administrative authority to have occurred in the course of any personnel action.

"(b) The Special Counsel shall make no investigation of any allegation of any prohibited activity referred to in subsection (a)(5), if the Special Counsel determines that the allegation may be resolved more appropriately under an administrative appeals procedure.

"(c)(1) If an investigation by the Special Counsel under subsection (a)(1) substantiates an allegation relating to any activity prohibited under section 7324, the Special Counsel may petition the Merit Systems Protection Board for any penalties provided for under section 7325.

"(2) If the Special Counsel receives an allegation concerning any matter under paragraph (3), (4), or (5) of subsection (a), the Special Counsel may investigate and seek corrective action under section 1214 in the same way as if a prohibited personnel practice were involved.

"§ 1217. Transmittal of information to Congress

"The Special Counsel or any employee of the Special Counsel designated by the Special Counsel, shall transmit to the Congress on the request of any committee or subcommittee thereof, by report, testimony, or otherwise, information and the Special Counsel's views on functions, responsibilities, or other matters relating to the Office. Such information shall be transmitted concurrently to the President and any other appropriate agency in the executive branch.

"§ 1218. Annual report

"The Special Counsel shall submit an annual report to the Congress on the activities of the Special Counsel, including the number, types, and disposition of allegations of prohibited personnel practices filed with it, investigations conducted by it, and actions initiated by it before the Merit Systems Protection Board, as well as a description of the recommendations and reports made by it to other agencies pursuant to this subchapter, and the actions taken by the agencies as a result of the reports or recommendations. The report required by this section shall include whatever recommendations for legislation or other action by Congress the Special Counsel may consider appropriate.

"§ 1219. Public information

"(a) The Special Counsel shall maintain and make available to the public—

"(1) a list of noncriminal matters referred to heads of agencies under subsection (c) of section 1213, together with reports from heads of agencies under subsection (c)(1)(B) of such section relating to such matters;

"(2) a list of matters referred to heads of agencies under section 1215(c)(2);

"(3) a list of matters referred to heads of agencies under subsection (e) of section 1214, together with certifications from heads of agencies under such subsection; and

"(4) reports from heads of agencies under section 1213(g)(1).

"(b) The Special Counsel shall take steps to ensure that any list or report made available to the public under this section does not contain any information the disclosure of which is prohibited by law or by Executive order requiring that information be kept secret in the interest of national defense or the conduct of foreign affairs.

"SUBCHAPTER III—INDIVIDUAL RIGHT OF ACTION IN CERTAIN REPRISAL CASES

"§ 1221. Individual right of action in certain reprisal cases

"(a) Subject to the provisions of subsection (b) of this section and subsection 1214(a)(3), an employee, former employee, or applicant for employment may, with respect to any personnel action taken, or proposed to be taken, against such employee, former employee, or applicant for employment, as a result of a prohibited personnel practice described in section 2302(b)(8), seek corrective action from the Merit Systems Protection Board.

"(b) This section may not be construed to prohibit any employee, former employee, or applicant for employment from seeking corrective action from the Merit Systems Protection Board before seeking corrective action from the Special Counsel, if such employee, former employee, or applicant for employment has the right to appeal directly to the Board under any law, rule, or regulation.

"(c)(1) Any employee, former employee, or applicant for employment seeking corrective action under subsection (a) may request that the Board order a stay of the personnel action involved.

"(2) Any stay requested under paragraph (1) shall be granted within 10 calendar days (excluding Saturdays, Sundays, and legal holidays) after the date the request is made, if the Board determines that such a stay would be appropriate.

"(3)(A) The Board shall allow any agency which would be subject to a stay under this subsection to comment to the Board on such stay request.

"(B) Except as provided in subparagraph (C), a stay granted under this subsection shall remain in effect for such period as the Board determines to be appropriate.

"(C) The Board may modify or dissolve a stay under this subsection at any time, if the Board determines that such a modification or dissolution is appropriate.

"(d)(1) At the request of an employee, former employee, or applicant for employment seeking corrective action under subsection (a), the Board may issue a subpoena for the attendance and testimony of any person or the production of documentary or other evidence from any person if the Board finds that such subpoena is necessary for the development of relevant evidence.

"(2) A subpoena under this subsection may be issued, and shall be enforced, in the same manner as applies in the case of subpoenas under section 1204.

"(e)(1) Subject to the provisions of paragraph (2), in any case involving an alleged prohibited personnel practice as described under section 2302(b)(8), the Board shall order such corrective action as the Board considers appropriate if the employee, former employee, or applicant for employment has demonstrated that a disclosure described under section 2302(b)(8) was a contributing factor in the personnel action which was taken or is to be taken against such employee, former employee, or applicant.

"(2) Corrective action under paragraph (1) may not be ordered if the agency demonstrates by clear and convincing evidence that it would have taken the same personnel action in the absence of such disclosure.

"(f)(1) A final order or decision shall be rendered by the Board as soon as practicable after the commencement of any proceeding under this section.

"(2) A decision to terminate an investigation under subchapter II may not be considered in any action or other proceeding under this section.

"(g)(1) If an employee, former employee, or applicant for employment is the prevailing party before the Merit Systems Protection Board, and the decision is based on a finding of a prohibited personnel practice, the agency involved shall be liable to the employee, former employee, or applicant for reasonable attorney's fees and any other reasonable costs incurred.

"(2) If an employee, former emloyee, or applicant for employment is the prevailing party in an appeal from the Merit Systems Protection Board, the agency involved shall be liable to the employee, former employee, or applicant for reasonable attorney's fees and any other reasonable costs incurred, regardless of the basis of the decision.

"(h)(1) An employee, former employee, or applicant for employment adversely affected or aggrieved by a final order or decision of the Board under this section may obtain judicial review of the order or decision.

"(2) A petition for review under this subsection shall be filed with such court, and within such time, as provided for under section 7703(b).

"(i) Subsections (a) through (h) shall apply in any proceeding brought under section 7513(d) if, or to the extent that, a prohibited personnel practice as defined in section 2302(b)(8) is alleged.

"(j) In determining the appealability of any case involving an allegation made by an individual under the provisions of this chapter, neither the status of an individual under any retirement system established under a Federal statute nor any election made by such individual under any such system may be taken into account.

"§ 1222. Availability of other remedies

"Except as provided in section 1221(i), nothing in this chapter or chapter 23 shall be construed to limit any right or remedy available under a provision of statute which is outside of both this chapter and chapter 23.".

(b) CONFORMING AMENDMENTS.—(1) The table of chapters for part II of title 5, United States Code, is amended by striking the item relating to chapter 12 and inserting in lieu thereof the following:

(2) The heading for chapter 12 of title 5, United States Code, is amended to read as follows:

"CHAPTER 12—MERIT SYSTEMS PROTECTION BOARD, OFFICE OF SPECIAL COUNSEL, AND EMPLOYEE RIGHT OF ACTION".

(3) The table of sections for chapter 12 of title 5, United States Code, is amended to read as follows:

(4) Chapter 12 of title 5, United States Code, is further amended by inserting before section 1201 the following subchapter heading:

"SUBCHAPTER I—MERIT SYSTEMS PROTECTION BOARD".

SEC. 4. REPRISALS.

(a) AMENDMENTS TO SECTION 2302(b)(8).—Section 2302(b)(8) of title 5, United States Code, is amended—

(1) by inserting ", or threaten to take or fail to take," after "take or fail to take";

(2) by striking out "as a reprisal for" and inserting in lieu thereof "because of";

(3) in subparagraph (A) by striking out "a disclosure" and inserting in lieu thereof "any disclosure";

(4) in subparagraph (A)(ii) by inserting "gross" before "mismanagement";

(5) in subparagraph (B) by striking out "a disclosure" and inserting in lieu thereof "any disclosure"; and

(6) in subparagraph (B)(ii) by inserting "gross" before "mismanagement".

(b) AMENDMENT TO SECTION 2302(b)(9).—Section 2302(b)(9) of title 5, United States Code, is amended to read as follows:

"(9) take or fail to take, or threaten to take or fail to take, any personnel action against any employee or applicant for employment because of—

"(A) the exercise of any appeal, complaint, or grievance right granted by any law, rule, or regulation;

"(B) testifying for or otherwise lawfully assisting any individual in the exercise of any right referred to in subparagraph (A);

"(C) cooperating with or disclosing information to the Inspector General of an agency, or the Special Counsel, in accordance with applicable provisions of law; or

"(D) for refusing to obey an order that would require the individual to violate a law;".

SEC. 5. PREFERENCE IN TRANSFERS FOR WHISTLEBLOWERS.

(a) IN GENERAL.—Subchapter IV of chapter 33 of title 5, United States Code, is amended by adding at the end thereof the following new section:

"§ 3352. Preference in transfers for employees making certain disclosures

"(a) Subject to the provisions of subsections (d) and (e), in filling a position within any Executive agency, the head of such agency may give preference to any employee of such agency, or any other Executive agency, to transfer to a position of the same status and tenure as the position of such employee on the date of applying for a transfer under subsection (b) if—

"(1) such employee is otherwise qualified for such position;

"(2) such employee is eligible for appointment to such position; and

"(3) the Merit Systems Protection Board makes a determination under the provisions of chapter 12 that a prohibited personnel action described under section 2302(b)(8) was taken against such employee.

"(b) An employee who meets the conditions described under subsection (a) (1), (2), and (3) may voluntarily apply for a transfer to a position, as described in subsection (a), within the Executive agency employing such employee or any other Executive agency.

"(c) If an employee applies for a transfer under the provisions of subsection (b) and the selecting official rejects such application, the selecting official shall provide the employee with a written notification of the reasons for the rejection within 30 days after receiving such application.

"(d) An employee whose application for transfer is rejected under the provisions of subsection (c) may request the head of such agency to review the rejection. Such request for review shall be submitted to the head of the agency within 30 days after the employee receives notification under subsection (c). Within 30 days after receiving a request for review, the head of the agency shall complete the review and provide a written statement of findings to the employee and the Merit Systems Protection Board.

"(e) The provisions of subsection (a) shall apply with regard to any employee—

"(1) for no more than 1 transfer;

"(2) for a transfer from or within the agency such employee is employed at the time of a determination by the Merit Systems Protection Board that a prohibited personnel action as described under section 2302(b)(8) was taken against such employee; and

"(3) no later than 18 months after such a determination is made by the Merit Systems Protection Board.

"(f) Notwithstanding the provisions of subsection (a), no preference may be given to any employee applying for a transfer under subsection (b), with respect to a preference eligible (as defined under section 2108(3)) applying for the same position.".

(b) TECHNICAL AMENDMENT.—The table of sections for chapter 33 of title 5, United States Code, is amended by inserting after the item relating to section 3351 the following:

"3352. Preference in transfers for employees making certain disclosures.".

SEC. 6. INTERIM RELIEF.

Section 7701 of title 5, United States Code, is amended—

(1) by redesignating subsection (b) as paragraph (1) of subsection (b); and

(2) by adding at the end thereof the following new paragraph:

"(2)(A) If an employee or applicant for employment is the prevailing party in an appeal under this subsection, the employee or applicant shall be granted the relief provided in the decision effective upon the making of the decision, and remaining in effect pending the outcome of any petition for review under subsection (e), unless—

"(i) the deciding official determines that the granting of such relief is not appropriate; or

"(ii)(I) the relief granted in the decision provides that such employee or applicant shall return or be present at the place of employment during the period pending the outcome of any petition for review under subsection (e); and

"(II) the employing agency, subject to the provisions of subparagraph (B), determines that the return or presence of such employee or applicant is unduly disruptive to the work environment.

"(B) If an agency makes a determination under subparagraph (A)(ii)(II) that prevents the return or presence of an employee at the place of employment, such employee shall receive pay, compensation, and all other benefits as terms and conditions of employment during the period pending the outcome of any petition for review under subsection (e).

"(C) Nothing in the provisions of this paragraph may be construed to require any award of back pay or attorney fees be paid before the decision is final.".

SEC. 7. SAVINGS PROVISIONS.

(a) ORDERS, RULES, AND REGULATIONS.—All orders, rules, and regulations issued by the Merit Systems Protection Board or the Special Counsel before the effective date of this Act shall continue in effect, according to their terms, until modified, terminated, superseded, or repealed.

(b) ADMINISTRATIVE PROCEEDINGS.—No provision of this Act shall affect any administrative proceeding pending at the time such provisions take effect. Orders shall be issued in such proceedings, and appeals shall be taken therefrom, as if this Act had not been enacted.

(c) SUITS AND OTHER PROCEEDINGS.—No suit, action, or other proceeding lawfully commenced by or against the members of the Merit Systems Protection Board, the Special Counsel, or officers or employees thereof, in their official capacity or in relation to the discharge of their official duties, as in effect immediately before the effective date of this Act, shall abate by reason of the enactment of this Act. Determinations with respect to any such suit, action, or other proceeding shall be made as if this Act had not been enacted.

SEC. 8. AUTHORIZATION OF APPROPRIATIONS; RESTRICTION RELATING
          TO APPROPRIATIONS UNDER THE CIVIL SERVICE REFORM
          ACT OF 1978; TRANSFER OF FUNDS.

(a) AUTHORIZATION OF APPROPRIATIONS.—There are authorized to be appropriated, out of any moneys in the Treasury not otherwise appropriated—

(1) for each of fiscal years 1989, 1990, 1991, 1992, 1993, and 1994, such sums as necessary to carry out subchapter I of chapter 12 of title 5, United States Code (as amended by this Act); and

(2) for each of fiscal years 1989, 1990, 1991, and 1992, such sums as necessary to carry out subchapter II of chapter 12 of title 5, United States Code (as amended by this Act).

(b) RESTRICTION RELATING TO APPROPRIATIONS UNDER THE CIVIL SERVICE REFORM ACT OF 1978.—No funds may be appropriated to the Merit Systems Protection Board or the Office of Special Counsel pursuant to section 903 of the Civil Service Reform Act of 1978 (5 U.S.C. 5509 note).

(c) TRANSFER OF FUNDS.—The personnel, assets, liabilities, contracts, property, records, and unexpended balances of appropriations, authorizations, allocations, and other funds employed, held, used, arising from, available or to be made available to the Special Counsel of the Merit Systems Protection Board are, subject to section 1531 of title 31, United States Code, transferred to the Special Counsel referred to in section 1211 of title 5, United States Code (as added by section 3(a) of this Act), for appropriate allocation.

SEC. 9. TECHNICAL AND CONFORMING AMENDMENTS.

(a)(1) Section 2303(c) of title 5, United States Code, is amended by striking "the provisions of section 1206" and inserting "applicable provisions of sections 1214 and 1221".

(2) Sections 7502, 7512(E), 7521(b)(C), and 7542 of title 5, United States Code, are amended by striking "1206" and inserting "1215".

(3) Section 1109(a) of the Foreign Service Act of 1980 (22 U.S.C. 4139(a)) is amended by striking "1206" and inserting "1214 or 1221".

(b) Section 3393(g) of title 5, United States Code, is amended by striking "1207" and inserting "1215".

SEC. 10. BOARD RESPONDENT.

Section 7703(a)(2) of title 5, United States Code, is amended to read as follows:

"(2) The Board shall be named respondent in any proceeding brought pursuant to this subsection, unless the employee or applicant for employment seeks review of a final order or decision on the merits on the underlying personnel action or on a request for attorney fees, in which case the agency responsible for taking the personnel action shall be the respondent.".

SEC. 11. EFFECTIVE DATE.

This Act and the amendments made by this Act shall take effect 90 days following the date of enactment of this Act.

Approved April 10, 1989.

* * * * *

Note on Chapter 12 of Title 5, U.S.C., and the WPA

The Whistleblower Protection Act was enacted just as this book was going into print. Therefore, the Act is not yet codified. As a result, the reader will have to do some cross referencing in order to fully understand the effective provisions. The Act amended the previously existing sections of 5 U.S.C. 1201–1209 by adding and deleting various provisions and by renumbering the sections 1201 through 1206. The Act then added Subchapters II and III to title 5 of the U.S. Code and amended Subchapter IV of Chapter 33 of title 5 and sections 7701, 7703, and other more minor conforming amendments.

* * * * *

TITLE 5—GOVERNMENT ORGANIZATION AND EMPLOYEES

"CHAPTER 12—MERIT SYSTEMS PROTECTION BOARD AND SPECIAL COUNSEL

"Sec.

"1201.   Appointment of members of the Merit Systems Protection Board.
"1202.   Term of office; filling vacancies; removal.
"1203.   Chairman; Vice Chairman.
"1204.   Special Counsel; appointment and removal.
"1205.   Powers and functions of the Merit Systems Protection Board and Special Counsel.
"1206.   Authority and responsibilities of the Special Counsel.
"1207.   Hearings and decisions on complaints filed by the Special Counsel.
"1208.   Stays of certain personnel actions.
"1209.   Information.

"§ 1201. Appointment of members of the Merit Systems Protection Board

"The Merit Systems Protection Board is composed of 3 members appointed by the President, by and with the advice and consent of the Senate, not more than 2 of whom may be adherents of the same political party. The Chairman and members of the Board shall be individuals who, by demonstrated ability, background, training, or experience are especially qualified to carry out the functions of the Board. No member of the Board may hold another office or position in the Government of the United States, except as otherwise provided by law or at the direction of the President. The Board shall have an official seal which shall be judicially noticed. The Board shall have its principal office in the District of Columbia and may have field offices in other appropriate locations.

"§ 1202. Term of office, filling vacancies; removal

"(a) The term of office of each member of the Merit Systems Protection Board is 7 years.

"(b) A member appointed to fill a vacancy occurring before the end of a term of office of his predecessor serves for the remainder of that term. Any appointment to fill a vacancy is subject to the requirements of section 1201 of this title.

"(c) Any member appointed for a 7-year term may not be reappointed to any following term but may continue to serve beyond the expiration of the term until a successor is appointed and has qualified, except that such member may not continue to serve for more than one year after the date on which the term of the member would otherwise expire under this section.

"(d) Any member may be removed by the President only for inefficiency, neglect of duty, or malfeasance in office.

"§ 1203. Chairman; Vice Chairman

"(a) The President shall from time to time, appoint, by and with the advice and consent of the Senate, one of the members of the Merit Systems Protection Board as the Chairman of the Board. The Chairman is the chief executive and administrative officer of the Board.

"(b) The President shall from time to time designate one of the members of the Board as Vice Chairman of the Board. During the absence or disability of the Chairman, or when the office of Chairman is vacant, the Vice Chairman shall perform the functions vested in the Chairman.

"(c) During the absence or disability of both the Chairman and Vice Chairman, or when the offices of Chairman and Vice Chairman are vacant, the remaining Board member shall perform the functions vested in the Chairman.

"§ 1204. Special Counsel; appointment and removal

"The Special Counsel of the Merit Systems Protection Board shall be appointed by the President from attorneys, by and with the advice and consent of the Senate, for a term of 5 years. A Special Counsel appointed to fill a vacancy occurring before the end of a term of office of his predecessor serves for the remainder of the term. The Special Counsel may be removed by the President only for inefficiency, neglect of duty, or malfeasance in office.

"§ 1205. Powers and functions of the Merit Systems Protection Board and Special Counsel

"(a) The Merit Systems Protection Board shall—

"(1) hear, adjudicate, or provide for the hearing or adjudication, of all matters within the jurisdiction of the Board under this title, section 2023 of title 38, or any other law, rule, or regulation, and, subject to otherwise applicable provisions of law, take final action on any such matter;

"(2) order any Federal agency or employee to comply with any order or decision issued by the Board under the authority granted under paragraph (1) of this subsection and enforce compliance with any such order;

"(3) conduct, from time to time, special studies relating to the civil service and to other merit systems in the executive branch, and report to the President and to the Congress as to whether the public interest in a civil service free of prohibited personnel practices is being adequately protected; and

"(4) review, as provided in subsection (e) of this section, rules and regulations of the Office of Personnel Management.

"(b)(1) Any member of the Merit Systems Protection Board, the Special Counsel, any administrative law judge appointed by the Board under section 3105 of this title, and any employee of the Board designated by the Board may administer oaths, examine witnesses, take depositions, and receive evidence.

"(2) Any member of the Board, the Special Counsel, and any administrative law judge appointed by the Board under section 3105 of this title may—

"(A) issue subpenas requiring the attendance and testimony of witnesses and the production of documentary or other evidence from any place in the United States or any territory or possession thereof, the Commonwealth of Puerto Rico, or the District of Columbia; and

"(B) order the taking of depositions and order responses to written interrogatories.

"(3) Witnesses (whether appearing voluntarily or under subpena) shall be paid the same fee and mileage allowances which are paid subpenaed witnesses in the courts of the United States.

"(c) In the case of contumacy or failure to obey a subpena issued under subsection (b)(2) of this section, the United States district court for the judicial district in which the person to whom the subpena is addressed resides or is served may issue an order requiring such person to appear at any designated place to testify or to produce documentary or other evidence. Any failure to obey the order of the court may be punished by the court as a contempt thereof.

"(d)(1) In any proceeding under subsection (a)(1) of this section, any member of the Board may request from the Director of the Office of Personnel Management an advisory opinion concerning the interpretation of any rule, regulation, or other policy directive promulgated by the Office of Personnel Management.

"(2) In enforcing compliance with any order under subsection (a) (2) of this section, the Board may order that any employee charged with complying with such order, other than an employee appointed by the President by and with the advice and consent of the Senate, shall not be entitled to receive payment for service as an employee during any period that the order has not been complied with. The Board shall certify to the Comptroller General of the United States that such an order has been issued and no payment shall be made out of the Treasury of the United States for any service specified in such order.

"(3) In carrying out any study under subsection (a)(3) of this section, the Board shall make such inquiries as may be necessary and, unless otherwise prohibited by law, shall have access to personnel records or information collected by the Office and may require additional reports from other agencies as needed.

"(e)(1) At any time after the effective date of any rule or regulation issued by the Director in carrying out functions under section 1103 of this title, the Board shall review any provision of such rule or regulation—
"(A) on its own motion;
"(B) on the granting by the Board, in its sole discretion, of any petition for such review filed with the Board by any interested person, after consideration of the petition by the Board; or
"(C) on the filing of a written complaint by the Special Counsel requesting such review.
"(2) In reviewing any provision of any rule or regulation pursuant to this subsection the Board shall declare such provision—
"(A) invalid on its face, if the Board determines that such provision would, if implemented by any agency, on its face, require any employee to violate section 2302(b) of this title; or
"(B) invalidly implemented by any agency, if the Board determines that such provision, as it has been implemented by the agency through any personnel action taken by the agency or through any policy adopted by the agency in conformity with such provision, has required any employee to violate section 2302 (b) of this title.
"(3)(A) The Director of the Office of Personnel Management, and the head of any agency implementing any provision of any rule or regulation under review pursuant to this subsection, shall have the right to participate in such review.
"(B) Any review conducted by the Board pursuant to this subsection shall be limited to determining—
"(i) the validity on its face of the provision under review; and
"(ii) whether the provision under review has been validly implemented.
"(C) The Board shall require any agency—
"(i) to cease compliance with any provisions of any rule or regulation which the Board declares under this subsection to be invalid on its face; and
"(ii) to correct any invalid implementation by the agency of any provision of any rule or regulation which the Board declares under this subsection to have been invalidly implemented by the agency.
"(f) The Board may delegate the performance of any of its administrative functions under this title to any employee of the Board.
"(g) The Board shall have the authority to prescribe such regulations as may be necessary for the performance of its functions. The Board shall not issue advisory opinions. All regulations of the Board shall be published in the Federal Register.
"(h) Except as provided in section 518 of title 28, relating to litigation before the Supreme Court, attorneys designated by the Chairman of the Board may appear for the Board, and represent the Board, in any civil action brought in connection with any function carried out by the Board pursuant to this title or as otherwise authorized by law.
"(i) The Chairman of the Board may appoint such personnel as may be necessary to perform the functions of the Board. Any appointment made under this subsection shall comply with the provisions of this title, except that such appointment shall not be subject to the

approval or supervision of the Office of Personnel Management or the Executive Office of the President (other than approval required under section 3324 or subchapter VIII of chapter 33 of this title).

"(j) The Board shall prepare and submit to the President, and, at the same time, to the appropriate committees of Congress, an annual budget of the expenses and other items relating to the Board which shall, as revised, be included as a separate item in the budget required to be transmitted to the Congress under section 201 of the Budget and Accounting Act, 1921 (31 U.S.C. 11).

"(k) The Board shall submit to the President, and, at the same time, to each House of the Congress, any legislative recommendations of the Board relating to any of its functions under this title.

"§ 1206. Authority and responsibilities of the Special Counsel

"(a)(1) The Special Counsel shall receive any allegation of a prohibited personnel practice and shall investigate the allegation to the extent necessary to determine whether there are reasonable grounds to believe that a prohibited personnel practice has occurred, exists, or is to be taken

"(2) If the Special Counsel terminates any investigation under paragraph (1) of this subsection, the Special Counsel shall prepare and transmit to any person on whose allegation the investigation was initiated a written statement notifying the person of the termination of the investigation and the reasons therefor.

"(3) In addition to authority granted under paragraph (1) of this subsection, the Special Counsel may, in the absence of an allegation, conduct an investigation for the purpose of determining whether there are reasonable grounds to believe that a prohibited personnel practice has occurred, exists, or is to be taken.

"(b)(1) In any case involving—

"(A) any disclosure of information by an employee or applicant for employment which the employee or applicant reasonably believes evidences—

"(i) a violation of any law, rule, or regulation; or

"(ii) mismanagement, a gross waste of funds, an abuse of authority, or a substantial and specific danger to public health or safety;

if the disclosure is not specifically prohibited by law and if the information is not specifically required by Executive order to be kept secret in the interest of national defense or the conduct of foreign affairs; or

"(B) a disclosure by an employee or applicant for employment to the Special Counsel of the Merit Systems Protection Board, or to the Inspector General of an agency or another employee designated by the head of the agency to receive such disclosures of information which the employee or applicant reasonably believes evidences—

"(i) a violation of any law, rule, or regulation; or

"(ii) mismanagement, a gross waste of funds, an abuse of authority, or a substantial and specific danger to public health or safety;

the identity of the employee or applicant may not be disclosed without the consent of the employee or applicant during any investigation under subsection (a) of this section or under paragraph (3) of this subsection, unless the Special Counsel determines that the disclosure of the identity of the employee or applicant is necessary in order to carry out the functions of the Special Counsel.

"(2) Whenever the Special Counsel receives information of the type described in paragraph (1) of this subsection, the Special Counsel shall promptly transmit such information to the appropriate agency head.

"(3) (A) In the case of information received by the Special Counsel under paragraph (1) of this section, if, after such review as the Special Counsel determines practicable (but not later than 15 days after the receipt of the information), the Special Counsel determines that there is a substantial likelihood that the information discloses a violation of any law, rule, or regulation, or mismanagement, gross waste of funds, abuse of authority, or substantial and specific danger to the public health or safety, the Special Counsel may, to the extent provided in subparagraph (B) of this paragraph, require the head of the agency to—

"(i) conduct an investigation of the information and any related matters transmitted by the Special Counsel. to the head of the agency; and

"(ii) submit a written report setting forth the findings of the head of the agency within 60 days after the date on which the information is transmitted to the head of the agency or within any longer period of time agreed to in writing by the Special Counsel.

"(B) The Special Counsel may require an agency head to conduct an investigation and submit a written report under subparagraph (A) of this paragraph only if the information was transmitted to the Special Counsel by—

"(i) any employee or former employee or applicant for employment in the agency which the information concerns; or

"(ii) any employee who obtained the information in connection with the performance of the employee's duties and responsibilities.

"(4) Any report required under paragraph (3)(A) of this subsection shall be reviewed and signed by the head of the agency and shall include—

"(A) a summary of the information with respect to which the investigation was initiated;

"(B) a description of the conduct of the investigation;

"(C) a summary of any evidence obtained from the investigation;

"(D) a listing of any violation or apparent violation of any law, rule, or regulation; and

"(E) a description of any corrective action taken or planned as a result of the investigation, such as—

"(i) changes in agency rules, regulations, or practices;

"(ii) the restoration of any aggrieved employee;

"(iii) disciplinary action against any employee; and

"(iv) referral to the Attorney General of any evidence of a criminal violation.

"(5) (A) Any such report shall be submitted to the Congress, to the President, and to the Special Counsel for transmittal to the complainant. Whenever the Special Counsel does not receive the report of the agency head within the time prescribed in paragraph (3)(A)(ii) of this subsection, the Special Counsel may transmit a copy of the information which was transmitted to the agency head to the President and to the Congress together with a statement noting the failure of the head of the agency to file the required report.

"(B) In any case in which evidence of a criminal violation obtained by an agency in an investigation under paragraph (3) of this subsection is referred to the Attorney General—

"(i) the report shall not be transmitted to the complainant; and

"(ii) the agency shall notify the Office of Personnel Management and the Office of Management and Budget of the referral.

"(6) Upon receipt of any report of the head of any agency required under paragraph (3)(A)(ii) of this subsection, the Special Counsel shall review the report and determine whether—

"(A) the findings of the head of the agency appear reasonable; and

"(B) the agency's report under paragraph (3)(A)(ii) of this subsection contains the information required under paragraph (4) of this subsection.

"(7) Whenever the Special Counsel transmits any information to the head of the agency under paragraph (2) of this subsection but does not require an investigation under paragraph (3) of this subsection, the head of the agency shall, within a reasonable time after the information was transmitted, inform the Special Counsel, in writing, of what action has been or is to be taken and when such action will be completed. The Special Counsel shall inform the complainant of the report of the agency head.

"(8) Except as specifically authorized under this subsection, the provisions of this subsection shall not be considered to authorize disclosure of any information by any agency or any person which is—

"(A) specifically prohibited from disclosure by any other provision of law: or

"(B) specifically required by Executive order to be kept secret in the interest of national defense or the conduct of foreign affairs.

"(9) In any case under subsection (b)(1)(B) of this section involving foreign intelligence or counterintelligence information the disclosure of which is specifically prohibited by law or by Executive order, the Special Counsel shall transmit such information to the Permanent Select Committee on Intelligence of the House of Representatives and the Select Committee on Intelligence of the Senate.

"(c)(1)(A) If, in connection with any investigation under this section, the Special Counsel determines that there are reasonable grounds to believe that a prohibited personnel practice has occurred, exists, or is to be taken which requires corrective action, the Special Counsel shall report the determination together with any findings or recommendations to the Board, the agency involved, and to the Office, and may report the determination. findings, and recommendations to the President. The Special Counsel may include in the report recommendations as to what corrective action should be taken.

"(B) If, after a reasonable period, the agency has not taken the corrective action recommended. the Special Counsel may request the

Board to consider the matter. The Board may order such corrective action as the Board considers appropriate, after opportunity for comment by the agency concerned and the Office of Personnel Management.

"(2)(A) If, in connection with any investigation under this section, the Special Counsel determines that there is reasonable cause to believe that a criminal violation by an employee has occurred, the Special Counsel shall report the determination to the Attorney General and to the head of the agency involved, and shall submit a copy of the report to the Director of the Office of Personnel Management and the Director of the Office of Management and Budget.

"(B) In any case in which the Special Counsel determines that there are reasonable grounds to believe that a prohibited personnel practice has occurred, exists, or is to be taken, the Special Counsel may proceed with any investigation or proceeding instituted under this section notwithstanding that the alleged violation has been reported to the Attorney General.

"(3) If, in connection with any investigation under this section, the Special Counsel determines that there is reasonable cause to believe that any violation of any law, rule, or regulation has occurred which is not referred to in paragraph (1) or (2) of this subsection, the violation shall be reported to the head of the agency involved. The Special Counsel shall require, within 30 days of the receipt of the report by the agency, a certification by the head of the agency which states—

"(A) that the head of the agency has personally reviewed the report; and

"(B) what action has been, or is to be, taken, and when the action will be completed.

"(d) The Special Counsel shall maintain and make available to the public a list of noncriminal matters referred to heads of agencies under subsections (b)(3)(A) and (c)(3) of this section, together with—

"(1) reports by the heads of agencies under subsection (b)(3) (A) of this section, in the case of matters referred under subsection (b); and

"(2) certifications by heads of agencies under subsection (c) (3), in the case of matters referred under subsection (c).

The Special Counsel shall take steps to ensure that any such public list does not contain any information the disclosure of which is prohibited by law or by Executive order requiring that information be kept secret in the interest of national defense or the conduct of foreign affairs.

"(e)(1) In addition to the authority otherwise provided in this section, the Special Counsel shall, except as provided in paragraph (2) of this subsection, conduct an investigation of any allegation concerning—

"(A) political activity prohibited under subchapter III of chapter 73 of this title, relating to political activities by Federal employees;

"(B) political activity prohibited under chapter 15 of this title, relating to political activities by certain State and local officers and employees;

"(C) arbitrary or capricious withholding of information prohibited under section 552 of this title, except that the Special Counsel shall make no investigation under this subsection of any withholding of foreign intelligence or counterintelligence information the disclosure of which is specifically prohibited by law or by Executive order;

"(D) activities prohibited by any civil service law, rule, or regulation, including any activity relating to political intrusion in personnel decisionmaking; and

"(E) involvement by any employee in any prohibited discrimination found by any court or appropriate administrative authority to have occurred in the course of any personnel action.

"(2) The Special Counsel shall make no investigation of any allegation of any prohibited activity referred to in paragraph (1)(D) or (1)(E) of this subsection if the Special Counsel determines that the allegation may be resolved more appropriately under an administrative appeals procedure.

"(f) During any investigation initiated under this section, no disciplinary action shall be taken against any employee for any alleged prohibited activity under investigation or for any related activity without the approval of the Special Counsel.

"(g)(1) Except as provided in paragraph (2) of this subsection, if the Special Counsel determines that disciplinary action should be taken against any employee—

"(A) after any investigation under this section, or

"(B) on the basis of any knowing and willful refusal or failure by an employee to comply with an order of the Merit Systems Protection Board,

the Special Counsel shall prepare a written complaint against the employee containing his determination, together with a statement of supporting facts, and present the complaint and statement to the employee and the Merit Systems Protection Board in accordance with section 1207 of this title.

"(2) In the case of an employee in a confidential, policy-making, policy-determining, or policy-advocating position appointed by the President, by and with the advice and consent of the Senate (other than an individual in the Foreign Service of the United States), the complaint and statement referred to in paragraph (1) of this subsection, together with any response by the employee, shall be presented to the President for appropriate action in lieu of being presented under section 1207 of this title.

"(h) If the Special Counsel believes there is a pattern of prohibited personnel practices and such practices involve matters which are not otherwise appealable to the Board under section 7701 of this title, the Special Counsel may seek corrective action by filing a written complaint with the Board against the agency or employee involved and the Board shall order such corrective action as the Board determines necessary.

"(i) The Special Counsel may as a matter of right intervene or otherwise participate in any proceeding before the Merit Systems Protection Board, except that the Special Counsel shall comply with the rules of the Board and the Special Counsel shall not have any right of judicial review in connection with such intervention.

"(j)(1) The Special Counsel may appoint the legal, administrative, and support personnel necessary to perform the functions of the Special Counsel.

"(2) Any appointment made under this subsection shall comply with the provisions of this title, except that such appointment shall not be subject to the approval or supervision of the Office of Personnel Management or the Executive Office of the President (other than approval required under section 3324 or subchapter VIII of chapter 33 of this title).

"(k) The Special Counsel may prescribe regulations relating to the receipt and investigation of matters under the jurisdiction of the Special Counsel. Such regulations shall be published in the Federal Register.

"(l) The Special Counsel shall not issue any advisory opinion concerning any law, rule, or regulation (other than an advisory opinion concerning chapter 15 or subchapter III of chapter 73 of this title).

"(m) The Special Counsel shall submit an annual report to the Congress on the activities of the Special Counsel, including the number, types, and disposition of allegations of prohibited personnel practices filed with it, investigations conducted by it, and actions initiated by it before the Board, as well as a description of the recommendations and reports made by it to other agencies pursuant to this section, and the actions taken by the agencies as a result of the reports or recommendations. The report required by this subsection shall include whatever recommendations for legislation or other action by Congress the Special Counsel may deem appropriate.

"§ 1207. Hearings and decisions on complaints filed by the Special Counsel

"(a) Any employee against whom a complaint has been presented to the Merit Systems Protection Board under section 1206(g) of this title is entitled to—

"(1) a reasonable time to answer orally and in writing and to furnish affidavits and other documentary evidence in support of the answer;

"(2) be represented by an attorney or other representative;

"(3) a hearing before the Board or an administrative law judge appointed under section 3105 of this title and designated by the Board;

"(4) have a transcript kept of any hearing under paragraph (3) of this subsection; and

"(5) a written decision and reasons therefor at the earliest practicable date, including a copy of any final order imposing disciplinary action.

"(b) A final order of the Board may impose disciplinary action consisting of removal, reduction in grade, debarment from Federal employment for a period not to exceed 5 years, suspension, reprimand, or an assessment of a civil penalty not to exceed $1,000.

"(c) There may be no administrative appeal from an order of the Board. An employee subject to a final order imposing disciplinary action under this section may obtain judicial review of the order in the United States court of appeals for the judicial circuit in which the employee resides or is employed at the time of the action.

"(d) In the case of any State or local officer or employee under chapter 15 of this title. the Board shall consider the case in accordance with the provisions of such chapter.

"§ 1208. Stays of certain personnel actions

"(a)(1) The Special Counsel may request any member of the Merit Systems Protection Board to order a stay of any personnel action for 15 calendar days if the Special Counsel determines that there are reasonable grounds to believe that the personnel action was taken, or is to be taken, as a result of a prohibited personnel practice.

"(2) Any member of the Board requested by the Special Counsel to order a stay under paragraph (1) of this subsection shall order such stay unless the member determines that, under the facts and circumstances involved, such a stay would not be appropriate.

"(3) Unless denied under paragraph (2) of this subsection, any stay under this subsection shall be granted within 3 calendar days (excluding Saturdays, Sundays, and legal holidays) after the date of the request for the stay by the Special Counsel.

"(b) Any member of the Board may, on the request of the Special Counsel, extend the period of any stay ordered under subsection (a) of this section for a period of not more than 30 calendar days.

"(c) The Board may extend the period of any stay granted under subsection (a) of this section for any period which the Board considers appropriate, but only if the Board concurs in the determination of the Special Counsel under such subsection, after an opportunity is provided for oral or written comment by the Special Counsel and the agency involved.

"§ 1209. Information

"(a) Notwithstanding any other provision of law or any rule, regulation or policy directive, any member of the Board, or any employee of the Board designated by the Board, may transmit to the Congress on the request of any committee or subcommittee thereof, by report, testimony, or otherwise, information and views on functions, responsibilities, or other matters relating to the Board, without review, clearance, or approval by any other administrative authority.

"(b) The Board shall submit an annual report to the President and the Congress on its activities, which shall include a description of significant actions taken by the Board to carry out its functions under this title. The report shall also review the significant actions of the Office of Personnel Management, including an analysis of whether the actions of the Office of Personnel Management are in accord with merit system principles and free from prohibited personnel practices.".

*   *   *   *   *

CHAPTER 15—POLITICAL ACTIVITY OF CERTAIN STATE AND LOCAL EMPLOYEES

Sec.
1501. Definitions.
1502. Influencing elections; taking part in political campaigns; prohibitions; exceptions.
1503. Nonpartisan political activity permitted.
1504. Investigations; notice of hearing.
1505. Hearings; adjudications; notice of determinations.
1506. Orders; withholding loans or grants; limitations.
1507. Subpenas and depositions.
1508. Judicial review.

§1501. Definitions

For the purpose of this chapter —

(1) "State" means a State or territory or possession of the United States;

(2) "State or local agency" means the executive branch of a State, municipality, or other political subdivision of a State, or an agency or department thereof;

(3) "Federal agency" means an executive agency or other agency of the United States, but does not include a member bank of the Federal Reserve System;

(4) "State or local officer or employee" means an individual employed by a State or local agency whose principal employment is in connection with an activity which is financed in whole or in part by loans or grants made by the United States or a Federal agency, but does not include —

(A) an individual who exercises no functions in connection with that activity; or

(B) an individual employed by an educational or research institution, establishment, agency, or system which is supported in whole or in part by a State or political subdivision thereof, or by a recognized religious, philanthropic, or cultural organization; and

(5) the phrase "an active part in political management or in political campaigns" means those acts of political management or political campaigning which were prohibited on the part of employees in the competitive service before July 19, 1940, by determinations of the Civil Service Commission under the rules prescribed by the President.

§1502. Influencing elections; taking part in political campaigns; prohibitions; exceptions

(a) A State or local officer or employee may not —

(1) use his official authority or influence for the purpose of interfering with or affecting the result of an election or a nomination for office;

(2) directly or indirectly coerce, attempt to coerce, command, or advise a State or local officer or employee to pay, lend, or contribute anything of value to a party, committee, organization, agency, or person for political purposes; or

(3) take an active part in political management or in political campaigns.

(b) A State or local officer or employee retains the right to vote as he chooses and to express his opinions on political subjects and candidates.

(c) Subsection (a) (3) of this section does not apply to—

(1) the Governor or Lieutenant Governor of a State or an individual authorized by law to act as Governor;

(2) the mayor of a city;

(3) a duly elected head of an executive department of a State or municipality who is not classified under a State or municipal merit or civil-service system; or

(4) an individual holding elective office.

§1503. Nonpartisan political activity permitted

Section 1502(a) (3) of this title does not prohibit political activity in connection with—

(1) an election and the preceding campaign if none of the candidates is to be nominated or elected at that election as representing a party any of whose candidates for presidential elector received votes in the last preceding election at which presidential electors were selected; or

(2) a question which is not specifically identified with a National or State political party.

For the purpose of this section, questions relating to constitutional amendments, referendums, approval of municipal ordinances, and others of a similar character, are deemed not specifically identified with a National or State political party.

§1504. Investigations; notice of hearing

When a Federal agency charged with the duty of making a loan or grant of funds of the United States for use in an activity by a State or local officer or employee has reason to believe that the officer or employee has violated section 1502 of this title, it shall report the matter to the Special Counsel. On receipt of the report or on receipt of other information which seems to the Special Counsel to warrant an investigation, the Special Counsel shall investigate the report and such other information and present his findings and any charges based on such findings to the Merit Systems Protection Board, which shall—

(1) fix a time and place for a hearing; and

(2) send, by registered or certified mail, to the officer or employee charged with the violation and to the State or local agency employing him a notice setting forth a summary of the alleged violation and giving the time and place of the hearing.

The hearing may not be held earlier than 10 days after the mailing of the notice.

§1505. Hearings; adjudications; notice of determinations

Either the State or local officer or employee or the State or local agency employing him, or both, are entitled to appear with counsel at

TEXT OF RELEVANT STATUTES

the hearing under section 1504 of this title, and be heard. After this hearing, the Merit Systems Protection Board shall—
(1) determine whether a violation of section 1502 of this title has occurred;
(2) determine whether the violation warrants the removal of the officer or employee from his office or employment; and
(3) notify the officer or employee and the agency of the determination by registered or certified mail.

§1506. Orders; withholding loans or grants; limitations

(a) When the Merit Systems Protection Board finds—
(1) that a State or local officer or employee has not been removed from his office or employment within 30 days after notice of a determination by the Board that he has violated section 1502 of this title and that the violation warrants removal; or
(2) that the State or local officer or employee has been removed and has been appointed within 18 months after his removal to an office or employment in the same State in a State or local agency which does not receive loans or grants from a Federal agency;
the Board shall make and certify to the appropriate Federal agency an order requiring that agency to withhold from its loans or grants to the State or local agency to which notice was given an amount equal to 2 years' pay at the rate the officer or employee was receiving at the time of the violation. When the State or local agency to which appointment within 18 months after removal has been made is one that receives loans or grants from a Federal agency, the Board order shall direct that the withholding be made from that State or local agency.

(b) Notice of the order shall be sent by registered or certified mail to the State or local agency from which the amount is ordered to be withheld. After the order becomes final, the Federal agency to which the order is certified shall withhold the amount in accordance with the terms of the order. Except as provided by section 1508 of this title, a determination of order of the Board becomes final at the end of 30 days after mailing the notice of the determination or order.

(c) The Board may not require an amount to be withheld from a loan or grant pledged by a State or local agency as security for its bonds or notes if the withholding of that amount would jeopardize the payment of the principal or interest on the bonds or notes.

§1507. Subpenas and depositions

(a) The Merit Systems Protection Board may require by subpena the attendance and testimony of witnesses and the production of documentary evidence relating to any matter before it as a result of this chapter. Any member of the Board may sign subpenas, and members of the Board and its examiners when authorized by the Board may administer oaths, examine witnesses, and receive evidence. The attendance of witnesses and the production of documentary evidence may be required from any place in the United States at the designated place of hearing. In case of disobedience to a subpena, the Board may invoke the aid of a court of the United States in requiring the attendance and testimony of witnesses and the production of documentary evidence. In case of contumacy or refusal to obey a subpena issued to a person, the United States District Court within whose jurisdiction the inquiry is carried on may issue an order requiring him to appear before the Board, or to produce documentary evidence if so ordered, or to give evidence concerning the matter in question; and any failure to obey the order of the court may be punished by the court as a contempt thereof.

(b) The Board may order testimony to be taken by deposition at any stage of a proceeding or investigation before it as a result of this chapter. Depositions may be taken before an individual designated by the Board and having the power to administer oaths. Testimony shall be reduced to writing by the individual taking the deposition, or under his direction, and shall be subscribed by the deponent. Any person may be compelled to appear and depose and to produce documentary evidence before the Board as provided by this section.

(c) A person may not be excused from attending and testifying or from producing documentary evidence or in obedience to a subpena on the ground that the testimony or evidence, documentary or otherwise required of him may tend to incriminate him or subject him to a penalty or forfeiture for or on account of any transaction, matter, or thing concerning which he is compelled to testify, or produce evidence, documentary or otherwise, before the Board in obedience to a subpena issued by it. A person so testifying is not exempt from prosecution and punishment for perjury committed in so testifying.

§1508. Judicial review

A party aggrieved by a determination or order of the Merit Systems Protection Board under section 1504, 1505, or 1506 of this title may, within 30 days after the mailing of notice of the determination or order, institute proceedings for review thereof by filing a petition in the United States District Court for the district in which the State or local officer or employee resides. The institution of the proceedings does not operate as a stay of the determination or order unless —

(1) the court specifically orders a stay; and

(2) the officer or employee is suspended from his office or employment while the proceedings are pending.

A copy of the petition shall immediately be served on the Board, and thereupon the Board shall certify and file in the court a transcript of the record on which the determination or order was made. The court shall review the entire record including questions of fact and questions of law. If application is made to the court for leave to adduce additional evidence, and it is shown to the satisfaction of the court that the additional evidence may materially affect the result of the proceedings and that there were reasonable grounds for failure to adduce this evidence in the hearing before the Board, the court may direct that the additional evidence be taken before the Board in the manner and on the terms and conditions fixed by the court. The Board may modify its findings of fact or its determination or order in view of the additional evidence and shall file with the court the modified findings, determination, or order; or the modified findings of fact, if supported by substantial evidence, are conclusive. The court shall affirm the determination or order, or the modified determination or order, if the court determines that it is in accordance with law. If the court determines that the determination or order, or the modified determination or order, is not in accordance with law, the court shall remand the proceeding to the Board with directions either to make a determination or order determined by the court to be lawful or to take such further proceedings as, in the opinion of the court, the law requires. The judgment and decree of the court are final, subject to review by the appropriate United States Court of Appeals as in other cases, and the judgment and decree of the court of appeals are final, subject to review by the Supreme Court of the United States on certiorari or certification as provided by section 1254 of title 28. If a provision of this section is held to be invalid as applied to a party by a determination or order of the Board, the determination or order becomes final and effective as to that party as if the provision had not been enacted.

* * * * *

Subpart A—General Provisions

CHAPTER 21—DEFINITIONS

Sec.
2101. Civil service; armed forces; uniformed services.
2101a. The Senior Executive Service.
2102. The competitive service.
2103. The excepted service.
2104. Officer.
2105. Employee.
2106. Member of Congress.
2107. Congressional employee.
2108. Veteran; disabled veteran; preference eligible.
2109. Air traffic controller.

§ 2101. Civil service; armed forces; uniformed services

For the purpose of this title—

(1) the "civil service" consists of all appointive positions in the executive, judicial, and legislative branches of the Government of the United States, except positions in the uniformed services;

(2) "armed forces" means the Army, Navy, Air Force, Marine Corps, and Coast Guard; and

(3) "uniformed services" means the armed forces, the commissioned corps of the Public Health Service, and the commissioned corps of the National Oceanic and Atmospheric Administration.

(Pub. L. 89–554, Sept. 6, 1966, 80 Stat. 408, amended Pub. L. 90–83, § 1(4), Sept. 11, 1967, 81 Stat. 196; Pub. L. 96–54, Aug. 14, 1979; 93 Stat. 381.)

§ 2101a. The Senior Executive Service

The "Senior Executive Service" consists of Senior Executive Service positions (as defined in section 3132(a)(2) of this title). (Pub. L. 95–454, Oct. 13, 1978, 92 Stat. 1154.)

§ 2102. The competitive service

(a) The "competitive service" consists of—
    (1) all civil service positions in the executive branch, except—
        (A) positions which are specifically excepted from the competitive service by or under statute;
        (B) positions to which appointments are made by nomination for confirmation by the Senate, unless the Senate otherwise directs; and
        (C) positions in the Senior Executive Service;
    (2) civil service positions not in the executive branch which are specifically included in the competitive service by statute; and
    (3) positions in the government of the District of Columbia which are specifically included in the competitive service by statute.

(b) Notwithstanding subsection (a)(1)(B) of this section, the "competitive service" includes positions to which appointments are made by nomination for confirmation by the Senate when specifically included therein by statute.

(c) As used in other Acts of Congress, "classified civil service" or "classified service" means the "competitive service". (Pub. L. 89–554, Sept. 6, 1966, 80 Stat. 408; amended Pub. L. 95–454, Oct. 13, 1978, 92 Stat. 1154.)

§ 2103. The excepted service

(a) For the purpose of this title, the "excepted service" consists of those civil service positions which are not in the competitive service or the Senior Executive Service.

(b) As used in other Acts of Congress, "unclassified civil service" or "unclassified service" means the "excepted service". (Pub. L. 89–554, Sept. 6, 1966, 80 Stat. 408; amended Pub. L. 95–454, Oct. 13, 1978, 92 Stat. 1154.)

§ 2104. Officer

(a) For the purpose of this title, "officer", except as otherwise provided by this section or when specifically modified, means a justice or judge of the United States and an individual who is—
    (1) required by law to be appointed in the civil service by one of the following acting in an official capacity—
        (A) the President;
        (B) a court of the United States;
        (C) the head of an Executive agency; or
        (D) the Secretary of a military department;
    (2) engaged in the performance of a Federal function under authority of law or an Executive act; and

(3) subject to the supervision of an authority named by paragraph (1) of this section, or the Judicial Conference of the United States, while engaged in the performance of the duties of his office.

(b) Except as otherwise provided by law, an officer of the United States Postal Service or of the Postal Rate Commission is deemed not an officer for purposes of this title. (Pub. L. 89–554, Sept. 6, 1966, 80 Stat. 408, amended Pub. L. 91–375, § 6(c)(3), Aug. 12, 1970, 84 Stat. 775.)

§ 2105. Employee

(a) For the purpose of this title, "employee", except as otherwise provided by this section or when specifically modified, means an officer and and individual who is—

(1) appointed in the civil service by one of the following acting in an official capacity—

(A) the President;

(B) a Member or Members of Congress, or the Congress;

(C) a member of a uniformed service;

(D) an individual who is an employee under this section;

(E) the head of a Government controlled corporation; or

(F) an adjutant general designated by the Secretary concerned under section 709(c) of title 32;

(2) engaged in the performance of a Federal function under authority of law or an Executive act; and

(3) subject to the supervision of an individual named by paragraph (1) of this subsection while engaged in the performance of the duties of his position.

(b) An individual employed at the United States Naval Academy in the midshipmen's laundry, the midshipmen's tailor shop, the midshipmen's cobbler and barber shops, and the midshipmen's store, except an individual employed by the Academy dairy, is deemed an employee.

(c) An employee paid from nonappropriated funds of the Army and Air Force Exchange Service, Army and Air Force Motion Picture Service, Navy Ship's Stores Ashore, Navy exchanges, Marine Corps exchanges, Coast Guard exchanges, and other instrumentalities of the United States under the jurisdiction of the armed forces conducted for the comfort, pleasure, contentment, and mental and physical improvement of personnel of the armed forces is deemed not an employee for the purpose of—

(1) laws (other than subchapter IV of chapter 53 and sections 5550 and 7204 of this title) administered by the Office of Personnel Management; or

(2) subchapter I of chapter 81 and section 7902 of this title.

This subsection does not affect the status of these nonappropriated fund activities as Federal instrumentalities.

(d) A Reserve of the armed forces who is not on active duty or who is on active duty for training is deemed not an employee or an individual holding an office of trust or profit or discharging an official function under or in connection with the United States because of his appointment, oath, or status, or any duties or functions performed or pay or allowances received in that capacity.

(e) Except as otherwise provided by law, an employee of the United States Postal Service or of the Postal Rate Commission is deemed not an employee for purposes of this title. (Pub. L. 89–554, Sept. 6, 1966, 80 Stat. 409, amended Pub. L. 90–486, § 4, Aug. 13, 1968, 82 Stat. 757; Pub. L. 91–375, § 6(c) (4), Aug. 12, 1970, 84 Stat. 775; Pub. L. 92–392, § 2, Aug. 19, 1972, 86 Stat. 573; Pub. L. 95–454, Oct. 13, 1978, 92 Stat. 1217 and 1224; Pub. L. 96–54, Aug. 14, 1979, 93 Stat. 381.)

§ 2106. Member of Congress

For the purpose of this title, "Member of Congress" means the Vice President, a member of the Senate or the House of Representatives, a Delegate to the House of Representatives, and the Resident Commissioner from Puerto Rico (Pub. L. 89–554, Sept. 6, 1966, 80 Stat. 409, amended Pub. L. 91–405, § 204(b), Sept. 22, 1970, 84 Stat. 852; Pub. L. 96–54, Aug. 14, 1979, 93 Stat. 381.)

§ 2107. Congressional employee

For the purpose of this title, "Congressional employee" means—

(1) an employee of either House of Congress, of a committee of either House, or of a joint committee of the two Houses;

(2) an elected officer of either House who is not a Member of Congress;

(3) the Legislative Counsel of either House and an employee of his office;

(4) a member of the Capitol Police;

(5) an employee of a Member of Congress if the pay of the employee is paid by the Secretary of the Senate or the Clerk of the House of Representatives;

(6) Repealed. Pub. L. 90–83, § 1(5) (A), Sept. 11, 1967, 81 Stat. 196;

(7) the Architect of the Capitol and an employee of the Architect of the Capitol;

(8) an employee of the Botanic Garden; and

(9) an employee of the Capitol Guide Service.

(Pub. L. 89–554, Sept. 6, 1966, 80 Stat. 409, amended Pub. L. 90–83, § 1(5), Sept. 11, 1967, 81 Stat. 196; Pub. L. 91–510, § 442(a), Oct. 26, 1970, 84 Stat. 1191.)

§ 2108. Veteran; disabled veteran; preference eligible

For the purpose of this title—

(1) "veteran" means an individual who—

(A) served on active duty in the armed forces during a war, in a campaign or expedition for which a campaign badge has been authorized, or during the period beginning April 28, 1952, and ending July 1, 1955; or

(B) served on active duty as defined by section 101(21) of title 38 at any time in the armed forces for a period of more than 180 consecutive days any part of which occurred after January 31, 1955, and before the date of the enactment of the Veterans' Education and Employment Assistance Act of 1976, not including service under section 511(d) of title 10 pursuant to an enlistment in the Army National Guard or the Air National Guard or as a Reserve for service in the Army Reserve, Naval Reserve, Air Force Reserve, Marine Corps Reserve, or Coast Guard Reserve;
and who has been separated from the armed forces under honorable conditions;

(2) "disabled veteran" means an individual who has served on active duty in the armed forces, has been separated therefrom under honorable conditions, and has established the present existence of a service-connected disability or is receiving compensation, disability retirement benefits, or pension because of a public statute administered by the Veterans' Administration or a military department;

(3) "preference eligible" means, except as provided in paragraph (4) of this section—

(A) a veteran as defined by paragraph (1)(A) of this section;

(B) a veteran as defined by paragraph (1)(B) of this section;

(C) a disabled veteran;

(D) the unmarried widow or widower of a veteran as defined by paragraph (1)(A) of this section;

(E) the wife or husband of a service-connected disabled veteran if the veteran has been unable to qualify for any appointment in the civil service or in the government of the District of Columbia;

(F) the mother of an individual who lost his life under honorable conditions while serving in the armed forces during a period named by paragraph (1)(A) of this section, if—

(i) her husband is totally and permanently disabled;

(ii) she is widowed. divorced. or separated from the father and has not remarried: or

(iii) she has remarried but is widowed. divorced. or legally separated from her husband when preference is claimed: and

(G) the mother of a service-connected permanently and totally disabled veteran, if

(i) her husband is totally and permanently disabled;

(ii) she is widowed, divorced, or separated from the father and has not remarried; or

(iii) she has remarried but is widowed, divorced, or legally separated from her husband when preference is claimed;

but does not include applicants for, or members of, the Senior Executive Service, the Defense Intelligence Senior Executive Service, the Senior Cryptologic Executive Service, the Federal Bureau of Investigation and Drug Enforcement Administration Senior Executive Service, or the General Accounting Office;

(4) except for the purposes of chapters 43 and 75 of this title, "preference eligible" does not include a retired member of the armed forces unless—

(A) the individual is a disabled veteran: or

(B) the individual retired below the rank of major or its equivalent; and

(5) "retired member of the armed forces" means a member or former member of the armed forces who is entitled. under statute, to retired, retirement, or retainer pay on account of service as a member.

(Pub L. 89–554, Sept. 6, 1966, 80 Stat. 410, amended Pub. L. 90–83, § 1(6), Sept. 11, 1967, 81 Stat. 196; Pub. L. 90–623, § 1(2), Oct. 22, 1968, 82 Stat. 1312; Pub. L. 92–187, § 1 Dec. 15, 1971, 85 Stat. 644; Pub. L. 94–50, Oct. 15, 1976, 90 Stat. 2405; Pub. L. 95–454, Oct. 13, 1978, 92 Stat. 1147, 1154; Pub. L. 96–54, Aug. 14, 1979, 93 Stat. 381; Pub. L. 96–191, § 8(a), Feb. 15, 1980, 94 Stat. 33; Pub. L. 97–89, Title VIII, § 801, Dec. 4, 1981, 95 Stat. 1161; Pub. L. 100–325, § 2(a), May 30, 1988, 102 Stat. 581.)

§ 2109. Air traffic controller; Secretary

For the purpose of this title—

(1) "air traffic controller" or "controller" means a civilian employee of the Department of Transportation or the Department of Defense who, in an air traffic control facility or flight service station facility—

(A) is actively engaged—

(i) in the separation and control of air traffic; or

(ii) in providing preflight, inflight, or airport advisory service to aircraft operators; or

(B) is the immediate supervisor of any employee described in subparagraph (A); and

(2) "Secretary", when used in connection with "air traffic controller" or "controller", means the Secretary of Transportation with respect to controllers in the Department of Transportation, and the Secretary of Defense with respect to controllers in the Department of Defense.

(As amended Pub. L. 96–347, § 1(a), Sept. 12, 1980, 94 Stat. 1150; Pub. L. 99–335, Title II, § 207(b), June 6, 1986, 100 Stat. 594.)

* * * * *

CHAPTER 23—MERIT SYSTEM PRINCIPLES

2304. Responsibility of the General Accounting Office.
2305. Coordination with certain other provisions of law.

§ 2301. Merit system principles

(a) This section shall apply to—
(1) an Executive agency;
(2) the Administrative Office of the United States Courts; and
(3) the Government Printing Office.

(b) Federal personnel management should be implemented consistent with the following merit system principles:

(1) Recruitment should be from qualified individuals from appropriate sources in an endeavor to achieve a work force from all segments of society, and selection and advancement should be determined solely on the basis of relative ability, knowledge, and skills, after fair and open competition which assures that all receive equal opportunity.

(2) All employees and applicants for employment should receive fair and equitable treatment in all aspects of personnel management without regard to political affiliation, race, color, religion, national origin, sex, marital status, age, or handicapping condition, and with proper regard for their privacy and constitutional rights.

(3) Equal pay should be provided for work of equal value, with appropriate consideration of both national and local rates paid by employers in the private sector, and appropriate incentives and recognition should be provided for excellence in performance.

(4) All employees should maintain high standards of integrity, conduct, and concern for the public interest.

(5) The Federal work force should be used efficiently and effectively.

(6) Employees should be retained on the basis of the adequacy of their performance, inadequate performance should be corrected, and employees should be separated who cannot or will not improve their performance to meet required standards.

(7) Employees should be provided effective education and training in cases in which such education and training would result in better organizational and individual performance.

(8) Employees should be—
(A) protected against arbitrary action, personal favoritism, or coercion for partisan political purposes, and
(B) prohibited from using their official authority or influence for the purpose of interfering with or affecting the result of an election or a nomination for election.

(9) Employees should be protected against reprisal for the lawful disclosure of information which the employees reasonably believe evidences—
(A) a violation of any law, rule, or regulation, or

(B) mismanagement, a gross waste of funds, an abuse of authority, or a substantial and specific danger to public health or safety.

(c) In administering the provisions of this chapter—

(1) with respect to any agency (as defined in section 2302(a)(2)(C) of this title), the President shall, pursuant to the authority otherwise available under this title, take any action, including the issuance of rules, regulations, or directives; and

(2) with respect to any entity in the executive branch which is not such an agency or part of such an agency, the head of such entity shall, pursuant to authority otherwise available, take any action, including the issuance of rules, regulations, or directives;

which is consistent with the provisions of this title and which the President or the head, as the case may be, determines is necessary to ensure that personnel management is based on and embodies the merit system principles. (Pub. L. 95–454, Oct. 13, 1978, 92 Stat. 1113.)

§ 2302. Prohibited personnel practices

(a)(1) For the purpose of this title, "prohibited personnel practice" means any action described in subsection (b) of this section.

(2) For the purpose of this section—

(A) "personnel action" means—

(i) an appointment;

(ii) a promotion;

(iii) an action under chapter 75 of this title or other disciplinary or corrective action;

(iv) a detail, transfer, or reassignment;

(v) a reinstatement;

(vi) a restoration;

(vii) a reemployment;

(viii) a performance evaluation under chapter 43 of this title;

(ix) a decision concerning pay, benefits, or awards, or concerning education or training if the education or training may reasonably be expected to lead to an appointment, promotion, performance evaluation, or other action described in this subparagraph; and

(x) any other significant change in duties or responsibilities which is inconsistent with the employee's salary or grade level;

with respect to an employee in, or applicant for, a covered position in an agency;

(B) "covered position" means any position in the competitive service, a career appointee position in the Senior Executive Service, or a position in the excepted service, but does not include—

(i) a position which is excepted from the competitive service because of its confidential, policy-determining, policy-making, or policy-advocating character; or

(ii) any position excluded from the coverage of this section by the President based on a determination by the President that it is necessary and warranted by conditions of good administration.

(C) "agency" means an Executive agency, the Administrative Office of the United States Courts, and the Government Printing Office, but does not include—

(i) a Government corporation;

(ii) the Federal Bureau of Investigation, the Central Intelligence Agency, the Defense Intelligence Agency, the National Security Agency, and, as determined by the President, any Executive agency or unit thereof the principal function of which is the conduct of foreign intelligence or counterintelligence activities; or

(iii) the General Accounting Office.

(b) Any employee who has authority to take, direct others to take, recommend, or approve any personnel action, shall not, with respect to such authority—

(1) discriminate for or against any employee or applicant for employment—

(A) on the basis of race, color, religion, sex, or national origin, as prohibited under section 717 of the Civil Rights Act of 1964 (42 U.S.C. 2000e–16);

(B) on the basis of age, as prohibited under sections 12 and 15 of the Age Discrimination in Employment Act of 1967 (29 U.S.C. 631, 633a);

(C) on the basis of sex, as prohibited under section 6(d) of the Fair Labor Standards Act of 1938 (29 U.S.C. 206(d));

(D) on the basis of handicapping condition, as prohibited under section 501 of the Rehabilitation Act of 1973 (29 U.S.C. 791); or

(E) on the basis of marital status or political affiliation, as prohibited under any law, rule, or regulation;

(2) solicit or consider any recommendation or statement, oral or written, with respect to any individual who requests or is under consideration for any personnel action unless such recommendation or statement is based on the personal knowledge or records of the person furnishing it and consists of—

(A) an evaluation of the work performance, ability, aptitude, or general qualifications of such individual; or

(B) an evaluation of the character, loyalty, or suitability of such individual;

(3) coerce the political activity of any person (including the providing of any political contribution or service), or take any action against any employee or applicant for employment as a reprisal for the refusal of any person to engage in such political activity;

(4) deceive or willfully obstruct any person with respect to such person's right to compete for employment;

(5) influence any person to withdraw from competition for any position for the purpose of improving or injuring the prospects of any other person for employment;

(6) grant any preference or advantage not authorized by law, rule, or regulation to any employee or applicant for employment (including defining the scope or manner of competition or the requirements for any position) for the purpose of improving or injuring the prospects of any particular person for employment;

(7) appoint, employ, promote, advance, or advocate for appointment, employment, promotion, or advancement, in or to a civilian position any individual who is a relative (as defined in section 3110(a)(3) of this title) of such employee if such position is in the agency in which such employee is serving as a public official (as defined in section 3110(a)(2) of this title) or over which such employee exercises jurisdiction or control as such an official;

(8) take or fail to take a personnel action with respect to any employee or applicant for employment as a reprisal for—

(A) a disclosure of information by an employee or applicant which the employee or applicant reasonably believes evidences—

(i) a violation of any law, rule, or regulation, or

(ii) mismanagement, a gross waste of funds, an abuse of authority, or a substantial and specific danger to public health or safety,

if such disclosure is not specifically prohibited by law and if such information is not specifically required by Executive order to be kept secret in the interest of national defense or the conduct of foreign affairs; or

(B) a disclosure to the Special Counsel of the Merit Systems Protection Board, or to the Inspector General of an agency or another employee designated by the head of the agency to receive such disclosures, or information which the employee or applicant reasonably believes evidences—

(i) a violation of any law, rule, or regulation, or

(ii) mismanagement, a gross waste of funds, an abuse of authority, or a substantial and specific danger to public health or safety;

(9) take or fail to take any personnel action against any employee or applicant for employment as a reprisal for the exercise of any appeal right granted by any law, rule, or regulation;

(10) discriminate for or against any employee or applicant for employment on the basis of conduct which does not adversely affect the performance of the employee or applicant or the performance of others; except that nothing in this paragraph shall prohibit an agency from taking into account in determining suitability or fitness any conviction of the employee or applicant for any crime under the laws of any State, of the District of Columbia, or of the United States; or

(11) take or fail to take any other personnel action if the taking of or failure to take such action violates any law, rule, or regulation implementing, or directly concerning, the merit system principles contained in section 2301 of this title.

This subsection shall not be construed to authorize the withholding of information from the Congress or the taking of any personnel action against an employee who discloses information to the Congress.

(c) The head of each agency shall be responsible for the prevention of prohibited personnel practices, for the compliance with and enforcement of applicable civil service laws, rules, and regulations, and other aspects of personnel management. Any individual to whom the head of an agency delegates authority for personnel management, or for any aspect thereof, shall be similarly responsible within the limits of the delegation.

(d) This section shall not be construed to extinguish or lessen any effort to achieve equal employment opportunity through affirmative action or any right or remedy available to any employee or applicant for employment in the civil service under—

(1) section 717 of the Civil Rights Act of 1964 (42 U.S.C. 2000e–16), prohibiting discrimination on the basis of race, color, religion, sex, or national origin;

(2) sections 12 and 15 of the Age Discrimination in Employment Act of 1967 (29 U.S.C. 631, 633a), prohibiting discrimination on the basis of age;

(3) under section 6(d) of the Fair Labor Standards Act of 1938 (29 U.S.C. 206(d)), prohibiting discrimination on the basis of sex;

(4) section 501 of the Rehabilitation Act of 1973 (29 U.S.C. 791), prohibiting discrimination on the basis of handicapping condition; or

(5) the provisions of any law, rule, or regulation prohibiting discrimination on the basis of marital status or political affiliation.

(Pub. L. 95–454, Oct. 13, 1978, 92 Stat. 1114.)

2303. Prohibited personnel practices in the Federal Bureau of Investigation

(a) Any employee of the Federal Bureau of Investigation who has authority to take, direct others to take, recommend, or approve any personnel action, shall not, with respect to such authority, take or fail to take a personnel action with respect to any employee of the Bureau as a reprisal for a disclosure of information by the employee to the Attorney General (or an employee designated by the Attorney General for such purpose) which the employee or applicant reasonably believes evidences—

(1) a violation of any law, rule, or regulation, or

(2) mismanagement, a gross waste of funds, an abuse of authority, or a substantial and specific danger to public health or safety.

For the purpose of this subsection, "personnel action" means any action described in clauses (i) through (x) of section 2302(a) (2) (A) of this title with respect to an employee in, or applicant for, a position in the Bureau (other than a position of a confidential, policy-determining, policymaking, or policy-advocating character).

(b) The Attorney General shall prescribe regulations to ensure that such a personnel action shall not be taken against an employee of the Bureau as a reprisal for any disclosure of information described in subsection (a) of this section.

(c) The President shall provide for the enforcement of this section in a manner consistent with the provisions of section 1206 of this title.

(Pub. L. 95–454, Oct. 13, 1978, 92 Stat. 1117.)

§ 2304. Responsibility of the General Accounting Office

(a) If requested by either House of the Congress (or any committee thereof), or if considered necessary by the Comptroller General, the General Accounting Office shall conduct audits and reviews to assure compliance with the laws, rules, and regulations governing employment in the executive branch and in the competitive service and to assess the effectiveness and soundness of Federal personnel management.

(b) the General Accounting Office shall prepare and submit an annual report to the President and the Congress on the activities of the Merit Systems Protection Board and the Office of Personnel Management. The report shall include a description of—

(1) significant actions taken by the Board to carry out its functions under this title; and

(2) significant actions of the Office of Personnel Management, including an analysis of whether or not the actions of the Office are in accord with merit system principles and free from prohibited personnel practices.

(Pub. L. 95–454, Oct. 13, 1978, 92 Stat. 1118.)

§ 2305. Coordination with certain other provisions of law

No provision of this chapter, or action taken under this chapter, shall be construed to impair the authorities and responsibilities set forth in section 102 of the National Security Act of 1947 (61 Stat, 495; 50 U.S.C. 403), the Central Intelligence Agency Act of 1949 (63 Stat. 208; 50 U.S.C. 403a and following), the Act entitled "An Act to provide certain administrative authorities for the National Security Agency, and for other purposes", approved May 29, 1959 (73 Stat. 63; 50 U.S.C. 402 note), and the Act entitled "An Act to amend the Internal Security Act of 1950", approved March 26, 1964 (78 Stat. 168; 50 U.S.C. 831–835). (Pub. L. 95–454, Oct. 13, 1978, 92 Stat. 1118.)

*   *   *   *   *

CHAPTER 43—PERFORMANCE APPRAISAL

SUBCHAPTER I—GENERAL PROVISIONS

SUBCHAPTER I—GENERAL PROVISIONS

§ 4301. Definitions

For the purpose of this subchapter—

(1) "agency" means—

(A) an Executive agency;

(B) the Administrative Office of the United States Courts; and

(C) the Government Printing Office;

but does not include—

(i) a Government corporation;

(ii) the Central Intelligence Agency, the Defense Intelligence Agency, the National Security Agency, or any Executive agency or unit thereof which is designated by the President and the principal function of which is the conduct of foreign intelligence or counterintelligence activities; or

(iii) the General Accounting Office;

(2) "employee" means an individual employed in or under an agency, but does not include—

(A) an employee outside the United States who is paid in accordance with local native prevailing wage rates for the area in which employed;

(B) an individual in the Foreign Service of the United States;

(C) a physician, dentist, nurse, or other employee in the Department of Medicine and Surgery, Veterans' Administration whose pay is fixed under chapter 73 of title 38;

(D) an administrative law judge appointed under section 3105 of this title;

(E) an individual in the Senior Executive Service or the Federal Bureau of Investigation and Drug Enforcement Administration Senior Executive Service;

(F) an individual appointed by the President; or

(G) an individual occupying a position not in the competitive service excluded from coverage of this subchapter by regulations of the Office of Personnel Management; and

(3) "unacceptable performance" means performance of an employee which fails to meet established performance standards in one or more critical elements of such employee's position.

(Pub. L. 95–454, Oct. 13, 1978, 92 Stat. 1132; Pub. L. 100–325, May 30, 1988, 102 Stat. 581.)

§ 4302. Establishment of performance appraisal systems

(a) Each agency shall develop one or more performance appraisal systems which—

(1) provide for periodic appraisals of job performance of employees;

(2) encourage employee participation in establishing performance standards; and

(3) use the results of performance appraisals as a basis for training, rewarding, reassigning, promoting, reducing in grade, retaining, and removing employees;

(b) Under regulations which the Office of Personnel Management shall prescribe, each performance appraisal system shall provide for—

(1) establishing performance standards which will, to the maximum extent feasible, permit the accurate evaluation of job performance on the basis of objective criteria (which may include the extent of courtesy demonstrated to the public) related to the job in question for each employee or position under the system;

(2) as soon as practicable, but not later than October 1, 1981, with respect to initial appraisal periods, and thereafter at the beginning of each following appraisal period, communicating to each employee the performance standards and the critical elements of the employee's position;

(3) evaluating each employee during the appraisal period on such standards;

(4) recognizing and rewarding employees whose performance so warrants;

(5) assisting employees in improving unacceptable performance; and

(6) reassigning, reducing in grade, or removing employees who continue to have unacceptable performance but only after an opportunity to demonstrate acceptable performance.

(Pub. L. 95–454, Oct. 13, 1978, 92 Stat. 1132.)

§ 4302a. Establishment of performance appraisal systems for performance management and recognition system employees

(a) Each agency shall develop one or more performance appraisal systems for employees covered by chapter 54 of this title which—

(1) provide for periodic appraisals of job performance of such employees;

(2) require the joint participation of the supervising official and the employee in developing performance standards with authority for establishing standards resting with the supervising official; and
(3) use the results of performance appraisals as a basis—
    (A) for adjusting the base pay and making performance award decisions with respect to any such employee in accordance with the applicable provisions of such chapter 54; and
    (B) for training, rewarding, reassigning, promoting, reducing in grade, retaining, and removing any such employee.
  (b) Under regulations which the Office of Personnel Management shall prescribe, each performance appraisal system under this section shall provide for—
    (1) five levels of summary performance ratings as follows:
      (A) two levels which are above the fully successful level;
      (B) a fully successful level; and
      (C) two levels which are below the fully successful level;
    (2) establishing, in writing, the critical elements of each employee's position and the performance standards for the fully successful level for each such element which will, to the maximum extent feasible, permit accurate evaluation of job performance on the basis of objective criteria related to the job in question;
    (3) communicating, at the beginning of each appraisal period and in writing, to each employee who is covered by chapter 54 of this title the performance standards and critical elements of the employee's position;
    (4) evaluating each such employee during the appraisal period on the basis of such standards;
    (5) assisting any such employee in improving performance rated at a level below the fully successful level; and
    (6) reassigning, reducing in grade, or removing any employee who continues to perform at the level which is 2 levels below the fully successful level, after such employee has been provided with written notice of such employee's rating and afforded reasonable opportunity to raise such employee's level of performance to the fully successful level or higher.
  (c)(1) Appraisals of performance under this section—
    (A) shall take into account individual performance and may take into account organizational accomplishment;
    (B) shall be based on factors such as—
      (i) any improvement in efficiency, productivity, and quality of work or service, including any significant reduction in paperwork;
      (ii) cost efficiency;
      (iii) timeliness of performance;
      (iv) other indications of the effectiveness, productivity, and quality of performance of the employees for whom the employee is responsible; and
      (v) meeting affirmative action goals and achievement of equal employment opportunity requirements;
    (C) may be reviewed by an employee of the agency in accordance with procedures established by the Office of Personnel Management;

(D) shall, on request of the employee whose performance is appraised, by [sic] reconsidered by an employee of the agency in accordance with procedures established by the Office; and

(E) may not be appealed outside the agency.

(2) Reconsideration of an appraisal under paragraph (1)(D) of this subsection may be made only by an employee who is in a higher position in the agency than each employee who made, reviewed, or approved the appraisal.

(d)(1) In order to promote the purposes of this section, there shall be established within each agency a performance standards review board (hereinafter in this subsection referred to as the "board"), consisting of at least six members, all of whom shall be chosen by the agency head from individuals employed in or under such agency. Of the members, at least one-half shall be employees who are covered by chapter 54 of this title and who are in the competitive service. A board shall be chaired by the member of the board designated for that purpose by the agency head.

(2) It shall be the function of each board—

(A) to assess, by the use of representative sampling techniques, the appropriateness of performance standards developed and used by the agency under this section;

(B) to study the feasibility of an awards program based on the collective performance of units or other groups of employees who are covered by chapter 54 of this title, and to submit as part of its annual report under paragraph (3) of this subsection recommendations for any actions which the board considers appropriate with respect to any such program; and

(C) to provide technical assistance with respect to any demonstration projects which may relate to performance standards of the agency under this section.

(3) A board shall report to the head of the agency on its activities under this subsection annually.

(e) In carrying out this section, neither the Office nor any other agency may prescribe a distribution of levels of performance ratings for employees covered by chapter 54 of this title.

(f) The Office may not prescribe, or require an agency to prescribe, any specific performance standard or element for purposes of this section.

(g) This section and any regulations prescribed under this section shall cease to be effective as of the date on which chapter 54 of this title ceases to be effective.

(Added Pub. L. 98–615, Title II, § 202(a), Nov. 8, 1984, 98 Stat. 3214.)

§ 4303. Actions based on unacceptable performance

(a) Subject to the provisions of this section, an agency may reduce in grade or remove an employee for unacceptable performance.

(b) (1) An employee whose reduction in grade or removal is proposed under this section is entitled to—

(A) 30 days' advance written notice of the proposed action which identifies—

(i) specific instances of unacceptable performance by the employee on which the proposed action is based; and

(ii) the critical elements of the employee's position involved in each instance of unacceptable performance;

(B) be represented by an attorney or other representative;

(C) a reasonable time to answer orally and in writing; and

(D) a written decision which—

(i) in the case of a reduction in grade or removal under this section, specifies the instances of unacceptable performance by the employee on which the reduction in grade or removal is based, and

(ii) unless proposed by the head of the agency, has been concurred in by an employee who is in a higher position than the employee who proposed the action.

(2) An agency may, under regulations prescribed by the head of such agency, extend the notice period under subsection (b)(1)(A) of this section for not more than 30 days. An agency may extend the notice period for more than 30 days only in accordance with regulations issued by the Office of Personnel Management.

(c) The decision to retain, reduce in grade, or remove an employee—

(1) shall be made within 30 days after the date of expiration of the notice period, and

(2) in the case of a reduction in grade or removal, may be based only on those instances of unacceptable performance by the employee—

(A) which occurred during the 1-year period ending on the date of the notice under subsection (b)(1)(A) of this section in connection with the decision; and

(B) for which the notice and other requirements of this section are complied with.

(d) If, because of performance improvement by the employee during the notice period, the employee is not reduced in grade or removed, and the employee's performance continues to be acceptable for 1 year from the date of the advance written notice provided under subsection (b)(1)(A) of this section, any entry or other notation of the unacceptable performance for which the action was proposed under this section shall be removed from any agency record relating to the employee.

(e) Any employee who is a preference eligible or is in the competitive service and who has been reduced in grade or removed under this section is entitled to appeal the action to the Merit Systems Protection Board under section 7701 of this title.

(f) This section does not apply to—

(1) the reduction to the grade previously held of a supervisor or manager who has not completed the probationary period under section 3321(a)(2) of this title,

(2) the reduction in grade or removal of an employee in the competitive service who is serving a probationary or trial period under an initial appointment or who has not completed 1 year of current continuous employment under other than a temporary appointment limited to 1 year or less, or

(3) the reduction in grade or removal of an employee in the excepted service who has not completed 1 year of current continuous employment in the same or similar positions.
(Pub. L. 95–454, Oct. 13, 1978, 92 Stat. 1133.)

§ 4304. Responsibilities of the Office of Personnel Management

(a) The Office of Personnel Management shall make technical assistance available to agencies in the development of performance appraisal systems.

(b) (1) The Office shall review each performance appraisal system developed by any agency under this section and determine whether the performance appraisal system meets the requirements of this subchapter.

(2) The Comptroller General shall from time to time review on a selected basis performance appraisal systems established under this subchapter to determine the extent to which any such system meets the requirements of this subchapter and shall periodically report its findings to the Office and to the Congress.

(3) If the Office determines that a system does not meet the requirements of this subchapter (including regulations prescribed under section 4305), the Office shall direct the agency to implement an appropriate system or to correct operations under the system, and any such agency shall take any action so required. (Pub. L. 95–454, Oct. 13, 1978, 92 Stat. 1134.)

§ 4305. Regulations

The Office of Personnel Management may prescribe regulations to carry out the purpose of this subchapter. (Pub. L. 95–454, Oct. 13, 1978, 92 Stat. 1134.)

* * * * *

SUBCHAPTER II—PERFORMANCE APPRAISAL IN THE SENIOR EXECUTIVE SERVICE

§ 4311. Definitions

For the purpose of this subchapter, "agency", "senior executive", and "career appointee" have the meanings set forth in section 3132(a) of this title. (Pub. L. 95–454, Oct. 13, 1978, 92 Stat. 1167.)

§ 4312. Senior Executive Service performance appraisal systems

(a) Each agency shall, in accordance with standards established by the Office of Personnel Management, develop one or more performance appraisal systems designed to—

(1) permit the accurate evaluation of performance in any position on the basis of criteria which are related to the position and which specify the critical elements of the position;

(2) provide for systematic appraisals of performance of senior executives;

(3) encourage excellence in performance by senior executives; and

(4) provide a basis for making eligibility determinations for retention in the Senior Executive Service and for Senior Executive Service performance awards.

(b) Each performance appraisal system established by an agency under subsection (a) of this section shall provide—

(1) that, on or before the beginning of each rating period, performance requirements for each senior executive in the agency are established in consultation with the senior executive and communicated to the senior executive;

(2) that written appraisals of performance are based on the individual and organizational performance requirements established for the rating period involved; and

(3) that each senior executive in the agency is provided a copy of the appraisal and rating under section 4314 of this title and is given an opportunity to respond in writing and have the rating reviewed by an employee or (with the consent of the senior executive) a commissioned officer in the uniformed services serving on active duty, in a higher level in the agency before the rating becomes final.

(c) (1) The Office shall review each agency's performance appraisal system under this section, and determine whether the agency performance appraisal system meets the requirements of this subchapter.

(2) The Comptroller General shall from time to time review performance appraisal systems under this section to determine the extent to which any such system meets the requirements under this subchapter and shall periodically report its findings to the Office and to each House of the Congress.

(3) If the Office determines that an agency performance appraisal system does not meet the requirements under this subchapter (including regulations prescribed under section 4315), the agency shall take such corrective action as may be required by the Office.

(d) A senior executive may not appeal any appraisal and rating under any performance appraisal system under this section. (Pub. L. 95–454, Oct. 13, 1978, 92 Stat. 1167, and amended Pub. L. 98–615, Nov. 8, 1984, 98 Stat. 3220.)

§ 4313. Criteria for performance appraisals

Appraisals of performance in the Senior Executive Service shall be based on both individual and organizational performance, taking into account such factors as—

(1) improvements in efficiency, productivity, and quality of work or service, including any significant reduction in paperwork;

(2) cost efficiency;

(3) timeliness of performance;

(4) other indications of the effectiveness, productivity, and performance quality of the employees for whom the senior executive is responsible; and

(5) meeting affirmative action goals and achievement of equal employment opportunity requirements.

(Pub. L. 95–454, Oct. 13, 1978, 92 Stat. 1168.)

§ 4314. Ratings for performance appraisals

(a) Each performance appraisal system shall provide for annual summary ratings of levels of performance as follows:

(1) one or more fully successful levels,

(2) a minimally satisfactory level, and

(3) an unsatisfactory level.

(b) Each performance appraisal system shall provide that—

(1) any appraisal and any rating under such system—

(A) are made only after review and evaluation by a performance review board established under subsection (c) of this section;

(B) are conducted at least annually, subject to the limitation of subsection (c)(3) of this section;

(C) in the case of a career appointee, may not be made within 120 days after the beginning of a new Presidential administration; and

(D) are based on performance during a performance appraisal period the duration of which shall be determined under guidelines established by the Office of Personnel Management, but which may be terminated in any case in which the agency making the appraisal determines that an adequate basis exists on which to appraise and rate the senior executive's performance;

(2) any career appointee receiving a rating at any of the fully successful levels under subsection (a)(1) of this section may be given a performance award under section 5384 of this title;

(3) any senior executive receiving an unsatisfactory rating under subsection (a)(3) of this section shall be reassigned or transferred within the Senior Executive Service, or removed from the Senior Executive Service, but any senior executive who receives 2 unsatisfactory ratings in any period of 5 consecutive years shall be removed from the Senior Executive Service; and

(4) any senior executive who twice in any period of 3 consecutive years receives less than fully successful ratings shall be removed from the Senior Executive Service.

(c)(1) Each agency shall establish, in accordance with regulations prescribed by the Office, one or more performance review boards, as appropriate. It is the function of the boards to make recommendations to the appropriate appointing authority of the agency relating to the performance of senior executives in the agency.

(2) The supervising official of the senior executive shall provide to the performance review board, an initial appraisal of the senior executive's performance. Before making any recommendation with respect to the senior executive, the board shall review any response by the senior executive to the initial appraisal and conduct such further review as the board finds necessary.

(3) Performance appraisals under this subchapter with respect to any senior executive shall be made by the appointing authority only after considering the recommendations by the performance review board with respect to such senior executive under paragraph (1) of this subsection.

(4) Members of performance review boards shall be appointed in such a manner as to assure consistency, stability, and objectivity in performance appraisal. Notice of the appointment of an individual to serve as a member shall be published in the Federal Register.

(5) In the case of an appraisal of a career appointee, more than one-half of the members of the performance review board shall consist of career appointees. The requirement of the preceding sentence shall not apply in any case in which the Office determines that there exists an insufficient number of career appointees available to comply with the requirement.

(d) The Office shall include in each report submitted to each House of the Congress under section 3135 of this title a report of—

(1) the performance of any performance review board established under this section,

(2) the number of individuals removed from the Senior Executive Service under subchapter V of chapter 35 of this title for less than fully successful executive performance, and

(3) the number of performance awards under section 5384 of this title.

(Pub. L. 95–454, Oct. 13, 1978, 92 Stat. 1169.)

§ 4315. Regulations

The Office of Personnel Management shall prescribe regulations to carry out the purpose of this subchapter. (Pub. L. 95–454, Oct. 13, 1978, 92 Stat. 1170.)

*   *   *   *   *

CHAPTER 55—PAY ADMINISTRATION

SUBCHAPTER 9 – SEVERANCE PAY AND BACK PAY

* * *

§ 5596. Back pay due to unjustified personnel action

(a) For the purpose of this section, "agency" means—

(1) an Executive agency;

(2) the Administrative Office of the United States Courts;

(3) the Library of Congress;

(4) the Government Printing Office. and

(5) the government of the District of Columbia.

(b)(1) An employee of an agency who. on the basis of a timely appeal or an administrative determination (including a decision relating to an unfair labor practice or a grievance) is found by appropriate authority under applicable law, rule, regulation, or collective bargaining agreement, to have been affected by an unjustified or unwarranted personnel action which has resulted in the withdrawal or reduction of all or part of the pay, allowances, or differentials of the employee—

    (A) is entitled, on correction of the personnel action, to receive for the period for which the personnel action was in effect—

        (i) an amount equal to all or any part of the pay, allowances, or differentials, as applicable which the employee normally would have earned or received during the period if the personnel action had not occurred, less any amounts earned by the employee through other employment during that period; and

        (ii) reasonable attorney fees related to the personnel action which, with respect to any decision relating to an unfair labor practice or a grievance processed under a procedure negotiated in accordance with chapter 71 of this title, or under chapter 11 of title I of the Foreign Service Act of 1980, shall be awarded in accordance with standards established under section 7701(g) of this title; and

    (B) for all purposes, is deemed to have performed service for the agency during that period, except that—

        (i) annual leave restored under this paragraph which is in excess of the maximum leave accumulation permitted by law shall be credited to a separate leave account for the employee and shall be available for use by the employee within the time limits prescribed by regulations of the Office of Personnel Management, and

        (ii) annual leave credited under clause (i) of this subparagraph but unused and still available to the employee under regulations prescribed by the Office shall be included in the lump-sum payment under section 5551 or 5552(1) of this title but may not be retained to the credit of the employee under section 5552(2) of this title.

    (2)(A) An amount payable under paragraph (1)(A)(i) of this subsection shall be payable with interest.

    (B) Such interest—

        (i) shall be computed for the period beginning on the effective date of the withdrawal or reduction involved and ending on a date not more than 30 days before the date on which payment is made;

        (ii) shall be computed at the rate or rates in effect under section 6621(a)(1) of the Internal Revenue Code of 1986 during the period described in clause (i); and

        (iii) shall be compounded daily.

    (C) Interest under this paragraph shall be paid out of amounts available for payments under paragraph (1) of this subsection.

    (3) This subsection does not apply to any reclassification action nor authorize the setting aside of an otherwise proper promotion by a selecting official from a group of properly ranked and certified candidates.

(4) For the purpose of this subsection, "grievance" and "collective bargaining agreement" have the meanings set forth in section 7103 of this title and (with respect to members of the Foreign Service) in sections 1101 and 1002 of the Foreign Service Act of 1980, "unfair labor practice" means an unfair labor practice described in section 7116 of this title and (with respect to members of the Foreign Service) in section 1015 of the Foreign Service Act of 1980, and "personnel action" includes the omission or failure to take an action or confer a benefit.

(c) The Office of Personnel Management, shall prescribe regulations to carry out this section. However, the regulations are not applicable to the Tennessee Valley Authority and its employees. (Added Pub. L. 90-83, § 1(34)(C). Sept. 11. 1967. 81 Stat. 203. amended Pub. L. 94-172, § 1(a). Dec. 23. 1975. 89 Stat. 1025: Pub. L. 95-454. Oct. 13. 1978. 92 Stat. 1216: Pub. L. 96-54. Aug. 14. 1979, 93 Stat. 382.)

(As amended Pub. L. 96-465, Oct. 17, 1980, 94 Stat. 2165; Pub. L. 100-202, Dec. 22, 1987, 101 Stat. ___.)

* * * * *

Subpart F—Labor-Management and Employee Relations

CHAPTER 71—LABOR-MANAGEMENT RELATIONS

SUBCHAPTER I—GENERAL PROVISIONS

SUBCHAPTER II—RIGHTS AND DUTIES OF AGENCIES AND LABOR ORGANIZATIONS

SUBCHAPTER III—GRIEVANCES, APPEALS, AND REVIEW

SUBCHAPTER IV—ADMINISTRATIVE AND OTHER PROVISIONS

7133. Compilation and publication of data.
7134. Regulations.
7135. Continuation of existing laws, recognitions, agreements, and procedures.

SUBCHAPTER I—GENERAL PROVISIONS

§ 7101. Findings and purpose

(a) The Congress finds that—

(1) experience in both private and public employment indicates that the statutory protection of the right of employees to organize, bargain collectively, and participate through labor organizations of their own choosing in decisions which affect them—

(A) safeguards the public interest,

(B) contributes to the effective conduct of public business, and

(C) facilitates and encourages the amicable settlements of disputes between employees and their employers involving conditions of employment; and

(2) the public interest demands the highest standards of employee performance and the continued development and implementation of modern and progressive work practices to facilitate and improve employee performance and the efficient accomplishment of the operations of the Government.

Therefore, labor organizations and collective bargaining in the civil service are in the public interest.

(b) It is the purpose of this chapter to prescribe certain rights and obligations of the employees of the Federal Government and to establish procedures which are designed to meet the special requirements and needs of the Government. The provisions of this chapter should be interpreted in a manner consistent with the requirement of an effective and efficient Government. (Pub. L. 95–454, Oct. 13, 1978, 92 Stat. 1192.)

§ 7102. Employees' rights

Each employee shall have the right to form, join, or assist any labor organization, or to refrain from any such activity, freely and without fear of penalty or reprisal, and each employee shall be protected in the exercise of such right. Except as otherwise provided under this chapter, such right includes the right—

(1) to act for a labor organization in the capacity of a representative and the right, in that capacity, to present the views of the labor organization to heads of agencies and other officials of the executive branch of the Government, the Congress, or other appropriate authorities, and

(2) to engage in collective bargaining with respect to conditions of employment through representatives chosen by employees under this chapter.

(Pub. L. 95–454, Oct. 13, 1978, 92 Stat. 1192.)

§ 7103. Definitions; application

(a) For the purpose of this chapter—

(1) "person" means an individual, labor organization, or agency;

(2) "employee" means an individual—

(A) employed in an agency; or

(B) whose employment in an agency has ceased because of any unfair labor practice under section 7116 of this title and who has not obtained any other regular and substantially equivalent employment, as determined under regulations prescribed by the Federal Labor Relations Authority;

but does not include—

(i) an alien or noncitizen of the United States who occupies a position outside the United States;

(ii) a member of the uniformed services;

(iii) a supervisor or a management official;

(iv) an officer or employee in the Foreign Service of the United States employed in the Department of State, the International Communication Agency, the United States International Development Cooperation Agency, the Department of Agriculture, or the Department of Commerce; or

(v) any person who participates in a strike in violation of section 7311 of this title;

(3) "agency" means an Executive agency (including a nonappropriated fund instrumentality described in section 2105(c) of this title and the Veterans' Canteen Service, Veterans' Administration), the Library of Congress, and the Government Printing Office, but does not include—

(A) the General Accounting Office;

(B) the Federal Bureau of Investigation;

(C) the Central Intelligence Agency;

(D) the National Security Agency;

(E) the Tennessee Valley Authority;

(F) the Federal Labor Relations Authority; or

(G) the Federal Service Impasses Panel;

(4) "labor organization" means an organization composed in whole or in part of employees, in which employees participate and pay dues, and which has as a purpose the dealing with an agency concerning grievances and conditions of employment, but does not include—

(A) an organization which, by its constitution, bylaws, tacit agreement among its members, or otherwise, denies membership because of race, color, creed, national origin, sex, age, preferential or nonpreferential civil service status, political affiliation, marital status, or handicapping condition;

(B) an organization which advocates the overthrow of the constitutional form of government of the United States:

(C) an organization sponsored by an agency; or

(D) an organization which participates in the conduct of a strike against the Government or any agency thereof or imposes a duty or obligation to conduct, assist, or participate in such a strike;

(5) "dues" means dues, fees, and assessments;

(6) "Authority" means the Federal Labor Relations Authority described in section 7104(a) of this title;

(7) "Panel" means the Federal Service Impasses Panel described in section 7119(c) of this title;

(8) "collective bargaining agreement" means an agreement entered into as a result of collective bargaining pursuant to the provisions of this chapter;

(9) "grievance" means any complaint—

(A) by any employee concerning any matter relating to the employment of the employee;

(B) by any labor organization concerning any matter relating to the employment of any employee; or

(C) by any employee, labor organization, or agency concerning—

(i) the effect or interpretation, or a claim of breach, of a collective bargaining agreement; or

(ii) any claimed violation, misinterpretation, or misapplication of any law, rule, or regulation affecting conditions of employment;

(10) "supervisor" means an individual employed by an agency having authority in the interest of the agency to hire, direct, assign, promote, reward, transfer, furlough, layoff, recall, suspend, discipline, or remove employees, to adjust their grievances, or to effectively recommend such action, if the exercise of the authority is not merely routine or clerical in nature but requires the consistent exercise of independent judgment, except that, with respect to any unit which includes firefighters or nurses, the term "supervisor" includes only those individuals who devote a preponderance of their employment time to exercising such authority;

(11) "management official" means an individual employed by an agency in a position the duties and responsibilities of which require or authorize the individual to formulate, determine, or influence the policies of the agency;

(12) "collective bargaining" means the performance of the mutual obligation of the representative of an agency and the exclusive representative of employees in an appropriate unit in the agency to meet at reasonable times and to consult and bargain in a good-faith effort to reach agreement with respect to the conditions of employment affecting such employees and to execute, if requested by either party, a written document incorporating any collective bargaining agreement reached, but the obligation referred to in this paragraph does not compel either party to agree to a proposal or to make a concession:

(13) "confidential employee" means an employee who acts in a confidential capacity with respect to an individual who formulates or effectuates management policies in the field of labor-management relations;

(14) "conditions of employment" means personnel policies, practices, and matters, whether established by rule, regulation, or otherwise, affecting working conditions, except that such term does not include policies, practices, and matters—

(A) relating to political activities prohibited under subchapter III of chapter 73 of this title;

(B) relating to the classification of any position; or

(C) to the extent such matters are specifically provided for by Federal statute;

(15) "professional employee" means—

(A) an employee engaged in the performance of work—

(i) requiring knowledge of an advanced type in a field of science or learning customarily acquired by a prolonged course of specialized intellectual instruction and study in an institution of higher learning or a hospital (as distinguished from knowledge acquired by a general academic education, or from an apprenticeship, or from training in the performance of routine mental, manual, mechanical, or physical activities) ;

(ii) requiring the consistent exercise of discretion and judgment in its performance;

(iii) which is predominantly intellectual and varied in character (as distinguished from routine mental, manual, mechanical, or physical work) ; and

(iv) which is of such character that the output produced or the result accomplished by such work cannot be standardized in relation to a given period of time; or

(B) an employee who has completed the courses of specialized intellectual instruction and study described in subparagraph (A)(i) of this paragraph and is performing related work under appropriate direction or guidance to qualify the employee as a professional employee described in subparagraph (A) of this paragraph;

(16) "exclusive representative" means any labor organization which—

(A) is certified as the exclusive representative of employees in an appropriate unit pursuant to section 7111 of this title; or

(B) was recognized by an agency immediately before the effective date of this chapter as the exclusive representative of employees in an appropriate unit—

(i) on the basis of an election, or

(ii) on any basis other than an election,

and continues to be so recognized in accordance with the provisions of this chapter;

(17) "firefighter" means any employee engaged in the performance of work directly connected with the control and extinguishment of fires or the maintenance and use of firefighting apparatus and equipment; and

(18) "United States" means the 50 States, the District of Columbia, the Commonwealth of Puerto Rico, Guam, the Virgin Islands, the Trust Territory of the Pacific Islands, and any territory or possession of the United States.

(b) (1) The President may issue an order excluding any agency or subdivision thereof from coverage under this chapter if the President determines that—

(A) the agency or subdivision has as a primary function intelligence, counterintelligence, investigative, or national security work, and

(B) the provisions of this chapter cannot be applied to that agency or subdivision in a manner consistent with national security requirements and considerations.

(2) The President may issue an order suspending any provision of this chapter with respect to any agency, installation, or activity located outside the 50 States and the District of Columbia, if the President determines that the suspension is necessary in the interest of national security. (Pub. L. 95–454, Oct. 13, 1978, 92 Stat. 1192; as amended Pub. L. 96–465, Oct. 17, 1980, 94 Stat. 2168.)

§ 7104. Federal Labor Relations Authority

(a) The Federal Labor Relations Authority is composed of three members, not more than 2 of whom may be adherents of the same political party. No member shall engage in any other business or employment or hold another office or position in the Government of the United States except as otherwise provided by law.

(b) Members of the Authority shall be appointed by the President by and with the advice and consent of the Senate, and may be removed by the President only upon notice and hearing and only for inefficiency, neglect of duty, or malfeasance in office. The President shall designate one member to serve as Chairman of the Authority.

(c) A member of the Authority shall be appointed for a term of 5 years. An individual chosen to fill a vacancy shall be appointed for the unexpired term of the member replaced. The term of any member shall not expire before the earlier of—

(1) the date on which the member's successor takes office, or

(2) the last day of the Congress beginning after the date on which the member's term of office would (but for this paragraph) expire.

(d) A vacancy in the Authority shall not impair the right of the remaining members to exercise all of the powers of the Authority.

(e) The Authority shall make an annual report to the President for transmittal to the Congress which shall include information as to the cases it has heard and the decisions it has rendered.

(f)(1) The General Counsel of the Authority shall be appointed by the President, by and with the advice and consent of the Senate, for a term of 5 years. The General Counsel may be removed at any time by the President. The General Counsel shall hold no other office or position in the Government of the United States except as provided by law.

(2) The General Counsel may—

(A) investigate alleged unfair labor practices under this chapter,

(B) file and prosecute complaints under this chapter, and

(C) exercise such other powers of the Authority as the Authority may prescribe.

(3) The General Counsel shall have direct authority over, and responsibility for, all employees in the office of General Counsel, including employees of the General Counsel in the regional offices of the Authority. (Pub. L. 95-454, Oct. 13, 1978, 92 Stat. 1196; as amended Pub. L. 98-224, Mar. 2, 1984, 98 Stat. 47.)

§ 7105. Powers and duties of the Authority

(a)(1) The Authority shall provide leadership in establishing policies and guidance relating to matters under this chapter, and, except as otherwise provided, shall be responsible for carrying out the purpose of this chapter.

(2) The Authority shall, to the extent provided in this chapter and in accordance with regulations prescribed by the Authority—

(A) determine the appropriateness of units for labor organization representation under section 7112 of this title;

(B) supervise or conduct elections to determine whether a labor organization has been selected as an exclusive representative by a majority of the employees in an appropriate unit and otherwise administer the provisions of section 7111 of this title relating to the according of exclusive recognition to labor organizations;

(C) prescribe criteria and resolve issues relating to the granting of national consultation rights under section 7113 of this title;

(D) prescribe criteria and resolve issues relating to determining compelling need for agency rules or regulations under section 7117(b) of this title;

(E) resolves issues relating to the duty to bargain in good faith under section 7117(c) of this title;

(F) prescribe criteria relating to the granting of consultation rights with respect to conditions of employment under section 7117(d) of this title;

(G) conduct hearings and resolve complaints of unfair labor practices under section 7118 of this title;

(H) resolve exceptions to arbitrator's awards under section 7122 of this title; and

(I) take such other actions as are necessary and appropriate to effectively administer the provisions of this chapter.

(b) The Authority shall adopt an official seal which shall be judicially noticed.

(c) The principal office of the Authority shall be in or about the Distric' of Columbia, but the Authority may meet and exercise any or all of its powers at any time or place. Except as otherwise expressly provided by law, the Authority may, by one or more of its members or by such agents as it may designate, make any appropriate inquiry necessary to carry out its duties wherever persons subject to this chapter are located. Any member who participates in the inquiry shall not be disqualified from later participating in a decision of the Authority in any case relating to the inquiry.

(d) The Authority shall appoint an Executive Director and such regional directors, administrative law judges under section 3105 of this title, and other individuals as it may from time to time find necessary for the proper performance of its functions. The Authority may delegate to officers and employees appointed under this subsection authori:y to perform such duties and make such expenditures as may be necessary.

(e)(1) The Authority may delegate to any regional director its authority under this chapter—

(A) to determine whether a group of employees is an appropriate unit;

(B) to conduct investigations and to provide for hearings;

(C) to determine whether a question of representation exists and to direct an election; and

(D) to supervise or conduct secret ballot elections and certify the results thereof.

(2) The Authority may delegate to any administrative law judge appointed under subsection (d) of this section its authority under section 7118 of this title to determine whether any person has engaged in or is engaging in an unfair labor practice.

(f) If the Authority delegates any authority to any regional director or administrative law judge to take any action pursuant to subsection (e) of this section, the Authority may, upon application by any interested person filed within 60 days after the date of the action, review such action, but the review shall not, unless specifically ordered by the Authority, operate as a stay of action. The Authority may affirm, modify, or reverse any action reviewed under this subsection. If the Authority does not undertake to gran⁺ review of the action under this subsection within 60 days after the later of—

(1) the date of the action; or

(2) the date of the filing of any application under this subsection for review of the action;

the action shall become the action of the Authority at the end of such 60-day period.

(g) In order to carry out its functions under this chapter, the Authority may—

(1) hold hearings;

(2) administer oaths, take the testimony or deposition of any person under oath, and issue subpenas as provided in section 7132 of this title; and

(3) may require an agency or a labor organization to cease and desist from violations of this chapter and require it to take any remedial action it considers appropriate to carry out the policies of this chapter.

(h) Except as provided in section 518 of title 28, relating to litigation before the Supreme Court, attorneys designated by the Authority may appear for the Authority and represent the Authority in any civil action brought in connection with any function carried out by the Authority pursuant to this title or as otherwise authorized by law.

(i) In the exercise of the functions of the Authority under this title, the Authority may request from the Director of the Office of Personnel Management an advisory opinion concerning the proper interpretation of rules, regulations, or policy directives issued by the Office of Personnel Management in connection with any matter before the Authority. (Pub. L. 95–454, Oct. 13, 1978, 92 Stat. 1196.)

§ 7106. Management rights

(a) Subject to subsection (b) of this section, nothing in this chapter shall affect the authority of any management official of any agency—

(1) to determine the mission, budget, organization, number of employees, and internal security practices of the agency; and

(2) in accordance with applicable laws—

(A) to hire, assign, direct, layoff, and retain employees in the agency, or to suspend, remove, reduce in grade or pay, or take other disciplinary action against such employees;

(B) to assign work, to make determinations with respect to contracting out, and to determine the personnel by which agency operations shall be conducted;

(C) with respect to filling positions, to make selections for appointments from—

(i) among properly ranked and certified candidates for promotion; or

(ii) any other appropriate source; and

(D) to take whatever actions may be necessary to carry out the agency mission during emergencies.

(b) Nothing in this section shall preclude any agency and any labor organization from negotiating—

(1) at the election of the agency, on the numbers, types, and grades of employees or positions assigned to any organizational subdivision, work project, or tour of duty, or on the technology, methods, and means of performing work;

(2) procedures which management officials of the agency will observe in exercising any authority under this section; or

(3) appropriate arrangements for employees adversely affected

by the exercise of any authority under this section by such management officials.
(Pub. L. 95-454, Oct. 13, 1978, 92 Stat. 1198.)

SUBCHAPTER II—RIGHTS AND DUTIES OF AGENCIES AND LABOR ORGANIZATIONS

§ 7111. Exclusive recognition of labor organizations

(a) An agency shall accord exclusive recognition to a labor organization if the organization has been selected as the representative, in a secret ballot election, by a majority of the employees in an appropriate unit who cast valid ballots in the election.

(b) If a petition is filed with the Authority—

    (1) by any person alleging—

        (A) in the case of an appropriate unit for which there is no exclusive representative, that 30 percent of the employees in the appropriate unit wish to be represented for the purpose of collective bargaining by an exclusive representative, or

        (B) in the case of an appropriate unit for which there is an exclusive representative, that 30 percent of the employees in the unit allege that the exclusive representative is no longer the representative of the majority of the employees in the unit; or

    (2) by any person seeking clarification of, or an amendment to, a certification then in effect or a matter relating to representation;

the Authority shall investigate the petition, and if it has reasonable cause to believe that a question of representation exists, it shall provide an opportunity for a hearing (for which a transcript shall be kept) after reasonable notice. If the Authority finds on the record of the hearing that a question of representation exists, the Authority shall supervise or conduct an election on the question by secret ballot and shall certify the results thereof. An election under this subsection shall not be conducted in any appropriate unit or in any subdivision thereof within which, in the preceding 12 calendar months, a valid election under this subsection has been held.

(c) A labor organization which—

    (1) has been designated by at least 10 percent of the employees in the unit specified in any petition filed pursuant to subsection (b) of this section;

    (2) has submitted a valid copy of a current or recently expired collective bargaining agreement for the unit; or

    (3) has submitted other evidence that it is the exclusive representative of the employees involved;

may intervene with respect to a petition filed pursuant to subsection (b) of this section and shall be placed on the ballot of any election under such subsection (b) with respect to the petition.

(d) The Authority shall determine who is eligible to vote in any election under this section and shall establish rules governing any such election, which shall include rules allowing employees eligible to vote the opportunity to choose—

(1) from labor organizations on the ballot, that labor organization which the employees wish to have represent them; or

(2) not to be represented by a labor organization.

In any election in which no choice on the ballot receives a majority of the votes cast, a runoff election shall be conducted between the two choices receiving the highest number of votes. A labor organization which receives the majority of the votes cast in an election shall be certified by the Authority as the exclusive representative.

(e) A labor organization seeking exclusive recognition shall submit to the Authority and the agency involved a roster of its officers and representatives, a copy of its constitution and bylaws, and a statement of its objectives.

(f) Exclusive recognition shall not be accorded to a labor organization—

(1) if the Authority determines that the labor organization is subject to corrupt influences or influences opposed to democratic principles;

(2) in the case of a petition filed pursuant to subsection (b)(1)(A) of this section, if there is not credible evidence that at least 30 percent of the employees in the unit specified in the petition wish to be represented for the purpose of collective bargaining by the labor organization seeking exclusive recognition;

(3) if there is then in effect a lawful written collective bargaining agreement between the agency involved and an exclusive representative (other than the labor organization seeking exclusive recognition) covering any employees included in the unit specified in the petition, unless—

(A) the collective bargaining agreement has been in effect for more than 3 years, or

(B) the petition for exclusive recognition is filed not more than 105 days and not less than 60 days before the expiration date of the of the collective bargaining agreement; or

(4) if the Authority has. within the previous 12 calendar months, conducted a secret ballot election for the unit described in any petition under this section and in such election a majority of the employees voting chose a labor organization for certification as the unit's exclusive representative.

(g) Nothing in this section shall be construed to prohibit the waiving of hearings by stipulation for the purpose of a consent election in conformity with regulations and rules or decisions of the Authority. (Pub. L. 95–454, Oct. 13, 1978, 92 Stat. 1199.)

§ 7112. Determination of appropriate units for labor organization representation

(a) (1) The Authority shall determine the appropriateness of any unit. The Authority shall determine in each case whether, in order to ensure employees the fullest freedom in exercising the rights guaranteed under this chapter, the appropriate unit should be established on an agency, plant, installation, functional, or other basis and shall determine any unit to be an appropriate unit only if the determination will ensure a clear and identifiable community of interest among the employees in the unit and will promote effective dealings with, and efficiency of the operations of, the agency involved.

(b) A unit shall not be determined to be appropriate under this section solely on the basis of the extent to which employees in the proposed unit have organized, nor shall a unit be determined to be appropriate if it includes—

(1) except as provided under section 7135 (a) (2) of this title, any management official or supervisor;

(2) a confidential employee;

(3) an employee engaged in personnel work in other than a purely clerical capacity;

(4) an employee engaged in administering the provisions of this chapter;

(5) both professional employees and other employees, unless a majority of the professional employees vote for inclusion in the unit;

(6) any employee engaged in intelligence, counterintelligence, investigative, or security work which directly affects national security; or

(7) any employee primarily engaged in investigation or audit functions relating to the work of individuals employed by an agency whose duties directly affect the internal security of the agency, but only if the functions are undertaken to ensure that the duties are discharged honestly and with integrity.

(c) Any employee who is engaged in administering any provision of law relating to labor-management relations may not be represented by a labor organization—

(1) which represents other individuals to whom such provision applies; or

(2) which is affiliated directly or indirectly with an organization which represents other individuals to whom such provision applies.

(d) Two or more units which are in an agency and for which a labor organization is the exclusive representative may, upon petition by the agency or labor organization, be consolidated with or without an election into a single larger unit if the Authority considers the larger unit to be appropriate. The Authority shall certify the labor organization as the exclusive representative of the new larger unit. (Pub. L. 95–454, Oct. 13, 1978, 92 Stat. 1200.)

§ 7113. National consultation rights

(a)(1) If, in connection with any agency, no labor organization has been accorded exclusive recognition on an agency basis, a labor organization which is the exclusive representative of a substantial number of the employees of the agency, as determined in accordance with criteria prescribed by the Authority, shall be granted national consultation rights by the agency. National consultation rights shall terminate when the labor organization no longer meets the criteria prescribed by the Authority. Any issue relating to any labor organization's eligibility for, or continuation of, national consultation rights shall be subject to determination by the Authority.

(b)(1) Any labor organization having national consultation rights in connection with any agency under subsection (a) of this section shall—

(A) be informed of any substantive change in conditions of employment proposed by the agency, and

(B) be permitted reasonable time to present its views and recommendations regarding the changes.

(2) If any views or recommendations are presented under paragraph (1) of this subsection to an agency by any labor organization—

(A) the agency shall consider the views or recommendations before taking final action on any matter with respect to which the views or recommendations are presented; and

(B) the agency shall provide the labor organization a written statement of the reasons for taking the final action.

(c) Nothing in this section shall be construed to limit the right of any agency or exclusive representative to engage in collective bargaining. (Pub. L. 95–454, Oct. 13, 1978, 92 Stat. 1201.)

§ 7114. Representation rights and duties

(a)(1) A labor organization which has been accorded exclusive recognition is the exclusive representative of the employees in the unit it represents and is entitled to act for, and negotiate collective bargaining agreements covering, all employees in the unit. An exclusive representative is responsible for representing the interests of all employees in the unit it represents without discrimination and without regard to labor organization membership.

(2) An exclusive representative of an appropriate unit in an agency shall be given the opportunity to be represented at—

(A) any formal discussion between one or more representatives of the agency and one or more employees in the unit or their representatives concerning any grievance or any personnel policy or practices or other general condition of employment; or

(B) any examination of an employee in the unit by a representative of the agency in connection with an investigation if—

(i) the employee reasonably believes that the examination may result in disciplinary action against the employee; and

(ii) the employee requests representation.

(3) Each agency shall annually inform its employees of their rights under paragraph (2) (B) of this subsection.

(4) Any agency and any exclusive representative in any appropriate unit in the agency, through appropriate representatives, shall meet and negotiate in good faith for the purposes of arriving at a collective bargaining agreement. In addition, the agency and the exclusive representative may determine appropriate techniques, consistent with the provisions of section 7119 of this title, to assist in any negotiation.

(5) The rights of an exclusive representative under the provisions of this subsection shall not be construed to preclude an employee from—

(A) being represented by an attorney or other representative, other than the exclusive representative, of the employee's own choosing in any grievance or appeal action; or

(B) exercising grievance or appellate rights established by law, rule, or regulation;

except in the case of grievance or appeal procedures negotiated under this chapter.

(b) The duty of an agency and an exclusive representative to negotiate in good faith under subsection (a) of this section shall include the obligation—

(1) to approach the negotiations with a sincere resolve to reach a collective bargaining agreement;

(2) to be represented at the negotiations by duly authorized representatives prepared to discuss and negotiate on any condition of employment;

(3) to meet at reasonable times and convenient places as frequently as may be necessary, and to avoid unnecessary delays;

(4) in the case of an agency, to furnish to the exclusive representative involved, or its authorized representative, upon request and, to the extent not prohibited by law, data—

(A) which is normally maintained by the agency in the regular course of business;

(B) which is reasonably available and necessary for full and proper discussion, understanding, and negotiation of subjects within the scope of collective bargaining; and

(C) which does not constitute guidance, advice, counsel, or training provided for management officials or supervisors, relating to collective bargaining; and

(5) if agreement is reached, to execute on the request of any party to the negotiation a written document embodying the agreed terms, and to take such steps as are necessary to implement such agreement.

(c) (1) An agreement between any agency and an exclusive representative shall be subject to approval by the head of the agency.

(2) The head of the agency shall approve the agreement within 30 days from the date the agreement is executed if the agreement is in accordance with the provisions of this chapter and any other appli-

cable law, rule, or regulation (unless the agency has granted an exception to the provision).

(3) If the head of the agency does not approve or disapprove the agreement within the 30-day period, the agreement shall take effect and shall be binding on the agency and the exclusive representative subject to the provisions of this chapter and any other applicable law, rule, or regulation.

(4) A local agreement subject to a national or other controlling agreement at a higher level shall be approved under the procedures of the controlling agreement or, if none, under regulations prescribed by the agency. (Pub. L. 95–454, Oct. 13, 1978, 92 Stat. 1202.)

§ 7115. Allotments to representatives

(a) If an agency has received from an employee in an appropriate unit a written assignment which authorizes the agency to deduct from the pay of the employee amounts for the payment of regular and periodic dues of the exclusive representative of the unit, the agency shall honor the assignment and make an appropriate allotment pursuant to the assignment. Any such allotment shall be made at no cost to the exclusive representative or the employee. Except as provided under subsection (b) of this section, any such assignment may not be revoked for a period of 1 year.

(b) An allotment under subsection (a) of this section for the deduction of dues with respect to any employee shall terminate when—

(1) the agreement between the agency and the exclusive representative involved ceases to be applicable to the employee; or

(2) the employee is suspended or expelled from membership in the exclusive representative.

(c)(1) Subject to paragraph (2) of this subsection, if a petition has been filed with the Authority by a labor organization alleging that 10 percent of the employees in an appropriate unit in an agency have membership in the labor organization, the Authority shall investigate the petition to determine its validity. Upon certification by the Authority of the validity of the petition, the agency shall have a duty to negotiate with the labor organization solely concerning the deduction of dues of the labor organization from the pay of the members of the labor organization who are employees in the unit and who make a voluntary allotment for such purpose.

(2)(A) The provisions of paragraph (1) of this subsection shall not apply in the case of any appropriate unit for which there is an exclusive representative.

(B) Any agreement under paragraph (1) of this subsection between a labor organization and an agency with respect to an appropriate unit shall be null and void upon the certification of an exclusive representative of the unit. (Pub. L. 95–454, Oct. 13, 1978, 92 Stat. 1203.)

§ 7116. Unfair labor practices

(a) For the purpose of this chapter, it shall be an unfair labor practice for an agency—

(1) to interfere with, restrain, or coerce any employee in the exercise by the employee of any right under this chapter;

(2) to encourage or discourage membership in any labor organization by discrimination in connection with hiring, tenure, promotion, or other conditions of employment;

(3) to sponsor, control, or otherwise assist any labor organization, other than to furnish, upon request, customary and routine services and facilities if the services and facilities are also furnished on an impartial basis to other labor organizations having equivalent status;

(4) to discipline or otherwise discriminate against an employee because the employee has filed a complaint, affidavit, or petition, or has given any information or testimony under this chapter;

(5) to refuse to consult or negotiate in good faith with a labor organization as required by this chapter;

(6) to fail or refuse to cooperate in impasse procedures and impasse decisions as required by this chapter;

(7) to enforce any rule or regulation (other than a rule or regulation implementing section 2302 of this title) which is in conflict with any applicable collective bargaining agreement if the agreement was in effect before the date the rule or regulation was prescribed; or

(8) to otherwise fail or refuse to comply with any provision of this chapter.

(b) For the purpose of this chapter, it shall be an unfair labor practice for a labor organization—

(1) to interfere with, restrain, or coerce any employee in the exercise by the employee of any right under this chapter;

(2) to cause or attempt to cause an agency to discriminate against any employee in the exercise by the employee of any right under this chapter;

(3) to coerce, discipline, fine, or attempt to coerce a member of the labor organization as punishment, reprisal, or for the purpose of hindering or impeding the member's work performance or productivity as an employee or the discharge of the member's duties as an employee;

(4) to discriminate against an employee with regard to the terms or conditions of membership in the labor organization on the basis of race, color, creed, national origin, sex, age, preferential or nonpreferential civil service status, political affiliation, marital status, or handicapping condition;

(5) to refuse to consult or negotiate in good faith with an agency as required by this chapter;

(6) to fail or refuse to cooperate in impasse procedures and impasse decisions as required by this chapter;

(7)(A) to call, or participate in, a strike, work stoppage, or slowdown, or picketing of an agency in a labor-management dispute if such picketing interferes with an agency's operations, or

(B) to condone any activity described in subparagraph (A) of this paragraph by failing to take action to prevent or stop such activity; or

(8) to otherwise fail or refuse to comply with any provision of this chapter.

Nothing in paragraph (7) of this subsection shall result in any informational picketing which does not interfere with an agency's operations being considered as an unfair labor practice.

(c) For the purpose of this chapter it shall be an unfair labor practice for an exclusive representative to deny membership to any employee in the appropriate unit represented by such exclusive representative except for failure—

(1) to meet reasonable occupational standards uniformly required for admission, or

(2) to tender dues uniformly required as a condition of acquiring and retaining membership.

This subsection does not preclude any labor organization from enforcing discipline in accordance with procedures under its constitution or bylaws to the extent consistent with the provisions of this chapter.

(d) Issues which can properly be raised under an appeals procedure may not be raised as unfair labor practices prohibited under this section. Except for matters wherein, under section 7121 (e) and (f) of this title, an employee has an option of using the negotiated grievance procedure or an appeals procedure, issues which can be raised under a grievance procedure may, in the discretion of the aggrieved party, be raised under the grievance procedure or as an unfair labor practice under this section, but not under both procedures.

(e) The expression of any personal view, argument, opinion or the making of any statement which—

(1) publicizes the fact of a representational election and encourages employees to exercise their right to vote in such election,

(2) corrects the record with respect to any false or misleading statement made by any person, or

(3) informs employees of the Government's policy relating to labor-management relations and representation,

shall not, if the expression contains no threat of reprisal or force or promise of benefit or was not made under coercive conditions, (A) constitute an unfair labor practice under any provision of this chapter, or (B) constitute grounds for the setting aside of any election conducted under any provisions of this chapter. (Pub. L. 95-454, Oct. 13, 1978, 92 Stat. 1204.)

§ 7117. Duty to bargain in good faith; compelling need; duty to consult

(a)(1) Subject to paragraph (2) of this subsection, the duty to bargain in good faith shall. to the extent not inconsistent with any Federal law or any Government-wide rule or regulation, extend to matters which are the subject of any rule or regulation only if the rule or regulation is not a Government-wide rule or regulation.

(2) The duty to bargain in good faith shall. to the extent not inconsistent with Federal law or any Government-wide rule or regulation, extend to matters which are the subject of any agency rule or regulation referred to in paragraph (3) of this subsection only if the Authority has determined under subsection (b) of this section that no compelling need (as determined under regulations prescribed by the Authority) exists for the rule or regulation.

(3) Paragraph (2) of the subsection applies to any rule or regulation issued by any agency or issued by any primary national subdivision of such agency. unless an exclusive representative represents an appropriate unit including not less than a majority of the employees in the issuing agency or primary national subdivision, as the case may be, to whom the rule or regulation is applicable.

(b)(1) In any case of collective bargaining in which an exclusive representative alleges that no compelling need exists for any rule or regulation referred to in subsection (a)(3) of this section which is then in effect and which governs any matter at issue in such collective bargaining, the Authority shall determine under paragraph (2) of this subsection, in accordance with regulations prescribed by the Authority, whether such a compelling need exists.

(2) For the purpose of this section, a compelling need shall be determined not to exist for any rule or regulation only if—

(A) the agency, or primary national subdivision, as the case may be, which issued the rule or regulation informs the Authority in writing that a compelling need for the rule or regulation does not exist; or

(B) the Authority determines that a compelling need for a rule or regulation does not exist.

(3) A hearing may be held. in the discretion of the Authority, before a determination is made under this subsection. If a hearing is held. it shall be expedited to the extent practicable and shall not include the General Counsel as a party.

(4) The agency, or primary national subdivision, as the case may be, which issued the rule or regulation shall be a necessary party at any hearing under this subsection.

(c)(1) Except in any case to which subsection (b) of this section applies, if an agency involved in collective bargaining with an exclusive representative alleges that the duty to bargain in good faith does not extend to any matter. the exclusive representative may appeal the allegation to the Authority in accordance with the provisions of this subsection.

(2) The exclusive representative may, on or before the 15th day after the date on which the agency first makes the allegation referred to in paragraph (1) of this subsection, institute an appeal under this subsection by—

(A) filing a petition with the Authority: and

(B) furnishing a copy of the petition to the head of the agency.

(3) On or before the 30th day after the date of the receipt by the head of the agency of the copy of the petition under paragraph (2) (B) of this subsection, the agency shall—
   (A) file with the Authority a statement—
     (i) withdrawing the allegation; or
     (ii) setting forth in full its reasons supporting the allegation; and
   (B) furnish a copy of such statement to the exclusive representative.

(4) On or before the 15th day after the date of the receipt by the exclusive representative of a copy of a statement under paragraph (3) (B) of this subsection, the exclusive representative shall file with the Authority its response to the statement.

(5) A hearing may be held, in the discretion of the Authority, before a determination is made under this subsection. If a hearing is held. it shall not include the General Counsel as a party.

(6) The Authority shall expedite proceedings under this subsection to the extent practicable and shall issue to the exclusive representative and to the agency a written decision on the allegation and specific reasons therefor at the earliest practicable date.

(d) (1) A labor organization which is the exclusive representative of a substantial number of employees, determined in accordance with criteria prescribed by the Authority, shall be granted consultation rights by any agency with respect to any Government-wide rule or regulation issued by the agency effecting any substantive change in any condition of employment. Such consultation rights shall terminate when the labor organization no longer meets the criteria prescribed by the Authority. Any issue relating to a labor organization's eligibility for, or continuation of, such consultation rights shall be subject to determination by the Authority.

(2) A labor organization having consultation rights under paragraph (1) of this subsection shall—
   (A) be informed of any substantive change in conditions of employment proposed by the agency, and
   (B) shall be permitted reasonable time to present its views and recommendations regarding the changes.

(3) If any views or recommendations are presented under paragraph (2) of this subsection to an agency by any labor organization—
   (A) the agency shall consider the views or recommendations before taking final action on any matter with respect to which the views or recommendations are presented; and
   (B) the agency shall provide the labor organization a written statement of the reasons for taking the final action.
(Pub. L. 95–454, Oct. 13, 1978, 92 Stat. 1205.)

§ 7118. Prevention of unfair labor practices

(a) (1) If any agency or labor organization is charged by any person with having engaged in or engaging in an unfair labor practice, the General Counsel shall investigate the charge and may issue and cause to be served upon the agency or labor organization a complaint. In any case in which the General Counsel does not issue a complaint because the charge fails to state an unfair labor practice, the General Counsel shall provide the person making the charge a written statement of the reasons for not issuing a complaint.

(2) Any complaint under paragraph (1) of this subsection shall contain a notice—

(A) of the charge;

(B) that a hearing will be held before the Authority (or any member thereof or before an individual employed by the authority and designated for such purpose) ; and

(C) of the time and place fixed for the hearing.

(3) The labor organization or agency involved shall have the right to file an answer to the original and any amended complaint and to appear in person or otherwise and give testimony at the time and place fixed in the complaint for the hearing.

(4) (A) Except as provided in subparagraph (B) of this paragraph, no complaint shall be issued based on any alleged unfair labor practice which occurred more than 6 months before the filing of the charge with the Authority.

(B) If the General Counsel determines that the person filing any charge was prevented from filing the charge during the 6-month period referred to in subparagraph (A) of this paragraph by reason of—

(i) any failure of the agency or labor organization against which the charge is made to perform a duty owed to the person, or

(ii) any concealment which prevented discovery of the alleged unfair labor practice during the 6-month period,

the General Counsel may issue a complaint based on the charge if the charge was filed during the 6-month period beginning on the day of the discovery by the person of the alleged unfair labor practice.

(5) The General Counsel may prescribe regulations providing for informal methods by which the alleged unfair labor practice may be resolved prior to the issuance of a complaint.

(6) The Authority (or any member thereof or any individual employed by the Authority and designated for such purpose) shall conduct a hearing on the complaint not earlier than 5 days after the date on which the complaint is served. In the discretion of the individual or individuals conducting the hearing, any person involved may be allowed to intervene in the hearing and to present testimony. Any such hearing shall, to the extent practicable, be conducted in accordance with the provisions of subchapter II of chapter 5 of this title, except that the parties shall not be bound by rules of evidence, whether statutory, common law, or adopted by a court. A transcript shall be kept of the hearing. After such a hearing the Authority, in its discretion, may upon notice receive further evidence or hear argument.

(7) If the Authority (or any member thereof or any individual employed by the Authority and designated for such purpose) deter-

mines after any hearing on a complaint under paragraph (5) of this subsection that the preponderance of the evidence received demonstrates that the agency or labor organization named in the complaint has engaged in or is engaging in an unfair labor practice, then the individual or individuals conducting the hearing shall state in writing their findings of fact and shall issue and cause to be served on the agency or labor organization an order—

    (A) to cease and desist from any such unfair labor practice in which the agency or labor organization is engaged;

    (B) requiring the parties to renegotiate a collective bargaining agreement in accordance with the order of the Authority and requiring that the agreement, as amended, be given retroactive effect;

    (C) requiring reinstatement of an employee with backpay in accordance with section 5596 of this title; or

    (D) including any combination of the actions described in subparagraphs (A) through (C) of this paragraph or such other action as will carry out the purpose of this chapter.

If any such order requires reinstatement of an employee with backpay, backpay may be required of the agency (as provided in section 5596 of this title) or of the labor organization, as the case may be, which is found to have engaged in the unfair labor practice involved.

    (8) If the individual or individuals conducting the hearing determine that the preponderance of the evidence received fails to demonstrate that the agency or labor organization named in the complaint has engaged in or is engaging in an unfair labor practice, the individual or individuals shall state in writing their findings of fact and shall issue an order dismissing the complaint.

    (b) In connection with any matter before the Authority in any proceeding under this section, the Authority may request, in accordance with the provisions of section 7105(i) of this title, from the Director of the Office of Personnel Management an advisory opinion concerning the proper interpretation of rules, regulations, or other policy directives issued by the Office of Personnel Management. (Pub. L. 95–454, Oct. 13, 1978, 92 Stat. 1207.)

§ 7119. Negotiation impasses; Federal Service Impasses Panel

    (a) The Federal Mediation and Conciliation Service shall provide services and assistance to agencies and exclusive representatives in the resolution of negotiation impasses. The Service shall determine under what circumstances and in what manner it shall provide services and assistance.

    (b) If voluntary arrangements, including the services of the Federal Mediation and Conciliation Service or any other third party mediation, fail to resolve a negotiation impasse—

    (1) either party may request the Federal Service Impasses Panel to consider the matter, or

    (2) the parties may agree to adopt a procedure for binding arbitration of the negotiation impasse, but only if the procedure is approved by the Panel.

(c) (1) The Federal Service Impasses Panel is an entity within the Authority, the function of which is to provide assistance in resolving negotiation impasses between agencies and exclusive representatives.

(2) The Panel shall be composed of a Chairman and at least six other members, who shall be appointed by the President, solely on the basis of fitness to perform the duties and functions involved, from among individuals who are familiar with Government operations and knowledgeable in labor-management relations.

(3) Of the original members of the Panel, 2 members shall be appointed for a term of 1 year, 2 members shall be appointed for a term of 3 years, and the Chairman and the remaining members shall be appointed for a term of 5 years. Thereafter each member shall be appointed for a term of 5 years, except that an individual chosen to fill a vacancy shall be appointed for the unexpired term of the member replaced. Any member of the Panel may be removed by the President.

(4) The Panel may appoint an Executive Director and any other individuals it may from time to time find necessary for the proper performance of its duties. Each member of the Panel who is not an employee (as defined in section 2105 of this title) is entitled to pay at a rate equal to the daily equivalent of the maximum annual rate of basic pay then currently paid under the General Schedule for each day he is engaged in the performance of official business of the Panel, including travel time, and is entitled to travel expenses as provided under section 5703 of this title.

(5) (A) The Panel or its designee shall promptly investigate any impasse presented to it under subsection (b) of this section. The Panel shall consider the impasse and shall either—

(i) recommend to the parties procedures for the resolution of the impasse; or

(ii) assist the parties in resolving the impasse through whatever methods and procedures, including factfinding and recommendations, it may consider appropriate to accomplish the purpose of this section.

(B) If the parties do not arrive at a settlement after assistance by the Panel under subparagraph (A) of this paragraph, the Panel may—

(i) hold hearings;

(ii) administer oaths, take the testimony or deposition of any person under oath, and issue subpenas as provided in section 7132 of this title; and

(iii) take whatever action is necessary and not inconsistent with this chapter to resolve the impasse.

(C) Notice of any final action of the Panel under this section shall be promptly served upon the parties, and the action shall be binding on such parties during the term of the agreement, unless the parties agree otherwise. (Pub. L. 95–454, Oct. 13, 1978, 92 Stat. 1208.)

§ 7120. Standards of conduct for labor organizations

(a) An agency shall only accord recognition to a labor organization that is free from corrupt influences and influences opposed to basic democratic principles. Except as provided in subsection (b) of this section, an organization is not required to prove that it is free from such influences if it is subject to governing requirements adopted by the organization or by a national or international labor organization or federation of labor organizations with which it is affiliated, or in which it participates, containing explicit and detailed provisions to which it subscribes calling for—

    (1) the maintenance of democratic procedures and practices including provisions for periodic elections to be conducted subject to recognized safeguards and provisions defining and securing the right of individual members to participate in the affairs of the organization, to receive fair and equal treatment under the governing rules of the organization, and to receive fair process in disciplinary proceedings;

    (2) the exclusion from office in the organization of persons affiliated with communist or other totalitarian movements and persons identified with corrupt influences;

    (3) the prohibition of business or financial interests on the part of organization officers and agents which conflict with their duty to the organization and its members; and

    (4) the maintenance of fiscal integrity in the conduct of the affairs of the organization, including provisions for accounting and financial controls and regular financial reports or summaries to be made available to members.

    (b) Notwithstanding the fact that a labor organization has adopted or subscribed to standards of conduct as provided in subsection (a) of this section, the organization is required to furnish evidence of its freedom from corrupt influences or influences opposed to basic democratic principles if there is reasonable cause to believe that—

    (1) the organization has been suspended or expelled from, or is subject to other sanctions, by a parent labor organization, or federation of organizations with which it had been affiliated, because it has demonstrated an unwillingness or inability to comply with governing requirements comparable in purpose to those required by subsection (a) of this section; or

    (2) the organization is in fact subject to influences that would preclude recognition under this chapter.

    (c) A labor organization which has or seeks recognition as a representative of employees under this chapter shall file financial and other reports with the Assistant Secretary of Labor for Labor Management Relations, provide for bonding of officials and employees of the organization, and comply with trusteeship and election standards.

    (d) The Assistant Secretary shall prescribe such regulations as are necessary to carry out the purposes of this section. Such regulations shall conform generally to the principles applied to labor organizations in the private sector. Complaints of violations of this section shall be filed with the Assistant Secretary. In any matter arising under this section, the Assistant Secretary may require a labor organization to cease and desist from violations of this section and require it to take such actions as he considers appropriate to carry out the policies of this section.

(e) This chapter does not authorize participation in the management of a labor organization or acting as a representative of a labor organization by a management official, a supervisor, or a confidential employee, except as specifically provided in this chapter, or by an employee if the participation or activity would result in a conflict or apparent conflict of interest or would otherwise be incompatible with law or with the official duties of the employee.

(f) In the case of any labor organization which by omission or commission has willfully and intentionally, with regard to any strike, work stoppage, or slowdown, violated section 7116(b)(7) of this title, the Authority shall, upon an appropriate finding by the Authority of such violation—

　　(1) revoke the exclusive recognition status of the labor organization, which shall then immediately cease to be legally entitled and obligated to represent employees in the unit; or

　　(2) take any other appropriate disciplinary action.

(Pub. L. 95–454, Oct. 13, 1978, 92 Stat. 1210.)

SUBCHAPTER III—GRIEVANCES, APPEALS, AND REVIEW

§ 7121. Grievance procedures

(a)(1) Except as provided in paragraph (2) of this subsection, any collective bargaining agreement shall provide procedures for the settlement of grievances, including questions of arbitrability. Except as provided in subsections (d) and (e) of this section, the procedures shall be the exclusive procedures for resolving grievances which fall within its coverage.

(2) Any collective bargaining agreement may exclude any matter from the application of the grievance procedures which are provided for in the agreement.

(b) Any negotiated grievance procedure referred to in subsection (a) of this section shall—

　　(1) be fair and simple,

　　(2) provide for expeditious processing, and

　　(3) include procedures that—

　　　　(A) assure an exclusive representative the right, in its own behalf or on behalf of any employee in the unit represented by the exclusive representative, to present and process grievances;

　　　　(B) assure such an employee the right to present a grievance in the employee's own behalf, and assure the exclusive representative the right to be present during the grievance proceeding; and

　　　　(C) provide that any grievance not satisfactorily settled under the negotiated grievance procedure shall be subject to binding arbitration which may be invoked by either the exclusive representative or the agency.

(c) The preceding subsections of this section shall not apply with respect to any grievance concerning—

(1) any claimed violation of subchapter III of chapter 73 of this title (relating to prohibited political activities) ;

(2) retirement, life insurance, or health insurance;

(3) a suspension or removal under section 7532 of this title;

(4) any examination, certification, or appointment; or

(5) the classification of any position which does not result in the reduction in grade or pay of an employee.

(d) An aggrieved employee affected by a prohibited personnel practice under section 2302(b)(1) of this title which also falls under the coverage of the negotiated grievance procedure may raise the matter under a statutory procedure or the negotiated procedure, but not both. An employee shall be deemed to have exercised his option under this subsection to raise the matter under either a statutory procedure or the negotiated procedure at such time as the employee timely initiates an action under the applicable statutory procedure or timely files a grievance in writing, in accordance with the provisions of the parties' negotiated procedure, whichever event occurs first. Selection of the negotiated procedure in no manner prejudices the right of an aggrieved employee to request the Merit Systems Protection Board to review the final decision pursuant to section 7702 of this title in the case of any personnel action that could have been appealed to the Board, or, where applicable, to request the Equal Employment Opportunity Commission to review a final decision in any other matter involving a complaint of discrimination of the type prohibited by any law administered by the Equal Employment Opportunity Commission.

(e)(1) Matters covered under sections 4303 and 7512 of this title which also fall within the coverage of the negotiated grievance procedure may, in the discretion of the aggrieved employee, be raised either under the appellate procedures of section 7701 of this title or under the negotiated grievance procedure, but not both. Similar matters which arise under other personnel systems applicable to employees covered by this chapter may, in the discretion of the aggrieved employee, be raised either under the appellate procedures, if any, applicable to those matters, or under the negotiated grievance procedure, but not both. An employee shall be deemed to have exercised his option under this subsection to raise a matter either under the applicable appellate procedures or under the negotiated grievance procedure at such time as the employee timely files a notice of appeal under the applicable appellate procedures or timely files a grievance in writing in accordance with the provisions of the parties' negotiated grievance procedure, whichever event occurs first.

(2) In matters covered under sections 4303 and 7512 of this title which have been raised under the negotiated grievance procedure in accordance with this section, an arbitrator shall be governed by section 7701(c)(1) of this title, as applicable.

(f) In matters covered under sections 4303 and 7512 of this title which have been raised under the negotiated grievance procedure in accordance with this section, section 7703 of this title pertaining to judicial review shall apply to the award of an arbitrator in the same manner and under the same conditions as if the matter had been decided by the Board. In matters similar to those covered under sections 4303 and 7512 of this title which arise under other personnel systems and which an aggrieved employee has raised under the negotiated grievance procedure, judicial review of an arbitrator's award may be obtained in the same manner and on the same basis as could be obtained of a final decision in such matters raised under applicable appellate procedures. (Pub. L. 95–454, Oct. 13, 1978, 92 Stat. 1211; amended Pub. L. 96–54, Aug. 14, 1979, 93 Stat. 383.)

§ 7122. Exceptions to arbitral awards

(a) Either party to arbitration under this chapter may file with the Authority an exception to any arbitrator's award pursuant to the arbitration (other than an award relating to a matter described in section 7121(f) of this title). If upon review the Authority finds that the award is deficient—

   (1) because it is contrary to any law, rule, or regulation; or
   (2) on other grounds similar to those applied by Federal courts in private sector labor-management relations;
the Authority may take such action and make such recommendations concerning the award as it considers necessary, consistent with applicable laws, rules, or regulations.

(b) If no exception to an arbitrator's award is filed under subsection (a) of this section during the 30-day period beginning on the date the award is served on the party, the award shall be final and binding. An agency shall take the actions required by an arbitrator's final award. The award may include the payment of backpay (as provided in section 5596 of this title). (Pub. L. 95–454, Oct. 13, 1978, 92 Stat. 1212; as amended Pub. L. 98–224, Mar. 2, 1984, 98 Stat. 48.)

§ 7123. Judicial review; enforcement

(a) Any person aggrieved by any final order of the Authority other than an order under—

   (1) section 7122 of this title (involving an award by an arbitrator), unless the order involves an unfair labor practice under section 7118 of this title, or
   (2) section 7112 of this title (involving an appropriate unit determination),
may, during the 60-day period beginning on the date on which the order was issued, institute an action for judicial review of the Authority's order in the United States court of appeals in the circuit in which the person resides or transacts business or in the United States Court of Appeals for the District of Columbia.

(b) The Authority may petition any appropriate United States court of appeals for the enforcement of any order of the Authority and for appropriate temporary relief or restraining order.

(c) Upon the filing of a petition under subsection (a) of this section for judicial review or under subsection (b) of this section for enforcement, the Authority shall file in the court the record in the proceedings, as provided in section 2112 of title 28. Upon the filing of the petition, the court shall cause notice thereof to be served to the parties involved, and thereupon shall have jurisdiction of the proceeding and of the question determined therein and may grant any temporary relief (including a temporary restraining order) it considers just and proper, and may make and enter a decree affirming and enforcing, modifying and enforcing as so modified, or setting aside in whole or in part the order of the Authority. The filing of a petition under subsection (a) or (b) of this section shall not operate as a stay of the Authority's order unless the court specifically orders the stay. Review of the Authority's order shall be on the record in accordance with section 706 of this title. No objection that has not been urged before the Authority, or its designee, shall be considered by the court, unless the failure or neglect to urge the objection is excused because of extraordinary circumstances. The findings of the Authority with respect to questions of fact, if supported by substantial evidence on the record considered as a whole, shall be conclusive. If any person applies to the court for leave to adduce additional evidence and shows to the satisfaction of the court that the additional evidence is material and that there were reasonable grounds for the failure to adduce the evidence in the hearing before the Authority, or its designee, the court may order the additional evidence to be taken before the Authority, or its designee, and to be made a part of the record. The Authority may modify its findings as to the facts, or make new findings by reason of additional evidence so taken and filed. The Authority shall file its modified or new findings, which, with respect to questions of fact, if supported by substantial evidence on the record considered as a whole, shall be conclusive. The Authority shall file its recommendations, if any, for the modification or setting aside of its original order. Upon the filing of the record with the court, the jurisdiction of the court shall be exclusive and its judgment and decree shall be final, except that the judgment and decree shall be subject to review by the Supreme Court of the United States upon writ of certiorari or certification as provided in section 1254 of title 28.

(d) The Authority may, upon issuance of a complaint as provided in section 7118 of this title charging that any person has engaged in or is engaging in an unfair labor practice, petition any United States district court within any district in which the unfair labor practice in question is alleged to have occurred or in which such person resides or transacts business for appropriate temporary relief (including a restraining order). Upon the filing of the petition, the court shall cause notice thereof to be served upon the person, and thereupon shall have jurisdiction to grant any temporary relief (including a temporary restraining order) it considers just and proper. A court shall not grant any temporary relief under this section if it would interfere with the ability of the agency to carry out its essential functions or if the

Authority fails to establish probable cause that an unfair labor practice is being committed. (Pub. L. 95–454, Oct. 13, 1978, 92 Stat. 1213.)

SUBCHAPTER IV—ADMINISTRATIVE AND OTHER PROVISIONS

§ 7131. Official time

(a) Any employee representing an exclusive representative in the negotiation of a collective bargaining agreement under this chapter shall be authorized official time for such purposes, including attendance at impasse proceeding, during the time the employee otherwise would be in a duty status. The number of employees for whom official time is authorized under this subsection shall not exceed the number of individuals designated as representing the agency for such purposes.

(b) Any activities performed by any employee relating to the internal business of a labor organization (including the solicitation of membership, elections of labor organization officials, and collection of dues) shall be performed during the time the employee is in a non-duty status.

(c) Except as provided in subsection (a) of this section, the Authority shall determine whether any employee participating for, or on behalf of, a labor organization in any phase of proceedings before the Authority shall be authorized official time for such purpose during the time the employee otherwise would be in a duty status.

(d) Except as provided in the preceding subsections of this section—

(1) any employee representing an exclusive representative, or

(2) in connection with any other matter covered by this chapter, any employee in an appropriate unit represented by an exclusive representative,

shall be granted official time in any amount the agency and the exclusive representative involved agree to be reasonable, necessary, and in the public interest. (Pub. L. 95–454, Oct. 13, 1978, 92 Stat. 1214.)

§ 7132. Subpenas

(a) Any member of the Authority, the General Counsel, or the Panel, any administrative law judge appointed by the Authority under section 3105 of this title, and any employee of the Authority designated by the Authority may—

(1) issue subpenas requiring the attendance and testimony of witnesses and the production of documentary or other evidence from any place in the United States; and

(2) administer oaths, take or order the taking of depositions, order responses to written interrogatories, examine witnesses, and receive evidence.

No subpena shall be issued under this section which requires the disclosure of intramanagement guidance, advice, counsel, or training within an agency or between an agency and the Office of Personnel Management.

(b) In the case of contumacy or failure to obey a subpena issued under subsection (a) (1) of this section, the United States district court for the judicial district in which the person to whom the subpena is addressed resides or is served may issue an order requiring such person to appear at any designated place to testify or to produce documentary or other evidence. Any failure to obey the order of the court may be punished by the court as a contempt thereof.

(c) Witnesses (whether appearing voluntarily or under subpena) shall be paid the same fee and mileage allowances which are paid subpenaed witnesses in the courts of the United States. (Pub. L. 95–454, Oct. 13, 1978, 92 Stat. 1214.)

§ 7133. Compilation and publication of data

(a) The Authority shall maintain a file of its proceedings and copies of all available agreements and arbitration decisions, and shall publish the texts of its decisions and the actions taken by the Panel under section 7119 of this title.

(b) All files maintained under subsection (a) of this section shall be open to inspection and reproduction in accordance with the provisions of sections 552 and 552a of this title. (Pub. L. 95–454, Oct. 13, 1978, 92 Stat. 1215.)

§ 7134. Regulations

The Authority, the General Counsel, the Federal Mediation and Conciliation Service, the Assistant Secretary of Labor for Labor Management Relations, and the Panel shall each prescribe rules and regulations to carry out the provisions of this chapter applicable to each of them, respectively. Provisions of subchapter II of chapter 5 of this title shall be applicable to the issuance, revision, or repeal of any such rule or regulation. (Pub. L. 95–454, Oct. 13, 1978, 92 Stat. 1215.)

§ 7135. Continuation of existing laws, recognitions, agreements, and procedures

(a) Nothing contained in this chapter shall preclude—

(1) the renewal or continuation of an exclusive recognition, certification of an exclusive representative, or a lawful agreement between an agency and an exclusive representative of its employees, which is entered into before the effective date of this chapter; or

(2) the renewal, continuation, or initial according of recognition for units of management officials or supervisors represented by labor organizations which historically or traditionally represent management officials or supervisors in private industry and which hold exclusive recognition for units of such officials or supervisors in any agency on the effective date of this chapter.

(b) Policies, regulations, and procedures established under and decisions issued under Executive Orders 11491, 11616, 11636, 11787, and 11838, or under any other Executive order, as in effect on the effective date of this chapter, shall remain in full force and effect until revised or revoked by the President, or unless superseded by specific provisions of this chapter or by regulations or decisions issued pursuant to this chapter. (Pub. L. 95–454, Oct. 13, 1978, 92 Stat. 1215.)

* * * * *

CHAPTER 72—ANTIDISCRIMINATION; RIGHT TO PETITION CONGRESS

SUBCHAPTER I—ANTIDISCRIMINATION IN EMPLOYMENT

SUBCHAPTER I—ANTIDISCRIMINATION IN EMPLOYMENT

§ 7201. Antidiscrimination policy; minority recruitment program

(a) For the purpose of this section—

(1) "underrepresentation" means a situation in which the number of members of a minority group designation (determined by the Equal Employment Opportunity Commission in consultation with the Office of Personnel Management, on the basis of the policy set forth in subsection (b) of this section) within a category of civil service employment constitutes a lower percentage of the total number of employees within the employment category than the percentage that the minority constituted within the labor force of the United States, as determined under the most recent decennial or mid-decade census, or current population survey, under title 13, and

(2) "category of civil service employment" means—

(A) each grade of the General Schedule described in section 5104 of this title;

(B) each position subject to subchapter IV of chapter 53 of this title;

(C) such occupational, professional, or other groupings (including occupational series) within the categories established under subparagraphs (A) and (B) of this paragraph as the Office determines appropriate.

(b) It is the policy of the United States to insure equal employment opportunities for employees without discrimination because of race, color, religion, sex, or national origin. The President shall use his existing authority to carry out this policy.

(c) Not later than 180 days after the date of the enactment of the Civil Service Reform Act of 1978, the Office of Personnel Management shall, by regulation, implement a minority recruitment program which shall provide, to the maximum extent practicable—

(1) that each Executive agency conduct a continuing program for the recruitment of members of minorities for positions in the agency to carry out the policy set forth in subsection (b) in a manner designed to eliminate underrepresentation of minorities in the various categories of civil service employment within the Federal service, with special efforts directed at recruiting in minority communities, in educational institutions, and from other sources from which minorities can be recruited; and

(2) that the Office conduct a continuing program of—

(A) assistance to agencies in carrying out programs under paragraph (1) of this subsection, and

(B) evaluation and oversight and such recruitment programs to determine their effectiveness in eliminating such minority underrepresentation.

(d) Not later than 60 days after the date of the enactment of the Civil Service Reform Act of 1978, the Equal Employment Opportunity Commission shall—

(1) establish the guidelines proposed to be used in carrying out the program required under subsection (c) of this section; and

(2) make determinations of underrepresentation which are proposed to be used initially under such program; and

(3) transmit to the Executive agencies involved, to the Office of Personnel Management, and to the Congress the determinations made under paragraph (2) of this subsection.

(e) Not later than January 31 of each year, the Office shall prepare and transmit to each House of the Congress a report on the activities of the Office and of Executive agencies under subsection (c) of this section, including the affirmative action plans submitted under section 717 of the Civil Rights Act of 1964 (42 U.S.C. 2000e–16), the personnel data file maintained by the Office of Personnel Management, and any other data necessary to evaluate the effectiveness of the program for each category of civil service employment and for each minority group designation, for the preceding fiscal year, together with recommendations for administrative or legislative action the Office considers appropriate. (Pub. L. 89–554, Sept. 6, 1966, 80 Stat. 523; amended, Pub. L. 95–454, Oct. 13, 1978, 92 Stat. 1152, 1216.)

§ 7202. Marital status

(a) The President may prescribe rules which shall prohibit, as nearly as conditions of good administration warrant, discrimination because of marital status in an Executive agency or in the competitive service.

(b) Regulations prescribed under any provision of this title, or under any other provision of law, granting benefits to employees, shall provide the same benefits for a married female employee and her spouse and children as are provided for a married male employee and his spouse and children.

(c) Notwithstanding any other provision of law, any provision of law providing a benefit to a male Federal employee or to his spouse or family shall be deemed to provide the same benefit to a female Federal employee or to her spouse or family. (Pub. L. 89–554, Sept. 6, 1966, 80 Stat. 523, amended Pub. L. 92–187, § 3, Dec. 15, 1971, 85 Stat. 644; Pub. L. 95–454, Oct. 13, 1978, 92 Stat. 1216.)

§ 7203. Handicapping condition

The President may prescribe rules which shall prohibit, as nearly as conditions of good administration warrant, discrimination because of handicapping condition in an Executive agency or in the competitive service with respect to a position the duties of which, in the opinion of the Office of Personnel Management, can be performed efficiently by an individual with a handicapping condition, except that the employment may not endanger the health or safety of the individual or others. (Pub. L. 89–554, Sept. 6, 1966, 80 Stat. 523, amended, Pub. L. 95–454, Oct. 13, 1978, 92 Stat. 1118, 1216, and 1224.)

§ 7204. Other prohibitions

(a) Repealed. Pub. L. 90–83, § 1(44), Sept. 11, 1967, 81 Stat. 208.

(b) In the administration of chapter 51, subchapters III and IV of chapter 53, and sections 305 and 3324 of this title, discrimination because of race, color, creed, sex, or marital status is prohibited with respect to an individual or a position held by an individual.

(c) The Office of Personnel Management may prescribe regulations necessary for the administration of subsection (b) of this section. (Pub L. 89–554, Sept. 6, 1966, 80 Stat. 523, amended Pub. L. 90–83, § 1(44), Sept. 11, 1967, 81 Stat. 208; Pub. L. 92–392, § 8, Aug. 19, 1972, 86 Stat. 573; Pub. L. 95–454, Oct. 13, 1978, 92 Stat. 1216 and 1224.)

SUBCHAPTER II—EMPLOYEES' RIGHT TO PETITION CONGRESS

§ 7211. Employees' right to petition Congress

The right of employees, individually or collectively, to petition Congress or a Member of Congress, or to furnish information to either House of Congress, or to a committee or Member thereof, may not be interfered with or denied. (Pub. L. 95–454, Oct. 13, 1978, 92 Stat. 1217.)

* * * * *

CHAPTER 73—SUITABILITY, SECURITY, AND CONDUCT

SUBCHAPTER II – EMPLOYMENT LIMITATIONS

SUBCHAPTER II—EMPLOYMENT LIMITATIONS

§7311. Loyalty and striking

An individual may not accept or hold a position in the Government of the United States or the government of the District of Columbia if he—

(1) advocates the overthrow of our constitutional form of government;

(2) is a member of an organization that he knows advocates the overthrow of our constitutional form of government;

(3) participates in a strike, or asserts the right to strike, against the Government of the United States or the government of the District of Columbia; or

(4) is a member of an organization of employees of the Government of the United States or of individuals employed by the government of the District of Columbia that he knows asserts the right to strike against the Government of the United States or the government of the District of Columbia.

§7312. Employment and clearance; individuals removed for national security

Removal under section 7532 of this title does not affect the right of an individual so removed to seek or accept employment in an agency of the United States other than the agency from which removed. However, the appointment of an individual so removed may be made only after the head of the agency concerned has consulted with the Office of Personnel Management. The Office, on written request of the head of the agency or the individual so removed, may determine whether the individual is eligible for employment in an agency other than the agency from which removed.

§7313. Riots and civil disorders

(a) An individual convicted by any Federal, State, or local court of competent jurisdiction of—

(1) inciting a riot or civil disorder;

(2) organizing, promoting, encouraging, or participating in a riot or civil disorder;

(3) aiding or abetting any person in committing any offense specified in clause (1) or (2); or

(4) any offense determined by the head of the employing agency to have been committed in furtherance of, or while participating in, a riot or civil disorder;

shall, if the offense for which he is convicted is a felony, be ineligible to accept or hold any position in the Government of the United States or in the government of the District of Columbia for the five years immediately following the date upon which his conviction becomes final. Any such individual holding a position in the Government of the United States or the government of the District of Columbia on the date his conviction becomes final shall be removed from such position.

(b) For the purposes of this section, "felony" means any offense for which imprisonment is authorized for a term exceeding one year.

SUBCHAPTER III—POLITICAL ACTIVITIES

§7321. Political contributions and services

The President may prescribe rules which shall provide, as nearly as conditions of good administration warrant, that an employee in an Executive agency or in the competitive service is not obliged, by reason of that employment, to contribute to a political fund or to render political service, and that he may not be removed or otherwise prejudiced for refusal to do so.

§7322. Political use of authority or influence; prohibition

The President may prescribe rules which shall provide, as nearly as conditions of good administration warrant, that an employee in an Executive agency or in the competitive service may not use his official authority or influence to coerce the political action of a person or body.

§7323. Political contributions; prohibition

An employee in an Executive agency (except one appointed by the President, by and with the advice and consent of the Senate) may not request or receive from, or give to, an employee, a Member of Congress, or an officer of a uniformed service a thing of value for political purposes. An employee who violates this section shall be removed from the service.

§7324. Influencing elections; taking part in political campaigns; prohibitions; exceptions

(a) An employee in an Executive agency or an individual employed by the government of the District of Columbia may not—

(1) use his official authority or influence for the purpose of interfering with or affecting the result of an election; or

(2) take an active part in political management or in political campaigns.

For the purpose of this subsection, the phrase "an active part in political management or in political campaigns" means those acts of political management or political campaigning which were prohibited on the part of employees in the competitive service before July 19, 1940, by determinations of the Civil Service Commission under the rules prescribed by the President.

(b) An employee or individual to whom subsection (a) of this section applies retains the right to vote as he chooses and to express his opinion on political subjects and candidates.

(c) Subsection (a) of this section does not apply to an individual employed by an educational or research institution, establishment, agency, or system which is supported in whole or in part by the District of Columbia or by a recognized religious, philanthropic, or cultural organization.

(d) Subsection (a) (2) of this section does not apply to—

(1) an employee paid from the appropriation for the office of the President;

(2) the head or the assistant head of an Executive department or military department;

(3) an employee appointed by the President, by and with the advice and consent of the Senate, who determines policies to be pursued by the United States in its relations with foreign powers or in the nationwide administration of Federal laws;

(4) the Commissioners of the District of Columbia; or

(5) the Recorder of Deeds of the District of Columbia.

§7325. Penalties

An employee or individual who violates section 7324 of this title shall be removed from his position, and funds appropriated for the position from which removed thereafter may not be used to pay the employee or individual. However, if the Merit Systems Protection Board finds by unanimous vote that the violation does not warrant removal, a penalty of not less than 30 days' suspension without pay shall be imposed by direction of the Board.

§7326. Nonpartisan political activity permitted

Section 7324(a) (2) of this title does not prohibit political activity in connection with—

(1) an election and the preceding campaign if none of the candidates is to be nominated or elected at that election as representing a party any of whose candidates for presidential elector received votes in the last preceding election at which presidential electors were selected; or

(2) a question which is not specifically identified with a National or State political party or political party of a territory or possession of the United States.

§7327. Political activity permitted; employees residing in certain municipalities

The Office of Personnel Management may prescribe regulations permitting employees and individuals to whom section 7324 of this title applies to take an active part in political management and political campaigns involving the municipality or other political subdivision in which they reside, to the extent the Office considers it to be in their domestic interest, when—

(1) the municipality or political subdivision is in Maryland or Virginia and in the immediate vicinity of the District of Columbia, or is a municipality in which the majority of voters are employed by the Government of the United States; and

(2) the Office determines that because of special or unusual circumstances which exist in the municipality or political subdivision it is in the domestic interest of the employees and individuals to permit that political participation.

(Amended Pub. L. 97–468, Jan. 14, 1983, 96 Stat. 2578.)

* * * * *

CHAPTER 75—ADVERSE ACTIONS

SUBCHAPTER I—SUSPENSION FOR 14 DAYS OR LESS

SUBCHAPTER I—SUSPENSION FOR 14 DAYS OR LESS

§ 7501. Definitions

For the purpose of this subchapter—

(1) "employee" means an individual in the competitive service who is not serving a probationary or trial period under an initial

appointment or who has completed 1 year of current continuous employment in the same or similar positions under other than a temporary appointment limited to 1 year or less; and

(2) "suspension" means the placing of an employee, for disciplinary reasons, in a temporary status without duties and pay. (Pub. L. 95–454, Oct. 13, 1978, 92 Stat. 1134.)

§ 7502. Actions covered

This subchapter applies to a suspension for 14 days or less, but does not apply to a suspension under section 7521 or 7532 of this title or any action initiated under section 1206 of this title. (Pub. L. 95–454, Oct. 13, 1978, 92 Stat. 1135.)

§ 7503. Cause and procedure

(a) Under regulations prescribed by the Office of Personnel Management, an employee may be suspended for 14 days or less for such cause as will promote the efficiency of the service (including discourteous conduct to the public confirmed by an immediate supervisor's report of four such instances within any one-year period or any other pattern of discourteous conduct).

(b) An employee against whom a suspension for 14 days or less is proposed is entitled to—

(1) an advance written notice stating the specific reasons for the proposed action;

(2) a reasonable time to answer orally and in writing and to furnish affidavits and other documentary evidence in support of the answer:

(3) be represented by an attorney or other representative; and

(4) a written decision and the specific reasons therefor at the earliest practicable date.

(c) Copies of the notice of proposed action, the answer of the employee if written, a summary thereof if made orally, the notice of decision and reasons therefor, and any order effecting the suspension, together with any supporting material, shall be maintained by the agency and shall be furnished to the Merit Systems Protection Board upon its request and to the employee affected upon the employee's request. (Pub. L. 95–454, Oct. 13, 1978, 92 Stat. 1135.)

§ 7504. Regulations

The Office of Personnel Management may prescribe regulations to carry out the purpose of this subchapter. (Pub. L. 95–454, Oct. 13, 1978, 92 Stat. 1135.)

SUBCHAPTER II—REMOVAL, SUSPENSION FOR MORE THAN 14 DAYS, REDUCTION IN GRADE OR PAY, OR FURLOUGH FOR 30 DAYS OR LESS

§ 7511. Definitions; application

(a) For the purpose of this subchapter—

(1) "employee" means—

(A) an individual in the competitive service who is not serving a probationary or trial period under an initial appointment or who has completed 1 year of current continuous employment under other than a temporary appointment limited to 1 year or less; and

(B) a preference eligible in an Executive agency in the excepted service, and a preference eligible in the United States Postal Service or the Postal Rate Commission, who has completed 1 year of current continuous service in the same or similar positions;

(2) "suspension" has the meaning as set forth in section 7501(2) of this title;

(3) "grade" means a level of classification under a position classification system;

(4) "pay" means the rate of basic pay fixed by law or administrative action for the position held by an employee; and

(5) "furlough" means the placing of an employee in a temporary status without duties and pay because of lack of work or funds or other nondisciplinary reasons.

(b) This subchapter does not apply to an employee—

(1) whose appointment is made by and with the advice and consent of the Senate;

(2) whose position has been determined to be of a confidential, policy-determining, policy-making or policy-advocating character by—

(A) the Office of Personnel Management for a position that it has excepted from the competitive service; or

(B) the President or the head of an agency for a position which is excepted from the competitive service by statute.

(c) The Office may provide for the application of this subchapter to any position or group of positions excepted from the competitive service by regulation of the Office (Pub. L. 95-454, Oct. 13, 1978, 92 Stat. 1135.)

§ 7512. Actions covered

This subchapter applies to—

(1) a removal;

(2) a suspension for more than 14 days;

(3) a reduction in grade;

(4) a reduction in pay; and

(5) a furlough of 30 days or less:

but does not apply to—

(A) a suspension or removal under section 7532 of this title,

(B) a reduction-in-force action under section 3502 of this title,

(C) the reduction in grade of a supervisor or manager who has not completed the probationary period under section 3321 (a) (2) of this title if such reduction is to the grade held immediately before becoming such a supervisor or manager,

(D) a reduction in grade or removal under section 4303 of this title, or

(E) an action initiated under section 1206 or 7521 of this title.

(Pub L. 95–454, Oct. 13, 1978, 92 Stat. 1136.)

§ 7513. Cause and procedure

(a) Under regulations prescribed by the Office of Personnel Management, an agency may take an action covered by this subchapter against an employee only for such cause as will promote the efficiency of the service.

(b) An employee against whom an action is proposed is entitled to—

(1) at least 30 days' advance written notice, unless there is reasonable cause to believe the employee has committed a crime for which a sentence of imprisonment may be imposed, stating the specific reasons for the proposed action;

(2) a reasonable time, but not less than 7 days, to answer orally and in writing and to furnish affidavits and other documentary evidence in support of the answer;

(3) be represented by an attorney or other representative; and

(4) a written decision and the specific reasons therefor at the earliest practicable date.

(c) An agency may provide, by regulation, for a hearing which may be in lieu of or in addition to the opportunity to answer provided under subsection (b) (2) of this section.

(d) An employee against whom an action is taken under this section is entitled to appeal to the Merit Systems Protection Board under section 7701 of this title.

(e) Copies of the notice of proposed action, the answer of the employee when written, a summary thereof when made orally, the notice of decision and reasons therefor, and any order effecting an action covered by this subchapter, together with any supporting material, shall be maintained by the agency and shall be furnished to the Board upon its request and to the employee affected upon the employee's request. (Pub. L. 95–454, Oct. 13, 1978, 92 Stat. 1136.)

§ 7514. Regulations

The Office of Personnel Management may prescribe regulations to carry out the purpose of this subchapter, except as it concerns any matter with respect to which the Merit Systems Protection Board may prescribe regulations. (Pub. L. 95–454, Oct. 13, 1978, 92 Stat. 1137.)

SUBCHAPTER III—ADMINISTRATIVE LAW JUDGES

§ 7521. Actions against administrative law judges

(a) An action may be taken against an administrative law judge appointed under section 3105 of this title by the agency in which the administrative law judge is employed only for good cause established and determined by the Merit Systems Protection Board on the record after opportunity for hearing before the Board.

(b) The actions covered by this section are—
(1) a removal;
(2) a suspension;
(3) a reduction in grade;
(4) a reduction in pay; and
(5) a furlough of 30 days or less;
but do not include—
(A) a suspension or removal under section 7532 of this title;
(B) a reduction-in-force action under section 3502 of this title; or
(C) any action initiated under section 1206 of this title.

(Pub. L. 95–454, Oct. 13, 1978, 92 Stat. 1137.)

SUBCHAPTER IV—NATIONAL SECURITY

§ 7531. Definitions

For the purpose of this subchapter, "agency" means—
(1) the Department of State;
(2) the Department of Commerce;
(3) the Department of Justice;
(4) the Department of Defense;
(5) a military department;
(6) the Coast Guard;
(7) the Atomic Energy Commission;
(8) the National Aeronautics and Space Administration; and
(9) such other agency of the Government of the United States as the President designates in the best interests of national security.

The President shall report any designation to the Committees on the Armed Services of the Congress. (Pub. L. 89–554, Sept. 6, 1966, 80 Stat. 528.)

§ 7532. Suspension and removal

(a) Notwithstanding other statutes, the head of an agency may suspend without pay an employee of his agency when he considers that action necessary in the interests of national security. To the extent that the head of the agency determines that the interest of national security permit, the suspended employee shall be notified of the reasons for the suspension. Within 30 days after the notification, the suspended employee is entitled to submit to the official designated by the head of the agency statements or affidavits to show why he should be restored to duty.

(b) Subject to subsection (c) of this section, the head of an agency may remove an employee suspended under subsection (a) of this section when, after such investigation and review as he considers necessary, he determines that removal is necessary or advisable in the interests of national security. The determination of the head of the agency is final.

(c) An employee suspended under subsection (a) of this section who—

(1) has a permanent or indefinite appointment;

(2) has completed his probationary or trial period; and

(3) is a citizen of the United States;

is entitled, after suspension and before removal, to—

(A) a written statement of the charges against him within 30 days after suspension, which may be amended within 30 days thereafter and which shall be stated as specifically as security considerations permit;

(B) an opportunity within 30 days thereafter, plus an additional 30 days if the charges are amended, to answer the charges and submit affidavits;

(C) a hearing, at the request of the employee, by an agency authority duly constituted for this purpose;

(D) a review of his case by the head of the agency or his designee, before a decision adverse to the employee is made final; and

(E) a written statement of the decision of the head of the agency.

(Pub. L. 89–554, Sept. 6, 1966, 80 Stat. 529.)

§ 7533. Effect on other statutes

This subchapter does not impair the powers vested in the Atomic Energy Commission by chapter 23 of title 42, or the requirement in section 2201(d) of title 42 that adequate provision be made for administrative review of a determination to dismiss an employee of the Atomic Energy Commission. (Pub. L. 89–554, Sept. 6, 1966, 80 Stat. 529.)

SUBCHAPTER V—SENIOR EXECUTIVE SERVICE

§ 7541. Definitions

For the purpose of this subchapter—

(1) "employee" means a career appointee in the Senior Executive Service who—

(A) has completed the probationary period prescribed under section 3393(d) of this title; or

(B) was covered by the provisions of subchapter II of this chapter immediately before appointment to the Senior Executive Service; and

(2) "suspension" has the meaning set forth in section 7501(2) of this title.

(Added Pub. L. 95-454, Title IV, § 411(2), Oct. 13, 1978, 92 Stat. 1174.)

§ 7542. Actions covered

This subchapter applies to a removal from the civil service or suspension for more than 14 days, but does not apply to an action initiated under section 1206 of this title, to a suspension or removal under section 7532 of this title, or to a removal under section 3592 of this title.
(Added Pub. L. 95–454, Title IV, § 411(2), Oct. 13, 1978, 92 Stat. 1174.)

§ 7543. Cause and procedure

(a) Under regulations prescribed by the Office of Personnel Management, an agency may take an action covered by this subchapter against an employee only for misconduct, neglect of duty, malfeasance, or failure to accept a directed reassignment or to accompany a position in a transfer of function.

(b) An employee against whom an action covered by this subchapter is proposed is entitled to—

(1) at least 30 days' advance written notice, unless there is reasonable cause to believe that the employee has committed a crime for which a sentence of imprisonment can be imposed, stating specific reasons for the proposed action;

(2) a reasonable time, but not less than 7 days, to answer orally and in writing and to furnish affidavits and other documentary evidence in support of the answer;

(3) be represented by an attorney or other representative; and

(4) a written decision and specific reasons therefor at the earliest practicable date.

(c) An agency may provide, by regulation, for a hearing which may be in lieu of or in addition to the opportunity to answer provided under subsection (b)(2) of this section.

(d) An employee against whom an action is taken under this section is entitled to appeal to the Merit Systems Protection Board under section 7701 of this title.

(e) Copies of the notice of proposed action, the answer of the employee when written, and a summary thereof when made orally, the notice of decision and reasons therefor, and any order effecting an action covered by this subchapter, together with any supporting material, shall be maintained by the agency and shall be furnished to the Merit Systems Protection Board upon its request and to the employee affected upon the employee's request.
(Added Pub. L. 95–454, Title IV, § 411(2), Oct. 13, 1978, 92 Stat. 1174; as amended Pub. L. 97–35, Title XVII, § 1704(d)(2), Aug. 13, 1981, 95 Stat. 768; Pub. L. 98–615, Title III, § 304(c), Nov. 8, 1984, 98 Stat. 3219.)

* * * * *

CHAPTER 77—APPEALS

§ 7701. Appellate procedures

(a) An employee, or applicant for employment, may submit an appeal to the Merit Systems Protection Board from any action which is appealable to the Board under any law, rule, or regulation. An appellant shall have the right—

(1) to a hearing for which a transcript will be kept; and

(2) to be represented by an attorney or other representative.

Appeals shall be processed in accordance with regulations prescribed by the Board.

(b) The Board may hear any case appealed to it or may refer the case to an administrative law judge appointed under section 3105 of this title or other employee of the Board designated by the Board to hear such cases, except that in any case involving a removal from the service, the case shall be heard by the Board, an employee experienced in hearing appeals, or an administrative law judge. The Board, administrative law judge, or other employee (as the case may be) shall make a decision after receipt of the written representations of the parties to the appeal and after opportunity for a hearing under subsection (a) (1) of this section. A copy of the decision shall be furnished to each party to the appeal and to the Office of Personnel Management.

(c) (1) Subject to paragraph (2) of this subsection, the decision of the agency shall be sustained under subsection (b) only if the agency's decision—

(A) in the case of an action based on unacceptable performance described in section 4303 of this title, is supported by substantial evidence, or

(B) in any other case, is supported by a preponderance of the evidence.

(2) Notwithstanding paragraph (1), the agency's decision may not be sustained under subsection (b) of this section if the employee or applicant for employment—

(A) shows harmful error in the application of the agency's procedures in arriving at such decision;

(B) shows that the decision was based on any prohibited personnel practice described in section 2302(b) of this title; or

(C) shows that the decision was not in accordance with law.

(d) (1) In any case in which—

(A) the interpretation or application of any civil service law, rule, or regulation, under the jurisdiction of the Office of Personnel Management is at issue in any proceeding under this section; and

(B) the Director of the Office of Personnel Management is of the opinion that an erroneous decision would have a substantial impact on any civil service law, rule, or regulation under the jurisdiction of the Office:

the Director may as a matter of right intervene or otherwise participate in that proceeding before the Board. If the Director exercises his right to participate in a proceeding before the Board, he shall do so as early in the proceeding as practicable. Nothing in this title shall be construed to permit the Office to interfere with the independent decisionmaking of the Merit Systems Protection Board.

(2) The Board shall promptly notify the Director whenever the interpretation of any civil service law, rule, or regulation under the jurisdiction of the Office is at issue in any proceeding under this section.

(e) (1) Except as provided in section 7702 of this title, any decision under subsection (b) of this section shall be final unless—

(A) a party to the appeal or the Director petitions the Board for review within 30 days after the receipt of the decision; or

(B) the Board reopens and reconsiders a case on its own motion.

The Board, for good cause shown, may extend the 30-day period referred to in subparagraph (A) of this paragraph. One member of the Board may grant a petition or otherwise direct that a decision be reviewed by the full Board. The preceding sentence shall not apply if, by law, a decision of an administrative law judge is required to be acted upon by the Board.

(2) The Director may petition the Board for a review under paragraph (1) of this subsection only if the Director is of the opinion that the decision is erroneous and will have a substantial impact on any civil service law, rule, or regulation under the juridiction of the Office.

(f) The Board, or an administrative law judge or other employee of the Board designated to hear a case, may—

(1) consolidate appeals filed by two or more appellants, or

(2) join two or more appeals filed by the same appellants and hear and decide them concurrently,

if the deciding official or officials hearing the cases are of the opinion that the action could result in the appeals being processed more expeditiously and would not adversely affect any party.

(g) (1) Except as provided in paragraph (2) of this subsection, the Board, or an administrative law judge or other employee of the Board designated to hear a case, may require payment by the agency involved of reasonable attorney fees incurred by an employee or applicant for employment if the employee or applicant is the prevailing party and the Board, administrative law judge, or other employee (as the case may be) determines that payment by the agency is warranted in the interest of justice, including any case in which a prohibited personnel practice was engaged in by the agency or any case in which the agency's action was clearly without merit.

(2) If an employee or applicant for employment is the prevailing party and the decision is based on a finding of discrimination prohibited under section 2302(b)(1) of this title, the payment of attorney fees shall be in accordance with the standards prescribed under section 706(k) of the Civil Rights Act of 1964 (42 U.S.C. 2000e–5(k)).

(h) The Board may, by regulation, provide for one or more alternative methods for settling matters subject to the appellate jurisdiction of the Board which shall be applicable at the election of an applicant for employment or of an employee who is not in a unit for which a labor organization is accorded exclusive recognition, and shall be in lieu of other procedures provided for under this section. A decision under such a method shall be final, unless the Board reopens and reconsiders a case at the request of the Office of Personnel Management under subsection (e) of this section.

(i)(1) Upon the submission of any appeal to the Board under this section, the Board, through reference to such categories of cases, or other means, as it determines appropriate, shall establish and announce publicly the date by which it intends to complete action on the matter. Such date shall assure expeditious consideration of the appeal, consistent with the interests of fairness and other priorities of the Board. If the Board fails to complete action on the appeal by the announced date, and the expected delay will exceed 30 days, the Board shall publicly announce the new date by which it intends to complete action on the appeal.

(2) Not later than March 1 of each year, the Board shall submit to the Congress a report describing the number of appeals submitted to it during the preceding fiscal year, the number of appeals on which it completed action during that year, and the number of instances during that year in which it failed to conclude a proceeding by the date originally announced, together with an explanation of the reasons therefor.

(3) The Board shall by rule indicate any other category of significant Board action which the Board determines should be subject to the provisions of this subsection.

(4) It shall be the duty of the Board, an administrative law judge, or employee designated by the Board to hear any proceeding under this section to expedite to the extent practicable that proceeding.

(j) The Board may prescribe regulations to carry out the purpose of this section. (Pub. L. 95–454, Oct. 13, 1978, 92 Stat. 1138; amended Pub. L. 96–54, Aug. 14, 1979, 93 Stat. 384; as amended Pub. L. 99–386, Aug. 22, 1986, 100 Stat. 824.)

§ 7702. Actions involving discrimination

(a)(1) Notwithstanding any other provision of law, and except as provided in paragraph (2) of this subsection, in the case of any employee or applicant for employment who—

(A) has been affected by an action which the employee or applicant may appeal to the Merit Systems Protection Board, and

(B) alleges that a basis for the action was discrimination prohibited by—

(i) section 717 of the Civil Rights Act of 1964 (42 U.S.C. 2000e–16),

(ii) section 6(d) of the Fair Labor Standards Act of 1938 (29 U.S.C. 206(d)),

(iii) section 501 of the Rehabilitation Act of 1973 (29 U.S.C. 791),

(iv) sections 12 and 15 of the Age Discrimination in Employment Act of 1967 (29 U.S.C. 631, 633a), or

(v) any rule, regulation, or policy directive prescribed under any provision of law described in clauses (i) through (iv) of this subparagraph,
the Board shall, within 120 days of the filing of the appeal, decide both the issue of discrimination and the appealable action in accordance with the Board's appellate procedures under section 7701 of this title and this section.

(2) In any matter before an agency which involves—
(A) any action described in paragraph (1)(A) of this subsection; and
(B) any issue of discrimination prohibited under any provision of law described in paragraph (1)(B) of this subsection;
the agency shall resolve such matter within 120 days. The decision of the agency in any such matter shall be a judicially reviewable action unless the employee appeals the matter to the Board under paragraph (1) of this subsection.

(3) Any decision of the Board under paragraph (1) of this subsection shall be a judicially reviewable action as of—
(A) the date of issuance of the decision if the employee or applicant does not file a petition with the Equal Employment Opportunity Commission under subsection (b)(1) of this section, or
(B) the date the Commission determines not to consider the decision under subsection (b)(2) of this section.

(b)(1) An employee or applicant may, within 30 days after notice of the decision of the Board under subsection (a)(1) of this section, petition the Commission to consider the decision.

(2) The Commission shall, within 30 days after the date of the petition, determine whether to consider the decision. A determination of the Commission not to consider the decision may not be used as evidence with respect to any issue of discrimination in any judicial proceeding concerning that issue.

(3) If the Commission makes a determination to consider the decision, the Commission shall, within 60 days after the date of the determination, consider the entire record of the proceedings of the Board and, on the basis of the evidentiary record before the Board, as supplemented under paragraph (4) of this subsection, either—
(A) concur in the decision of the Board; or
(B) issue in writing another decision which differs from the decision of the Board to the extent that the Commission finds that, as a matter of law—
(i) the decision of the Board constitutes an incorrect interpretation of any provision of any law, rule, regulation, or policy directive referred to in subsection (a)(1)(B) of this section, or
(ii) the decision involving such provision is not supported by the evidence in the record as a whole.

(4) In considering any decision of the Board under this subsection, the Commission may refer the case to the Board, or provide on its own,

for the taking (within such period as permits the Commission to make a decision within the 60-day period prescribed under this subsection) of additional evidence to the extent it considers necessary to supplement the record.

(5)(A) If the Commission concurs pursuant to paragraph (3)(A) of this subsection in the decision of the Board, the decision of the Board shall be a judicially reviewable action.

(B) If the Commission issues any decision under paragraph (3)(B) of this subsection, the Commission shall immediately refer the matter to the Board.

(c) Within 30 days after receipt by the Board of the decision of the Commission under subsection (b)(5)(B) of this section, the Board shall consider the decision and—

(1) concur and adopt in whole the decision of the Commission; or

(2) to the extent that the Board finds that, as a matter of law, (A) the Commission decision constitutes an incorrect interpretation of any provision of any civil service law, rule, regulation or policy directive, or (B) the Commission decision involving such provision is not supported by the evidence in the record as a whole—

(i) reaffirm the initial decision of the Board; or

(ii) reaffirm the initial decision of the Board with such revisions as it determines appropriate.

If the Board takes the action provided under paragraph (1), the decision of the Board shall be a judicially reviewable action.

(d)(1) If the Board takes any action under subsection (c)(2) of this section, the matter shall be immediately certified to a special panel described in paragraph (6) of this subsection. Upon certification, the Board shall, within 5 days (excluding Saturdays, Sundays, and holidays), transmit to the special panel the administrative record in the proceeding, including—

(A) the factual record compiled under this section,

(B) the decisions issued by the Board and the Commission under this section, and

(C) any transcript of oral arguments made, or legal briefs filed, before the Board or the Commission.

(2)(A) The special panel shall, within 45 days after a matter has been certified to it, review the administrative record transmitted to it and, on the basis of the record, decide the issues in dispute and issue a final decision which shall be a judicially reviewable action.

(B) The special panel shall give due deference to the respective expertise of the Board and Commission in making its decision.

(3) The special panel shall refer its decision under paragraph (2) of this subsection to the Board and the Board shall order any agency to take any action appropriate to carry out the decision.

(4) The special panel shall permit the employee or applicant who brought the complaint and the employing agency to appear before the

panel to present oral arguments and to present written arguments with respect to the matter.

(5) Upon application by the employee or applicant, the Commission may issue such interim relief as it determines appropriate to mitigate any exceptional hardship the employee or applicant might otherwise incur as a result of the certification of any matter under this subsection, except that the Commission may not stay, or order any agency to review on an interim basis, the action referred to in subsection (a) (1) of this section.

(6)(A) Each time the Board takes any action under subsection (c) (2) of this section, a special panel shall be convened which shall consist of—

    (i) an individual appointed by the President, by and with the advice and consent of the Senate, to serve for a term of 6 years as chairman of the special panel each time it is convened;

    (ii) one member of the Board designated by the Chairman of the Board each time a panel is convened; and

    (iii) one member of the Commission designated by the Chairman of the Commission each time a panel is convened.

The chairman of the special panel may be removed by the President only for inefficiency, neglect of duty, or malfeasance in office.

(B) The chairman is entitled to pay at a rate equal to the maximum annual rate of basic pay payable under the General Schedule for each day he is engaged in the performance of official business on the work of the special panel.

(C) The Board and the Commission shall provide such administrative assistance to the special panel as may be necessary and, to the extent practicable, shall equally divide the costs of providing the administrative assistance.

(e)(1) Notwithstanding any other provision of law, if at any time after—

    (A) the 120th day following the filing of any matter described in subsection (a)(2) of this section with an agency, there is no judicially reviewable action under this section or an appeal under paragraph (2) of this subsection;

    (B) the 120th day following the filing of an appeal with the Board under subsection (a)(1) of this section, there is no judicially reviewable action (unless such action is not as the result of the filing of a petition by the employee under subsection (b) (1) of this section); or

    (C) the 180th day following the filing of a petition with the Equal Employment Opportunity Commission under subsection (b) (1) of this section, there is no final agency action under subsection (b), (c), or (d) of this section;

an employee shall be entitled to file a civil action to the same extent and in the same manner as provided in section 717(c) of the Civil Rights Act of 1964 (42 U.S.C. 2000e–16(c)), section 15(c) of the Age Discrimination in Employment Act of 1967 (29 U.S.C. 633a(c)), or section 16(b) of the Fair Labor Standards Act of 1938 (29 U.S.C. 216(b)).

(2) If, at any time after the 120th day following the filing of any matter described in subsection (a)(2) of this section with an agency, there is no judicially reviewable action, the employee may appeal the matter to the Board under subsection (a)(1) of this section.

(3) Nothing in this section shall be construed to affect the right to trial de novo under any provision of law described in subsection (a)(1) of this section after a judicially reviewable action, including the decision of an agency under subsection (a)(2) of this section.

(f) In any case in which an employee is required to file any action, appeal, or petition under this section and the employee timely files the action, appeal, or petition with an agency other than the agency with which the action, appeal, or petition is to be filed, the employee shall be treated as having timely filed the action, appeal, or petition as of the date it is filed with the proper agency. (Pub. L. 95–454, Oct. 13, 1978, 92 Stat. 1140; amended Pub. L. 96–54, Aug. 14, 1979, 93 Stat. 384.)

§ 7703. Judicial review of decisions of the Merit Systems Protection Board

(a)(1) Any employee or applicant for employment adversely affected or aggrieved by a final order or decision of the Merit Systems Protection Board may obtain judicial review of the order or decision.

(2) The Board shall be the named respondent in any proceeding brought pursuant to this subsection, unless the employee or applicant for employment seeks review of a final order or decision issued by the Board under section 7701. In review of a final order or decision issued under section 7701, the agency responsible for taking the action appealed to the Board shall be the named respondent.

(b)(1) Except as provided in paragraph (2) of this subsection, a petition to review a final order or final decision of the Board shall be filed in the United States Court of Appeals for the Federal Circuit. Notwithstanding any other provision of law, any petition for review must be filed within 30 days after the date the petitioner received notice of the final order or decision of the Board.

(2) Cases of discrimination subject to the provisions of section 7702 of this title shall be filed under section 717(c) of the Civil Rights Act of 1964 (42 U.S.C. 2000e–16(c)), section 15(c) of the Age Discrimination in Employment Act of 1967 (29 U.S.C. 633a(c)), and section 16(b) of the Fair Labor Standards Act of 1938, as amended (29 U.S.C. 216(b)), as applicable. Notwithstanding any other provision of law, any such case filed under any such section must be filed within 30 days after the date the individual filing the case received notice of the judicially reviewable action under such section 7702.

(c) In any case filed in the United States Court of Appeals for the Federal Circuit, the court shall review the record and hold unlawful and set aside any agency action, findings, or conclusions found to be—

(1) arbitrary, capricious, an abuse of discretion, or otherwise not in accordance with law;

(2) obtained without procedures required by law, rule, or regulation having been followed; or

(3) unsupported by substantial evidence;

except that in the case of discrimination brought under any section referred to in subsection (b) (2) of this section, the employee or applicant shall have the right to have the facts subject to trial de novo by the reviewing court.

(d) The Director of the Office of Personnel Management may obtain review of any final order or decision of the Board by filing a petition for judicial review in the United States Court of Appeals for the Federal Circuit if the Director determines, in his discretion, that the Board erred in interpreting a civil service law, rule, or regulation affecting personnel management and that the Board's decision will have a substantial impact on a civil service law, rule, regulation, or policy directive. If the Director did not intervene in a matter before the Board, the Director may not petition for review of a Board decision under this section unless the Director first petitions the Board for a reconsideration of its decision, and such petition is denied. In addition to the named respondent, the Board and all other parties to the proceedings before the Board shall have the right to appear in the proceeding before the Court of Appeals. The granting of the petition for judicial review shall be at the discretion of the Court of Appeals.

(Pub. L. 95–454, Oct. 13, 1978, 92 Stat. 1143; as amended Pub. L. 97–164, Apr. 2, 1982, 96 Stat. 45.)

* * * * *

TITLE 29—LABOR

CHAPTER 8—FAIR LABOR STANDARDS

* * *

§204(f) Employees of Library of Congress; administration of provisions by Office of Personnel Management

The Secretary is authorized to enter into an agreement with the Librarian of Congress with respect to individuals employed in the Library of Congress to provide for the carrying out of the Secretary's functions under this chapter with respect to such individuals. Notwithstanding any other provision of this chapter, or any other law, the Civil Service Commission is authorized to administer the provisions of this Act with respect to any individual employed by the United States (other than an individual employed in the Library of Congress, United States Postal Service, Postal Rate Commission, or the Tennessee Valley Authority). Nothing in this subsection shall be construed to affect the right of an employee to bring an action for unpaid minimum wages, or unpaid overtime compensation, and liquidated damages under section 216(b) of this Title.

* * *

§206. Minimum wage

(d) Prohibition of sex discrimination

(1) No employer having employees subject to any provisions of this section shall discriminate, within any establishment in which such employees are employed, between employees on the basis of sex by paying wages to employees in such establishment at a rate less than the rate at which he pays wages to employees of the opposite sex in such establishment for equal work on jobs the performance of which requires equal skill, effort, and responsibility, and which are performed under similar working conditions, except where such payment is made pursuant to (i) a seniority system; (ii) a merit system; (iii) a system which measures earnings by quantity or quality of production; or (iv) a differential based on any other factor other than sex: *Provided*, That an employer who is paying a wage rate differential in violation of this subsection shall not, in order to comply with the provisions of this subsection, reduce the wage rate of any employee.

(2) No labor organization, or its agents, representing employees of an employer having employees subject to any provisions of this section shall cause or attempt to cause such an employer to discriminate against an employee in violation of paragraph (1) of this subsection.

(3) For purposes of administration and enforcement, any amounts owing to any employee which have been withheld in violation of this subsection shall be deemed to be unpaid minimum wages or unpaid overtime compensation under this chapter.

(4) As used in this subsection, the term "labor organization" means any organization of any kind, or any agency or employee representation committee or plan, in which employees participate and which exists for the purpose, in whole or in part, of dealing with employers concerning grievances, labor disputes, wages, rates of pay, hours of employment, or conditions of work.

* * *

§216. Penalties

(a) Fines and imprisonment

Any person who willfully violates any of the provisions of section 215 of this title shall upon conviction thereof be subject to a fine of not more than $10,000, or to imprisonment for not more than six months, or both. No person shall be imprisoned under this subsection except for an offense committed after the conviction of such person for a prior offense under this subsection.

(b) Damages; right of action; attorney's fees and costs; termination of right of action

Any employer who violates the provisions of section 206 or section 207 of this title shall be liable to the employee or employees affected in the amount of their unpaid minimum wages, or their unpaid overtime compensation, as the case may be, and in an additional equal amount as liquidated damages. Any employer who violates the provisions of section 215(a)(3) of this title shall be liable for such legal or equitable relief as may be appropriate to effectuate the purposes of section 215(a)(3) of this title, including without limitation employment, reinstatement, promotion, and the payment of wages lost and an additional equal amount as liquidated damages. An action to recover the liability prescribed in either of the preceding sentences may be maintained against any employer (including a public agency) in any Federal or State court of competent jurisdiction by any one or more employees for and in behalf of himself or themselves and other employees similarly situated. No employee shall be a party plaintiff to any such action unless he gives his consent in writing to become such a party and such consent is filed in the court in which such action is brought. The court in such action shall, in addition to any judgment awarded to the plaintiff or plaintiffs, allow a reasonable attorney's fee to be paid by the defendant, and costs of the action. The right provided by this subsection to bring an action by or on behalf of any employee, and the right of any employee to become a party plaintiff to any such action, shall terminate upon the filing of a complaint by the Secretary of Labor in an action under section 217 of this title in which (1) restraint is sought of any further delay in the payment of unpaid minimum wages, or the amount of unpaid overtime compensation, as the case may be, owing to such employee under section 206 or section 207 of this title by an employer liable therefor under the provisions of this subsection or (2) legal or equitable relief is sought as a result of alleged violations of section 215(a)(3) of this title.

(c) **Payment of wages and compensation; waiver of claims; actions by the Secretary; limitation of actions**

The Secretary is authorized to supervise the payment of the unpaid minimum wages or the unpaid overtime compensation owing to any employee or employees under section 206 or section 207 of this title, and the agreement of any employee to accept such payment shall upon payment in full constitute a waiver by such employee of any right he may have under subsection (b) of this section to such unpaid minimum wages or unpaid overtime compensation and an additional equal amount as liquidated damages. The Secretary may bring an action in any court of competent jurisdiction to recover the amount of unpaid minimum wages or overtime compensation and an equal amount as liquidated damages. The right provided by subsection (b) of this section to bring an action by or on behalf of any employee to recover the liability specified in the first sentence of such subsection and of any employee to become a party plaintiff to any such action shall terminate upon the filing of a complaint by the Secretary in an action under this subsection in which a recovery is sought of unpaid minimum wages or unpaid overtime compensation under sections 206 and 207 of this title or liquidated or other damages provided by this subsection owing to such employee by an employer liable under the provisions of subsection (b) of this section, unless such action is dismissed without prejudice on motion of the Secretary. Any sums thus recovered by the Secretary of Labor on behalf of an employee pursuant to this subsection shall be held in a special deposit account and shall be paid, on order of the Secretary of Labor, directly to the employee or employees affected. Any such sums not paid to an employee because of inability to do so within a period of three years shall be covered into the Treasury of the United States as miscellaneous receipts. In determining when an action is commenced by the Secretary of Labor under this subsection for the purposes of the statutes of limitations provided in section 255(a) of this title, it shall be considered to be commenced in the case of any individual claimant on the date when the complaint is filed if he is specifically named as a party plaintiff in the complaint, or if his name did not so appear, on the subsequent date on which his name is added as a party plaintiff in such action.

(d) Savings provisions

In any action or proceeding commenced prior to, on, or after August 8, 1956, no employer shall be subject to any liability or punishment under this chapter or the Portal-to-Portal Act of 1947 [29 U.S.C. 251 et seq.] on account of his failure to comply with any provision or provisions of this chapter or such Act (1) with respect to work heretofore or hereafter performed in a workplace to which the exemption in section 213(f) of this title is applicable, (2) with respect to work performed in Guam, the Canal Zone or Wake Island before the effective date of this amendment of subsection (d), or (3) with respect to work performed in a possession named in section 206(a)(3) of this title at any time prior to the establishment by the Secretary, as provided therein, of a minimum wage rate applicable to such work.

(e) Civil penalties for child labor violations

Any person who violates the provisions of section 212 of this title, relating to child labor, or any regulation issued under that section, shall be subject to a civil penalty of not to exceed $1,000 for each such violation. In determining the amount of such penalty, the appropriateness of such penalty to the size of the business of the person charged and the gravity of the violation shall be considered. The amount of such penalty, when finally determined, may be —

(1) deducted from any sums owing by the United States to the person charged;

(2) recovered in a civil action brought by the Secretary in any court of competent jurisdiction, in which litigation the Secretary shall be represented by the Solicitor of Labor; or

(3) ordered by the court, in an action brought for a violation of section 215(a)(4) of this title, to be paid to the Secretary.

Any administrative determination by the Secretary of the amount of such penalty shall be final, unless within fifteen days after receipt of notice thereof by certified mail the person charged with the violation takes exception to the determination that the violations for which the penalty is imposed occurred, in which event final determination of the penalty shall be made in an administrative proceeding after opportunity for hearing in accordance with section 554 of title 5, and regulations to be promulgated by the Secretary. Sums collected as penalties pursuant to this section shall be applied toward reimbursement of the costs of determining the violations and assessing and collecting such penalties, in accordance with the provisions of section 9a of this title.

* * * * *

CHAPTER 14—AGE DISCRIMINATION IN EMPLOYMENT

633a. Nondiscrimination on account of age in Federal Government employment.
(a) Federal agencies affected.
(b) Enforcement by Equal Employment Opportunity Commission and by Librarian of Congress in the Library of Congress; remedies; rules, regulations, orders, and instructions of Commission; compliance by Federal agencies; powers and duties of Commission; notification of final action on complaint of discrimination; exemptions; bona fide occupational qualification.
(c) Civil actions; jurisdiction; relief.
(d) Notice to Commission; time of notice; Commission notification of prospective defendants; Commission elimination of unlawful practices.
(e) Duty of Government agency or official.
(f) Applicability of statutory provisions to personnel action of Federal departments, etc.
(g) Study and report to President and Congress by Equal Employment Opportunity Commission; scope.
634. Authorization of appropriations.

§621. Congressional statement of findings and purpose

(a) The Congress hereby finds and declares that—

(1) in the face of rising productivity and affluence, older workers find themselves disadvantaged in their efforts to retain employment, and especially to regain employment when displaced from jobs;

(2) the setting of arbitrary age limits regardless of potential for job performance has become a common practice, and certain otherwise desirable practices may work to the disadvantage of older persons;

(3) the incidence of unemployment, especially long-term unemployment with resultant deterioration of skill, morale, and employer acceptability is, relative to the younger ages, high among older workers; their numbers are great and growing; and their employment problems grave;

(4) the existence in industries affecting commerce, of arbitrary discrimination in employment because of age, burdens commerce and the free flow of goods in commerce.

(b) It is therefore the purpose of this chapter to promote employment of older persons based on their ability rather than age; to prohibit arbitrary age discrimination in employment; to help employers and workers find ways of meeting problems arising from the impact of age on employment.

§622. Education and research program; recommendation to Congress

(a) The Secretary of Labor shall undertake studies and provide information to labor unions, management, and the general public concerning the needs and abilities of older workers, and their potentials for continued employment and contribution to the economy. In order to achieve the purposes of this chapter, the Secretary of Labor shall carry on a continuing program of education and information, under which he may, among other measures—

(1) undertake research, and promote research, with a view to reducing barriers to the employment of older persons, and the promotion of measures for utilizing their skills;

(2) publish and otherwise make available to employers, professional societies, the various media of communication, and other inter-

ested persons the findings of studies and other materials for the promotion of employment;

(3) foster through the public employment service system and through cooperative effort the development of facilities of public and private agencies for expanding the opportunities and potentials of older persons;

(4) sponsor and assist State and community informational and educational programs.

(b) Not later than six months after the effective date of this chapter, the Secretary shall recommend to the Congress any measures he may deem desirable to change the lower or upper age limits set forth in section 631 of this title

§623. Prohibition of age discrimination

(a) Employer practices

It shall be unlawful for an employer—

(1) to fail or refuse to hire or to discharge any individual or otherwise discriminate against any individual with respect to his compensation, terms, conditions, or privileges of employment, because of such individual's age;

(2) to limit, segregate, or classify his employees in any way which would deprive or tend to deprive any individual of employment opportunities or otherwise adversely affect his status as an employee, because of such individual's age; or

(3) to reduce the wage rate of any employee in order to comply with this chapter.

(b) Employment agency practices

It shall be unlawful for an employment agency to fail or refuse to refer for employment, or otherwise to discriminate against, any individual because of such individual's age, or to classify or refer for employment any individual on the basis of such individual's age.

(c) Labor organization practices

It shall be unlawful for a labor organization—

(1) to exclude or to expel from its membership, or otherwise to discriminate against, any individual because of his age;

(2) to limit, segregate, or classify its membership, or to classify or fail or refuse to refer for employment any individual, in any way which would deprive or tend to deprive any individual of employment opportunities, or would limit such employment opportunities or otherwise adversely affect his status as an employee or as an applicant for employment, because of such individual's age;

(3) to cause or attempt to cause an employer to discriminate against an individual in violation of this section.

(d) Opposition to unlawful practices; participation in investigations, proceedings, or litigation

It shall be unlawful for an employer to discriminate against any of his employees or applicants for employment, for an employment agency to discriminate against any individual, or for a labor organization to discriminate against any member thereof or applicant for membership, because such individual, member or applicant for membership has opposed any practice made unlawful by this section, or because such individual, member or applicant for membership has made a charge, testified, assisted, or participated in any manner in an investigation, proceeding, or litigation under this chapter.

(e) Printing or publication of notice or advertisement indicating preference, limitation, etc.

It shall be unlawful for an employer, labor organization, or employment agency to print or publish, or cause to be printed or published, any notice or advertisement relating to employment by such an employer or membership in or any classification or referral for employment by such a labor organization, or relating to any classification or referral for employment by such an employment agency, indicating any preference, limitation, specification, or discrimination, based on age.

(f) Lawful practices; age an occupational qualification; other reasonable factors; seniority system; employee benefit plans; discharge or discipline for good cause

It shall not be unlawful for an employer, employment agency, or labor organization —

(1) to take any action otherwise prohibited under subsections (a), (b), (c), or (e) of this section where age is a bona fide occupational qualification reasonably necessary to the normal operation of the particular business, or where the differentiation is based on reasonable factors other than age;

(2) to observe the terms of a bona fide seniority system or any bona fide employee benefit plan such as a retirement, pension, or insurance plan, which is not a subterfuge to evade the purposes of this chapter, except that no such employee benefit plan shall excuse the failure to hire any individual, and no such seniority system or employee benefit plan shall require or permit the involuntary retirement of any individual specified by section 631(a) of this title because of the age of such individual; or

(3) to discharge or otherwise discipline an individual for good cause.

(g) Entitlement to coverage under group health plan

(1) For purposes of this section, any employer must provide that any employee aged 65 or older, and any employee's spouse aged 65 or older, shall be entitled to coverage under any group health plan offered to such employees under the same conditions as any employee, and the spouse of such employee, under age 65.

(2) For purposes of paragraph (1), the term "group health plan" has the meaning given to such term in section 162(i)(2) of Title 26.

(h) Practices of foreign corporations controlled by American employers; foreign persons not controlled by American employers; factors determining control

(1) If an employer controls a corporation whose place of incorporation is in a foreign country, any practice by such corporation prohibited under this section shall be presumed to be such practice by such employer.

(2) The prohibitions of this section shall not apply where the employer is a foreign person not controlled by an American employer.

(3) For the purpose of this subsection, the determination of whether an employer controls a corporation shall be based upon the—

(A) interrelation of operations,

(B) common management,

(C) centralized control of labor relations, and

(D) common ownership or financial control, of employer and the corporation.

(i) Firefighters and law enforcement officers attaining hiring or retiring age under State or local law on March 3, 1983

It shall not be lawful for an employer which is a State, a political subdivision of a State, an agency or instrumentality of a State or a political subdivision of a State, or an interstate agency to fail, refuse to hire or to discharge any individual because of such individual's age if such action is taken—

(1) with respect to the employment of an individual as a firefighter or as a law enforcement officer and the individual has attained the age of hiring or retirement in effect under applicable State or local law on March 3, 1983, and

(2) pursuant to a bona fide hiring or retirement plan that is not a subterfuge to evade the purposes of this chapter.

(i)[1] Employee pension benefit plans; cessation or reduction of benefit accrual or of allocation to employee account; distribution of benefits after attainment of normal retirement age; compliance; highly compensated employees

(1) Except as otherwise provided in this subsection, it shall be unlawful for an employer, an employment agency, a labor organization, or any combination thereof to establish or maintain an employee pension benefit plan which requires or permits—

(A) in the case of defined benefit plan, the cessation of an employee's benefit accrual, or the reduction of the rate of an employee's benefit accrual, because of age, or

(B) in the case of a defined contribution plan, the cessation of allocations to an employee's account, or the reduction of the rate at which amounts are allocated to an employee's account, because of age.

(2) Nothing in this section shall be construed to prohibit an employer, employment agency, or labor organization from observing any provision

---

[1]So in original.

of an employee pension benefit plan to the extent that such provision imposes (without regard to age) a limitation on the amount of benefits that the plan provides or a limitation on the number of years of service or years of participation which are taken into account for purposes of determining benefit accrual under the plan.

(3) In the case of any employee who, as of the end of any plan year under a defined benefit plan, has attained normal retirement age under such plan—

(A) if distribution of benefits under such plan with respect to such employee has commenced as of the end of such plan year, then any requirement of this subsection for continued accrual of benefits under such plan with respect to such employee during such plan year shall be treated as satisfied to the extent of the actuarial equivalent of in-service distribution of benefits, and

(B) if distribution of benefits under such plan with respect to such employee has not commenced as of the end of such year in accordance with section 1056(a)(3) of this Title [the Employee Retirement Income Social Security Act of 1974] and section 401(a)(14)(C) of Title 26, and the payment of benefits under such plan with respect to such employee is not suspended during such plan year pursuant to section 1053(a)(3)(B) of this Title or section 411(a)(3)(B) of Title 26, then any requirement of this subsection for continued accrual of benefits under such plan with respect to such employee during such plan year shall be treated as satisfied to the extent of any adjustment in the benefit payable under the plan during such plan year attributable to the delay in the distribution of benefits after the attainment of normal retirement age.

The provisions of this paragraph shall apply in accordance with regulations of the Secretary of the Treasury. Such regulations shall provide for the application of the preceding provisions of this paragraph to all employee pension benefit plans subject to this subsection and may provide for the application of such provisions, in the case of any such employee, with respect to any period of time within a plan year.

(4) Compliance with the requirements of this subsection with respect to an employee pension benefit plan shall constitute compliance with the requirements of this section relating to benefit accrual under such plan.

(5) Paragraph (1) shall not apply with respect to any employee who is a highly compensated employee (within the meaning of section 414(q) of Title 26), to the extent provided in regulations prescribed by the Secretary of the Treasury for purposes of precluding discrimination in favor of highly compensated employees within the meaning of subchapter D of chapter 1 of Title 26.

(6) A plan shall not be treated as failing to meet the requirements of paragraph (1) solely because the subsidized portion of any early retirement benefit is disregarded in determining benefit accruals.

(7) Any regulations prescribed by the Secretary of the Treasury pursuant to clause (v) of section 411(b)(1)(H) of Title 26 and subparagraphs (C) and (D) of section 411(b)(2) of Title 26 shall apply with respect to the requirements of this subsection in the same manner and to the same extent as such regulations apply with respect to the requirements of such sections 411(b)(1)(H) and 411(b)(2) of Title 26.

(8) A plan shall not be treated as failing to meet the requirements of this section solely because such plan provides a normal retirement age described in section 1002(24)(B) of this Title and section 411(a)(8)(B) of Title 26.

(9) For purposes of this subsection—

(A) The terms "employee pension benefit plan", "defined benefit plan", "defined contribution plan", and "normal retirement age" have the meanings provided such terms in section 1002 of this Title.

(B) The term "compensation" has the meaning provided by section 414(s) of Title 26.

(As amended Pub. L. 99–272, Title IX, § 9201(b)(1), (3), Apr. 7, 1986, 100 Stat. 171; Pub. L. 99–509, Title IX, § 9201, Oct. 21, 1986, 100 Stat. 1973; Pub. L. 99–592, §§ 2(a), (b), 3(a), Oct. 31, 1986, 100 Stat. 3342.)

§624. Study by Secretary of Labor; reports to President and Congress; scope of study; implementation of study; transmittal date of reports

(a)(1) The Secretary of Labor is directed to undertake an appropriate study of institutional and other arrangements giving rise to involuntary retirement, and report his findings and any appropriate legislative recommendations to the President and to the Congress. Such study shall include—

(A) an examination of the effect of the amendment made by section 3(a) of the Age Discrimination in Employment Act Amendments of 1978 in raising the upper age limitation established by section 631(a) of this title to 70 years of age;

(B) a determination of the feasibility of eliminating such limitation;

(C) a determination of the feasibility of raising such limitation above 70 years of age; and

(D) an examination of the effect of the exemption contained in section 631(c) of this title, relating to certain executive employees, and the exemption contained in section 631(d) of this title, relating to tenured teaching personnel.

(2) The Secretary may undertake the study required by paragraph (1) of this subsection directly or by contract or other arrangement.

(b) The report required by subsection (a) of this section shall be transmitted to the President and to the Congress as an interim report not later than January 1, 1981, and in final form not later than January 1, 1982.

§625. Administration

The Secretary shall have the power—

(a) Delegation of functions; appointment of personnel; technical assistance

to make delegations, to appoint such agents and employees, and to pay for technical assistance on a fee for service basis, as he deems necessary to assist him in the performance of his functions under this chapter;

(b) Cooperation with other agencies, employers, labor organizations, and employment agencies

to cooperate with regional, State, local, and other agencies, and to cooperate with and furnish technical assistance to employers, labor organizations, and employment agencies to aid in effectuating the purposes of this chapter.

§626. Recordkeeping, investigation, and enforcement

(a) Attendance of witnesses; investigations, inspections, records, and homework regulations

The Equal Employment Opportunity Commission shall have the power to make investigations and require the keeping of records necessary or appropriate for the administration of this chapter in accordance with the powers and procedures provided in sections 209 and 211 of this title.

(b) Enforcement; prohibition of age discrimination under fair labor standards; unpaid minimum wages and unpaid overtime compensation; liquidated damages; judicial relief; conciliation, conference, and persuasion

The provisions of this chapter shall be enforced in accordance with the powers, remedies, and procedures provided in sections 211(b), 216 (except for subsection (a) thereof), and 217 of this title, and subsection (c) of this section. Any act prohibited under section 623 of this title shall be deemed to be a prohibited act under section 215 of this title. Amounts owing to a person as a result of a violation of this chapter shall be deemed to be unpaid minimum wages or unpaid overtime compensation for purposes of sections 216 and 217 of this title: *Provided*, That liquidated damages shall be payable only in cases of willful violations of this chapter. In any action brought to enforce this chapter the court shall have jurisdiction to grant such legal or equitable relief as may be appropriate to effectuate the purposes of this chapter, including without limitation judgments compelling employment, reinstatement or promotion, or enforcing the liability for amounts deemed to be unpaid minimum wages or unpaid overtime compensation under this section. Before instituting any action under this section, the Equal Employment Opportunity Commission shall attempt to eliminate the discriminatory practice or practices alleged, and to effect voluntary compliance with the requirements of this chapter through informal methods of conciliation, conference, and persuasion.

(c) Civil actions; persons aggrieved; jurisdiction; judicial relief; termination of individual action upon commencement of action by Commission; jury trial

(1) Any person aggrieved may bring a civil action in any court of competent jurisdiction for such legal or equitable relief as will effectuate the purposes of this chapter: *Provided*, That the right of any person to bring such action shall terminate upon the commencement of an action

by the Equal Employment Opportunity Commission to enforce the right of such employee under this chapter.

(2) In an action brought under paragraph (1), a person shall be entitled to a trial by jury of any issue of fact in any such action for recovery of amounts owing as a result of a violation of this chapter, regardless of whether equitable relief is sought by any party in such action.

(d) Filing of charge with Commission; timeliness; conciliation, conference, and persuasion

No civil action may be commenced by an individual under this section until 60 days after a charge alleging unlawful discrimination has been filed with the Equal Employment Opportunity Commission. Such a charge shall be filed —

(1) within 180 days after the alleged unlawful practice occurred; or

(2) in a case to which section 633(b) of this title applies, within 300 days after the alleged unlawful practice occurred, or within 30 days after receipt by the individual of notice of termination of proceedings under State law, whichever is earlier.

Upon receiving such a charge, the Commission shall promptly notify all persons named in such charge as prospective defendants in the action and shall promptly seek to eliminate any alleged unlawful practice by informal methods of conciliation, conference, and persuasion.

(e) Statute of limitations; reliance in future on administrative ruling, etc.; tolling

(1) Sections 255 and 259 of this title shall apply to actions under this chapter.

(2) For the period during which the Equal Employment Opportunity Commission is attempting to effect voluntary compliance with requirements of this chapter through informal methods of conciliation, conference, and persuasion pursuant to subsection (b) of this section, the statute of limitations as provided in section 255 of this title shall be tolled, but in no event for a period in excess of one year.

§627. Notices to be posted

Every employer, employment agency, and labor organization shall post and keep posted in conspicuous places upon its premises a notice to be prepared or approved by the Equal Employment Opportunity Commission setting forth information as the Commission deems appropriate to effectuate the purposes of this chapter.

§628. Rules and regulations; exemptions

In accordance with the provisions of subchapter II of chapter 5 of title 5, the Equal Employment Opportunity Commission may issue such rules and regulations as it may consider necessary or appropriate for carrying out this chapter, and may establish such reasonable exemptions to and from any or all provisions of this chapter as it may find necessary and proper in the public interest.

§629. Criminal penalties

Whoever shall forcibly resist, oppose, impede, intimidate or interfere with a duly authorized representative of the Equal Employment Opportunity Commission while it is engaged in the performance of duties under this chapter shall be punished by a fine of not more than $500 or by imprisonment for not more than one year, or by both: *Provided, however*, That no person shall be imprisoned under this section except when there has been a prior conviction hereunder.

§630. Definitions

For the purposes of this chapter —

(a) The term "person" means one or more individuals, partnerships, associations, labor organizations, corporations, business trust, legal representatives, or any organized groups of persons.

(b) The term "employer" means a person engaged in an industry affecting commerce who has twenty or more employees for each working day in each of twenty or more calendar weeks in the current or preceding calendar year: *Provided*, That prior to June 30, 1968, employers having fewer than fifty employees shall not be considered employers. The term also means (1) any agent of such a person, and (2) a State or political subdivision of a State and any agency or instrumentality of a State or a political subdivision of a State, and any interstate agency, but such term does not include the United States, or a corporation wholly owned by the Government of the United States.

(c) The term "employment agency" means any person regularly undertaking with or without compensation to procure employees for an employer and includes an agent of such a person; but shall not include an agency of the United States.

(d) The term "labor organization" means a labor organization engaged in an industry affecting commerce, and any agent of such an organization, and includes any organization of any kind, any agency, or employee representation committee, group, association, or plan so engaged in which employees participate and which exists for the purpose, in whole or in part, of dealing with employers concerning grievances , labor disputes, wages, rates of pay, hours, or other terms or conditions of employment, and any conference, general committee, joint or system board, or joint council so engaged which is subordinate to a national or international labor organization.

(e) A labor organization shall be deemed to be engaged in an industry affecting commerce if (1) it maintains or operates a hiring hall or hiring office which procures employees for an employer or procures for employees opportunities to work for an employer, or (2) the number of its members (or, where it is a labor organization composed of other labor organizations or their representatives, if the aggregate number of the members of such other labor organization) is fifty or more prior to July 1, 1968, or twenty-five or more on or after July 1, 1968, and such labor organization —

(1) is the certified representative of employees under the provisions of the National Labor Relations Act, as amended [29 U.S.C. 151

et seq.], or the Railway Labor Act, as amended [45 U.S.C. 151 et seq.]; or

(2) although not certified, is a national or international labor organization or a local labor organization recognized or acting as the representative of employees of an employer or employers engaged in an industry affecting commerce; or

(3) has chartered a local labor organization or subsidiary body which is representing or actively seeking to represent employees of employers within the meaning of paragraph (1) or (2); or

(4) has been chartered by a labor organization representing or actively seeking to represent employees within the meaning of paragraph (1) or (2) as the local or subordinate body through which such employees may enjoy membership or become affiliated with such labor organization; or

(5) is a conference, general committee, joint or system board, or joint council subordinate to a national or international labor organization, which includes a labor organization engaged in an industry affecting commerce within the meaning of any of the preceding paragraphs of this subsection.

(f) The term "employee" means an individual employed by any employer except that the term "employee" shall not include any person elected to public office in any State or political subdivision of any State by the qualified voters thereof, or any person chosen by such officer to be on such officer's personal staff, or an appointee on the policymaking level or an immediate adviser with respect to the exercise of the constitutional or legal powers of the office. The exemption set forth in the preceding sentence shall not include employees subject to the civil service laws of a State government, governmental agency, or political subdivision.

(g) The term "commerce" means trade, traffic, commerce, transportation, transmission, or communication among the several States; or between a State and any place outside thereof; or within the District of Columbia, or a possession of the United States; or between points in the same State but through a point outside thereof.

(h) The term "industry affecting commerce" means any activity, business, or industry in commerce or in which a labor dispute would hinder or obstruct commerce or the free flow of commerce and includes any activity or industry "affecting commerce" within the meaning of the Labor-Management Reporting and Disclosure Act of 1959 [29 U.S.C. 401 et seq.].

(i) The term "State" includes a State of the United States, the District of Columbia, Puerto Rico, the Virgin Islands, American Samoa, Guam, Wake Island, the Canal Zone, and Outer Continental Shelf lands defined in the Outer Continental Shelf Lands Act [43 U.S.C. 1331 et seq.].

(j) The term "firefighter" means an employee, the duties of whose position are primarily to perform work directly connected with the control and extinguishment of fires or the maintenance and use of firefighting apparatus and equipment, including an employee engaged in this activity who is transferred to a supervisory or administrative position.

(k) The term "law enforcement officer" means an employee, the duties of whose position are primarily the investigation, apprehension, or detention of individuals suspected or convicted of offenses against the criminal laws of a State, including an employee engaged in this activity who is transferred to a supervisory or administrative position. For the purpose of this subsection, "detention" includes the duties of employees assigned to guard individuals incarcerated in any penal institution.
(As amended Pub. L. 99–592, § 4, Oct. 31, 1986, 100 Stat. 3343.)

§631. Age limits

(a) Individuals at least 40

The prohibitions in this chapter (except the provisions of section 623(g) of this title) shall be limited to individuals who are at least 40 years of age.

(b) Employees or applicants for employment in Federal Government

In the case of any personnel action affecting employees or applicants for employment which is subject to the provisions of section 633a of this title, the prohibitions established in section 633a of this title shall be limited to individuals who are at least 40 years of age.

(c) Bona fide executives or high policymakers

(1) Nothing in this chapter shall be construed to prohibit compulsory retirement of any employee who has attained 65 years of age and who, for the 2-year period immediately before retirement, is employed in a bona fide executive or a high policymaking position, if such employee is entitled to an immediate nonforfeitable annual retirement benefit from a pension, profit-sharing, savings, or deferred compensation plan, or any combination of such plans, of the employer of such employee, which equals, in the aggregate, at least $44,000.

(2) In applying the retirement benefit test of paragraph (1) of this subsection, if any such retirement benefit is in a form other than a straight life annuity (with no ancillary benefits), or if employees contribute to any such plan or make rollover contributions, such benefit shall be adjusted in accordance with regulations prescribed by the Equal Employment Opportunity Commission, after consultation with the Secretary of the Treasury, so that the benefit is the equivalent of a straight life annuity (with no ancillary benefits) under a plan to which employees do not contribute and under which no rollover contributions are made.

(d) Tenured employee at institution of higher education

Nothing in this chapter shall be construed to prohibit compulsory retirement of any employee who has attained 70 years of age, and who is serving under a contract of unlimited tenure (or similar arrangement providing for unlimited tenure) at an institution of higher education (as defined by section 1141(a) of Title 20).
(As amended Pub. L. 99–272, Title IX, § 9201(b)(2), Apr. 7, 1986, 100 Stat. 171; Pub. L. 99–592, § 2(c), § 6(a), Oct. 31, 1986, 100 Stat. 3342, 3344.)

§632. Annual report to Congress

The Equal Employment Opportunity Commission shall submit annually in January a report to the Congress covering its activities for the preceding year and including such information, data and recommendations for further legislation in connection with the matters covered by this chapter as it may find advisable. Such report shall contain an evaluation and appraisal by the Commission of the effect of the minimum and maximum ages established by this chapter, together with its recommendations to the Congress. In making such evaluation and appraisal, the Commission shall take into consideration any changes which may have occurred in the general age level of the population, the effect of the chapter upon workers not covered by its provisions, and such other factors as it may deem pertinent.

§633. Federal-State relationship

(a) Federal action superseding State action

Nothing in this chapter shall affect the jurisdiction of any agency of any State performing like functions with regard to discriminatory employment practices on account of age except that upon commencement of action under this chapter such action shall supersede any State action.

(b) Limitation of Federal action upon commencement of State proceedings

In the case of an alleged unlawful practice occurring in a State which has a law prohibiting discrimination in employment because of age and establishing or authorizing a State authority to grant or seek relief from such discriminatory practice, no suit may be brought under section 626 of this title before the expiration of sixty days after proceedings have been commenced under the State law, unless such proceedings have been earlier terminated: *Provided*, That such sixty-day period shall be extended to one hundred and twenty days during the first year after the effective date of such State law. If any requirement for the commencement of such proceedings is imposed by a State authority other than a requirement of the filing of a written and signed statement of the facts upon which the proceeding is based, the proceeding shall be deemed to have been commenced for the purposes of this subsection at the time such statement is sent by registered mail to the appropriate State authority.

§633a. Nondiscrimination on account of age in Federal Government employment

(a) Federal agencies affected

All personnel actions affecting employees or applicants for employment who are at least 40 years of age (except personnel actions with regard to aliens employed outside the limits of the United States) in military departments as defined in section 102 of title 5, in executive agencies as defined in section 105 of title 5 (including employees and applicants for employment who are paid from nonappropriated funds), in the

United States Postal Service and the Postal Rate Commission, in those units in the government of the District of Columbia having positions in the competitive service, and in those units of the legislative and judicial branches of the Federal Government having positions in the competitive service, and in the Library of Congress shall be made free from any discrimination based on age.

(b) Enforcement by Equal Employment Opportunity Commission and by Librarian of Congress in the Library of Congress; remedies; rules, regulations, orders, and instructions of Commission: compliance by Federal agencies; powers and duties of Commission; notification of final action on complaint of discrimination; exemptions: bona fide occupational qualification

Except as otherwise provided in this subsection, the Equal Employment Opportunity Commission is authorized to enforce the provisions of subsection (a) of this section through appropriate remedies, including reinstatement or hiring of employees with or without backpay, as will effectuate the policies of this section. The Equal Employment Opportunity Commission shall issue such rules, regulations, orders, and instructions as it deems necessary and appropriate to carry out its responsibilities under this section. The Equal Employment Opportunity Commission shall—

(1) be responsible for the review and evaluation of the operation of all agency programs designed to carry out the policy of this section, periodically obtaining and publishing (on at least a semiannual basis) progress reports from each department, agency, or unit referred to in subsection (a) of this section;

(2) consult with and solicit the recommendations of interested individuals, groups, and organizations relating to nondiscrimination in employment on account of age; and

(3) provide for the acceptance and processing of complaints of discrimination in Federal employment on account of age.

The head of each such department, agency, or unit shall comply with such rules, regulations, orders, and instructions of the Equal Employment Opportunity Commission which shall include a provision that an employee or applicant for employment shall be notified of any final action taken on any complaint of discrimination filed by him thereunder. Reasonable exemptions to the provisions of this section may be established by the Commission but only when the Commission has established a maximum age requirement on the basis of a determination that age is a bona fide occupational qualification necessary to the performance of the duties of the position. With respect to employment in the Library of Congress, authorities granted in this subsection to the Equal Employment Opportunity Commission shall be exercised by the Librarian of Congress.

(c) Civil actions; jurisdiction; relief

Any person aggrieved may bring a civil action in any Federal district court of competent jurisdiction for such legal or equitable relief as will effectuate the purposes of this chapter.

(d) Notice to Commission; time of notice; Commission notification of prospective defendants; Commission elimination of unlawful practices

When the individual has not filed a complaint concerning age discrimination with the Commission, no civil action may be commenced by any individual under this section until the individual has given the Commission not less than thirty days' notice of an intent to file such action. Such notice shall be filed within one hundred and eighty days after the alleged unlawful practice occurred. Upon receiving a notice of intent to sue, the Commission shall promptly notify all persons named therein as prospective defendants in the action and take any appropriate action to assure the elimination of any unlawful practice.

(e) Duty of Government agency or official

Nothing contained in this section shall relieve any Government agency or official of the responsibility to assure nondiscrimination on account of age in employment as required under any provision of Federal law.

(f) Applicability of statutory provisions to personnel action of Federal departments, etc.

Any personnel action of any department, agency, or other entity referred to in subsection (a) of this section shall not be subject to, or affected by, any provision of this chapter, other than the provisions of section 631(b) of this title and the provisions of this section.

(g) Study and report to President and Congress by Equal Employment Opportunity Commission; scope

(1) The Equal Employment Opportunity Commission shall undertake a study relating to the effects of the amendments made to this section by the Age Discrimination in Employment Act Amendments of 1978, and the effects of section 631(b) of this title.

(2) The Equal Employment Opportunity Commission shall transmit a report to the President and to the Congress containing the findings of the Commission resulting from the study of the Commission under paragraph (1) of this subsection. Such report shall be transmitted no later than January 1, 1980.

§634. Authorization of appropriations

There are hereby authorized to be appropriated such sums as may be necessary to carry out this chapter.

* * * * *

CHAPTER 16—VOCATIONAL REHABILITATION AND OTHER REHABILITATION SERVICES

§ 701. Congressional declaration of purpose

The purpose of this chapter is to develop and implement, through research, training, services, and the guarantee of equal opportunity, comprehensive and coordinated programs of vocational rehabilitation and independent living, for individuals with handicaps in order to maximize their employability, independence, and integration into the workplace and the community.

*   *   *

§ 706. Definitions

For purposes of this chapter:

*   *   *

(6) The term "employability," with respect to an individual, means a determination that, with the provision of vocational rehabilitation services, the individual is likely to enter or retain, as a primary objective, full-time employment, and when appropriate, part-time employment, consistent with the capacities or abilities of the individual in the competitive labor market or any other vocational outcome the Secretary may determine consistent with this Act.

*   *   *

(8)(A) Except as otherwise provided in subparagraph (B), the term "individual with handicaps" means any individual who (i) has a physical or mental disability which for such individual constitutes or results in a substantial handicap to employment and (ii) can reasonably be expected to benefit in terms of employability from vocational rehabilitation services provided pursuant to subchapters I and III of this chapter.

(B) Subject to the second sentence of this subparagraph, the term "individual with handicaps" means, for purposes of subchapters IV and V of this chapter, any person who (i) has a physical or mental impairment which substantially limits one or more of such person's major life activities, (ii) has a record of such an impairment, or (iii) is regarded as having such an impairment. For purposes of sections 793 and 794 of this Title as such sections relate to employment, such term does not include any individual who is an alcoholic or drug abuser whose current use of alcohol or drugs prevents such individual from performing the duties of the job in question or whose employment, by reason of such current alcohol or drug abuse, would constitute a direct threat to property or the safety of others.

(C) For the purpose of sections 793 and 794 of this Title, as such sections relate to employment, such term does not include an individual who has a currently contagious disease or infection and who, by reason of such disease or infection, would constitute a direct threat to the health or safety of other individuals or who, by reason of the currently contagious disease or infection, is unable to perform the duties of the job.

*   *   *

(15)(A) Except as provided in subparagraph (B), for purposes of this chapter the term "individual with severe handicaps" means an individual with handicaps (as defined in paragraph (8))—

(i) who has a severe physical or mental disability which seriously limits one or more functional capacities (such as mobility, communication, self-care, self-direction, interpersonal skills, work tolerance, or work skills) in terms of employability;

(ii) whose vocational rehabilitation can be expected to require multiple vocational rehabilitation services over an extended period of time; and

(iii) who has one or more physical or mental disabilities resulting from amputation, arthritis, autism, blindness, burn injury, cancer, cerebral palsy, cystic fibrosis, deafness, head injury, heart disease, hemiplegia, hemophilia, respiratory or pulmonary dysfunction, mental retardation, mental illness, multiple sclerosis, muscular dystrophy, musculo-skeletal disorders, neurological disorders (including stroke and epilepsy), paraplegia, quadriplegia, and other spinal cord conditions, sickle cell anemia, specific learning disability, end-stage renal disease, or another disability or combination of disabilities determined on the basis of an evaluation of rehabilitation potential to cause comparable substantial functional limitation.

(B) For purposes of subchapter VII of this chapter the term "individual with severe handicaps" means an individual whose ability to function independently in family or community or whose ability to engage or continue in employment is so limited by the severity of his or her physical or mental disability that independent living rehabilitation services are required in order to achieve a greater level of independence in functioning in family or community or engaging or continuing in employment.

*   *   *   *   *

SUBCHAPTER V—MISCELLANEOUS PROVISIONS

§ 791. Employment of individuals with handicaps

(a) Interagency Committee on Handicapped Employees; establishment; membership; co-chairmen; availability of other Committee resources; purpose and functions

There is established within the Federal Government an Interagency Committee on Handicapped Employees (hereinafter in this section referred to as the "Committee"), comprised of such members as the President may select, including the following (or their designees whose positions are Executive Level IV or higher): the Chairman of the Equal Employment Opportunity Commission (hereinafter in this section referred to as the "Commission"), the Administrator of Veterans' Affairs, and the Secretary of Labor, the Secretary of Education, and the Secretary of Health and Human Services. The Secretary of Education and the Chairman of the Commission shall serve as co-chairpersons of the Committee. The resources of the President's Committees on Employment of People With Disabilities and on Mental Retardation shall be made fully available to the Committee. It shall be the purpose and function of the

Committee (1) to provide a focus for Federal and other employment of individuals with handicaps, and to review, on a periodic basis, in cooperation with the Commission, the adequacy of hiring, placement, and advancement practices with respect to individuals with handicaps, by each department, agency, and instrumentality in the executive branch of Government, and to insure that the special needs of such individuals are being met; and (2) to consult with the Commission to assist the Commission to carry out its responsibilities under subsections (b), (c), and (d). of this section. On the basis of such review and consultation, the Committee shall periodically make to the Commission such recommendations for legislative and administrative changes as it deems necessary or desirable. The Commission shall timely transmit to the appropriate committees of Congress any such recommendations.

(b) Federal agencies; affirmative action program plans

Each department, agency, and instrumentality (including the United States Postal Service and the Postal Rate Commission) in the executive branch shall, within one hundred and eighty days after September 26, 1973, submit to the Commission and to the Committee an affirmative action program plan for the hiring, placement, and advancement of individuals with handicaps in such department, agency, or instrumentality. Such plan shall include a description of the extent to which and methods whereby the special needs of employees with handicaps are being met. Such plan shall be updated annually, and shall be reviewed annually and approved by the Commission if the Commission determines, after consultation with the Committee, that such plan provides sufficient assurances, procedures and commitments to provide adequate hiring, placement, and advancement opportunities for individuals with handicaps.

(c) State agencies; rehabilitated individuals, employment

The Commission, after consultation with the Committee, shall develop and recommend to the Secretary for referral to the appropriate State agencies, policies and procedures which will facilitate the hiring, placement, and advancement in employment of individuals who have received rehabilitation services under State vocational rehabilitation programs, veterans' programs, or any other program for individuals with handicaps, including the promotion of job opportunities for such individuals. The Secretary shall encourage such State agencies to adopt and implement such policies and procedures.

(d) Report to Congressional committees

The Commission, after consultation with the Committee, shall, on June 30, 1974, and at the end of each subsequent fiscal year, make a complete report to the appropriate committees of the Congress with respect to the practices of and achievements in hiring, placement, and advancement of individuals with handicaps by each department, agency, and instrumentality and the effectiveness of the affirmative action programs required by subsection (b) of this section, together with recommendations as to legislation which have been submitted to the Commission under subsection (a) of this section, or other appropriate action to insure the adequacy of such practices. Such report shall also include an evaluation by the Committee of the effectiveness of the activities of the Commission under subsections (b) and (c) of this section.

(e) Federal work experience without pay; non-Federal status

An individual who, as a part of an individualized written rehabilitation program under a State plan approved under this chapter, participates in a program of unpaid work experience in a Federal agency, shall not, by reason thereof, be considered to be a Federal employee or to be subject to the provisions of law relating to Federal employment, including those relating to hours of work, rates of compensation, leave, unemployment compensation, and Federal employee benefits.

(f) Federal agency cooperation; special consideration for positions on President's Committee on Employment of People With Disabilities

(1) The Secretary of Labor and the Secretary of Education are authorized and directed to cooperate with the President's Committee on Employment of People With Disabilities in carrying out its functions.

(2) In selecting personnel to fill all positions on the President's Committee on Employment of People With Disabilities, special consideration shall be given to qualified individuals with handicaps.
(As amended Pub. L. 99–506, Title I, § 103(d)(2)(C), Title X, §§ 1001(f)(1), 1002(e)(1), (2)(A), Oct. 21, 1986, 100 Stat. 1810, 1843, 1844; Pub. L. 100–630, Title II, § 206(a), Nov. 7, 1988, 102 Stat. 3311.)

*   *   *

§794a. Remedies and attorney fees

(a)(1) The remedies, procedures, and rights set forth in section 717 of the Civil Rights Act of 1964 (42 U.S.C. 2000e-16), including the application of sections 706(f) through 706(k) (42 U.S.C. 2000e-5(f) through (k)), shall be available, with respect to any complaint under section 791 of this title, to any employee or applicant for employment aggrieved by the final disposition of such complaint, or by the failure to take final action on such complaint. In fashioning an equitable or affirmative action remedy under such section, a court may take into account the reasonableness of the cost of any necessary work place accommodation, and the availability of alternatives therefor or other appropriate relief in order to achieve an equitable and appropriate remedy.

(2) The remedies, procedures, and rights set forth in title VI of the Civil Rights Act of 1964 [42 U.S.C. 2000d et seq.] shall be available to any person aggrieved by any act or failure to act by any recipient of Federal assistance or Federal provider of such assistance under section 794 of this title.

(b) In any action or proceeding to enforce or charge a violation of a provision of this subchapter, the court, in its discretion, may allow the prevailing party, other than the United States, a reasonable attorney's fee as part of the costs.

*   *   *   *   *

TITLE 42—THE PUBLIC HEALTH AND WELFARE

CHAPTER 21—CIVIL RIGHTS

SUBCHAPTER VI—EQUAL EMPLOYMENT OPPORTUNITIES
* * *

§2000e-16. Employment by Federal Government

(a) Discriminatory practices prohibited; employees or applicants for employment subject to coverage

All personnel actions affecting employees or applicants for employment (except with regard to aliens employed outside the limits of the United States) in military departments as defined in section 102 of Title 5, in executive agencies as defined in section 105 of Title 5 (including employees and applicants for employment who are paid from nonappropriated funds), in the United States Postal Service and the Postal Rate Commission, in those units of the Government of the District of Columbia having positions in the competitive service, and in those units of the legislative and judicial branches of the Federal Government having positions in the competitive service, and in the Library of Congress shall be made free from any discrimination based on race, color, religion, sex, or national origin.

(b) Enforcement powers of Commission; issuance of rules, regulations, etc.; annual review and approval of national and regional equal employment opportunity plans; review and evaluation of equal employment opportunity programs and publication of progress reports; consultations with interested parties; compliance with rules, regulations, etc.; contents of national and regional equal employment opportunity plans; authority of Librarian of Congress

Except as otherwise provided in this subsection, the Equal Employment Opportunity Commission shall have authority to enforce the provisions of subsection (a) of this section through appropriate remedies, including reinstatement or hiring of employees with or without back pay, as will effectuate the policies of this section, and shall issue such rules, regulations, orders and instructions as it deems necessary and appropriate to carry out its responsibilities under this section. The Equal Employment Opportunity Commission shall—

(1) be responsible for the annual review and approval of a national and regional equal employment opportunity plan which each department and agency and each appropriate unit referred to in subsection (a) of this section shall submit in order to maintain an affirmative program of equal employment opportunity for all such employees and applicants for employment;

(2) be responsible for the review and evaluation of the operation of all agency equal employment opportunity programs, periodically obtaining and publishing (on at least a semiannual basis) progress reports from each such department, agency, or unit; and

(3) consult with and solicit the recommendations of interested individuals, groups, and organizations relating to equal employment opportunity.

The head of each such department, agency, or unit shall comply with such rules, regulations, orders, and instructions which shall include a provision that an employee or applicant for employment shall be notified of any final action taken on any complaint of discrimination filed by him thereunder. The plan submitted by each department, agency, and unit shall include, but not be limited to—

(1) provision for the establishment of training and education programs designed to provide a maximum opportunity for employees to advance so as to perform at their highest potential; and

(2) a description of the qualifications in terms of training and experience relating to equal employment opportunity for the principal and operating officials of each such department, agency, or unit responsible for carrying out the equal employment opportunity program and of the allocation of personnel and resources proposed by such department, agency, or unit to carry out its equal employment opportunity program.

With respect to employment in the Library of Congress, authorities granted in this subsection to the Equal Employment Opportunity Commission shall be exercised by the Librarian of Congress.

(c) Civil action by employee or applicant for employment for redress of grievances; time for bringing of action; head of department, agency, or unit as defendant

Within thirty days of receipt of notice of final action taken by a department, agency, or unit referred to in subsection (a) of this section, or by the Equal Employment Opportunity Commission upon an appeal from a decision or order of such department, agency, or unit on a complaint of discrimination based on race, color, religion, sex or national origin, brought pursuant to subsection (a) of this section, Executive Order 11478 or any succeeding Executive orders, or after one hundred and eighty days from the filing of the initial charge with the department, agency, or unit or with the Equal Employment Opportunity Commission on appeal from a decision or order of such department, agency, or unit until such time as final action may be taken by a department, agency, or unit, an employee or applicant for employment, if aggrieved by the final disposition of his complaint, or by the failure to take final action on his complaint, may file a civil action as provided in section 2000e-5 of this title, in which civil action the head of the department, agency, or unit, as appropriate, shall be the defendant.

(d) Section 2000e-5(f) through (k) of this title applicable to civil sections

The provisions of section 2000e-5(f) through (k) of this title, as applicable, shall govern civil actions brought hereunder.

(e) Government agency or official not relieved of responsibility to assure nondiscrimination in employment or equal employment opportunity

Nothing contained in this Act shall relieve any Government agency or official of its or his primary responsibility to assure nondiscrimination in employment as required by the Constitution and statutes or of its or his responsibilities under Executive Order 11478 relating to equal employment opportunity in the Federal Government.

* * * * *

CHAPTER 6A

SUBCHAPTER III-A—ALCOHOL, DRUG ABUSE, AND MENTAL HEALTH PROGRAMS

PART D—MISCELLANEOUS PROVISIONS RELATING TO ALCOHOL ABUSE AND ALCOHOLISM AND DRUG ABUSE

§290dd-1. Programs for government and other employees

* * *

(b) Prior alcohol abuse no bar to federal employment; exceptions

(1) No person may be denied or deprived of Federal civilian employment or a Federal professional or other license or right solely on the ground of prior alcohol abuse or prior alcoholism.

(2) This subsection shall not apply to employment (A) in the Central Intelligence Agency, the Federal Bureau of Investigation, the National Security Agency, or any other department or agency of the Federal Government designated for purposes of national security by the President, or (B) in any position in any department or agency of the Federal Government, not referred to in clause (A), which position is determined pursuant to regulations prescribed by the head of such agency or department to be a sensitive position.

(c) Dismissal for incapacity unaffected

This section shall not be construed to prohibit the dismissal from employment of a Federal civilian employee who cannot properly function in his employment.

(July 1, 1944, c. 373, Title V, §542, formerly Pub. L. 91-616, Title II, §201, Dec. 31, 1970, 84 Stat. 1849; Pub. L. 96-180, §6(a), (b)(1), Jan. 2, 1980, 93 Stat. 1302; Pub. L. 97-35, Title IX, §§961, 966(d), (e), Aug. 13, 1981, 95 Stat. 592, 595; renumbered §521 and amended Pub. L. 98-24, §2(b)(13), Apr. 26, 1983, 97 Stat. 181, as amended Pub. L. 98-509, Title III, §301(c)(2), Oct. 19, 1984, 98 Stat. 2364; Pub. L. 99-570, Title VI,

§6002(b)(1), Oct. 27, 1986, 100 Stat. 3207-158, 3207-159; renumbered §542, Pub. L. 100-77, Title VI, §611(2), July 22, 1987, 101 Stat. 516.)

§290ee-1. Drug abuse among government and other employees

* * *

(b) Disqualification solely on ground of prior drug abuse prohibited; certain agencies, national security employment, and sensitive positions excepted from restriction

(1) No person may be denied or deprived of Federal civilian employment or a Federal professional or other license or right solely on the ground of prior drug abuse.

(2) This subsection shall not apply to employment (A) in the Central Intelligence Agency, the Federal Bureau of Investigation, the National Security Agency, or any other department or agency of the Federal Government designated for purposes of national security by the President, or (B) in any position in any department or agency of the Federal Government, not referred to in clause (A), which position is determined pursuant to regulations prescribed by the head of such department or agency to be a sensitive position.

(c) Dismissal for functional disability

This section shall not be construed to prohibit the dismissal from employment of a Federal civilian employee who cannot properly function in his employment.

(July 1, 1944, c. 373, Title V, §546, formerly Pub. L. 92-255, Title IV, §413, Mar. 21, 1972, 86 Stat. 84; Pub. L. 96-181, §8(a), (b)(1), Jan. 2, 1980, 93 Stat. 1313, 1314; Pub. L. 97-35, Title IX, §973(e), Aug. 13, 1981, 95 Stat. 598; renumbered §525 and amended Pub. L. 98-24, §2(b)(16)(A), Apr. 26, 1983, 97 Stat. 182; Pub. L. 99-570, Title VI, §6002(b)(2), Oct. 27, 1986, 100 Stat. 3207-159; renumbered §546, Pub. L. 100-77, Title VI, §611(2), July 22, 1987, 101 Stat. 516, amended Pub. L. 100-607, Title VIII, §813(4), Nov. 4, 1988, 102 Stat. 3171; Pub. L. 100-628, Title VI, §613(4), Nov. 7, 1988, 102 Stat. 3243.)

2. Addresses of National and Field Offices

Office of Personnel Management

Central Office: 1900 E Street, NW
Washington, DC 20415

Atlanta Region: Richard B. Russell Federal Building
75 Spring Street, SW
Atlanta, GA 30303

Area Offices:

Alabama: 3322 Memorial Parkway, Suite 341
Huntsville, AL 35801

Florida: Commodore Building, Suite 150
3444 McCrory Place
Orlando, FL 32803

Georgia: Richard B. Russell Federal Building
75 Spring Street, SW, Suite 956
Atlanta, GA 30303

Kentucky: (serviced by Memphis Area Office)

Mississippi: (serviced by Huntsville Area Office)

North Carolina: Temporary address: 4505 Falls-of-the Neuse Road
Raleigh, NC 27609

South Carolina: (serviced by Raleigh Area Office)

Tennessee: 200 Jefferson Avenue, Suite 1312
Memphis, TN 38103

Chicago Region: John C. Kluczynski Building
230 South Dearborn Street
Chicago, IL 60604

Area Offices:

Illinois: 175 W. Jackson Boulevard, 5th Floor
Chicago, IL 60604

Indiana: Minton-Capehart Federal Building
575 North Pennsylvania
Indianapolis, IN 46204

Michigan: 477 Michigan Avenue, Room 565
Detroit, MI 48226

Minnesota:	Federal Building, Room 501 Fort Snelling, MN 55111
Ohio:	U.S. Courthouse and Federal Building 200 West 2nd Street, Room 507 Dayton, OH 45402
Dallas Region:	1100 Commerce Street Dallas, TX 75242

Area Offices:

Louisiana:	1515 Poydras, Suite 600 New Orleans, LA 70112
New Mexico:	421 Gold Avenue, SW Albuquerque, NM 87102
Oklahoma/ Arkansas:	200 N.W. 5th Street Oklahoma City, OK 73102
Texas:	1100 Commerce Street Dallas, TX 75242

Philadelphia Region:	600 Arch Street Philadelphia, PA 19106

Area Offices:

Maryland:	Edward A. Garmatz Federal Building and Courthouse 101 W. Lombard Street Baltimore, MD 21201
Philadelphia:	William J. Green, Jr. Federal Building 600 Arch Street Philadelphia, PA 19106
Pittsburgh:	Federal Building 1000 Liberty Avenue Pittsburgh, PA 15222
Virginia:	Federal Building 200 Granby Mall Norfolk, VA 23510

San Francisco Region:	211 Main Street, 7th Floor San Francisco, CA 94105

Area Offices:

Arizona:	522 North Central Avenue Phoenix, AZ 85004

California: 845 South Figueroa Street
                Los Angeles, CA 90017
                1029 J Street, Room 202
                Sacramento, CA 95814
                800 Front Street
                San Diego, CA 92188
                211 Main Street, 7th Floor
                San Francisco, CA 94105
Hawaii: 300 Ala Moana Boulevard, P.O. Box 50028
                Honolulu, HI 96850

Equal Employment Opportunity Commission

National Office: 2401 E Street, NW
                       Washington, DC 20506

District Offices:

Atlanta: 75 Piedmont Avenue, NE, Suite 1100
                Atlanta, GA 30335
Baltimore: 109 Market Place, Suite 4000
                Baltimore, MD 21202
Birmingham: 2121 Eighth Avenue, North
                Birmingham, AL 35203
Charlotte: 5500 Central Avenue
                Charlotte, NC 28212
Chicago: 536 South Clark Street, Room 930 A
                Chicago, IL 60605
Cleveland: 1375 Euclid Avenue
                Room 600
                Cleveland, OH 44115
Dallas: 8303 Elmbrook Drive
                Dallas, TX 75247
Denver: 1845 Sherman Street, 2nd Floor
                Denver, CO 80203
Detroit: 477 Michigan Avenue, Room 1540
                Detroit, MI 48226
Houston: 1919 Smith Street, 7th Floor
                Houston, TX 77002
Indianapolis: 46 East Ohio Street, Room 456
                Indianapolis, IN 46204
Los Angeles: 3660 Wilshire Blvd., 5th Floor
                Los Angeles, CA 90010

Memphis:	1407 Union Avenue, Suite 621 Memphis, TN 38104
Miami:	1 Northeast First Street, 6th Floor Miami, FL 33131
Milwaukee:	310 West Wisconsin Avenue, Suite 800 Milwaukee, WI 53203
New Orleans:	701 Loyola Avenue, Suite 600 New Orleans, LA 70113
New York:	90 Church Street, Room 1501 New York, NY 10007
Philadelphia:	1421 Cherry Street, 10th Floor Philadelphia, PA 19102
Phoenix:	4520 N. Central Avenue, Suite 300 Phoenix, AZ 85012
San Antonio:	5410 Fredricksburg Road, Suite 200 San Antonio, TX 78229
San Francisco:	901 Market Street, Suite 500 San Francisco, CA 94103
Seattle:	1321 Second Avenue, 7th Floor Seattle, WA 98101
St. Louis:	625 North Euclid Street St. Louis, MO 63108

Area Offices which provide complaints examiners for federal sector cases:

San Diego:	880 Front Street, Room 4S21 San Diego, CA 92188
Washington:	1400 L Street, NW, Suite 200 Washington, DC 20005

Merit Systems Protection Board

Headquarters Office:	1120 Vermont Avenue, 8th Floor Washington, DC 20419

Regional Offices:

Atlanta:	1365 Peachtree Street, NE, Suite 500 Atlanta, GA 30309
Boston:	150 Causeway Street, Room 1122 Boston, MA 02114
Chicago:	230 South Dearborn Street, 31st Floor Chicago, IL 60604

Dallas:	1100 Commerce Street, Room 6F20 Dallas, TX 75242
Denver:	730 Simms Street, Room 301 Golden, CO 80401
New York:	26 Federal Plaza, Room 2339 New York, NY 10278
Philadelphia:	U.S. Customhouse, Room 501 2nd and Chestnut Streets Philadelphia, PA 19106
St. Louis:	1520 Market Street, FOB 1740 St. Louis, MO 63103
San Francisco:	525 Market Street, Room 2800 San Francisco, CA 94105
Seattle:	915 Second Avenue, FOB 1840 Seattle, WA 98174
Washington:	5203 Leesburg Pike, Suite 1109 Falls Church, VA 22041

Office of the Special Counsel

Headquarters Office: 1120 Vermont Avenue, NW, Room 818
Washington, DC 20419

Field Offices:

Atlanta:	1365 Peachtree Street, Room 317 Atlanta, GA 30309
Dallas:	1100 Commerce Street, Room 2B29 Dallas, TX 75242
Philadelphia:	325 Chestnut Street, Room 505 Philadelphia, PA 19106
San Francisco:	50 United Nations Plaza Room 505 San Francisco, CA 94102

Federal Labor Relations Authority

National Office: 500 C Street, SW
Washington, DC 20424

Regional Offices:

Region I:	10 Causeway Street, Room 1017 Boston, MA 02222

Region II:	26 Federal Plaza, Room 3700 New York, NY 10278
Subregion:	105 S. 7th Street Fifth Floor Philadelphia, PA 19106
Region III:	1111 18th Street, NW, Room 700 P.O. Box 33758 Washington, DC 10033-0758
Region IV:	1371 Peachtree Street, NE Suite 501, North Wing Atlanta, GA 30367
Region V:	175 W. Jackson Blvd., Suite 1359-A Chicago, IL 60604
Subregion:	1375 E. 9th Street 1 Cleveland Center, Suite 850 Cleveland, OH 44114
Region VI:	525 Griffin Street, Suite 926 Dallas, TX 75202
Region VII:	535 16th Street, Suite 310 Denver, CO 80202
Region VIII:	350 South Figueroa Street, Suite 370 Los Angeles, CA 90071
Region IX:	901 Market Street San Francisco, CA 94103

Federal Service Impasses Panel

500 C Street, SW
Washington, DC 20424

Table of Cases

Court Decisions

537

E

East Tex. Motor Freight Sys., Inc. v. Rodriguez, 431 U.S. 395, 14 FEP Cases 1505 (1977)   159

Edmondson v. Simon, 24 FEP Cases 1031 (N.D. Ill. 1978)   38

EEOC v. Radiator Specialty Co., 610 F.2d 178, 21 FEP Cases 272 (4th Cir. 1979)   161, 162

EEOC v. Universal Underwriters Ins. Co., 653 F.2d 1243, 26 FEP Cases 775 (8th Cir. 1981)   181

Egger v. Phillips, 710 F.2d 292 (7th Cir.), cert. denied, 464 U.S. 918 (1983)   202

Eisen v. Carlisle & Jacquelin, 417 U.S. 156, 9 FEP Cases 1302 (1974)   168

Elliott v. Perez, 751 F.2d 1472 (5th Cir. 1985)   208, 209

Elliott v. Weinberger, 564 F.2d 1219 (9th Cir. 1977), aff'd in part and rev'd on other grounds, 441 U.S. 682 (1977)   159, 160

Ellis v. Postal Serv., 784 F.2d 835 (7th Cir. 1986)   201

Ellis v. United States, 610 F.2d 760 (Ct.Cl. 1980)   116

Elmore v. Hampton, 373 F. Supp. 360 (E.D. Tenn. 1973)   106

Elrod v. Burns, 427 U.S. 347 (1976)   123

Englehart v. United States, 125 Ct.Cl. 603 (1983)   83

Espanola Way Corp. v. Meyerson, 690 F.2d 827 (11th Cir. 1982)   207

Espelding v. Thornhill, 13 EPD ¶ 11,463 (E.D. Mich. 1976)   174

Espenschied v. MSPB, 804 F.2d 1233 (Fed. Cir. 1984)   105

Ethnic Employees of the Library of Congress v. Boorstin, 751 F.2d 1405, 36 FEP Cases 1216 (D.C. Cir. 1985)   153

Eubanks v. Pickens-Bond Constr. Co., 635 F.2d 1341, 24 FEP Cases 897 (8th Cir. 1981)   161, 162

Evans v. Wright, 582 F.2d 20 (5th Cir. 1978)   190

Expeditions Unlimited Aquatic Enters. v. Smithsonian Inst., 566 F.2d 298 (D.C. Cir. 1977), cert. denied, 438 U.S. 915 (1978)   190

F

Facer v. Dept. of the Air Force, 836 F.2d 535 (Fed. Cir. 1988)   96

Fairall v. VA, 844 F.2d 775 (Fed. Cir. 1987)   100

Federal Labor Relations Auth. v. Aberdeen Proving Ground, 127 LRRM 3137 (1988)   232, 244

Felton v. EEOC, 820 F.2d 391 (Fed. Cir. 1987)   89

Ferris v. Dept. of the Navy, 810 F.2d 1121 (Fed. Cir. 1987)   91

Ferrone v. Dept. of Labor, 797 F.2d 962 (Fed. Cir. 1986)   88

Filiberti & Dysthe v. MSPB, 804 F.2d 1504, 86 FMSR 7097 (9th Cir. 1986)   125

Finch v. United States, 179 Ct.Cl. 1 (1967)   108

Finfer v. Kaplan, 344 F.2d 38 (2d Cir. 1965)   87

Fiorillo v. Dept. of Justice, 795 F.2d 1544 (Fed. Cir. 1986)   94, 126

Fitzgerald v. Hampton, 467 F.2d 755 (D.C. Cir. 1972)   110

Ford v. HUD, 450 F. Supp. 559 (N.D. Ill. 1978)   89

Forrester v. White, 484 U.S. 219, 45 FEP Cases 1112 (1988)   204

Forsyth v. Kleindienst, 599 F.2d 1203 (3d Cir.), cert. denied sub nom. Mitchell v. Forsyth, 453 U.S. 913 (1981)   203

Fort Knox Dependent Schools v. FLRA, 875 F.2d 1179 (6th Cir. 1989)   278

Fort Stewart Schools v. FLRA, 860 F.2d 396 (11th Cir. 1988), petition for cert. filed, 57 USLW 3025 (1989)   285

Foster v. Ripley, 645 F.2d 1142 (D.C. Cir. 1981)   94

Franks v. Nimmo, 796 F.2d 1230 (10th Cir. 1986)   202

Frazier v. MSPB, 672 F.2d 150 (D.C. Cir. 1982)   97, 139, 151, 152, 350

Freier v. New York Life Ins. Co., 679 F.2d 780 (9th Cir. 1982)   187

Fugate v. LeBaube, 372 F. Supp. 1208 (N.D. Tex. 1974)   86

Johnson—*cont'd*
—v. Lehman, 679 F.2d 918, 28 FEP Cases 1485 (D.C. Cir. 1982)   365
—v. MSPB, 812 F.2d 705 (Fed. Cir. 1987)   116
—v. Orr, 747 F.2d 1352 (10th Cir. 1984)   85
—v. Pettibone Corp., 755 F.2d 1484 (11th Cir. 1985)   190
Jones v. Lee Way Motor Freight, Inc., 431 F.2d 245, 2 FEP Cases 895 (10th Cir. 1970)   157
Jordan v. Dept. of Justice, 691 F.2d 514 (D.C. Cir. 1982)   381
Jordan v. Hudson, 47 FEP Cases 583 (E.D. Va. 1988)   32, 369
Joseph v. CSC, 554 F.2d 1140 (D.C. Cir. 1977)   143
Judge v. Marsh, 649 F. Supp. 770, 42 FEP Cases 1003 (D.D.C. 1986)   154
Justice, Dept. of, Justice Mgmt. Div. v. FLRA, No. 88-1316 (D.C. Cir. Apr. 22, 1988)   276, 277

K

Kalkines v. United States, 473 F.2d 1391 (Ct.Cl. 1973)   84
Karohalios v. NFFE, Local 1263, 130 LRRM 2737 (1989)   266
Katz v. Dole, 709 F.2d 251, 31 FEP Cases 1521 (4th Cir. 1983)   157, 158
Keely v. MSPB, 760 F.2d 246, 85 FMSR 7027 (Fed. Cir. 1985)   361, 362, 363
Keely v. MSPB, 793 F.2d 1273, 86 FMSR 7058 (Fed. Cir. 1986)   370
Keim v. United States, 177 U.S. 290 (1900)   343
Kendall v. Stokes, 44 U.S. (3 How.) 87 (1845)   191
Kennedy v. Whitehurst, 690 F.2d 951, 29 FEP Cases 1373 (D.C. Cir. 1982)   173
Kerr v. National Endowment for the Arts, 726 F.2d 730 (Fed. Cir. 1984)   117
King v. Greenblatt, 560 F.2d 1024 (1st Cir. 1977), cert. denied, 438 U.S. 916 (1978)   374, 375
Kissner v. OPM, 792 F.2d 133 (Fed. Cir. 1986)   89

Kizas v. Webster, 737 F.2d 524, 31 FEP Cases 905 (D.C. Cir. 1983), cert. denied, 464 U.S. 1042, 33 FEP Cases 1084 (1984)   153, 198
Kletschka v. Driver, 411 F.2d 436 (2d Cir. 1969)   96
Knuckles v. Bolger, 654 F.2d 25 (8th Cir. 1981)   86
Kochanny v. BATF, 694 F.2d 698 (Fed. Cir. 1982)   84
Korte v. OPM, 797 F.2d 967 (Fed. Cir. 1985)   89
Kotarski v. Cooper, 799 F.2d 1342 (9th Cir.), judgment vacated, 56 USLW 3879 (1988), rev'd on other grounds, 866 F.2d 311 (9th Cir. 1989)   198, 199, 201, 202
Krodel v. Young, 576 F. Supp. 390, 33 FEP Cases 701 (D.D.C. 1983)   173, 365
Krohn v. United States, 742 F.2d 24 (1st Cir. 1984)   209
Kumferman v. Dept. of the Navy, 785 F.2d 286 (Fed. Cir. 1986)   89, 95

L

Laffey v. Northwest Airlines, 567 F.2d 429, 13 FEP Cases 1068 (D.C. Cir. 1976), cert. denied, 434 U.S. 1086, 16 FEP Cases 998 (1978)   181, 182
Langster v. Schweiker, 565 F. Supp. 407, 36 FEP Cases 1623 (N.D. Ill. 1983)   153
Lanphear v. Prokop, 703 F.2d 1311, 31 FEP Cases 671 (D.C. Cir. 1983)   155
Laugesen v. Anaconda Co., 510 F.2d 307, 10 FEP Cases 567 (9th Cir. 1975), cert. denied, 422 U.S. 1045 (1975)   171
Lawrence v. Acree, 665 F.2d 1319 (D.C. Cir. 1981)   204
Leedom v. Kyne, 358 U.S. 8, 43 LRRM 2222 (1958)   338
Lehman v. Nakshian, 453 U.S. 156, 26 FEP Cases 65 (1981)   168, 174
Lewis v. Dept. of the Navy, 674 F.2d 714, 82 FMSR 7043 (8th Cir. 1982)   360

Overseas Educ. Ass'n v. FLRA, 824 F.2d 61 (D.C. Cir. 1987)   74

Owens v. United States, 822 F.2d 408, 44 FEP Cases 247 (3d Cir. 1987), after remand sub nom. Owens v. Turnage, 681 F. Supp. 1095, 46 FEP Cases 528 (D.N.J. 1988)   159, 170

Oyler v. National Guard Ass'n, 743 F.2d 545 (7th Cir. 1984)   191

P

Palermo v. Rorex, 806 F.2d 1266 (5th Cir.), cert. denied, 56 USLW 3243 (1988)   190, 191, 195, 199

Palmer v. GSA, 787 F.2d 300, 40 FEP Cases 630 (8th Cir. 1986)   173

Panama Canal Comm'n v. FLRA, 867 F.2d 905, 130 LRRM 2430 (5th Cir. 1989)   301

Parker v. Matthews, 411 F. Supp. 1059 (D.D.C. 1976), aff'd sub nom. Parker v. Califano, 561 F.2d 320 (D.C. Cir. 1977)   352, 353

Parker v. Postal Serv., 819 F.2d 1113 (Fed. Cir. 1987)   91

Parks v. United States, 147 F. Supp. 261 (Ct.Cl. 1957)   106

Paroczay v. Hodges, 219 F. Supp. 89 (D.D.C. 1963)   98

Parsons v. Dept. of the Air Force, 707 F.2d 1406 (D.C. Cir. 1983)   95, 96

Paterson v. United States, 319 F.2d 882 (Ct.Cl. 1963)   86

Paterson v. United States, 436 F.2d 438 (Ct.Cl. 1971)   116

Paton v. LaPrade, 524 F.2d 862 (3d Cir. 1975)   197

Paul v. Davis, 424 U.S. 693 (1976)   208

Payne v. Panama Canal Co., 607 F.2d 155 (5th Cir. 1979)   346

Pearce v. Wichita City, City of Wichita Falls, Tex. Hosp. Bd., 590 F.2d 128, 19 FEP Cases 339 (5th Cir. 1979)   181, 182, 183

Pearson v. Western Elec., 542 F.2d 1150, 13 FEP Cases 1202 (10th Cir. 1976)   168

Peltier v. City of Fargo, 533 F.2d 374, 12 FEP Cases 945 (8th Cir. 1976)   182

Pena v. Brattleboro Retreat, 702 F.2d 322, 31 FEP Cases 198 (2d Cir. 1983)   171

Pennsylvania v. Delaware Valley Citizens' Council, 478 U.S. 546 (1986), rev'd, 483 U.S. 711, 45 FEP Cases 1750 (1987)   374, 376, 377, 379

People of Three Mile Island v. Nuclear Regulatory Comm'rs, 747 F.2d 139 (3d Cir. 1984)   206

Perry v. Sindermann, 408 U.S. 593 (1972)   94, 197

Peter v. United States, 534 F.2d 232 (Ct.Cl. 1975)   343

Pettis v. HHS, 803 F.2d 1176 (Fed. Cir. 1986)   109

Pettway v. American Cast Iron Co., 494 F.2d 211, 7 FEP Cases 1115 (5th Cir. 1974)   168

Pfaehler v. MSPB, 783 F.2d 187, 86 FMSR 7012 (Fed. Cir. 1986)   347

Pfeiffer v. Essex Wire Corp., 682 F.2d 684, 29 FEP Cases 420 (7th Cir.), cert. denied, 459 U.S. 1039, 30 FEP Cases 440 (1982)   173

Phillips v. Bergland, 586 F.2d 1007 (4th Cir. 1978)   90

Phillips v. Martin Marietta Corp., 400 U.S. 542, 3 FEP Cases 40 (1971)   165

Piccone v. United States, 407 F.2d 866 (Ct.Cl. 1969)   118

Pickering v. Board of Educ., 391 U.S. 563 (1968)   94, 126, 197

Pinar v. Dole, 747 F.2d 899 (4th Cir.), cert. denied, 471 U.S. 1016 (1985)   199, 202

Polcover v. Dept. of the Treasury, 477 F.2d 1223 (D.C. Cir. 1973)   85, 86

Poolman v. Nelson, 802 F.2d 304 (8th Cir. 1986)   192

Poorsina v. MSPB, 726 F.2d 507 (9th Cir. 1984)   82

Postal Serv. Bd. of Governors v. Aikens, 460 U.S. 711, 31 FEP Cases 609 (1983)   160, 163, 167

Prandini v. National Tea Co., 557 F.2d 1015 (3d Cir. 1077)   378

Pratte v. NLRB, 683 F.2d 1041 (7th Cir. 1982)   82

V

Van Fossen v. MSPB, 788 F.2d 748, 86 FMSR 7031 (Fed. Cir. 1986)   361

Van Hoomissen v. Xerox Corp., 503 F.2d 1131 (9th Cir. 1974)   352, 353

Vasquez v. Eastern Air Lines, 579 F.2d 107, 17 FEP Cases 1116 (1st Cir. 1978)   173

Veterans Admin. Medical Center, Minneapolis v. FLRA, 705 F.2d 953 (9th Cir. 1983)   307

Veterans Admin. Medical Center, Northport v. FLRA, 732 F.2d 1128 (2d Cir. 1984)   307

Vitarelli v. Seaton, 359 U.S. 535 (1959)   83

Vukonich v. CSC, 589 F.2d 494 (10th Cir. 1978)   82

W

Wade v. Dept. of the Navy, 829 F.2d 1106 (Fed. Cir. 1987)   93

Walker v. Weinberger, 600 F. Supp. 757 (D.D.C. 1985)   178

Wallen v. Domm, 700 F.2d 124 (4th Cir. 1983)   191

Warren v. Dept. of the Army, 804 F.2d 654 (Fed. Cir. 1986)   103

Washington v. Davis, 426 U.S. 229, 12 FEP Cases 1415 (1976)   166

Washington v. Dept. of the Army, 813 F.2d 390 (Fed. Cir. 1987)   93, 94

Washington, County of v. Gunther, 452 U.S. 161, 25 FEP Cases 1521 (1981)   180, 181

Watson v. Fort Worth Bank & Trust, 487 U.S. __, 47 FEP Cases 102 (1988)   155, 160, 161, 163, 167

Watts v. OPM, 814 F.2d 1576 (Fed. Cir. 1987)   82

Weaver v. Dept. of the Navy, 2 MSPB 297, 80 FMSR 7012, aff'd, 669 F.2d 613 (9th Cir. 1982)   360

Webb v. Board of Educ., 471 U.S. 234, 37 FEP Cases 785 (1985)   349

Weeks v. Southern Bell Tel. & Tel. Co., 408 F.2d 228, 1 FEP Cases 656 (5th Cir. 1969)   164

Weirauch v. Dept. of the Army, 782 F.2d 1560 (Fed. Cir. 1986)   103

Weiss v. Postal Serv., 700 F.2d 754 (1st Cir. 1983)   95

West Point Elementary School Teachers Ass'n v. FLRA, 855 F.2d 936 (2d Cir. 1988)   278

Westfall v. Erwin, 484 U.S. 292, 56 USLW 4087 (1988)   170, 188, 189, 190, 191, 192, 193, 194, 195

Weston v. HUD, 724 F.2d 943 (Fed. Cir. 1983)   84

Whitaker v. MSPB, 784 F.2d 1109 (Fed. Cir. 1986)   43

White v. Bloomberg, 345 F. Supp. 133 (D. Md. 1973)   90

White v. Dept. of the Army, 720 F.2d 209 (D.C. Cir. 1983)   106

Whitlock v. Donovan, 598 F. Supp. 126, 36 FEP Cases 425 (D.D.C. 1984), aff'd sub nom. Whitlock v. Brock, 790 F.2d 964, 45 FEP Cases 520 (D.C. Cir. 1986)   178

Wiemers v. MSPB, 792 F.2d 1113 (Fed. Cir. 1986)   85

Wiggins v. Postal Serv., 653 F.2d 219 (5th Cir. 1981)   53

Wild v. HUD, 692 F.2d 1129, 82 FMSR 7054 (7th Cir. 1982)   90, 129

Wilderness Soc'y v. Morton, 495 F.2d 1026 (D.C. Cir. 1974), rev'd on other grounds sub nom. Alyeska Pipeline Serv. Co. v. Wilderness Soc'y, 421 U.S. 240 (1975)   379

Wilhelm v. Continental Title Co., 720 F.2d 1173, 33 FEP Cases 385 (10th Cir. 1983); cert. denied, 465 U.S. 1103, 34 FEP Cases 416 (1984)   187

Wilkes v. Postal Serv., 548 F. Supp. 642, 30 FEP Cases 20 (N.D. Ill. 1982)   174

Williams v. Dept. of the Army, 715 F.2d 1485 (Fed. Cir. 1983)   53

Williams v. IRS, 745 F.2d 702 (D.C. Cir. 1984)   201

Williams v. VA, 701 F.2d 764 (8th Cir. 1983)   88

Wilmot v. United States, 205 Ct.Cl. 686 (1974)   108

Wilson v. Califano, 473 F. Supp. 1350, 20 FEP Cases 1024 (D. Colo. 1979)   168

Merit Systems Protection Board Decisions

Federal Labor Relations Authority Decisions

Navy, Department of the—*cont'd*
—, Portsmouth Naval Shipyard, Portsmouth, N.H., 19 FLRA 586 (1985) 264
—, Puget Sound Naval Shipyard and Bremerton Metal Trades Council, 33 FLRA 56 (1988) 328
—, Trident Refit Facility, Bangor, Me. and Machinists, Dist. Local 282, 5 FLRA 606 (1981) 229
—, U.S. Naval Ordnance Station and Machinists, Local Lodge 830, 23 FLRA 671 (1986) 313
—, U.S. Naval Ordnance Station, Louisville, Ky. and Machinists, Local Lodge 830, 22 FLRA 382 (1986) 314
New Cumberland Army Depot and AFGE, Local 2004, 21 FLRA 968 (1986) 316, 328
New York State Nurses Ass'n and Veterans Admin. Bronx Medical Center, 30 FLRA 706 (1987) 275
Nuclear Regulatory Comm'n, 6 FLRA 18 (1981) 243
Nuclear Regulatory Comm'n, 21 FLRA 765 (1986) 257
Nuclear Regulatory Comm'n, and NTEU, 8 FLRA 715 (1982) 289
Office of Personnel Mgmt. and AFGE, 5 FLRA 238 (1981) 226
Overseas Educ. Ass'n
—and DOD Dependents Schools, 4 FLRA 98 (1980) 337
—and DOD Dependents School, 11 FLRA 377 (1983) 304
—and DOD Dependents Schools, 15 FLRA 358 (1984) 317
Overseas Fed'n of Teachers
—and DOD Dependents Schools, Mediterranean Region, 21 FLRA 757 (1986) 320
—and DOD Dependents Schools Mediterranean Region, 32 FLRA 410 (1988) 335
—and DOD Dependents Schools Mediterranean Region, 26 FLRA 362 (1987) 328
PATCO and Federal Aviation Admin., 5 FLRA 763 (1981) 311

PATCO, affiliated with MEBA, AFL-CIO (Federal Aviation Admin., Dept. of Transp.), 7 FLRA 34 (1981), enforced sub nom. PATCO v. FLRA, 685 F.2d 547, 110 LRRM 2676 (D.C. Cir. 1982) 267
Panama Canal Comm'n and Masters, Mates & Pilots, Panama Canal Pilots Branch, 26 FLRA 958 (1987) 337
Panama Canal Comm'n and Masters, Mates & Pilots, 27 FLRA 907 (1987) 310
Patent & Trademark Office, Dept. of Commerce and Patent Office Professional Ass'n, 21 FLRA 580 (1986) 296
Pension Benefit Guaranty Corp. and NTEU, Chapter 211, 32 FLRA 141 (1988) 337
Police Ass'n of the D.C. and National Park Serv., U.S. Park Police, 18 FLRA 348 (1985) 308
Production, Maintenance, & Pub. Employees, Local 1276 and Defense Logistics Agency, Defense Depot Tracy, Cal., 9 FLRA 919 (1982) 270
Sheet Metal Workers, Local 97 and Philadelphia Metal Trades Council and Robert Cosden, 7 FLRA 799 (1982) 303
Small Business Admin. and AFGE, Local 2532, 33 FLRA 28 (1988) 332
Social Sec. Admin., see Health & Human Servs., Dept. of
Southwestern Power Admin. and Electrical Workers (IBEW), Local 1002, 22 FLRA 475 (1986) 312
State, County & Mun. Employees, Local 2478 and Commission on Civil Rights, 26 FLRA 158 (1987) 314
State, County & Mun. Employees, Local 3097 and Department of Justice, 31 FLRA 322 (1988), petition for review filed sub nom. Department of Justice, Justice Mgmt. Div. v. FLRA, No. 88-1316 (D.C. Cir. Apr. 22, 1988) 276, 277, 323
Tidewater, Va., Federal Employees Metal Trades Council and Machinists, Local 441, 8 FLRA 217 (1982) 304

Federal Service Impasses Panel Decisions

Comptroller General Decisions

Equal Employment Opportunity Commission Decisions

Note: Only recently have decisions of the EEOC been published through a service.

Index

Federal Wage System   11, 62
Fifth Amendment   197, 198
Filing requirements
    appealable action cases   16–17
    attorney fee awards   347–348,
        366–367
    mixed cases   50–51
    negotiability appeals   268–270
    unfair labor practice charges   55–56
Final-offer arbitration   293–294
Firefighters   116, 224–225
First Amendment   197–198, 201, 267
Flexible and compressed work
    schedules   294–295
Foreign Service Act of 1980   288, 289,
    342
Foreign Service employees   60
Foreign Service Impasses Dispute
    Panel   288
Form No. 22 (FLRA)   54, 55
Form No. 23 (FLRA)   54, 55
Form 53 (FMCS)   287
Former employees   238
Fourth Amendment   197, 199
Fraud   91
Freedom of Information Act
    (FOIA)   119, 145, 150, 253
Fringe benefits (see Employee and fringe
    benefits)
Functus officio doctrine   335
Furloughs   82, 109, 111–112, 309

G

Gambling   89, 175
General Accounting Office   121
General Counsel   218n
General Services Administration   236
Good-faith bargaining (see Collective
    bargaining)
Government (see Federal government)
Government employment (see Federal
    employment)
Government Printing Office   60, 121
Grade reduction or removal   81, 103,
    184, 309, 384
Grade retention   59, 307
Grievance arbitration (see Arbitration)

Grievance procedures (see Agency
    administrative grievance
    procedure; Negotiated grievance
    procedure)

H

Handbilling   233
Handicap discrimination   174–179
    administrative and judicial
        forums   37n, 179
    alcohol or drug dependency   92,
        177–178
    attorney fee awards   365
    burden of proof   175–177
    remedies   389
    statutory prohibition   174–175, 179,
        522
    terms defined   175
Handicapped employees
    disability retirement   92–93
    excepted service   83n
    involuntary resignation   98
    substance abuse   92
Hardiman, Jerome P.   302
Harmful error   23n, 96, 317, 320, 386
Hatch Act   124, 142–145, 429, 488
Health insurance
    OPM review   11, 66–68, 307
    reinstatement remedy   387
Hearing
    appealable action cases   19, 21–22
    arbitration procedures   305–306,
        333–334
    EEO complaint cases   32–34, 41, 71
    mixed cases   46, 50
    position classification appeals   61
    prohibited personnel practice
        cases   136–137, 141
    Senior Executive Service actions   114
    unfair labor practice cases   55, 58
Height requirements   165
Hiring process
    prohibited practices   123–126
Homicide   90, 91
Homosexuality   90–91
Horn, Stuart R.   268

L

About the Authors

Ellen M. Bussey is a Washington, D.C., labor arbitrator and consulting economist. Her arbitration practice, developed since 1980, is broadly based, including the public and private sectors and service on permanent adjudicating panels as well as ad hoc hearings. Dr. Bussey conceived the idea for a volume of this nature after her appointment to the first Personnel Appeals Board for the General Accounting Office in 1980, when it became apparent while working on the official Rules required for such a body, that nothing comprehensive existed on overall federal civil service law and procedures. Dr. Bussey's career as an economist has included service with a number of international organizations, foundations, and the U.S. Government and has focused on problems of employment and unemployment and labor relations. She is the author of numerous articles and a book published by D.C. Heath in 1973, dealing with comparative international job-creation policies; and she is the editor of the first edition of *Federal Civil Service Law and Procedures*, published by BNA in 1984. She has contributed to, among others, the *Monthly Labor Review*, *Industrial Relations*, and *Labor Law Journal*. Dr. Bussey obtained her Ph.D. from American University in Washington, D.C.

Carl D. Moore is the General Counsel of the Personnel Appeals Board for the U.S. General Accounting Office. From 1978 to 1981, Mr. Moore was the Deputy Director for Civilian Personnel Law, Office of the General Counsel, U.S. Department of the Navy and Counsel for Civilian Personnel Law to the Chief of Naval Operations. From 1976 to 1978 he served as Executive Director and General Counsel for the Overseas Education Association/NEA. Mr. Moore is a regular instructor on federal personnel law for the Legal Education Institute of the U.S. Department of Justice, a course taught throughout the United States for attorneys representing the U.S. Government. He is the author of a number of articles on federal civilian personnel law including one on attorney's fees in the December 1982 issue of the *Arbitration Journal* of the American Arbitration Association and others on performance appraisals in the federal government in the December 1989 and January 1990 issues of

Federal Personnel Management Guideposts, published by the Labor Relations Press. Mr. Moore also contributed three chapters to the first edition of this book. He holds a 1971 J.D. from the University of Texas School of Law and is a member of the Texas and the District of Columbia Bars.

Sandra H. Shapiro is Associate General Counsel for Business and Administrative Law for the Office of General Counsel, U.S. Department of Health and Human Services. Prior to joining HHS in 1982, she was an Assistant General Counsel at the Office of Personnel Management. Ms. Shapiro is also an adjunct professor at the Georgetown University Law Center where she teaches public personnel law. She is an instructor and member of the curriculum committee for the Department of Justice Legal Education Institute course on the law of federal employment taught at government installations throughout the country. She was the author of the chapter on civil service law in *West's Federal Practice Manual* from 1972 to 1982. Ms. Shapiro also contributed a chapter to the first edition of this book. She received a J.D. from the University of Minnesota Law School in 1961 and is a member of the Bars of Minnesota, the District of Columbia, and the U.S. Supreme Court.

Kathryn A. Bleecker is an attorney with the Washington, D.C., law firm of Terris, Edgecombe, Hecker & Wayne, specializing in employment litigation. Prior to 1986 she served as an attorney with the Office of the Special Counsel, Merit Systems Protection Board, for more than five years. Six months of this time were spent in 1984 working with the U.S. Attorney's Office, litigating criminal cases in the Superior Court of the District of Columbia. She received a Master's Degree in Social Work from the University of Minnesoa in 1973 and her J.D. from Catholic University in Washington, D.C., in 1980. She is a member of the District of Columbia Bar.

Michael J. Riselli is a principal in the Washington, D.C., law firm of Riselli & Pressler, which conducts a general civil practice with a substantial proportion of federal sector labor and employment cases. Before entering private practice in 1981, Mr. Riselli was the Deputy Assistant General Counsel (Administration, Legislation, and Inspection) for the U.S. Department of the Treasury for approximately six years. Before his government service, he was General Counsel of the National Association of Government Employees and its affiliate, the International Brotherhood of Police Officers. Mr. Riselli has lectured widely and, since 1981, has annually contributed an article on significant MSPB decisions dealing with labor-management relations issues for the ABA's *The Labor*

Lawyer. Mr. Riselli received a J.D., cum laude, from Suffolk University Law School, Boston, Massachusetts, in 1972 and an L.L.M. from Georgetown University Law Center, Washington, D.C., in 1977. He is a member of the District of Columbia and Massachusetts Bars and is admitted to practice before various federal courts including the U.S. Supreme Court and the U.S. Court of Appeals for the Federal Circuit.

R. John Seibert has been associated with the U.S. Department of Justice for fifteen years, of which ten were in the Department's Civil Division, where he acquired considerable expertise defending federal officials and employees in constitutional tort actions. A former Associate Professor of Law at George Mason University in Virginia, Mr. Seibert also serves on the faculty of the Attorney General's Advocacy Institute which trains new Justice Department attorneys. He has lectured extensively for numerous federal agencies throughout the country with an emphasis on civil litigation and ethical issues confronting the government lawyer. In 1987 Mr. Seibert relocated to Honolulu where he serves as the Senior Assistant United States Attorney in charge of the Office's Organized Crime Strike Force unit. Mr. Seibert received his J.D. from Georgetown University Law Center in 1973 and is a member of the Virginia Bar.

Robert T. Simmelkjaer has been a professor of educational administration at the City College of New York Graduate School of Education since 1974. He has taught collective bargaining, law, and public finance and has also served as Vice Provost for Academic Administration and as Dean of the School of General Studies. Dr. Simmelkjaer is an attorney and labor arbitrator and is a member of several public and private sector labor arbitration panels, including the FMCS, AAA, New York PERB, N.J. PERC, and the New York City OCB. Dr. Simmelkjaer served as a Member and Vice Chair of the Personnel Appeals Board for the U.S. General Accounting Office for three years. He has been the Executive Director of the New York Governor's Advisory Commission for Black Affairs and the Deputy Chief Counsel, Joint Commission for Integrity in the Public Schools. He is the author of several articles on labor relations and public finance including "Finality of Arbitration Awards," which appeared in *The Arbitration Forum*, Fall, 1989. Mr. Simmelkjaer is a member of the National Academy of Arbitrators and sits on the board of directors of the Institute for Mediation and Conflict Resolution. He received M.B.A. and Ed.D. degrees from Columbia University and a J.D. from Fordham University's School of Law, June 1978. He is a member of the New York Bar.

?id L. Feder is the Assistant General Counsel for Legal Policy ?vice in the Office of the General Counsel, Federal Labor Relations ?ority. In this Senior Executive Service position, he is responsible for ?iewing the legal work of all the regional offices of the authority and for providing case handling advice. Prior to his appointment in 1981, he served in positions of increasing responsibility at the FLRA and its predecessor FLRC. Mr. Feder received a J.D. from Northeastern University School of Law in 1974 and an L.L.M. in labor law from New York University School of Law in 1975. He has published numerous articles concerning the federal service Labor Management Relations Statute. The most recent is "Pick a Forum—Any Forum: A Proposal for a Federal Dispute Resolution Board," *Labor Law Journal* (May 1989). Mr. Feder also contributed a chapter to the first edition of this book. He is a member of the Society of Federal Labor Relations Professionals, the American Bar Association, and the Pennsylvania Bar.

Stuart R. Horn is Chief Counsel to one of the three Members of the Federal Labor Relations Authority. Before the Authority was reorganized in 1986 to provide a separate staff for each Member, he was the Assistant Chief Counsel for Negotiability, that is, the principal advisor to the Authority concerning negotiability issues between federal management and federal unions. During most of the 1972 to 1979 period, he performed a similar function for the Federal Labor Relations Council, the predecessor of the FLRA. Mr. Horn has lectured extensively on negotiability matters at professional conferences and at both union- and management-sponsored training programs. He holds a J.D. from California Western Law School and is a member of the District of Columbia Bar.

Jerome P. Hardiman, currently an attorney and labor arbitrator specializing in the resolution of federal sector employee and labor-management relations problems, served with the Federal Labor Relations Authority from 1979 to 1988, in a number of senior executive positions including that of Assistant Chief Counsel for Arbitration. From 1972 to 1978, he was an attorney advisor with the Federal Labor Relations Council. Mr. Hardiman is the author of several articles on federal sector labor relations published between 1974 and 1989 and a forthcoming book, *A Practitioner's Guide to Negotiability in the Federal Sector* (Federal Personnel Management Institute, Inc., 1990). He received his J.D. degree from Georgetown University in 1971 and is a member of the District of Columbia Bar.